STEPHEN A. HIPP

"PERSON" IN CHRISTIAN TRADITION AND IN THE CONCEPTION OF SAINT ALBERT THE GREAT

A SYSTEMATIC STUDY OF ITS CONCEPT AS ILLUMINATED BY THE MYSTERIES OF THE TRINITY AND THE INCARNATION

ASCHENDORFF MÜNSTER

BEITRÄGE ZUR GESCHICHTE DER PHILOSOPHIE UND THEOLOGIE DES MITTELALTERS

Texte und Untersuchungen

Begründet von Clemens Baeumker
Fortgeführt von Martin Grabmann und Michael Schmaus

Im Auftrag der Görres-Gesellschaft
herausgegeben von Ludwig Hödl und Wolfgang Kluxen

Neue Folge
Band 57

Gedruckt mit Unterstützung
der Görres-Gesellschaft zur Pflege der Wissenschaft

© 2001 Aschendorffsche Verlagsbuchhandlung GmbH & Co., Münster

Druck: Druckhaus Aschendorff, Münster, 2001
Gedruckt auf säurefreiem, alterungsbeständigem Papier ∞

ISBN 3-402-04008-5

I would like to express my gratitude to Professor Dr. Jean-Pierre Torrell, O.P., who generously and patiently guided me throughout this work, and Professor Dr. Ruedi Imbach who kindly accepted to be the second reviser.

I especially wish to thank Professor Dr. Ludwig Hödl and Prof. Dr. Dr. h.c. mult. Wolfgang Kluxen for accepting this book in the Baeumker-Beiträge series.

Finally, I extend my appreciation to the Görres-Gesellschaft for their assistance in printing this work, as well as Dr. Dirk Paßmann, Director of Aschendorff, for his kind collaboration in the preparation of the manuscript.

TABLE OF CONTENTS

I. INTRODUCTION

II. THE NOTION OF PERSONALITY IN
SAINT ALBERT THE GREAT

I. INTRODUCTION

I.1. THE THEOLOGICAL QUESTION AND APPROACH

The problem

The *res* toward which every effort of Christian theology is directed is God the Father, the Son and Holy Spirit, a God who manifested and gave Himself to man in the flesh and blood of Jesus of Nazareth. The very heart of the Christian faith consists in the mysteries of the Trinity and Incarnation. The first consists of the essential unity proper to the Father, Son and Holy Spirit who are one God subsistent in three distinct persons. The second signifies the taking of human flesh, the uniting of human nature to the second person of the Trinity, the admirable union accomplished by the Trinity between the eternal divine nature they share in common and the created human nature in the unique person of Jesus Christ. On the one hand are three persons of one substance or nature; on the other, two natures substantially united in one person. For both, the relation obtaining between personal reality and natural reality constitutes the mystery in question. As a consequence, in the history of the theological explication of dogma, the Church has constantly articulated these beliefs and deepened her understanding of them by means of explicitating the meaning of "person" and "nature". An understanding of these concepts is indispensable to the construction of meaningful statements with regard to the divine mysteries of the Trinity and Christ, and a lack of conceptual rigor in their regard can only lead to a misapprehension of the central articles of Christian faith. It was precisely due to a limited perception of the relationship between person and nature that Nestorianism and Eutyches introduced two errors into the understanding of the Incarnation. Because each saw a reciprocal numerical correspondence between personhood and nature, believing that from natural number follows number in person and vice versa, one, affirming the duality of natures in Christ, asserted a duality of persons, while the other, affirming the unity of person, acknowledged only one nature in Christ. Both errors follow from the fact that neither was able to properly distinguish person from nature[1].

---

[1]   St. Albert the Great makes this observation when considering the unacceptable consequences of assigning personality to the nature Christ assumes: *"Nestorius enim et Eutyches invenerunt duos errores circa incarnationem. Unus enim videns, quod semper ad numerum naturarum sequitur numerus personarum, et videns Christum esse unam personam*

In order to combat the influence of heretical teaching which would repudiate the sense of revelation and destroy the work of salvation either by refusing the divinity and equal dignity of the Lord with respect to the Father or by refusing his consubstantiality with men, the Church had to develop its formulation of the deposit of faith by recourse to terminology of philosophical origin: "essence", "substance", "hypostasis", "person", "relation"[2]. As a result, the course of theological reflection on the Trinitarian and Christological mysteries was destined to take the form of a dialectical elaboration of these notions. Any study, therefore, of the Trinity and Christ is inevitably engaged in a speculative dissection of philosophical concepts employed in the elaboration of theological truths[3]. In effect, the development of a particular and original semantical application of philosophical language characteristically marks the early-Christian effort to clarify the kerygma[4]. For man's attention was drawn to the distinction between "person" and "nature" only because of the recognition of several persons within a single divinity, and only because of his encounter with the one and unique mediator between God and man. Thus it was Christian theology which shed light on the importance of the person, as much in light of its announcement of the fundamental value of the individual (whose dignity surpasses that of the universal nature), as in the fact that the distinction between person and nature at the anthropological level is simply not evident outside of its revelation in God Incarnate[5].

In the context of Trinitarian discourse, the Church has used the terms "substance", "nature" and "essence" to designate that which is common to the divine persons, the divine being in its unity, while the

---

tantum, dixit Christum etiam esse unius naturae... Alius autem considerans in Christo esse duas naturas, et idem supponens cum ipso, dixit etiam ibi esse duas personas. Et utriusque error provenit ex hoc quod nesciebant distinguere inter personam et naturam" – III Sent., d. 5, a. 12, sol., ed. Borgnet, vol. 28, p. 111. For the Arian confusion of hypostasis with οὐσία, and the relation between the two notions in general, see A. Milano, Persona in teologia, Edizione Dehoniane, Naples 1987, p. 112-119.

2   Cf. Catechism of the Catholic Church, §251.

3   Cf. A. M. Henry, The Historical and Mystical Christ, Fides, Chicago 1958, p. 78: "Regardless of the philosophy they may prefer, those who have the responsibility of preserving the deposit of faith must constantly make use of philosophical terms. It is only by laboriously considering the concept of the person that theology can, insofar as it is humanly possible, clarify the mystery of the Trinity... and the Incarnation".

4   Cf. A. Milano, Persona in teologia, Edizioni Dehoniane, Naples 1987, p. 35-41.

5   Cf. J. Galot, "La définition de la personne, relation et sujet", Gregorianum 75/2 (1994), p. 289. With regard to the overall relation of philosophy to theology, cf. in-

terms "person" or "hypostasis" are employed to signify the persons according to their real distinction, and "relation" to designate the distinctive character of that distinction [6]:

"While relatively three persons are asserted, we yet believe they are one nature or substance. We do not affirm three substances as we affirm three persons, but one substance and three persons" [7]. "Every one of the three persons is that reality, namely, substance, essence or divine nature... distinctions are in persons and unity in nature" [8].

The mystery of the Incarnation, equally based upon the paradoxical relation between person and nature (though in an inverse way [9]), expresses itself with the same terms:

"Although he is God and man, yet he is not two, but he is one Christ... one absolutely not by confusion of substance, but by unity of person" [10]. "One and the same Christ... acknowledged in two natures which undergo no confusion... but rather the property of both natures is preserved and comes together into a single person" [11].

But the dogma of the Incarnation (which especially because of the nature of its soteriological dimensions appears as sheer folly to the

fra, note 16, as well as the penultimate paragraph under "METHOD", p. 21, and note 1371 in the "FINAL CONCLUSION".

6   Cf. *Catechism of the Catholic Church*, §252.

7   Council of Toledo XI: "*In relativis vero personarum nominibus Pater ad Filium, Filius ad Patrem, Spiritus Sanctus ad utrosque refertur: quae cum relative tres personae dicantur, una tamen natura vel substantia creditur. Nec sicut tres personas, ita tres substantias praedicamus, sed unam substantiam, tres autem personas*" – DS 528, 15-16.

8   Lateran Council IV: "*quaelibet trium personarum est illa res, videlicet substantia, essentia seu natura divina... distinctiones sint in personis, et unitas in natura*" – DS 804; DEC, p. 232, 9-14; cf. *Catechism of the Catholic Church*, §253-4.

9   For a first testimony of this symmetry at the speculative level, cf. Gregory of Nazianzus, *Ep.* 101, 4, who points out that the mystery of the relationship between nature and person in Christ is to be conceived conversely from the way it is conceived in the Trinity: "ἄλλο καὶ ἄλλο... οὐκ ἄλλος δὲ καὶ ἄλλος, μὴ γένοιτο"; cf. Louis Ott, *Précis de théologie dogmatique*, trans. M. Grandclaudon, Éditions Salvator, Tournai/Paris 1954, p. 211-212.

10 Symbol *Quicumque*: "*qui licet Deus sit et homo, non duo tamen, sed unus est Christus... unus omnino, non confusione substantiae, sed unitate personae*" – DS 76, 34-36.

11 Council of Chalcedon: "ἕνα καὶ τὸν αὐτὸν Χριστὸν... ἐν δύο φύσεσιν ἀσυγχύτως... σωζομένης δὲ μᾶλλον τῆς ἰδιότητος ἑκατέρας φύσεως, καὶ εἰς ἓν πρόσωπον" ("*unum eundemque Christum... in duabus naturis inconfuse... magisque salva proprietate utriusque naturae et in unam personam*") – *Conciliorum Oecumenicorum Decreta*, ed. G. Alberigo, Istituto per le Scienze Religiose, Bologna 1973, in *Decrees of the Ecumenical Councils*, ed. N. P. Tanner, Sheed & Ward, Georgetown 1990 (hereafter referred to as DEC), p. 86, 31-39; DS 302.

human mind unenlightened by faith) presents the human intelligence with a compounded difficulty already at the ontological level. Not only must the notions of person and nature be distinguished in such a way as to make conceptual room for the possibility of a plurality of one without that of the other, but the very modality according to which two natures are able to be united in a single person must also be accounted for if the unity between God and man, between uncreated act and a purely contingent created nature, is to make any sense. In the person of Jesus Christ, human nature is united to divine nature in such a way that the singular person of the Word becomes the subject of attribution for both natures, in such a way that the human nature itself does not result in a second personal referent, in contrast to the fact that the natural production of every other human nature necessarily results in the constitution of a correspondingly distinct person. But, in just what "such a way" is this able to happen? How are we able to fully recognize the reality of the assumed human nature in Christ without compromising the unicity of person? How shall we provide a non-contradictory account of the existence of this humanity which is neither person nor subsistent in itself[12]? The answer to these questions rests primarily upon our understanding of the very notions employed in speaking about the Incarnation or "hypostatic union". As a result, the fruits of Christian reflection upon the mystery of the Trinity, preeminently aimed at explaining personhood and the principles of its multiplication in distinction from those of natural division, are the immediate seeds for reflection over the mystery interior to the Incarnation. No examination of the personal union in Christ can prescind from a consideration of the insights on personhood and nature gathered from the Church's reflection on the Trinitarian mystery. Indeed, the Trinity is the theologian's starting point in coming to understand every mystery in the economy of creation and salvation. Before the revealed mystery of a certain plurality in God, the first concern of the theologian consists in reconciling that number with the absolute simplicity of divine nature[13]. How is it possible that a plurality in God of concrete existents not result, as it does in creatures, in a numbering of nature? The unique response to this question lies in a conceptualization of personhood respectful of distinc-

---

[12]   The questions express, in particular, an apparent objection against the dogma of the hypostatic union *ex parte assumpti,* that is, in consideration of what is assumed.

[13]   Cf. A. Pompei, *La dottrina trinitaria di S. Alberto Magno, O. P.. Esposizione organica del Commentario delle Sentenze in rapporto al movimento teologico scolastico,* Diss., University of Fribourg (Switzerland), Rome 1953, p. 75.

tion while nonetheless not compromising the divine simplicity, a conceptualization which, while making room for the real distinction demanded by the divine hypostases, excludes any form of diversity whatsoever in the Godhead[14]. The quest for personhood is therefore situated within the context of coming to an understanding of the supreme truth constituting the heart of the theologian's speculation, namely the distinction of Persons within the unity of essence[15], and it is *ex intelligentia mysterii Trinitatis* that the very mystery of the Incarnation begins to make sense.

General aim of this study

In this treatise, we intend to examine the problem of personhood and the Christological issue at a philosophical level by investigating the terms employed in their articulation, something fully engaging us in the struggle to clarify the personal mystery in the Trinity, with the hopes of thus providing the basis for a series of conclusions able to be drawn concerning the modality of the hypostatic union. This study is ultimately a question of personality and, more precisely, of (the role of) the distinction between "nature", "person", "essence", and "subsistence" – inasmuch as the existential status of the human nature of Christ, as well as his personality, must be defined according to the categories which these notions are able to provide. We say "able" because the traditional understanding of these terms are perhaps not the only ones possible, especially when one considers that the reality of the Trinity and Incarnation shall play a normative role in the elaboration of their understanding (according as the truths of faith illuminate the truths of natural reason[16]). Our aim, therefore, is that

---

[14] Cf. Albert, *I Sent.*, d. 2, a. 19, ad 3, ed. Borgnet, vol. 25, p. 78.

[15] Cf. A. Pompei, op. cit., p. 79, 188; cf. Albert, *I Sent.*, d. 22, A, div. textus, ed. Borgnet, vol. 25, p. 565: "*pars illa quae est de nominum diversitate quae tota inducitur ad hoc ut accipiatur hoc nomen, 'persona', de quo maxime tractare intendit*".

[16] It is a presupposition here that the truths of theology are able to shed light upon philosophical considerations. Though nature is sometimes filled with more than sufficient clues about natural philosophical truths, we are not always able to reach those truths – fallen man being "blocked" as it were – without the aid of God's revelation. By this, we do not wish to espouse the idea that the world of miraculous phenomena impinges upon the world of nature (as though, for example, the eucharistic miracle were to have a normative value for chemistry), but believe that revelation is capable of signaling to us both accessible and inaccessible truths concerning the world around us (as when the doctrine of creation illumined philosophers as to the non-eternity of the world, or when the Decalogue opened men's eyes to certain fundamental aspects of the natural law). The fundamental formal

of an exposition of the metaphysical notions of essence, substance, nature, hypostasis, person and subsistence, in the context of contemplating the central mysteries of the Christian faith. And we do this according as they are discussed by certain representative early Christian and medieval theologians whose thought had a non-marginal influence on the question of personal unity in Christ[17]. Canvassing the theological contributions of several authors, we shall provide a historical preview aimed at preparing the context within which to evaluate the culminating perspectives exceptionally able to be drawn, in our opinion, from the works of Albert the Great.

The crux of our interrogation is expressed by the following questions. Just what is it that constitutes the perfection of personhood, what is it that gives to nature the crown of personality? And what is the definition of person? A large variety of works are dedicated to different elements of the historically emerging responses to these questions. Some – to name a few important examples –, such as M. Richard's, *L'Introduction du mot 'hypostase' dans la théologie de l'Incarnation*[18], report the birth and evolution of certain linguistic terms indispensable to discourse on the subject. Others aim at ascertaining

primacy of revelatory truth in its relation to philosophical reasoning is clearly formulated in *De fide et ratione* of the First Vatican Council (sess. 3, c. 4); cf., in particular, *Denz.* 3017-3018. Between philosophy and theology, however, we are fully aware of the existence of an organic mutual dependency. While the former is able to direct and even correct the latter, the latter permits the refinement and articulation of our understanding of the former. Reason is not derogated; it is presupposed and necessary to faith which can in no way mature and display its content without reason. As to the harmony and authentically scientific interdependency existing between faith and reason, see M. Scheeben, *The Mysteries of Christianity*, XXIX, §109; H. U. von Balthasar, *The Glory of the Lord*, vol. I, "Seeing the Form", I, §5-6; cf. also the recent encyclical letter by Pope John Paul II, *Fides et ratio*. In defense of an "open philosophy", characterized by the unpretentious submission of the rational spirit to the transcendence and plenitude of its object and to the diverse manners in which it is made known to man, cf. E. Forment, *Lecciones de Metafísica*, Ediciónes Rialp, Madrid 1992, p. 258-260; M. García Morente, "El clasicismo de Santo Tomás", in *Escritos desconocidos e inéditos*, M. García Morente (editor), BAC, Madrid 1987, p. 174-190.

[17] A historical approach to the evaluation of these concepts is inevitable, particularly in light of the finely nuanced and often new significations given to the linguistic terms used to signify them, terms the signification of which cannot be discerned outside of an understanding of the historical *use* which they acquired. For the importance of understanding the *use* of language, that is the function received by a linguistic term in a given context, in order to determine its signification, see A. Milano, *Persona in teologia*, Edizioni Dehoniane, Naples 1987, p. 25-26, 31-43.

[18] M. Richard, *L'Introduction du mot 'hypostase' dans la théologie de l'Incarnation*, Opera Minora, II, p. 243-270. Also along these lines is A. De Halleux, "'Hypostase' et 'Personne' dans la Formation du Dogme Trinitaire (ca 375-381)" in *Patrologie et oecuménisme*, University Press, Louvain 1990, p. 113-214).

the precise interpretation of related doctrines of different authorities such as Boethius, as for example, in P. Hadot, *La distinction de l'être et de l'étant dans le 'De hebdomadibus' de Boèce*[19]. Others present thematic considerations proper to a given period of thought, such as S. A. Turienzo's, *Aspectos del Problema de la Persona en el Siglo XII*[20] and E. H. Wéber's *La personne humaine au XIIIe siècle*[21]. While still others cover the broader historical development of the personal problem in works such as that of J. A. Sayes, *Jesucristo, Ser y Persona*[22], and A. Milano, *Persona in teologia*[23]. The modern concept of personality is not what we are interested in. This should be obvious from our metaphysical standpoint which sharply contrasts with the prevalent philosophical trend globally depicting personhood as some form or combination of

[19] P. Hadot, "La distinction de l'être et de l'étant dans le 'De hebdomadibus' de Boèce", in *Miscellanea Mediaevalia* 2, "Die Metaphysik im Mittelalter", Walter de Gruyter, Berlin 1963, p. 147-153. For patristical authorities such as Cyril of Alexandria and the Cappadocian Fathers, see especially J. N. D. Kelly, *Early Christian Doctrines*, Harper and Row, New York 1960, and A. Grillmeier, *Christ in Christian Tradition*, John Knox Press, Atlanta 1975; for Nestorius, see L. I. Scipioni, *Ricerche sulla Cristologia del "Libro di Eraclide" di Nestorio. La formulazione e il suo contesto filosofico*, Fribourg 1956. As for St. Albert, see: J. Saranyana, "Sobre la Contribución de Alberto Magno a la Doctrina del 'Actus Essendi'", in *Miscellanea Mediaevalia* 14, "Albert der Grosse. Seine Zeit, sein Werk, sein Wirkung", Walter de Gruyter, Berlin/New York 1981, p. 41-49; A. De Libera, *Albert le Grand et la philosophie*, Librairie Philosophique J. Vrin, Paris 1990; L. De Raeymaeker, "Albert le Grand, philosophe. Les lignes fondamentales de son système métaphysique", *Revue néoscolastique de philosophie* 35 (1933), p. 5-36; I. Craemer-Ruegenberg, *Albertus Magnus*, C. H. Beck, Munich 1980.

[20] S. A. Turienzo, "Aspectos del Problema de la Persona en el Siglo XII", in *Miscellanea Mediaevalia* 2, "Die Metaphysik im Mittelalter", Walter de Gruyter, Berlin 1963, p. 180-183.

[21] E. H. Wéber, *La personne humaine au XIIIe siècle*, Librairie Philosophique J. Vrin, Paris 1991.

[22] J. A. Sayes, *Jesucristo, Ser y Persona*, Ediciones Aldecoa, Burgos 1984. The work contains a historical analysis of the patristical development of dogma, accentuating the apparently contending perspectives resulting from the Cappadocian characterization of person as the "idiomatized" οὐσία and the Cyrillian intuition of person as subject of attribution and ultimate bearer of properties. Only a brief outline of the Boethian elaboration appears, followed by a catalogue of the contributions of historically successive thinkers from and including St. Thomas to various salient modern theologians on the notion of personality. Finally the author proposes his own theory of personal identity in Christ grounded on an understanding of the psychological foundation of intersubjectivity.

[23] A. Milano, *Persona in teologia*, Edizioni Dehoniane, Naples 1987. The concept of person and its historical evolution from the early patristical period through Boethius is discussed by the author with particular emphasis upon the linguistic origins and grammatical value of the terms surrounding the concept of personhood. Along similar lines, systematically elaborating the notion of person in its various theological contexts, cf. J. Auer, *Person. Ein Schlüssel zum christlichen Mysterium*, Pustet, Regensburg 1979.

self-consciousness, inter-subjectivity or autonomy[24]. We are concerned with the being of the person as such, its ontological structure, as discussed by the long and ancient tradition of the Church. It is rather a theologically necessitated philosophical reflection, one which is guided by the principles of our faith, which must determine the givens in an ontological study of personality: for it was theology which exalted the concept of person when Greek philosophy stood without it[25]. Such a reflection begins with the Church's effort to render a philosophically non-repugnant sense to the mystery of the Trinity, by distinguishing what the Father, Son and Holy Spirit share in common from what they have and are as three distinct identities within a single Godhead.

Note that an immediate analysis of the hypostatic union is not a goal of this study. That analysis is necessarily dependent on everything investigated here and we hope to adequately prepare for a direct confrontation with the problem of personal unity in Christ; but due to the limitations of space and the already broad scope of the current thesis, considerations of the mode of union in Christ shall be reserved for a second study intended as a follow-up to this work[26].

Method

Our theological study begins with the early Church's first formulation of Trinitarian dogma (Nicea) and proceeds to a reflection upon the Cappadocian Fathers, historically introducing the fundamental prob-

---

[24] Such a characterization, understood to adequately define person, represents a deviation from the systematic scholastic ontology to a psychologico-moral perspective as the basis for a philosophy of man. The confusions this has engendered in understanding the Trinity are significant, seeing as it would be utterly absurd to propose three centers of consciousness, or three centers of autonomous action, in the unique substance of the triune God.

[25] Cf. J. A. Sayes, *Jesucristo, Ser y Persona*, Ediciones Aldecoa, Burgos 1984, p. 88; A. Milano, *Persona in teologia*, Edizioni Dehoniane, Naples 1987, p. 21-22, 28; C. Vigna, "Sostanza e relazione", in *L'Idea di persona*, V. Melchiorre (editor), Vita e Pensiero, Milan 1996, p. 175-203.

[26] Nevertheless, the sense and orientation of this work consists not only in a reconsideration of the relation between person and nature (by means of a review of the tradition led by Saint Albert), but is manifested also in its tendency to open itself to Christological avenues. One will notice near the end of almost every section a question or paragraph consecrated to the application of certain preceding conclusions to the problem of the unique person of the two natures in Christ. For, as we have pointed out, the proper character of personality cannot be determined without responding to the demands presented by the Incarnation; and it is this last challenge which puts our concept of person to the greatest test.

lem of the distinction between person and nature. After a condensed recapitulation of the Church's official adaptation of language in the Council of Constantinople (381), we briefly explore the tensions between Cyril of Alexandria and Nestorius serving to specify the kind of response required by the personal dilemma. This is followed by a survey of the prevalent Christological statements of the third and fourth oecumenical councils and a preliminary consideration of the Latin term *"persona"*. With theses significant elements beneath our feet, we embark on a more systematic scrutiny of the issues surrounding personality with Boethius.

The necessity to study Boethius is self-evident. His metaphysical doctrine provides an indispensable structure within which to situate the problem of personhood in general and within which the governing principles of substance and subsistence may be accurately defined. In the chapter entitled "BOETHIUS AND A METAPHYSICS OF NORMATIVE VALUE", we shall analyze the thought of this Roman philosopher and develop our position with respect to major metaphysical factors entering into the concept of person. Because Boethius became, in a rather authoritative way, the central point of reference for later medieval reflection on personhood, and because his celebrated definition of person continues to occupy a privileged place in theological and anthropological discussions, a variety of comparisons to his particular explanation of personality shall be made throughout the course of this investigation, both in anticipation and retrospectively.

The chapter which follows unites the reflections of Gilbert of Poitiers along with those of Richard of St. Victor who, particularly in the case of Gilbert, oblige us to carefully nuance the use of our vocabulary in order to adequately respect the different levels at which distinction and identity may be affirmed in the Trinity[27]. In particular, we shall encounter in this section certain fundamental characteristics of person emphatically brought under light by Richard of St. Victor.

Finally, we have centered our attention on Albert the Great, since he, perhaps better than any other medieval author, synthesizes the many metaphysical facets involved in the consideration of person and, while faithful to the Boethian elaboration, opens the door to a radically unique explanation for the unity of person in Christ. With the

---

[27] Note that one of the principal reasons for including an elementary reflection on Gilbert of Poitiers consists in the fact that Albert the Great, with whom we are more immediately concerned, frequently refers to him in the process of developing his own conception of personality. Cf. infra, "GILBERT OF POITIERS AND RICHARD OF SAINT-VICTOR", p. 150.

opening chapter on Albert ("ONTOLOGICAL DIVISIONS AND SIGNIFICATION OF TERMS") we begin to build a coherent understanding of the person and the kind of unity in Christ, illuminated by the mystery of the Trinity, based upon the systematic exposition of St. Albert. This chapter is dedicated to the major ontological distinctions of being, assigning the ontic status of person and situating the signification of the term "person" with respect to the notions of substance, hypostasis and nature. The successive chapters are also thematically divided, each one elaborating a particular issue related to personhood, following the investigation of St. Albert.

We conclude the entire study with an integrative and comparative profile of the historical thought on personality, condensing the insight of thinkers both anterior and posterior to Albert, in an effort to show the perennial value and rational solidity of the Albertinian doctrine. In this "SYNTHESIS AND OVERVIEW" we shall quickly glance at the theological systems of Scotus, Capreolus, Cajetan and Suárez, as well as consider a modern ontological approach to personality, in order better place in light the contributions of the Universal Doctor.

Naturally, there are many other authors worthy of consideration, but the scope of this work cannot begin to take them all into account. We have chosen these authors because of the reasons given above and because they, in particular, remain historical benchmarks in the reflection over person.

Our procedure for analyzing the works of these authors follows a relatively linear examination after the manner of a commentary, structured however according to thematic concerns (whence the many subtitles) and selectively narrowing the passages considered. But, far from aiming to give an exhaustive account of this or that author's personal perspective, and far from attempting to estimate the motives for or the precise historical sources of their thought, we have set out to directly confront the philosophical and theological question with which these authors were themselves concerned. It is the theological issue itself which holds our primary attention, and the entire aim of this work is to come to a better understanding of the personal mystery in the Trinity and Christ[28]. These authors are important to us pre-

---

[28]   "The study of philosophy is not destined to making known what men have thought, but what is really the truth of things" – Aquinas, *De Caelo*, L. 1, lect. 22, n. 8, ed. Leonine, vol. 3, p. 91: *"studium philosophiae non est ad hoc quod sciatur quid homines senserint, sed qualiter se habeat veritas rerum"*.

cisely for their contribution to this understanding. Where they have left a relevant question unresolved (and to the degree that this has been perceived), we have attempted to address the issue; where they diverge from the presuppositions or givens germane to our topic, we have diverged from them; where they supply conceptual instruments for pushing their own speculation to newer conclusions, we have endeavored to exploit the opportunity. In particular, our thesis represents a theological development of elements especially present in the writings of St. Albert. Though "the thought of St. Albert" *as such* is not our ultimate concern, that thought is certainly of central importance to this thesis, and we have tried to accurately present his views (as likewise with respect to the other authors) [29].

As a result, the operative method consists as much in a personal reflection as in a critical historical exposition. Because, in the spirit of Saint Thomas, it is not the literary origin of the ideas of this or that author nor their respective personal intentions which occupy the foreground of our investigation, but the scientific object itself and the truth of things, our approach is guided by thematic considerations the arrangement of which obeys a logical order interior to the question of the person. We have commented the principal passages concerning personality in order to extract the conclusive (and original, in the sense of adding new notes to our image of the person being constructed) elements which play a determinate role in the conceptualization of person. We say "conceptualization" since it is not only a question of the definition of person, but equally of how we grasp this reality, a dimension which requires a proper understanding of a variety of principles not necessarily intrinsic to the essence of the person in itself – such as the use of language (with its properties of signification and supposition), and the metaphysical foundations of natural philosophy (including the distinction between substance and accident, subsistence and dependent being, the necessary and the possible, the notion of origin, of priority according to its diverse orders, of individuality and of numeration *in fieri*, as well as an appreciation of

---

[29]   Without having originally aimed at an exposition of his doctrine in itself, nor of the historical factors which influenced him, Albert became the foundation and term of our reflection, for the depth and breadth of his speculation suffices to provide every element necessary both for a precise definition of person as well as a refined appreciation of its components. In particular, and as we shall see, there is an *open character* to his thought which permits the adopting of different approaches to the questions rooted in the difficult problem of the relation between being and essence, such as the difficulty posed by the humanity of Christ, the being of the individual as such, and even the distinction between supposit and nature.

the predicamental hierarchy in consideration of relation). We have attempted, to the degree to which it has been possible, to coordinate all of these factors without which a position regarding personality would lack in coherence. As an inevitable result, we oscillate between an interpretive commentary, often interpolative, and the direct exposition of a text. Nevertheless, we have indicated our point of departure when it is a question of a development thoroughly independent of the thought of the author in consideration.

One will observe that our method in studying the mentioned figures is largely restricted to the primary literature. For the authors addressed in our introduction, this deliberate choice is grounded on two reasons: (1) our intention to provide but a succinct historical backdrop, by means of direct familiarity with the language and arguments of the selected writers, against which to measure the contribution of the Universal Doctor (the relative importance of which authors is structurally reflected by their restriction to the introduction); and (2) the simple fact that much of the secondary literature either too frequently skews the original thrust or comparative implications of an author's thought (a point which is especially evident in the case of Boethius), or amounts to a needless and tiresome repetition of what a small handful of experts have already said once and for all. Nevertheless, our work is not without reference to nor capable of standing independently of the most important secondary literature. Ultimately, we have supplied a condensed inventory of the pertinent bibliography in this regard.

The same methodological approach is justified for St. Albert in a more fundamental and less circumstantial way. We have preferred to inspect his thought according to the primary literature not only in light of the vast amounts of unexplored territory in the Albertinian corpus, but especially because of the lamentably sparse treatment which his notion of personality has received by modern scholars[30].

We would like to draw the reader's attention to the fact that an *a priori* to the overall elaboration of this thesis is an Aristotelio-Thomistic metaphysics. This, however, is not a filter through which we interpret the intent of St. Albert or Boethius, for example, but rather a back-

---

[30]   Cf. infra, "PRINCIPAL STUDIES", p. 183, in regard to the poverty of major investigations dealing with Albert's understanding of personality.

ground against which to estimate the implication of their insights and a frame of reference within which we shall borrow their thought for further speculative development. With reference once more to our philosophical approach, it must be kept in mind that we are dealing with theological issues unenunciable outside of the language of philosophy. Inversely, the earlier acknowledged fact that theology obliges us to correct and direct our philosophical viewpoint should not be seen as presenting any serious problems, neither for the scientific object under discussion nor for the relationship between faith and reason in general. It is not revelation in itself that imposes a sort of governance over our philosophical investigation, but our *reflection upon* that revelation in the effort to make reasoned sense out of the divine mysteries. In effect, we are engaged in a *dialogue* between philosophy and theology precisely in order to deepen our comprehension of a supremely difficult mystery. In the case at hand, we are concerned with the precise theme of the triune God in his personal reality, a mystery the knowledge of which can only be received in faith and whose parameters burst the categories of an exclusively philosphical mindset[31].

Finally, one will note that different sections of our treatise often reiterate conclusions and premises from preceding sections. This repetition of principles is inevitable, not only because the nature of the mystery requires a constant awareness of the doctrines set out in advance, but also, and especially, because its different aspects are so tightly interwoven that to selectively analyze one means to concomitantly exhibit the other. "I assert", concludes M. J. Scheeben, "one single principle taken from the revealed doctrine of the Trinity is sufficient for reason to construct and develop the dogma in its entire rich content. The dogma is so symmetrical... that starting with any thread at random we can trace the whole pattern from one end to another"[32].

---

[31]   Cf. supra, "THE PROBLEM", p. 9 (especially p. 10); cf. note 16.

[32]   M. J. Scheeben, *The Mysteries of Christianity*, trans. C. Vollert, Herder, London 1947, p. 50. The habit of reiteration is advocated by St. Athanasius as well: "In dealing with this subject matter above all, we must not be afraid to frequently repeat the same things" – St. Athanasius, *First Letter to Serapion concerning the Holy Spirit* 19, §4 (PG 26, 573C).

A modern philosophical dimension

Over and above the theological necessity to define personhood, the importance of the notion of person in contemporary philosophy is incontestable; it plays a fundamental role in the consideration of man as well as in many modern ethical and juridical debates. As to the precise content of the notion of person we find a fundamental eluci-dation already in common language where "person" and "man" are practically synonymous. While these terms admit of diverse intension (that is, their content or explicitly indicated notes are different), they have traditionally been held to be identical in extension (referring to the same individuals or classes of individuals): every man, or every rational individual, to be more accurate, is said to be a person; and every person is a rational individual. The fact that every man has tra-ditionally been called a person, and that the very notion of person has been the result of a consideration of human nature, means that "per-son" was understood as a characterization of what a man is and as de-scribing this rational individual. "Person", then, has a descriptive role and is linked to the referents from which its notion was derived. As a consequence, "person" should not be understood as the hypostatiza-tion of an abstract property, but as a name for a certain referent[33]. Person, as we shall see, is not a property, but a subject which is signi-fied according to a certain property.

Though it be for different motivations, today, as was the case for the early Church before the mysteries of her faith, we witness a strong effort to differentiate the notion of person from that of nature. Now, the theological consideration of the Trinity and of the person of Christ, already prior to the fifth century, had led to philosophically distinguishing these notions, and it is precisely these theological is-sues, when analyzed in depth, which offer refined metaphysical crite-ria of distinction and unification for personhood and nature, in such a way that, while maintaining their distinctness at one level, human nature and person cannot be distinguished at another (except for the intension of their respective concepts).

The different levels of consideration to which we have alluded are, briefly, that of considering (and signifying) the human nature accord-ing as it is the formal (or, if one prefers, "qualifying") principle of the subject we recognize to exist and to which we attribute various proper-ties such as consciousness and dignity, and that of considering (and

---

[33] See in this regard: E. Agazzi, *"L'essere umano come persona"*, *Bioetica e Persona* 31 (1993), p. 137-157.

signifying) the human nature according to its complete individuality, that is, insofar as it is wholly singularized as a distinct referent. In the first case, nature and person are distinct from one another as formal constituent[34] and subject of that form, as *quo est* and *quod est*, the latter

---

[34] We say "constituent" instead of "part" since the case in question actually concerns the *forma totius*, that is, the human nature as the form of the whole supposit consisting in that nature and its act of existence. The human nature here is therefore not the abstract nature – which can only be a part of the whole nature composed of matter and form – but it is the concrete or individualized nature, considered however in precision from its existence and the subjectivality due to it in virtue of the personal principle of "complete individuation/singularization" from which its singular mode of existence is seen to derive. As is evident from these preliminary considerations, theological investigation of the notion of personality is strongly dependent upon a philosophy of individuation. The latter difficulty presents a topic beyond the scope of this thesis, though we inevitably deal with a variety of dimensions connected with it. For a rudimentary synopsis of the problem, cf. infra, "A WORD ABOUT INDIVIDUALITY AND THE 'PROBLEM OF INDIVIDUATION'", p. 51.

Equally evidenced in this excursus is the related and no less difficult question of isolating the proper character of nature in itself. The task requires not only the momentous enterprise of pinning down the relationship between quiddity and existence, but also establishing the footing for an underlying principle of unity or identity. Modern philosophical concerns with personality have tended for the most part to ignore the former issue altogether while but unsatisfactorily addressing the notion of unity. The modern approach to the question of personality typically formulates the problem in terms of "personal identity". The expression, however, receives two very different senses or applications. On the one hand, it is sometimes taken as an achievement of the characteristics of consciousness proper to man, in the sense that it is itself constituted by reason of the unifying act of intelligence and memory able to coherently relate past and present experience into a consistent whole (thus "personal identity" is a mind dependent phenomenon). On the other hand, "personal identity" is sometimes understood as the trans-phenomenal endurance of a subject which resists the changes and dissolution proper to its perceivable properties threatened by time. This latter understanding, of course, has no direct value for questions related to personality in the Trinity, since there is absolutely no change or succession in God (however, the notion of "subject" and the unity which this implies can be employed in an analogous way in accounting for divine personality). While the first sense of "personal identity" falls properly within the domain of psychology, the latter is nearly synonymous with the Scholastic conception of substance as the principle of unity for any given entity.

With respect to the "identity" of the persisting subject, however, modern philosophy has generally attempted to substitute the Scholastic account of its principle with a variety of other candidates. As alluded to above, memory is frequently advanced as the reason for "personal identity", since it alone manifests a temporally successive unity of experience to the human mind. But memory itself must stem from something more foundational to the very entity (man) of whom it is the memory. Ordinary experience teaches me not that I *am* a memory, but that I *have* a memory. Memory is something I *exercise*, it is an *operation* and, as such, requires a *principle* of operation. As a result, proposing memory as an explanation for "personal identity" merely begs the question. Another, less popular, opinion regards materiality itself (independent of the notions of "substance" or "nature" or "essence") as responsible for everything proper to men including their "personal identity". This position, as a consequence of its rejection of "nature", also denies the

possessing the former and alone properly said to subsist – for which reason it is also called the supposit. In the second case, nature and person are identified with one another (*in re* or extension) because the nature so signified *is* the concrete subject which, for reasons of connoting dignity, we also call "person"; here nature and person can be said to differ only in *mode of signification*. According to these distinctions, then, from an ontological point of view, the modern assertion that not every human individual be a person will be unacceptable, because the human *individual is* the subject; "human being" does not signify the nature as a formal constituent, but as the concrete singular existent.

The two concepts differ according to the articulation/explicitation of a certain property (or lack of such an articulation) accomplished by their respective modes of signifying. The properties each term singles out are different, but the subject to which these properties belong, and which is the referent of either term, is the same. Even if they are distinguished in such a way that *being man* does not of itself constitute personhood, this does not permit the affirmation that that which *is man* is not of itself a person, or that that which *has* a human nature is not necessarily a person. A distinction in concepts could never result in an affirmation that certain human beings are not persons; but neither does the fact that no human being can fail to be a person preclude a distinction between the two concepts.

As we shall see, it is not the individuals who might turn out not to be persons, but only the human nature (the individual humanity) of

---

reality of the soul. However, the problem with such a perspective is that the very empirical elements recognized to constitute this or that individual lose their *own* consistency on the basis of the premise presupposed. If there is no underlying (and unobservable) principle of unity for an observable reality, but only outwardly manifest properties, then this or that man, animal, plant or fluid is no longer one in reality, but only conventionally referred to as "one", since there is no unifying principle by which it is one total being. To the contrary, according to the materialistic point of view, such things are *conglomerates* of a multitude of empirically acknowledged material unities. What is even more destructive of the theory, however, is the fact that, if there can be no natures in the metaphysical sense of the term, then *even these aggregated constituents* lack an intrinsic unity (and we either continue to dissect the perceived individual *ad infinitem*, without ever knowing what it or any of its components are, or we deny that it is anything at all). If, on the other hand, we ascribe some sort of subsistent or enduring status to the perceivable qualities of a thing themselves – such as in the theory maintaining that such qualities are the only real things (whose existence we may legitimately affirm) – then we have either (a) returned to a concept of the substance, insofar as these *passiones* of a thing are now treated as existing in their own right and not within another as in a subject (i.e. as *per se* existents), or (b) reduced all reality to mere appearance (effectively restricting it to having but an intentional value, which is no ontological value at all).

those individuals. This is precisely the point of discussion raised by the theological problem concerning the human nature of Christ. It is not incorrect to affirm that every person is a certain nature, and that every human (or rational) nature is also a person, assuming, of course, that "nature" be taken concretely. To have defined personhood, then, in terms of nature – as is the case with Boethius – neither runs counter-intuitive to strictly anthropological nor to the purely theological traditions. If Boethius has been criticized for insufficiently accounting for Trinitarian personhood because of his overly "physical" definition of person[35], perhaps his critics may be criticized for failing to fully appreciate the fundamental identity Boethius was presupposing in the formulation of his definition of person.

Note on "modus significandi"

Many of the concepts we are forced to struggle with are related to one another both according to identity and alteriety depending upon the way in which they are signified. Moreover, the realities to which they are referred are frequently distinguishable only at the level of our understanding. As a result, this study is heavily laden with distinctions of the conceptual sort requiring careful attention to the linguistic value of a term. Though things might seem on occasion to be overwhelmed by the notion of distinction according to mode of signification[36], in individuals we nevertheless recognize a real distinction between form and matter, essence and existence (even were the concept of an essence to include its existence, for the whole would never be predicable of the part[37]), substance and accident, even nature and supposit.

---

[35] Cf., as the principal representative of Mediaeval efforts to define personhood at a non-physical level, Richard of Saint-Victor, *De Trinitate*, critical edition by J. Ribaillier, Vrin, Paris, 1958; and, as an example of a similarly inspired modern divergence from Boethius, J. Galot, *La personne du Christ*, Duculot-Lethielleux, Paris 1969.

[36] Cf. infra, "ON DISTINCTION ACCORDING TO MODE OF SIGNIFICATION", p. 207.

[37] Except for subjective parts, as when "man" is predicated of "this man". The idea of distinguishing being from essence as a part from a greater whole derives from a consideration of the *individual* nature, where existential factors may be appealed to for the source of numerical discreteness. Such a distinction is easy to maintain when intending being in an efficient sense as a predicamentally accidental relation responsible for the actualization of a substance, but from the point of view of being taken as the formal act of an actual essence perhaps there is not, even from the standpoint of an existential theory of individuation, a distinction of part to whole, if it may be said that the being of a substance is identical to the substance according as it is. It may be argued: the white of Socrates *is* Socrates insofar as white; the relation of a substance is the substance insofar as related; and the bigness of Tom is

But of these parts, many can be considered otherwise, and not as parts at all, and may thus oblige the understanding to affirm another kind of distinction based upon how we view or comprehend the object of our concern. Here, at the level of the mystery of the individual, we are confronted with a flurry of distinctions dependent upon our manner of understanding and speaking. Naturally, therefore, a study of the most dignified thing of nature, the most perfect individual which is the person, will lead us into the delicate twists and turns of a linguistic metaphysical approach[38].

Tom insofar as big (that is, insofar as looked at in his accidental nature, which accidental nature is nothing other than his bigness, the bigness of Tom). From this perspective, the being of a substance is the substance insofar as it is, or viewed according to its *natura essendi* (i.e. according to its *ens*ness). But perhaps substance insofar as it *is* is not *all* that an actual substance is, such that the actual essence can still represent a whole greater in some fashion from its being as such (according as the actual essence further include the notion of a certain and specific quality). But such a quality is nothing at all if not actualized by being, and the being in question, namely of this essence, is necessarily the being of this quality, whence "the being of the substance" is simultaneously the being of this quality and, therefore, that very quality according as it is (though it does not seem to be equivalent to that quality according as it delimits the *ens*). Even the quality (i.e. the specification of nature) is unable to distinguish itself from the being (*esse*) except when considered either (a) according as it is not, or (b) according as it is but a delimitation of being (taken in abstraction from its existence). In the latter case, the essence (which is the essence *qua* specification) is nothing other than a potential principle. But that potency is a potency to being, whence it seems that such a potentiality is nothing at all. It is nothing considered strictly in itself; however, it is a real potency taken according to its reality, which is to consider it according as it is actualized by *esse* (in which case it is no longer *in* potency, but remains *a* potency insofar as abstracted from the very act by which its potentiality is real). The difficult issue of ascertaining the relationship between essence and existence cannot be taken up here. We shall certainly come against it in various other places within this treatise, particularly when discussing the thought of Francis Suárez, but reserve a technical analysis of the problem for another occasion (that of our forthcoming work on the Incarnation) when we will be directly concerned with the problem of individuation where *esse* and its causes have a fundamental role to play.

[38] Note that careful attention to language is essential to the task of the theologian. Adherence to the knowledge of faith itself can only occur by means of the transmission of the propositions of the Creed. Grammatical exactitude is not a matter of theological purism; to the contrary, errors in mode of expression can easily amount to or lead to heresy.

I.2. THE FIRST OECUMENICAL COUNCIL

Along with the development in the articulation of the concepts of person and nature in the contexts of Trinitarian and Incarnation theology, we witness a corresponding evolution in the authoritative expressions of faith represented by the general ecclesial councils; the achievements of the Fathers in their struggle to eradicate the scandals of heresy and expound the living word of faith find their definitive canonization in the decrees of the oecumenical councils. A brief survey of the pertinent synodal teachings regarding the Trinity and personal unity in Christ will not only help to chart the historical advancement in understanding the mystery of the Incarnation, but, more importantly, provides us with the ultimate source of authority against which to check the principles operative in our examination of personality; for the magisterium alone is both guarantor of the apostolic teaching and the authentic interpreter of revelation, and "it is well known that it redounds to the great benefit of the catholic Church that its authority... to which all are obliged to submit, should be manifested frequently and the attention of all should be drawn to it"[39]. We begin our study, therefore, with the doctrinal decrees of the first oecumenical council, first universal and normative symbol of the faith which the post-Nicene Fathers incessantly strove to uphold. Note that our analysis, here and in subsequent conciliar surveys, situates the conciliar declarations in successive order, according as they are related in the *actus conciliorum*. Only certain passages directly relevant to the theological problem of personality are considered, and we have attempted not to repeat content when already taken into account in a preceding council. In general, we adhere to the original texts on account of the technical terminology. These conciliar "synopses", we would like to emphasize, are in no way intended to represent an in-depth study of the development of dogma, but should serve simply as useful points of reference for evaluating the status of the historical progression of theological reflection on personhood[40].

---

[39] *Concilium Basiliense (- Ferrariense - Florentinum - Romanum)*, Session 18: DEC 477, 28-31 (note: from this point onward, references to the DEC will first indicate the page number followed by line numbers).

[40] For a superb analysis of the general councils dealing with the Christological controversies as well as an appreciation of the overall dogmatic tradition of the Church, we refer the reader to Bernard Sesboüé, *Jésus-Christ dans la tradition de l'Église*, Desclée, Paris 1982.

Concilium Nicaenum (325)

FAITH, AND A QUESTION OF LANGUAGE

(1) Πιστεύομεν εἰς ἕνα Θεὸν... καὶ εἰς ἕνα κύριον Ἰησοῦν Χριστὸν τὸν υἱὸν τοῦ θεοῦ γεννηθέντα... τουτέστιν ἐκ τῆς οὐσίας τοῦ πατρός... ὁμοούσιον τῷ πατρί... τὸν δι' ἡμᾶς τοὺς ἀνθρώπους καὶ διὰ τὴν ἡμετέραν σωτηρίαν κατελθόντα καὶ σαρκωθέντα, ἐνανθρωπήσαντα[41].

"We believe in one God... and in one Lord Jesus Christ, the Son of God, the only begotten, begotten of the Father, that is from the substance of the Father... consubstantial with the Father... who for us men and for our salvation came down and became incarnate, became man".

This is the essence of Christianity, and the first oecumenical profession of faith, in relation to which *all* other Christology is the development (or a deviation). Person and nature are already implicitly distinguished, inasmuch as the Son is not the Father, and yet they are one in substance (ὁμοούσιος); if "person" signifies the substance, it cannot do so in an unqualified way. The expression "one Lord, Jesus Christ, the Son of God, only begotten of the Father... who for us men... became man" represents, arguably[42], a primitive enunciation of the unity of subject characteristic of the person, a subjective unity to be reiterated in more explicit terms by the Council of Chalcedon.

(2) Τοὺς δὲ λέγοντας... ἢ ἐξ ἑτέρας ὑποστάσεως ἢ οὐσίας... ἀναθεματίζει ἡ καθολικὴ καὶ ἀποστολικὴ ἐκκλησία[43].

"Those who say... that he came to be from another hypostasis or substance... these the apostolic church anathematises".

The passage is a first demonstration of the ever prevalent problem of semantics in speaking about persons and nature. Here the notion of hypostasis possesses nothing of a notional value. "The Word cannot be said to have come from another ὑπόστασις or substance". In this anti-Arian rebuttal, ὑπόστασις is used synonymously with substance. The word group is translated *substantia* in the Latin. Thus, at the time of Ni-

---

[41] Profession of Faith of the 318 fathers: DEC 5, 2-15.
[42] Cf. J. Galot, "La définition de la personne, relation et sujet", *Gregorianum* 75/2 (1994), p. 291-292.
[43] DEC 5, 20-27.

cea, ὑπόστασις is not yet distinguished in its designation from οὐσία. When the same anti-Arian argumentation is repeated in the First Council of Constantinople (381), thanks to the speculative labors of the Cappadocian Fathers, the term ὑπόστασις is dropped from the vocabulary and only οὐσία and φύσις occur, as it is evidently a question of essence or nature as distinguished from the concrete distinct *entitas* which it becomes the task of ὑπόστασις to signify[44].

---

[44] DEC 28, 33-38.

I.3. THE CAPPADOCIANS

Basil the Great, Gregory of Nazianzus and Gregory of Nyssa

Basil of Cesarea (330-379) was a man of action, a profound spiritual master and a theologian of far-reaching speculative capacity. Formed in Athens and Constantinople, he became bishop of Cesarea in 370 after twelve years of monastic solitude. Firmly convinced that the Arian heresy could only be combated by adherence to the Nicene creed, St. Basil prevails over tritheism and subordinationism with his concept of one οὐσία and three ὑποστάσεις, a formula developed in his effort to make peace between contentious churches[45]. As a result of that formulation, the orthodox sense of a previously floating vocabulary is established in a paradigmatic way for the rest of Christian tradition.

Like Basil, Gregory of Nazianzus (†390) was a brilliant and highly cultured theologian, educated in the schools of Cesarea, Alexandria and Athens (where he developed an indissoluble friendship with Basil). Gregory, who devoted his life to study, ascetic virtue and solitude, was, moreover, a first rank poet and orator, known for the eloquence with which he fought against the threats of Arianism, Apollinarianism and Sabellianism. Bishop of Constantinople and champion of the faith of the fourth century Greek Church, Gregory upheld with particular clarity the distinction between οὐσία and ὑπόστασις, promoted an anti-Sabellian employment of the term πρόσωπον, and defended the personal unicity of Christ in recognizing a distinction between natural elements and subject and in supplying the classical doctrine of the communication of idioms.

Gregory of Nyssa (c. 335-394), brother to Basil the Great, consecrated himself to serving the Church first as a lector, then as a professor and a married man, and finally as member of the clergy after the death of his spouse. He too undertook the strict monastic discipline of asceticism and study until he allowed his brother to consecrate him bishop of Nyssa in 371. Present at the general council of Constantinople, with special theological authority he reaffirmed the Nicene faith. As much a philosopher as a theologian, and demonstrating an exceptional aptitude for metaphysical speculation, Gregory defended the dogma of the Trinity in an exceptional way, fervently maintaining

---

[45] Cf. A. Milano, *Persona in teologia*, Edizioni Dehoniane, Naples 1987, p. 127-128.

a Trinity of persons in a numerical unity of nature, and going beyond his brother and Gregory of Nazianzus by carefully distinguishing the originative mode of the Holy Spirit from that of the Son. In comparison with the other Cappadocians, Gregory stands out for his surpassing systematization and more scientific treatment of the great problems in theology and philosophy. He also applied his understanding of personhood to the singular person of Christ; however, as equally for the other Cappadocians, for want of decisive language and precise doctrinal definition, that effort does not enjoy the far-reaching achievements of Cappadocian Trinitarian doctrine.

All of the Cappadocians were influenced by both Stoic and neo-Platonic philosophical elements. Though particularly influenced by the latter in their spiritual reflection (notably in the exegetical wake of Origin), it is rather the content of Stoic philosophy which, as we shall see, contributed to shaping their understanding of the individual existent and, therefore, of the person.

Initial conceptual clarifications

The concept of "nature"

The concept of nature, along with that of person, is of the greatest importance in Trinitarian and Christological discussions. To distinguish them, we first note that "nature" is broader in extension than "person", as is evident from the fact that every person is (or has) a nature, while not every nature is or has a person. Historically, the term "nature" has its roots in early Greek philosophical reflection over the ultimate principles or active sources of natural processes. The underlying active origin of natural movement was given the name "φύσις", specifically implying a source from which something proceeds, toward the possession of some end or goal. The various dimensions of the concept are expressed in Latin by the term *"natura"* (whence the English "nature"), deriving from *"nasci"* which signifies "coming to be through generation"[46]. Used to express the principle

---

[46]   Cf. J. Weisheipl, "The Concepts of 'Nature' and 'Person'", in *Commentary on the Gospel of St. John of St. Thomas Aquinas*, Magi Books, New York 1980, I, appendix, p. 458-468; "The Concept of Nature: Avicenna and Aquinas", *Thomistic Papers* 1 (1984), p. 65-81. Cf. *Enciclopedia Filosofica*, "NATURA", Centro di Studi Filosofici di Gallarate, Stampa Romagraf, Rome 1979, p. 1014-1015; Y.-E. Masson, "NATURE (ÉTATS DE)", *DTC* 11, p. 36.

of generation, "nature" designated something intrinsic to the living creature, according as the source of a new generated life is contained within the living generator. By extension, the term was applied to every intrinsic principle of movement or change.

The concept of nature properly pertains to natural philosophy, and it is in this context that Aristotle's "φύσις" is defined and explained[47]. In all experienced coming to be, one observes the confluence of several factors, some passive some active. While the pre-Socratics had already strongly emphasized the reduction of change to certain fundamental material principles, accurately identifying a source of continuity in natural processes, there remained the need to explain the *active* principle according to which the structural building blocks of the world were put together. Matter, as a passive recipient under the influence of active principles certainly explains why a thing is the way it is and behaves the way it does; for this reason, it rightly receives the name "nature". But, as is clear from the passivity of a material principle, it is the active principle which far more accounts for the what of a thing and its behavior. Thus the active principle of a thing, with even greater reason, receives the name "nature". "Φύσις" or "nature", therefore, has both an active and a passive sense. To "φύσις" taken in the active sense, Aristotle gave the name "form", while "φύσις" as a passive principle is called "matter". "Φύσις" or "nature" in general is defined as the "source or cause of activity and rest in those things to which it belongs properly and not incidentally"[48]. Note that the mode according to which a thing is generated, that from which it derives and the goal with respect to which its generation occurs, determine what the thing itself *is*, its essence. This essence (specifically common to the generator and what is generated) is nature precisely inasmuch as principle of generation (or operation in general). "Essence" and "nature" designate the same thing, but according to diverse modes of signification. They signify the fundamental character of a substance from different points of view. For, the same substance can be envisaged either according to what it is in itself, that is, from the point of view of being, or according to its operation. Viewed in respect of its very being, its most intimate constitution as such, substance is called an essence; considered in respect of its activity, that is, as the principle of action and passion, substance is called nature. "Nature" thus, properly speaking, includes a certain

---

[47]   Aristotle, *Physics*, II, 1.
[48]   Aristotle, *Physics*, II, 1: 192b, 22-23.

dynamism in its concept, signifying the essence precisely in its relation to operation[49].

Because it is defined as a *source* of action or passion, "nature" is a relative term; because "nature" properly signifies the principle of observable properties and operations, its notion includes the relationship of origin[50]. This is very important for understanding nature in its comparison to person. Nature is not a *nomen absolutum*, but a *nomen relativum*. Thus "nature is not really a thing, but an origin or "source" from which (*a quo*) other things proceed"[51]. Even when nature is taken in an extended sense as simply indicating whatever it is that makes a thing to be what it is, such that it is applicable even to realities lacking a principle of motion (as in the case of mathematical objects), "nature" retains a sense of "source", inasmuch as "nature" thus understood is the *quod quid est* (the what of a thing) *formally* speaking, and not simply speaking. "Nature" in this sense is identical to the *essence* of a thing; but the essence (in the present sense of specific constitution, i.e. *forma totius*) is that *of which* an individual thing is constituted, a *quo est formalis* or a formal "source". In every case, that which possesses an essence or nature is a substantial *quod est*, a *res absoluta*, and this is "οὐσία" in the primary sense as expounded by Aristotle, not "φύσις". "Οὐσία", taken in the secondary sense as the complete specific constitution of a thing, is identical to the concept of "essence" possessing a certain static signification (in contrast to the dynamic/processional signification of "φύσις" or "nature" properly understood). But "secondary οὐσία" – or "secondary substance" – does not exist of itself, but only in a subject, which is the proper subject of existence. Existence, therefore, is not directly attributed to "οὐσία" so signified.

Οὐσία taken as secondary substance is identical to the composite form, that is, the *forma totius* composed of the two partial φύσεις of matter and substantial form. It is distinct from "primary οὐσία" as active principle (or, more precisely, formal principle – since the passive material principle is also included in the notion of the *forma totius*) to the subjective *res* of which it is the principle, as *quo est* to *quod est*. "Φύσις", originally, is a simpler notion than οὐσία. In fact, even secondary οὐσία implies a composition between two reciprocally re-

---

[49] Cf. Aristotle, *Met.*, V, c. 4: 1015ᵃ, 2-19.
[50] Cf. Aquinas, In II *Phys.*, Lect. 1, n. 5.
[51] J. Weisheipl, "The Concepts of 'Nature' and 'Person'", in *Commentary on the Gospel of St. John of St. Thomas Aquinas*, Magi Books, New York, 1980, I, appendix, p. 464.

lated principles. These, however, taken as a composite principle, are also φύσις – here φύσις is identical to secondary οὐσία. The philosophical tradition will contrast "οὐσία" understood as an undifferentiated or common element with the particular existent dependent upon it. "Οὐσία" in this context must be understood as secondary οὐσία, synonymous with "φύσις" or "essence" as a formal principle. In God, however, the common οὐσία is not a secondary substance, but is itself concrete and identical to the three of whom it is the quiddity. Nevertheless, οὐσία and ὑπόστασις are distinct notions even in God. One fruit of the inexhaustible labor of the Cappadocian Fathers was to abolish the long-standing synonymy between οὐσία and ὑπόστασις, a synonymy retained by the Council of Nicea and which did not help to assure the faith it proclaimed[52].

The term "hypostasis": nascent vocabulary problems

The Greek "hypostasis" originally signifies a base or "foundation" which stands beneath other things. In a very general sense, "hypostasis" can be said to stand for that which has an objective reality, in contrast with what is merely a subjective or illusory phenomenon[53]. Such is the sense of the term as found in the Bible and as used by a number of Fathers of the early Church. "Hypostasis" in these cases, and especially with respect to the Fathers, has a value synonymous with Aristotle's prime substance. Over the centuries, however, the term "hypostasis" was applied in theological contexts in a variety of ways and according to very different intensions. The fact that "hypostasis" represented the self-contained existent reality made it the most fitting term for defining the most perfect and consistent reality of all, namely person[54]. The result of this transposition, however, meant that

---

[52] Cf. A. Milano, *Persona in teologia*, Edizioni Dehoniane, Naples 1987, p. 112-119, especially 114-115.

[53] Cf. A. Michel, "HYPOSTASE", *DTC* 7, p. 369. Etymologically, "hypostasis" derives from the verb ὑφίστημι (= ὑπό-ἴστημι), and corresponds most frequently to the passive form: ὑφίσταμαι. According as the verbal root signifies (1) "standing-under", (2) "to be placed beneath", and (3) "to be deposited as a foundation or sediment" (where separation occurs, corresponding philosophically to "to exist" or "to be"), the substantive "hypostasis" stands for "support", "foundation", "existence" or "reality". Cf. A. Milano, *Persona in teologia*, Edizioni Dehoniane, Naples 1987, p. 98-99.

[54] Origen was the first to employ the term "hypostasis" in theological discussions of the divine persons. In the polemic against Monarchianism, Origen emphasized the reality of the distinction within the Triad, describing the error of the Monarchians as a failure to admit numerical distinction, recognizing a distinction of reason only

"hypostasis" could be used to designate either the divine substance or the several persons of the Trinity. Already the theological language stood in need of clarification. The accusation of tritheism leveled against Dionysius of Alexandria because he professed τρεῖς ὑποστά-σεις stemmed from an understanding of "hypostasis" as essence or substantial nature. But "hypostasis", as it was commonly employed among the Alexandrian Fathers (including Origen and Athanasius), stood for the personal reality, over and against the common οὐσία of the Trinity. Such a specialized sense of the term, remarks A. Milano, has little or nothing to do with the Biblical use of the term and represents an evolving use of language characteristic of the Christian culture. "Hypostasis" here, in contrast to οὐσία, accentuates the individuality of a thing, that is, its objective distinction with respect to others, while οὐσία indicates its singular being and inner unity.

The Latin equivalent of "hypostasis" used to designate the personal subject is *"persona"*. It was Tertullian who coined the Latin formula *"una substantia tres personae"*. The Trinitarian dictum has its Christological counterpart in the formulas expressing the double *substantia* and singular *persona* of Christ[55]. But "hypostasis" could not always be translated with *"persona"*, and was consistently translated in Latin philosophy as *"substantia"* (understood in the primary sense)[56]. Moreover, the Greeks had another name for the designation of concrete individuals and which was for a long time considered to be a direct etymon of *"persona"*, namely πρόσωπον. But because this latter term – according to a prevailing modern opinion – retained in the Greek world the sense of "roll", "mask" or "cynosure", its use for the designation of a plurality of persons in the Trinity appears to have run the risk of being understood in a Sabellian way. On the other hand, the

---

among the three: "ἐν οὐ μόνον οὐσία αλλά καὶ ὑποκειμένο" – *In Io.* 10, 37 (PG 14, 376B).

[55] These formulae with respect to Trinitarian and Christological doctrine provided the foundation for western orthodoxy and were more or less explicitly incorporated in the expressions of the great ecumenical councils. Cf., in particular, Tertullian, *Adv. Prax.*, c. 2, 11, 13, 18, 21, 24, 27, 31: CCL II, 1161-1204.

[56] Even the Council of Nicea continues to employ the term ὑπόστασις synonymously with οὐσία: "τοὺς δὲ λέγοντας... ἢ ἐξ ἑτέρας ὑποστάσεως ἢ οὐσίας... ἀναθε-ματίζει ἡ καθολικὴ καὶ ἀποστολικὴ ἐκκλησία" (DEC 5, 20-27). The Word cannot be said to have come from another ὑπόστασις or οὐσία. In this anti-Arian rebuttal, ὑπόστασις is identical with substance. The word group is translated *substantia* in the Latin. Thus, at the time of Nicea, ὑπόστασις is not yet distinguished in its designation from οὐσία. When the same anti-Arian argumentation is repeated in the First Council of Constantinople (381), the term ὑπόστασις is

expression τρεῖς ὑπόστασεις could be accused, as we have seen, of distinguishing within the Trinity three different substances. It is entirely understandable, therefore, why, in 376, St. Jerome felt the need to address Pope Damascene requesting terminological clarification[57]. Similar needs for clarification will continue to make themselves felt until a precise understanding of the metaphysical differences between substance, supposit, hypostasis and person is had in the Middle Ages. Naturally, therefore, one will observe the presence of linguistic uncertainties and a measure of ambiguity in the early Christian works examined in this section. Subsequent chapters, aimed at precisely delineating the sense of each term, will overcome these points of confusion.

The term πρόσωπον

As alluded to above, "prosopon" is reported to have originally signified a mask and, by extension, the external appearance of a thing and its concrete manifestation. Such a contention, however, represents a veritable deformation of the true original use of the term, according to A. Milano[58]. In its most foundational use, πρόσωπον had the function of designating "that which falls within one's sight", "that which one sees". It signified the face and aspect of a man, and only as a consequence of this fundamental meaning came to be used to designate a mask and even the role of an actor. In the New Testament, πρόσω-πον is never used to indicate a mask, but refers to the aspect or presence of someone, and is even used to stand for the individual[59]. It is in this sense, in order to signify the concrete existent, and never in the sense of a theatrical mask, that the term is taken up by the early Christian writers up through Basil the Great. In 451, the term shall be assumed in the Chalcedonian formula in order to designate, along with ὑπόστασις, the singular subject which Christ is. The first use of the term in Trinitarian theology appears to be that of Hippolytus who speaks with respect to the Father and Son as two πρόσωπα having a

---

dropped from the vocabulary and only οὐσία and φύσις occur, as it is evidently a question of essence or nature (cf. DEC 28, 33-38).

[57] Cf. *Ad Damasum Epist.*, 15, n. 3-4: PL 22, 356-357. A brief but insightful discussion of these general terminological difficulties is given by J. A. Sayes, *Jesucristo, Ser y Persona*, Aldecoa, Burgos 1984, p. 17-22.

[58] Cf. A. Milano, *Persona in teologia*, Edizioni Dehoniane, Naples 1987, p. 57.

[59] Cf. A. Milano, *Persona in teologia*, Edizioni Dehoniane, Naples 1987, p. 59.

single power[60]. But the definitive introduction of its employment in speaking about the Trinity is attributed to the Cappadocian Fathers.

General philosophical perspective

In the effort to articulate unity and trinity in the Godhead, the Cappadocians, as well as Nestorius, employ, in particular, the concepts of οὐσία, ὑπόστασις and πρόσωπον, in a way characteristic of typical patterns of (Aristotelio-) Stoic speculation[61]. In Stoic thought, the existence of natural realities is explained according to a certain logical movement from what is more simple and indeterminate to the complex and determined[62]. Οὐσία, the common and undifferentiated element at the base of all entities is realized and multiplied into distinct singular beings through particularizing active causes which determine it. For the Stoics, being was understood as an infinite primordial matter out of which, as a physical process of emerging, finite things came to exist. Οὐσία was thus being according to its infinite possibility. Starting with undetermined matter, οὐσία ὕλη, something is specified and individuated by a determinate set of qualities or active principles, τὰ ποιά, which posit it in concrete reality. We begin with indeterminate, passive[63] and undefined[64] matter having the sole quality of being an ultimate subject, πρῶτον ὑποκείμενον. Over and against this are the qualifying or formal, characterizing elements, τὰ ἄλλα τὰ ποιά. As pure passivity and subject, the οὐσία ὕλη receives its first determination from the specifying quality, κοινὴ ποιότης, by which it becomes a species, a κοινῶς ποιός. The κοινῶς ποιός is correspondingly particularized by the ἰδία ποιότης through which it is rendered an individual, ἰδίως ποιός:

---

[60] Cf. Hippolytus, *Contra Noet.* 7, ed. P. Nautin, Paris 1949, p. 247.

[61] See J. N. D. Kelly, *Early Christian Doctrines*, Harper and Row, 1960, p. 9-28; L. I. Scipioni, *Ricerche sulla Cristologia del "Libro di Eraclide" di Nestorio. La formulazione e il suo contesto filosofico*, Fribourg 1956, p. 45-67, 98-109; A. Grillmeier, *Christ in Christian Tradition*, John Knox Press, Atlanta 1975, I, p. 372-375; A. Milano, *Persona in teologia*, Edizioni Dehoniane, Naples 1987, p. 99-100, 130.

[62] For a succinct exposition of the Stoic physic, see L. I. Scipioni, op. cit., p. 98-109 and A. Grillmeier, op. cit., p. 372-375.

[63] παθητόν.

[64] ἀόριστον.

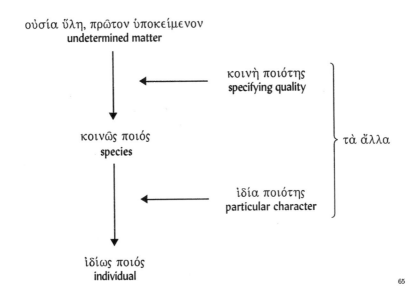

That which has come to be according to singular concrete existence also received from the Stoics the name ὑπόστασις (representing a transferal of the term from its original residence in the natural sciences to the technical philosophical domain) [66]. "Hypostasis" thus designates a being or nature according to its concrete manifestation. But the original "matter" is distinguishable from its objective actuality according to quality and particularity in thought only; for the ὑπόστασις is not one thing and the οὐσία another, but ὑπόστασις *is* the οὐσία insofar as concretized in objective reality.

Integration of these concepts in the writings of Basil the Great ~ Gregory of Nyssa

These concepts become very important for the Cappadocian understanding of individuality and explanation of the Trinity, a fact most

---

[65] Compare this pattern with Boethius infra, "ONTOLOGICAL PRINCIPLES BEHIND 'SUBSISTENTIA' AND 'SUBSTANTIA'", p. 116. The κοινὴ ποιότης is equivalent to "form", and thus in turn implies *esse*, since form gives being. Ἰδία ποιότης is equivalent to "*materia designata*", which is exactly *particularitates*.

[66] Cf. A. Milano, *Persona in teologia*, Edizioni Dehoniane, Naples 1987, p. 99.

clearly revealed by *Epistle 38* attributed to Basil[67]. In this letter, Basil (or Gregory of Nyssa[68]) develops his doctrine on οὐσία and ὑπόστασις. There he begins as well with the universal nature common to the individual members of a species which must be differentiated or determined according to a certain quality or character in order to account for the particular. The community of substance must be distinguished from the principle of the hypostases: "τὸ κοινὸν τῆς οὐσίας... ἀπὸ τοῦ τῶν ὑποστάσεων λόγου"[69], which principle is the determinate circumscription of a thing, ἡ πραγματός τινος περιγραφή[70]. Through a particularizing element (τὸ ἰδίαζον) the universal nature (κοινὴν φύσιν, ἡ κοινότης τῆς φύσεως) becomes a ὑπόστασις particularly set off from all other individuals[71]. Ὑπόστασις, then, indicates that which is signified by a proper name and not what is common to many individuals of the same nature[72].

Earlier in the *Contra Eunomium*, Basil explains how a personal name does not signify the essence, but the particular property of the individual to whom it is attached[73]. Hypostasis too, on the basis of its connection with the personal name, must therefore signify something other than the unique essence or substance of the divinity. It signifies rather at another level, namely that of the particularities. In the *Contra Eun.*, these latter traits, these distinguishing features, are closely associated with the notion of relation (*schésis*), the application of which to the Trinity constitutes, according to A. Milano[74], a guiding principle in the entirety of Basil's reflection on the Trinity.

The author of *Ep. 38* describes the individuality signified by ὑπόστασις as the reality beneath any veritable instantiation of a nature: "τὸ δὲ ὑφεστὸς καὶ δηλούμενον ἰδίως ὑπὸ τοῦ ὀνόματος"[75].

---

[67]   Ps-Basil (= Basil the Great and/or Gregory of Nyssa), *Ep. 38*, Γρηγορίῳ ἀδελφῷ περὶ διαφορᾶς οὐσίας καὶ ὑποστάσεως, ed. Y. Courtonne, *Saint Basile, Lettres*, Collection des Universités de France, Paris 1957 (= *Lettres*, to which our citations shall refer when not otherwise indicated), vol. I, p. 81-92 (= PG 32, 325-342).

[68]   The letter is quite possibly the composition of Gregory of Nyssa. Cf. A. Milano, *Persona in teologia*, Edizioni Dehoniane, Naples 1987, p. 140; J. N. D. Kelly, *Early Christian Doctrines*, Harper and Row, New York 1960, p. 275, note 76.

[69]   Ps.-Basil, *Ep. 38: Lettres*, I, p. 81, 1-2.

[70]   Ps.-Basil, *Ep. 38: Lettres*, I, p. 82, 14.

[71]   "ἐπὶ τὰ ἰδιάζοντα τρέψῃ τὴν θεωρίαν δι' ὧν ξωρίζεται τοῦ ἑτέρου τὸ ἕτερον" – Ps.-Basil, *Ep. 38: Lettres*, I, p. 82, 12-28.

[72]   "τὸ ἰδίως λεγόμενον τῷ τῆς ὑποστάσεως δηλοῦσθαι ῥήματι" – Ps.-Basil, *Ep. 38: Lettres*, I, p. 82, 1-5.

[73]   Cf. Basil, *Contra Eun.* 2, 9; 2, 12; 2, 28; PG 29, 588; 593; 637.

[74]   Cf. A. Milano, *Persona in teologia*, Edizioni Dehoniane, Naples 1987, p. 131.

[75]   Ps.-Basil, *Ep. 38: Lettres*, I, p. 82, 2-6.

In this way, he is asserting the concrete reality of ὑπόστασις as distinguished from the indefinite universal nature. Basil (or Gregory) characterizes this concrete reality as subsistent; for when one calls something by its proper name, "one shows the subsistent nature in the thing named. This is ὑπόστασις: it is not the indefinite notion of οὐσία, which finds no stability in the community of the thing signified, but this notion which delimits and defines that which is common and indeterminate in a certain particular object, through its manifesting properties"[76]:

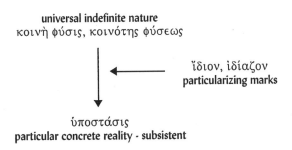

universal indefinite nature
κοινὴ φύσις, κοινότης φύσεως

ἴδιον, ἰδιάζον
particularizing marks

ὑποστάσις
particular concrete reality - subsistent

The same contraposition between subsistent reality – that is, the real thing according to its act of concrete existence – and the same reality according as it is commonly possessed by the subsisting thing is verified in various writings of Basil. According to the particular mode of existence, each member of the Triad is distinct (εἷς καὶ εἷς); according however to the common nature (τὸ κοινόν τῆς φύσεως), they are a single thing (ἕν)[77]. The divine οὐσία is equally possessed by all three hypostases[78], the particularity of which hypostases results in the fact that the οὐσία is become the what of this and that singular thing[79]. Note that the simultaneous insistence upon (1) the distinc-

[76] Ps.-Basil, *Ep. 38: Lettres*, I, p. 82-83, 6-12: "Ὁ δὲ Παῦλον εἰπὼν ἔδειξεν ἐν τῷ δηλουμένῳ ὑπὸ τοῦ ὀνόματος πράγματι ὑφεστῶσαν τὴν φύσιν. Τοῦτο οὖν ἐστιν ἡ ὑπόστασις, οὐχ ἡ ἀόριστος τῆς οὐσίας ἔννοια μηδεμίαν ἐκ τῆς κοινότητος τοῦ σημαινομένου στάσιν εὑρίσκουσα, ἀλλ' ἡ τὸ κοινόν τε καὶ ἀπερίγραπτον ἐν τῷ τινὶ πράγματι διὰ τῶν ἐπιφαινομένων ἰδιωμάτων παριστῶσα καὶ περιγράφουσα".

[77] Cf. Basil, *De Sp. S.* 18, 45: PG 32, 142.

[78] Cf. Basil, *Hom.* 24, 4: PG 31, 605B; *Ep. 9*, 3: PG 32, 272A.

[79] Cf. A. Milano, *Persona in teologia*, Edizioni Dehoniane, Naples 1987, p. 131. Basil also clarifies the fact that the commonality of the divine οὐσία should not be considered in a way analogous to that proper to created individuals of a common nature; it should not be understood as something "superior" (in the sense of broader in extension by way of universality) to the persons or divided amongst them (cf.

tion between οὐσία and hypostasis and (2) the subsistent reality of
the hypostasis understood as existence according to a concrete mode
assures the real distinctive consistency of hypostasis, at once a distinct
thing in its own right as well as a concrete real entity (and not just a
perceivable aspect of that reality). In this way hypostasis says much
more (or is at least much more explicit) than πρόσωπον. Whence: "it
is not enough to enumerate the differences of the πρόσωπα, but it is
furthermore necessary to recognize that every πρόσωπον exists in a
true hypostasis"[80].

The author of *Ep. 38* continues by applying this understanding of
distinction between οὐσία and ὑπόστασις when transposing the respective concepts to the divinity[81]. In the Trinity, the particularizing
marks shall furnish us with the necessary distinction: "διὰ τῶν ἰδιαζόντων σημείων ἀσύγχυτον ἐπὶ τῆς Τριάδος τὴν διάκρισιν
ἕξειν"[82]. *Secundum* the particularity of that by which they are known,
the Persons share nothing in common ("οὐδεμίαν κατὰ τὸ ἰδιάζον
τῶν γνωρισμάτων τὴν κοινωνίαν ἕξει"[83]), and the distinctive marks
are described as inconciliable and incommunicable[84]. Thus Basil (or
Gregory) characterizes the notion of ὑπόστασις according as a particularization of a commonly shared nature, incommunicably distinguishing it from every other ὑπόστασις. We are in certain respects
speculatively further than the reflections brought to bear on these
questions by Boethius himself. For Basil (or Gregory) explicitly introduces the notion of incommunicability, momentous in the concept of
personhood, while Boethius, as we shall see, only intimates this notion, implicitly at best, in discussing the independence proper to subsistences. For Basil (as for Boethius) the particularity of the Persons is
constituted by the distinctive marks (*particularitates*)[85]. The commu-

---

Basil, *Hom.* 24, 4: PG 31, 605B; *Ep.* 52, 1: PG 32, 393A; *De Sp. S.* 18, 47: PG 32, 153;
cf. A. Milano, *Persona in teologia*, Edizioni Dehoniane, Naples 1987, p. 141). The resulting unity is a real and concrete ontological unity. The same observation is made
by Gregory of Nyssa (*Oratio* 31, 15: PG 36, 149B) who emphasizes the objective
reality of the unity, in contrast to the purely mental unity holding for a community
of men.

80   Basil, *Ep. 210*, 5: PG 32, 776C.
81   Ps.-Basil, *Ep. 38*: *Lettres*, I, p. 83, 30-33.
82   Ps.-Basil, *Ep. 38*: *Lettres*, I, p. 84, 41-43.
83   Ps.-Basil, *Ep. 38*: *Lettres*, I, p. 85, 32-33.
84   "ἀσύμβατά φαμεν εἶναι καὶ ἀκοινώνητα τὰ ἐπιθεωρούμενα τῇ Τριάδι γνω-
     ρίσματα" – Ps.-Basil, *Ep. 38*: *Lettres*, I, p. 85, 39-40.
85   "δι' ὧν ἡ ἰδιότης παρίσταται τῶν ἐν τῇ πίστει παραδεδομένων προσώπων,
     ἑκάστου τοῖς ἰδίοις γνωρίσμασι διακεκριμένως καταλαμβανομένου, ὥστε διὰ

nity of substance (τῆς κατὰ τὴν οὐσίαν κοινότης) stands in contrast to the ἰδιάζον τῶν γνωρισμάτων, the particularity of the distinctive marks, the *proprietates individuales* which constitute for Basil (or Gregory) the persons of the Trinity[86].

Ὑπόστασις is then defined as the concourse of the particular properties: "ὑπόστασιν ἀποδεδώκαμεν εἶναι τὴν συνδρομὴν τῶν περὶ ἕκαστον ἰδιωμάτων"[87]. Strictly speaking, persons are distinguished according to their respective particularities and are not themselves the particularities through which they are distinguished[88]. The particular characters permit one individual to be separated from another: "ἐπὶ τὰ ἰδιάζοντα τρέψῃ τὴν θεωρίαν δι᾽ ὧν χωρίζεται τοῦ ἑτέρου τὸ ἕτερον"[89]. Through the particularities we have the distinction[90], and Basil will refer to them as the principle (τὸν λόγον) of separation[91], but a principle of separation is not identical with the thing separated. Nonetheless, because we are dealing with the Trinity, the particularities *are* the very Persons (the subsistent relations), however this does not mean that "person" is the particularities. In fact, the divine Persons are not equated with the (relational) particularities insofar as *persons* but only insofar as *divine* Persons[92].

Nevertheless, despite apparently speaking of the particularities as "signs" enabling us to distinguish the ὑπόστασις, Basil seems to want

---

τῶν εἰρημένων σημείων τὸ κεχωρισμένον τῶν ὑποστάσεων ἐξευρεθῆναι." – Ps.-Basil, *Ep. 38: Lettres*, I, p. 85, 41-44.

[86] Ps.-Basil, *Ep. 38*: PG 32, 333A; *Lettres*, I, p. 87, 83-87.

[87] Ps.-Basil, *Ep. 38*: PG 32, 336C; *Lettres*, I, p. 89, 4-6.

[88] This is already plain in Basil's first definition of ὑπόστασις, as expressed by the "διὰ τῶν": "τὸ κοινόν τε καὶ ἀπερίγραπτον ἐν τῷ τινὶ πράγματι διὰ τῶν ἐπιφαινομένων ἰδιωμάτων παριστῶσα καὶ περιγράφουσα" (Ps.-Basil, *Ep. 38: Lettres*, I, p. 82-83, 10-12).

[89] Ps.-Basil, *Ep. 38*: PG 32, 328A; *Lettres*, I, p. 82, 27-28.

[90] "Διὰ τῶν ἰδιαζόντων σημείων ἀσύγχυτον ἐπὶ τῆς Τριάδος τὴν διάκρισιν ἕξειν" – Ps.-Basil, *Ep. 38*: PG 32, 329A; *Lettres*, I, p. 84, 41-45.

[91] Ibid. The use of the term separation (χωρίζεται: p. 82, 28; διάκρισιν, κρίσιν: passim), to the extent that Basil intends more than mere distinction (and Basil insists upon the concreteness and clarity of the διάκρισις [ἀσύγχυτον: p. 84, 42; ἀσύμβατά φαμεν εἶναι καὶ ἀκοινώνητα: p. 85, 39-40; κἂν ὁ τῆς πίστεως λόγος ἀσύγχυτον καὶ διῃρημένην τὴν τῶν ὑποστάσεων διδάσκῃ διαφοράν: p. 91, 33-35]), may be significant. Basil can speak of a "separation" of hypostases precisely because they are considered as subsistences (ὑφεστῶσαν, στάσιν: p. 82, 5-10; ὑπάρξεως: p. 90, 12-14).

[92] Hence we remark, with regard to the work *La Personne du Christ* by J. Galot, that while the divine Persons are nothing other than (subsistent) relations, it does not follow from that that what it is to be a person is to be a relation, in relation or "relational" (cf. especially p. 27-34: *La Personne du Christ*, Duculot-Lethielleux, Paris 1969). Cf. infra, "THE RELATIVE CONCEPTUALIZATION OF J. GALOT", p. 502.

to treat ὑπόστασις as the signs themselves, and not as the person of which the particularities are the sign[93]. This is evident in the definition: "ὑπόστασιν ἀποδεδώκαμεν εἶναι τὴν συνδρομὴν τῶν περὶ ἕκαστον ἰδιωμάτων" and already manifest in "ἡ δὲ ὑπόστασις τὸ ἰδιάζον ἑκάστου σημεῖόν ἐστιν"[94]. Further, Basil affirms that ὑπόστασις is the particular sign of the existence of each person: "ἡ ὑπόστασις τὸ ἰδιάζον τῆς ἑκάστου ὑπάρξεως σημεῖόν ἐστι"[95] (this latter statement holds the positive content of indicating existence, carrying us back to the beginning of the epistle where Basil avers the subsistence of a ὑπόστασις). If ὑπόστασις is sometimes described as the conflux of the particularizing characters or as the *sign* of certain properties ascribed to an individual, it cannot be ignored that ὑπόστασις equally intends the individuals which are particularized and is likewise the object of the signification achieved by the particular marks, just as the ὑπόστασις of the Son serves (as sign) to reveal the ὑπόστασις of the Father[96]. We must remember that Basil is concerned with the Trinity, where the identifying particularity (ἀγεννητός, γεννητός, ἐκπορευτῶς[97]) is identical with the person for whom it is the particularizing mark. The linguistic complications are enormous, as, for example, the Son is *in* a ὑπόστασις: "οὐχ ὡς [ὁ Μονογένος] οὐκ ὄντος ἐν ὑποστάσει"[98]; the particularities are considered *in* the persons of the Trinity: "τῆς ἐπιθεωρουμένης αὐτοῖς ἰδιότητος"[99]; the persons *are* the concourse of the distinctive marks: "ὑπόστασιν ἀποδεδώκαμεν εἶναι τὴν συνδρομὴν τῶν περὶ ἕκαστον ἰδιωμάτων"[100]; the characters make known or *reveal* the ὑπόστασις: "τοῦ Πατρὸς ὑπόστασις ἐν τῇ τοῦ Υἱοῦ μορφῇ ἐπιγνώσκεται"[101]; etc.. But this complexity in no way detracts from the conceptual contributions Basil makes with regard to the notions of person and nature.

[93]   Except to the degree that the identity between the relative signs and the persons in God would likewise equate hypostasis with the person *in re.*

[94]   Ps.-Basil, *Ep. 38: Lettres,* I, p. 89, 62-63.

[95]   Ps.-Basil, *Ep. 38: Lettres,* I, p. 90, 12-14.

[96]   "Ὥστε ἡ τοῦ Υἱοῦ ὑπόστασις οἱονεὶ μορφὴ καὶ πρόσωπον γίνεται τῆς τοῦ Πατρὸς ἐπιγνώσεως, καὶ ἡ τοῦ Πατρὸς ὑπόστασις ἐν τῇ τοῦ Υἱοῦ μορφῇ ἐπιγινώσκεται, μονούσης αὐτοῖς τῆς ἐποθεωρουμένης ἰδιότητος εἰς διάκρισιν ἐναργῆ τῶν ὑποστάσεων" – Ps.-Basil, *Ep. 38. Lettres,* I, p. 92, 26-30.

[97]   See especially Gregory of Nazianzus, *Oratio XXXIX:* PG 36, 345-347.

[98]   Ps.-Basil, *Ep. 38: Lettres,* I, p. 91, 37.

[99]   Ps.-Basil, *Ep. 38: Lettres,* I, p. 91, 43.

[100] Ps.-Basil, *Ep. 38: Lettres,* I, p. 89, 4-6.

[101] Ps.-Basil, *Ep. 38: Lettres,* I, p. 92, 28-29.

A brief consideration of *Epistle 236*[102] provides a clear reaffirmation of the content of *Epistle 38.* In *Epistle 236*, οὐσία and ὑπόστασις are distinguished one from another as the common from the particular, universal nature from the determinate individual[103]. The ὑποστάσεις are particular, and for each distinctive characters have been defined[104]. Here the characters are distinguished from the persons (inasmuch as περὶ ἕκαστον). Moreover, the particular properties are *attributed to* each person[105]. Later, however, Basil effaces much of the distinction in declaring that that which is particular is the *distinctive character* (e.g., paternity): "κοινὸν ἡ θεότης, ἴδιον ἡ πατρότης"[106]. If this distinctive character is identical with the ὑπόστασις, then there remains only a logical distinction (which would account for the mental act of attribution[107]); if they are not identical, then both are simply particular. This is not problematic to the idea that one operate as a principle of determination responsible for the other's particularity; as we shall see in Boethius, the very particularizing principles are themselves particular, as, for example, humanity becomes *this* man via an individuating principle which is none other than *materia designata*, and not some *common* matter, or the Persons of the Trinity are particularized by particular and subsistent relations. In any event, the particularizing aspect, even if particular, never *exists* apart from the existence of the particular individual, and we shall later examine more closely this "unicity of act"[108]. The ensemble of these Basilian considerations furnishes us with the following summarical representation:

---

[102] Basil, *Ep. 236,* Ἀμφιλοχίῳ Ἐπισκόπῳ: PG 32, 875-886; *Lettres*, III, p. 47-55.

[103] "Οὐσία δὲ καὶ ὑπόστασις ταύτην ἔχει τὴν διαφορὰν ἥν ἔχει τὸ κοινὸν πρὸς τὸ καθ᾽ ἕκαστον, οἷον ὡς ἔχει τὸ ζῷον πρὸς τὸν δεῖνα ἄνθρωπον"; and "ὑπόστασιν δὲ ἰδιάζουσαν" – Basil, *Ep. 236: Lettres*, III, p. 53, 1-3.

[104] "τοὺς ἀφωρισμένους περὶ ἕκαστον χαρακτῆρας, οἷον πατρότητα καὶ υἱότητα καὶ ἁγιασμόν" – Basil, *Ep. 236: Lettres*, III, p. 53, 8-9.

[105] "καὶ τὸ τῶν προσώπων ἰδιάζον ὁμολογεῖσθαι ἐν τῷ ἀφορισμῷ τῶν περὶ ἕκαστον νοουμένων ἰδιωμάτων" – Basil, *Ep. 236: Lettres*, III, p. 54, 20-22.

[106] Basil, *Ep. 236, Lettres*, III, p. 53, 12-13.

[107] Y. Courtonne translates the passage: "*ce qui est particulier aux personnes sera confessé dans la distinction des propriétés particulières que la pensée attribue à chacune*" (*Lettres*, III, p. 54).

[108] Cf. infra, "ONTOLOGICAL PRINCIPLES BEHIND 'SUBSISTENTIA' AND 'SUBSTANTIA'", p. 115; cf. graph to "A POSSIBLE DIVISIVE CHRISTOLOGICAL ARGUMENT", p. 133.

οὐσία κοινὴ
common/universal, undetermined

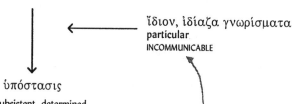

ἴδιον, ἰδίαζα γνωρίσματα
particular
INCOMMUNICABLE

ὑπόστασις

particular/concrete - subsistent, determined
sometimes defined as the concourse of the ἰδιωμάτα, whence an identification with
INCOMMUNICABLE, since at least part of what constitutes it is incommunicable

Gregory of Nazianzus

The same reasoning characteristic of Stoicism is found in both Gregory of Nazianzus and Gregory of Nyssa. In *Oratio XLII* of Gregory of Nazianzus, we read: *"Nimirum tria esse, quae dividantur, non naturis, sed proprietatibus"*[109]. The members of the Trinity are distinguished exclusively by the *proprietates*. These *proprietates*, according to Gregory, are themselves distinct but not diversified from the common essence of the divinity, and they constitute the several hypostases whom we call persons[110]. More than Basil, Gregory of Nazianzus emphasizes the completeness and subsistence *in se* proper to persons as well as the numerical distinctness of each of the divine persons[111]. Gregory, more clearly than Basil, further elucidates the distinction between the divine persons in terms of relations of origin[112]. Of particular importance, Gregory of Nazianzus is the first oriental theologian to have applied the conclusions of Trinitarian theological reflection to the mystery of the Incarnation[113]. Distinguishing "whatness" from "subject

---

[109] "Τὸ τρία εἶναι τὰ διαιρούμενα, οὐ φύσεσιν, ἀλλ᾽ ἰδιότησιν" – Gregory of Nazianzus, *Orat. 42: Supremum Vale*. PG 36, 477B.

[110] *"Deum porro cum dico, uno eodemque triplici lumine perstringamini: triplici quidem, quantum ad proprietates, sive hypostases, si cui hoc verbum magis arridet, sive personas"* ("Θεοῦ δὲ ὅταν ἔπω, ἑνὶ φωτὶ περιαστράφθητε καὶ τρισί· τρισὶ μὲν, κατὰ τὰς ἰδιότητας, εἴτουν ὑποστάσεις, ἔι τινι φίλον καλεῖν, εἴτε πρόσωπα") – Gregory of Nazianzus, *Orat. 39: In Sancta Lumina*: PG 36, 345CD; *Sources Chrétiennes*, 358, p. 170-172.

[111] Cf. Gregory of Nazianzus, *Orat.* 33, 16: PG 36, 236.

[112] Cf. Gregory of Nazianzus, *Orat.* 31, 34; *Orat.* 41: PG 36, 165B; 352A; 441C; cf. A. Milano, *Persona in teologia*, Edizioni Dehoniane, Naples 1987, p. 137.

[113] Cf. A. Grillmeier, *Christ in Christian Tradition*, John Knox Press, Atlanta 1975, I, p. 368-371; M. Richard, "L'introduction du mot 'hypostase' dans la théologie de

of a whatness", Gregory declares: "If I must speak synthetically, the Savior is constituted of one thing and another (ἄλλο μὲν καὶ ἄλλο), since the invisible is not identical to the visible... but not of one subject and another (ἄλλος δε καὶ ἄλλος). That is beyond discussion! ... I say: one thing and another (ἄλλο καὶ ἄλλο), the inverse of what occurs in the Trinity. There, in fact, there is subject and subject (ἄλλος καὶ ἄλλος), given that we must not confound the ὑποστάσεις, but not one thing and another (ἄλλο δε καὶ ἄλλο), since the Three are one and the same with respect to the divinity"[114]. There are "two φύσεις which come together in a single Son, and not two"[115].

Gregory of Nyssa

With greater speculative adeptness, Gregory of Nyssa develops a more lucid and logical elaboration of Trinitarian unity and division than either of the other Cappadocians. Besides the content of *Epistle 38* examined above, in the *Contra Eunomium*[116], Gregory asserts: *"in ratione substantiae unum et idem sunt inter se mutuo... sed in proprietatibus hypostaticis, minime conveniunt"*[117]. The first part states the non-multiplicity of the οὐσία while the second the non-commonality in the properties of the ὑποστάσεις. The persons share very much in common (the fullness of the divine nature) but nothing *insofar as* distinguished, whence Gregory asserts that nothing concurs in what is proper to the hypostases. *"Hypostases suis idiomatis et proprietatibus a se mutuo secernat"*[118]. It is through, or from (ἀπό), the ἰδιώμα that hypostases are separated[119].

When elucidating his understanding of the *ratio substantiae*[120], Gregory stresses the necessity of the ἰδιώμα for *complete substantiality*.

---

l'incarnation", *Mélanges de science religieuse* 2 (1945) p. 29-32, 189-190; A. Milano, *Persona in teologia*, Edizioni Dehoniane, Naples 1987, p. 138-139.

[114] Gregory of Nazianzus, *Ep.* 101: PG 37, 180AB.

[115] Gregory of Nazianzus, *Orat.* 37, 2: PG 36, 284.

[116] Gregory of Nyssa, *Contra Eunomium*, I: PG 45, 320.

[117] "Πέτρος γὰρ καὶ Ιακὼβ, καὶ Ιωάννης ἐν μὲν τῷ λόγῳ τῆς ὁσίας, οἱ αὐτοὶ ἦσαν ἀλλήλοις... ἐν δὲ τοῖς ἰδιώμασι τῆς ἑκάστου αὐτῶν ὑποστάσεως, ἀλλήλοις οὐ συνεφέροντο" – Gregory of Nyssa, *Contra Eunomium*, I: PG 45, 320BC.

[118] "τὰς ὑποστάσεις ἀπ' ἀλλήλων τοῖς ἐπιθεωρουμένοις ἰδιώμασι διακρίνων" – Gregory of Nyssa, *Contra Eunomium*, I: PG 45, 320C.

[119] Here there seems to be clearer distinction between the determining principles and the determined thing than found in Basil.

[120] Cf. Gregory of Nyssa, *Contra Eunomium*, I: PG 45, 301-312.

A substance's very existence is at stake taken away the properties of which it is the subject[121]: *"cum eum proprie esse negat, deberet etiam negare eum minus esse"*[122]. Once again we encounter the same movement from a rather universal notion of nature to its concrete substantiality provided it is combined with its particularizing characteristics; if the ἰδιώμα are denied the οὐσία, it lacks in completeness[123].

An inevitable problem inherent in this reasoning finally emerges when Gregory has to account for the non-subsistence (*in se*) of Christ's human nature when defending himself against the Apollinarian charge that he upheld a twofold Sonship in Christ. According as ὑπόστασις is characterized as concrete, existing, subsistent reality (in opposition to universal, abstract nature), we are faced, in the case of Christ, with the dilemma of having either to admit of a human subsistence or to render account of its absence. Yet the only means to preserve this humanity from subsistence seems to lie, from what has been said, in denying either the role of or the very existence of the particularizing principles which apparently necessarily produce the completed substance, the ὑπόστασις, the *omnino substantialis*. Consequently, we find Gregory reverting to an explanation founded upon the negation in Christ of the manifestation of what would be his human particularizing qualities[124]. The insufficiency of Gregory's solution is a somewhat vindicating anticipation of the path sought by Nestorius in attempting to unite the duality of the concrete individualized natures.

Note that, like Gregory of Nazianzus, Gregory of Nyssa employs the terms πρόσωπον and ὑπόστασις rather indifferently[125]. This situates ὑπόστασις closer to πρόσωπον (taken as "person") than what is perhaps typical of the later and philosophically more developed tradition

---

[121] *"Ipso subjecto, cui proprie nomen substantiae competit"* – Gregory of Nyssa, *Contra Eunomium*, I: PG 45, 305C.

[122] Gregory of Nyssa, *Contra Eunomium*, I: PG 45, 320D.

[123] "Ὡς γὰρ οὐκ ἔστιν ἄνθρωπον εἶναι, ᾧ μὴ τελείως ὁ κατὰ τὸ ὄνομα λόγος ἐφήρμοσται· τῷ δὲ ἐλλείποντι τῶν ἰδιωμάτων, ὅλος ὁ τῆς οὐσίας αὐτῷ συνδιαγράφεται λόγος·" (*"Quod autem proprietatibus rei caret, ei tota substantiae illius ratio abjudicatur"*) – Gregory of Nyssa, *Contra Eunomium*, I: PG 45, 320D.

[124] Cf. Gregory of Nyssa, *Ad Theoph. adv. Apoll.*: PG 45, 1276-1277. *"Primitiae vero naturae humanae... sunt illae quidem in divinitate, non tamen in peculiaribus suis proprietatibus"* ("Ἡ δὲ προσληφθεῖσα τῆς ἀνθρωπίνης φύσεως"): 1275CD (1276C). *"Quod in humanum est, non in proprietatibus naturae esse ostenditur":* 1278B.

[125] *"Ecclesia doceat fidem minime sciendendam et dividendam in pluralitatem substantiarum, sed in tribus personis et hypostasibus nihil secundum essentiam differentiae credendum esse"* ("Τῆς γὰρ Ἐκκλησίας δογματιζούσης, μὴ εἰς πλῆθος οὐσιῶν διασχίζειν τὴν πίστιν, ἀλλ᾽ ἐν τρισὶ προσώποις καὶ ὑποστάσεσι μηδεμίαν τὴν κατὰ τὸ εἶαι διαφορὰν πιστεύειν") – Gregory of Nyssa, *Contra Eunomium*, I: PG 45, 320D.

represented by Boethius[126], but since the Cappadocians are treating ὑπόστασις in the sense of "person" (distinguished from οὐσία), and because, as we have seen in Basil, it is identified as *subsistentia*, it follows that ὑπόστασις and πρόσωπον share virtually identical significations, and may therefore be used interchangeably[127].

Conclusion

In their explanation of the paradox of the Trinitarian unity and multiplicity, the Cappadocian Fathers demonstrate with superb limpidity that these are to be sought at different levels of consideration. Settling the terminological fluidity which nourished the Arian crisis, Basil specifies the concept of hypostasis attaching its signification to the concrete act of subsistence, thus distancing the notion of hypostasis from that of secondary substance and determining it to primary substance. In this way, to move from a concept of οὐσία to one of ὑπόστασις is to pass from the abstract to an act of existing *in se*: hypostasis is "that which properly, and in a perfect way, exists in itself"[128]. "Advancing the formula μία οὐσία - τρεῖς ὑποστάσεις, Basil salvaged both the ontological realism and the saving power of the Trinitarian mystery. He chose ὑπόστασις and adapted it to his designs, because, as much for its etymology as for its philosophical density, that term defended the possibility of designating the subsistence of a substantial being"[129].

The originality of the Cappadocians lies in using the word ὑπόστασις to designate the person in distinction from substance[130]. The distinction between ὑπόστασις and οὐσία had not been instituted during apostolic times; the Greek Fathers are the first to articulate it in order to resist the heretical temptation to advocate three distinct Gods or a single divine Person. This distinction between οὐσία

---

[126] Cf. infra, "RELATIVE ARCHITECTURE OF THE ONTOLOGICAL NOTIONS", p. 127.

[127] The complexity of the relation between these terms cannot be labored here; we shall re-encounter an important aspect of that relation when summarily considering pertinent elements of the philosophical framework of Nestorius.

[128] Basil, *Ep.* 210, 4: PG 32, 773; cf. A. Milano, *Persona in teologia*, Edizioni Dehoniane, Naples 1987, p. 144.

[129] A. Milano, *Persona in teologia*, Edizioni Dehoniane, Naples 1987, p. 144-145.

[130] "Substance", however, taken as uncircumscribed/undetermined, since they are evidently not distinguishing the strict (and Boethian) sense of substance (*substantia*) from ὑπόστασις taken as person in a way not identifying "person" with "concretized individual", that is primary substance from hypostasis understood as adding something to the notion of the former.

and ὑπόστασις (integrated into the Council of Constantinople in 381) represents a cultural and philosophical rupture with the ancient Greek perspective, inasmuch as it places a primordial (and ontological) value upon the individual, in contrast to the Greek philosophical conviction that universals have the preeminent claim to "truth"[131], and upholds the profoundly Christian vision of the intrinsic worth (i.e. perfection) of every person. Nevertheless, the concepts which prevail in the Cappadocian explanation of personality do not entirely transcend the physical order. A shortcoming resides in the fact that their effective understanding (i.e. their articulation) of the notions being distinguished partially defeats the results of the distinction. Οὐσία or φύσις, to follow the logic of their arguments and analogies, is mostly presented as the universal, undetermined nature, whereby it is set off from ὑπόστασις, expressing the concrete individualized nature. Besides the difficulty this presents with respect to the divine nature, the unity of which cannot be that of a universal (a point observed by both Basil and Gregory of Nyssa[132]), another consequence is that both terms (οὐσία and ὑπόστασις) refer to *nature*, according to its degree of ontological completeness or actualization. Ὑπόστασις or person delineates the individual subsistent (i.e. existent); and, aside from the acuity of the Boethian distinction we shall encounter between *subsistentia* and *substantia*[133], "person" is already confined to the very same category as the Boethian *persona*/πρόσωπον. Faced with the existing human nature of Jesus Christ, it would seem that we continue to stand in need of an adequate distinction between "person" and "nature" capable of distinguishing *concrete individuality* from personhood. As we shall see, it is precisely this difficulty which stood at the root of the maladroitness, as well as a certain astuteness, of Nestorius' resolution of the unity in Christ. For, equally influenced by Stoic philosophy,

---

[131] Universals here are understood in the ontologico-metaphysical sense, and truth is intended not in its gnoseological sense, but according to its identity with being; cf. G. Reale, *Storia della filosofia antica*, Vita e Pensiero, Milan 1992, vol. 5, p. 142, 282-283, 290-291.

[132] As mentioned above (note 79), Basil refuses to view the divine οὐσία as something "superior" (i.e. more extensive by way of universality) to the persons and divided amongst them (cf. Basil, *Hom.* 24, 4: PG 31, 605B; *Ep.* 52, 1: PG 32, 393A; *De Sp. S.* 18, 47: PG 32, 153; cf. A. Milano, *Persona in teologia*, Edizioni Dehoniane, Naples 1987, p. 141). The unity is rather real and concrete. Gregory of Nyssa (*Oratio* 31, 15: PG 36, 149B) likewise insists upon the objective reality of the unity, contrasting it with the purely logical communion of many men.

[133] Cf. infra, "SUBSISTENCE AND ITS RELATION TO SUBSTANCE", p. 110; "SPECIFIC ASPECTS OF SUBSTANTIA AND SUBSISTENTIA", p. 121.

Nestorius' proponing of the "prosopon of union"[134] and the "natural prosopa"[135], insofar as fully acknowledging the ontological plenitude of the humanity of Christ, demonstrates a profound awareness of and fidelity to the dictates of the metaphysics at issue. Unfortunately, at the time, those concerned with the mystery of the Incarnation were unable to see how these metaphysics might surmount the difficulty of providing for the conceptualization of a complete substance which does not subsist *in se*.

A word about individuality and the "problem of individuation"

As should be quite clear by now (and as will only become clearer), the notion of individuality appears most extensively throughout the historical discussion of personality, in every treatise dedicated to the ontology of person. Questions of individuality, naturally therefore, saturate the present work. The problem of the person – as we intend to show – is fundamentally a problem of individuation, since individuation (understood as embracing the aspects of incommunicability, subsistence, completeness and singularity) constitutes personhood[136]. In fact, the response to the basic Christological problem largely resides in an analysis of individuation[137].

The so-called "problem of individuation" concerns establishing the causes and principles of individuality (in the effort to acquire scientific knowledge of the fundamental makeup of the individual thing). An enormous amount of literature, both ancient and contemporary, is devoted to the question of individuation. Already in the Aristotelio-Stoic philosophical currents at the time of the Cappadocian Fathers the problem surfaces; Boethius consecrates explicit attention to individuation especially in his *De Trinitate* and his *Commentary on Porphyry's Isagoge*, works destined to have a tremendous influence throughout the Middle Ages[138]; and the Middle Ages witness a prolific occupation with questions concerning individuation in works by John Eriugena,

---

[134] See Nestorius, *Liber Heraclidis*, ed. Nau, 212, 214, 224-225, 242-243, 349, 411-412.

[135] Nestorius, *Liber Heraclidis*, ed. Nau, 230, 240, 242-244, 252, 267, 290, 297-299, 361.

[136] Person, as we shall see, can be defined as the most perfect of all individuals, or the most perfectly individual thing, and is constituted as such by the perfection of individuality, implying an indivisible intrinsic structure as well as divisibility or, more precisely, distinction, from all others.

[137] The truth of this affirmation shall be made clear in our subsequent study dedicated to the singular concrete subject of Christ.

[138] Not to mention the landmark inclusion of "individual" in Boethius' famous definition of person occurring in the *Contra Eutychen et Nestorium*.

Ordo of Tournai, Anselm of Aosta, Adelard of Bath, Clarembald of
Arras, William of Champeaux, Thierry of Chartres, Gilbert of Poitiers,
John of Salisbury, Peter Abelard, Avicenna, Averroes, Moses Maimon-
ides, Gersonides, Bedersi, Albert the Great, Roger Bacon, Bonaven-
ture, Thomas Aquinas, Henry of Ghent, Giles of Rome, Godfrey of
Fontaines, Peter of Auvergne, John Baconthorpe, James of Viterbo,
John Duns Scotus, Hervaeus Natalis, Richard of Mediavilla, Durand of
Saint Pourçain, Henry of Harclay, Walter Burley, William of Ockham,
Jean Buridan, Cajetan, Chrysostom Javellus, Francis Sylvester Ferrara,
Francis Suárez, and John of Saint Thomas.

At a general level, and as a presupposition to the various competing doctrines, individuality implies above all the concept of unity or
indivisibility. The individual, *ens indivisum in se*, enjoys a single act of
existence, in virtue of which singularity it remains undivided, or un-
distributed as it were to more than one existent. This indivision
proper to the existent thing (and the corresponding unicity of its existence) has traditionally been understood to have two very different
modes of realization: either in virtue of the simplicity of the individual
thing, or in virtue of a composition of diverse principles by which the
being is constituted one. In the first case, pertaining to purely spiritual beings, individuality is understood to be rooted in the simple
spiritual form itself, for which reason it is said to be "individuated by
itself". In the second case, individuality is considered to derive from
one or another of the collaborating intrinsic principles, and this principle receives the designation "principle of individuation". It was
primarily with respect to corporal substances that respective theories
of individuation were worked out. The vastly ranging theories span a
broad spectrum of often incompatible metaphysical standpoints. But
the common objective was to determine which of the essential or inhering components of a given body was responsible for its being this
individual among many[139]. Was it the matter? Was it the form? Or
was it the particular collection of accidents? Or some combination of
the foregoing?

For obvious reasons, we cannot attempt within these pages a synthetic overview of the historical development of the problem. The

---

[139] The object of investigation was the principle of numerical unity amongst natural
substances, what makes this individual to be this individual, and not simply a principle by which we can account for a substance's distinction from individuals of another species. Note, moreover, that what we are looking for is a metaphysical principle capable of *explaining* individuality, and this is not to be confused with seeking,
by conceptually descending as it were through the predicable grades, a logical
means of designating the ultimate singularity of a thing.

inherent difficulties of the issue – complicated by the further requirement of resolving questions on the concepts of being and relation (since either are advanced as legitimate candidates for principles of individuation) as well as the indissociable question of universals and their relation to particulars – suffice to make it a thesis unto itself. We simply draw attention to the paramount importance of the concept of individuality inseparably tied to our discussion of personality and destined to shape the formulation of Catholic dogma, and outline its most basic parameters as the question weaves its way into the heart of our investigation and plays a pivotal role in the doctrine of the men we have set out to study[140].

---

[140] We refer the reader to the following publications for a thorough introduction to the problem: M. McCORD ADAMS, *William Ockham*, 2 vols., University of Notre Dame Press, Notre Dame (IN) 1987, revised edition 1989; "Ockham on Identity and Distinction", *Franciscan studies* 36 (1976), p. 5-74; E. B. ALLAIRE, "Bare Particulars", *Philosophical Studies* 14 (1963), p. 1-7; M. M. ANAWATI, "St. Thomas et la métaphysique d'Avicenne", in *St. Thomas Aquinas*, E. Gilson (editor), Pontifical Institute of Medieval Studies, Toronto 1974, vol. I, p. 449-465; G. E. M. ANSCOMBE, "The Principle of Individuation", *Berkeley and Modern Problems, Proceedings of the Aristotelian Society*, suppl. vol. 27, 1953, p. 83-96; H. ANZULEWICZ, "Grundlagen von Individuum und Individualität in der Anthropologie des Albertus Magnus", in Aertsen, J. A./Speer, A. (editors), *Individuum und Individualität im Mittelalter*, Walter de Gruyter, Berlin/New York 1996 (*Miscellanea Mediaevalia* 24), p. 124-160; A. J. AYER, "Individuals", in *Philosophical Essays*, Macmillian and Company, London 1954, p. 1-25; "The Identity of Indiscernibles", in *Philosophical Essays*, Macmillian and Company, London 1954, p. 26-35; A. BÄCK, "The Islamic Background: Avicenna (B. 980; D. 1037) and Averroes (B. 1126; D. 1198)", in *Individuation in Scholasticism, The Later Middle Ages and the Counter-Reformation, 1150-1650*, J. J. E. Gracia (editor), State University of New York Press, New York 1994, p. 39-67; C. BÉRUBÉ, *La connaissance de l'individuel au Moyen Age*, Presses de l'université de Montréal/Presses universitaires de France, Montréal/Paris 1964; J. BOBIK, "Dimensions in the Individuation of Bodily Substance", *Philosophical Studies* (Maynooth) 4 (1954), p. 66-79; "La doctrine de saint Thomas sur l'individuation des substances corporelles", *Revue philosophique de Louvain* 51 (1953), p. 5-41; "The 'Materia Signata' of Cajetan", *NSchol* 30 (1956), p. 127-153; O. BOULNOIS, "Genèse de la théorie scotiste de l'individuation", in Mayaud, Pierre-Noël (editor), *Le problème de l'individuation*, J. Vrin, Paris 1991, p. 51-77; O. J. BROWN, "Individuation and Actual Existence in Scotistic Metaphysics. A Thomistic Assessment", *NSchol* 53 (1979), p. 347-361; H.-N. CASTAÑEDA, "Individuation and Non-Identity", *American Philosophical Quarterly* 12 (1975), p. 131-140; W. CHARLTON, "Aristotle and the Principle of Individuation", *Phronesis* 17 (1972), p. 239-249; K. C. CLATTERBAUGH, "Individuation in the Ontology of Duns Scotus", *Fransican Studies* 32 (1972), p. 65-73; G. J. COULTER, "St. Thomas Aquinas on explaining individuality", *ACPQ* 65 (1991), p. 169-178; J. F. COURTINE, "Le principe d'individuation chez Suárez et chez Leibniz", *Studia Leibnitiana*, suppl. 23 (1983), p. 174-190; C. D A ALTARI, "Individuo e principio d'individuazione in S. Bonaventura", *Studi Francescani* 58 (1961), p. 264-286; L. DE RAEYMAEKER, *Metaphysica generalis*, revised edition, E. Warney, Louvain 1935; A. F. DE VOS, "L'aristotélisme de Suárez et sa théorie de l'individuation", in *Actas. Congreso Internacional de Filosofía, Barcelona, 1948*, Istituto Luis Vives de Filosofía, Madrid 1949, vol. 3, p. 505-514; U. DEGL'INNOCENTI, "Animadversiones in Caietani doctrinam de corporum individua-

tione", *Divus Thomas* (Piacenza) 51 (1948), p. 19-45; "Del Gaetano e del principio d'individuazione", *Divus Thomas* (Piacenza) 52 (1949), p. 202-208; "Il pensiero di San Tommaso sul principio d'individuazione", *Divus Thomas* (Piacenza) 45 (1942), p. 35-81; "Il principio d'individuazione dei corpi e Giovanni di S. Tommaso", *Aquinas* 12 (1969), p. 59-99; A. GAZZANA, "La *materia signata* di S. Tommaso secondo la diversa interpretazione del Gaetano o del Ferrarese", *Gregorianum* 24 (1943), p. 78-85; A. M. GOICHON, *La philosophie d'Avicenne et son influence en Europe médiévale,* Adrien-Maisonneuve, Paris 1944; N. GOODMAN, "A World of Individuals", in *The Problem of Universals,* Charles Landesman (editor), Notre Dame University Press, Notre Dame (IN) 1956, p. 293-306; J. J. E. GRACIA, "Individuals as Instances", *Review of Metaphysics* 37 (1983), p. 39-59; "Suárez' Criticism of the Thomistic Principle of Individuation", in *Atti. Congresso di S. Tommaso d'Aquino nel suo VII Centenario,* Rome 1977, p. 563-568; "The Centrality of the Individual in the Philosophy of the Fourteenth Century", *History of Philosophy Quarterly* 8, no. 3 (1991), p. 235-251; "The Problem of Individuation", in *Individuation in Scholasticism. The Later Middle Ages and the Counter-Reformation 1150-1650,* J. J. E. Gracia (editor), State University of New York Press, New York 1994, p. 1-20; "What the Individual Adds to the Common Nature According to Suárez", *NSchol* 53 (1979), p. 221-233; *Individuality: An Essay on the Foundations of Metaphyics,* State University of New York Press, Albany 1988; *Individuation in Scholasticism, The Later Middle Ages and the Counter-Reformation, 1150-1650,* J. J. E. Gracia (editor), State University of New York Press, New York 1994; *Introduction to the Problem of Individuation in the Early Middle Ages,* 2nd revised edition, Philosophia Verlag, Munich/Vienna 1988; *Suárez on Individuation,* Marquette University Press, Milwaukee 1982; J. HACKETT, "Albert the Great", in *Individuation in Scholasticism,* J. J. E. Gracia (editor), University of N.Y. Press, New York 1994, p. 97-115; HOFFMANN, TOBIAS, "Individuation bei Duns Scotus und bei dem jungen Leibniz", *Medioevo* 24 (1998), p. 31-87; P. O. KING, "Jean Buridan", in *Individuation in Scholasticism. The Later Middle Ages and the Counter-Reformation 1150-1650,* J. J. E. Gracia (editor), State University of New York Press, New York 1994, p. 397-430; I. KLINGER, *Das Prinzip der Individuation bei Thomas von Aquin,* Münsterschwarzacher studien, No. 2, Vier-Türme Verlag, Münsterschwarzach 1964; N. KRETZMANN and E. STUMP (translators), *The Cambridge Translations of Medieval Philosophical Texts,* vol 1: *Logic and the Philosophy of Language,* Cambridge University Press, New York 1988; A. C. LLOYD, "Aristotle's Principle of Individuation", *Mind* 79 (1970), p. 519-529; M. J. LOUX (editor), *Universals and Particulars: Readings in Ontology,* 2nd edition, Notre Dame University Press, Notre Dame (IN) 1976; J. LUKASIEWICZ, "The Principle of Individuation", *Proceedings of the Aristotelian Society,* suppl. vol. 27 (1953), p. 69-82; B. J. MARTINE, *Individuation and Individuality,* State University of New York Press, Albany 1984; A. A. MAURER, "William of Ockham", in *Individuation in Scholasticism. The Later Middle Ages and the Counter-Reformation 1150-1650,* J. J. E. Gracia (editor), State University of New York Press, New York 1994, p. 373-396; L. B. MCCULLOUGH, "Leibniz's Principle of Individuation in His Disputatio metaphysica de principio individui of 1663", in *Individuation and Identity in Early Modern Philosophy. Descartes to Kant,* K. F. Barber and J. J. E. Gracia (editors), State University of New York Press, Albany 1994, p. 201-217; *The Early Philosophy of Leibniz on Individuation: A study of the "Disputatio metaphysica de principio individui" of 1663,* Diss., University of Texas, Austin 1976; R. MCINERNY, "Albert on Universals", in *Albert the Great Commemorative Essays,* F. Kovach and R. Shahan (editors), University of Oklahoma Press, Norman (OK) 1980, p. 3-18; J. W. MEILAND, "Do Relations Individuate?", *Philosophical Studies* 17 (1966), p. 65-69; W. O'MEARA, "Actual Existence and the Individual according to Duns Scotus", *Monist* 49 (1965), p. 659-669; J. OWENS, "Thomas Aquinas", in *Individuation in Scholasticism, The Later Middle Ages and the Counter-Reformation, 1150-1650,* J. J. E. Gracia (editor), State University of New York Press, New York 1994,

p. 173-194; "Thomas Aquinas: Dimensive Quantity as Individuating Principle", *Medieval Studies* 50 (1988), p. 279-310; R. PANIKAR, "Singularity and individuality. The double principle of individuation", *RIPh* 29 (1975), p. 141-166; W. PARK, "Common Nature and Haecceitas", *Franziskanische Studien* (West Germany) 71 (1989), p. 188-192; "Haecceitas and the Bare Particular", *Review of Metaphysics* 46 (1990), p. 375-398; "The Problem of Individuation for Scotus: A Principle of Indivisibility or A Principle of Distinction?", *Franciscan Studies* 48 (1988), p. 105-123; L. PETERSON, "Cardinal Cajetan (Thomas De Vio) (B. 1468; D. 1534) and Giles of Rome (B. CA. 1243/47; D. 1316)", in *Individuation in Scholasticism, The Later Middle Ages and the Counter-Reformation, 1150-1650*, J. J. E. Gracia (editor), State University of New York Press, New York 1994, p. 431-455; K. R. POPPER, "The Principle of Individuation", *Proceedings of the Aristotelian Society* 27 (1953), p. 107-112; E. PORTALUPI, "Das Lexicon der Individualität bei Thomas von Aquin", in Aertsen, J. A./Speer, A. (editors), *Individuum und Individualität im Mittelalter*, Walter de Gruyter, Berlin/New York 1996 (*Miscellanea Mediaevalia* 24), p. 57-73; W. V. QUINE, "Identity, Ostention and Hypostasis", *Journal of Philosophy* 47 (1950), p. 621-633; M.-D. ROLAND-GOSSELIN, *Le "De ente et essentia" de S. Thomas d'Aquin*, J. Vrin, Paris 1948, p. 49-134; J. ROSANAS, "El principio de individuación, según Suárez", *Ciencia y Fe* 6 (1950), p. 69-86; J. R. ROSENBERG, *The Principle of Individuation: A Comparative Study of St. Thomas, Scotus, and Suárez*, Catholic University of America Press, Washington D.C. 1950; T. M. RUDAVSKY, "The Jewish Tradition: Maimonides, Gersonides, and Bedersi", in *Individuation in Scholasticism, The Later Middle Ages and the Counter-Reformation, 1150-1650*, J. J. E. Gracia (editor), State University of New York Press, New York 1994, p. 69-96; V. P. SPADE, *Five Texts on the Mediaeval Problem of Universals: Porphyry, Boethius, Abelard, Duns Scotus, Ockham*, Hackett, Indianapolis 1994; R. SPECHT, *Francisco Suárez, Über die Individualität und das Individuationsprinzip*, 2 vols., Meiner, Hamburg 1976; P. F. STRAWSON, *Individuals*, Methuen and Company, London 1959; I. TONNA, "The Problem of Individuation in Scotus and other Franciscan Thinkers of Oxford in the 13th Century", in *De doctrina Ioannis Duns Scoti, Acta Congressus Scotistici Internationalis Oxonii et Edimburgi 11-17 sept. 1966 celebrati*, vol. 1, Rome 1968, p. 257-270; F. VAN STEENBERGHEN, *La philosophie au XIIIe siècle*, Publications Universitaires de Louvain, Louvain 1966; H. VEATCH, "Essentialism and the Problem of Individuation", *Proceedings of the American Catholic Philosophical Association* 47 (1974), p. 64-73; C. VOLLER, *Francis Suárez, On the Various Kinds of Distinctions*, Marquette University Press, Milwaukee 1947, reprint 1976; J. A. WEISHEIPL, "Albertus Magnus and Universal Hylomorphism", in *Albert the Great Commemorative Essays*, F. Kovach and R. Shahan (editors), University of Oklahoma Press, Norman (OK) 1980, p. 239-260; K. WHITE, "Individuation in Aquinas's Super Boethium de Trinitate, Q. 4", *ACPQ* 69 (1995), p. 543-556; D. WIGGINS, *Sameness and Substance*, Basil Blackwell, Oxford 1980; D. WINIEWICZ, "A Note on *Alteritas* and Numerical Diversity in St. Thomas Aquinas", *Dialogue* 16 (1977), p. 693-707; J. F. WIPPEL, "Godfrey of Fontaines: Disputed Questions 9, 10 and 12", *Franciscan Studies* 33 (1973), p. 351-372; "Godfrey of Fontaines, Peter of Auvergne, and John Baconthorpe", in *Individuation in Scholasticism, The Later Middle Ages and the Counter-Reformation, 1150-1650*, J. J. E. Gracia (editor), State University of New York Press, New York 1994, p. 221-256; "James of Viterbo", in *Individuation in Scholasticism, The Later Middle Ages and the Counter-Reformation, 1150-1650*, J. J. E. Gracia (editor), State University of New York Press, New York 1994, p. 257-269; *The Metaphysical Thought of Godfrey of Fontaines: A Study in Late Thirteenth-Century Philosophy*, The Catholic University of America Press, Washington D.C. 1981; A. B. WOLTER, "Duns Scotus on Intuition, Memory and Our Knowledge of Individuals", in *History of Philosophy in the Making*, L. J. Thro (editor), University Press of America, Washington D.C. 1982, p. 81-104; *Duns Scotus' Early Oxford Lecture on Individuation*, Old Mission Santa Barbara, Santa Barbara (CA) 1992;

"John Duns Scotus", in *Individuation in Scholasticism, The Later Middle Ages and the Counter-Reformation, 1150-1650*, J. J. E. Gracia (editor), State University of New York Press, New York 1994, p. 271-298; *The Philosophical Theology of John Duns Scotus*, M. McCord Adams (editor), Cornell University Press, Ithaca (NY) 1990; M. J. WOODS, "Identity and Individuation", in *Analytical Philosophy*, R. J. Butler (editor), 2nd series, Oxford 1965, p. 120-130.

I.4. SECOND OECUMENICAL COUNCIL

Concilium Constantinopolitanum (381)
TRINITARIAN ORTHODOXY, AND A SPECIFICATION OF LANGUAGE

(1) ἐν τρισὶ τελειοτάταις ὑποστάσεσιν, ἤγουν τρισὶ τελεί-
οις προσώποις [141].

"In three most perfect hypostases, or three perfect persons".

Of broad significance, from this council on, ὑπόστασις possesses its new signification as *person*, collated and identified
with πρόσωπον. Ὑπόστασις designates the subsistent thing,
the particular of a distinctive act of subsistence. Nevertheless,
despite its propinquity to *"subsistentia"*, the Latin tradition
continued until the time of Chalcedon to translate ὑπόστασις as *substantia* [142]. On one hand, this manifests a certain
conceptual behindedness on the part of the Latin church at
the time; on the other hand, the polyvalent semantical character of *"substantia"*, able to be taken in very different senses,
helped none to restrict its application in order to remove ambiguity. The distance between ὑπόστασις's acceptation as
substantia and its acceptation as *subsistentia* is indistinctly
marked, and this on account of important philosophical reasons (the nature of which we examine in Boethius [143]). This
must be kept in mind when exploring subsequent elabora-
tions, in particular, the conciliar acts of Chalcedon and the
personal letters of Leo the Great [144].

---

[141] DEC 28, 25-27.
[142] To eliminate the possibility of confusion in the Latin version of the Chalcedonian
definition, the deacon Rusticus translated the Greek ὑπόστασις with Rufinus of
Aquileia's *subsistentia*; cf. A. Grillmeier, *Christ in Christian Tradition*, John Knox
Press, Atlanta 1975, I, p. 538-539. In general, from the time of Rufinus of Aquileia,
in the second half of the fourth century, the Latins used *subsistentia* to translate
ὑπόστασις; cf. Rufinus, *Hist. eccl* I, 29: PL 21, 499-500; cf. A. Milano, *Persona in teologia*, Edizioni Dehoniane, Naples 1987, p. 365. The contribution of Rusticus to
the discussion of personality, particularly in Christology, has passed relatively unno-
ticed. Most noteworthy, however, is the fact that he identifies personality with subsistent act and the subsistence of the human nature in Christ with the person of the
Word! – cf. Rusticus, *Contra Aceph*: PL 67, 1198B; 1239B; cf. A. Milano, *Persona in teologia*, Edizioni Dehoniane, Naples 1987, p. 374.
[143] Cf. infra, on Boethius, "SUBSISTENCE AND ITS RELATION TO SUBSTANCE", p. 110; "SPECIFIC ASPECTS OF
SUBSTANTIA AND SUBSISTENTIA", p. 121.
[144] Cf. infra, *Concilium Chalcedonense*, §2, p. 86.

(2) ὡς μήτε τὴν Σαβελλίου νό-
σον χώραν λαβεῖν συγχεο-
μένων τῶν ὑποστάσεων εἴτ᾽
οὖν τῶν ἰδιοτήτων ἀναιρου-
μένων[145].

"There is no place for Sabelius's
diseased theory in which the
hypostases are confused and
thus their proper characteristics
detroyed".

The Council of Constantinople leaves no place for Sabellius'
diseased theory in which the ὑποστάσεις are confused and
thus their proper differences destroyed. A confusion of the
ὑποστάσεις eliminates the differences because, as we have
seen in Cappadocian theology[146], the differences necessarily
distinguish the ὑποστάσεις. The implicit argument, claiming
that to deny the distinction of the ὑποστάσεις results in the
destruction of the differences, abides by the principles of material implication, for it consists in the simple and logically
valid operation of "denying the consequent" of the condi-
tional already explicitly drawn out elsewhere by the Cappadocians and generically expressed by the axiom "difference
causes number". This confirmation of the ontological role
ascribed to the *particularitates* offers a significant touchstone
for Boethius as well.

(3) μήτε μὴν τὴν εὐομιανῶν καὶ
ἀρειανῶν καὶ πνευματομά-
χων βλασφημίαν ἰσχύειν, τῆς
οὐσίας ἢ τῆς φύσεως ἢ τῆς
θεότητος τεμνομένης[147].

"Nor may the blasphemy of
Eunomians and Arians and
Pneumatomachi prevail, with its
division of substance or of nature or of Godhead".

The passage insists that there be no division of sub-
stance/essence/nature. The terms οὐσία and φύσις seem to
be well established and identified or at least coextensive with
one another. We must be cautious however, since the terms
are not always employed identically, as is manifest with Nestorius and as Cyril of Alexandria's theology attests when describing the union in Christ κατὰ φύσιν[148]. Φύσις, as we shall see,

---

[145] DEC 28, 27-30.
[146] See especially supra, "INTEGRATION OF THESE CONCEPTS IN THE WRITINGS OF BASIL THE GREAT ~
GREGORY OF NYSSA", p. 39; "GREGORY OF NYSSA", p. 47.
[147] DEC 28, 30-34.
[148] "ἀλλ᾽ ἑνωθεὶς κατὰ φύσιν" (DEC 52, 12-13); "οὐκ ἀπόχρη γὰρ τοῦτο πρὸς
ἕνωσιν φυσικήν" (DEC 52, 27-28); "τῇ καθ᾽ ἕνωσιν φυσικήν" (DEC 59, 28-29).
Cf. infra, *Concilium Ephesinum*, §4, p. 82.

must in certain respects retain its distinction from οὐσία, as for example, the concretized nature is distinguished in thought from its abstract essentiality. Nestorius, as we intend to show, might have had a poignant insight in this regard[149].

(4)   Καὶ τὸν τῆς ἐνανθρωπήσεως   "And we preserve undistorted
      δὲ τοῦ κυρίου λόγον ἀδιά-   the accounts of the Lord's tak-
      στροφον σῴζομεν[150].   ing of humanity".

The mystery of the Incarnation is somehow wholly expressed by the term ἐνανθρωπήνιν signifying both the act (becoming) and object (the taken substantial form) of the assumption. The breadth of that substantial form, the nature "in which" the Logos comes to be, though certainly including, is not explicitly restricted to an individual nature. The Lord's "taking of humanity" carries with it much more than simply becoming a particular man, "for by his incarnation the Son of God united himself in some sense with every human being"[151]. It is worth observing that patristical and conciliar language, from the first pronunciation in Nicea, never narrows the extension and profound implication of Christ's ἐνανθρωπήνιν. We intend to comment on the mystery of the extension of the assumption when considering the assumptive act itself in our study of the Incarnation planned as a sequel to this thesis.

---

[149] Cf. infra, "CORRESPONDENCE BETWEEN THE PHILOSOPHY OF NESTORIUS AND THE CAPPADOCIANS", p. 62; "AXIS PLACED IN RELIEF BY CYRIL.", notes 210 & 216.
[150] DEC 28, 38-40.
[151] Concilium Vaticanum II, Constitutio pastoralis de ecclesia in mundo huius temporis, 22 (DEC 1082, 2-3): "Ipse enim, Filius Dei, incarnatione sua cum omni homine quodammodo se univit". Cf. infra, Concilium Ephesinum, §1, p. 81.

I.5. NESTORIUS AND CYRIL OF ALEXANDRIA

Nestorius and Nestorianism

Bishop of Constantinople (†451), Nestorius belonged to a philosophical culture dominated by realism and naturalistic tendencies. Probably a disciple of Theodore of Mopsuestia, Nestorius was formed in the Antiochian "school" characterized in Christology by what has been referred to as the "Logos-anthropos schema", a perspective emphasizing the proper concrete reality of each of the two natural elements in Christ, the human and the divine. After becoming patriarch of Constantinople in 428, Nestorius engendered extensive scandal by rejecting the already popular expression "Mary mother of God" (which he substituted with "mother of Christ"[152]). The real motive for that rejection seems to have been a legitimate concern for the Christian kerygma, inasmuch as the title "Theotokos" had become a prop for the Arians and Apollinarians who defended it in attacking the true divinity of Christ, understood as compromised by its intimate unity with the flesh[153]. From the whole of his theology, including the *Liber Heraclidis* (which comes only after the Council of Ephesus and plays no role in that discussion), it is doubtful that Nestorius professed the heretical position concerning the dihypostasism attributed to him by Cyril of Alexandria[154]. However, the formal condemnation of the Council of Ephesus in 431 was entirely appurtenant for what concerns Nestorius' refusal of the exchange of predicates with respect, in particular, to his human generation[155]. The Nestorian heresy, as it came to be called, and as it evolved from the actual teaching of the patriarch, maintained, among other things, that: a) Christ is a perfect man like each of us, wherefore his human nature possesses its own subsis-

---

[152] "τὴν ἁγίαν παρθένον Χριστοτόκον, οὐ θεοτόκον" – Nestorius, Ἐπιστολὴ δευτέρα πρὸς Κύριλλον (DEC 47, 36-37). Such a refusal of the exchange of predicates, demonstrates Nestorius' radically false understanding of the person of the Word.

[153] Cf. A. Grillmeier, *Christ in Christian Tradition*, John Knox Press, Atlanta 1975, I, p. 447-448 & note 3, 451-452; cf. J. A. Sayes, *Jesucristo, Ser y Persona*, Aldecoa, Burgos 1984, p. 26.

[154] Cf. A. Grillmeier, *Christ in Christian Tradition*, John Knox Press, Atlanta 1975, I, p. 447-463; A. Milano, *Persona in teologia*, Edizioni Dehoniane, Naples 1987, p. 176-178.

[155] Cf. B. Sesboüé, *Histoire des Dogmes*, tome I: *Le Dieu du Salut*, Desclée, Paris 1994, p. 390-392.

tence and its own autonomy; b) the Word dwells in the humanity as in
a temple; c) Christ as man and Christ as divine are two distinct subjects, forming a union in a moral sense alone; d) because the union
between the subjects is accidental, the properties of one cannot be
attributed to the other, whence; e) Mary is not the mother of God
(θεοτόκος), but the mother of Christ. It was particularly the latter
issue which sparked the heated controversies between Nestorius and
Cyril of Alexandria. The Alexandrians, who especially insisted upon
the unity of Christ, taking as a point of theological departure the divine person of the Word instead of the empirical reality of the human
nature, affirmed that Mary was the mother of God and that God had
suffered. In the opinion of Nestorius, such expression was inappropriate (whence the substitution *Christotokos*), since the Word of God
(which Nestorius seems to have confused with the divine nature) cannot have been born, suffered and died on the cross, but the man
Christ underwent change, birth, suffering and death. In so arguing,
Nestorius successfully maintained the inalterable character and distinctness of each of the natures in the union, but effectively misses the
concept of union according to hypostasis between the natures, reducing the union to that of a non-substantial "conjunction" in his effort
to avoid every possibility of a confusion of natures.

In his opposition to Apollinarius, Nestorius is pushed to emphasize
the distinction between the natures. Nevertheless, he acknowledges a
certain unity which takes place at the level of the "πρόσωπον"[156]. Far
from fostering "division at all cost", Nestorius is legitimately concerned with finding an ontological basis for unity. His inability to
properly conceptualize the *mode* of union, however, results in an explanation laden with inconsistency.

Correspondence between the philosophy of Nestorius and the Cappadocians

The Christological position of Nestorius and its philosophical expression, which provoked the fiery controversies leading to the arduously
formulated definition of Chalcedon[157], is equally stamped with Stoic

---

[156] The key term "prosopon" indicates for Nestorius the collectivity of the properties
possessed by the complete οὐσία which is a ὑπόστασις. A closer look at these
terms is had in what follows.

[157] Particularly as a result of the *mia physis* formula employed by Cyril of Alexandria in
defense of the unity of Christ against Nestorian dualism. In Constantinople, the
monk and archimandrite Eutyches, of grand reputation both for his holiness and
political influence, never ceased repeating the Cyrillian formula "a single nature of

elements. For Nestorius as well, nature is the indeterminate reality which receives its qualification or determination through the totality of the particular differences or properties [158]. This prior concept of nature, called essence or οὐσία, is the incomplete nature, indistinct, and unknowable, and is rendered complete, distinct and knowable by the properties, the *notae individuantes*. Essence, then, is the nature prior to any determination. Most commonly however, when Nestorius speaks of nature, he intends the completed nature, the terminated nature. Nature in this sense, φύσις, indicates the same essence under the aspect of determination, according as the essence receives a *mutatio*: "the things that have been altered from their primordial essence, uniquely possess the nature in which they have been altered" [159]. Nestorius' distinction between the determined and undetermined senses of nature clarifies his contention with Monophysitism. Nestorius is determined to oppose a union *in natura* advocated by those who confess that "after the union the two natures are no longer considered because they have been united in essence, the two having become one" [160]. For Nestorius, union *in essentia* is based not on the nature insofar as particularized or on the determining particularities, but on what is purely essential to the nature aside from its concrete determination [161]. Nature qualified as completed, designates the concrete entity, as opposed to abstract or formal reality.

---

the Word incarnate", to which he added his own heterodox theology according to which the human nature was absorbed by and even converted into the divine nature in the union. The polemics triggered by this led to the requested intervention of Pope Leo and a series of rather boorish conciliar convocations harmoniously concluded by the Council of Chalcedon.

[158] Cf. in this regard L. I. Scipioni, op. cit., p. 45-67, 99-109; and M. Richard, *L'Introduction du Mot "Hypostase" dans la Théologie de l'Incarnation*, Opera Minora, II, p. 243-270.

[159] Nestorius, *Liber Heraclidis*, 25 (all citations of this work correspond to the edition by F. Nau, *Le Livre d'Héraclide de Damas*, Paris, 1910). Note that the term φύσις has acquired a more concrete, more "substantial" sense than οὐσία (an acceptation which stands behind the ordinary use of our "physical" to refer to *tangible* realities). This has its roots in the efficient causality originally connected with the Aristotelian notion of φύσις and is contrasted to the formal causality proper to οὐσία taken as secondary substance. The distinction currently being made by Nestorius between essence (οὐσία) and nature (φύσις) loosely corresponds to the later Boethian distinction between *natura* and *subsistentia*.

[160] Nestorius, *Liber Heraclidis*, 128.

[161] L. I. Scipioni remarks that *"il valore formale del termine 'essenza' sia quello di contenuto sostanziale e essere specifico della natura"* – op. cit., p. 53. It is important to keep in mind that πρόσωπον – a predominant explanatory reality in Nestorius' system – extends from the nature (as completed essence) and not from the essence prescinding from determination.

A remarkable similarity exists between the metaphysical independence attributed to "nature" (φύσις) by Nestorius and that attributed to the corresponding notion of *subsistentia* as it shall be defined by Boethius. For Nestorius, "the completed nature does not need another nature in order to be and to live; because it possesses in itself and has received all that is required to exist"[162], and "in a natural composite, we see that neither of the natures contributing to its formation is complete, but they need each other in order to live and to subsist"[163]. Boethius will employ a nearly identical expression: "for a thing has subsistence when it does not require accidents in order to be... for they do not depend on accidents for their being; for they are already provided with their proper and specific differences"[164]. Now, man is a complete nature, and the Incarnation consists in the union between two complete natures. Nestorius is about to run against the same metaphysical wall which stood more than a century later in the course of Boethius. But before we consider the difficult consequences of legitimately recognizing the concrete reality of Christ's humanity, we must first, as has been óur procedure until now, examine the principles responsible for the completion of that nature.

These are, of course, none other than the "differences", the "properties", the "distinctions", the "definitions". These "differences" are what determine the nature, constituting its recognizability, and distinguishing it from every other nature. Repeating Gregory of Nyssa's insistence upon the *proprietates* for the completion of the substance/ὑπόστασις, Nestorius affirms that if any of these *notae individuantes* are removed or excluded, the nature remains incomplete; and where the nature is incomplete, there is no real union between it and another, nor can it be said to remain after the union[165]. Because the Incarnation involves the assumption of a perfect human nature, Nestorius is wont to consider the assumed nature as complete in itself and as therefore possessing every property ascribed to an individual

---

[162] Nestorius, *Liber Heraclidis*, 418.
[163] Ibid.
[164] Boethius, *Contra Eutychen*, III, 45-46; 52-54: "*Subsistit enim quod ipsum accidentibus, ut possit esse, non indiget... nam neque ipsa indigent accidentibus ut sint; informata enim sunt iam propriis et specificis differentiis*". Cf. infra, "SPECIFIC ASPECTS OF SUBSTANTIA AND SUBSISTENTIA", p. 121.
[165] "If every difference is suppressed, there is no more union... If every delimitation of the nature is cut away, how could the union not entail the elimination of the differences of the natures?" – Nestorius, *Liber Heraclidis*, 226.

man[166]. Taken in an exaggerated way, this seems to suggest the *assumptus homo*, but the properties to which Nestorius is referring need not include those by which an individual man is *this* man, but simply everything proper to him as *man* (though it is doubtful Nestorius saw the importance of this distinction, as is evidenced in his lack of appreciation for the one πρόσωπον of Cyril of Alexandria). Accordingly, Nestorius will praise those "conserving without confusion the natures and their properties"[167]. However, with regard to those who would negate the differences in denying the πρόσωπον of the nature, Nestorius is less adulating: for Nestorius, Cyril of Alexandria would eliminate the very reality of the humanity by denying its own πρόσωπον precisely inasmuch as he discerns but a single πρόσωπον for both the divine and the human[168]. Cyril would destroy the humanity because to deny the πρόσωπον is to deny the essence as well; because if the essence is truly an existing nature, then the collectivity of its distinctive properties – and this is the πρόσωπον[169] – cannot be absent.

Πρόσωπον *and* ὑπόστασις

"I divide the properties of the union between each of the natures, in such a way that each of the natures subsists in its hypostasis"[170]. If the natures are particularized, then they are necessarily in a hypostasis, which signifies exactly the *concrete* reality, *natura completa*. A. Grillmeier makes a meaningful observation about the sense of the term hypostasis as revealed in the Latin translation of Nestorius' sermon of 25 March 431 by Marius Mercator[171]. There ὑπόστασις is translated by *substantia* and simply means real and concrete particularity. The hypostasis is the *natura completa*, the οὐσία insofar as determined by its entire set of particular properties which themselves constitute the

---

[166] "The Incarnation has not come to us as something incomplete... but because the humanity is considered in a full sense the nature of man, it possesses in a complete way the properties of men" – Nestorius, *Liber Heraclidis*, 302-303.

[167] Nestorius, *Liber Heraclidis*, 254.

[168] "The differences subsist because there is no confusion or destruction because you [Cyril] would attribute the diversity of the natures, naturally, to one single nature and to one sole πρόσωπον of this nature, and eliminate that which is without πρόσωπον and without its very essence, namely the humanity" – Nestorius, *Liber Heraclidis*, 339-340.

[169] Cf. Nestorius, *Liber Heraclidis*, 321-322; Grillmeier, op. cit., p. 506-507.

[170] Nestorius, *Liber Heraclidis*, 291.

[171] "*Coniunctionis igitur confiteamur dignitatem unam, naturam autem substantias duplices*": cf. F. Loofs, *Nestoriana*, Halle 1905, 340[17f]; cf. A. Grillmeier, op. cit., p. 458.

πρόσωπον[172]. It is through this πρόσωπον that the ὑπόστασις is known. Any particularized nature, then, is furthermore also with its πρόσωπον which is the recognizable expression of its concreteness[173]. The first sense of πρόσωπον is that which indicates the form, image and appearance of the nature; hence the one prosopon of Christ is the "figure of his hypostasis"[174]. Yet, more than mere appearance, it is the ensemble of the totality of the properties, and is in precisely this sense that which distinguishes, terminates, the natures (whence the impossibility of its denial). According to L. I. Scipioni[175], when speaking of πρόσωπον in the concrete sense, Nestorius identifies it with the *natura completa*, ὑπόστασις; formally speaking, however, πρόσωπον performs the *causal role* of completing the nature, its final effectuation[176]. Such an understanding of the relation between the *notae individuantes* and the ὑπόστασις was already evidenced in Basil[177]. Ὑπόστασις, then, names the nature insofar as completed; it is the term of the determining role of the properties[178]. With regard to the human nature of Christ, complete and in possession of all the properties and differences accruing to men, who can deny that the flesh "is in its hypostasis"[179]? For this reason, Nestorius will criticize the Manicheans who claim "that the change of form (from God to man) has terminated in a form without hypostasis"[180], Sabellius who posits "the prosopa without hypostasis and without essence"[181], and any who call the body of Christ "a form[182] without hypostasis"[183]. In Christ, the natures

---

[172] Cf. Nestorius, *Liber Heraclidis*, 80, 116, 131, 230, 242, 297, 299, 321-322.
[173] "It is not without hypostasis and without prosopon that each of them [the natures in Christ] is known in the diversities of the natures" – Nestorius, *Liber Heraclidis*, 304. Thus "hypostasis" names the same thing as does "physis" when the latter is taken according as it expresses the nature in its concreteness (in which regard it is distinct in signification from "οὐσία").
[174] Nestorius, *Liber Heraclidis*, 229.
[175] Cf. L. I. Scipioni, op. cit., p. 67.
[176] Cf. ibid.: "'due prosopa naturali' nel senso concreto di 'due nature complete e distinte'... 'prosopon naturale' è l'elemento che determina e costituisce la natura come completa e distinta".
[177] Cf. supra, "INTEGRATION OF THESE CONCEPTS IN THE WRITINGS OF BASIL THE GREAT ~ GREGORY OF NYSSA", p. 39.
[178] It is therefore equivalent to "physis" taken as concretely signifying the essence, though its name, contrary to physis, does not directly say or signify the essence.
[179] Nestorius, *Liber Heraclidis*, 233.
[180] Nestorius, *Liber Heraclidis*, 22-23.
[181] Nestorius, *Liber Heraclidis*, 316.
[182] σχῆμα.
[183] Nestorius, *Liber Heraclidis*, 127.

are not without hypostasis, precisely because they really, concretely, exist.

Consequences for Nestorius' interpretation of the unity in Christ

Every nature therefore has its own characteristics, appearances and individuality, its own πρόσωπον. Πρόσωπον is the collectivity of properties which brings the ὑπόστασις into real existence (starting from οὐσία) and equally the outward expression of the concrete nature. Representing the final point in the analysis of nature, it becomes for Nestorius the basis of his attempt to explain the union of the natures in Christ. Since the union cannot be effected according to essence, there remains for Nestorius only the realm of the πρόσω-πον[184]. Πρόσωπα can be united, natures (essences) cannot. Πρόσω-πον stands for the *ens concretum*, for the task is to account for the unity between two concrete natures. The exclusion of a union of "natures" intends to exclude union in the line of essences, that is, a unity based upon the physis *qua* essence (as opposed to physis *insofar as* concretized, i.e., according to its distinctive properties, which pertains to the ὑπόστασις *qua* ὑπόστασις[185]). The sphere of the individual properties alone can provide Nestorius with an ontic basis for grounding the unity in Christ, because, outside of the οὐσία, there remains only the *notae individuantes* in the ontic structure of a concrete reality. The fundamental deficiency in continuing with this approach is obvious – for, the unity is inevitably expressed as the coming together or summation of the properties of both natures; however, given Nestorius' metaphysical starting points, it is difficult to see where else he might have sought a ground for the union. The structure and status of the natures which emerges from the foregoing discussion can be condensed in the following way:

---

[184] "Not that the Son be one and the Word God another; the first signifies the union, the second the essence... one indicates the πρόσωπον, the other the nature" – Nestorius, *Liber Heraclidis*, 361-362. The term "Word", for Nestorius, signifies only the divine nature as such, and not the Person of the union.

[185] Φύσις *is* the essence but signified according to its concreteness. Thus the essence in its completed state is really the same as physis, though the proper notion of the essence *as such* does not include that determination. Note that the concrete realm of the hypostasis constitutes the Nestorian basis for union, for "that which is only according to hypostasis belongs also to several" – Nestorius, *Liber Heraclidis*, 233.

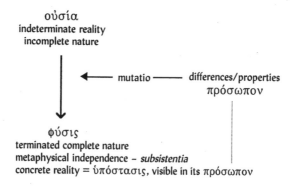

As regards the particularities of the mode of union proposed by Nestorius, without going into detail, we simply observe that, rather than expressing that unity in terms of the Logos as the unique subject, in contrast with Cyril of Alexandria, Nestorius speaks of "the Christ" in which the πρόσωπα of both natures come together[186]. That unity is described in terms of a conjunction (*synapheia* or *coniunctio*), in contrast to "union" (ἕνωσις), suggesting an exteriority which would reduce the Incarnation to a moral union between the natures. However, as A. Grillmeier remarks, Nestorius' aversion for the term "ἕνωσις" stemmed from its proximity to the natural union of the Apollinarians[187]. Given the level at which unity may be affirmed in the Nestorian framework, the πρόσωπον of each nature is united to the other in a "πρόσωπον of union"[188]. In his struggle to find an ontic basis for the unity of the one πρόσωπον, Nestorius finally speaks, in the *Liber Heraclidis*, of the "compensation" of the πρόσωπα, each natural πρόσωπον making use of the other[189]. Unfortunately, because the "giving and taking"[190] between the natures is restricted exclusively to their πρόσωπα (understood as the marks of the οὐσία and that by

[186] Cf. in this regard, A. Grillmeier, *Christ in Christian Tradition*, John Knox Press, Atlanta 1975, I, p. 453-454; F. Loofs, *Nestoriana*, Halle 1905, 295⁷⁻⁹.

[187] Cf. A. Grillmeier, *Christ in Christian Tradition*, John Knox Press, Atlanta 1975, I, p. 459.

[188] Cf. Nestorius, *Liber Heraclidis*, 144, 151, 194, 218; A. Grillmeier, *Christ in Christian Tradition*, John Knox Press, Atlanta 1975, I, p. 507, 510-512.

[189] Cf. Nestorius, *Liber Heraclidis*, 194, 233-234; A. Grillmeier, *Christ in Christian Tradition*, John Knox Press, Atlanta 1975, I, p. 462; J. A. Sayes, *Jesucristo, Ser y Persona*, Aldecoa, Burgos 1984, p. 28.

[190] Nestorius, *Liber Heraclidis*, 223, 233.

which it is made known), the natures as such seem to abide unaffected by that "compensation" and to remain external to one another ontologically speaking. Of course, the πρόσωπα are not to be understood as separable accidents of the real natures; they are not mere appearances or roles, but something substantial inasmuch as they belong to the realm of the ἰδίως ποιόν responsible for the completion of the individual nature[191]. The idea of their "mutual compensation" is moreover expanded by the notion of the real interpenetration of the natures or perichoresis[192]. The natures are not intended by Nestorius as existing apart from one another[193]; rather a substantial unity is sought which nevertheless respects the concrete individual integrity of both. Operating from within the current metaphysical view of the *ens concretum*, besides the essences, there are only the individual notes with which to build a concept of the personal unity in Christ. *Unless*, perhaps, one steps outside of the perspective of the individual natures themselves, in order to regard the principle of their individuality as a possible source of community, something Nestorius never did. If, however, all of the elements involved in the analysis of the *ens concretum* – the dynamic or causal principles as well as the static or completed thing and all of its properties – can provide no ontological basis for the union, then the solution indeed lies in another direction. According to A. Grillmeier, Nestorius' ultimate limitation consisted in the fact that "he had no idea of going beyond the individuality of the concrete nature and asking for a deeper analysis of the independence of the concrete spiritual being"[194]. The apparent implication, however, of such a conclusion is that individuality and independence are separable notions; but, as we shall see, the latter may be understood as but an expression of the former when realized to the fullest[195], thus replanting the problem of personal ontology on ancient Stoic soil.

---

[191] Cf. A. Grillmeier, *Christ in Christian Tradition,* John Knox Press, Atlanta 1975, I, p. 512.

[192] Cf. Nestorius, *Liber Heraclidis,* 184; cf. A. Grillmeier, *Christ in Christian Tradition,* John Knox Press, Atlanta 1975, I, p. 515.

[193] Cf. Nestorius, *Liber Heraclidis,* 141; A. Grillmeier, *Christ in Christian Tradition,* John Knox Press, Atlanta 1975, I, p. 516.

[194] A. Grillmeier, *Christ in Christian Tradition,* John Knox Press, Atlanta 1975, I, p. 517-518.

[195] Cf. especially, F. L. B. Cunningham (editor), *Christ and His Sacraments,* from *Theology: A Basic Synthesis for the College,* 3 vol., vol III, Priory Press, Dubuque (Iowa) 1958, p. 104-106.

Cyril of Alexandria

If Nestorius distinguishes the natures to the point that he cannot find
a suitable means to unite them, Cyril of Alexandria (c. 370-444) prevails in showing their substantial union, even if the ambiguities of his
language tends to obscure their distinction. Bishop of Alexandria and
heir to a theological tradition stressing the unity between the divine
and human natures in the unique subject of the Logos[196], Cyril of Alexandria fought vigorously against both of the great heresies, Arianism and Nestorianism. With a certain degree of politico-religious tension already subsisting between the imperial city, the "New Rome",
and the metropolitan Alexandria, Cyril unhesitatingly and precipi-
tously intervened against Nestorius, rapidly becoming his adversary.
The conflictive exchange took the form of a series of letters of progressive doctrinal vigor, ultimately reproduced in the Council of
Ephesus, and in which Cyril demonstrates a profound sense of the
Nicene faith which he brilliantly associates with biblical references to
the existence, origin and identity of Christ[197]. Against the deleterious
heresy of Nestorianism, Cyril was defending the *real unity* of Christ.
While the battle between Cyril and Nestorius was exacerbated by terminological imprecisions (with respect to the semantic value of οὐσία, φύσις and ὑπόστασις), the struggle was more than a discussion
of language. Cyril knew what he was defending: the real substantial
unity between the divine and human natures in a single person.
Nonetheless, while he affirmed the integrity of the human nature
along with that of the divine nature, Cyril, in his struggle for unity,
frequently spoke of "a single nature of the incarnate Logos". Cyril was
convinced that this expression had its origin with Athanasius[198]; however, its true source was Apollinarius of Laodicea[199]. Unfortunately,
such a use of language lent itself to equivocation and opened a door

---

[196] A tradition which has received the appellation "Logos-sarx" and which has its speculative starting point in a recognition of the Logos as the indivisible center of unity
in the God-man and primordial principle of his saving works. Because the Alexandrian school tended frequently to exalt the preeminence of the divine nature with
respect to the human, its obvious liability consisted in impairing the perfection of
Christ's manhood, as clearly evidenced in the case of Apollinarianism.

[197] Cf. B. Sesboüé, *Histoire des* dogmes, tome I, *Le Dieu du salut*, Desclée, Paris 1994,
p. 375-378.

[198] Cf. Athanasius, *Rect. fid. ad Reg.* 1, 9: PG 76, 1212-1213.

[199] Cf. A. Grillmeier, *Christ in Christian Tradition*, John Knox Press, Atlanta 1975, I,
p. 333-336; A. Milano, *Persona in teologia*, Edizioni Dehoniane, Naples 1987,
p. 169-170; J. Quasten, *Patrology*, Newman Press, Westminster (MD) 1953, III,
p. 381-383.

to Monophysitism. Scholars generally agree that Cyril's intention in employing the *mia physis* formula was to indicate the unique subsistent or, as one author puts it, "the subsistence of the divine being in the concrete subject which Christ is"[200] – to which we should add that, if it is to be something unique pertaining to both natures, then it must be the subsistence for both (which is naturally referred to as the divine subsistence, since the unique person is the pre-existent person of the Word). As a result, φύσις, for Cyril (here in the context of his Christology), is not equivalent to the Cappadocian οὐσία; φύσις stands rather for the personal subject which the Cappadocians designated with ὑπόστασις[201]. More than the "what", Cyril's intuition places a finger on the "who", i.e. the subsisting subject.

Axis placed in relief by Cyril

Like Nestorius, Cyril endorses the concrete integrity of each nature. The idea that the union takes place between two ὑποστάσεις, taken as concrete realities, is not foreign to Cyril. This is explicit in a passage from his *Adversus Theodoretum* where Cyril condemns treating the unified natures as though they were pure forms without a concrete mode of existence. The natures are not unhypostatized forms somehow related to one another, but complete substances, "hypostases"[202]. Ὑπόστασις signifies the substantial reality, the concrete entity be-

---

[200] A. Milano, *Persona in teologia*, Edizioni Dehoniane, Naples 1987, p. 173.

[201] It is important to keep in mind that we are speaking here of Cyril's language as it pertains to the problem of the singular person of Christ. Qualifying the sense of φύσις employed by Cyril as indicative of the hypostatic subject is valid only in the context of his Christological discussions. The term takes on an entirely different sense in Cyril's Trinitarian discourse where φύσις is rather opposed to the notion of hypostasis as handed to us by the Cappadocians. In his *Thesaurus* (Ἡ Βίβλος τῶν θησαυρῶν περὶ τῆς ἁγιάς καὶ ὁμοουσίου Τριάδος), and especially his *De consubstantiali Trinitate* (Περὶ ἁγίας τε καὶ ὁμοουσίου Τριάδος), Cyril demonstrates an unequivocal adherence to the language of the Cappadocians for whom φύσις or οὐσία is clearly distinguished from ὑπόστασις, manifested in such expressions as "naturally proceeding from the Father" (ἐκ Πατρὸς φυσικῶς) and "a single divine nature" (μία γάρ ἡ θεότητος).

[202] "It is because he says that the form of a servant was assumed by the form of God, that he continues to teach us as if it were without the hypostases, alone and in themselves, that the forms were united one to another. I think that he also rejects [this error] from this point. In effect, they are not simply similitudes or forms ἀνυπόστατοι which are united one to another according to a union of economy (οἰκονομικὴν), but there has been a conjunction of the things themselves or ὑποστάσεις" – Cyril of Alexandria, *Adversus Theodoretum*: Acta Conciliorum Oecumenicorum (= ACO), ed. Schwartz, 1927, I, 1, 6, p. 112, 12-16 = col. 396 C.

neath the μορφή. Here there is no difference between Cyril and Nestorius[203]. But, as A. Milano points out, the concrete natures are not to
be taken as independently subsisting: the human nature, composed of
a rational soul and a body subsists *in the Logos* and not by itself.
Consequently, it would be a misrepresentation of Cyril's thought to
speak (in a manner fostered by the Saint's expression) of two real natures prior to the union subsequently united into one φύσις after the
union[204].

In the bishop of Alexandria's third letter to Nestorius, an alternate
principle, sharply contrasting with the duality of hypostases, is maintained. With respect to what is ascribed by the Gospel to Christ, the
referent, Cyril tells us, of every expression is the unique hypostasis of
the God-man[205]. At first sight, this thesis seems irreconcilable with the
first which maintained a duality of ὑπόστασεις characterized by a
certain subsistence. If M. Richard's opinion[206] is correct, Cyril will
adamantly insist on the unicity of ὑπόστασις (even φύσις) in Christ
in order to avoid the impious result of admitting two subjects of attribution[207]. Ὑπόστασις, in this context, therefore, should be taken in
the sense of "subject of attribution", and not simply as concrete reality
or thing (as in the previous statement affirming "a conjunction of the
things themselves or ὑποστασεις"). The apparent opposition in declarations is perhaps less troublesome if Cyril intends, and this is the
opinion of M. Richard, that the assumed humanity subsist somehow
after the union, though not as a subject of attribution[208]. Accordingly,
the hypostasis of the humanity (when "hypostasis" is taken in the weak

---

[203] M. Richard remarks, furthermore, that *"pour Cyrille* φύσις *et* ὑπόστασις *sont syn-
onymes"* – *Introduction du Mot "Hypostase" dans la Théologie de l'Incarnation*, p. 42,
note 8.

[204] Cf. A. Milano, *Persona in teologia*, Edizioni Dehoniane, Naples 1987, p. 173.

[205] "All the expressions, therefore, that occur in the gospels are to be referred to one
person, the one enfleshed hypostasis of the Word. For there is one Lord Jesus
Christ, according to the scriptures" – Cyril of Alexandria, Ἐπιστολὴ Κυρίλλου
πρὸς Νεστόριον τρίτη: DEC 56, 8-13; ACO, I, 1, 1, p. 38, 21 = col. 116 C: "ἑνὶ τοιγαροῦν προσώπῳ τὰς ἐν τοῖς εὐαγγελίοις πάσας ἀναθετέον φωνάς, ὑποστάσει
μιᾷ τῇ τοῦ λόγου σεσαρκωμένῃ· κύριος γὰρ εἷς Ἰησοῦς Χριστὸς κατὰ τὰς
γραφάς".

[206] See M. Richard, op. cit., p. 248.

[207] According to A. Grillmeier, the whole of Cyrillian Christology is motivated by opposition to Nestorius, in such a way that all of his effort is directed toward defending
the unity in Christ. This characteristic of Cyril's thought explains his emphasizing
the Apollinarian μία φύσις formula, as a result of which, the term φύσις is limited
in content to expressing the individual existent. Cf. A. Grillmeier, *Christ in Christian
Tradition*, I, p. 480-483.

first sense of the term according to which each nature, insofar as complete in itself, is a substance or hypostasis in its own right) may be recognized because we admit its subsistence, while the humanity is united in the unique hypostasis of the Word (when "hypostasis" is taken precisely as designating the subject of attribution). However, two very different senses of "hypostasis" emerge from this perspective, the latter of which seems to be limited to the logical function of receiving the reference of predication. Moreover, the former sense of "hypostasis" distributed to each of the natures remains an ontological enigma to the extent that it admit of subsistence and concrete individuality while nevertheless failing to be a subject of operation. Nevertheless, Cyril himself employs the term differently, and this is a reflection of the ambiguity inherent in this term used to signify a substance, an ambiguity which, as we shall see, can be eliminated only by careful attention to the modes according to which substance may be signified. The important point, however, is the introduction of the notion of subject of attribution and its ascription to the concept of person. The categorical extension of "hypostasis" thus taken remains to be explored, however it seems Cyril inserts a new dimension into the concept of "hypostasis", the intension of which must include the independence proper to a subject of attribution.

If such was the intent of the bishop of Alexandria, then he must be credited with having uncovered the crucial and pivotal issue in articulating the unity of being in the hypostatic union, for not only does such an acceptation of ὑπόστασις (as subject of attribution) permit its distinction (in at least a verbal way at this point) from the individualized concrete nature as such, but it additionally raises the question of how some really existing, substantial *thing* not be a subject of attribution[209]. Cyril, it seems, succeeds in distinguishing the critical sense of the term ὑπόστασις as *person*, subject of attribution, in distinction from distinct, concretized natural reality (even if this distinction were to ultimately result in being purely logical[210]).

---

[208] "*L'humanité assumée par le Verbe a subsisté sans confusion après l'union, mais comme chose, non comme sujet d'attribution*" – M. Richard, op. cit., p. 248.

[209] It does not appear that the notion of the *quod est* can assist us in conceptualizing that difference. The same problem will be encountered in Boethius; cf. infra, "A POSSIBLE DIVISIVE CHRISTOLOGICAL ARGUMENT", p. 132. We shall later attempt to circumscribe this difficulty by explaining how the human nature of Christ as such is not a subject of attribution; cf. infra, "PRELIMINARY REMARK ON THE PERSONAL PRINCIPLE: A TENTATIVE HYPOTHESIS", p. 269; "CONSIDERATIONS ON THE SEPARATED SOUL AND THE HUMANITY OF CHRIST; THE CRITERION OF THE OMNINO INCOMMUNICABILIS", p. 365.

[210] And this is *not* equivalent to the possible logical distinction operated by Nestorius between φύσις and ὑπόστασις, the latter being nothing more than φύσις accord-

The result is that there can be no second or independent human ὑπόστασις: "οὔτε ὑποστάσεσι δυσὶν οὔτε μὴν προσώποις"²¹¹. Πρόσωπον is here used identically with ὑπόστασις. An incisive light is cast by Cyril's use of the term πρόσωπον in his second letter to Nestorius. In speaking against the two Sons in Christ, Cyril places "one πρόσωπον" in refutational contrast with "two sons". There cannot be two sons, because there cannot be two πρόσωπα; indeed, it is illicit to speak of two πρόσωπα²¹². The treatment of terms, commensurating "πρόσωπον" with "Son", means that "πρόσωπον" is "person" in the *full sense* of the term, just as a son is a person. Shortly later, Cyril continues (and here is the acute statement): "οὐ γὰρ εἴρηκεν ἡγραφὴ ὅτι ὁ λόγος ἀνθρώπου πρόσωπον ἥνωσεν ἑαυτῷ, ἀλλ᾽ ὅτι γέγονε σάρξ·"²¹³. The λόγος could not have united the πρόσωπον of a man to himself; this would be some sort of adoptionism, because, Cyril could argue, πρόσωπον implies an already existing and complete subject, which is, therefore, the personal *bearer* of a nature²¹⁴. Cyril's conception of πρόσωπον is completely different from that of Nestorius. This is behind the reasons for which Nestorius makes the blasphemous assertion: "τὴν ἁγίαν παρθένον Χριστοτόκον, οὐ θεοτόκον"²¹⁵, thinking that to bear God at all is to bear his divine nature. Following Cyril's inclination, one could reasonably conclude that the πρόσωπον is distinguished from the divine nature *per se*, as *bearer* of the natures; Nestorius sees only the concrete divine *nature* or φύσις²¹⁶.

---

ing as φύσις signifies the nature *concretely* (and not according as φύσις signifies the essence or οὐσία), hypostasis too, for Nestorius, designating nothing other than the nature *insofar as/qua* concretized, differentiated. Physis = the nature *qua* concrete; hypostasis = the concrete thing (or physis) *qua* concrete; physis alone directly expresses the nature. The insight of Cyril, however, would explicitly add the concept of subjectivity to either. Cf. Nestorius, supra, "πρόσωπον AND ὑπόστασις", p. 65; "CONSEQUENCES FOR NESTORIUS' INTERPRETATION OF THE UNITY IN CHRIST", p. 67.

211 Cyril of Alexandria, Ἐπιστολὴ Κυρίλλου πρὸς Νεστόριον τρίτη: DEC 55, 13-15.
212 "Οὐ... υἱοὺς δύο...κἂν εἰ προσώπων ἕνωσιν ἐπιφημίζωσί τινες·" – Cyril, Κυρίλλου ἐπιστολὴ δευτέρα πρὸς Νεστόριον: DEC 43, 24-29.
213 Cyril, Κυρίλλου ἐπιστολὴ δευτέρα πρὸς Νεστόριον: DEC 43, 30-32.
214 In explicit opposition to adoptionism, see Cyril, *Ep.* 45: PG 77, 236A.
215 Nestorius, Νεστορίου ἐπιστολὴ δευτέρα πρὸς Κύριλλον: DEC 47, 36-37.
216 If this latter is not identical to the concrete hypostasis which bears an essence, then it must be the nature as such, even if viewed in its individuality and from the point of view of its being concretized. It is not so much Nestorius' treatment of φύσις which errs, as his failure to carry that intuition further. In some respects, Nestorius perhaps better seizes the status of the individualized concretized nature; for even if it is to differ from its concrete bearer, it cannot do so as a really distinct form abstractly considered. The nature *per se* said to be distinguished from πρόσωπον in the Cyrillian context can refer to either the abstract nature or the concrete indi-

Πρόσωπον, then, is distinguished from the concretized nature, as its bearer, and as the subject of its operations.

Another text from Cyril's third letter to Nestorius expresses the same ideas. "We do not divide up the words of our Saviour in the gospels among two hypostases or persons, for the one and only Christ is not dual, even though he be considered to be from two distinct realities (ἐκ δύο νοῆται καὶ διαφόρων πραγμάτων)"[217]. Are we not here invited to recognize a difference between these "distinct realities" and "person"? The Latin translation of the critical phrase, "ex duabus diversisque rebus" signals an essential delicacy; for the sense of "res" determines everything. Since we are dealing with substantial natures, that is, primary substances or supposits (alone properly said to exist), our normal expectation would give "res subsistens"[218]. If "ἐκ δύο νοῆται καὶ διαφόρων πραγμάτων" means ex duabus rebus in this sense, then the natures are demarcated as subsisting substances, and when the completed nature is understood as such, it is not so clear as to how it could be understood not to be a subject of attribution. If one is to adhere to a double sense of subsisting indicated above, it appears the notion of subsistence itself need perhaps be expanded in such a way as to account for different forms of real existence, as might be achieved, for example, by a distinction between subsistentia in se

vidualized nature. In the latter case, however, it does not have its concrete reality except insofar as enhypostatized or "enprosoponized", for which reason it is only conceptually distinct from the unique hypostasis when so signified (this shall become clear in our study of St. Albert). If Cyril intends to maintain a distinction between the πρόσωπον and the individualized real human nature, then he shall have to do so otherwise than by ascribing a non-hypostatic status to that nature, since that nature is indeed hypostatized. That hypostatized nature, however, as shall become clear in our study of Albert, can be signified according to its natural reality as such – which is not exactly the concrete thing but rather that which is actually undergoing concretization – or according to its identity in hypostasis which is this concrete thing of such a nature. This is why the πρόσωπον can be said to differ from the concretized human nature (existing in a hypostasis), but not the concrete nature which subsists as the hypostasis in that nature. Nestorius' φύσις much more accurately describes the concretized nature distinguishable from the person; unfortunately, he treats it as the concrete (as opposed to the concretized) nature, thereby multiplying πρόσωπα. Cf. infra, "HYPOSTASIS", p. 218 (especially p. 222); "THE PRECISE DENOTATION OF 'HYPOSTASIS', ITS DISTINCTIVE MODE OF SIGNIFICATION", p. 233 (especially p. 237).

217 Cyril of Alexandria, Ἐπιστολὴ Κυρίλλου πρὸς Νεστόριον τρίτη (DEC 55, 12-18): "Τὰς δέ γε ἐν τοῖς εὐαγγελίοις τοῦ σωτῆρος ἡμῶν φωνὰς οὔτε ὑποστάσεσι δυσὶν οὔτε μὴν προσώποις καταμερίζομεν· οὐ γάρ ἐστι διπλοῦς ὁ εἷς καὶ μόνος Χριστός, κἂν ἐκ δύο νοῆται καὶ διαφόρων πραγμάτων εἰς ἑνότητα τὴν ἀμέριστον συνενηνεγμένος".

218 Cf. J. A. Weisheipl, "The Concepts of 'Nature' and 'Person'", in Commentary on the Gospel of St. John of St. Thomas Aquinas, Magi, 1980, appendix III, p. 458-468; cf. Aristotle, Categories, c. 5, 2ᵃ-3ᵇ.

and *subsistentia in alio*. In any case, the necessary distinction (and the necessary kind of distinction) between ὑπόστασις (as subject of attribution) and the completed nature (φύσις) was absent among the Cappadocians and Nestorius. While Cyril may be credited with having intimated its importance, we still find no theological elaboration of the problem even through the Council of Chalcedon. Boethius, as we shall see, was himself ill-equipped for grappling with the issue, and it will not be until the Scholastic period that the difficulty be more adequately appreciated.

There remains one unprecedented Cyrillian proposition we cannot overlook (and which perhaps points toward a later historical articulation of the issue[219]): "We must not think that it is the flesh of a man like us (for how can the flesh of a man be life-giving by its own nature?)"[220]. The point is, there is something different about (the subsistence of) the human nature in Christ! Here is the result of the Cyrillian orthodoxy:

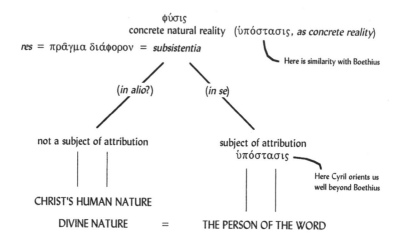

---

[219] We are alluding to the later doubts raised during the Scholastic period as to the type of "being" we may or may not be able to attribute to Christ's humanity.

[220] "Οὐχ ὡς ἀνθρώπου τῶν καθ' ἡμᾶς ἑνὸς καὶ αὐτὴν εἶναι λογιούμεθα (πῶς γὰρ ἡ ἀνθρώπου σὰρξ ζωοποιὸς ἔσται κατὰ φύσιν τὴν ἑαυτῇ)" – Cyril of Alexandria, Ἐπιστολὴ Κυρίλλου πρὸς Νεστόριον τρίτη: DEC 55, 4-6.

Conclusion

Nestorius, despite the inevitable impasse in his doctrine caused by overestimating the consequences of having to recognize the concrete reality of each of the natures in Christ (thinking that the proper concreteness of each entailed a duality of non-identifiable *prosopa*), hands to theology, in our opinion, an important and subtle distinction between nature as abstract and nature as concrete, and this without reducing that distinction to one between abstract nature and person as such. For φύσις, which is the concrete nature signified according to its natural reality, is not entirely identical to person, which is the concrete subsistent nature according to its personal reality (the latter qualification expressible in terms either of attributive subjectivality or of individuality *as such*)[221]. Overly focused upon the – admittedly necessary – hypostatic reality of both natures, Nestorius failed to perceive the true unique principle of union. Looking almost exclusively at the outer manifestation of the concreteness of the natures (the multiplicity of properties), he passed over the fundamental cause of their concreteness. What Nestorius does do, and very correctly, is affirm the intrinsic concreteness of each nature, that is, the necessary singularity which must enter into the structure of each nature in order even to exist. Perhaps because he is vigorously committed to avoiding any melding of natures in his opposition to Apollinarianism, he cannot envision that something intimately constitutive of one nature's singularity be shared with the other; indeed, he never discovered the constitutive cause of that singularity (and nor will anyone else until the late Scholastic debates over the principle of individuation).

Guarding the concrete integrity of the natures, Nestorius adamantly opposes the idea of a "natural union" and rightly discloses the distinctive feature of union according to essence. By appealing to the *prosopa* in his search for an ontological basis for union, Nestorius demonstrates an awareness of the crucial need to look for a point of conjunction transcending the boundaries of the essence as such. Because the essence is the undifferentiated οὐσία, the point of union between the natures must consist rather in a particular, concrete factor. For this reason, Nestorius advances his theory of the conjoining of the concretizing properties as a basis for union in Christ. These properties, however, belong to every *ens concretum physicum*, whence Nestorius must recognize for every real nature its own *prosopon* (the

---

[221] The relevance of this distinction will become clear later; cf. infra, "ʜʏᴘᴏsᴛᴀsɪs", p. 218; "'ᴘᴇʀsᴏɴ'", p. 240 (especially p. 243).

collection of these properties). From this, it follows that there are two *prosopa* in Christ. At this point alone, we can only credit Nestorius for having affirmed the true concrete perfection of both natures. The crucial step to be taken would be to equate the two *prosopa* at the level of the *principle* of the *prosopon*, but that is precisely the step which Nestorius misses. Inasmuch as these properties are the *notae individuantes*, Nestorius is in some ways not far from the pathway toward resolving the problem of the mode of union. His great limitation, which seems also to have been that of Cyril, consists in failing (1) to identify the principal and essential individuating element in distinction from the accidental notes which necessarily accompany it in created natures, and (2) to have recognized that this principle is itself the basis for substantial union and is identical for both of the natures[222].

Cyril too had spoken of "two hypostases" in Christ, but later insists upon the "μία ὑπόστασις" to demonstrate the unity of subject. Both expressions are absolutely right, provided either: (a) the term "hypostasis" be used in two distinct senses, or (b) the two hypostases recognized in the first formula be understood as identical in some respect, namely as regards their individuality, i.e. their concreteness and corresponding act of subsisting – wherefore the two are identical precisely *qua individual* (which is not equivalent to *qua natures*). Cyril's merit, however, consists especially in having shifted the semantic sense of hypostasis from concrete reality to subject of attribution. This is not to affirm that the concrete instantiation of a nature – i.e. prime substance, which is the supposit in the genus of substance – is not a subject of attribution. Cyril has rather explicitated a fundamental aspect of the supposit, namely its subjective status, and as a result has instituted an absolute preclusion of a duality of supposits. A distressing tension lingers over how to evaluate the concrete reality of

---

[222] N. B.: Such a thesis (which is our personal perspective) does not have to imply an intrinsic substantial modification of the nature, depending, precisely, upon the nature of the distinctive principle – a principle which in all likeliness pertains to the *existential* order and, it is our belief, the relative dimensions of that order (concerning a contingent nature's dependence for *esse*). As a result, the humanity of Christ suffers no *absolute* modification, and the concept of an ultimate individuating factor, contrary to the opposition of J.-H. Nicolas (cf. *Synthèse dogmatique*, 2nd edition, Éditions Universitaires, Fribourg 1986, §279), might arguably provide the basis for substantial union in Christ. The nature, we may maintain, is only affected according to *esse ad alio*, and not absolutely. And if one claims that this is, nevertheless, a real modification of (or accident within) the essence, we observe that the modification in indeed only accidental (and we may differ from Christ in every accidental way). From the point of view of his individuality, moreover, he *must* be different (since no two individuals are the same as such); the relative alteration only affects (according to formal perfection) the nature taken as this individual nature.

the human nature. How can it be concrete and "in its hypostasis" if it is not also a subject of attribution? The fact that the subsistence of the humanity depends upon that of the Word – something Cyril seems to have maintained [223] – already orients us in the right direction, toward identifying the subsistence/concrete mode of existence of the human nature with that of the divine nature as hypostatized in the Word. There must remain a sense, however, in which even the *concrete* human nature may be considered in itself, if a discussion of the difference between concrete nature and person is to make sense. That sense cannot abstract from the nature's hypostatization, lest the nature not be concrete and real, but must rather attain to the hypostatized reality *according* to its *natural* constitution. That is, the concrete natural reality, if (1) it is not to be conceived according to its subjective quality by which it is a hypostasis (and in this case identical to the unique hypostasis of the Word), and if (2) it is nevertheless to be conceived according to its concrete reality, necessarily including the notion of its hypostatization (in the subsistence of the Word), then it can only be conceived as the hypostatized reality viewed precisely in its *natural* makeup, that is, as the concrete nature *qua nature* as opposed to the concrete nature *qua concrete*. Such a series of formal distinctions (to which we shall later return in more detail) is certainly not contained in the thought of Cyril. The bishop of Alexandria's thought nevertheless makes an indelible contribution to discerning the proper character of personhood, perhaps more in the logical domain of reference, evidencing its status as *qui*, than in the ontological domain of its *quid*.

While it is true that Cyril safeguards the communication of idioms stubbornly refused by Nestorius in virtue of his conception of the Logos as the unique subject of attribution, we do not agree with J. A. Sayes that this Cyrillian intuition, ontologically speaking, represents a radical departure from the older Antiochian conception of person as forged by the Cappadocian Fathers [224]. One may simplistically conclude in adulation of Cyril for "leading the unity of Christ to personal terrain", but the problem is entirely unresolved to the extent that a technical conception of person is lacking, and the ontological headway made by Cyril is not so clear if the "personal terrain" turns out to be nothing other than that of the individual nature. Sayes places the notion of attributive subjectivity in opposition to what he considers to be the dead-end approach of the Cappadocians to which "Nestorius remained prisoner" [225].

---

[223] Cf. Cyril, *Ep. 40 ad Acac.*: PG 77, 177A; cf. A. Milano, *Persona in teologia*, Edizioni Dehoniane, Naples 1987, p. 173.

[224] Cf. J. A. Sayes, *Jesucristo, Ser y Persona*, Aldecoa, Burgos 1984, p. 28, 30, 38.

[225] J. A. Sayes, op. cit., p. 28; cf. id., p. 38.

Such a characterization is unnecessary, and, as we hope to demonstrate, both conceptualizations converge in a complementary fashion at the very level of the person, the one expressing the intuitive and experiential encounter with the unique Saviour whom we declare to be "one and the same", the other expressing in a technical and more abstract way the ontological foundation for that affirmation as well as the real structure of the subject.

I.6. THE THIRD AND FOURTH OECUMENICAL COUNCILS

Concilium Ephesinum (431)

DEFENSE OF THE KERYGMA, AND THE ONE AND UNIQUE SAVIOR

(1) γέγονεν ἄνθρωπος... ἀλλ᾽ οὐ-
δὲ ὡς ἐν προσλήψει προσώ-
που μόνου²²⁶.

"Became man... not by the assumption of a person alone".

Ephesus proclaims, above all, the *substantial* union of natures
in Christ. Not the assumption of a person alone (as if Christ
were to have assumed an already existing individual), for such
a union could be nothing other than moral and accidental.
The emphatic μόνος (προσώπου μόνου) suggests that defining the Incarnation as attaining to but one somehow limits
the perfusive dimensions of the Incarnation. Against union
with a single person, the council affirms a union of the natures, perhaps not only to refuse adoptionism or accidental
union, but also to imply that in the human nature is contained in some sense all of humanity²²⁷.

(2) Οὐ... υἱοὺς δύο... κἂν εἰ προσώπων ἔνωσιν ἐπιφημίζωσί
τινες²²⁸.

"Not split into two sons... even
though some do speak of a union of persons".

We have already seen this statement determining the sense of
πρόσωπον as person²²⁹.

(3) οὐ γὰρ εἴρηκεν ἡγραφὴ ὅτι ὁ
λόγος ἀνθρώπου πρόσωπον
ἥνωσεν ἑαυτῷ, ἀλλ᾽ ὅτι γέγονε σάρξ²³⁰.

"For scripture does not say that
the Word united the person of a
man to himself, but that he became flesh".

---

²²⁶ DEC 41, 29-33.
²²⁷ Perhaps this is how we should interpret the repeated affirmations: "he united to
himself hypostatically the human" – "ἐνώσας ἑαυτῷ καθ᾽ ὑπόστασιν τὸ ἀνθρώπινον" (DEC 42, 11-12); "καθ᾽ ὑπόστασιν ἐνώσας ἑαυτῷ τὸ ἀνθρώπινον"
(DEC 58, 17-18).
²²⁸ DEC 43, 24-29.
²²⁹ Cf. supra, "AXIS PLACED IN RELIEF BY CYRIL", p. 71 (especially p. 74); cf. infra, *Concilium
Ephesinum*, §5, p. 82.
²³⁰ DEC 43, 30-32.

Indeed, the Word did not unite himself with a πρόσωπον because πρόσωπον implies the already complete existing subject, which must be the bearer of its nature(s).

(4)	ἀλλ᾿ ἐνωθεὶς κατὰ φύσιν...	"But he was united by nature...
	Οὔτε μὴν κατὰ παράθεσιν	Niether do we understand the
	τὸν τῆς συναφείας νοοῦμεν	manner of conjunction to be
	τρόπον (οὐκ ἀπόχρη γὰρ τοῦ-	one of juxtaposition for this is
	το πρὸς ἕνωσιν φυσικήν)[231].	not enough for natural union".

In the Council of Ephesus, the linguistic value of terms is far
from settled. The sense of φύσις here cannot be equivalent to
οὐσία but is analogous to the Cappadocian concept of
ὑπόστασις. "If anyone divides in the one Christ the hypostases after the union... and not rather by a coming together in a
union by nature, let him be anathema"[232]. For Cyril, there is
only one hypostasis after the union, yet in some sense he
spoke of two hypostases. Is the one hypostasis the μία φύσις?
A significant lack of clarity and linguistic fluidity resides in the
bishop of Alexandria's canonized statements, a limitation to
have impending results upon the Christian flock. Not even
the effort of Chalcedon to rectify the use of language and define its right interpretation will succeed to allay the controversies nourished by the Cyrillian formulation and which endure
to the present day.

(5)	οὔτε ὑποστάσεσι δυσὶν οὔτε	"We do not divide up the words
	μὴν προσώποις[233].	of our Saviour in the gospels
		among two hypostases or per-
		sons".

There is no second or human hypostasis distinct from that of
the Logos. The concept of hypostasis, again synonymized
with πρόσωπον, refers to the subject of attribution and operations. The human nature of itself, therefore, can never more
receive the designation "hypostasis", even if it is a completed

---

[231] Ἐπιστολὴ Κυρίλλου πρὸς Νεστόριον τρίτη: DEC 52, 12-13; 27-28.
[232] "Εἴ τις ἐπὶ τοῦ ἑνὸς Χριστοῦ διαιρεῖ τὰς ὑποστάσεις μετὰ τὴν ἕνωσιν... καὶ
οὐχὶ δὴ μᾶλλον συνόδῳ τῇ καθ᾿ ἕνωσιν φυσικήν, ἀνάθεμα ἔστω" – Ἐπιστολὴ
Κυρίλλου πρὸς Νεστόριον τρίτη: DEC 59, 23-29.
[233] DEC 55, 13-15.

natural reality: nature and person have been definitively distinguished by means of the special concept of subjectivity.

(6) οὐ γάρ ἐστι διπλοῦς ὁ εἶς καὶ μόνος Χριστός, κἂν ἐκ δύο νοῆται καὶ διαφόρων πραγμάτων εἰς ἑνότητα τὴν ἀμέριστον συνενηνεγμένος[234].

"For the one and only Christ is not dual, even though he be considered to be from two distinct realities, brought together into an unbreakable union".

Christ is said to be from two distinct realities, but he is not double. Additionally, the sentence before excluded a duality of hypostases, hence these "realities"/"*res*" cannot (both) be hypostatic (in themselves). The status of the human nature, then, is clearly non-hypostatic (in itself); consequently, our notion of what constitutes a hypostasis must adjust to this standard (if hypostasis is to mean person in the full sense intended by Cyril). When, and if, we can determine that which constitutes a hypostasis, *as a subject of attribution and bearer of a nature*, then, and only then, will we gain some insight into what it is that differentiates our human natures from the σάρξ of Jesus Christ[235].

(7) καθάπερ ἀμέλει καὶ ἄνθρωπος ἐκ ψυχῆς νοεῖται καὶ σώματος καὶ οὐ διπλοῦς μᾶλλον, ἀλλ' εἶς ἐξ ἀμφοῖν[236].

"In the same way as any man, though composed of soul and body, he is not considered to be dual, but rather one out of the two".

Already church tradition makes use of the body-soul analogy.

(8) ἑνὶ τοιγαροῦν προσώπῳ τὰς ἐν τοῖς εὐαγγελίοις πάσας ἀναθετέον φωνάς, ὑποστάσει μιᾷ τῇ τοῦ λόγου σεσαρκωμένῃ[237].

"All of the expressions, therefore, that occur in the gospels are to be referred to one person, the one enfleshed hypostasis of the Word".

---

[234] DEC 55, 15-18.
[235] Cf. supra, "AXIS PLACED IN RELIEF BY CYRIL.", p. 71 (especially p. 73, 74-76); cf. infra, in the chapter on Boethius, "A POSSIBLE DIVISIVE CHRISTOLOGICAL ARGUMENT", p. 132; "OBJECTION AND ALTERNATIVES TO THE ARGUMENT", p. 133.
[236] DEC 55, 18-21.
[237] DEC 56, 8-11.

The one hypostasis is the *subject of attribution*, for it is *to* this one πρόσωπον that every action is referred. (Note that, again, πρόσωπον = ὑπόστασις, and this becomes a standard equivalence consistently reaffirmed).

(9) καὶ ἔστιν ἐν ὑποστάσει τὸ πνεῦμα ἰδικῇ καὶ δὴ καὶ νοεῖται καθ᾽ ἑαυτο, καθὸ πνεῦμά ἐστιν καὶ οὐχ υἱός[238].

"The Spirit exists in his own hypostasis and is thought of on his own, according as he is Spirit and not the Son".

This is a lucid pronouncement of the *individuality/distinctness* of hypostasis.

(10) θεὸν τέλειον καὶ ἄνθρωπον τέλειον[239] ... ὁμοούσιον τῷ πατρὶ τὸν αὐτὸν κατὰ τὴν θεότητα καὶ ὁμοούσιον ἡμῖν κατὰ τὴν ἀνθρωπότητα. Δύο γὰρ φύσεων ἕνωσις γέγονεν·[240] ... τέλειος ὢν ἐν θεότητι καὶ τέλειος ὁ αὐτὸς ἐν ἀνθρωπότητι καὶ ὡς ἐν ἑνὶ προσώπῳ νοούμενος[241].

"Perfect God and perfect man... one and the same consubstantial with the Father in Godhead and consubstantial with us in humanity, for a union of two natures took place... being both perfect in Godhead and perfect in humanity and thought of as in one person".

The perfect integrity of Christ's human and divine natures is affirmed here; he is man like us, and God like the Father.

(11) ἡ τῶν φύσεων μὴ ἀγνοῆται διαφορά, ἐξ ὧν τὴν ἀπόρρητον ἕνωσιν πεπρᾶχθαι φαμέν[242].

"We do not ignore the differences of natures, out of which we say that the ineffable union was effected".

We do not ignore the difference of the natures, *out of which* the union is said to be effected. The expression "out of which" was the object of much controversy, since it seemed to imply a transformation or alteration of the united elements after the effected union. The necessity for linguistic precision

---

[238] DEC 57, 26-29.
[239] DEC 69, 41-02.
[240] DEC 70, 8-11.
[241] DEC 72, 21-23.
[242] DEC 72, 25-28.

will lead the Council of Chalcedon to a more prudential choice of expression (as shall be accomplished, for example, by the formulation "in which", as opposed to "out of which").

Concilium Chalcedonense (451)
UNION IN THE PERSON AND THE PARADOX OF SUBSTANTIAL PLENITUDE

(1) *Salva igitur proprietate utriusque naturae et in unam coeunte personam*[243].

"The proper character of both natures was maintained and came together in a single person".

As evidenced in this proclamation of Leo the Great, in the Chalcedonian speculative analysis, the concept of the *proprietas* continues, as it did in Cappadocian theology, to play a distinctive role. However, the Stoic presupposition that the ὑπόστασις comes about through the addition of the ἰδιότης to the οὐσία does not conform with the message and language of Chalcedon, for which the concrete realization of two different sets of natural properties come together in *a single* person or hypostasis. We appear to incur an inconsistency if we say that, on the one hand, each nature retains that which makes it a ὑπόστασις, and on the other assert that there is only one ὑπόστασις. Therefore, it seems either the Stoic presupposition is incorrect, or *persona* means something other than ὑπόστασις (taken in the Stoic sense). The Chalcedonian declaration breaks new territory, inasmuch as its concept of ὑπόστασις and πρόσωπον require a different metaphysical understanding than hitherto recognized. Leo's proclamation demonstrates the tension existing between the implications of Greco-Roman philosophy and Incarnation theology. A unique quote from an earlier sermon shows a certain tendency not to forego the discernments of that philosophy: "because neither substance so retained their properties that there could be any division of persons in them"[244]. In such a way, the unity of person would be preserved on account of the fact that the natures forfeit their "hypostatizing" characteristics.

---

[243] DEC 78B, 7-9.
[244] Leo the Great, *Ser. 23*, I: PL 54, 200A.

Of course, Leo will permit absolutely nothing to be subtracted from the natural constitution of the natures, as is made clear in the *Tomus ad Flavianum*[245]; however, the text serves to illustrate that the *proprietates* are commonly understood to personalize a nature. The emphasis should be placed upon the word "so", in which case the sense would be that while both substances or natures retained their properties, neither did so *in such a way* as to entail a division of persons.

(2) *Natura inviolabilis naturae est*   "Invulnerable nature was united
     unita passibili[246].   to a nature that could suffer".

Again, the terms of the relation of union are the natures, which union itself is terminated in the person. This is important for understanding the ontological structure of the union in itself. At this point, however, we draw the reader's attention to a crucial observation. Throughout the *Tomus ad Flavianum*, the term *substantia* is consistently avoided. This is peculiar since some of the expressions are recurrences of previously expressed views (various sermons) in which Leo employs the term *substantia*[247]. Moreover, the absence of *substantia* seems strange for a response directed against the heresy of Eutyches who denied Christ's consubstantiality (ὁμοούσιος) with us. If the discrepancy in case may be attributed to the hand of the redactor, Prosper of Aquitaine, we are still left with the question as to what motivated these linguistic preferences. Now, besides the advantage of avoiding the difficulty which might have arisen from the acknowledgment of one ὑπόστασις (translated as *substantia*) and two *substantiae*, the use of *natura* may indicate the recognition of a fundamental difference between *substantia* and *natura*. Three terms are at issue: *natura, substantia, subsistentia*. The first and last are clearly distinct one from another; the problem lies with our

---

[245] Cf. infra, *Concilium Chalcedonense* §3-4, p. 87.

[246] DEC 78B, 13-14.

[247] J. Gaidoz shows us (in "Saint Prosper d'Aquitaine et le Tome a Flavien", *RevSR* 23, 1949, p. 282-288) that several passages of the *Tomus* are taken from earlier sermons in which the originally occurring term *substantia* is replaced by *natura*. At face value, one might be inclined to conclude: *"De la sorte, pas une seule fois dans la lettre à Flavien, ne se rencontre le terme 'substantia', jamais il n'est question de la substance humaine du Christ"* (J. Gaidoz, op. cit., p. 283). Cf. A. Grillmeier, op. cit., p. 538-539.

acceptation of the second, whether to situate it beside *natura* or *subsistentia*. We might ask ourselves the *raison d'être* for the Latin translation of the Chalcedonian profession of faith: *"magisque salva proprietate utriusque naturae, et in unam personam atque subsistentiam concurrente"*[248]. Was *natura* preferable to *substantia* because *substantia* is co-signifying with *subsistentia*[249]? Was *subsistentia* used instead of *substantia* to translate ὑπόστασις because *substantia* restricts itself to the level of *natura*? If we are respectful of the existential independence proper to substance (as understood in Aristotelian terms of prime substance), then substance, it would seem, possesses the character of subsistence. And if we find ourselves hard pressed to conceive of a subsisting thing failing to be a subject of attribution, it would seem reasonable to shun speaking about two substances in Christ. Perhaps this is the motivation behind the exclusive use of *natura* in the *Tomus ad Flavianum*[250].

(3)	*In integra ergo veri hominis perfectaque natura verus natus est deus, totus in suis, totus in nostris*[251].	"Thus was true God born in the undiminished and perfect nature of a true man, complete in what is his and complete in what is ours".

Here he emphasizes the integrity of the human nature, undiminished, perfect and complete.

(4)	*Tenet enim sine defectu proprietatem suam utraque natura*[252].	"Each nature kept its proper character without loss".

The human nature united to the divine nature is no different from our own with respect to what constitutes it in an absolute sense; no element essential to our concrete human nature can be lacking in that of Christ. For this reason, that nature

---

[248] DEC 86, 37-40; cf. infra, §4.
[249] Cf. infra, in the chapter on Boethius, "SUBSISTENCE AND ITS RELATION TO SUBSTANCE", p. 110. By "co-signifying" we mean "used to signify the same thing", since the terms can remain nevertheless different in meaning (cf. infra, "SPECIFIC ASPECTS OF SUBSTANTIA AND SUBSISTENTIA", p. 121).
[250] Cf. infra, *Concilium Chalcedonense* §5, p. 88.
[251] DEC 78B, 18-21.
[252] DEC 78B, 40-41.

(along with the divine) is described as "without loss"; for "uniquely wondrous and wondrously unique as that act of generation was, it is not to be understood as though the proper character of its kind was taken away by the sheer novelty of its creation"[253]. *Nothing* can be subtracted from the constitution of Christ's humanity, which brings us back to the conclusion above that either something other than the Stoic sense of hypostasis constitutes personhood, or the human nature in Christ *is* somehow a person (though the latter alternative does not have to mean that it be a person *in itself*).

(5)
Agit enim utraque forma cum alterius communione quod proprium est, verbo scilicet operante quod verbi est, et carne exequente quod carnis est[254].	"The activity of each form is what is proper to it in communion with the other: that is, the Word performs what belongs to the Word, and the flesh accomplishes what belongs to flesh".

From *agit utraque forma*, it might appear that the *forma*, i.e. the nature, is made the subject of the actions. But we should not misinterpret these words as suggesting separate *agentes*; Leo, in his concern to counter Eutychian confusion, wants to accentuate the distinction of the two natural principles of operation with their respective *actiones*. He distinguishes the *principium quo* from the *principium quod* which had until then held the exclusive theological attention since Cyril of Alexandria. But if it is true, as A. Grillmeier contends, that "Leo allows the two natures to strive, each in its own way, to the term of their activity"[255], then Leo does seem to verge upon making each nature an *agens*. Perhaps greater care could have been exercised in its formulation; the statement nevertheless displays the immense tension between unity of person and duality of nature. Although for Leo, there is never a question of the possibility of a human person (of itself) – and this is stressed throughout his sermons and letters (as the citation of the following paragraph confirms) –, his formulation of the *principia quibus* seems to leave room for a possession of a cer-

---

[253] "*Sed non ita intelligenda est illa generatio singulariter mirabilis et mirabiliter singularis, ut per novitatem creationis proprietas remota sit generis*" (DEC 78A, 39-43).

[254] DEC 79B, 3-5.

[255] A. Grillmeier, *Christ in Christian Tradition. From the Apostolic Age to Chalcedon (451)*, trans. J. Bowden, John Knox Press, 2nd edition, Atlanta 1975, p. 534.

tain autonomy on the part of the natures. Clearly there is no
problem in recognizing an autonomy for the divine nature,
which is strictly identified with the person of the Word, but if
a similar admission with regard to the human nature is smack-
ingly precarious, perhaps that is reason enough for having
avoided the use of the term *substantia*[256], which implies an independence, and having opted rather for *natura*, which distinction from the *principium quod* is more transparent[257].

(6)   *Quamvis enim in domino Iesu*   "For although there is in the
       Christo dei et hominis una persona   Lord Jesus Christ a single per-
       sit, aliud tamen est unde in utro-   son who is of God and of man,
       que communis est contumelia, ali-   the insults shared by both have
       ud unde communis est gloria[258].   their source in one thing, and
                                               the glory that is shared in an-
                                               other".

The choice of the neuter (*aliud*) demonstrates that the distinction recognized between the natures refuses separate subjects or persons[259].

(7)   *Propter hanc ergo unitatem per-*   "It is on account of this oneness
       sonae in utraque natura intelle-   of person, which must be un-
       gendam[260].   derstood in both natures".

The mode of the unity in Christ is "personal": person is the
distinct ontological seat of the unity. While the natures are

---

[256] See supra, *Concilium Chalcedonense*, §2, p. 86.

[257] Cf. the Council of Florence: "*Amplectitur etiam... tertiam Constantinopolitanam syn-
odum... in qua... diffinitum est in domino nostro Ihesu Christo duas esse perfectas inte-
grasque naturas et duas operationes, duas etiam voluntates, licet esset una eademque persona,
cui utriusque nature competerent actiones, deitate agente que Dei sunt, et humanitate, que
hominis sunt*" – DEC 580, 20-38. Though the unity of subject be affirmed according
as there is but one single subject of attribution "to whom the actions of each nature
belong", the natures themselves seem to receive *in some manner* an attribution of action, since it is somehow *their* actions which belong to the Word. Perhaps even the
notion of a *quo est* requires of itself something proprietary. Nevertheless, it is quite
possible that the genitive expression only intends to accentuate the natural origin
of operation (the natures *from which* actions proceed). In fact, in virtue of the subsequent ablatives, the statement reads: "*through* the divinity doing what is of God,
through the humanity what is of man".

[258] DEC 80A, 19-24.

[259] With regard to linguistic conventions in the use of gender, cf. infra, "THE PREDICAMENTS
OF 'WHO', 'HOW' AND 'WHAT'", p. 297.

[260] DEC 80A, 26-28.

maintained in their distinction – *"in eo proprietas divinae humanaeque naturae individua permanere"*[261] –, the unity attributed to the person, within which the diverse natures endure, entails its distinction from natural reality as such.

(8) τέλειον τὸν αὐτὸν ἐν θεότητι καὶ τέλειον τὸν αὐτὸν ἐν ἀνθρωπότητι, θεὸν ἀληθῶς καὶ ἄνθρωπον ἀληθῶς τὸν αὐτόν, ἐκ ψυχῆς λογικῆς καὶ σώματος, ὁμοούσιον τῷ πατρὶ κατὰ τὴν θεότητα καὶ ὁμοούσιον ἡμῖν τὸν αὐτὸν κατὰ τὴν ἀνθρωπότητα... ἕνα καὶ τὸν αὐτὸν... ἐν δύο φύσεσιν ἀσυγχύτως, ἀτρέπτως, ἀδιαιρέτως, ἀχωρίστως γνωριζόμενον, οὐδαμοῦ τῆς τῶν φύσεων διαφορᾶς ἀνῃρημένης διὰ τὴν ἕνωσιν, σῳζομένης δὲ μᾶλλον τῆς ἰδιότητος ἑκατέρας φύσεως καὶ εἰς ἕν πρόσωπον καὶ μίαν ὑπόστασιν συντρεχούσης, οὐκ εἰς δύο πρόσωπα μεριζόμενον ἢ διαιρούμενον, ἀλλ᾽ ἕνα καὶ τὸν αὐτον υἱὸν μονογενῆ θεὸν λόγον κύριον Ἰησοῦν Χριστόν"[262].

"The same perfect in divinity and perfect in humanity, the same truly God and truly man, of a rational soul and a body; consubstantial with the Father as regards his divinity, and the same consubstantial with us as regards his humanity... one and the same... acknowledged in two natures which undergo no confusion, no change, no division, no separation; at no point was the difference between the natures taken away through the union, but rather the property of both natures is preserved and comes together into a single person and a single subsistent being or hypostasis; he is not parted or divided into two persons, but is one and the same only-begotten Son, God, Word, Lord Jesus Christ".

Chalcedon integrates the technical term *consubstantialem* to express the perfection of each nature in Christ: the man Christ-Jesus is as fully and really and concretely human as every other man; Christ the Son of God possesses the complete divinity in just the same way as the Father himself. The expression ἐν δύο φύσεσιν marks an advancement from the Cyrillian ἐκ δύο φύσεων[263]. Misunderstood, ἐκ δύο φύσεων intimates union at the natural level, as though two elements of equal ontological status were thought of as coming together. Moreover, the preposition "in" operates better with

---

[261] DEC 81A, 6-8.
[262] DEC 86, 18-24; 31-43.
[263] See supra, "AXIS PLACED IN RELIEF BY CYRIL.", p. 71 (especially p. 75); *Concilium Ephesinum*, §11, p. 84.

regard to expressions of subsistence, as when it is said that the person of Jesus Christ subsists in two natures. Finally, integrating the formula of St. Irenaeus of Lyons – "one and the same"[264] –, the council especially emphasizes the unity of subject proper to Christ who is a single person, illustrating the subjective character of personality[265]. To the concrete phenomenological recognition of this unicity of subject, the expression "a single hypostasis" gives a more reflected metaphysical value, signifying the unique subject or person in the ontological order[266].

[264] Cf. Irenaeus, *Adv. haer.*, I, 9, 2; III, 16, 2; cf. A. Grillmeier, *Christ in Christian Tradition. From the Apostolic Age to Chalcedon (451)*, trans. J. Bowden, John Knox Press, 2nd edition, Atlanta 1975, p. 102; A. Benoit, *St. Irénée. Introduction à l'étude de sa théologie*, Paris 1960, p. 212-214.

[265] Cf. J. Galot, "La définition de la personne, relation et sujet", *Gregorianum* 75/2 (1994), p. 292.

[266] Cf. J. Galot, "La définition de la personne, relation et sujet", *Gregorianum* 75/2 (1994), p. 292-293.

I.7. THE TERM *"PERSONA"* – PREAMBLE TO THE LATIN ELABORATION

Its etymology

The many discussions of the etymological origin of *"persona"* have yet to reach a consensus. While an ancient tradition associated its derivation with the term "prosopon", recent study strongly discourages this interpretation[267]. *"Persona"* seems rather to have its roots in the names of certain divinities associated with Etruscan rituals. Probably as a result of the influence of these rituals on the Roman theater, *"persona"* came to be used to designate the theatrical mask, role and character[268]. The term underwent rapid semantic development, so much so that, by the time of Cicero, *"persona"* could simultaneously express all of the senses mentioned above and soon came to be considered as semantically equivalent to "prosopon", particularly as indicative of individual concrete *men*. Prior to the Christian era, therefore, *"persona"* already possessed a signification expressing individuality (at least with respect to and over and against the general notion of man)[269].

Assumption of the term *"persona"* in Trinitarian theology: Tertullian

It was Tertullian who provided the West with the basis for its formulation of Trinitarian orthodoxy according to the expression *"una substantia – tres personae"*. In Tertullian, *"persona"* acquires a technical

---

[267] Cf. F. Chiereghin, "Le ambiguità del concetto di persona e l'impersonale", in *L'Idea di persona*, V. Melchiorre (editor), Vita e Pensiero, Milan 1996, p. 65-86; A. Milano, *Persona in teologia*, Edizioni Dehoniane, Naples 1987, p. 68; M. Nédoncelle, "Prósopon et persona dans l'antiquité classique. Essai de bilan linguistique", *RevSR* 22 (1948), p. 277-299.

[268] Cf. H. U. von Balthasar, "On the Concept of Person", *Communio* 13 (Spring 1986), p. 20; A. Milano, *Persona in teologia*, Edizioni Dehoniane, Naples 1987, p. 69-70; K. Schmitz, "Selves and persons: A difference in loves?", *Communio* 18 (Summer 1991), p. 196-198; "The Geography of the Human Person", *Communio* 13 (Spring 1986), p. 29-30.

[269] Cf. A. Milano, *Persona in teologia*, Edizioni Dehoniane, Naples 1987, p. 70-71; K. Schmitz, "The Geography of the Human Person", *Communio* 13 (Spring 1986), p. 29-32. On the semantical transformations undergone by the term as a result of Christian faith in the Word of God, see J. Ratzinger, "Concerning the Notion of Person in Theology", *Communio* 17 (Fall 1990), p. 441-443.

sense able to be placed in opposition to the notion of substance, in such a way that person and substance, while contra-distinguished from each other, retain something in common with respect to their very quiddity[270]. Such an equality and distinction is able to be established on the basis of principles inherent in Stoic philosophy, in particular, the concept of the *ens concretum physicum*. In accordance with its etymology, *"substantia"* possesses for Tertullian a concrete value and signifies the fundamental/foundational thing of which something is made. This fundamental aspect of an entity's overall reality is that quality by which it is classed within the hierarchy of beings and distinguished among the grades of perfection. It is not, however, that element by which a singular thing is distinguished from another singular thing of equal hierarchical status. Individuals are distinguished from one and other on another basis which is responsible for the presence of *tres personae* in God, notwithstanding the *unitas substantiae*[271]. Conjoined in a single real concrete substance, the persons of the Trinity are *one*, while nevertheless numerically distinct and three according to person. Tertullian thus furnishes Latin Christendom with the means for expressing the paradox of unity and distinction in the Godhead, *"substantia"* naming that which unites the three in indivisible being, *"persona"* that in which the three are three. With the latter term, Tertullian intends the concrete existent as characterized by a unique existence *in se*: "certainly it does not signify for him an exterior appearance, a role or simple function, but rather signifies the object of a judgment of existence, the effective and manifest presence of someone who exists *in se*... thus manifesting the person's proper individuality"[272].

For Tertullian, *"person"* signifies more the manifestation of the singular existent than the ontological value of existing *in se* or the singular existent as such. It is the subsisting being or supposit according as it is perceived and manifested to us in action[273]. Though the underlying ontological subject of such outward manifestations is certainly implicit in the name designating the latter, the precise value of "person" as signifying the *per se* subsisting individual according to distinction is

[270] For the importance of Tertullian in the development of the notion of *"persona"* in theology, see A. Grillmeier, *Christ in Christian Tradition*, trans. J. Bowden, John Knox Press, Atlanta 1975, I, p. 117-131; A. Milano, *Persona in teologia*, Edizioni Dehoniane, Naples 1987, p. 65-97.

[271] Cf. Tertullian, *Adv. Prax.* 6, 1; 12, 3; 12, 7; 18, 2: CCL 2, 1165; 1173; 1173; 1183.

[272] A. Milano, *Persona in teologia*, Edizioni Dehoniane, Naples 1987, p. 89.

[273] Cf. J. Moingt, *Théologie trinitaire de Tertullien*, 4 vol., Paris 1966-1969, II, p. 644; A. Milano, *Persona in teologia*, Edizioni Dehoniane, Naples 1987, p. 90-92.

not explicitly present in Tertullian. This insufficiency prevents Tertullian from being able to articulate the concept of person as itself able to provide an explanation for the very unity of substance to which it is opposed, that is, as positing a plurality in God at a level uniquely pertaining to the distinctive property of existence, and thus indifferently with respect to the substantial level. As a result, *"persona"* does not signify the divine substance insofar as subsisting in a determinate individual, but rather the substance according as it has been "distributed" to the Son via generation, according as it has been "parceled" so to speak to this determinate individual in whom a separate existence is rendered manifest. In this sense, A. Milano affirms the presence in Tertullian of a pluralistic unity based upon an "interior organization of the divine substance" [274], in distinction from a plurality founded upon subsistent or supposital acts. This speculative weakness inherent in the doctrine of Tertullian impedes his understanding of the perichoresis of the divine persons (to affirm the total presence of the Father in the Son and the Son in the Father according to being jeopardizing in his eyes their distinctive property) and ultimately leads him to patropassionist terrain (seeing the Father as somehow incarnate in Christ, since [a "portion" of] the divine substance is incarnate in Christ). All of this means that Tertullian remained ill-equipped to lucidly conceive the identity between substance and person in the Trinity despite the distinction of persons, or the proper distinction between substance and person in Christ. Nevertheless, tremendous historical merit is due to Tertullian for having accurately exposed the distinctive levels of consideration with respect to which the Trinitarian and Christological paradoxes are expressed, as well as for having coined the terminology adopted by the Church in order to define them. What is more, Tertullian prepared the future of theological discourse by indicating the orthodox pathway toward specifying the sense of person/hypostasis in contradistinction from substance/ousia, and demonstrated the correspondence between Trinitarian and Christological theology.

---

[274] A. Milano, *Persona in teologia,* Edizioni Dehoniane, Naples 1987, p. 93.

Boethius

It is with Anicius Manlius Severinus Boethius (c. 480-526) that Christian antiquity, in the process of determining the signification of person, attains for the first time a formal speculative definition of the term. Boethius represents, from this point of view, a culmination in the genesis of the concept of person, and the point of departure for its semantical future in the West. Educated in Rome according to the classical, rhetorico-philosophical model, and completing his studies in Athens, Boethius was one of the principal channels whereby the philosophy of the ancient world was passed on to the Middle Ages. His vast cultural program included the translation and interpretation of all of the works of Plato and Aristotle and a demonstration of their fundamental concordance, though only a small part of this project was realized. As a statesman of high magisterial office under the Ostrogoth king, Theodoric, Boethius was the inspiration of the political synthesis between the Roman and Germanic people. Later accused of treason, he was imprisoned and put to death. During the period of his imprisonment, Boethius composed the work for which he is most famous, his *De consolatione philosophiae*. In the course of the complicated post-Chalcedonian politico-religious hostilities waged between the Nestorian and Monophysite factions in Constantinople, Boethius composed his so called "theological tractates" (*Opuscula sacra*): *De Trinitate, Utrum Pater et Filius et Spiritus Sanctus substantialiter praedicentur, De hebdomadibus (Quomodo substantiae in eo quod sint bonae...), De fide catholica, Contra Eutychen et Nestorium*. The latter work, consisting of a personal reexamination of the Christological problem, contains Boethius' celebrated definition of person.

While Boethius does not enter with extreme depth into the grammatical issues of signification through which one may attempt to resolve the apparent contradiction inherent in the dogma of the Incarnation – where the individual human nature of Christ does not constitute of itself a human person as in the case of all other men – he nevertheless situates personhood within the ontological order in a way becoming standard for the majority of thinkers throughout the Middle-Ages and even until our day. The "classical" Boethian definition of person has been countlessly cited and often authoritatively employed as a premise in argumentation. Unfortunately, a wealth of other valuable Boethian insights surrounding the very pages in which he treats of person seems sometimes to be overlooked on account of (what may be a simplistic) enthusiasm and eagerness to employ his definition of person. It is this author's opinion that an enormous amount of attention has been given to the Boethian definition of person without sufficiently examining the metaphysical presuppositions and groundwork within which that definition emerges and is meant to be fitted. Amongst the philosophical concepts indispensable for understanding both personhood as well as the broader context within which Boethius develops his definition is the crucial notion of subsistence.

As the entire issue centers upon the affirmation that an existing human nature as such does not constitute a human person, it is our necessary first concern to define the terms "nature" and "person", distinguishing them according to their proper differences and indicating the logico-ontological relationship between them. This task becomes the special concern of Boethius in his treatise *Contra Eutychen et Nestorium*, where he formulates the definition of "person" to influence the entirety of subsequent western thought. In this chapter we intend to examine Boethius' philosophical unpackaging of that notion and the metaphysical infrastructures responsible for its distinctive character. Consequently, we are equally interested in the notions of "substance" and "subsistence". The analysis shall proceed especially from a logical point of view, with the end of better uncovering the Boethian position in the face of personhood and subsistence while exposing what we consider to be a more coherent notion of subsistence all together, when compared with what the tradition has perhaps ironically retained until now.

As will become clear, traditional use of these terms has frequently contributed toward obscuring their various senses and weakening their illuminating power. Consider the fact that the very Boethian doctrine which so many Medievals took for granted actually succeeds in raising a serious problem insofar as his notion of a concrete nature effectively demands that it also be subsistent (a difficulty already vigorously present in the doctrinal treatises of the Cappadocian Fathers). If we regard (relatively) modern attempts to better seize the mystery in question, expressed, for example, in terms of an "integration of the being of the Word" or "immediate participation in uncreated being", or of a "secondary being" (as in an exceptional passage of St. Thomas[275]), or a "termination of the nature" (by some non-essential aspect called "subsistence"); or, to complicate the semantics even more, we hear that "the human nature subsists in the person of the Word", but "it is the Word who subsists in his human nature (as well as in his divine nature)", etc., how can one avoid thinking that we ought to return to a discussion of the basic principles according to which one would be capable of affirming such propositions? There is obviously no single univocal notion of subsistence, but what is worse is to employ the term without having previously defined it or even having situated it amongst its neighboring concepts like that of existence.

It is precisely in this regard that a special clarity shall be sought from Boethius' exposition. We will begin our analysis by rapidly sketching the Boethian concept of nature, which shall conduct us to more subtle considerations connected with personhood[276].

---

[275] The idea of an *"esse secundarium"* which is not an accidental being but inscribed in the very substantial constitution of a subject posterior to its *esse simpliciter* is considered by St. Thomas in the *De Unione Verbi Incarnati* The concept is arguably extraneous to Thomas' general metaphysical views and represents in certain respects a discontinuity with the metaphysical commitments characteristic of the Thomistic synthesis. For an in-depth comparison of the *De Unione* with the rest of the Thomistic corpus directly related to the hypostatic union, cf. A. Patfoort, *L'Unité d'être dans le Christ d'après S. Thomas*, Desclée, Tournai 1964, especially p. 150-189.

[276] Our goal is to illustrate (and exploit) certain philosophical underpinnings of Boethius' philosophy of the concrete subsistent or person. Studies on this subject are numerous. Amongst the most important literature we refer the reader to R. BEINHAUER, *Untersuchungen zu philosophisch-theologischen Termini in "De Trinitate" des Boethius*, VWGÖ, Vienna 1990; K. BRUDER, *Die philosophischen Elemente in den Opuscula Sacra des Boethius: ein Beitrag zur Quellengeschichte der Philosophie der Scholastik*, F. Meiner, Leipzig 1928; P. COURCELLE, "Étude critique sur les Commentaires de Boèce (IX-XV siècles)", *AHDLMA* 13 (1939), p. 5-140; I. CRAEMER-RUEGENBERG, *Die Substanzmetaphysik des Boethius in den Opuscula sacra*, Diss., University of Cologne, 1969; A. CROCCO, *Introduzione a Boezio*, Empireo, Naples 1975; K. DÜRR, *The Propositional Logic of Boethius*, North-Holland Publishing Co., Amsterdam 1951 (reprinted in 1969 and in 1980 by Greenwood Press, Westport, Conn.); ELSÄSSER, M., *Anicius Manlius Severinus Boethius, Die theologischen Traktate*, Felix Meiner Verlag, Hamburg 1988; *Das Person-Verständnis des Boethius*, Diss., Julius-Maximilians-Universität zu Würzburg, Münster 1973; JORGE J. E. GRACIA, "Boethius and the Problem of Individuation in the Commentaries on the 'Isagoge' ", in *Atti, Congresso internazionale di studi boeziani* (Pavia, 5-8 Ottobre 1980), edited by L. Obertello, Editrice Herder, Rome 1981, p. 169-182; P. HADOT, "Forma essendi. Interpretation philologique et interpretation philosophique d'une formule de Boèce", *Les études classiques* 38 (1970), p. 143-156; "La distinction de l'être et de létant dans le "De hebdomadibus" de Boèce", in *Miscellanea Mediaevalia* 2, "Die Metaphysik im Mittelalter", Walter de Gruyter, Berlin 1963, p. 147-153; D. C. HALL, *The Trinity: an Analysis of St. Thomas Aquinas' "Expositio" of the "De Trinitate" of Boethius*, E. J. Brill, Leiden/New York 1992; M. LLUCH-BAIXAULI, *La teologia de Boecio en la transición del mundo clásico al mundo medieval*, Ediciones Universidad de Navarra, Pamplona 1990; M. LUTZ-BACHMANN, "'Natur' und 'Person' in den 'Opuscula Sacra' des A.M.S. Boethius", *Theologie und Philosophie* 58 (1983), p. 48-70; C. MICAELLI, "'Natura' e 'Persona' nel 'Contra Eu-

A definition of "nature"

Following the divisions in the order of beings, Boethius, in the *Contra Eutychen et Nestorium*[277], establishes four definitions of nature operating on Aristotelian principles[278]. First, "nature belongs to those things

tychen et Nestorium' di Boezio: osservazioni su alcuni problemi filosofici e linguistici", in *Atti, Congresso internazionale di studi boeziani* (Pavia, 5-8 Ottobre 1980), edited by L. Obertello, Editrice Herder, Rome 1981, p. 327-336; *Studi sui trattati teologici di Boezio*, M. D'Auria, Naples 1988; M. MILANI, *Boezio: l'ultimo degli antichi*, Camunia, Milan 1994 [focussing on the personality, history and cultural impact of Boethius]; A. MILANO, *Persona in teologia*, Edizioni Dehoniane, Naples 1987; M. NÉDONCELLE, "Les variations de Boèce sur la personne", *RevSR* 29 (1955), p. 201-238; L. OBERTELLO, *Severino Boezio*, 2 vols., Accademia ligure di scienze e lettere, Genova 1974 [this work, representing the leading word in Boethian studies, contains an ample bibliography]; L. M. DE RIJK, "Boèce logicien et philosophe: ses positions sémantiques et sa métaphysique de l'être", in *Atti, Congresso internazionale di studi boeziani* (Pavia, 5-8 Ottobre 1980), edited by L. Obertello, Editrice Herder, Rome 1981, p. 141-156; J. J. ACOSTA RODRIGUEZ, "Los conceptos esse e id quod est en Boecio", *Ciudad de Dios* 202 (1989), p. 613-656; S. A. TURIENZO, "Aspectos del Problema de la Persona en el Siglo XII", in *Miscellanea Mediaevalia* 2, "Die Metaphysik im Mittelalter", Walter de Gruyter, Berlin 1963, p. 180-183; B. WALD, "Aristoteles, Boethius und der Begriff der Person im Mittelalter", *Archiv für Begriffsgeschichte* 39 (1996), p. 161-179; "'Rationalis naturae individua substantia'. Aristoteles, Boethius und der Begriff der Person im Mittelalter", in Aertsen, J. A./Speer, A. (editors), *Individuum und Individualität im Mittelalter*, Walter de Gruyter, Berlin/New York 1996 (*Miscellanea Mediaevalia* 24), p. 371-388. For an indication of the editions as well as the existing translations of the Boethian treatises, see L. Obertello (editor), *Boezio, La consolazione della filosofia. Gli opuscoli teologici*, Milan 1979; cf. also M. Lluch-Baixauli, "Bibliografia commemorativa de Manlio Severino Boecio", *Scripta Theol.* 21 (1989), p. 213-225. Noteworthy Thomistic studies related to our investigation of Boethius include J. R. CATAN, "Aristotele e S. Tommaso intorno all' 'actus essendi'", *Rivista di Filosofia Neoscolastica* 73 (1981), p. 639-695; M. GRABMANN, "Die Schrift 'De ente et essentia', und die Seinsmetaphysik des heiligen Thomas von Aquin", in *Mittelalterliches Geistesleben*, M. Grabmann/Max Hüber (editors), Munich 1926 (reprinted in 1956), vol. 1, p. 314-331; D. LORENZ, *I fondamenti dell'ontologia tomista, Il trattato "De ente et essentia"*, Edizioni studio domenicano, Bologna 1992; R. MCINERNY, *Boethius and Aquinas*, Catholic University of America Press, Washington D.C. 1990; M. D. ROLAND-GOSSELIN, *Le "De ente et essentia" de Saint Thomas d'Aquin*, Vrin, Paris 1948; T. TYN, *Metafisica della sostanza, partecipazione e analogie entis*, Edizioni studio domenicano, Bologna 1991.

[277] Anicius Manlius Severinus Boethius, *Contra Eutychen et Nestorium*, I. We cite the theological treatises of Boethius according to the Loeb edition, ed. H. F. Stewart - E. K. Rand, *Boethius, The Theological Tractates, The Consolation of Philosophy*, London-Cambridge 1953.

[278] According to A. Milano, the first, third and fourth definitions clearly derive from Aristotle, while the second should be ascribed to Plato and Proclus (cf. A. Milano, *Persona in teologia*, Edizioni Dehoniane, Naples 1987, p. 358). For the sources of Boethius in general, see L. Obertello, *Severino Boezio*, 2 vols., Genova 1974, I, p. 386-562; for strictly neo-Platonic influences, see P. Courcelle, *La Consolation de la philosophie dans la tradition littéraire. Antécedents et posterité de Boèce*, Études Augustiniennes, Paris 1967; for an appreciation of the Porphyrian influence on Boethius,

which, since they exist, can in some way be apprehended by the intellect"[279]; second, "nature is either that which is able to act or be acted upon"[280]; third, "nature is a *per se* and non-accidental principle of movement"[281]; and fourth, "nature is the specific difference that gives form to anything"[282]. As remarked by A. Milano[283], the successive definitions, more than a mere collocation of different intensions, represent a logical passage from the less determined to the more determined, from a wider signification to a more restricted signification, as is typical of the Porphyrian hierarchical structure of ideas, ordered from top to bottom according to decreasing extension and increasing comprehension. Such is the Boethian methodology in discovering the signification of person.

The first, second and fourth definitions can be applied to both the divinity and humanity of Christ while the third, confined by Boethius to corporal substances alone[284], refers only to the humanity. The fourth definition designates something essential, as when in common speech we would ask "what is the nature of man?" and reply "rationality" which is that which makes us to be what we are. Similarly, the term "nature" can refer to the whole form of something (*forma totius*[285]), and is the essence properly speaking in this sense. Both instances of the fourth definition indicate therefore that through which and in which a thing has being, for "nothing is said to be[286] because of

see A. Milano, op. cit., p. 334-361. Cf. also, M. Elsässer, *Das Person-Verständnis des Boethius*, Diss., Julius-Maximilians-Universität zu Würzburg, Münster 1973, p. 13-28.

[279] Boethius, *Contra Eut.*, I, 8-10, ed. Loeb, p. 78: *"natura est earum rerum quae, cum sit, quoquo modo intellectu capi possunt"*. Cf. Aristotle, *Metaphysics* VII, 6, 1031b7; Aquinas, In VII *Met.*, Lect. 5 (ed. Cathala, No. 1365); In V *Met.*, Lect. 2 (ed. Cathala, No. 764); *De ente et ess.*, I; *De princ. nat.*, II, 14; *De veritate*, q. 1, a. 1c; q. 7, a. 8c; *Sum. theol.*, I, 34, 1 ad 3.

[280] Boethius, *Contra Eut.*, I, 25-26, ed. Loeb, p. 78: *"natura est vel quod facere vel quod pati possit"*.

[281] Boethius, *Contra Eut.*, I, 41-42, ed. Loeb, p. 80: *"natura est motus principium per se non per accidens"*.

[282] Boethius, *Contra Eut.*, I, 57-58, ed. Loeb, p. 80: *"natura est unam quamque rem informans specifica differentia"*.

[283] Cf. A. Milano, *Persona in teologia*, Edizioni Dehoniane, Naples 1987, p. 335, 358.

[284] Cf. Boethius, *Contra Eut.*, I, 34-37, ed. Loeb, p. 78-80: *"quod si naturae nomen relictis incorporeis substantiis ad corporales usque contrahitur, ut corporeae tantum substantiae naturam habere videantur, sicut Aristoteles"*.

[285] We distinguish the *whole form* from the proper form of the whole which is none other than the formal cause taken alone, for, the *forma totius*, in natural substances, is the matter and form taken together as essential causes. Cf. Aquinas, *De ente et ess.*, II.

[286] It is interesting to note that the translation of Stewart-Rand – as well as the French translation by H. Merle, *Boèce, Courts traités de théologie*, Cerf, Paris 1991 – give "to exist" in place of "to be" (for *"esse"*). This interpretation poses no problem, as long as

"being" should be taken in the strong Aristotelian sense of the term, that is, as signifying the reality of a thing with respect to act (cf. *Metaphysics*, Bk. IX, especially c. 6 & 8). While it is difficult to determine the quality of Boethius' Aristotelianism, and the degree of his "Platonism" is debated, for those who oppose to interpreting "being" in the sense of "to exist", we consecrate the following remarks. Let it be noted, first of all, that whatever the acceptation of the sense of *"esse"* in Boethius, this does not affect the principal object of our investigation – which is the relation between "substance" and "subsistence", "nature" and "person". It is what is proper to the notion of "subsistence" in itself that changes according to the sense given to *"esse"* – here taking an essential character, there an existential character –, but in this skirmish it is only the coherence of the idea of "subsistent universals" which is affected. This latter category is of little importance for our study, but we have taken it into account in our schematization in order to better respect the different possible points of view.

In his *Metaphysics* (especially IV, 2 & VI, 2), Aristotle observes that we use the word "being" in diverse ways: to deny as well as to affirm, to attribute properties as well as to attribute existence. There are, in particular, two radically different manners of considering being, namely, being insofar as the being of propositions, that is logical being, which does not attribute existence to the essence it serves to describe, and real or ontological being which makes a thing to be outside of nothing, that it be real.

The same rudimentary distinction is articulated by Aristotle (*Met.* V, 7) when he differentiates the senses of accidental being, essential being, being as true, and being insofar as potency or act (as for what concerns us, we shall only consider essential being – not being interested in that which is only accidentally called being – that is, real being which is divided according to the ten categories). Now, it is of primary importance to note that Aristotle does not attribute being to a thing (taking into account the fact that, for Aristotle, being, taken in the sense of *"ens"* [τὸ ὄv], is not a predicate – for which reason it would be better to say that, for Aristotle, a thing is not said "to be") except insofar as it is related to that which is said to be in the strong and essential sense of the term (which sends us to the categories and, in the final analysis, to "substance", the only thing properly said to be – cf. *Met.* IV,2; V,7; 8; VI,4; *Cat.* 3; 5).

But this thing which "is", how are we to understand it? For J. Tricot, Aristotle directly intends the existent subject: *"le sujet existant... parce que le prédicat est un accident du sujet existant... à la fois être et substance... parce que le sujet... lui-même existe"* (citation from the text of Aristotle following the translation given by Tricot: Aristote, *La Métaphysique*, t. I, p. 269-70, J. Vrin, Paris, 1986). Unless we are to situate ourselves within the problematic perspective of the *Sophist*, where being (εἶναι) is reduced to the stability of the essence, where οὐσία ("substance") is that which truly possesses being because it remains what it is, unless we are to adopt an ontology unable ever to exit from essentiality, there is no other way to take it, and it is not for nothing that Thomas Aquinas developed his thesis of the "act of existence" on the basis of an Aristotelian metaphysics (even if filtered by Peripatetism) without having indicated a particular divergence from the thought of the "Philosopher" in this regard. But St. Thomas is not the only one to have interpreted Aristotle (such as he received him) in this manner: consider Albert the Great, Alexander of Hales and Gilbert of Poitiers, to give a few examples. All of these authors effectively treated the being attributed by Boethius to the nature as designating the fact of existing (something which becomes manifest if one considers the perspective of these authors on the hierarchy of acquired perfections, where the first perfection is "being", after which the perfections of action and the goodness deriving from second act may be attributed, perfections which presuppose the actual existence of a nature; the same perspective is evidenced in their notion of the dependence of contingent being for its being, that is for its existence).

That Boethius himself could have had in mind a sense of "being" – in this context where he says that a nature "is" (where the verb "to be" is not envisaged substantively like the *quo est* which composes with the *quod est*) – which not be purely logical but which would not imply existence seems doubtful to us. To say that Boethius would have exclusively attached himself to an essentialist idea of *esse* is inadmissible in light as much of the hardiness of his distinction between being and that which is, as of the fact that such a thesis renders in some fashion inexistent the very natures to which Boethius most wants to ascribe existence – such as the human nature of Christ (natures which undergo change). Though the thought of Boethius on subsistent universals, i.e. universals which possess being and which have no need for accidents in order to be, leaves a place for being insofar as an expression of the immutability of an essence, one must recognize in Boethius the full importance of being as "act of an essence" (existential sense of *"forma essendi"* and *"esse suscipere"* of *Quomodo sub.*, II, 28-34), that is, the act which poses a nature in reality. Peremptorily, A. Milano declares: *"Lo stato di esistenza attuale è espresso da Boezio con la formula: 'Ciò che è, recevuta la forma dell'essere, è e sussiste'... È evidente che il risultato finale dell'accoglimento della forma essendi da parte della sostanza o 'ciò che è' è uno stato di esistenza attuale"* – A. Milano, *Persona in teologia*, Edizioni Dehoniane, Naples 1987, p. 344.

Since there is room for both conceptualizations of being in Boethius, one can reasonably ask whether the being he attributes to universals does not suggest that they exist in the Platonic sense. In fact, if we were to restrict ourselves exclusively to the essentialist position proper to the *Sophist*, we would have no distinction between the universal essence which is not (in the Aristotelian sense) and the universal essence which is, all of the reality of the "being" being contained in the essence as such. The major obstacle to this position, however, is the fact that this being is effectively undifferentiated from a logical or purely intentional being inasmuch as the being of a thing is inseparable from (even dependent upon) the intelligibility of the essence, an intelligibility deriving from a stability which is assured only to the extent that the essence is separated from the reality known by experience – it is a stability by way of abstraction or evacuation of intentional content, which amounts to the inalterability of its notion. If, on the other hand, we admit the realism of the Boethian being, the universal which is but which is not yet *"substantia"* becomes nothing other than the universal in the Platonic sense.

According to the rather realist Boethian perspective, one should minimize the sense of *"esse"* and *"est"* taken as expressions of essential immutability and give to them a sense expressing a veritable property (that of actuality) attributed to the nature of which they are said. From this point of view, we find it difficult to conceive that an essence have being (in the real sense of the term) but not exist. What does it mean to have being for a thing which does not exist? One can speak, we repeat, of what an essence is from the point of view of its proper definitional constitution, and here one remains indeed at the "essential" level (in opposition to the "existential" level), but the being of which we are speaking here is nothing other than the logical or intentional being proper to our consideration of what is said to be "this" or "that", but this is not the being attributed to an essence when one says simply that "it is" or *"esse habet"*. In this latter case, one is speaking of real being, and real being confers existence, implies existence. Every nature, therefore, which really is exists. This represents in no way a projection of Thomas Aquinas on Boethius, but rather the simple acceptation of the sense of the term such as it imposes itself, such as it presented itself to the thought of Thomas Aquinas and other Scholastics. It is also the reason for which the only French translation of this treatise of Boethius as

matter, but because of its distinctive form"[287], and "man has essence...
because he is"[288]. That this latter definition appears to occupy the
central role in distinguishing nature from person becomes manifest
when contending with Nestorius, where Boethius re-emphasizes the

well as the English translation of the critical edition by Loeb were legitimately able
to render the word *"esse"* with "existence", and *"est"* with "exist". We are in agreement with this interpretation, because the veritable being of a thing implies its existence (just as its existence is the sign and immediate effect of its being) – interior to
a realist and not exclusively essentialist metaphysic, the choice between these terms
is not of first importance.

Within this perspective (where to truly be is to exist), it should be noted that to
say that an essence "is", as in the phrase "humanity is", does not mean that it "is" in
itself or as such. When one says that "man is", this does not mean that "man" is
something existing by itself outside of nothingness; nor, however, does it simply
mean that "man" is above change and invariable. What is signified is indeed the
veritable existence of humanity and of man, but according, precisely, as it is possible to attribute true being or existence to this humanity, that is according as this
humanity is said to be real and existent, which is insofar as realized in this or that
individual. This removes nothing from the essential reality of "man", which still
remains some *thing* by itself: by itself, it "is something" (where the copula expresses
the truth of the proposition). But this "humanity" considered in itself does not
possess "being": by itself, it "is" not. In the first case, we signify the thing according
to its concept; in the second, according to its actuality. One can say, it is true, that
"man is" in actuality, that "man exists", but at this moment one no longer signifies
this humanity such as it is in itself, but one signifies it according as it exists. Thus
the mode of signification proper to (and determinate of the sense of) the subject
depends upon the intension of the predicate (affair of supposition): from the moment one attributes "being" to an essence or nature, one is already in the process of
intellecting and signifying it according to the modality proper to it insofar as existing, that is, according as it is found in particular existents. It therefore no longer
represents the abstract or universal essence but the concrete nature with which it is
identified. The only difference between the essence in itself and the concrete nature which exists and which represents its instantiation is the mode of signification.
To say, therefore, that "humanity is" is not to attribute "being" to it without admitting (or in a manner indifferent to) existence, for humanity is not said "to be" except insofar as it is identified with that to which one attributes existence, namely
the individual existent (for that nature is found or realized in the individual precisely as identifiable with it *in re*); already by affirming the nature "to be", we signify
it according as it is concretely (inasmuch as it is identified with the individual in
which it is realized), thus indicating the essence insofar as it is individualized. This
identity *in re* of the nature insofar as it is (i.e. viewed from the point of view of the
individual conditions by which it is) and the subject of its instantiation, of the particular nature and the existent, is, as we shall have the occasion to see later, the explanatory thread for the fundamental identification to be made by Maximus Confessor between the human nature of Christ concretely considered and the humano-
divine person which it is.

[287] Boethius, *De Trin.*, II, 28-29, ed. Loeb, p. 10: *"nihil igitur secundum materiam esse dicitur sed secundum propriam formam"*.

[288] *"Est igitur et hominis quidem essentia... quoniam est"* – Boethius, *Contra Eut.*, III, 79-82,
ed. Loeb, p. 90.

definition of nature as "the specific property of any substance"[289], thereby restricting nature to the essence. The respective assignments of these denominations of "nature" to things, according to Boethius' thought, yields:

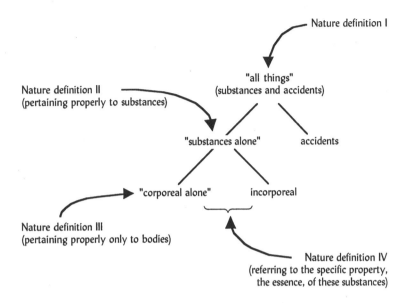

Defining "person"

Boethius first situates "person" within the divisions of beings (to which belongs nature[290]) in order to ascribe its distinctive genus and species. "One thing is clear, namely, that nature is a [logical] substrate of person, and that person cannot be predicated apart from nature"[291].

---

289 *"Hoc interim constet quod inter naturam personamque differre praediximus, quoniam natura est cuiuslibet substantiae specificata proprietas, persona vero rationabilis naturae individua substantia"* – Boethius, *Contra Eut.,* IV, 5-9, ed. Loeb, p. 92.

290 This implies the distinction between a thing and its nature, *id quod est, id quo est,* or the existent and its essence (for which even in God, as with essence and existence, there is logical distinction). It is important to be attentive to the fact that the difference between *id quo est* and *id quod est* is not the same as that between essence and existence but pertains more precisely to that between a thing, that is, the "existent" and its essence. Cf. Boethius, *Quomodo sub.,* II-VIII, ed. Loeb, p. 40-42.

291 *"Manifestum est personae subiectam esse naturam nec praeter naturam personam posse praedicari"* – Boethius, *Contra Eut.,* II, 10-11, ed. Loeb, p. 82.

Now, since natures are either substances or accidents[292], and person is nowise predicated of accidents, it remains that "person is properly predicated of substances"[293]. And, while substances can be either particular or universal, "person cannot anywhere be predicated of universals but only of particulars and individuals"[294]. Hence:

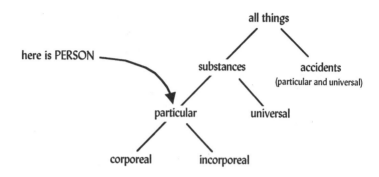

whence the definition of person: *"naturae[295] rationabilis individua[296] substantia"[297]*.

---

[292] *"Naturae aliae sunt substantiae, aliae accidentes"* – Boethius, *Contra Eut.*, II, 14-15, ed. Loeb, p. 82.

[293] Boethius, *Contra Eut.*, II, 18, ed. Loeb, p. 82: *"personam in substantiis dici conveniat"*.

[294] Boethius, *Contra Eut.*, II, 47-49, ed. Loeb, p. 84: *"nusquam in universalibus persona dici potest, sed in singularibus tantum atque in individuis"*.

[295] In light of the analogicity of the term "nature", said of matter and form and even of the term of generation (by which it is extended to the essence, in the sense that the essence of anything is called nature), and in light of the relativity of its concept implying a respect toward operation, the use of the term in defining person, particularly because person is predicated of both creatures and God, may seem inappropriate. If we follow St. Thomas (*Sum. theol.*, I, 29, 1, ad 4), however, Boethius' use of the term *naturae* in the definition of person is entirely fitting; for "nature", in that context, is taken as signifying essence inasmuch as essence is what is completed by the form (which is most fully "nature" as the active principle of operation) which specifies it. Since that which is commonly called nature (namely form) specifies and determines the essence – that is, makes the essence what it is –, then that essence itself is called nature (since that which is nature is its very constitution). Nature is extended to essence, then, insofar as the natural form performs a specifying role (which is why Boethius calls nature "the specific property" or specific difference, according as this latter completes the definition and is derived from the special form of a thing). "Nature", in this context, therefore, signifies the essence as specified, and is not wholly equivalent to "essence" simply taken, that is, according to its proper mode of signification only, which pertains to being (which is broader as such than this or that kind of being). Because, according to St. Thomas, person signifies the singular in a determined genus, it is more fitting to use the term "nature" (according as it signifies essence in the sense just described) than "essence" in

The definition consists in various elements, all of which we shall examine in depth later. But what, briefly, does this definition affirm about persons? Besides the obvious point of rationality, Boethius declares that every person has a nature. There cannot be a person which is not also a nature, for "person" cannot be predicated in precision from "nature"[298]. The converse, however, is not true; many natures are not persons. "Nature" is broader in extension than "person" and includes "person", for which reason Boethius proceeds to a notion of "person" by means of conceptual restriction corresponding to the Porphyrian rules of logic[299]. Person is said to be an *individual* substance. The concept of individuality intended by Boethius when defining "person" as an "individual" is not easy to determine, not only because of the extreme difficulty in distinguishing his own opinion from that of the author from whom he borrows the notion, but also because of the different and apparently contending theories his analysis brings into discussion. Despite a tendency, when commenting the *Isagoge*, to reduce a substance's individuality to an effect of the collection of its accidents[300], elsewhere, when confronted with the speculative implications of his Christian faith, Boethius seems to confess a substantial concept of individuality. Individuality for Boethius,

its definition, since the specificity connoted in the *modus significandi* of the former better indicates the determination expressed in the concept of person, while the indetermination of the latter expresses nothing of generic limitation.

[296] As opposed to a universal substance such as genus, species, etc. (i.e., secondary substances). This is the minimum sense of the term. It can also be argued that the term "individual" is intended to signify a more pregnant sense of individuality, such as that associated with the notion of self-possession of being, or self-possession of subsistence whereby the nature is a self-contained subject of attribution and operation. A critical look at this crucial aspect of person, namely individuality, would befit a subsequently thorough examination of "substance". Cf. supra, "A WORD ABOUT INDIVIDUALITY AND THE 'PROBLEM OF INDIVIDUATION'", p. 51; cf. infra, "BOETHIUS' DEFINITION AND THE PRINCIPAL CONSTITUENT OF PERSONALITY", p. 341; "THE INCOMMUNICABILITY IMPORTED BY 'INDIVIDUAL'", p. 347.

[297] Boethius, *Contra Eut.*, III, 4-5, ed. Loeb, p. 84.

[298] On the unique manner in which "nature" may be predicated of the person, and the distinction to be observed between nature so taken and nature as distinguishable from the person (when the latter is understood as *possessing* the former or – as expressed in the Boethian formula – as "*of* a nature"), cf. M. Elsässer, *Das Person-Verständnis des Boethius*, Diss., Julius-Maximilians-Universität zu Würzburg, Munster 1973, p. 63-66.

[299] Cf. A. Milano, *Persona in teologia*, Edizioni Dehoniane, Naples 1987, p. 357-358.

[300] Cf. Boethius, *In Isag.* III: PL 64, 111C-112A; cf. Jorge J. E. Gracia, "Boethius and the Problem of Individuation in the Commentaries on the 'Isagoge' ", in *Atti, Congresso internazionale di studi boeziani* (Pavia, 5-8 Ottobre 1980), edited by L. Obertello,

according to A. Milano, though made visible by means of the accidents, nevertheless consists in a *quid proprium* of the substantial order[301]. If such an interpretation is correct, then the notion of individuality employed by Boethius in his definition will more readily adapt itself to analogous predication across the entire spectrum of persons, from men, to angels, to God. Now, the individual which the person is is an individual *substance.* Boethius takes up the classical Aristotelian distinction between substance and accident, recognizing, along with Aristotle, that that which truly is, in an absolute and unqualified way, is substance or οὐσία. Person is the *per se* existent, and it is the *perseity* of substance (with respect to the act of being – which we may legitimately call existence[302]) which is signified by its predication of persons in general. While it is true that Boethius radically amplifies the Aristotelian doctrine of substance, it is perhaps not exact to affirm that he modifies it in a sense implying that he dispenses with the Aristotelian concept, substituting it with a Christian notion of the created subject in distinction from its being[303]. The Boethian "transformation", which would be better designated "amplification", consists in specifying the signification of substance in such a way as to (1) allow for a distinction between substantiality as such and its act of existence, between *id quod est* and *esse*[304], and (2) allow for a distinction

Editrice Herder, Rome 1981, p. 169-182; cf. A. Milano, *Persona in teologia,* Edizioni Dehoniane, Naples 1987, p. 336.

[301] Cf. A. Milano, *Persona in teologia,* Edizioni Dehoniane, Naples 1987, p. 358. The texts which Milano basis this conclusion on are: *"persona accidentibus non posse constitui... persona in substantiis dici conveniat"* – Boethius, *Contra Eut.* II, 15-18 (ed. Loeb, p. 82); and *"individua principaliter substantiae sunt, et propriae et maximae... Individua igitur aequaliter substantiae sunt"* – *In Cat. Arist.* I: PL 64, 188C. The passages, however, can easily be taken in another way and as wholly conforming to the concept of individuality as expressed in the *Commentary on the Isagoge.*

[302] Cf. supra, note 286 (on right acceptation of the Boethian *"esse").*

[303] The criticisms of A. Milano with regard to the Boethian use of the term *"substantia"* to designate persons in both the natural and supernatural order, seem to reflect a certain speculative inelasticity, inasmuch as they restrictively envisage "substance" according to but one of its modes of signifying, namely that according to which it is contra-distinguished from *"subsistentia".*

[304] On the various ways in which the distinction as well as the sense of the explicitly distinguished terms are inteneded to be taken, see L. B. Geiger, *La participation dans la philosophie de St. Thomas d'Aquin,* Paris 1942, p. 36-73; P. Hadot, "Forma essendi. Interpretation philologique et interpretation philosophique d'une formule de Boèce", *Les études classiques* 38 (1970), p. 143-156; "La distinction de l'être et de létant dans le "De hebdomadibus" de Boèce", in *Miscellanea Mediaevalia* 2, "Die Metaphysik im Mittelalter", Walter de Gruyter, Berlin 1963, p. 147-153; B. Maioli, *Gilberto Porretano: dalla grammatica speculativa alla metafisica del concreto,* Bulzoni, Rome 1979, p. 184-192, 214-215; M. D. Roland-Gosselin, *Le "De ente et essentia" de Saint Thomas d'Aquin,* Vrin, Paris 1948, p. 142-145.

between substance and subsistence, that is, between existents which are the subjects of accidents and those which are not. The latter division is especially sanctioned by the fact that Boethius treats of existents of both the natural and the supernatural order. Since Aristotle was not concerned with substances not belonging to the natural order, a distinction within οὐσία between accident-subjective and non-accident-subjective kinds was not opportune. The former distinction (number one above) is certainly not present in Aristotle. However, much of the Boethian discussion of substance concerns the divine substance where the distinction does not apply; and, given that his definition of person aims at embracing every person of any sort, the concept of substance retained in the definition cannot imply any real distinction between *id quod est* and *esse*. Person, in the end, can accurately be defined according to substance, provided: (1) that "substance" not be intended in the sense in which it signifies a real distinction from being; and (2) that it signify in a way indifferent to the possible division of Aristotelian substance (οὐσία broadly speaking) into "substance" (taken as a predicably inferior type of οὐσία) and "subsistence". Though we have defended a sense in which substance may be legitimately employed by Boethius in defining person, this does not mean that a better term or a better definition was not available. We shall address this and other questions in what follows.

A question of language

Once having systematically defined "person", Boethius is ready to examine and compare the Greek and Latin uses of language turning about its notion. However, the translational difficulties, of which Boethius himself is aware [305], tend to complicate the issue: "the Greeks far more clearly called the individual subsistence of a rational nature by the name ὑπόστασις... giving the name ὑπόστασις to the individual subsistence" [306]. It appears as though the term subsistence has replaced the term substance in the proposed definition of person. Is Boethius equivocating on the meanings of these terms? Have the Greeks attached the name ὑπόστασις to a reality somehow different from that to which Boethius attaches *persona*? There is an alteration in vocabulary between what Boethius ultimately uses in his own defini-

---

[305] Cf. Boethius, *Contra Eut.*, III, 23-29, ed. Loeb, p. 86.
[306] Ibid.: *"longe vero illi signatius naturae rationabilis individuam subsistentiam* ὑπο-στάσεως *nomine vocaverunt...* ὑπόστασιν *vocat individuam subsistentiam".*

tion and what he claims belongs to the long-standing Greek tradition. Yet, in respect of the definition of person, Boethius is apparently indifferent to the shift, as his subsequent use of the Greek expression to support his own reasoning suggests. Although he uses the term *substantia*, we need not consider that as having been "chosen" over *subsistentia*; indeed Boethius makes no comment as to the favorableness of either term. It is our opinion that the term *subsistentia* ultimately presents itself as the superior, and this resting upon the distinctions that Boethius himself elaborates[307]. It remains somewhat perplexing that he employs the term *substantia* when the entirety of his treatise is examined, yet the context from which his definition of person emerges explains perhaps why it does not include the term *subsistentia*, since the definition occurs prior to Boethius' establishing the difference between *substantia* and *subsistentia*.

Subsistence and its relation to substance

Subsistence, according to Boethius' exposition, can be interpreted, as we shall see, such that subsistence is substance (in the sense that they are predicable of one another, according to a precise mode of supposition[308]), that is, a subsistence is a "substance" once the subsistence (which is nothing other than an existing essence[309]) has been "substantiated" through the medium of particularization or individuation[310]. Thus substance is a kind or manner of being of a subsistence. Any interpretation, therefore, which, while recognizing the distinction between essence, subsistence and substance, nevertheless dismisses the notion of subsistence from the Boethian understanding of person[311] misses a very important point: it is precisely the notion of

---

[307] M. Elsässer is equally sensitive to the discrepancy; cf. *Das Person-Verständnis des Boethius*, Diss., Julius-Maximilians-Universität zu Würzburg, Munster 1973, p. 76-78.

[308] The term supposition designates the role exercised by a word in a proposition when that word stands for a determinate object; it is thus the linguistic mode according to which the substantive term denotes the object (according to precise sense and extension as determined by the context). The logical notion is especially important when speaking about God and applies in Trinitarian theology to the various names by which the substance or one or more persons is able to be designated. Cf. Albert, *I Sent.*, d. 2, a. 18 & 25; d. 4, a. 1 & 6.

[309] See Boethius, *Contra Eut.*, III, 31-39, ed. Loeb, p. 86-88.

[310] Cf. Boethius, *Contra Eut.*, III, 36-39, ed. Loeb, p. 88.

[311] S. A. Turienzo, "Aspectos del Problema de la Persona en el Siglo XII", in *Miscellanea Mediaevalia* 2, "Die Metaphysik im Mittelalter", Walter de Gruyter, Berlin 1963, p. 180-183. It seems that the author oversimplifies the dynamics of the scenario. Recognizing that *"hay que distinguir entre essentia, subsistentia y substantia. La esencia*

"subsistences" laid out by Boethius which can afford an adequate understanding of person aimed at satisfying both Trinitarian and non-Trinitarian demands. This, however, only becomes possible with reference to Boethius' other "theological" tractates[312].

A discerning statement gives us an important insight into the issue: "essences can indeed be in universals, but they 'substand' in individuals and particulars alone"[313]. The English translation given in the Loeb seems dangerously inaccurate: "essences... *subsist* in individuals". The verb employed is *substare* (*"substant"*) which Boethius is soon to explicitly distinguish from *subsistere*. "Wherefore since subsistences themselves are present in universals but acquire substance in particulars they rightly gave the name ὑπόστασις to subsistences which acquired substance through the medium of particulars. For to no one looking at it with any care or penetration will subsistence and substance appear identical"[314]. We have essences which are present in both universals and particulars and subsistences which are also in both universals and particulars. The latter acquire substance in particulars, through which (or "in which") they *substant*. This does not necessarily mean that once particularized, a subsistent is necessarily or has necessarily acquired substance but rather asserts that a subsistent, if it is to acquire substance, does so through the medium of particulars. That is, a subsistent is capable of being particular without thereby being identified with substance. Now, the "equivalents of the Greek terms οὐσίωσις οὐσιῶσθαι are respectively *subsistentia* and *subsistere*, while their ὑπόστασις ὑφίστασθαι are represented by our *substantia* and *substare*"[315]. "Subsistence", then, is indetachable from

es abstracta; subsistencia y sustancia son concretas", he proceeds to eliminate the (Boethian) notion of subsistence from the Boethian understanding of personhood: *"Prescindiendo del lado platónico de la explicación, que afecta sobre todo al término subsistencia, la explicación del ser de la persona surge en relación con el concepto aristotélico de sustancia".*

312 *De Trinitate, Utrum Pater et Filius, Quomodo substantiae.*

313 Boethius, *Contra Eut.*, III, 31-35, ed. Loeb, p. 86: *"αἱ οὐσίαι ἐν μὲν τοῖς καθόλου εἶναι δύνανται· ἐν δὲ τοῖς ἀτόμοις καὶ κατὰ μέρος μόνοις ὑφίστανται, id est: essentiae in universalibus quidem esse possunt, in solis vero individuis et particularibus substant".*

314 Boethius, *Contra Eut.*, III, 36-41, ed. Loeb, p. 88: *"quocirca cum ipsae subsistentiae in universalibus quidem sint, in particularibus vero capiant substantiam, iure subsistentias particulariter substantes* ὑποστάσεις *appelaverunt. Neque enim pensius subtiliusque intuenti idem videbitur esse subsistentia quod substantia".*

315 Boethius, *Contra Eut.*, III, 42-45, ed. Loeb, p. 88: *"nam quod Graeci* οὐσίωσιν *vel* οὐσιῶσθαι *dicunt, id nos subsistentiam vel subsistere appellamus; quod vero illi* ὑπόστασιν *vel* ὑφίστασθαι, *id nos substantiam vel substare interpretamur".* (The verbal οὐσιῶσθαι would render: "to be existing as an essence").

the notions of "being", "substance" and "essence" (broadly understood). We have seen how a subsistence is an essence in as much as they are equally distributed over existing universals and particulars[316]. But subsistence is not identical to every kind of essence, according as it is distinguished from that kind of essence which is purely universal or non-real (in the Aristotelian sense) and from every "secondary" substance[317]. Whence its inseparable relation to being, since these subsistences really exist, whether or not they are understood in the Platonic sense as existing universals (genera, etc.) or as particulars. Let us schematize these observations:

---

[316] Boethius, *Contra Eut.*, III, 33-39, ed. Loeb, p. 86-88: *"essentiae in universalibus quidem esse possunt... ipsae subsistentiae in universalibus quidem sint, in particularibus vero..."*. Obviously, simple correspondence in extension is far from sufficient for asserting identity between "subsistence" and "essence", but it is evident from the context that a certain coextensivity is intended to suggest mutual predicability (no particular mode of supposition presupposed).

[317] As for the existence of Platonic universals, see P. Hadot, "La distinction de l'être et de l'étant dans le 'De hebdomadibus' de Boèce", in *Miscellanea Mediaevalia* 2, "Die Metaphysik im Mittelalter", Walter de Gruyter, Berlin 1963, p. 147-153, as an example of attempting to establish the importance of neo-Platonist elements in the writings of Boethius. Cf. also M. Elsässer, *Das Person-Verständnis des Boethius*, Diss., Julius-Maximilians-Universität zu Würzburg, Munster 1973, p. 13-25. Although our exposition will continue to take into consideration the possibility of Platonic categories of beings in interpreting Boethius, Boethian realism would tend to minimize their significance, as *"formae vero subiectae esse non possunt"* – Boethius, *De Trin.*, II, 43, ed. Loeb, p. 10 (and this holds for an essence's composition with being as well, the distinctiveness for which Boethius explicitly argues: cf. *Quomodo sub.*, II-VIII, ed. Loeb, p. 40-42).

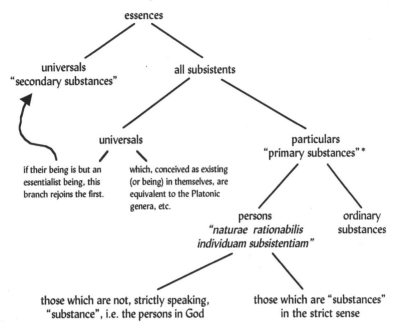

essences

universals
"secondary substances"

all subsistents

universals

if their being is but an
essentialist being, this
branch rejoins the first.

which, conceived as existing
(or being) in themselves, are
equivalent to the Platonic
genera, etc.

particulars
"primary substances" *

persons
"naturae rationabilis
individuam subsistentiam"

ordinary
substances

those which are not, strictly speaking,
"substance", i.e. the persons in God

those which are "substances"
in the strict sense

* We say "primary substance" in the broad sense in order simply to indicate a distancing from secondary substance, for it is the primary substances which possess being in the full sense and are truly existent (which exist in themselves). The proper character of "substance" (which has not yet been articulated), however is not the aim of this branch, the accent being placed rather upon particularity. This particularity implies for Boethius, as for the entire Christian tradition since the reflections of the Cappadocian Fathers on the particularity/community relation at the heart of the Trinity, the fact of standing beneath a common nature. But this is not to be confused with the sense of "standing under" attributed to the notion of *"substantia"* taken in the strict sense. There are two distinct acts of "standing under": one belonging to the hypostasis insofar as "supposit" of a nature (whether the nature be identical to the supposit or not); the other belonging to the substance insofar as subject of accidents. From this point of view, to assign to "ὑπόστασις" the sense of our *"substantia"* alone would be to forget its other application of signifying according to the act of the supposit as such.

That Boethius spoke in a manner leaving room for an interpretation of universals in the Platonic sense (an interpretation with regard to which we maintain our distance) should not be surprising (he is certainly not the only Aristotelian of the Middle Ages to have done so). The explanation for this resides at once in the confusion inherent in his metaphysics of being[318], as well as – and this is what is most inter-

---

318 See note 286 (on legitimate interpretation of the Boethian *"esse"*); cf. L. M. De Rijk, "Boèce logicien et philosophe: ses positions sémantiques et sa métaphysique de l'être", in *Atti, Congresso internazionale di studi boeziani* (Pavia, 5-8 Ottobre 1980), edited by L. Obertello, Editrice Herder, Rome 1981, p. 141-156.

esting – in the fact that he envisaged a personal category that escapes every effort of conceptualization which is tied to terrestrial analogues, namely, that of the divinity. It is quite possible that the status of the universals which possess being, that is, the non-particulars which nevertheless are, allows for an intimation of the divine persons to the extent that, on the one hand, the latter do not admit of "particularity" in the strict sense of the term, which would indicate a "contraction" with respect to something common[319], and, on the other hand, these divine persons fully subsist[320]. In the diagram, the three end terms designated under particular subsistences are all "substances"[321] (even the persons of the Trinity *are* the divine substance[322]), though not univocally ("substance in Him is not really substantial but supersubstantial"[323]), whereas they are all "subsistents" in a virtually univocal sense

---

[319] Particularity is compared to universality, but since universality in the strict sense is to be excluded from God, the particularity of the divine persons must be understood differently than in creatures. One will speak of the persons which are "particular" with respect to the common nature the community of which is not a "universality from" (strict sense where the universal is derived *from* several individuals), but a "universality in" (that is, in several). The sense of "particular" and "individual" in God is in any case always analogical. Cf. infra, "COMMUNITY OF PROPORTION", p. 320; "THE TERMS 'SINGULAR', 'INDIVIDUAL' AND 'PARTICULAR' IN GOD", p. 373.

[320] Cf., for example, Boethius, *De Trin.*, II, ed. Loeb, p. 8-12, for a direct comparison of *formae praeter materiam* and God.

[321] Taken in a broad sense intending primary substances, in contradistinction from secondary substances.

[322] Boethius, however, has been reproached for speaking of a multiplicity of substances in God in virtue of his substantial definition of personhood, expressly visible in *Contra Eut.* III, 87-101 (ed. Loeb, p. 90-92); cf. A. Milano, *Persona in teologia*, Edizioni Dehoniane, Naples 1987, p. 370, 373, 375; M. Nédoncelle, "Les variations de Boèce sur la personne", *RevSR* 39 (1965), p. 257. The criticism is sound; however, it must be noted that Boethius, despite the use of expressions mentioning "three substances", nowise proposes a formal multiplication of substance and, in fact, speaks against such an understanding, even if his explanation of how the divine persons may be called "substance" leaves much to be desired (concluding with the idea that God is the "substance" of the world inasmuch as the foundation or principle beneath all things according as he is the source of their being) and fails to articulate an analogical concept of substance able to be attributed to God because of its ability to have the value of subsistence. Moreover, even while limited in its signification to naming the essence or "foundation" (as opposed to the existent of an essence), "substance" may still function to define person even in the context of the Trinity; for, to say that there are three persons does not necessarily imply that there are three individual substances of a rational nature, but rather that there are three things that are an individual substance of a rational nature, that is, three things each of which is an individual substance of a rational nature. Whether or not the substance which each necessarily is is distinct from that of the other depends upon factors entirely extrinsic to the definition.

[323] *"Substantia in illo non est vere substantia sed ultra substantiam"* – Boethius, *De Trin.*, IV, 10-11, ed. Loeb, p. 16. The meaning of "suprasubstantial" will become clearer when Boethius explains the difference between "substance" and "subsistence" as a

(insofar as the use of the term *"subsistentia"* admits of less variation in supposition and is able to be employed or predicated in a more perfect analogical sense, that is, according to a strict analogy of proportion [324]). The explanation for this lies in the unique manner in which Boethius distinguishes subsistence from substance.

Ontological principles behind *"subsistentia"* and *"substantia"*

First, it would be helpful to delineate some dynamics of the active principles involved in the logical progression from the more simple or general order to the specific order, that is, from top to bottom in the foregoing diagram. Limiting ourselves to particular subsistents, we have acknowledged an inseparability with "being", for it is precisely on account of an essence's reception of its actuality that the subsistent (being nothing other than the same essence with its *actus essendi* [325]) subsists. This subsistent then may exist according as a substance, with all that is proper to substance (through the medium of its particularizing aspect), or as a subsistent which fails to admit of substantial property (i.e., a non-substantial subsistent such as God [326]). With horizontal arrows representing active or determining principles, we obtain:

consequence of which the notion of substance may only metaphorically be applied to the Trinity.

[324] While "substance", depending on whether it is used to signify according to the substrative act of standing beneath accidents or to signify according to the independent act of existence (due to it, as we shall see, in virtue of its being a subsistent), is either predicated of God in an entirely metaphorical sense (if signifying in the first way) or according to an imperfect analogicity (if signifying in the second way), since signification according to the act of independent existence is not proper to the concept of "substance" as such, but insofar as it is a subsistence (it is a question, therefore, of universal commensurability in attributing denotation to a term, or signification to a concept) – a point, however, which only makes sense if we adequately distinguish between "substance" and "subsistence", or, more precisely, between their respective denotations. [For a broad outline of the notion of analogicity, cf. infra, note 842 in the section entitled "SHARING IN THE COMMON NOTION OF PERSON"].

[325] Cf. Boethius, *Quomodo sub.*, II, 28-30, ed. Loeb, p. 40. *"Actus essendi"* quite acceptably renders the sense of *"esse"* the role of which is to make something to be, actualizing the being of an essence: *"est autem aliquid, cum esse susceperit"* (*Quomodo sub.*, II, 33-34, ed. Loeb, p. 40). It must be noted, nevertheless, that the sense of *"actus"* does not necessarily situate us at the existential level, for an essence is also "actualized" to the extent that it receives its proper "consistency" from a form, making it to be what it is.

[326] We are fully aware of the fact that God is not an essence in the same way as are created essences. Essence in the strict sense presupposes a real distinction between essence and existence, where the former plays a passive or receptive role with respect to the latter. Essence then, taken in this sense, may only be said of God metaphorically. A logical essence cannot be determined in God because no rela-

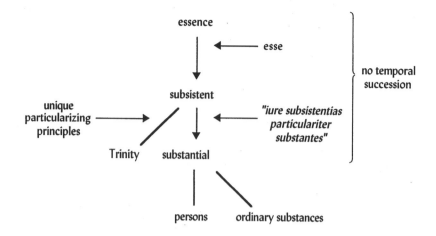

These ideas of Boethius shed light on several aspects of the problem of personhood in the Trinity and in men. The "particularizing aspect", as we have labeled it, provides us with a way in which to distinguish "personhood" in the Trinity from other forms of personhood, since what particularizes amongst the three Persons of the Godhead is purely relation (whence the appellation "subsistent relations"). Attending to our schema, then, just as relation (as a principle of difference[327]) accounts for a plurality of persons in the Trinity without dragging "subsistence" into the limitations/dependencies of "substance", so the principles of individuation in man are precisely what result in his "substantiality"[328]. Indeed, it is via the "principle of individuation" that particular men come to exist[329]. That is, the versatility

---

tion of genus to species and specific difference can be established between the divine attributes, though a metaphysical essence, taken from the fundamental attribute of existence, is metaphorically ascribed to God.

[327] See Boethius, De Trin., I, 9-19; III, 50-55, ed. Loeb, p. 6; 16. Cf. Aquinas, De ente et ess., IV.

[328] The principles of actuation or determination hitherto referred to are not to be thought of in temporal succession, as though being were to first come to essence followed by particularities; rather they consist in one action positing a nature in existence.

[329] This is evident from the fact that such principles are nothing other than ultimate ontological determinants accounting for a things numerical unity, without which determination, nothing would be particular. Though we do not encounter in Boethius an explicit elaboration of the principle of individuation in terms of "designated matter", his ultimate reduction of individuation to bodily properties, and his explanation of the reception of such properties or accidents on the basis of matter, immediately moves us in such a direction (see Boethius, De Trin., I-II, ed.

of the "particularizing aspect" succeeds both in multiplying the divine persons in the context of pure subsistence and in accounting for a plurality of human individuals in the material context of substantiality.

Brief comparison with the "classical" notion of subsistence

An ontologically important parallel to this schema must be drawn. The vertical movement from essence to the subsistent corresponds to and is a transliteration of the passage of a secondary substance, *id quo est*, to *id quod est*, in virtue of the *actus essendi*. The *subsistent* is understood as *id quod est*, which, according to other determining factors, is or is not "substantial". Consequently, a significantly other semantic than that of the "classical" expression is adopted when speaking about "subsistence". For, the "classical" explication[330] defines "subsistence" as a principle responsible for the determination of a substance as self-subsistent, that is, a principle which adds to the perfection possessed by what is already considered substantial (as opposed to accidental) a final perfection rendering the substance wholly autonomous and incommunicable. In the case of rational substances, such a perfection entails personhood. The flexibility of the Boethian exposition results in a radically different use of language if not understanding. In contrast to the aforementioned logical progression from essence to subsistence to substance, via *esse* and particularizing aspects, the "classical" characterization runs from essence to substance to person, via an "individuating principle" and "subsistence", which supply the ontological preparation for the crowning perfection of existence:

Loeb, p. 4-12). Cf. Aristotle, *De anima* III; *Met.* VII; and, as an example of a coherent development of such a notion of individuation, Aquinas, *In Boet. de Trin.*, q. IV, a. 2; *De ente et ess.*, II; *In I Sent.*, d. VIII, q. 5, a. 2; *De princ. nat.*, II.

[330] We are referring to the Cajetanian understanding of subsistence, commonly accepted amongst so many Thomists. A closer look at this theory shall be taken when comparing it with the effective Boethian sense of "subsistence" in note 358 of the section on "SPECIFIC ASPECTS OF SUBSTANTIA AND SUBSISTENTIA".

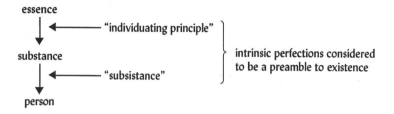

In essence, the final term of the so called "classical" progression is nothing other than the middle term of the preceding Boethian schema. In the Boethian structure, the reception (or simple Act) of *esse* and the determination accomplished by the particularizing principles are a simultaneous event; they are two distinguishable aspects of the same realization of a thing's actuality, the former (*esse*) being "conditioned" or specified by the latter. Consequently, the subsistent is necessarily either "supra-substantial" or substantial, and no "second step" is required for the realization of its mode of existence (or mode of subsistence). In the Cajetanian exposition, the final term of the progression in this series of ontological perfections represents the ultimate intrinsic disposition of the subsistent essence considered in abstraction from its existence. That is, they represent perfections of the fully individualized essence considered in itself, even if these perfections cannot pertain (i.e. belong in actuality) to such an essence outside of the act of existence. The particular modality according to which the subsistent thing is going to exist is not articulated, since (and this agrees with everything we have said about Boethius until now) the notion of subsistence is indifferent as to whether a thing be substance (in the strict sense of the term) or not.

An important difference, however, must be observed. For Boethius, there can be no difference, as there appears to be for Cajetan, between the individuated substance and the subsistent, for an individual substance naturally subsists in virtue of the very being it has received and fully possesses because of its substantiality. Cajetan is compelled, on the other hand, since he is concerned to explain how it is that the human nature of Christ – which is individual and exists – fails to be self-subsistent, to posit subsistence as an ulterior perfection added to that of substantiality by which the substance is rendered incommunicable, subsistent, personal. But even if it must be admitted that Christ's human nature does not subsist in itself, it certainly does not follow that it is not subsistent on another account[331], nor does there necessarily follow a distinction between the substantially existing and the subsistent. Moreover, precisely what kind of existence shall we ascribe to a non-subsistent but existing individual nature? For Boethius, the only really existing thing is the subsistent[332].

Finally, because the human nature of Christ, ontologically speaking, cannot differ from our own in any way beside the fact that it constitutes no human person, defenders of the Cajetanian formulation[333] have stressed the fact that the, albeit "intrinsic", perfection of subsistence does not affect the essence of the nature. "Subsistence" is described as a non-essential determination of an essence, "terminating" or "completing" it in the line of being[334].

Subsistentia est id quod est; subsistentia est "esse"

What, then, returning to Boethius, shall we conclude about subsistence? The subsistent is an essence[335] which subsists, i.e., which has subsistence. Subsistence, then, is just that which differentiates the "subsistent" from other essences, which is precisely "being"[336]. Subsistence *is* being. This we assert in an entirely strict and *per se* sense, since there are other things whose "being" can only be spoken of in a derived sense, such as that of accidents which we do not call subsis-

---

[331] A Cajetanian will not deny this, but the subsistence typically attributed to Christ's humanity will be understood as a particular kind of subsistence, the status of which is not entirely clear.

[332] The exact degree to which these positions diverge cannot be studied in detail here. A possible conceptual instrument of conciliation between them could be the different (strong and weak) senses of "subsistent" entailed in the Cajetanian doctrine. These senses are briefly revisited later (cf. especially infra, note 358).

[333] Cf., for example, F. L. B. Cunningham, *Christ and His Sacraments*, Priory Press, Dubuque (Iowa) 1958, p. 97-137.

[334] The idea that a nature or substance becomes or is rendered a person on account of a certain *non-essential* determining principle needed for its completion or "termination" is extraneous to the prior philosophical tradition (compare Aquinas, *Sum. theol.*, I, 29, 2); the language incompatibility offers itself as an indication of possible vocabulary superfluity (i.e., inventiveness) or an alteration in traditional acceptations of grounded philosophical concepts. In any event, this idea of subsistence should be treated in its own right on another occasion. We refer the reader to the insights offered by Eudaldo Forment Giralt in *Persona y Modo Substancial*, PPU, Barcelona 1983.

[335] Cf. Boethius, *Contra Eut.*, III, 33-38, ed. Loeb, p. 86-88: *"essentiae... in solis vero individuis et particularibus substant... subsistentiae... in particularibus vero capiant substantiam"*.

[336] This is our "substantial being" (not accidental or intentional). Cf. Aquinas, *De princ. nat.*, I, 1.

tent[337]. It might be argued that accidents are also modes of subsistence inasmuch as they exist, however they do not "have" existence properly speaking (as is the case for every self-contained substance, or subsistence), which is why they are described as *"inessendi"*.

Finally, the subsistent, as distinguished from accidents, implies a non-accidental mode of being, which allows us to regard subsistence itself as a mode of being (although in this instance, the term "being", because it pertains even to accidents, is not entirely univocal, whence the possibility of identifying subsistence with being when being is taken in its propermost sense; that is, depending on how one takes the sense of being, it either *is* or is a mode of being).

Boethius most expressly deals with "being" in the *Quomodo substantiae*[338]. There he is careful to distinguish *"esse"* from *"id quod est"*: "Being and 'that which is' are different; being itself awaits manifestation, but 'that which is', once having received its 'form of being', is and exists... in every composite thing, being is one thing, and 'that which is' is another"[339]. The distinction here iterated (between *esse* and *id quod est)* is no different than distinguishing "subsistence" from the "subsistent", the latter being exactly *id quod est*[340].

Substance is correspondingly a mode of subsistence (as indeed substance is a mode of existence). This is why Boethius can affirm that "οὐσία is identical with essence, οὐσίωσις with subsistence, ὑπόστασις with substance, πρόσωπον with person"[341]. Clearly a ὑπόστασις is a type of οὐσία, and πρόσωπον a type of substance or subsistence. That substance be a more determined notion than subsistence is clear from the locution: "but individuals have not only subsistence but also substance..."[342]. Though, at this point, subsistence and substance have been described and situated in relation one to another according to the universality of their ontological determina-

---

[337] Cf. Aquinas, *De princ. nat.*, I, 4; I, 2; VI, 38; *De ente et ess.*, I; VI.

[338] *Quomodo sub.*, especially I-VIII, ed. Loeb, p. 40-42; cf. *De Trin.*, IV, 31-36, ed. Loeb, p. 18.

[339] Boethius, *Quomodo sub.*, II & VIII: *"diversum est esse et id quod est; ipsum enim esse nondum est, at vero quod est accepta essendi forma est atque consistit... Omni composito aliud est esse, aliud ipsum est"*. Note the vocabulary: *"nondum est"*, *"essendi forma"*, with respect to the active/determining principles mentioned above in the section on "ONTOLOGICAL PRINCIPLES BEHIND 'SUBSISTENTIA' AND 'SUBSTANTIA'".

[340] *"Quocirca* εἶναι *atque* οὐσιῶσθαι *esse atque subsistere"* – Boethius, *Contra Eut.*, III, 56, ed. Loeb, p. 88.

[341] Boethius, *Contra Eut.*, III, 69-71, ed. Loeb, p. 90: *"idem est igitur* οὐσίαν *esse quod essentiam, idem* οὐσίωσιν *quod subsistentiam, idem* ὑπόστασιν *quod substantiam, idem* πρόσωπον *quod personam"*. Cf. Aquinas, *De ente et ess.*, II.

tion, it remains to single out the characterizing or distinctive difference between the notions.

Specific aspects of substantia and subsistentia

"A thing has subsistence[343] when it does not require accidents in order to be, but that thing has substance which supplies to other things, accidents to wit, a substrate enabling them to be"[344]. Here have the crucial elements been stated. It is the perspective of independence which isolates subsistence (at least logically) from substance and that of "standing under" accidents which identifies substance. Hence, although the two terms are frequently co-signifying (may be used to signify one and the same thing), they are different in meaning. Subsistence, taken in precision from substance, indicates independence from accidents; substance, prescinding from subsistence, designates being placed under accidents as a substrate[345]. Neither term is exclusive of the other, however, substance, now delimited in strict understanding, delineates a distinctive class of subsistents (to wit, all those besides genera and species[346] and God).

That subsistence means a certain independence with regard to accidents must be understood correctly. *"Subsistit enim quod ipsum accidentibus, ut possit esse, non indiget... Est igitur et hominis quidem... vero atque subsistentia quoniam in nullo subiecto est"*[347]. The first affirmation concerning subsistence is refined by the second. The first states that a subsistent does not require accidents in order that it be (precisely: that thing subsists which, in order to exist, is not in need of accidents). This may be taken simply to mean that if something exists without needing accidents it is subsistent (such is obviously the case with non-substantial subsistences; nonetheless it is true also of individual substances insofar as "they are already provided with their

---

[342] Boethius, *Contra Eut.*, III, 51-52, ed. Loeb, p. 88: *"individua vero non modo subsistunt verum etiam substant..."*.

[343] In the narrow sense which distinguishes from "substance" and is therefore not simply "being" but a certain type of being.

[344] Boethius, *Contra Eut.*, III, 45-48, ed. Loeb, p. 88: *"subsistit enim quod ipsum accidentibus, ut possit esse, non indiget. Substat autem id quod aliis accidentibus subiectum quoddam, ut esse valeant, subministrat".*

[345] *"Sub illis enim stat, dum subiectum est accidentibus"* – Boethius, *Contra Eut.*, III, 48-49, ed. Loeb, p. 88.

[346] *"Itaque genera vel species subsistunt tantum; neque enim accidentia generibus speciebusve contingunt"* – Boethius, Contra *Eut.*, III, 49-51, ed. Loeb, p. 88. We leave angelic considerations aside.

[347] Boethius, *Contra Eut.*, III, 45-46; 79-83; ed. Loeb, p. 88; 90.

proper and specific differences"[348]). But, as the "essentiality" of this last point (regarding individual substances) hints at, the affirmation may imply that accidental being is not what makes it (the subsistent) to be, which is equivalent to ascribing what we would call "substantial being" (for "a subject does not have an act of existing from that which accrues to it, but possesses complete being by itself"[349]). Thus the second statement more exactly introduces the propriety of "subsistence": man subsists precisely because he does not reside in a subject[350].

Now, this seems to echo the popular definition of substance: "that which exists in itself and not in another as in a subject"[351]. But, does not this definition leave out something central to the notion of substance as Boethius expounds it? For substance must well satisfy the requirements of "subsistence" according as we have structured their relation above, but it differs precisely in that substance "is subject to the other things which are not subsistences"[352]. Drawing upon what we have recently established above, those things other than subsistences are none other than accidents, and is it not just these to which substance is subject? So, there is no incoherence in attaching the common definition of substance (that which exists in itself and not in another as in subject) to the Boethian "subsistence". Rather a more precise system of designation results, since substance is really a particular limited mode of subsistence, all of which subsistences possess their existence *per se* and not through another or in another, but of which only some are subject to the limitations inherent in the status of *substantia*[353]. Every subsistent (and therefore every substance), then,

---

[348]   Boethius, *Contra Eut.*, III, 52-54, ed. Loeb, p. 88: *"nam neque ipsa indigent accidentibus ut sint; informata enim sunt iam propriis et specificis differentiis"*. Compare: "a subject does not have an act of existing from that which accrues to it, but possesses of itself complete being" – Aquinas, *De princ. nat.*, I, 2; ed. Leonine, vol. 43, p. 4, §1, 28-29: *"subiectum est quod non habet esse ex eo quod aduenit, sed per se habet esse completum"*.

[349]   Aquinas, *De princ. nat.*, I, 2; ed. Leonine, vol. 43, p. 4, §1, 28-29: *"subiectum est quod non habet esse ex eo quod aduenit, sed per se habet esse completum"*.

[350]   Compare this with Aquinas, *Sum. theol.*, I, 29, 2.

[351]   As A. Milano observes, *subsistentia* thus understood signifies the *"in subiecto esse"*, that is, what is proper to substance in general in the Aristotelian and Porphyrian sense of the term (cf. A. Milano, *Persona in teologia*, Edizioni Dehoniane, Naples 1987, p. 364). Boethius is aware of the equivalency; cf. Boethius, *In Cat. Arist.*: PL 64, 191B; cf. C. Micaelli, "'Natura' e 'Persona' nel 'Contra Eutychen et Nestorium' di Boezio: osservazioni su alcuni problemi filosofici e linguistici", in *Atti, Congresso internazionale di studi boeziani* (Pavia, 5-8 Ottobre 1980), edited by L. Obertello, Editrice Herder, Rome 1981, p. 333.

[352]   Boethius, *Contra Eut.*, III, 84-85, ed. Loeb, p. 90: *"vero atque substantia, quoniam subest ceteris quae subsistentiae non sunt"*.

[353]   Compare with the scholastic definitions of these terms: *"subsistentia dicitur, cujus actus est subsistere, id est, per se existere... substantia, subsistentia et essentia, distinguuntur*

enjoys that independence proper to those things which exist *in se*. Every subsistent, however, is not free from accidents, and these are substances, which are, in a certain sense, passive and acted upon (through the accidental mode) and therefore not entirely independent. God alone (leaving universal ideas aside[354]) possesses that unique form of absolute independence proper only to non-substantial subsistence[355]. Subsistence, then, carries with it the notion of independence. But that independence necessarily connected with subsistence is not evidently identical with that understood to be achieved in personal incommunicability[356] by way of "subsistence" as a principle of determination. That independence is, however, characterized by self-contained being and ontological unicity.

This, then, is the originality of the Boethian conception of *subsistentia*. Taken in the sense of that which distinguishes the "subsistent" from other (non-subsistent) natures, "subsistence" is not some extra-essential determination of a nature said to "complete" it in the line of existence, but a thing's *esse* itself, the principle of a nature's act of existence[357], rendering a nature existent in the full (and subjectival)

---

secundum triplicem actum: scilicet substare, subsistere et esse: quorum esse est commune omni enti, sed substare et subsistere est commune tantum substantiae" – Tabula Aurea, Thomae Aquinatis Opera Omnia, ed. Vives, vol. 33-34, p. 219-220; *Sum. theol.*, I, 29; *In I Sent.*, d. XXIII, q. 1; and "ens per subsistentiam complementum dicitur suppositum... substantia generatim est ens per se subsistens... etsi ulterius possit perfici in ordine accidentali" – Lexicon Scholasticorum Verborum, *Sum. theol.*, ed. Marietti, vol. 6, p. 35-36.

It is worth noting that the term substance can be signified either according to that which is proper to it in virtue of its subsistence or according to what pertains to it insofar as "substanding", that is, insofar as it is subject to the inherence of accidents (that is, according to its substantiality strictly understood). This difference accounts for some of the confusion in the application of definitions which name or signify a thing according to but one of several points of view. A close examination of substance and the different ways in which it may be signified is made in the second part of this thesis under "ONTOLOGICAL DIVISIONS AND SIGNIFICATION OF TERMS", p. 189 (see especially p. 196, 203).

[354] Cf. supra, note 317.

[355] Even in the case of angels there remains an ontological dependence ("from above") on the part of the subsistent, for every subsistent beside God exists in virtue of something other than itself, i.e., in virtue of principles outside of its own essence. Cf. Boethius, *Quomodo sub.*, II-VIII, ed. Loeb, p. 40-42; cf. Aquinas, *De ente et ess.*, IV-V.

[356] Whether this notion should be extended to substances/subsistences in general, and how it might be understood to be limited to persons (at the level of intelligence) or supposits as such must be examined. See especially Aquinas, *Sum. theol.*, I, 29. Cf. infra, "BOETHIUS' DEFINITION AND THE PRINCIPAL CONSTITUENT OF PERSONALITY", p. 341; "THE INCOMMUNICABILITY IMPORTED BY 'INDIVIDUAL'", p. 347.

[357] In a certain sense, it is not simply the act of existence, because the act of existence is said to be *exercised* by the nature (according as the nature "exerts itself in reality") in virtue of that nature's possession of being. Being (*esse*) is what makes a thing exist.

sense of the term[358]. Taken in the sense of that which itself possesses subsistence, that which is said to "subsist", *"subsistentia"* designates

Existence, then, is nothing other than the very realization of being according as it is possessed. For a more profound consideration of this distinction, see J. Maritain, *Court traité de l'existence et de l'existant*, c. 1, 3-8.

[358] Adherents to the Cajetanian formulation have emphasized the fact that their notion of subsistence is intended to operate in the entitative (and not in the qualitative) order. Precisely what it might add to the ontological act of an existing substance is not so clear, and a commonly adopted strategy is that of ascribing to subsistence the roll of conferring perfect independence to the substance, in such a way as to maintain that "subsistence" is, in fact, a certain mode of being, namely, independent being (in the fullest sense of the term). First of all, we must assume that the independence in question is an ontological independence (and *not* the property of "self-determination" so often elected to fulfill this roll); otherwise we are outside the entitative order and considering independence as a kind of perfection accruing to a thing over and above its act of existence, as a perfection, therefore, of a thing in "second act", that is, according to operations which are accidents added to its essence (as opposed to "first act" which concerns the perfections proper to a thing as it is in itself, whether or not it actually operate or be operated upon). Secondly we must consider that, amongst created substances, the degrees of ontological dependence are limited to two: depending for one's existence upon *esse* alone (as in the case of separated subsistences); and depending for one's existence, not only upon a "composition" with being (*quo est*), but also upon a composition between matter and form (as is the case for all natural substances). There are other degrees of dependence, such as that which we ascribe to accidents and integral parts of the body, but these are not substances, and every substance is free from these dependencies.

What kind of ontological independence might an individual substance be in potency to receive? (Already it seems strange to speak about receiving independence, since *in*dependence is precisely the negation of some dependency). It certainly cannot be freed from its dependency on matter and form (or it would cease to be the substance that it is), and even less from being. It seems that every *ontological* independence proper to any kind of substance pertains to it insofar as *substance* – not existing in another as in a subject, and existing as a complete individual (a kind of independence insofar as every individual is a unity distinct from every other and incapable of being found in its entirety in more than one); such independence is already inherent in the notion of the individual substance itself. The notion of a "completion" conferring ontological independence to what is already sufficiently constituted as an existent or an independent subject in its own right is superfluous. The "Cajetanian" would respond, of course, that first substance is not necessarily a subject (even if it happens to be in every case except for Christ), that we have failed to take one kind of ontological independence into account, namely, that of incommunicability.

This incommunicability is understood as something transcending the constitution of the individual or primary substance, an independence not already implied by what is contained in the notion of primary substance. In other words, primary substances as such are communicable, because the notion of primary substance does not include that of subsistence, and, therefore, an individual substance might not be an independent subject, precisely if it is communicated to another subject. Another kind of ontological dependence must, then, be recognized, namely, that belonging exclusively to the human nature of Christ, which is dependent upon the person of the Word for its subsistence, or for its subjectivization. "Subsistence" here indicates something more than the existential act of a first substance; it also implies that substance's incommunicability (a distinction sometimes expressed in terms of "actual subsistence" and "habitual subsistence", respectively).

Every substance, however, is incommunicable – indeed, no first substance exists without subsisting (otherwise it remains an abstract entity or a partial or non-real entity). What the Cajetanian notion of subsistence wants to add, then, to be more precise, is the fact that the nature's subsistence (or existence) is realized through a modality proper to its own constitution, and not according to a property belonging to another. If the nature's subsistence (in the Boethian sense of "being") is possessed according to a modality deriving from the particularity of another (and it must be possessed from somewhere if it is to truly exist) then the nature is not *self*-subsisting, and for this reason, even though it subsists (as it necessarily must – and in this case through another), we do not call it "subsistent" in the full (Cajetanian) sense of the term (which really implies self-subsistence). "Subsistence", then, in this full sense as "self-subsistence", is a modality of subsistence taken in the looser sense identifiable with the act of real existence proper to every individual substance. That self-subsistent modality simply means that the subsistent is incommunicable. The communicable subsistent possesses another modality of subsisting, namely, through the particularization of another.

A "mode of subsisting" means to exist according to the particularizing aspect distinguishing the nature as a numerical individual. This particularizing aspect conditions the *esse* received by the nature; it is itself a modality of being. The modality, therefore, to which we are referring when we use the term communicable (or incommunicable) is a new modality; it is a modality according to which the particularizing aspect is possessed by a nature. Communicability, then, is not so much the recognition of another kind of ontological dependence, as the identification of a new modality according to which (or through which) a nature's ontological dependency upon *esse* (the first kind of ontological dependence we mentioned above) is realized. Cajetan's subsistence thus labels the particularizing aspect; but, depending on whether the particularization is had in virtue of the constitution of the individualized essence itself or in virtue of a participation in the particularity of another, the nature so particularized is either self-subsistent or subsistent through another, respectively. It must be noted, however, that even when the particularizing aspect derives from another, it nevertheless enters into (even establishes) the constitution of the nature insofar as particular/individuated. The humanity of Christ is made individual (and subsistent) by something proper to the person of the Word, but that something truly individuates (particularizes) the humanity in conjunction with designated matter and, just like designated matter, forms part of that human nature *qua* particularized, *qua* subsistent. In ordinary men, designated matter, or the principle of individuation, and the essential particularity deriving from that, is enough – when posited in existence by *esse* – to constitute the supposit, the subsistent subject. Here the totality of individuality is clearly rooted in the concretized nature itself. Christ's (concrete) humanity was not posited in existence in this way, but somehow through the particularity of the Word, such that the realization of its *esse* occurred in a way dependent upon that particularity, which is precisely why that particularity forms part of the principle of individuation in Christ (since principles of individuation, particularizing aspects, may be described as modes *via* which substantial being is conferred upon or possessed by a nature).

If, in the entitative dynamic described by the defenders of Cajetan, the "extra-essential reality" responsible for conferring personal or supposital independence may be understood to be extra-essential in the sense of being outside the notion of the essence considered abstractly, then the entire schema can be fitted into a Boethian understanding of things. If what is meant by extra-essential means something outside of the universal essence, such as, for example, this or that designated matter, and does not mean something outside of the essence of the individual, then the schematic descent from nature to substance to subsistent or person can be seen as parallel to the Boethian descent from nature to subsistence, despite the vast disparity of language. The apparent double passage in the Cajetanian formulation, moving first from nature to substance and from substance to person, finally to be crowned by the act of existence, must be understood as a temporally simultaneous event where any priority may only be logically ascribed. Thus, *esse* and "subsistence" do not each actualize a nature in separate ways, but must be understood as two aspects of a single act positing a nature in reality.

Just, then, as the particularizing aspect is the mode according to which substantial or supposital being is received or possessed by a nature, so "subsistence", in the Cajetanian sense, is the mode according to which being is received or possessed by an essence. For Boethius, the (logical) "movement" from nature, via *esse* and the particularizing aspect, to the subsistent is clear enough: the active/determining principles result in this subsisting thing (substance or otherwise). And that subsistence (or substance) is recognized to be a person strictly on the basis of an independent (i.e. additional) verification of rationality. The "particularizing aspect" signifies any particularizing/individuating property whatsoever – it is understood as a term predicable of the distinctive personal properties or principles of individuation possessed by every subsistence, and in this way as predicable according to strict analogy of proportion. Cajetan's particularizing aspect, "subsistence", when taken in the narrow sense designating self-subsistence, indicates an incommunicable mode of existence; it is a particular kind of particularizing aspect (or the mode of possessing such a particularizing aspect). It too is predicable according to an analogy of proportion which is simply more limited in extension than that of the broader notion of the Boethian "particularizing aspect". This "subsistence", while indeed outside of the concept of the universal essence, cannot be extraneous to the concept of the individual essence which it constitutes as subject or person, for every particularizing aspect is what is most specific to an individual person and is the most determinate part of that person's essence. In fact, the principle of individuation, regardless of the particular theory one adopts in its regard, is always expressed as the ultimate ontological element capable of explaining, as an *intrinsic* cause, the numerical distinctness of an individual. If what is intended by the locution "extra-essential" implies that the "determinant" be something which does not even pertain to the individual essence (φύσις), then the entire "line-point analogy" theory of subsistence seems to fall apart. If, on the other hand, all that is meant is that the completion or "termination" called "subsistence" is a determination not included in the abstract notion of nature, then the theory can be made to work, but is encumbered by unorthodox linguistic ambiguity and seems to say little more than what was said 1000 years earlier. The theory must be credited, in any case, with having expressed, in an explanatory way, the different senses in which a subsistent (i.e. substantially existing) reality exercises its substantial act of existence; and this is more than to have merely indicated that substantial realities exercise their existence according to diverse principles of individuation or particularization.

[As to the capacity for self-determination, it is simply rooted in the nature itself and has no source in an extra-essential determination (though it does have a source in something extra-essential, namely *esse*, which is the extra-essential actualization of the entire essence)].

A general but direct analysis of the Cajetanian theory of personality is presented later: cf. infra, "CAJETAN AND SUBSISTENCE AS SUBSTANTIAL MODE", p. 487.

every entity which really exists, the *per se* and independently existing nature[359]. In this sense, "subsistence" is placed along with "substance" in the order of being (*ens*), but is a broader notion than "substance" which it embraces along with every other ontological subject. Boethius multiplies no realities, but points instead to the identity between what has alternately been called "being" (in the full sense of the term not including accidents) and subsistence[360]. Accordingly, the subsistent is the subject in possession of subsistence, and such a being (*ens*) is realized or manifested in either a substantial or supra-substantial mode according to which it exercises its existence.

Commenting on the final paragraph of chapter III, we should summarily orient the various terms that have, perhaps vexatiously, floated around until now.

Relative architecture of the ontological notions

Man is an οὐσία or an essence because he exists (or "is"); this, because essence designates that by which and in which a thing is said to exist (or "to be")[361]. He is οὐσίωσις or subsistence because he is not in any subject, since that which really exists *in se* does not exist in another as in a subject. Man is ὑπόστασις or substance because subject of certain things which are not subsistences, namely, accidents (which do not possess their own being[362]). Ὑπόστασις is here identified with

---

[359] *"Si può fondatamente sostenere che la subsistentia, come meglio dirà in sequito Tommaso d'Aquino (S. Th., I, q. 29, a. 2), non designa l'essere indeterminato, ma un modo d'essere determinato. Il subsistere equivale all'essere in-sé e per-sé, all'esistere autonomo, all'autosussistenza, e include ora il senso astratto di natura specifica ora quello di esistenza"* – A. Milano, *Persona in teologia*, Edizioni Dehoniane, Naples 1987, p. 366-367.

[360] Such an identification is characteristic of the metaphysical perspective advocated by Billot in his *De Verbi Incarnati*, q. 2, and can already be interpreted in Capreolus' *Defens. theol. divi Thomae de Aq.*, III, d. 5, q. 3.

[361] Cf. Boethius, *De Trin.*, II, 28-29; 44-46, ed. Loeb, p. 10-12; cf. Aquinas, *De ente et ess.*, I: "but 'essence' is used inasmuch as it designates that through which and in which a being has the act of existing" (*"sed essentia dicitur secundum quod per eam et in ea ens habet esse"*: ed. Leonine, vol. 43. p. 370, I, 50-52); cf. *De princ. nat.*, I, 2-3. If one were to object that the *forma propria* mentioned in the *De Trinitate* is not equivalent to *essentia*, it is enough to recall the broader sense of *forma* embracing the entire formal reality of a being which is not limited to but the formal *part* of the being (the sense of *forma totius* is clear in Boethius use of "humanity" in the following lines).

[362] Cf. Aquinas, *Sum. theol.*, I, 28, 2; *De princ. nat.*, I, 1-3: "the subject, however, makes an accident exist" (*"simpliciter loquendo... dat esse... subiectum accidenti"*: ed. Leonine, vol. 43, p. 4, §1, 32-33); I, 4: "when, however, an accidental form is introduced, something is said not to have come into being, but to have become this" (*"quando autem*

substance because "ὑποστάσεις... underlie the rest and are put under and subject to certain things such as accidents"[363]. This perhaps does not perfectly coincide with the statement *"naturae rationabilis individuam subsistentiam* ὑποστάσεως *nomine vocaverunt"*[364], as the denomination according to etymology ("put under") seems to suggest that "ὑπόστασις" be limited to wholly substantial subsistents. "Ὑπόστασις", thus taken, would not extend to all individual subsistents (rational or otherwise, since this is not what specifies "ὑπόστασις") but only to substances. On the other hand, the act of standing under can also be understood as the subjectival act of a supposit with respect to a common nature (οὐσία) which it hypostatizes, and this is the sense of "standing under" implied by the etymological structure of the term (as well as the reason for its frequent confusion with *"substantia"*). Finally, man is "πρόσωπον" or person on account of rationality, without which specification we would remain in the sphere of ordinary substances[365].

When ascribing πρόσωπον to man, nowhere does Boethius declare πρόσωπον to be a division of substance. To the contrary, πρόσωπον is characterized as a rational individual[366], thereby admitting of extension to any rational subsistent[367]. "Πρόσωπον", then, presents itself as the aptmost term for "person" understood in both Trinitarian and non-Trinitarian conceptual fields. If the historical development of speculative understanding has favored and ultimately insisted upon the use of "ὑπόστασις" in referring to the "personal", that success is

---

introducitur forma accidentalis, non dicitur aliquid fieri simpliciter sed fieri hoc": ed. Leonine, vol. 43, p. 4, §1, 52-54); VI, 38; *De ente et ess.*, I; *De ente et ess.*, VI: "they [accidents] do not, of themselves, have the act of existing independently" (*"non habent esse per se absolutum"*: ed. Leonine, vol. 43, p. 379, VI, 9).

[363] Boethius, *Contra Eut.*, III, 62-65, ed. Loeb, p. 88: "ὑποστάσεις... *subsunt et quibusdam quasi accidentibus subpositae subiectaeque sunt"*.

[364] Boethius, *Contra Eut.*, III, 23-25, ed. Loeb, p. 86; cf. supra, "SUBSISTENCE AND ITS RELATION TO SUBSTANCE", p. 110.

[365] *"Est igitur et hominis quidem essentia, id est* οὐσία, *et subsistentia, id est* οὐσίωσις, *et* ὑπόστασις, *id est substantia, et* πρόσωπον, *id est persona;* οὐσία *quidem atque essentia quoniam est,* οὐσίωσις *vero atque subsistentia quoniam in nullo subiecto est,* ὑπόστασις *vero atque substantia, quoniam subest ceteris quae subsistentiae non sunt, id est* οὐσιώσεις; *est* πρόσωπον *atque persona, quoniam est rationabile individuum"* – Boethius, *Contra Eut.*, III, 79-87, ed. Loeb, p. 90.

[366] *"Est* πρόσωπον *atque persona, quoniam est rationabile individuum"* – Boethius, *Contra Eut.*, III, 86-87, ed. Loeb, p. 90.

[367] It is important that πρόσωπον is never made a sub-division of substance, since if it were, it could never be equated with *persona*. The logical content of πρόσωπον indicates rationality (and not substantiality); that of *persona*, both rationality and *subsistentia*; that of ὑπόστασις, substantiality.

due in large part to the lack of linguistic and often conceptual uniformity in theological discourse between different individuals and their philosophical backgrounds[368]. Wrestling with differences in the meanings of terms, their connotative theological implications and varying philosophical orientations cannot be avoided, as we have already observed. In any event, that the Greeks give the name "ὑπόστασις", according to Boethius, to the individual *subsistent* of a rational nature represents a superiority over the traditional and very definition of person proposed by Boethius inasmuch as it does not suggest a plurality of substances in the Trinity but only of subsistences[369]. To say that "person" or "ὑπόστασις" is the individual *substance* of a rational nature is, from the point of view of natural philosophy, correct (which lies perhaps at the root of the long-standing translation of "ὑπόστασις" by *substantia*); yet, in consideration of the Trinity, the definition "individual subsistent..." remains preferable:

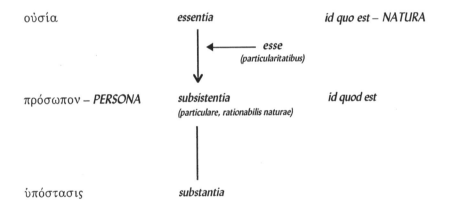

οὐσία	*essentia*	*id quo est – NATURA*
πρόσωπον – *PERSONA*	*subsistentia* (*particulare, rationabilis naturae*)	*id quod est*
ὑπόστασις	*substantia*	

esse
(particularitatibus)

According to this schema, every πρόσωπον is a nature or οὐσία. In the Trinity are three πρόσωπα, each a nature uniquely particularized; but the nature is the same one divine nature. The differences lie in the particularizations, but since these (the relations) are in God, they *are* God. That is, the πρόσωπα *are* the divine οὐσία (indeed, the *id*

---

[368] For an insightful discussion of this, see A. Grillmeier, *Christ in Christian Tradition*, I, p. 76-557.

[369] Provided the act of substanding be understood as referring to common nature, and not to accidental forms.

quod est and the *id quo est* are identical in God whose essence is his existence).

Some observations

As evidenced in our classification, the *id quod est* (figuring at the level of particularized subsistence) is the concrete existing nature (which in our case is rational). It is identified with πρόσωπον or person – for every person is a rational *quod est*, and every rational *quod est* is a person; they are particular subsistences of a rational nature. Human nature, then, is distinguishable from person only at the level of the οὐσία (*quo est*). Consequently (and this should have implications in the ethical domain), it cannot be affirmed that certain human individuals are not persons, precisely because such an individual is the concrete existent[370]. As was already alluded to, the οὐσία of which we are speaking does not necessarily refer to an abstract nature but can even signify the concrete nature[371] when taken in precision from its act of existence, that is, abstracting from its subjectivity, i.e. when it is no longer considered as a subject of attribution – which is to abstract from the existential mode proper to it in virtue of the entitative act of *esse* received according to the modality of the particularizing aspect[372].

---

[370] In fact, the term "human" already denotes rationality, and "individual" the particular subsistent, which are the precise boundaries of "person".

[371] Which, when still considered in distinction from and as more simple than person, is called φύσις, as opposed to οὐσία taken abstractly. Οὐσία taken in the broad sense can be used to signify either abstractly or concretely, in the latter of which cases it is more accurately substituted by the term φύσις. Cf. supra, in the section on Nestorius, "πρόσωπον AND ὑπόστασις", p. 65; "CONSEQUENCES FOR NESTORIUS' INTERPRETATION OF THE UNITY IN CHRIST", p. 67 (especially, p. 67).

[372] In other words, an existential mode is proper to it in virtue of the act received from being, namely, subsistence (which is an existential mode, or a mode of existing, if we extend the notion of existence to non-subsisting entities, or even intentional entities, as well). If, on the other hand, we restrict the notion of existence to those things *properly* said to exist, i.e. subsistents, then it is unnecessary to speak about an abstraction from an existential mode proper to the concrete nature, since there is only one veritable mode of existence and, in this case, we would simply abstract from its existence *simpliciter*. We have, however, designated an existential mode pertaining to the nature in virtue of the act received from *esse*, since it is the reality of *esse* which makes a thing exist, and if that *esse* is more than just a "derived *esse*" (which is proper to accidents) and is "self-possessed", then it will result in an existential mode which we call subsistence, or real existence (which is the most noble kind of existence). But this highest form of existence (which, to repeat, is the only real form of existence, strictly speaking) is realized amongst the diverse grades of being in different ways, and even quite diversely amongst the different individuals of a common grade of being. This is because the entitative act or being which is

This is not to suggest that it is possible to be concrete and not be fully actuated through a particularized *esse*; we are simply considering that concrete (and, therefore, fully singularized and existing) nature exclusively *in itself*, and not according to what is proper to it in virtue of its singularity by which it exists. We are at the level of considering an *individual* essence, or, to be precise, a *forma totius individualis*, and the concept of this, considered *in itself*, does not comprehend the subjectival act of existing and remains an *id quo est*[373].

received (or, in the case of God, simply possessed) by a nature (which is now the supposit because of its actualization and possession of being) is received (or possessed) according to a particular property by which the nature (supposit) is uniquely distinguished from every other supposit – this is the "particularizing aspect" we spoke about earlier. This is why we here speak of the entitative act of *esse* as being received/possessed according to the modality of the particularizing aspect. It is a second modality clamped onto the existential modality, and it is the unique way in which every supposit is distinct from every other. Moreover, it is precisely *via* this distinguishing modality (denominated *proprietas personalis* by various theologians including Albert the Great, who are careful not to confuse the concept with the ordinary notion of "property") that *esse* is received or possessed. This is manifest in the Trinity, where the Son, for example, possesses the same unique divine nature necessarily *according to* Filiation, and in man, where one exists as this man, i.e. as a real *quod est*, on account of his being existentially realized *through* the principle of individuation. With regard, then, to the concrete nature considered in distinction from person, and therefore no longer considered as a *quod est*, we are abstracting from the entitative actuality possessed by the concrete nature in virtue of its being and through a personal property. This is not to abstract from the personal property (i.e. the particularizing aspect) since that pertains to the essence of the individual concrete nature. We are simply indicating that the thing from which we abstract, namely existence, is itself possessed in virtue of such a personal property.

373 The speculation of Duns Scotus on the notion of *"haecceitas"* is related to just this issue. The idea is already present in the exchange of writings between Nestorius and Cyril of Alexandria, and the term φύσις is nuanced in such a way as to provide for the conceptualization of what might be called an "in-between realm", somewhere between the abstract nature (οὐσία) and the subsistent (ὑπόστασις or πρόσωπον), which is precisely the domain of the individual nature insofar as *quo est*, that is, the οὐσία as concrete but unhypostatized, or the ὑπόστασις prescinding from its existence. The concept is analogous to an essence such as "Socratesness" which includes all the concrete notes proper to this man and, therefore, designated matter, since that matter makes Socrates to be Socrates and is essential to "Socratesness". The essence character proper to the secondary intention of "Socratesness" derives not from the fact that we abstract from designated matter (which would give us a universal nature), but from the fact that the individual nature is abstracted from its existence. From the moment we unite in our concept actual existence to the individual essence, we no longer have "Socratesness" but Socrates himself, the concrete nature as supposit, with the subjectival act of exercising existence.
The use of the term φύσις to designate this "in-between" reality, we might add, corresponds with its more concrete mode of signification when compared with οὐσία. Φύσις (whence "physical") expresses, in a certain way, something concrete, inasmuch as it is a name for nature insofar as a principle of operation, as *motor intrinsecus*, a concreteness which derives from the empiricalness of the operations as-

A possible divisive Christological argument

A series of difficulties arises when Boethius attempts to explain the unity of person in Christ. Most important, Boethius cannot explain how it is that the human nature fails to constitute a person of its own. The entire seventh chapter of the *Contra Eutychen et Nestorium*, dedicated to explaining the *via media* between the great heresies, merely *affirms* the unicity of person and duality of natures[374], treating the two natures in a rather symmetrical way, as though the person were to result from their union[375]. What is lacking is not so much an "asymmetrical" account of the natures[376] as an intuition concerning where and in what (and with respect to what part of the definition) the natures are united. The human nature, in all of its concreteness, necessarily presents itself as another person if its concreteness is not identified with the personal concreteness of the Word. In all respects, the human nature appears to be a subject of being in its own right.

In Christ, it might be argued, the πρόσωπον of the Word is a subsistent (in precision from substance), the humanity a substance. Insofar as both are ranged among subsistences (or "substances" taken broadly), each one presents itself as an *id quod est*[377]. When we speak about the substantial character of the human nature, that is, when we recognize it as a first substance, we note the fact that it is a certain kind of subsistence in possession of being. Therefore, whether declaring the human nature to be a concrete particular substance or simply affirming that it *has* its own act of existence, we attribute to it the particular mode of being proper only to the *quod est*[378].

cribed to a nature. Φύσις, then, signifies the nature according as it is a principle of operation, while οὐσία signifies the same thing according as it is the formal reality of a thing. Φύσις derives from a consideration of nature according to (or under the formality of) the efficient order; οὐσία according to (or under the formality of) the formal order.

[374] Cf. especially *Contra Eut.* IV, 62-67; VII, 70-74: ed. Loeb, p. 96; 120.

[375] Cf. *Contra Eut.* VII, 28-31, ed. Loeb, p. 116.

[376] Which is what A. Milano maintains to be the primary weakness in Boethius' Christological response (cf. A. Milano, *Persona in teologia*, Edizioni Dehoniane, Naples 1987, p. 381).

[377] We are merely drawing out the implications of the philosophical system; recall that it is an aim of this essay to indicate the theological problem and to distinguish the philosophical terms employed in its consideration.

[378] Is such a characterization very far from speaking, as did certain Scholastic theologians such as Thomas Aquinas (*De unione Verbi incarnati*, q. 1, a. 4) about a "secondary" being in Christ? In effect, what can a secondary being imply if not an *id quod est*? For if the humanity of Christ *has* being then it is an *existent*, and the *id quod est* is precisely that which, through the *id quo est*, is said to exist. Little alternative occurs unless the humanity may be said to have being in some secondary sense as when we

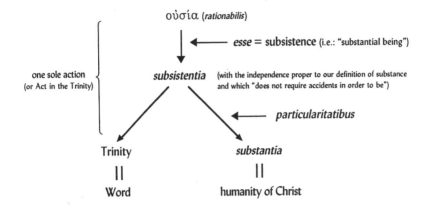

Objection and alternatives to the argument

Nevertheless, this entire argument (though licitly able to be constructed from the Boethian doctrine) is subject to serious objection since the sense of the word *"substantia"* here applied to the humanity of Christ belongs, one may argue, only to the person of the Word which subsistence in recent times became substance for the sake of all rational substances, the same *id quod est* both one (non-substantial) subsistence and one same substance[379]. In the Boethian schema, either a union must be worked out between Christ's human *substantia* and his divine *subsistentia*, in which case either a πρόσωπον must be

predicate being of accidents, for accidents do not properly speaking *have* being; rather their being is had from the being of the substance in which they inhere. It is the nature of an accident to inhere, making that which is to be such, as redness makes a book to be red. But, in the example, red – it may be maintained – does not (of itself) exist but is rather that which makes the existing book to be such, i.e., that through which the book is red. On this account, an accident is not an *id quod est* (except perhaps in some equivocal sense, as when it is said to have being) but an *id quo est* insofar as it is something through which a thing has (qualified) being. It is therefore an essence (since essence is defined as that through which and in which a thing has existence) but cannot be said properly speaking to have an essence except in as much as it is said to essentially inhere, but this is not an *id quod est*

[379] This is the heart of the sense of the unity of being in the person of Christ: "τέλειος ὢν ἐν θεότητι καὶ τέλειος ὁ αὐτὸς ἐν ἀνθρωπότητι καὶ ὡς ἐν ἑνὶ προσώπῳ νοούμενος" (Cyril of Alexandria, *Ep. 39 [ad Joannem Antiochenum]*: PG 77, 180B) and finds its only explanation in an articulation of the modes of signification and supposition attributed to the words we use to designate the divine and human realities, and this because of the epistemic limitation inherent in a language dependent discursive ratiocination.

communicable or an identity between the human substance and the divine subsistence must be affirmed at the level of the *quod est*[380], and accidental union must be avoided, or the humanity in Christ must be different from our own in such a way that it is not a "subsistent"[381], in which case the only place to account for this lies in the ontological dynamic occurring between οὐσία and *subsistentia*, i.e., in the actualization of the nature. Either there is something more than *esse substantialis* that accounts for being an *id quod est* or in the case of the humanity of Christ something contained in our *esse/subsistentia* is lacking, or, with regard to the same human nature, no distinction *in re* can obtain between it and the person when that nature is considered in its complete (and actual) individuality/singularity[382]. In all of these situations, unless we attempt to account for the unity of being either according to immediate participation in the uncreated being of the Word[383] or according to an "integration of singularity"[384], we are invited to grapple with the issue in a way similar to that which engendered the "classical" theory of subsistence outlined above.

Conclusion

The parallel between the thinking of Boethius and the that of the Fathers we have already examined is unmistakable:

---

[380] Which is more than simply to say "at the level of primary substance", since we are referring to the subjectival role (i.e. the role as a subject of attribution) of the substance being signified.

[381] And therefore neither truly substance according to the strict sense exposed above. This implication is crucial; for we have seen that a thing may be subsistent without being a substance, but how could it be possible to have (or to conceive of) an existing substance which does not subsist?

[382] And this latter case seems to be the implication of the relationships Boethius establishes between οὐσία, πρόσωπον and ὑπόστασις, in contraposition to any attempt to separate person and human nature. The last possibility, we might add, is exceptionally articulated in the writings of Maximus Confessor affirming that Christ the person *is* his natures, maintaining an identity between the person and the natures "from which, in which and which Christ is" – cf. Maximus Confessor, *Amb. ad Th.* 5, PG 91, 1045D-1060; *Amb. ad Io.* 27, 1268C-1272A; *Ep.* 15, 544D-576B.

[383] A theory which, despite its proclivity to Monophysitism, should not be prematurely dismissed and which ought perhaps to be revisited with special attention to what has been affirmed in these last pages.

[384] Where the individuation by which the human nature is actuated and singularized is nothing other than the individuating or particularizing aspect (to use the term which emerged from our discussion) of the Word himself, a perspective developed especially by St. Albert the Great and which offers itself as a justification for the rare expressions of identity we have just encountered as enounced by Maximus Confessor.

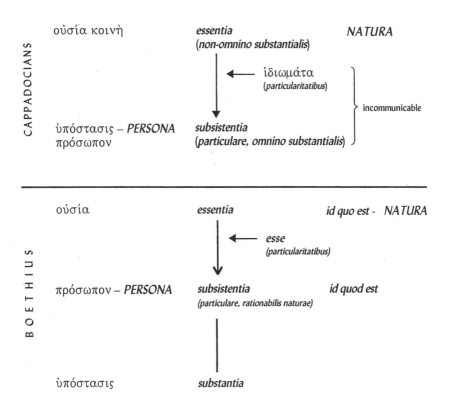

While understandably unable to integrate the entirety of preceding reflections upon the notions of person and nature, such as the fullness of the notion of "incommunicability" as perceived by Basil and that of "subject of attribution" as intimated by Cyril, Boethius nonetheless proposes the first systematic definition of person, at once capable of incorporating the preceding insights, in no way contradictory with orthodoxy, and open, perhaps in virtue of its certain ineluctable residual ambiguity, to accommodating subsequent history's advancement in the understanding of the relation between *persona* and *natura*. Particularly attentive to semantical ambiguities, Boethius establishes a linguistic correspondence between Greek and Latin vocabulary, noting all the while the inadequacy of Latin in rendering the Greek. Of eminent value is the Boethian distinction between substance strictly taken and subsistence. With this, Boethius effectively distinguishes between the two characteristics proper to the Aristotelian notion of the individual substance – perseity, and being a subject of others – and dissociates the eventual realization of the latter aspect from that of the former. Consequently, the concept of "substance" can signify in different ways, and in such a way that it may indeed be predicated of God without thereby also predicating subjectivity. Such a distinction between *"substare accidentibus"* and *"in subiecto esse sine substare accidentibus"* was hitherto unknown. Yet Boethius emphasizes less the distinction between them than he does their equivalence, for the individual substance is indeed an individual subsistence.

Uncovering the key notion of subsistence, the center of personality is recognized to consist in an ontological stability and independence; person is situated in the substantial category, i.e. that of the particularized nature. On the other hand, like Augustine, Boethius, affirming the identity between the divine persons and the singular substance of the divinity, ascribes personal distinction and the constitutive principle of personality in the Trinity to the reference of one to another: *"substantia continet unitatem, relatio multiplicat trinitatem"*[385]. Thus, accentuating, on the one hand, the substantial character of personality in the *Contra Eutychen et Nestorium*, and on the other hand, the relative structure of personality in the *De Trinitate* (and *De hebdomadibus*), Boethius offers two fundamental elements in solving the mystery of personality in theology: *relatio* and *subsistentia*[386]. In sum, the concepts of *per se* existence and a source for the multiplication of acts of *per se* existence are inseparable from the notion of personality. Never had such an ontologically precise understanding of person, loaded with enormous virtuality, been attained in prior thought. Gathering diverse elements into a systematic whole, Boethius furnishes us with the paradigmatic basis for reflection on personhood for the ages to come.

---

[385] Boethius, *De Trin.* VI, 7-9, ed. Loeb, p. 28-30.

[386] Cf. A. Milano, *Persona in teologia*, Edizioni Dehoniane, Naples 1987, p. 376-378, 386. Milano sees the different approaches to personhood in Boethius as antithetical and inconsistently developed. The apparent opposition, however, is easily dispelled by recognizing that the relative principles of personality in the Trinity are the principles of substantial particularity, whence the two concepts of personality convene.

I.9. THE FIFTH, SIXTH AND EIGHTH OECUMENICAL COUNCILS

Concilium Constantinopolitanum II (553)
THE HYPOSTATIC PROPERTY AND A UNIQUE ACT OF SUBSISTENCE

(1) Εἴ τις οὐκ ὁμολογεῖ πατρὸς καὶ υἱοῦ καὶ ἁγίου πνεύματος μίαν φύσιν, ἤτοι οὐσίαν... μίαν θεότητα ἐν τρισὶν ὑποστάσεσιν, ἤγουν προσώποις... ὁ τοιοῦτος ἀνάθεμα ἔστω [387].

"If anyone will not confess that the Father, Son and Holy Spirit have one nature or substance... one deity to be adored in three subsistences or persons: let him be anathema".

This is the clearest collation yet between the terms φύσις and οὐσία and ὑπόστασις and πρόσωπον. The Latin use of *"subsistentia"* to translate the hypostatic reality conforms to the Boethian concept of subsistence as a *per se* mode of being. *"Substantia"*, incidentally, would also have to be taken in respect of its subsistent act, and not in the sense in which it is a narrower *kind* of subsistence characterized by being the subject of inhering realities.

(2) Εἴ τις τὴν μίαν ὑπόστασιν τοῦ κυρίου ἡμῶν Ἰησοῦ Χριστοῦ οὕτως ἐκλαμβάνει, ὡς ἐπιδεχομένην πολλῶν ὑποστάσεων σημασίαν καὶ διὰ τούτου εἰσάγειν ἐπιχειρεῖ ἐπὶ τοῦ κατὰ Χριστὸν μυστηρίου δύο ὑποστάσεις, ἤτοι δύο πρόσωπα... ἀλλὰ μὴ ἀμολογεῖ τὸν τοῦ θεοῦ λόγον σαρκὶ καθ᾽ ὑπόστασιν ἐνωθῆναι, καὶ διὰ τοῦτο μίαν αὐτοῦ τὴν ὑπόστασιν, ἤτοι ἕν πρόσωπον· οὕτως τε καὶ τὴν ἁγίαν ἐν Καλχηδόνι σύνοδον μίαν ὑπόστασιν τοῦ κυρίου ἡμῶν Ἰησοῦ Χριστοῦ ὁμολογῆσαι, ὁ τοιοῦτος ἀνάθεμα ἔστω [388].

"If anyone understands by the single subsistence of our Lord Jesus Christ that it covers the meaning of many subsistences, and by this argument tries to introduce into the mystery of Christ two subsistences or two persons... and if he does not acknowledge that the Word of God is united with human flesh by subsistence, and that on account of this there is only one subsistence or one person... let him be anathema".

---

[387] DEC 114, 1-8.
[388] DEC 116, 1-4; 15-22.

While Cyril indeed used the expression "ἕνωσις καθ' ὑπόστασιν", it is not clear to what extent he differentiated the notion of ὑπόστασις from οὐσία, whence the value of the expression lies primarily in its affirmation, against the accidentality of the Nestorian union, of a substantial union between the natures in Christ. It was not until the Second Council of Constantinople that the phrase "hypostatic union" was adopted as the adequate expression of the Catholic doctrine concerning the unity of the two natures in the single person of Christ[389]. Union καθ' ὑπόστασιν may not be understood in a way admitting hypostatic or self-subsistent reality to more than one subject. There can be but one subsistent reality, because there can be but one subject of attribution, i.e. one person, and persons or hypostases alone subsist. No matter what status is ascribed to the human nature in Christ, whether concretely signified or strictly according to nature as such, it cannot introduce another subsistence, but must participate somehow in the unique subsistence of the Word[390]. The term subsistence here is formally distinct from that of sheer existence, but implies a particular mode of existing proper to complete hypostases alone.

(3) Οὔτε γὰρ προσθήκην προσώ-πον, ἤγουν ὑποστάσεως, ἐπε-δέξατο ἡ ἁγία τριάς, καὶ σαρκωθέντος τοῦ ἑνὸς τῆς ἁγίας τριάδος θεοῦ λόγου[391].

"There has been no addition of person or subsistence to the Holy Trinity even after one of its members, God the Word, becoming human flesh".

---

[389] Cf. Louis Ott, *Précis de théologie dogmatique*, trans. M. Grandclaudon, Éditions Salvator, Tournai/Paris 1954, p. 210.

[390] Cf. the Council of Florence: "*Anethematizat etiam Theodorum Mopsuestenum atque Nestorium asserentes humanitatem Dei Filio unitam esse per gratiam, et ob id duas in Christo esse personas, sicut duas fatentur esse naturas, cum intelligere non valerent unionem humanitatis ad verbum hypostaticam extitisse, et propterea negarent Verbi subsistentiam accepisse*" – DEC 574, 23-33. To claim that the humanity of Christ "*Verbi subsistentiam accepisse*" is possibly the boldest conciliar statement made with respect to the onto-logical constitution of that nature. Advocates of either the "classical" theory of the ecstasy of being or that of the integration of being ought most fruitfully exploit the declaration (satisfactory account being had of the council's questionable status). Note that, according to the locution, what the heretic denies is "that the humanity had received the *subsistence* of the Word", ≠ the *being* of the Word (at least not *necessarily*) — *supposital* being ≠ *esse simpliciter*.

[391] DEC 116, 24-26.

An unqualified exclusion of any new subsistence might raise an eyebrow. If there is no addition of subsistence at all, how correct is it to say that *the two natures subsist in the Word*, or that *the human nature has its subsistence through the Word?* Incontrovertibly, we exclaim that the Word subsists in his human nature and that the Word has a human subsistence, that is, his subsistence is also human. Now, even if the being one might ascribe to Christ's human nature is described as "secondary", and even if that nature is said to possess its subsistence (necessitated by its substantiality) through the Word, does it not remain a subsistence not originally proper to the Word? In response to this, we should note that the same subsistence can take different natural modalities without itself being multiplied. In this way, the exclusion of an addition of subsistence does not exclude a new modality of the unique subsistence of the Word (something we shall see elaborated by Albert and Thomas in terms of a new relation on the part of the same supposit to another substantial form). The Greek text, we should note, goes no further than to exclude another *subsistent*, and this is obvious enough. Nevertheless, the passage touches upon a serious issue residing in the difference between the commonly employed expressions: "the divine and human natures subsist in the person of the Word" and "the person of the Word subsists in his divine and human natures" [392]. The first does not spell any difficulties for a theory of secondary being or integration but might create tension with certain conciliar definitions; the second is theologically incontrovertible but lends no immediate support to a theory of secondary being.

(4) μένει γὰρ ἑκάτερον ὅπερ ἐστὶ   "Each remained what it is as a
     τῇ φύσει καὶ γενομένης τῆς   nature, because the union was
     ἑνώσεως καθ᾽ ὑπόστασιν [393].   made according to subsistence".

The statement that each one remains what it is notwithstanding the union tends to suggest that the reality (at least constitutionally) of each nature is independent of the union; for

---

[392] The reality signified by this latter locution (the Word existing *as human*) is comparable to the relation expressed between a substance and an accidental form in which it subsists, the substance existing *as such*.

[393] DEC 117, 20-22.

the natural tendency is to see the union as threatening the constitution of the natures, not as establishing them. But, the fact that subsistence must play an integral role in the concrete realization of every substantial nature, even if that subsistence not pertain to the nature *in se*, implies that the union itself, insofar as responsible for the subsistence ascribed to the concrete human nature, contributes somehow to its very actualization as such. From this point of view, the humanity of Christ depends upon the hypostatic act of the Word for its very being. From the point of view, however, of the formal reality of the nature *qua* nature, it seems the humanity is independent of the union which cannot affect its *formal* integrity. The equilibrium established by maintaining both points of view is responsible for asserting the analogy (i.e. the similarity and dissimilarity) between the humanity of Christ and an accident[394].

(5) ἀλλ' ἐπὶ διαιρέσει τῇ ἀνὰ μέρος τὴν τοιαύτην λαμβάνει φωνὴν ἐπὶ τοῦ κατὰ Χριστὸν μυστηρίου· ἢ τὸν ἀριθμὸν τῶν φύσεων ὁμολογῶν ἐπὶ τοῦ αὐτοῦ ἑνὸς κυρίου ἡμῶν Ἰησοῦ Χριστοῦ τοῦ θεοῦ λόγου σαρκωθέντος, μὴ τῇ θεωρίᾳ μόνῃ τὴν διαφορὰν τούτων λαμβάνει, ἐξ ὧν καὶ συνετέθη, οὐκ ἀναιρουμένην διὰ τὴν ἕνωσιν, (εἷς γὰρ ἐξ ἀμφοῖν καὶ δι' ἑνὸς ἀμφότερα) ἀλλ' ἐπὶ τούτῳ κέχρηται τῷ ἀριθμῷ, ὡς κεχωρισμένας καὶ ἰδιοϋποστάτους ἔχει τὰς φύσεις, ὁ τοιοῦτος ἀνάθεμα ἔστω[395].

"And if anyone understands the two natures in the mystery of Christ in the sense of a division into parts, or if he expresses his belief in the plural natures in the same Lord Jesus Christ, God the Word made flesh, but does not consider the difference of those natures, of which he is composed, to be only in the onlooker's mind, a difference which is not compromised by the union (for he is one from both and the two exist through the one) but uses the plurality to suggest that each nature is possessed separately and has a subsistence of its own: let him be anathema".

---

[394] Comparing Christ's humanity with an accident constitutes one of the three principle analogical explanatory devices common to the Scholastic tradition and plainly set forth by St. Thomas. The other two points of analogy consist in the relation between a substance and its integral parts, and the relation between the body and soul.

[395] DEC 117, 22-35.

The council affirms "not a division into parts", since the two natures do not come together after the manner of symmetrical addition, but the composition in question concerns the joining of the humanity to the subsistent act of the Word, who is nowise "part" (nor really composed) and in whom the humanity does not have an independent existence as a part which is conglomerately joined to another (indeed, the humanity, as later speculation will clarify, is rather a natural *principle* joined to the Word). The two are *through* the one (δι᾽ ἑνὸς ἀμφότερα)! The sense of this points toward the hypostatic act according to which a thing truly is, since the hypostasis alone properly *possesses* being as a subject. The divine nature certainly *is* whether or not we consider the "one" (hypostasis); but it is only through the "one" that it is *hypostatically* – the hypostatic being (or subjective subsistence) for both natures derives from that which is proper to the "one" (the hypostasis) as such (an affirmation implicitly pointing toward the personal property by which the Son is Son). Indeed, the council reasserts: the two do not possess a separate subsistence of their own. Finally, and perhaps of dramatic though vague implication, one should consider the differences "to be only in the onlookers mind"[396]. Naturally, the natures are as really distinct from one another at the natural level as the uncreated from the created; therefore, the sense of the expression must lie elsewhere, namely at the level of the hypostasis *as such*, that is, at the level of the subsistent act according to which both natures may be signified (since the Word *is* a man, and the Word *is* God, according to substantial predication *in quid*). The real identity signaled by the insistence upon uniquely logical distinction can be nothing other than that of the person who is one and the same. But the identity here, if it is not itself to be tautological, must be an identity between two things which are not identical in every respect. And so it is in the example at hand, for the council speaks of the uniquely logical distinction between the *two natures*. The identity affirmed between them is that of personal identity; but this means that *each* of the natures (since it is an identity between two things) in some sense can be signified according to identity with the one person (and therefore with each

---

[396] Cf. infra, *Concilium Constantinopolitanum IV*, §2, p. 146.

other *in respect of the person,* i.e. *qua* concretely identical to the person, or, simply, *qua* personalized). Of course, one must exercise extreme caution in speaking about a certain identity between the concretely signified natures, but the council seems to sanction such an approach to the significance of the hypostatic union.

(6)   Καθ' ὑπόστασιν γὰρ λέγοντες τὸν μονογενῆ λόγον ἡνῶσθαι, οὐκ ἀνάχυσίν τινα τὴν εἰς ἀλλήλους τῶν φύσεων πεπρᾶχθαι φαμεν, μενούσης δὲ μᾶλλον ἑκατέρας ὅπερ ἐστίν... ὁμοούσιος τῷ πατρὶ κατὰ τὴν θεότητα, καὶ ὁμοούσιος ἡμῖν ὁ αὐτὸς κατὰ τὴν ἀνθρωπότητα[397].

"In saying that it was in respect of subsistence that the only-begotten God the Word was united, we are not alleging that there was a confusion made of each of the natures in to one another, but rather that each of the two remained what it was... consubstantial with the Father in respect of his divinity, and also consubstantial with us in respect of our humanity".

In this statement, the council explicitates the sense of "union according to hypostasis" (*"secundum subsistentiam"*) regarding its implication for the natures. This is what we mean by "καθ' ὑπόστασιν": *"non confusionem... sed magis permanente utraque hoc quod est".* The *what* of each nature remains unaltered; this is not an affirmation that each is a *quod est,* but rather of the fact that the whatness of each endures, such that each, considered strictly according to its natural (i.e. essential) reality as such, is a *quale quid* of the *quod est* (whence the unique *quod est,* or *quis est,* possesses the property of consubstantiality with the members of both natures).

Concilium Constantinopolitanum III (680-681)
PRINCIPIUM QUO OR THE BEING OF NATURE, AND THE SUBJECT OF NATURAL ACT

The Third Council of Constantinople, primarily aimed at eradicating the cancer of the Monothelite heresy, reiterates many of the major pronouncements from the Council of

---

[397] DEC 118, 6-10.

Chalcedon and the Second Council of Constantinople concerning the integrity of the natures in Christ. The territory under discussion is not only the number of natural operations in the God-man, but, as an immediate consequence, the kind of unity affirmed between those natures. If there are "two wills and two operations" in Christ, what is the consequent of the principle: "operation follows being"? Are we to recognize a duality of beings? If so, what sort of being should be ascribed to the distinctly indicated ontological foundations of the distinct operations? The Monothelite Macarius of Antioch (condemned by the council) will continue to protest against two wills in order, precisely, not to fall into Nestorianism. On account of a duality of operations one is perhaps compelled to admit that there are two "beings" in some sense of the term, minimally, at least, as modes of being of the one person who subsists, that is, the one person existing (and operating) both humanly and divinely. The "what" of the natures repeatedly defended by the previous oecumenical council concerns just such being, that is, the being which must be assigned to the natures as such.

(1) Καὶ δύο φυσικὰς θελήσεις ἤτοι θελήματα ἐν αὐτῷ, καὶ δύο φυσικὰς ἐνεργείας ἀδιαιρέτως, ἀτρέπτως, ἀμερίστως, ἀσυγχύτως κατὰ τὴν τῶν ἁγίων πατέρων διδασκαλίαν[398]. ·

"And we proclaim equally two natural volitions or wills in him and two natural principles of action which undergo no division, no change, no partition, no confusion, in accordance with the teaching of the holy Fathers".

Against the scandalous assertion of one will and one energy of the two natures (τὰ σκάνδαλα, ἑνὸς θελήματος καὶ μιᾶς ἐνεργείας ἐπὶ τῶν δύο φύσεων[399]), the council clearly sets forth the two wills and two kinds of operation in Christ in one to one correspondence with the existence of two *principles* of such operation, principles which distinctly retain their complete natural integrity. Though the precise sense of that integrity is not explicitly expressed, it is clear from the relation-

---

[398] DEC 128, 12-16; cf. *Tomus ad Flavianum*, especially supra, *Concilium Chalcedonense*, §4-5, p. 87-88; §8, p.90.
[399] DEC 126, 3-5.

ship established between operation and principle of operation that the perfect natures are understood to preserve their
distinct character *as principles of operation* (according as this is
required by a duality of operations). The Third Council of
Constantinople thus contributes to specifying the kind of being we must acknowledge for Christ's humanity: not a self-
subsistent being, but rather that which is proper to a *principium quo* (even if such a lucid affirmation concerning the
"unity of being" in Christ will not be formulated until much
later).

(2) ὥσπερ γὰρ ἡ αὐτοῦ σάρξ
σάρξ τοῦ θεοῦ λόγου λέγεται
καὶ ἔστιν, οὕτω καὶ τὸ φυσι-
κὸν τῆς σαρκὸς αὐτοῦ θέλη-
μα ἴδιον τοῦ θεοῦ λόγου λέγεται καὶ ἔστι[400].

"For just as his flesh is said to be
and is flesh of the Word of God,
so too the natural will of his
flesh is said to and does belong
to the Word of God

The "being" ascribed to the will corresponds to and is consequent upon the "being" ascribed to his human nature. Whatever is said, therefore, about the will (in respect, for example,
of its numerical property and existential status) infers something about the nature, and vice versa[401]. Because there are
two kinds of action in Christ, there must be *two* natures or
principles of that action: Δύο δὲ φυσικὰς ἐνεργείας... θείαν
ἐνέργειαν καὶ ἀνθρωπίνην ἐνέργειαν[402].

(3) ἑνὸς γὰρ καὶ τοῦ αὐτοῦ τά
τε θαύματα καὶ τὰ πάθη γι-
νώσκομεν κατ᾽ ἄλλο καὶ
ἄλλο τῶν ἐξ ὧν ἐστι φύσεων
καὶ ἐν αἷς τὸ εἶναι ἔχει, ὡς ὁ
θεσπέσιος ἔφησε Κύριλλος[403].

"For we acknowledge that the
miracles and the suffering are of
one and the same, according to
one or the other of the two natures out of which he is and in
which he has his being".

The unique subject of operation is the person to whom every
action and passion is referred. What is more, and what goes
beyond the logical implication of the communication of idi-

---

[400] DEC 128, 27-31.
[401] Cf. infra, *Concilium Constantinopolitanum IV*, §1, p. 146.
[402] DEC 129, 3-9.
[403] DEC 129, 22-26.

oms, is the fact that the very being proper to the natural principles is properly ascribed (i.e. according to possession) to the same hypostatic subject. The unique subject of attribution is also the unique "bearer of being" in the proper sense of the term; the natures contribute to the manner in which *he is* and are that in which *he is*: "ἐξ ὧν ἐστι φύσεων καὶ ἐν αἷς τὸ εἶναι ἔχει" (*"ex quibus est naturarum et in quibus habet esse"*).

(4)   φαμὲν δύο αὐτοῦ τὰς φύσεις   "We say that he has two natures
ἐν τῇ μιᾷ αὐτοῦ διαλαμπού-   in his one radiant subsistence in
σας ὑποστάσει, ἐν ᾗ τά τε   which he demonstrated the
θαύματα καὶ τὰ παθήματα...   miracles and the sufferings...
ἐπεδείξατο, τῆς φυσικῆς ἐν   the difference of the natures be-
αὐτῇ τῇ μιᾷ ὑποστάσει δια-   ing made known in the same
φορᾶς γνωριζομένης[404].   one subsistence".

It is the hypostasis which is seen ("radiant"), the concrete reality, (the *quod est*) in which the operations are "displayed", in which the differences of the natures are "made known". The hypostasis, therefore, is not only the subject of attribution for natural operation, but the concrete center of visibility and that which manifests the activity accomplished through the "hidden" principles of nature. In some sense, this very and phenomenologically concrete and even notional (making natural exertion known) characterization of hypostasis brings its signification close to the name prosopon understood as signifying an outward appearance; however, in the declaration at hand, the ontological structure by which such an outward appearing and its reference to a unified subject obtains is also presupposed[405].

---

[404]   DEC 129, 33-38.
[405]   The *"sub*-standing" function proper to a hypostasis – linguistically captured by the morpheme "ὑπό" – is taken for granted.

Concilium Constantinopolitanum IV (869-870)
CONTINUITY WITH THE PAST AND INTIMATIONS OVER THE MANIFOLD
STRUCTURE OF CONCRETE NATURE

(1)   *"In unius Christi duabus naturis*   "In the two natures of the one
      consequenter etiam duas opera-   Christ there are, as a conse-
      tiones ac totidem voluntates"[406].   quence, two principles of action
                                              and the same number of wills".

In the very same spirit of the Third Council of Constantinople, the Fourth Council of Constantinople maintains the in-
ferential correspondence between operation and nature: as a
consequence of the two natures there are two operations.
Again, nature is presented only as a principle of operation,
and not as a concrete existent.

(2)   *"Impendens utrique parti unius*   "Assigning to each part of the
      Christi distinctas invicem natu-   one Christ natural properties
      rales proprietates, per quas procul distinct from each other, by
      dubio significationes et notiones di- which the meanings and con-
      vinae ipsius et humanae naturae   ceptions of his divine nature
      inconfuse permanere creduntur"[407]. and of his human nature are be-
                                              lieved beyond all doubt to re-
                                              main without confusion".

The statement concerns the distinction to be recognized between the natures. Curiously, the emphasized non-confusion
is said to lie between the *"meanings and conceptions"* of his divine and human natures. This, of course, does not mean that
the natures differ only logically, for, from the point of view of
the natures as such, the distance is, ontologically speaking,
infinite. But perhaps the passage leaves room for recognizing
a merely logical distinction, or, to be more precise, one of
mode of signification, between the natures viewed not according to their meanings and conceptions (i.e. according to their
essential integrity), but according to their concrete hypostatic
act of existence. The properties of the natures are certainly
distinct, and the notion or essential structure of each nature is
likewise distinct beyond doubt, but neither of these are an
affirmation of a distinction between the concretely signified

---

[406]   DEC 161, 43-44.
[407]   DEC 162, 14-16.

(fully hypostatized) natures. The level at which distinction is necessarily to be affirmed (as is clear from this and the preceding council) is that of principle of operation, and this, perhaps, lends support to thinking of the humanity as such (in its distinction from the Word) only as an *id quo est*[408].

---

[408] Cf. supra, *Concilium Constantinopolitanum II*, §5, p. 140-142.

I.10. GILBERT OF POITIERS AND RICHARD OF SAINT-VICTOR

In this chapter we intend, amongst other things, to give a brief analysis of certain passages found in the writings of Gilbert of Poitiers which pertain to the conceptualization of some of the difficult notions relevant to our investigation of the ontology of the person and already brought into relief by Boethius[409]. After glancing at several theological hazards flagged by the Porretanian doctrine, we shall examine the thought of Richard of Saint-Victor whose concept of personality plays a role in the future of Trinitarian speculation second only to that of Boethius.

A cursory review of Gilbert of Poitiers is justified not only by the historical significance of his strong realism for what concerns the doctrine of distinc-

---

[409] The following remarks on Gilbert are purely summarical and not intended in the least to represent a systematic study of his doctrine. For more systematic discussions of that doctrine, see M. L. COLISH, "Gilbert, The Early Porretans, and Peter Lombard: Semantics and Theology", in J. Jolivet – A. De Libera (editors), *Gilbert de Poitiers et ses contemporains. Aux origines de la Logica modernorum: Actes du septième Symposium européen d'histoire de la logique et de la sémantique médiévales, Centre d'Études supérieures de civilisation médiévale de Poitiers, Poitiers, 17-22 juin 1985*, Bibliopolis, Naples 1987, p. 229-250 [this work represents an excellent account of the metaphysical difficulty encountered by Gilbert in his attempt to account for the kind of human nature assumed by Christ as well as in the broader issue of distinguishing human nature from human personality]; K. JACOBI, "Einzelnes – Individuum – Person. Gilbert von Poitiers' Philosophie des Individuellen", in J. A. Aertsen/A. Speer (editors), *Individuum und Individualität im Mittelalter (Miscellanea Mediaevalia 24)*, p. 3-21; J. JOLIVET, "Trois variations médiévales sur l'universel et l'individu: Roscelin, Abélard, Gilbert de la Porrée", *Rev. Méta. Morale* 97 (1992), p. 111-155; JOLIVET, J. – DE LIBERA, A. (editors), *Gilbert de Poitiers et ses contemporains. Aux origines de la Logica modernorum: Actes du septième Symposium européen d'histoire de la logique et de la sémantique médiévales, Centre d'Études supérieures de civilisation médiévale de Poitiers, Poitiers, 17-22 juin 1985*, Bibliopolis, Naples 1987; B. MAIOLI, *Gilberto Porretano: dalla grammatica speculativa alla metafisica del concreto*, Bulzoni, Rome 1979; J. MARENBON, "Gilbert of Poitiers", in *A History of Twelfth-Century Western Philsophy*, P. Dronke (editor), Cambridge University Press, Cambridge 1988; L. O. NIELSEN, *Theology and Philosophy in the Twelfth Century: A Study of Gilbert Porreta's Thinking and the Theological Expositions of the Doctrine of the Incarnation During the Period 1130-1180*, E. J. Brill, Leiden 1982; L. M. DE RIJK, "Gilbert de Poitiers: ses vues sémantiques et métaphysiques", in J. Jolivet – A. De Libera (editors), *Gilbert de Poitiers et ses contemporains. Aux origines de la Logica modernorum: Actes du septième Symposium européen d'histoire de la logique et de la sémantique médiévales, Centre d'Études supérieures de civilisation médiévale de Poitiers, Poitiers, 17-22 juin 1985*, Bibliopolis, Naples 1987, p. 147-171; M. A. SCHMIDT, *Gottheit und Trinität nach dem Kommentar des Gilberts Porreta zu Boethius De Trinitate*, Basel 1956; H. C. VAN ELSWIJK, *Gilbert Porreta: sa vie, son oeuvre, sa pensée*, Spicilegium sacrum Lovaniense, Louvain 1966.

tions, but by the simple fact that Albert makes frequent reference to his doctrine. In his explanation of the reality of personal distinction, Albert constructs his *via media*, moreover, precisely between Gilbert of Poitiers and Praepositinus[410]. The discussion of Gilbert of Poitiers enters, furthermore, into a Church council in the Synod of Reims of 1148 (where his alleged position is condemned), thus exposing the ecclesiastical importance and theological significance of his doctrine while making the Porretanus highly visible and representative for Trinitarian dogma.

Gilbert of Poitiers

A superb dialectician, Gilbert of Poitiers (1076-1154), theologian and philosopher formed in the school of Chartres where he later taught, and bishop of Poitiers from 1142 until his death, introduced (by means of a particular and original interpretation of Boethian axioms) a distinction in medieval philosophy which was to be the cause of much controversy. Constructing explanations on the basis of the rules of grammar[411], Gilbert distinguished between "the subsistent" and "subsistence" as signifying the concrete existent and the form *by which* the existent is what it is; he maintained that "divinity" signified the form according to which God was God, while the name "God" signified the supposit[412]. He furthermore argued that, because they are not formally signified according to inherence but only according to the mode of referentiality *ad aliud*, relations, unlike other accidents, are not signified according to being, but as "assisting" or accompanying a thing's being[413]. As a result of this teaching, Gilbert was under-

---

[410] Cf. infra, "Οὐσία AND ὑπόστασις AS 'SUBSTANCE' IN DIFFERENT WAYS", p. 203; the conclusion to "PROPRIETAS", p. 464 (especially p. 468); and our "CLOSING REMARKS", p. 527 (especially p. 529).

[411] Cf. H. C. Van Elswijk, *Gilbert Porreta: sa vie, son oeuvre, sa pensée*, Spicilegium sacrum Lovaniense, Louvain 1966, p. 144-147, 312.

[412] For a detailed analysis of these distinctions operative in the Porretan's thought at the philosophical level, see B. Maioli, *Gilberto Porretano: dalla grammatica speculativa alla metafisica del concreto*, Bulzoni, Rome 1979, p. 183-198; for an account of their application in Trinitarian theology, see L. O. Nielsen, *Theology and Philosophy in the Twelfth Century: A Study of Gilbert Porreta's Thinking and the Theological Expositions of the Doctrine of the Incarnation During the Period 1130-1180*, E. J. Brill, Leiden 1982, p. 142-163. Cf. B. Sesboüé, *Histoire des dogmes*, tome I, *Le Dieu du salut*, Desclée, Paris 1994, p. 310; L. M. De Rijk, "Gilbert de Poitiers: ses vues sémantiques et métaphysiques", in J. Jolivet – A. De Libera (editors), *Gilbert de Poitiers et ses contemporains. Aux origines de la Logica modernorum: Actes du septième Symposium européen d'histoire de la logique et de la sémantique médiévales, Centre d'Études supérieures de civilisation médiévale de Poitiers, Poitiers, 17-22 juin 1985*, Bibliopolis, Naples 1987, p. 147-171, especially 148-149; L. O. Nielsen, op. cit., p. 142-143, 158.

[413] Gilbert of Poitiers, *In De Trin*, I, 4, 18, ed. N. M. Häring (in *The Commentaries on Boethius by Gilbert of Poitiers*, Pontifical Institute of Mediaeval Studies, Toronto 1966),

stood to have affirmed a real distinction between the divinity and God, as well as between the divine relations and the persons and the same relations and divine nature. Such an interpretation, which was the object of the condemnations of the Council of Reims in 1148, would not have been shared by the Porretanus, though his ultra-realist tendencies with regard to universals (particularly visible in his anthropology[414]) would seem to fortify convictions that his doctrine confesses, latently at least, a distinction in things (*res*) and not just in the significations of their names (*signa*)[415].

Gilbert's principal works are his commentary on the *Opuscula sacra* of Boethius and the *Liber sex principiorum*. In the first of these, we find Gilbert's commentary on the all-important Boethian treatise *Contra Eutychen et Nestorium*. There, Gilbert's definition of *persona* is not what interests us; while his understanding of person principally emerges from his analysis of the distinction between the abstract form and the concrete being of a thing, commenting on the phrase: *"Essentiae in universalibus sunt, in particularibus substant"*, the effective result for personhood is a qualified case of the individual, a specially gifted nature, and thus explained in terms of physical categories, not unlike that of Boethius[416]. What does interest us, however, is that analysis of the distinction, as Gilbert sees it, between a specific form and its concrete subject. The interrelation between these two notions, their causal or

---

p. 118 (PL 64, 1282); I, 5, 2 & 5, ed. Häring, p. 139 (PL 64, 1291); I, 5, 10-11, ed. Häring, p. 140-141 (PL 64, 1292); I, 6, 1, ed. Häring, p. 151 (PL 64, 1297); II, 1, 3-4, ed. Häring, p. 163 (PL 64, 1303). Cf. B. Maioli, *Gilberto Porretano: dalla grammatica speculativa alla metafisica del concreto*, Bulzoni, Rome 1979, p. 89-94; L. M. De Rijk, "Gilbert de Poitiers: ses vues sémantiques et métaphysiques", in J. Jolivet – A. De Libera (editors), *Gilbert de Poitiers et ses contemporains. Aux origines de la Logica modernorum: Actes du septième Symposium européen d'histoire de la logique et de la sémantique médiévales, Centre d'Études supérieures de civilisation médiévale de Poitiers, Poitiers, 17-22 juin 1985*, Bibliopolis, Naples 1987, p. 156-160.

[414] Cf. Gilbert, *In Contra Eut.*, 5, 25-39, ed. N.-M. Häring (in *The Commentaries on Boethius by Gilbert of Poitiers*, Pontifical Institute of Mediaeval Studies, Toronto 1966), p. 319-322 (PL 64, 1393). (An earlier version of the same critical edition can be found in *AHDLMA* 29 (1954), Vrin, Paris 1955).

[415] Cf. M. L. Colish, "Gilbert, The Early Porretans, and Peter Lombard: Semantics and Theology", in J. Jolivet – A. De Libera (editors), *Gilbert de Poitiers et ses contemporains. Aux origines de la Logica modernorum: Actes du septième Symposium européen d'histoire de la logique et de la sémantique médiévales, Centre d'Études supérieures de civilisation médiévale de Poitiers, Poitiers, 17-22 juin 1985*, Bibliopolis, Naples 1987, p. 229-250, especially 232-235.

[416] For the Porretanian notion of personality, see L. O. Nielsen, *Theology and Philosophy in the Twelfth Century: A Study of Gilbert Porreta's Thinking and the Theological Expositions of the Doctrine of the Incarnation During the Period 1130-1180*, E. J. Brill, Leiden 1982, p. 62-64.

participatory roles, their degree of distinctness, etc., has not been fully spelled out.

The general distinction

One might speak of two forms of subsistence in Gilbert's treatises: one for genera and species existing in themselves without reference to accidents; another for those subsistences which are the support of accidents, which are called substances in the strict sense[417]. As subsistences, both may be ranged within the Aristotelian category of primary substances[418], but it seems that the first, for Gilbert, is nothing other than substance understood Platonically, and its reality is ambiguous when we consider the peculiar view held by Gilbert on the inner constitution of the individual[419].

The *individualized* essence or substance, in which the accidents inhere, is distinguished from the *formae substantialis* or *formae nativae*[420] to which Gilbert attributed universality[421]. The commonality attrib-

---

[417] Cf. B. Maioli, *Gilberto Porretano: dalla grammatica speculativa alla metafisica del concreto*, Bulzoni, Rome 1979, p. 271-273, 289-291; L. M. De Rijk, "Gilbert de Poitiers: ses vues sémantiques et métaphysiques", in J. Jolivet – A. De Libera (editors), *Gilbert de Poitiers et ses contemporains. Aux origines de la Logica modernorum: Actes du septième Symposium européen d'histoire de la logique et de la sémantique médiévales, Centre d'Études supérieures de civilisation médiévale de Poitiers, Poitiers, 17-22 juin 1985*, Bibliopolis, Naples 1987, p. 153-154.

[418] Cf. L. O. Nielsen, *Theology and Philosophy in the Twelfth Century: A Study of Gilbert Porreta's Thinking and the Theological Expositions of the Doctrine of the Incarnation During the Period 1130-1180*, E. J. Brill, Leiden 1982, p. 52.

[419] Cf. B. Maioli, *Gilberto Porretano: dalla grammatica speculativa alla metafisica del concreto*, Bulzoni, Rome 1979, p. 291-292; L. O. Nielsen, *Theology and Philosophy in the Twelfth Century: A Study of Gilbert Porreta's Thinking and the Theological Expositions of the Doctrine of the Incarnation During the Period 1130-1180*, E. J. Brill, Leiden 1982, p. 58-62.

[420] Cf. Gilbert, *In De Trin.*, I, 2, 26-30, ed. N.-M. Häring, p. 83-84 (PL 64, 1266-1267); I, 2, 52, ed. Häring, p. 89 (PL 64 1269); I, 2, 57-58, ed. Häring, p. 90-91 (PL 64, 1270); *In Contra Eut.*, 1, 58, ed. Häring, p. 254 (PL 64, 1364); 8, 16, ed. Häring, p. 357-358 (PL 64, 1409). For a study of the historical development of the notion of these *formae nativae* and their place within the Porretan doctrine, cf. B. Maioli, *Gilberto Porretano: dalla grammatica speculativa alla metafisica del concreto*, Bulzoni, Rome 1979, p. 259-268. For an analysis of the ontological distinction to be affirmed between the "subsistences" and the subsistent thing, cf. id., p. 273-278, 303304; H. C. Van Elswijk, *Gilbert Porreta: sa vie, son oeuvre, sa pensée*, Spicilegium sacrum Lovaniense, Louvain 1966, p. 153-164.

[421] Even if not in the same sense as the archetypal Ideas which cannot become immanent in the concrete reality and which are therefore distinguished somehow (according to the generative realization of the subsistent form) from the *formae nativae* (cf. B. Maioli, *Gilberto Porretano: dalla grammatica speculativa alla metafisica del concreto*, Bulzoni, Rome 1979, p. 263-268, 274275, 278279; L. O. Nielsen, *Theology and Philosophy in the Twelfth Century: A Study of Gilbert Porreta's Thinking and the Theological*

uted to these forms derives from the fact that they are alike in the diversity of individuals or species in which they are found, which similitude accounts for the real value of our concepts[422]. The mind can abstract these native forms or essential determinations from the matter by which they are concrete in order to consider the similar elements, which are called species and genus[423]. These are *subsistentiae* but not substantially existing things[424].

A being's particular mode of existence is distinguished from the essential realities (*subsistentia, id quo est*) possessed by it: *"itaque genera et species i.e. generales et speciales subsistentiae subsistunt tantum, non substant"*[425]. Now, Gilbert affirms that essences exist only in individuals and are numerically multiplied in a plurality of natural substances[426]. The form is individual in each individual, though common, or alike, in all the members of a species[427]. But, that a separate human form be multiplied in separate individuals means that there can be no real universal form[428] (the natural consequence of this is that Christ would only be *similar* to us). Moreover, if these *subsistentiae* are only similar amongst different beings, and are therefore not really universal, then they are already determined in some way; what individualizing determination, one might ask, need then be invoked in order that they *substant?*

Expositions of the Doctrine of the Incarnation During the Period 1130-1180, E. J. Brill, Leiden 1982, p. 72-74).

[422] Cf. Gilbert, *De Trin.*, I, 1, 27-28, ed. Häring, p. 76 (PL 64, 1263); *In Contra Eut.*, 3, 59, ed. Häring, p. 283-284 (PL 64, 1376). Cf. L. O. Nielsen, *Theology and Philosophy in the Twelfth Century: A Study of Gilbert Porreta's Thinking and the Theological Expositions of the Doctrine of the Incarnation During the Period 1130-1180*, E. J. Brill, Leiden 1982, p. 66-69; H. C. Van Elswijk, *Gilbert Porreta: sa vie, son oeuvre, sa pensée*, Spicilegium sacrum Lovaniense, Louvain 1966, p. 186-188.

[423] Cf. H. C. Van Elswijk, *Gilbert Porreta: sa vie, son oeuvre, sa pensée*, Spicilegium sacrum Lovaniense, Louvain 1966, p. 192-193.

[424] Cf. Gilbert, *In De Trin.*, I, 2, 28-31, ed. Häring, p. 84-85 (PL 64, 1267).

[425] Gilbert, *In Contra Eut.*, 3, 42, ed. Häring, p. 280 (PL 64, 1375C).

[426] *"Unus enim homo una singulari humanitate... ut pluribus humanitatibus plures homines et substantiae–* Gilbert, *In Contra Eut.*, 3, 69, ed. Häring, p. 286 (PL 64, 1378AB).

[427] On the notion of *conformitas naturalis*, see H. C. Van Elswijk, *Gilbert Porreta: sa vie, son oeuvre, sa pensée*, Spicilegium sacrum Lovaniense, Louvain 1966, p. 189-191, 194197, 203, 294.

[428] Accordingly, Gilbert's doctrine has been described as representing both nominalist tendencies and an extreme realism latent in his epistemological methodology; cf. M. Wulf, *Histoire de la philosophie médiévale*, vol. I, p. 205; A. Hayen, *Le concile de Reims et l'erreur théologique de Gilbert de la Porrée*, in *AHDLMA* 10-11 (1935-1936); H. C. Van Elswijk, *Gilbert Porreta: sa vie, son oeuvre, sa pensée*, Spicilegium sacrum Lovaniense, Louvain 1966, p. 200-203, 340-341.

Important questions raised by this distinction

There is no difficulty in admitting a distinction between the abstract form and the concrete subject in natural things; Gilbert writes: *"in naturalibus enim aliud est quod est, aliud quo est"*[429]. And here in the natural context there is nothing untoward with the idea of causality (whether in the formal or the efficient order), since it is a distinction, precisely, of effect to cause[430]. However, an important question must be raised: this distinction between the form and the *suppositum*, does it necessarily imply a relation of participation[431], or one of causality and dependence[432]? The question here hinges upon its consideration, on the one hand, in creatures, and, on the other hand, in God; just how this question would impose itself in the Incarnation is another matter, where it is a question of a *divine suppositum* and a *created* human nature. Does this question about the distinction of the form and the *suppositum*, when transposed to Christ, become that of the distinction between the abstract human form and the concrete individual human nature of Christ, or of that between the concrete human nature and the person, or of both[433]?

Application of the distinction to God

As regards the transferal of this distinction to God, it is uncertain as to whether Gilbert actually intended a real distinction between *Deus* and

---

[429]   Gilbert, *In De Trin.*, I, 3, 38, ed. Häring, p. 109 (PL 64, 1278D).

[430]   *"Nichil enim naturalium [quae sunt concreta] nisi per causam"* – Gilbert, *In Contra Eut.*, 1, 16, ed. Häring, p. 245 (PL 64, 1360B); cf. *In De Trin.*, I, 2, 27-29, ed. Häring, p. 83-84 (PL 64, 1267A).

[431]   As was the case for Clarembaud of Arras, partisan of those reproaching Gilbert for having introduced a distinction between God and his divinity (cf. Hayen, op. cit., p. 52-53; cf. H. C. Van Elswijk, *Gilbert Porreta: sa vie, son oeuvre, sa pensée*, Spicilegium sacrum Lovaniense, Louvain 1966, p. 77-124, 319-327 for the historical details surrounding the conflict and the judgment of the Council of Reims).

[432]   As was the case for St. Bernard (cf. Hayen, op. cit., p. 52-53; B. Maioli, *Gilberto Porretano: dalla grammatica speculativa alla metafisica del concreto*, Bulzoni, Rome 1979, p. 225; H. C. Van Elswijk, *Gilbert Porreta: sa vie, son oeuvre, sa pensée*, Spicilegium sacrum Lovaniense, Louvain 1966, p. 358). Concerning participative and causal relations, cf. B. Maioli, op. cit., p. 271-273, 278-279, 303-304; L. O. Nielsen, *Theology and Philosophy in the Twelfth Century: A Study of Gilbert Porreta's Thinking and the Theological Expositions of the Doctrine of the Incarnation During the Period 1130-1180*, E. J. Brill, Leiden 1982, p. 48-49; cf. also H. C. Van Elswijk, op. cit., p. 156-158.

[433]   For an explanation of the kind of response supplied by Gilbert (founded on his notion of composition, his understanding of specific forms, and his doctrine of individual subsistence), see H. C. Van Elswijk, *Gilbert Porreta: sa vie, son oeuvre, sa pensée*, Spicilegium sacrum Lovaniense, Louvain 1966, p. 386-402, 434-451.

divinitas[434]. Certainly no causal relation is intended between God and his divinity, and no causal role is being ascribed to the ablative *quo Deus est*. Nonetheless, Gilbert establishes a working parallel between the distinction of created beings from their composite forms and the distinction of God from his simple essence[435]. However, it remains difficult to conceive of that in which a real distinction of *id quod est* and *id quo est* within a wholly simple being could consist[436].

If it is the case that Gilbert has exaggerated the distinction between the individual essence and the common essence when he characterizes it as *really* distinct from the former, then it would have to be either on the grounds of its transferal to the realm of the Trinity or insofar as it fails to treat the individual concrete nature as a *logical* subject of attribution for the nature considered abstractly[437]. In any

---

[434] "*Atque ideo vere est unum et adeo simplex in se et sine his, quae adesse possunt, solitarium ut recte de hoc uno dicatur quod de ipso principio, cujus* οὐσία *est, dicitur, scilicet, est id quod est. Sicut enim non est quo Deus sit nisi simplex atque sola essentia, id est* οὐσία, *sic non est unde* οὐσία *ipsa sit, nisi quoniam ea simplex et solus Deus est. Unde etiam usus loquendi est, ut de Deo dicatur, non modo 'Deus est', verum etiam 'Deus est ipsa essentia'*" – Gilbert, *In De Trin.*, I, 2, 54-55, ed. Häring, p. 89-90 (PL 64, 1269D). Compare this text with *In Contra Eut.*, 3, 59-60, ed. Häring. p. 283-284 (PL 64, 1377B). Cf. B. Maioli, *Gilberto Porretano: dalla grammatica speculativa alla metafisica del concreto*, Bulzoni, Rome 1979, p. 207-211; H. C. Van Elswijk, *Gilbert Porreta: sa vie, son oeuvre, sa pensée*, Spicilegium sacrum Lovaniense, Louvain 1966, p. 320, 326-327, 340-343; M. L. Colish, "Gilbert, The Early Porretans, and Peter Lombard: Semantics and Theology", in J. Jolivet – A. De Libera (editors), *Gilbert de Poitiers et ses contemporains. Aux origines de la Logica modernorum: Actes du septième Symposium européen d'histoire de la logique et de la sémantique médiévales, Centre d'Études supérieures de civilisation médiévale de Poitiers, Poitiers, 17-22 juin 1985*, Bibliopolis, Naples 1987, p. 229-250, especially 232-236; L. O. Nielsen, *Theology and Philosophy in the Twelfth Century: A Study of Gilbert Porreta's Thinking and the Theological Expositions of the Doctrine of the Incarnation During the Period 1130-1180*, E. J. Brill, Leiden 1982, p. 158. Regarding the complexity and originality of the Porretanian understanding of the criteria of simplicity, see B. Maioli, op. cit., p. 301-306; cf. L. O. Nielsen, op. cit., p. 53-54, 65-66.

[435] Cf. Gilbert, *In De Trin.*, I, 2, 16-26, ed. Häring, p. 81-83 (PL 64, 1266). Cf. M. L. Colish, "Gilbert, The Early Porretans, and Peter Lombard: Semantics and Theology", in J. Jolivet – A. De Libera (editors), *Gilbert de Poitiers et ses contemporains. Aux origines de la Logica modernorum: Actes du septième Symposium européen d'histoire de la logique et de la sémantique médiévales, Centre d'Études supérieures de civilisation médiévale de Poitiers, Poitiers, 17-22 juin 1985*, Bibliopolis, Naples 1987, p. 233-234; L. O. Nielsen, *Theology and Philosophy in the Twelfth Century: A Study of Gilbert Porreta's Thinking and the Theological Expositions of the Doctrine of the Incarnation During the Period 1130-1180*, E. J. Brill, Leiden 1982, p. 146; H. C. Van Elswijk, *Gilbert Porreta: sa vie, son oeuvre, sa pensée*, Spicilegium sacrum Lovaniense, Louvain 1966, p. 286-292, 295.

[436] For an exposition of the Porretan account of divine simplicity, cf. H. C. Van Elswijk, *Gilbert Porreta: sa vie, son oeuvre, sa pensée*, Spicilegium sacrum Lovaniense, Louvain 1966, p. 293-296, 305; B. Maioli, *Gilberto Porretano: dalla grammatica speculativa alla metafisica del concreto*, Bulzoni, Rome 1979, p. 301-306.

[437] Secondary substance exists in the individual as in a *logical subject of attribution*. But it does not therefore become an *accident* of the primary substance with which it is in

event, his real distinction between the *id quod est* and the *id quo est* (taken according to the formal order) does not leave room for the possibility of a purely *logical* distinction between them (*secundum intelligentiae rationem*), the latter of which is a notion already able to be drawn from Boethius.

The same distinction between the divine persons and their properties

Whether Gilbert admits a real distinction in God which would compromise his simplicity depends not only on whether or not he really distinguishes between God and his essence but also upon whether he really distinguishes between the persons of the Trinity and their properties, since these two distinctions mutually imply one another[438]. We have already seen the importance of correctly understanding the relation between the divine persons and the *particularitates* in the previous chapters.

Based on the admission of divine simplicity, these properties cannot enter into composition with that essence after the manner of an accidental form. Nor can they be attributed substantially, since anything substantially attributed to God applies to each person of the Trinity equally[439]. Consequently they must be identified with the persons themselves. And here is where Gilbert's excessive realism leads him to making a real distinction where there should be none on account of the diversity of concepts he derives. Certain *praedicationes*, Gilbert affirms, supply the *ratio* for a thing, that is, determine what it is

reality perfectly *identical* as an essence or nature. Cf. F.-J. Thonnard, *Précis de Philosophie en Harmonie avec les Sciences Modernes*, Desclée & Cie, Tornaci (Belgium) 1950, §86.

[438] Cf. Hayen, op. cit., p. 55: *"Dans le porrétanisme, ces deux distinctions s'implique et se confirment mutuellement"*. Cf. B. Maioli, *Gilberto Porretano: dalla grammatica speculativa alla metafisica del concreto*, Bulzoni, Rome 1979, p. 293-294; L. O. Nielsen, *Theology and Philosophy in the Twelfth Century: A Study of Gilbert Porreta's Thinking and the Theological Expositions of the Doctrine of the Incarnation During the Period 1130-1180*, E. J. Brill, Leiden 1982, p. 152.

[439] *"Quicquid de Deo substantialiter praedicatur, id et de Patre et de Filio et de Spiritu sancto et divisim et simul suppositis singulariter dicitur: neque vero Pater neque Filius neque Spiritus sanctus de eisdem omnibus vel divisim vel simul suppositis dicitur"*– Gilbert, *In De Trin.*, II, 1, 57, ed. Häring, p. 174 (PL 64, 1308CD). Cf. L. M. De Rijk, "Gilbert de Poitiers: ses vues sémantiques et métaphysiques", in J. Jolivet – A. De Libera (editors), *Gilbert de Poitiers et ses contemporains. Aux origines de la Logica modernorum: Actes du septième Symposium européen d'histoire de la logique et de la sémantique médiévales, Centre d'Études supérieures de civilisation médiévale de Poitiers, Poitiers, 17-22 juin 1985*, Bibliopolis, Naples 1987, p. 156, 160.

in itself, while others do not pertain to the constitution of the thing but obtain rather to something extrinsic[440].

Gilbert is taking recourse to the predicaments of time, place, etc., the *circumstantiae* which, when taken as *principia quibus,* only pertain to objects in an extrinsic way, and not *secundum rem*[441]. Since no predicament *secundum rem* can account for the plurality of persons in the Trinity, this diversity must be explained in terms of the extrinsic predicament of relation (which, for Gilbert, will not compromise the divine simplicity, since that which cannot intrinsically effect the very constitution of a being cannot really enter into composition with it)[442].

Now, the same real distinction (emphasizing the difference between the concrete and the abstract) operated between God and the divinity is repeated for the persons of the Trinity and their properties or relations (on the basis of the distinction between that *of which* a quality or relation is predicated and the quality or relation itself which – from all

---

[440] *"Aliae quidem earum [praedicationum] quasi monstrant rem, id est, esse quidlibet eo quo est; aliae vero non rem, id est, non esse quicquam eo quo est, sed quasi quasdam circumstancias rei"* – Gilbert, *In De Trin.,* I, 4, 109, ed. Häring, p. 137 (PL 64, 1291A). Cf. B. Maioli, *Gilberto Porretano: dalla grammatica speculativa alla metafisica del concreto,* Bulzoni, Rome 1979, p. 89-94, 294-298; H. C. Van Elswijk, *Gilbert Porreta: sa vie, son oeuvre, sa pensée,* Spicilegium sacrum Lovaniense, Louvain 1966, p. 312; L. M. De Rijk, "Gilbert de Poitiers: ses vues sémantiques et métaphysiques", in J. Jolivet – A. De Libera (editors), *Gilbert de Poitiers et ses contemporains. Aux origines de la Logica modernorum: Actes du septième Symposium européen d'histoire de la logique et de la sémantique médiévales, Centre d'Études supérieures de civilisation médiévale de Poitiers, Poitiers, 17-22 juin 1985,* Bibliopolis, Naples 1987, p. 156, 160.

[441] *"Illa vero alia praedicantur quidem, sed non ita ut rem subsistentem eis esse aliquid ostendant, sed potius extrinsecus, id est ex aliorum collationibus, et diversae rationis consortiis accomodatum aliquid quodam modo affigant. Non igitur haec secundum rem, sed recte extrinsecus comparatae praedicationes dicuntur"* – Gilbert, *In De Trin.,* I, 5, 111-112, ed. Häring, p. 138 (PL 64, 1291B).

[442] *"Quandoquidem extrinsecus accessu comparato relatio praedicatur, igitur non potest dici praedicationem relativam, id est relationem praedicatam, vel addere secundum se quicquam rei de qua dicitur, vel minuere secundum se, vel mutare secundum se. Quae relativa praedicatio tota consistit... non in eo quod est esse (quoniam nulli confert aliquid esse), sed potius consistit in eo tantum quod est habere se ad aliud in comparatione alterius ad alterum"* – Gilbert, *In De Trin.,* I, 5, 10, ed. Häring, p. 140 (PL 64, 1292C); cf. especially Hayen, op. cit., p. 62 and note 2. Gilbert attempts to account for the plurality of persons by means of predicating "exterior" relations. But employing an opposition of *praedicatio extrinseca* to *praedicatio secundum rem* is not the same as to employ that of *praedicatio secundum mentem* to *praedicatio secundum rem;* the former opposition is insufficient to preserve perfect divine simplicity. Cf. B. Maioli, *Gilberto Porretano: dalla grammatica speculativa alla metafisica del concreto,* Bulzoni, Rome 1979, p. 94-98. For a general account of relation and personal constitution in God according to Gilbert, see L. O. Nielsen, *Theology and Philosophy in the Twelfth Century: A Study of Gilbert Porreta's Thinking and the Theological Expositions of the Doctrine of the Incarnation During the Period 1130-1180,* E. J. Brill, Leiden 1982, p. 149-156.

grammatical appearances – is not so qualified or related) [443]. Again, this real distinction between the persons and their properties is not one between effect and cause, yet it cannot have a purely nominal value in light of the realism of Gilbert's formulations. To temper our judgment in calling it an *objective* distinction between a thing and its form [444] leaves the problem unresolved, for, exaggerated realism will distinguish as many realities as it does concepts, and, if Gilbert's simultaneously alleged nominalist tendency is true, it would seem to either disavow the objectively distinguished form or implicitly recognize some individuating determination proper to the form itself (since it is not really universal but only similar in different individuals), if it really subsists.

Conclusion

Gilbert's confusing mix of the Platonic doctrine of Ideas and the Aristotelian doctrine of abstraction in his theory of knowledge ultimately leads him into theological precariousness. His distinction between the persons of the Trinity and their respective properties, as between God and the divinity, serve to forewarn us about false understandings of both the relationship between and the signification of *id quod est* and *id quo est*. He seems to maintain a real distinction between universals and concrete or particular substances [445]. As far as the created subject is concerned, this is fine; but with respect to God, there can be no such distinction, within whom there is, at most, a logical difference between the *quod est* and the *quo est*; and as regards the individual essence of the created subject, no such distinction holds, since it is not distinguished from the essence as secondary substance, except logi-

---

[443] *"Qualitas vero in mathematicis omnium qualitatum generalissimum est, et quantitas omnium quantitatum. Et sunt quod dicuntur, non a causis quae in ipsis intelliguntur, sed ab efficiendo ea in quibus sunt subsistentia, ille quidem qualia, iste vero quanta... Nulla namque relatio, sed id tantum de quo ipsa praedicatur, ea ad aliquid est. Sicut nulla qualitas qualis est, sed ea id tantum de quo dicitur ipsa"* – Gilbert, *In De Trin.*, I, 4, 7 & 9, ed. Häring, p. 116-117 (PL 64, 1281D).

[444] Cf. Hayen, op. cit., p. 64.

[445] *"Recte ergo cum dixisset 'essentiae in universalibus sunt, in particularibus substant', dicit etiam 'substantiae in universalibus sunt, in particularibus capiunt substantiam', id est substant. Et est sensus: universalia quae intellectus ex particularibus colligit, sunt quoniam particularium illud esse dicuntur quo ipsa particularia aliquid sunt"* – Gilbert, *In Contra Eut.*, 3, 34-35, ed. Häring, p. 279 (PL 64, 1374D). Cf. L. O. Nielsen, *Theology and Philosophy in the Twelfth Century: A Study of Gilbert Porreta's Thinking and the Theological Expositions of the Doctrine of the Incarnation During the Period 1130-1180*, E. J. Brill, Leiden 1982, p. 68-69.

cally. Transposed to the context of the Incarnation, things are not so clear. Can we call the created humanity in some sense a "subject" of the universal form? With regard to the person of the Word, who is certainly the *quod est*, is there a duality of *quibus est* on the part of the human nature considered abstractly on the one hand and concretely on the other[446]? Yet a principal passage in Gilbert seems to confess a more nominalist character in that the universal is but a *principle* of being and does not itself subsist (*"universalia, quae intellectus ex particularibus colligit, sunt quoniam particularium illud esse dicuntur quo ipsa particularia aliquid sunt"*[447]). At the same time, the universal, or essential determination, as we have seen, is common to its different species only according to a unity of *resemblance*. Consequently there cannot exist but singular forms; thus, the humanity of Peter is not that of Paul[448]. We have already commented on what this means for the Incarnation[449].

The theological difficulties encountered by Gilbert of Poitiers demonstrate the subtlety and delicacy with which we must approach the problem of distinguishing between the concrete subject and its essence considered at its various levels. It also calls to mind the certain (albeit limited, though not insignificant) relevance of the problem of universals, as well as indicates the ontological "layering" so complex in the case of the person of Christ. With this, we turn to the more thorough examination of the problem of personhood occasioned by Richard of Saint-Victor who, wholly unlike Gilbert of Poitiers, attempts to situate the problem of personhood outside of the familiar physical categories employed by Boethius.

---

[446] L. O. Nielsen takes up the closely related problem of the ontological status *at the subsistent level* to be attributed to the two natures in Christ: cf. *Theology and Philosophy in the Twelfth Century: A Study of Gilbert Porreta's Thinking and the Theological Expositions of the Doctrine of the Incarnation During the Period 1130-1180*, E. J. Brill, Leiden 1982, p. 170-184.

[447] Gilbert, *In Contra Eut.*, 3, 35, ed. Häring, p. 279 (PL 64, 1374D).

[448] *"Quaecumque res subsistens, alii collata, ab ea est alterutrius numero alia, nullo illorum est aliquid quorum quolibet illa, a qua est alia, aliquid est. Nam etsi utraque subsistunt aliquibus ad se invicem eiusdem similitudine, nunquam tamen eiusdem essentiae singularitate"* – Gilbert, *In De Trin.*, I, 5, 28, ed. Häring, p. 145 (PL 64, 1294CD).

[449] The simple fact that Christ's human nature would merely be *similar* to our own, with all of its appalling consequences (cf. supra, "THE GENERAL DISTINCTION", p. 152 (especially p. 153).

Richard of St. Victor

Richard of Saint-Victor (†1173) represents the speculative and innovative result of an epoch which flourished in the teaching of the schools of Laon, Chartres, Orléans and Paris. The thought of Gilbert of Poitiers continues to be a fruitful source for the reflection of commentators, Bernard of Clairvaux has passed on his brilliant prudential wisdom, and Peter Lombard is producing his far reaching theology at Notre Dame in Paris. The Abbot of Saint-Victor, finally, is moreover rooted in the glorious tradition of the memorable Hugh. Like his predecessor, Richard concerns himself especially with mystical theology, publishing two works on contemplation, the *Beniamin minor*, on the preparation of the soul, and the *Beniamin maior*, on the grace of contemplation. As a spiritual writer, Richard rivals his mentor, Hugh, but whereas Hugh insisted upon the inadequacy of reason and the necessity of faith, Richard's more scholastic style aims to support the authority of scripture and the Fathers by laying greater emphasis upon dialectical argumentation, zealously seeking "necessary reasons" for the faith[450], much like Anselm of Canterbury[451]. The *De Trinitate*, alone amongst Richard's works able to be situated within the wholly speculative order, must be singled out as Richard's most important contribution. Written probably sometime after the Council of Reims (1148) criticizing the doctrine of Gilbert of Poitiers[452], the *De Trinitate* proceeds, according to an original dialectic on mutual love, to show that a plurality of persons in the singular Godhead necessarily flows from the fact that God is Love[453]. While the Abbot's Trinitarian speculation had considerable influence upon later Scholastic theology, his philosophical contribution seems to have had greater import, and he is also credited as being the first medieval thinker to provide a proof for the existence of God on an empirical basis according to the principles of causality. Naturally, in the thesis at hand, we shall focus upon the *De Trinitate* treating the substantial unity and trinity of persons in God. In it, Richard elaborates an original and precise concep-

---

[450] Richard of Saint-Victor, *De Trin.*, I, c. 4. (Note: all references to this work shall correspond to the critical edition by J. Ribaillier, Vrin, Paris, 1958; the Migne references are also given for reasons of utility with regard to the French translation of this work found in *Sources Chrétiennes* 63, Cerf, Paris, 1959).

[451] In fact, Richard's work may be described as an expression of a living spiritual current having Augustine as its first inspiration and taking Saint Anselm as its rational springboard.

[452] Cf. G. Salet, *Richard de Saint-Victor, La Trinité* (*SC* 63), p. 7.

[453] Richard is known as the theorist of the degrees of love for his masterful account of unity and distinction in the Trinity based upon the supreme notion of charity.

tion of the notion of person, in an effort to situate the problem of personhood outside of physical categories of explanation and with a certain independence with regard to the concept of substance. A consideration of this work, then, is not only important from a chronological point of view, but is especially indispensable insofar as constitutive of a radically new attempt at demarcating personal ontology[454].

An attempt to situate personhood beyond the category of substance

In his examination of personhood, Richard abandons the Greek vocabulary "ὑπόστασις" which, according to St. Jerome, contains a certain poison[455] and, as a general rule, avoids the term "subsistence"

---

[454] With the exception of the recent systematic investigation of N. Den Bok, *Communicating the Most High. A Systematic Study of Person and Trinity in the Theology of Richard of St. Victor (†1173)*, Brepols, Paris–Turnhout 1996, studies on Richard's Trinitarian theology can be grouped for the most part into two general categories: those which focus primarily on the historico-literary influences shaping his doctrine, and those (more recent) characterized by a more philological or sociological approach (cf. Den Bok, op. cit., p. 90-91). To the first group belong, in particular: J. CHÂTILLON, "Richard de Saint-Victor", in *D.S.* XIII, Paris 1987, p. 593-654; E. COUSINS, *The Notion of Person in the "De Trinitate" of Richard of Saint Victor*, unpublished Diss., Fordham University 1966; A.-M. ÉTHIER, *Le De Trinitate de Richard de Saint-Victor*, Institut d'Etudes Médiévale, Ottawa/Paris 1939; J. RIBAILLIER (editor), *Textes philosophiiques du Moyen Age*, VI, Vrin, Paris 1958 (critical text of the *De Trinitate*); G. SALET, *Richard de Saint-Victor, La Trinité* (*Sources chrétiennes* 63). Unfortunately, none of these authors, with the exception of E. Cousins, devote much attention to the Victorine's understanding of personality (cf. Den Bok, op. cit., p. 83). As to the second group of authors (including H. U. VON BALTHASAR, *Theologik*, vol. 2: *Wahrheit Gottes*, Einsiedeln 1985; W. KASPER, *Der Gott Jesu Christi*, Mainz 1982; P. SCHOONENBERG, "Trinity – The Consummated Covenant: Theses on the Doctrine of the Trinitarian God", *Studies in Religion* 5, 1975, p. 111-116), the proclivities for social trinitarianism tend, as pointed out by Den Bok (cf. op. cit. p. 84-85), to prematurely modernize Richard's views or obfuscate the ontological foundations of the relational and personal realities considered. Even the unpublished work of Cousins appears to be guided (and therefore limited) in large measure by a predominant spirit of social trinitarianism. In our survey we are, nevertheless, indebted to the priceless work of Éthier, Ribaillier and Salet whose clarifications are indispensable for a precise grasp of the Victorine use of language. As to the modern literature directly pertinent to the notion of personality in Richard, also noteworthy is the contribution of P. HOFMANN, "Analogie und Person. Zur Trinitätsspekulation Richards von St.-Victor", *Theologie und Philosophie* 59 (1984), p. 191-234; M. PURWATMA, *The Explanation of the Mystery of the Trinity Based on the Attribute of God as Supreme Love: A Study on the "De Trinitate" of Richard of St. Victor*, Rome 1990; S. A. TURIENZO, "Aspectos del Problema de la Persona en el Siglo XII", in *Miscellanea Mediaevalia* 2, "Die Metaphysik im Mittelalter", Walter de Gruyter, Berlin 1963, p. 180-183. For a broad and up to date bibliography on the subject, see the mentioned study by Den Bok.

[455] Cf. Richard, *De Trin.*, IV, c. 4, ed. Ribaillier, 157a; PL 196, 932C; cf. St. Jerome, *Ad Damascum epist.* 15: PL 22, 356.

which is perhaps too subtle for the simplicity of his expression and inaccessible to the common reader[456]. Instead, Richard opts for the more familiar terms of "person" and "substance", to which he intends to apply novel definitions, though his concern for semantics, as we shall see, seems less than satisfactory. He rejects the definition of Boethius and the interpretation of Gilbert of Poitiers which distinguishes the personal properties from the names directly indicating the persons themselves[457]. Richard expresses his rejection of the Boethian definition as an effort to avoid the confusion occasioned by inconsistently employing the word "person" sometimes to signify substance, sometimes subsistence and at other times the personal properties[458]. The identification of person with the common term substance insufficiently accounts for the distinctive personal property, which is ultimately able to be signified by the name carried by the person[459].

Person, then, cannot be satisfactorily defined according to substance, unless it were to signify nothing more than substantial being, but it signifies something more, namely, as we shall see, the possession of its substantial being through a particular property[460]. To the person belongs, over and above being a rational *substance* (*"cum dicitur persona, pro certo intelligitur aliquis unus qui tamen sit rationalis substantia"*[461]), another qualification, which pertains only to one and which, unlike rationality, cannot be shared by a plurality of substances, and, for which reason, is incommunicable[462]. The notion of substance denotes the *proprietas communis*, while that of person the *proprietas individualis, singularis, incommunicabilis*. Note that according to this usage,

---

[456] Cf. Richard, *De Trin.*, IV, c. 4, ed. Ribaillier, 157b; PL 196, 932D - 933A. In other works, e.g. *De tribus personis appropriatis in Trinitate*, Richard is less consistent in this regard; cf. N. Den Bok, *Communicating the Most High. A Systematic Study of Person and Trinity in the Theology of Richard of St. Victor (†1173)*, Brepols, Paris–Turnhout 1996, p. 209.

[457] Cf. Richard, *De Trin.*, IV, c. 3, ed. Ribaillier, 157a; PL 196, 932C.

[458] *"Nam sunt qui dicant nomen persone aliquando substantiam, aliquando subsistentias, aliquando personarum proprietates significare"* – Richard, *De Trin.*, IV, c. 3, ed. Ribaillier, 156d; PL 196, 932B.

[459] Cf. Richard, *De Trin.*, IV, c. 6, ed. Ribaillier, 158ab; PL 196, 934.

[460] *"Timentes itaque ubi non est timor, recte timerent fateri personas secundum substantiam dici, si persona simpliciter substantiale esse significaret, nec aliquid consignificaret. Significat autem habentem substantiale esse ex aliqua singulari proprietate"* – Richard, *De Trin.*, IV, c. 19, ed. Ribaillier, 163d; PL 196, 942D.

[461] Richard, *De Trin.*, IV, c. 8, ed. Ribaillier, 158d; PL 196, 935B.

[462] *"Multum est tamen inter significationem unius et significationem alterius. ... cum intelligentia substantie... subintelligitur proprietas communis... sub nomine persone, similiter subintelligitur quaedam proprietas quae non convenit nisi uni soli... proprietas individualis, singularis, incommunicabilis"* – Richard, *De Trin.*, IV, c. 6, ed. Ribaillier, 158ab; PL 196, 934A-C.

the term *substantia* would seem to play the role of species and not that of substance understood as a particular *individual* (for substance in the later sense cannot be something common). This does not square very well (or is at least insufficiently compared), however, with the treatment of substance as an *individual* essence when Richard considers the questions *quale quid sit* and *unde habeat esse*[463]. Person, in any case, signifies the most determined, distinct and concrete reality: *"unus aliquis solus, ab omnibus aliis singulari proprietate discretus"*[464].

Now, directly concerning Christology, the difficulties with the Boethian definition surface in the tensions occasioning the question: *utrum Christus in quantum homo sit aliquid*. The current twelfth century opinion is well expressed by Peter Lombard. According to the Lombard, Christ as man, if he is anything at all, is also a person, since whatever "thing" he be, it cannot be other than substantial, and if substantial, certainly not irrational, whence *Christus in quantum homo* satisfies the said definition of person[465]. Richard is well aware of the terms of the problem and articulates its Trinitarian counterpart: if Boethius' definition of person is universally satisfactory, then every instance of individual rational substance will be a person; but because the divine substance is itself an individual rational substance, it ought therefore also constitute a person, which it does not[466]. The fundamental task lies therefore in dissociating, that is, more precisely identifying, the

---

[463]   Cf. infra, "HOW PERSONS CAN BE DISTINGUISHED WITHOUT ENTAILING A DISTINCTION OF NATURE", p. 168.

[464]   Richard, *De Trin.*, IV, c. 7, ed. Ribaillier, 158d; PL 196, 935B.

[465]   *"Si secundum quod homo aliquid est, vel persona, vel substantia, vel aliud est; sed aliud non; ergo persona vel substantia. Sed si substantia est, vel rationalis, vel irrationalis; sed non est irrationalis substantia; ergo rationalis. Si vero secundum quod homo est rationalis substantia, ergo persona, quia haec est definitio personae: 'substantia rationalis individuae naturae'. Si ergo secundum quod homo est aliquid, et secundum quod homo persona est"* – Peter Lombard, *III Sent.*, d. 10, c. 1; ed. Collegii S. Bonaventurae Ad Claras Aquas, Grottaferrata (Rome), 1971-1981, II, p. 72; cf. Héfelé, *Histoire des conciles*, V, p. 975-977, 1110-1111; cf. A.-M. Éthier, *Le De Trinitate de Richard de Saint-Victor*, Inst. d'Etudes Médiévale, Ottawa/Paris 1939, p. 31.

[466]   *"Est autem diffinitio Boecii de persona, quod sit 'rationalis nature individua substantia'. Ut itaque generalis sit atque perfecta, oportet ut rationalis nature omnis substantia individua sit persona, et e converso omnis persona sit rationalis nature individua substantia. ... Si igitur divina substantia dicenda est individua, aliqua rationalis nature individua substantia erit aliquid quod non est persona"* – Richard, *De Trin.*, IV, c. 21, ed. Ribaillier, 165ab; PL 196, 945A. With regard to the Incarnational problem, Richard expresses himself: *"Quid, quaeso, est in quo humanitas et Divinitas unitae sunt, ut una persona esse possint? Nunquid aliquid quod hominis est, vel aliquid quod Dei est, vel aliquid quod utriusque? Sed si utriusque non est, quomodo in eo uniri possunt quos alterutro alienum est? Si aliquid quod hominis est, ergo creatura est. Si aliquid quod Dei est, supra creaturam est, et jam creatura non est. Si aliquid quod Dei et hominis est, nunquid ipsum utrumque erit, et utrumque non erit, creatura scilicet et non creatura?"* – Richard, *Benj. major*, IV, c. 18: PL 196, 159AB.

concepts of rational substance and person, as was indicated above. Though person is typically said according to substance and taken indeed to signify substance, there exists, for Richard, a vast difference between their respective significations[467]: diversity of substance pertains to distinction in natural being (*esse aliud et aliud*), while alteriety in personality entails distinction at another level (*esse alium et alium*)[468]. This, of course, does not distance the definition of person from that of being a *kind* of substance, and Richard will have to attempt to characterize the notion of person such that it not be identified with the notion of substance and express a property indistinguishable from (the name of) the individual to which it belongs[469]. Person, Richard affirms, designates not so much the particular properties of the persons (some of which – to supply the reason which Richard does not give – might be shared in common with other persons) as the particularity inherent in their names[470]. Substance is indicated by responding to the question *"quid"*; person by responding to the question *"quis"*, which is always a proper name[471]. To the *quid* corresponds a common (natural) property; to the *quis* corresponds a singular property (*proprietas singularis*), by which the person is discretely set off from every other[472]. Person certainly means a rational substance, but for each distinct person it does not necessarily follow that

---

[467] "*Dicamus imprimis quod dictum est ab aliis, quod persona secundum substantiam dicitur et substantiam significare videtur. Nihilominus tamen multum est inter significationem unius et significationem alterius*" – ibid.

[468] "*In rationali natura esse aliud et aliud facit diversitas substantiarum, esse alium et alium facit alteritas personarum*" – Richard, *De Trin.*, IV, c. 9, ed. Ribaillier, 159b; PL 196, 936A; cf. I, c. 17, ed. Ribaillier, 131d; PL 196, 898D.

[469] Richard, *De Trin.*, IV, c. 1 & 3, ed. Ribaillier, 156b & 156d - 157a; PL 196, 931B; 932BC; cf. Éthier, op. cit., p. 33 and notes 3-4.

[470] "'*Non enim nomina tantummodo, sed etiam nominum proprietates, id est personas'... Hieronymus in his verbis non dicit personas esse proprietates personarum sed proprietates nominum, hoc est quod proprie significant nomina personarum*" – Richard, *De Trin.*, IV, c. 3, ed. Ribaillier, 157a; PL 196, 932C. We have adjusted the argument to give an account of the concept of person, and not of the name of a person. Note that Richard has the name of the person signifying the particular property of the name, as though to confer a self-referential value to the term. But this sheds no light on the concept of person as such, unless the content of the personal name, that is the particularity implicitly expressed by the name, be understood as that which constitutes personhood and, therefore, as the central *significatum* of "person". Person does not signify the *names* of the persons, but rather what is captured by these names; it signifies the particularity inherent in these names.

[471] Cf. Richard, *De Trin.*, IV, c. 7, ed. Ribaillier, 158b-d.

[472] "*Per quid itaque inquiritur de proprietate communi, per quis de proprietate singulari. ... Ad nomen autem persone, nunquam intelligitur nisi unus aliquis solus, ab omnibus aliis singulari proprietate discretus*" – Richard, *De Trin.*, IV, c. 7, ed. Ribaillier, 158cd; PL 196, 934D - 935B.

there is a correspondingly numerically distinct rational substance[473] (for the proper and direct signification of person is the *quis*). Where there are several persons, each is necessarily *alius, aliquis*, several substances, *aliud, aliquid*.

A distinction of common and incommunicable existence

The distinction between substance and person emerges within the context of distinguishing common existence and incommunicable existence[474]. There are, according to Richard, two fundamental kinds of existence: that which is common to many, and that which is strictly incommunicable[475]. The former is possessed through what is commonly shared, while the latter kind of existence, characterized by the fact that it cannot be possessed by more than a single individual, is had from an incommunicable *proprietas*[476]. As a result, the person is constituted by a personal property, which is (after the manner of a formal cause?) simply that which makes one to be a person[477]. This personal property is absolutely incommunicable (*omnino sit incommunicabilis*), otherwise one person could be several. Finally, this incom-

---

[473] "*Non sit necesse ubicumque sunt plures persone, etiam plures substantias credere*" – Richard, *De Trin.*, IV, c. 8, ed. Ribaillier, 159a; PL 196, 935D.

[474] Cf. Richard, *De Trin.*, IV, c. 16, ed. Ribaillier, 161d - 162c.

[475] The notion of existence, as we shall see, represents the pivotal explanatory device for Richard's doctrine of person. N. Den Bok offers a brief discussion of its function in Richard's *De Trinitate* indicating the dispersed but interdependent themes related to its notion (cf. *Communicating the Most High. A Systematic Study of Person and Trinity in the Theology of Richard of St. Victor (†1173)*, Brepols, Paris–Turnhout 1996, p. 175, 209-212).

[476] "*Existentia vero alia pluribus communis, alia autem omnino incommunicabilis. ... Existentia vero incommunicabilis est, que nonnisi uni alicui persone convenire potest... existentia designat substantiale esse, sed aliquando quod sit ex communi, aliquando quod sit ex incommunicabili proprietate. Communem autem existentiam dicimus, ubi intelligitur esse habens ex proprietate communi; incommunicabilem vero, ubi intelligitur esse habens ex proprietate incommunicabile. ... In uno autem intelligitur proprietas communis, in altero vero proprietas incommunicabilis. Commune est autem omnibus personis divinis esse substantia... idem est quod communis existentia*" – Richard, *De Trin.*, IV, c. 16, ed. Ribaillier, 162a-c; PL 196, 940. The divine nature is clearly not incommunicable; but communicability does not necessarily mean communicability to another *substance*, whence the divinity's "substantial incommunicability" may be affirmed, since personal and substantial incommunicability are not the same thing.

[477] "*Proprietas personalis est ex qua unusquisque habet esse is qui ipse est. Personalem proprietatem dicimus, per quam quilibit unus est ab omnibus aliis discretus*" – Richard, *De Trin.*, IV, c. 17, ed. Ribaillier, 162c; PL 196, 941B.

municability consists in what is not common and cannot be common[478].

Types of incommunicability

Richard first speaks of incommunicability, in the context of the divine perfections, as deriving from a thing's identification with the divine substance[479], that is, incommunicability stems from the singular substantial perfection of the divinity. Does this undermine the idea of incommunicability being something proper to a *person* independently of the possible incommunicability of that person's *nature?* It seems there must be a distinction of incommunicability, according as a thing can be either incommunicable to another substance or incommunicable to another person[480]. Richard demonstrates an awareness of this, though his speculation never avails itself of the possibilities afforded by this distinction.

The divine substance *a semetipsa* is not to be confused with the definition of the Father who additionally possesses the incommunicability proper to personhood. This divine entity is *per se subsistens* and incommunicable to any other substance, independently of personal existences[481]. One substance is always incommunicable to another substance: *"tam igitur non potest ipsa divinitas communicabilis esse, quam non possunt diverse substantie esse una et una diverse"*[482]. However, though the substantial unity of God renders the communicability of the divinity to other substances impossible[483], it does not mean that the divinity cannot be possessed by several persons. Consequently, the incommu-

---

[478]   *"Illud veraciter incommunicabile est quod commune quidem non est, sed nec esse potest... et cum nominamus personam, nunquam intelligimus nisi unam solam substantiam et singularem aliquam"* – Richard, *De Trin.*, IV, c. 17, ed. Ribaillier, 162c; PL 196, 941A; *De Trin.*, IV, c. 6, ed. Ribaillier, 158b; PL 196, 934B. Note that a distinction between the concepts of non-commonality and that of being *incapable* of communion, as pointed out by Den Bok, op. cit., p. 220-221, helps us to impregnate the sense of "individual" or "singular" used to designate the personal reality.

[479]   Cf. Richard, *De Trin.*, II, c. 12, ed. Ribaillier, 138d; PL 196, 908C.

[480]   A whole host of difficulties surrounds Richard's treatment of the divine substance, a substance which must be at once communicable and incommunicable, which is a *per se* existent in its own right but no person. For the complications which proliferate in connection with this, see N. Den Bok, *Communicating the Most High. A Systematic Study of Person and Trinity in the Theology of Richard of St. Victor (†1173)*, Brepols, Paris–Turnhout 1996, p. 266-268; cf. id., p. 181-182.

[481]   Cf. Richard, *De Trin.*, I, c. 14-17 (especially 17), ed. Ribaillier, 131a - 132a; II, c. 13-15, ed. Ribaillier, 138d - 139d; IV, c. 19, ed. Ribaillier, 163a -164a.

[482]   Richard, *De Trin.*, II, c. 12, ed. Ribaillier, 138d; PL 196, 908B.

[483]   Cf. Richard, *De Trin.*, I, c. 16-17, ed. Ribaillier, 131b - 132a.

nicability spoken of above must intend *personal* incommunicability, since there also exists substantial incommunicability – a difference which must be drawn out if in communicability is to serve as formally constitutive of the person.

Corollary for the definition of person

The affirmation that the divine substance is the common existence of the persons (*"idem est quod communis existentia"*[484]) hints at an interesting way of regarding the person, namely that the person be defined as "that *in which* a (rational) nature exists". And this conforms with Richard's use of the distinction between *sistere* and *existere*[485], inasmuch as, even though we say that the divine substance or nature exists, we do not consider it a fourth existent[486]. It is better to emphasize its existing *in three persons,* saying that the three persons are that *in which the nature exists* (and the three persons are, therefore, the *existents*). In the case of an ordinary man, the individual nature which exists is identical to the existent, i.e. the person, which is why we can say that that substance (or nature) exists of or in *itself.* For this reason, it remains consistent to speak of person as that *in which* a nature exists, as the human person which is the individual human nature, exists in itself. Such a conceptualization of person encounters no difficulties in the Trinity, where the three persons are precisely those realities in which the divine substance exists, nor would that substance be multiplied by the mere fact that it exists simultaneously in three different persons. And, as has been explained, nothing prevents the same definition from operating with respect to ordinary human persons, whence it remains only to see how it might function with respect to Christ. Here, again, the definition is confirmed by the fact that Christ's divine person is precisely that in which the divine and human natures exist, nor can it be said that the humanity is something within which another (rational) nature exists, for which reason it cannot be a person. How does this differ from Boethius? For Boethius, person *is* a rational nature; person, according to our corollary, is *that in which* a rational nature exists. There can be no doubt that, in the latter definition, person and substance are conceptually distinct in such a way that person, *insofar as person,* is removed from the category of substance (naturally signified) – which is why, with respect to a non-physical definition of person, it seems able to take us further than the notion of "subject of attribution" which, although very *close* to what is being said here about person, signaling person as the bearer of a nature and the subject of its operations, fails to accommodate, as such, the objective reality of Christ's humanity tending to leave it placed amongst subjects of attribution (inasmuch as the bearer of particularizing principles and possessing its own being somehow) and there-

---

[484] *"Commune est autem omnibus personis divinis esse substantia... idem est quod communis existentia"* – Richard, *De Trin.,* IV, c. 16, ed. Ribaillier, 162a-c; PL 196, 940.

[485] Cf. infra, "HOW PERSONS CAN BE DISTINGUISHED WITHOUT ENTAILING A DISTINCTION OF NATURE", p. 168.

[486] Cf. Richard, *De Trin.,* IV, c. 21, ed. Ribaillier, 165ab.

fore too close to person [487]. The definition proposed here is indifferent as to whether the objective reality of Christ's humanity entail some sort of subjectivity (operational or ontological), since the simple fact that it is not the subject of *another nature* [488] already excludes it from personhood.   Interestingly enough, Richard's thesis on the *modes of subsistence* [489] might provide, moreover, the precise remedy needed in order to avoid having to admit that the humanity of Christ be somehow a subject of attribution; we have already seen its intimation in the doctrine of Cyril of Alexandria, which lends itself to a distinction of *subsistentia in se* and *subsistentia in alio* [490]. Nevertheless, this simple definition of person cannot escape ultimately begging the question, for it does not respond to the question: "*just what is it* within which the nature exists?". Even if it turn out to be an *exact* definition of person, it discloses little about the constitution of a person; though perhaps precise, it remains inadequate.

How persons can be distinguished without entailing a distinction of nature

Richard elaborates his notion of person and the possibility of its plurality without a multiplication of substances [491] by means of a decomposition of the term *"existentia"* to which, as we have seen, he gives two significations, one common, one incommunicable [492]. The two senses correspond to the duality of questions: "*quale quid sit et unde habeat esse*" [493]. Every existing thing has a *modus essendi* and a *modus existendi* [494]. The first consists in *sistere* and refers to the essence or substantiality of a thing, and thus responds to the question *quale quid sit*, a diversity here would entail an *aliud.* The second, expressed by the prefix *ex*, consists in the *modus obtinentiae* which concerns the origin of a thing [495], that *from* which a thing's *sistere* derives (indicating the *way* in

---

[487]   Cf. supra, with respect to the Cappadocians, "GENERAL PHILOSOPHICAL PERSPECTIVE", p. 38; "INTEGRATION OF THESE CONCEPTS IN THE WRITINGS OF BASIL THE GREAT ~ GREGORY OF NYSSA", p. 39.

[488]   Obviously, in the sense of another *complete* nature.

[489]   Cf. infra, "HOW PERSONS CAN BE DISTINGUISHED WITHOUT ENTAILING A DISTINCTION OF NATURE", p. 168; "TERMINOLOGICAL SUBSTITUTIONS OR DIFFERENT CONCEPTUAL CONTENT?", p. 172.

[490-]   Cf. supra, "AXIS PLACED IN RELIEF BY CYRIL", p. 71-76.

[491]   "*Quomodo possit esse alteritas personarum sine alteritate substantiarum*" – Richard, *De Trin.*, IV, c. 10, ed. Ribaillier, 159d; PL 196, 937A.

[492]   Cf. supra, "A DISTINCTION OF COMMON AND INCOMMUNICABLE EXISTENCE", p. 165; cf. also N. Den Bok, *Communicating the Most High. A Systematic Study of Person and Trinity in the Theology of Richard of St. Victor (†1173)*, Brepols, Paris–Turnhout 1996, p. 191, 211-212.

[493]   Richard, *De Trin.*, IV, c. 11, ed. Ribaillier, 159d; PL 196, 937A.

[494]   Cf. Richard, *De Trin.*, IV, c. 16 & 19, ed. Ribaillier, 161d - 162c & 163a - 164a.

[495]   "*Obtinentiam dico hoc loco modum quo quisque obtinet quod substantialiter est vel naturaliter habet*" – Richard, *De Trin.*, IV, c. 11, ed. Ribaillier, 160b; PL 196, 937B.

which it possesses its being), thus responding to the question *unde habeat esse*, which diversity results in the *alius*[496].

According to the different possible responses to the questions *quale quid sit* and *unde habeat esse*, existence is observed to have three distinct modes: "*Existentia autem... tribus generaliter modis potest variari*"[497], distinguished either by reason of a diversity of nature amongst persons of identical origin (*secundum solam rei qualitatem*), a diversity of origin where several persons possess the very same nature (*secundum solam originem*), or a diversity in both substance and origin (*tam secundum rei qualitatem quam secundum ejus originem*)[498].

While the persons of the Trinity differ only as regards the *unde habeat esse*, that is according to origin alone, the response to both questions, *quale quid sit* and *unde habeat esse*, differs for individuals of a human nature who differ both *secundum qualitatem* and *secundum originem*[499]. Curiously, if the *quale quid sit* is different for different human individuals, then the substantiality in question cannot be the essence *humanity*, which is common to all men, but must concern the *individual* essence[500]. It would seem more consistent to adhere to an abstract or common use of the term substance, in order that the *modus obtinentiae* alone, insofar as it expresses a *manner* of possessing substantial existence, be able to sufficiently account for personal distinction, but Richard is not very clear in this regard[501]. In any case, wherever there is a difference in the response to these questions, there is plurality of either *aliud* or *alius*; difference with regard to the *modus obtinentiae* constitutes an incommunicable property and accounts for an *alius* whose existence is therefore incommunicable[502]. Now, if the personal property is that by which one is distinct from all others[503], incommunicable, then it must lie in either the *quale quid* or the *unde*

---

[496]   "*In uno itaque hoc verbo existere, vel sub uno nomine existentie datur subintelligi posse et illam considerationem que pertinet ad rei qualitatem, et illam que pertinet ad rei originem*" – Richard, *De Trin.*, IV, c. 12, ed. Ribaillier, 160c; PL 196, 938A; cf. id., *De Trin.*, IV, c. 19, ed. Ribaillier, 163ab; PL 196, 942AB.

[497]   Richard, *De Trin.*, IV, c. 13, ed. Ribaillier, 160d; PL 196, 938B.

[498]   Cf. Richard, *De Trin.*, IV, c. 13, ed. Ribaillier, 160c - 161a.

[499]   "*Quod in divina natura variatur existentiarum pluralitas secundum solam originem, in humana vero natura tam secundum qualitatem quam secundum originem*" – Richard, *De Trin.*, IV, c. 15, ed. Ribaillier, 161c; PL 196, 939CD.

[500]   Cf. supra, "AN ATTEMPT TO SITUATE PERSONHOOD BEYOND THE CATEGORY OF SUBSTANCE", p. 161 (especially p. 163).

[501]   Cf. infra, "TERMINOLOGICAL SUBSTITUTIONS OR DIFFERENT CONCEPTUAL CONTENT?", p. 172.

[502]   Cf. Richard, *De Trin.*, IV, c. 16, ed. Ribaillier, 162a-c; PL 196, 940.

[503]   "*Proprietas personalis est ex qua unusquisque habet esse is qui ipse est. Personalem proprietatem dicimus, per quam quilibit unus est ab omnibus aliis discretus*" – Richard, *De Trin.*, IV, c. 17, ed. Ribaillier, 162c; PL 196, 941A.

habet esse, according to which a difference is introduced[504]. If we set aside the *unde habet esse*, that is, the notion of origin which plays the entire role in Trinitarian distinction, the incommunicable property will have to reside in the *quale quid sit*, i.e. the essence. But this leaves the issue unresolved, for as much as one can still ask the question: what is it about the individual essence that *makes* it to be different, i.e. incommunicable, from every other? The answer to this could be supplied by recourse to the *modus obtinentiae* were it to be taken in the sense of mode of subsistence. In this way, even when substance is taken in the sense of primary substance and it is a question of *individual* essence, the explanation for personal incommunicability is found in the *modus obtinentiae*. Moreover, Richard, who does not fully exploit the possibility of understanding the *modus obtinentiae* in the above mentioned way (that is, as an essential mode of existence, i.e. a unique mode of being of the substance itself), speaks as if the *modus obtinentiae* (which signifies a relation of origin *from which* a thing acquires its being) results in the constitution of a person (*modus obtinentiae* → person); but it is rather simply the case that the incommunicable property, here (in the case of the Trinity), happens to be constituted by the *modus obtinentiae*, consequently, to be universally commensurate[505], we must assert that the incommunicable property is what makes a person (incommunicable property → person), and not the *modus obtinentiae per se*, for the *modus obtinentiae* constitutes personhood in the Trinity only indirectly, insofar as it *there* happens to constitute the incommunicable property, alone which can account for personhood (entering into the essence of the person as such); there the *unde sit* responds to the question as to what *founds* the personal, or incommunicable, property which itself founds personhood.

In any event, in the divinity, the unity is *secundum modum essentiae*, plurality *secundum modum obtinentiae*. The divine persons differ only as regards their modes of existence, that is, their modes of origin; the same unique divine substance is possessed in three different ways on

---

[504] *"Cette propriété ineffable, qui ne peut appartenir qu'à un seul individu, répond à la question "unde" et s'exprime par le préfixe "ex" du mot existence"* – Éthier, op. cit., p. 102.

[505] By this we mean: to assert a principle of some perfection at the same level of universality as that proper to the extension of the perfection in question. Non-universal commensurability would imply designating a specific perfection according to its generic mode of being or a generic perfection according to a specific mode of its realization; it is to assign a generic principle as responsible for a specific perfection (e.g. affirming that "this dog is a German Shepherd because it has short fur", or a specific principle as responsible for a generic perfection (as in "this is an animal because it is four-legged" – assigning the reason for a generic perfection to a specific attribute).

account of three distinct properties[506]. What is unfortunate about Richard's treatment is that the distinctions he provides between the various modes of existence do not distinguish between *personal* and *non-personal* (i.e. merely substantial) modes of existence; Richard's distinctions rather cut indifferently across the entire substantial realm.

Definition of the person as an incommunicable existence

As we have seen, every personal property, which is formal to personhood, is absolutely incommunicable ("*omnis proprietas personalis omnino est incommunicabilis*"[507]). Incommunicable existence, then, is what constitutes the persons of the Trinity: "*nichil aliud ibi est persona quam incommunicabilis existentia*"[508] (whence there are, in God, as many persons as incommunicable existences)[509]. Existence signifies both that something is and that it has being through a certain property: "*existentia igitur significat rei esse, et hoc ipsum ex aliqua proprietate*"[510]. If that property is incommunicable, then the existent is incommunicable, and it is precisely this kind of property which pertains to personhood, over and above the common notion of substance[511]. Person, for Richard, is an incommunicable existent. There are three divine persons in reason of the fact that there are three existents who share the same undifferentiated substantial being *ex differenti proprietate*, united in *modo essendi*, but diverse in *modo existendi*[512]. What accounts for the di-

---

[506] "*Nichil itaque aliud erit plures in una divinitate personas esse quam plures unam eamdemque, utpote summam, dilectionem habere, quin potius esse, ex differenti proprietate*" – Richard, *De Trin.*, V, c. 20, ed. Ribaillier, 178d; PL 196, 963D.

[507] Richard, *De Trin.*, IV, c. 18, ed. Ribaillier, 162d; PL 196, 941C; another formulation of the same definition: "*quod persona divina sit divine nature incommunicabilis existentia*" – id. *De Trin.*, IV, c. 22, ed. Ribaillier, 165c; PL 196, 945C.

[508] Richard, *De Trin.*, IV, c. 18, ed. Ribaillier, 162d; PL 196, 941C. Cf. N. Den Bok, *Communicating the Most High. A Systematic Study of Person and Trinity in the Theology of Richard of St. Victor (†1173)*, Brepols, Paris–Turnhout 1996, p. 265-266. For an explanation of Richard's treatment of the sources of incommunicability in terms of non-accidental and essential properties, cf. id., p. 269, 280-281.

[509] "*Non itaque videtur impossibile vel incredibile plures existentias, et quod consequens est, plures personas esse in divinitate*" – Richard, *De Trin.*, IV, c. 19, ed. Ribaillier, 163bc; PL 196, 942C.

[510] Richard, *De Trin.*, IV, c. 19, ed. Ribaillier, 163b; PL 196, 942B.

[511] Cf. supra, "AN ATTEMPT TO SITUATE PERSONHOOD BEYOND THE CATEGORY OF SUBSTANCE", p. 161; cf. N. Den Bok, *Communicating the Most High. A Systematic Study of Person and Trinity in the Theology of Richard of St. Victor (†1173)*, Brepols, Paris–Turnhout 1996, p. 280-281.

[512] "*Ideo ergo fidenter fatemur personas in divinitate secundum substantiam dictas et substantiam significare, et plures ibi personas, non plures substantias esse, quia sunt ibi plures habentes unum et indifferens esse ex differenti proprietate. Unitas itaque ibi est juxta modum essendi, pluralitas juxta modum existendi. Unitas essentie quia unum et indifferens esse, plures*"

versity of persons in God are the distinctive characters *through which* the persons possess the same substance. These distinctive characters constitute the *modus obtinentiae* which responds to the question *unde habeat esse*. In God, there can be no other source of difference (such as *modus essendi*) upon which to base the incommunicable differences, whence Richard can affirm *plures persone quia plures existentie*, in the sense of <u>existentie</u>, that is, existences differing only with regard to origin. Outside of the divine context, difference may be supplied by the *modus essendi*, that is, a qualitative or natural difference. Again it is a question of an incommunicable existence, but whose incommunicability is rooted in much more than a property of origin[513]; that incommunicability is rooted at once in the things <u>existere</u> as well as *sistere*, that is, in the entirety of its *existentia*. In anyone other than God, however, questions of origin are accidental. For this reason, differences of personal existences reside in the substantiality of the thing, that is, in the nature or substance[514]; consequently, the incommunicability is derived from the very substantial structure of the thing, and it becomes difficult to see just what difference, if any, exists between Richard's notion of an incommunicable property and the incommunicability absolutely proper to every primary substance[515], which we call individuality.

Terminological substitutions or different conceptual content?

If the person is not simply *substantia individua naturae rationalis*, it must be defined in other terms. In the end, Richard will substitute *existentia* for *substantia*, while incommunicable will stand in place of

---

persone quia plures existentie" – Richard, *De Trin.*, IV, c. 19, ed. Ribaillier, 163d; PL 942D - 943A.

[513] This is not equivalent to saying that the *modus obtinentiae* could not account for that incommunicability, if the *modus obtinentiae* be understood as the particular *mode* by which an individual possesses its nature, and not merely as indicating that *from which* the *sistere* or substantial being is received.

[514] Cf. supra, "HOW PERSONS CAN BE DISTINGUISHED WITHOUT ENTAILING A DISTINCTION OF NATURE", p. 168.

[515] The fact that every real first substance is incommunicable is implied in the very definition of substance furnished by Aristotle, for whom "substance" is that which neither is predicable of a subject nor present in a subject (*Cat*, c. 5: 2ª, 11-13). Non-predicability and incommunicability are mutually entailing if not synonymous. Both of these concepts have been put forth in the history of philosophy as formal definitions of individuality. The convertibility of the non-predicable with that which is individual is clearly affirmed by Aristotle (who, in order to distinguish a certain *kind* of individuality, namely subsistent individuality proper to first substances alone, adds the requirement of non-presence in a subject) – cf. *Cat*, c. 5: 1ᵇ, 3-9.

individual[516]. Insofar as the idea of substance as individual or primary substance disappears[517], the problem is reduced to an antithesis between essence-person, the first designating substance, that which is common, and the second designating that which exists incommunicably, the non-common. Individual is replaced by incommunicable, yet both terms are collated in the passage cited above – *"proprietas individualis, singularis, incommunicabilis"*[518] –, and it is not clear as to where the significations of these terms diverge[519].

A final consideration in this regard concerns the notion of substantiality and a revealing use of the term *subsistentia*, intended in a way akin to the neo-Platonic acceptation denoting specific and generic forms. Every substance, according to Richard, has its being from its substantiality[520]. The term "substantiality" (*substantialitas*) has a particular meaning here: it is the subsistence of the substance; but it is also the natural form of the substance, such as "humanity" in man. My substantiality, then, is my individual nature and my very subsistence (in the sense, it seems we must add, of that according to which I possess my being). Richard employs the word "substantiality" in the sense of "specificity", that is, as the formal characteristic distinguishing a thing's nature, *"diversa namque substantialitas facit substantiam diversam"*[521]. It is quite interesting that this specificity be called *subsistence*, as if to imply that one's specificity is, or corresponds to, one's subsistence, or that one's mode of subsisting is determined by one's

---

[516] Cf. Richard, *De Trin.*, IV, c. 18, ed. Ribaillier, 162d - 163a.

[517] Cf. supra, "AN ATTEMPT TO SITUATE PERSONHOOD BEYOND THE CATEGORY OF SUBSTANCE", p. 161 (especially p. 162-165).

[518] Richard, *De Trin.*, IV, c. 6, ed. Ribaillier, 158b; PL 196, 934C. Cf. supra, "AN ATTEMPT TO SITUATE PERSONHOOD BEYOND THE CATEGORY OF SUBSTANCE", p. 162 and note 462.

[519] For Den Bok (op. cit., p. 218-219 & 224 note 106) the terms are equivalent. Cf. M. Purwatma, *The Explanation of the Mystery of the Trinity Based on the Attribute of God as Supreme Love: A Study on the "De Trinitate" of Richard of St. Victor*, Rome 1990, p. 88.

[520] *"Sciendum itaque de omni substantia quod habeat esse ex substantialitate sua. Nam cui substantialitas nulla inest, substantia recte dici non potest. Substantialitatem namque dicimus illam proprietatem subsistentie ex qua habet substantia dici et esse. Humane substantie substantialitas est ipsa humanitas; substantia siquidem que humanitatem non habet, homo nisi falso dici non valet. ... Substantialitas vero alia generalis, alia specialis, alia individualis. ... Individualis autem est illa, que uni soli quidem individuo inest et pluribus substantiis omnino communis non potest. Ad designandam individualem aliquam substantialitatem, nomen in usu non habemus, sed ad majorem dicendorum evidentiam ponere et a proprio nomine trahere possumus. Dicatur itaque a Daniele danielitas, sicut ab homine humanitas"* – Richard, *De Trin.*, II, c. 12, ed. Ribaillier, 138bc; PL 196, 907C - 908A.

[521] Richard, *De Trin.*, II, c. 12, ed. Ribaillier, 138c; PL 196, 908B.

specificity[522]. Personhood, then, would be constituted by the subsistence of a single substance: *"incommunicabilis itaque est danielitas, ut diximus, quia sic est subsistentia substantie unius ut non possit esse alterius"*[523]. But every substantial thing is subsistent: *"substantiale in quantum tale quid est quod consistit in seipso"*[524]; whence personhood must further depend on the *way* of subsisting, a subsistence which is inseparably bound to a single substance and unable to be that of another[525].

Because there are three types of substantiality (generic, specific, and individual), there are three kinds of subsistence. Individual substantiality is that which is not able to be common to a plurality of substances (*"pluribus substantiis omnino communis non potest"*); this is precisely, then, an incommunicable substantiality or incommunicable subsistence (at least in the sense of incommunicable to another *substance*). If the incommunicability in question can be extended to include personal incommunicability (i.e. incommunicability to a plurality of persons), then incommunicable (or individual) substantiality and incommunicable (or individual) subsistence are equivalent to and interchangeable with *proprietas personalis* (even the term used to designate this reality, Richard tells us, is taken from the individual's proper name – *"ad designandam individualem aliquam substantialitatem... a proprio nomine trahere possumus"*[526]).

Based upon this and the particular vocabulary choice made by Richard in formulating his definition of person, it can be said that, within that perspective, consideration of the universal is transformed

---

[522] *"Danielitas itaque intelligatur illa substantialitas, vel, si magis placet, illa subsistentia ex qua Daniel esse habet illa substantia que ipse est et quam participare non potest aliqu alia"* – Richard, *De Trin.*, II, c. 12, ed. Ribaillier, 138c; PL 196, 908A.

[523] Richard, *De Trin.*, II, c. 12, ed. Ribaillier, 138c; PL 196, 908B.

[524] Richard, *De Trin.*, IV, c. 19, ed. Ribaillier, 163c; PL 942D.

[525] *"Qui est tellement la subsistence d'une seule substance qu'elle ne peut l'être d'une autre"*: *"quia sic est subsistentia substantie unius ut non possit esse alterius"* – Richard, *De Trin.*, II, c. 12; trans. G. Salet, *Sources Chrétiennes* 63, Paris, 1959, p. 131; Ribaillier, 138c; PL 196, 908B. Richard seems to be touching here on what late Scholastics describe in terms of a distinction between "actual subsistence" and "habitual subsistence", a discretion introduced in order to explain the paradox of having to deny personality of the humanity of Christ as such notwithstanding a recognition of its proper substantial actuality. Note that we have focussed here on what is required to be a person *simpliciter*, and not on what would be necessary for being this or that person. Den Bok considers the differing levels of specificity according to which Richard's *"substantialitas"* can be applied to individual properties (cf. op. cit., p. 221-224) – however, we would not say that there must be two levels of individual properties (op. cit., p. 223), but rather that there is a more or less abstract way of signifying the different properties belonging to a common order (namely that of individuality). Cf. also id., p. 264-265.

[526] Richard, *De Trin.*, II, c. 12, ed. Ribaillier, 138bc; PL 196, 907C - 908A.

into a consideration of the common, the particular into that of proper, and individual into single and unshared; in brief, individual substance is regarded as incommunicably self-possessed being[527]. Effectively, Richard's definition of person (and not necessarily the speculative horizon of his method opening new avenues for reflection) amounts to little more than substituting for the term substance its very definition, along with a certain qualification: *"existens per se solum juxta singularem quemdam rationalis existentie modum. ... unus aliquis solus a ceteris omnibus singulari proprietate discretus"*[528]. Besides the difference in vocabulary, this position is conceptually equivalent to that of Boethius; that of Richard insists upon what has been considered the mystical aspect of totality and incommunicability (taking St. Augustine as its source), that of Boethius centers rather on individuality[529].

Conclusion

Perhaps it can be said that Richard's definition of person *"brille beaucoup plus par sa rigueur logique que par une intégration totale de l'objective réalité"*[530]; nevertheless, Richard's position (that is, his explanatory apparatus, and not necessarily his definition) draws significant attention to certain fundamental and *distinctive* realities of personhood not clearly brought into relief by conceptualizations wholly limited to physical categories such as that of Boethius. Richard must be credited with having drawn out the importance of the notion of incommunicability as determinate of a personalized substantial reality. Already in the fourth century, Basil the Great had indicated the importance of incommunicability in identifying the constitutive property of the person as incommunicable. Operating from within a similar conceptual framework, focusing upon the opposition between common nature and the particularity of persons, Richard too affirms the incommunicability of the personal property, but he explicitly and emphatically moves from this affirmation to that of the incommunicability of personal existences themselves.

---

[527] Cf. S. A. Turienzo, "Aspectos del Problema de la Persona en el Siglo XII", in *Miscellanea Mediaevalia* 2, "Die Metaphysik im Mittelalter", Walter de Gruyter, Berlin 1963, p. 180-183.

[528] Richard, *De Trin.*, IV, c. 24, ed. Ribaillier, 166ab; PL 196, 946CD. The work of Den Bok supports this understanding (cf. op. cit., especially p. 212-218, 225-226).

[529] Cf. A. Turienzo, op. cit.; cf. G. Salet, op. cit., p. 10.

[530] Éthier, op. cit., p. 79.

Formally speaking, the person is no longer *aliquid* but *aliquis*; attention is no longer called to the specific quality of *rationality*, which is common to every person, but to the absolute uniqueness of each person designatable only by a proper name. Through an innovative use of the term *existere*, indicating at once a things essential constitution and its origin or *mode of substantially existing*, person is able to be defined in a way which breaks from the limitations of an essentialist viewpoint, that is, one which sees person only as a *kind* of substance, precisely because *existentia* permits a distinction between *alius* and *alius* independently of a distinction between *aliud* and *aliud*. If the *modus obtinentiae* is understood in the sense employed immediately above (*mode of substantially existing*), such that personal differences could be identified not only with an incommunicable property, but an incommunicable property consisting of a particular mode of subsisting, then Richard's *De Trinitate*, contrary to the remarks of Éthier, makes a solid ontological contribution to the historical understanding of the notion of personhood.

I.11. SAINT ALBERT AND THE UNCOVERING OF PERSONALITY

Albert the Great

Albert the Great was undoubtedly the predominant figure of his time, the most influential teacher and the most prolific writer of the century. Born sometime between 1193 and 1206, he entered the Dominican order in 1223, studied at Padua and Bologna and received his baccalaureate from the University of Paris in 1240. There he taught as master form 1245 to 1248 with St. Thomas as his pupil and assistant. Albert was later sent to Cologne to organize a center for Dominican studies and made bishop of Ratisbon in 1260. He died in Cologne in 1280. Described as a scientist, a philosopher and a theologian, his encyclopedic production stands out especially for its synthetic quality, drawing into a Christian unity a plurality of pagan philosophies, structuring and ordering the ideas expressed by Greek and Arabic thinkers according to a systematic world-view proper to Christendom.

It is Albert's astounding philosophical capacity to distinguish the many concepts involved in the analysis of personhood which is of most interest to us. Undoubtedly, he contributes enormous speculative insight into the issue, and supplies us, in the final analysis, with an unprecedented instrument for expressing the mode of union in the person of Christ.

Presentation

Our method in examining the thought of St. Albert shall consist in an exposition of the content of principal passages concerning the personal mystery of the Trinity and Incarnation. We approach these in a more or less linear commentary-like fashion, at times filling in entire arguments necessary for a smooth progression from one point to another, at times paraphrasing certain passages almost literally, with the object of rendering the Albertinian thought more accessible by placing it in clearer language and elaborating the issues more fully, sometimes reserving our interpretations and speculations until after the presentation of an entire passage, sometimes interpolating the various related aspects of our own perspectives as we pass from consideration to consideration[531]. Because the Trinitarian (and, therefore, personal) doctrine of Albert seems to have undergone no significant alteration across the different periods of his productivity, rather than chronologically separating the content of his works, we have integrated passages from his most important treatises in this regard, namely the *Commentary on the Sentences* and the *Summa theologiae*, into paragraphs organized according to thematic considerations[532].

---

[531] A fuller explanation and justification of the method we have adopted is provided in the section entitled "METHOD" in the opening chapter, p. 16.

[532] As we embark upon investigating Albert's treatment of this philosophically complicated theological dogma, one might wish to mention the existence, as maintained by L. Sturlese (*Die deutsche Philosophie im Mittelalter*, Verlag C. H. Beck, Munich 1993) and, to some extent, A. De Libera ("Philosophie et théologie chez Albert le Grand et dans l'école dominicaine allemande", in *Miscellanea Mediaevalia* 20, "Die Kölner Universität im Mittelalter", Walter de Gruyter, Berlin/New York, 1989, p. 49-67), of a fundamental shift to be observed in Albert regarding the principles of arguing philosophically about the objects of revealed truth. The significance of such a change in Albert's view on the relation between philosophy and theology is not immediately relevant to our goals nor impends upon our non-genetic approach. Were we discussing the development of Albert's philosophical attitude, or his understanding of scientificity, or his convictions about what constitutes the consumate human activity, a genetic approach would perhaps be necessitated. For a presentation of Albert's original and certainly consequential perspective on the essence of philosophy in its relation to the science of God, see A. De Libera, *Albert le Grand et la philosophie*, Vrin, Paris 1990, p. 37-78; "Philosophie et théologie chez Albert le Grand et dans l'école dominicaine allemande", in *Miscellanea Mediaevalia* 20, "Die Kölner Universität im Mittelalter", Walter de Gruyter, Berlin/New York 1989, p. 49-67. In our opinion, the work of De Libera has not specifically pointed to a significant change within the thought of Albert himself, but primarily to the evolution of a certain perspective concerning the relationship between philosophy and theology *proper to the Albertist school* as a result of the interpretative liberty inspired by his texts. Where development has been demonstrated in Albert, moreover, we should note that it pertains most especially to objects of philosophical consideration (cf. H. Anzulewicz, "Neuere Forschung zu Albertus Magnus, Bestandsaufnahme und Problemstellungen", *Recherches de théologie et philosophie médiévales* 66, 1999, p. 163-206). According to Anzulewicz, Sturlese and De Libera concern themselves almost exclusively with the philosophical subject matter of Albert's thought, the value of their observations resulting less applicable therefore to a discussion of a *theological* development in the master (cf. also H. Anzulewicz, "Zur Theorie des menschlichen Lebens nach Albertus Magnus. Theologische Grundlegung und ihre bioethischen Implikationen", *Studia Mediewistyczne* 33, 1998, p. 35-49). While a certain number of elements may be verifiable at one stage of Albert's work and not at another (such, for example, as Albert's position on embryonic animation), one must be careful not to draw from this a sweeping conclusion regarding an overall movement in Albert's thinking (all the more so with respect to the theological domain). The parallelism observed in our work between the early work of the *Sentences* and the later work of the *Summa* (visible, for example, in Albert's treatment of the predicament of relation as applied to God, his explanation of the basic senses according to which substance may be signified, his understanding of the signification of "hypostasis" and "person", his explication of substantial indifference to personal multiplication in the Trinity, his description of the different kinds of com-

We have wanted to make the important texts available to the reader, whence the sometimes lengthy Latin citations in the notes[533]. Where objections are cited, unless otherwise indicated, they represent philosophical principles accepted by Albert himself and in conformity with the arguments and responses he provides. In fact, the common error of many of these objections lies in the misapplication of or illicit reasoning from true principles rather than in the adoption of false principles; it is usually with regard to their application and implication that Albert's commentary is most useful in rectifying understanding.

The texts

As regards the texts of Albert, we have used the critical (Cologne) edition where this was possible. References to those works for which a critical edition does not yet exist refer to the *Opera omnia* edited by A. Borgnet. Those works of Albert which enter into our study in a fundamental way are the *Summa theologiae* and the *Commentary on the Sentences*. In a marginal way, the *Summa de creaturis*, *Super Dionysium De divinis nominibus*, *De praedicabilibus*, *De praedicamentis*, *De causis et processu universitatis a prima causa* and the *Metaphysica* also contribute to the development of our thesis.

During the earliest period of Albert's productivity (preceding the year 1246), Albert composed his first *Summa* of theology, a systematic work embracing a series of opuscules, including the so called *Summa de creaturis*[534]. This opuscule provides several insights into the notion of individuation and the constitution of the singularity of the person, with particular emphasis on the subjective function of *quod est* (or "matter") in the causes responsible for the *per se unum*.

Also among Albert's earliest works, the *Commentary on the Sentences* dates between 1243 and 1249 (the three last books certainly posterior

---

munity and the sources of distinction, as well as the status and role he ascribes to personal properties) would seem to suggest a more constant systematic conception on the the part of the Universal Doctor. H. Anzulewicz, let us note, has found no such change in the theological content or methodology of Albert.

[533] Because the non-critical (Borgnet) edition of Albert often uses colons and commas in an unintelligible manner, to render the sense more clear and more precise, we have adopted the custom of eliminating confusing colons and replacing them with either semicolons or commas as the case demands.

[534] Cf. A. De Libera, A., *Albert le Grand et la philosophie*, Librairie Philosophique J. Vrin, Paris 1990, p. 19-21.

to the *Summa de creaturis*, to which they frequently refer)[535]. Of the four books, the first predominantly occupies our attention, the principal content of which concerns the distinction of persons and the procession of one from another. Compared with the exposition of his pupil, Thomas, from a structural point of view, two things stand out in Albert's commentary: a much stronger tie to the texts of the Lombard, and an extensive multiplication of sub-unities within a given division. As pointed out by G. Emery[536], the latter trait, accompanied by extreme analytical depth availing itself of a vast range of theological and philosophical sources (often resulting in a diversity of ways of responding to the same question), renders the thought of Albert more difficult to grasp as a coherent whole and according to a logical movement. The consequences of these difficulties are not lacking in the following presentation of Albert, which, in addition to problems of interpretation, is also faced with the difficulty of providing adequate documentation from other studies directly germane to our inquiry.

Immediately after commenting the *Sentences*, during the latter part of which period he also completed his commentary on the Dionysian *Celestial Hierarchy*, Albert wrote his commentary *On the Divine Names* (between 1249 and 1250)[537]. The work contributes to our study for its intermittent remarks concerning the role of forms in constituting the numerical unity of the individual and "terminating" an essence.

Several years later, Albert produced a variety of commentaries on Aristotle and on the Isagoge of Porphyry[538]. The latter, or *De praedicabilibus*, is much more than just a work of logic, but includes extensive considerations of the problem of individuation from a metaphysical point of view. We refer to this work both for its analysis of the predicable hierarchy (relation between the second intentions, genus, species and individual) as well as its treatment of substantial individuation. The additional treatise entitled *De praedicamentis* is also valuable to us for the light it sheds on the notion of relation.

---

[535]   Cf. G. Emery, *La Trinité créatrice*, Vrin, Paris 1995, p. 28-29. For a detailed analysis of the chronology of the *Sentences*, see Dom O. Lottin, "Commentaire des Sentences et Somme théologique d'Albert le Grand", *RTAM* 8 (1936), p. 117-153; cf. also J. A. Weisheipl, "The Life and Works of St. Albert the Great", in *Albertus Magnus and the Sciences, Commemorative Essays*, Pontifical Institute of Mediaeval Studies, Toronto 1980, p. 13-51.

[536]   Cf. G. Emery, op. cit., p. 30, 40.

[537]   Cf. A. De Libera, *Albert le Grand et la philosophie*, Vrin, Paris 1990, p. 21.

[538]   Cf. J. Hackett, "Albert the Great", in Gracia Jorge, *Individuation in Scholasticism*, University of N.Y. Press, New York 1994, p. 97, 111-112; A. De Libera, A., *Albert le Grand et la philosophie*, Librairie Philosophique J. Vrin, Paris 1990, p. 19.

Composed sometime between 1265 and 1272, the *De causis et processu universitatis* develops, in particular, the characteristically Albertinian metaphysical doctrine of the procession of flux (explicating the act of being and its derivation in creatures)[539]. It is relevant to our study in a rather tangential way for its perspective on the primordial role of relation in accounting for the production of a multitude of natures (privileging the status of relation in the hierarchical divisions of being).

Also having a peripheral relation to our investigation, the *Metaphysica*, written between 1263 and approximately 1267[540], provides us with several valuable insights into the function of forms and the constitution of the perfected, fully "terminated" concrete existent.

Finally, Albert's last synthesis directly pertaining to the notion of personhood, particularly as manifested in the Trinity, is furnished in his *Summa theologiae*, dating after 1268, in the latter years of Albert's productivity[541]. In this opus, Albert re-presents the same considerations on essence and personality in God as found in the *Sentences*, only with greater systematization and structural organization, moving from a consideration of the Trinity as it is in itself according to essence, to considerations of the Trinity according to the distinction of the persons.

Sources

As is clear from the above, in studying the Albertinian concept of personality, two different kinds of works ought to be taken into account: theological (*Summa de creaturis, Commentary on the Sentences, On the Divine Names* and *Summa theologiae*), and philosophical (*De praedicabilibus, De causis et processu universitatis* and *Metaphysica*). Besides the diversity of scope and method which this division implies, there is the further

---

[539] Cf. in this regard L. Sweeney, "Esse primum creatum in Albert the Great's Liber de causis et processu universitatis", *The Thomist* 44 (1980), p. 599-646; "Are Plotinus and Albertus Magnus Neoplatonists?", in *Graceful Reason: Essays in Ancient and Medieval Philosophy Presented to Joseph Owens, CSSR*, L. P. Gerson (editor), Papers in Mediaeval Studies 4, Pontifical Institute of Mediaeval Studies, Toronto 1983, p. 177-202; G. Emery, op. cit., p. 31, 55-59; A. De Libera, *Albert le Grand et la philosophie*, p. 117-177.

[540] Cf. A. De Libera, *Albert le Grand et la philosophie*, Vrin, Paris 1990, p. 21.

[541] Cf. D. Siedler and P. Simon, *Prolegomena* to vol. 34/1 of the Cologne edition, p. XVI-XVII; S. Tugwell (translator and editor), *Albert and Thomas, Selected Writings*, "The Classics of Western Spirituality", Mahwah, New York 1988, p. 32; G. Emery, op. cit., p. 32; M.-D. Roland-Gosselin, *Le "De ente et essentia" de Saint Thomas d'Aquin*, Vrin, Paris 1948, p. 90.

consideration of the different kinds of sources employed in the respective domains. On the one hand stands the authority of theologians such as Augustine, Boethius, Richard of Saint-Victor, Gilbert of
Poitiers and Alexander of Hales; on the other, the influence of different currents of philosophy including Aristotle and Aristotelianism,
Plato and neo-Platonism, and the thought of various Arabic thinkers
(Algazel, Averroes, Avicenna). Of course, both kinds of sources, the
sacred and profane, are interwoven to varying degrees within both
theological and philosophical treatises.

Concerning the order of being, the Albertinian concept of *ens* un-
folds along Aristotelico-Averroist lines, though his doctrine of the
contingency of the creature and its *esse* is significantly influenced by
Avicenna. Albert's doctrine of relation, entailed by a reflection on
creation itself as well as the nature of distinction in the Trinity, is deci-
sively influenced by Aristotle, Augustine and, to a certain extent,
Boethius[542]. All of this comes together in a concept of personality
emerging from a consideration of the Trinity demonstrating a metaphysical adherence to Boethius, whose definition of person is defended by Albert for its analogically precise content, accompanied by
a methodological adherence to Richard of Saint-Victor, in respect of
Richard's dialectical skill and demand for a refinement of the
Boethian definition. While the influence of Alexander of Hales on
Albert is disputed, an extreme parallelism in textual organization (in
respect of the questions posed and arguments put forward) between
the *Summa fratris Alexandri* and Albert's *Commentary on the Sentences* and
Summa theologiae cannot be mistaken[543]. Nevertheless, Albert typically
goes beyond the affirmations of Alexander, demonstrating an independence of thought and broader speculative development[544].

Though the precise import of these different sources is least
amongst our concerns in exposing the thought of St. Albert, it is
worth observing that his integration of such vastly divergent philoso-

---

[542] Cf. P. D. Marinozzi, *La relazione in S. Alberto Magno*, Diss., University of Fribourg
(Switzerland), 1956, p. 69.

[543] Cf. B. Geyer, *Prolegomena* to the edition of the *De Bono*, ed. Colon., vol. 28, Münster 1951, p. XI-XII; V. Doucet, *Prolegomena* to *Alexandri de Hales Summa theologica seu
sic ab origine dicta "Summa fratris Alexandri"*, vol. 4, Quaracchi, 1948, p. CCXXXV-
CCXL; J. A. Weisheipl, "The Life and Works of St. Albert the Great", in *Albertus
Magnus and the Sciences, Commemorative Essays 1980*, "Studies and Texts, 49", Toronto
1980, p. 22; G. Emery, *La Trinité créatrice*, Vrin, Paris 1995, p. 29.

[544] Cf. A. Pompei, *La dottrina trinitaria di S. Alberto Magno, O. P.. Esposizione organica del
Commentario delle Sentenze in rapporto al movimento teologico scolastico*, Diss., University
of Fribourg (Switzerland), Rome 1953, p. 104-107; P. D. Marinozzi, *La relazione in S.
Alberto Magno*, Diss., University of Fribourg (Switzerland), 1956, p. 67-68.

phical currents into what he considered to be a single coherent whole already sets him off from his predecessors. The originality of Albertinian doctrine cannot be under-estimated. Because of the vast number of theological and philosophical resources employed, and because of Albert's superb depth of penetration (often tending to multiply problems), "it happens that he sometimes misses the conclusions of the principles he enunciates, [that] his opinions evolved over a long and fruitful career, [and that] he hesitates over certain important points and does not always succeed in gathering his ideas into a solid coherent whole. But it remains certain that the *Universal Doctor* not only possessed a grand erudition, but was not content to report the opinions of others. He seized the sense of Aristotelianism; he conceived the plan of Christian Peripatetism. With Saint Thomas, he made triumphant the eternal principles of Christian philosophy. He is a master, and the system which he has handed to us bears the mark of his strong personality"[545].

Principal studies

Current literature abounds with a vast number of publications on the philosophical thought of Albert. Unfortunately, in theological matters, the thought of the Universal Doctor has suffered relative neglect, examined only occasionally, and usually with respect to particular points alone, despite the fact that the most refined expression of that thought resides in his theological works. Without attempting to mention countless studies dedicated to evaluating Medieval currents of thought, in which Albert the Great certainly holds a privileged position and is frequently mentioned and compared to his contemporaries, a few works have more explicitly examined the theological work of Albert and his doctrine of the Trinity (where the problem of personality is fought out). Most of these remain comparative studies, and touch upon the concept of person only indirectly[546]. But two in par-

---

[545] L. De Raeymaeker, "Albert le Grand, philosophe. Les lignes fondamentales de son système métaphysique", *Revue néoscholastique de philosophie* 35 (1933), p. 36.

[546] Noteworthy studies include the comparative examination of the Trinitarian doctrines of Ulrich of Strasbourg, Thomas and Albert by A. Stohr, *Die Trinitätslehre Ulrichs von Strassburg mit besonderer Berücksichtigung ihres Verhältnisses zu Albert dem Grossen und Thomas von Aquin*, "Münsterische Beiträge zur Theologie, 13", Aschendorff, Münster 1928; a study of the procession of the Holy Spirit by the same, "Der heilige Albertus über den Ausgang des Heiligen Geistes", *Divus Thomas* (Fr.) 10 (1932), p. 109-123; the comparative compilation of M. Schmaus, *Der liber propugnatorius des Thomas Anglicus und die Lehrunterschiede zwischen Thomas von Aquin und*

ticular make an immediate and substantial contribution to the problem of understanding personhood and natural communication in
God as pertinent to our study: first, the recent work of G.

Emery, *La
Trinité créatrice*, Vrin, Paris 1995, especially helpful to us in conceptualizing the communication of nature in God and the terms according to
which it can be affirmed (particularly illuminating the notions of *principium* and *ordo* in God); and second, the crucial study of A. Pompei,
*La dottrina trinitaria di S. Alberto Magno, O. P.. Esposizione organica del
Commentario delle Sentenze in rapporto al movimento teologico scolastico*,
Diss., University of Fribourg (Switzerland), Rome 1953, which represents, in our opinion, a definitive expression of the Trinitarian
thought of Albert, coupled with penetrating personal insight, the
value of which goes well beyond the individual thought of the Universal Doctor. If A. Pompei has supplied us with a thorough and detailed
exposition of Albert's Trinitarian doctrine as present in the *Commentary on the Sentences*, the general focus of his labor, while undoubtedly
serving as a fundamental point of reference in the effort to construct

Duns Scotus, Münster 1930; a work by the same author focussing on the doctrine of
the Trinitarian image, "Die trinitarische Gottesebenbildlichkeit nach dem Senten-
zenkommentar Alberts des Grossen", in *Virtus politica*, Festgabe... A. Hufnagel, ed.
J. Möller and H. Kohlenberger, Bad Cannstatt, Stuttgart 1974, p. 277-306; a pneu-
matologically related study of love and the causality of the good by J. Schneider, *Das
Gute und die Liebe nach der Lehre Albert des Grossen*, "Veröffentlichungen des Grab-
mann-Instituts, N.F. 3", Munich/Paderborn/Vienna 1967; and several diverse
thematic studies by F. Ruello illustrating the influence had by Albert upon Thomas
including "Le commentaire inédit de saint Albert le Grand sur les *Noms divins*.
Présentation et aperçus de théologie trinitaire", *Traditio* 12 (1956), p. 231-314;
"Une source problable de la théologie trinitaire de saint Thomas", *RSR* 43 (1955),
p. 104-128. Cf. G. Emery, *La Trinité créatrice*, Vrin, Paris 1995, p. 21; A. Pompei, *La
dottrina trinitaria di S. Alberto Magno, O. P.. Esposizione organica del Commentario delle
Sentenze in rapporto al movimento teologico scolastico*, Diss., University of Fribourg (Switzerland), Rome 1953, p. 4. As evident from this inventory, very little attention is
given to the problem of personality in Albert, and direct concern for his Trinitarian
doctrine restricts itself almost exclusively to the German language. Among experts
on medieval thought at the time of St. Albert, A. De Libera, and others like E. H.
Wéber, to our knowledge, have not devoted special research to the Albertinian
concept of personality, or to Albert's theory of the hypostatic union, or to Albert's
teaching on the Trinity. In his book *Albert le Grand et la philosophie*, A. De Libera
presents rather the Albertinian notions on human understanding and on the divine
productive causality – a metaphysics of flux, and the idea of univocal cause –, with
consistent reference to Albert's vastly ranging sources. As concerns the recent work
of E. H. Wéber, *La personne humaine au XIIIᵉ siècle*, Vrin, Paris 1991, though the title
sounds most pertinent indeed to our study, the breadth of its focus is almost exclusively anthropological and consists more in an analysis of the components of substantial nature than in an effort to discern concepts of personality (though the issues are indissociably related). A final section does pick up the theme of the subsistent act proper to the person, but focuses especially on the subjective unfolding of
that first act in the order of operation.

a synthetic vision of the problems involved in the attribution of personality to God, has left room to develop Albert's Trinitarian doctrine along more specific lines.

The difference between our work and that of A. Pompei is one of scope as well as approach. While A. Pompei thoroughly presents the major lines of Albert's Trinitarian doctrine, particularly emphasizing the theological difficulty presented by the disparity between the supreme simplicity of the objective reality of the mystery and the limited human conceptual mode of its expression, the fundamental task of realistically recognizing distinction and the inconfoundability of different predicates in God while maintaining absolute unity and the real identity of all of the divine predicates, we have presented the same doctrine with a view to disentangling more fully the concept of personality and the kind of distinction to be affirmed between person and nature. Naturally, much of the same material is considered in both, however the points of emphasis and many of the implications drawn from that material orient our work in a more immediate way to the overall problem of personhood and an application of the Trinitarian doctrine to the analogous problem of the mode of personal union in Christ. In other respects, our study of Albert's thought on the Trinity is textually more encompassing than that of Pompei (restricted to the *Commentary on the Sentences*), forasmuch as we have included doctrinal material from the entire span of Albert's writing career, from his earliest works (the *Commentary on the Sentences*) to the *Summa theologiae* (for practical purposes conclusive of his productivity).

The scope of our work

Naturally, we are not the first to have explored questions centering on the theological problem of personality; we have simply taken up and bring to light again what a long tradition has handed down to us. We do not pretend to have presented an exhaustive account of personal ontology, nor an evaluation which is wholly satisfactory. Many points have had to be overlooked because of the limitations inherent in our study, and a variety of important issues left undetermined due to their sheer conceptual difficulty. Our work can only be conceived as an endeavor to cast another perspective on the ever obscure mystery of divine personality, with the modest hopes that, by applying the implications of certain metaphysical doctrines to that mystery, we might raise legitimate queries and stimulate a greater admiration for the

seamless continuity of the ontological structure of intellectual being
and its relation to God[547].

---

[547] Several subjects of intellectual being related according to substantial identity in the
Trinity, created intellectual being related to God according to personal identity in
Christ, and a multitude of created intellectual natures related in an essential way to
God for their very subjective singularity. Furthermore, for each of these cases,
more than demonstrating an essential relation to God, the very relation in question
is intrinsically constitutive of personal discretion. For, the persons of the Trinity *are*
divine relations; while the rational nature in Christ (manifesting in its personal
identity a seamless continuity between individual intellectual nature and God himself) possesses its completed substantial perfection through the principle of the
unique hypostatic act, which is none other than the *relation* of Filiation by which the
Son is Son – there personal identity is rooted in and founded upon a common
principle of hypostatic distinction which means that such a relation (since that
principle is a divine relation) is the cause of what the concrete human nature is, *insofar as* responsible for its enhypostatization; finally, for all created intellectual natures, relation to God (in the context of the efficient production of a thing's act)
may be understood to *constitute* the individuality of the nature, and therefore the
very nature itself insofar as individual. (The latter point is not treated in this thesis,
but represents a ramification of one of the fundamental objectives of our study to
appear on the Incarnation, namely the problem of individuation).

II. THE NOTION OF PERSONALITY IN
SAINT ALBERT THE GREAT

1. ONTOLOGICAL DIVISIONS AND SIGNIFICATION OF TERMS

2. TOWARD DEFINING PERSON

3. SHARING IN THE COMMON NOTION OF PERSON

4. DEFINITIONS OF PERSON

5. MULTIPLYING INDIVIDUALS AND THE ROLE OF RELATION IN
    THE TRINITY

6. NUMBER IN THE TRINITY AND IN MEN

7. *PROPRIETAS*

II.1. ONTOLOGICAL DIVISIONS AND SIGNIFICATION OF TERMS

Introduction

In a way similar to the systematic procedure of Boethius, we move from general to more specific categories in our effort to isolate the distinctive nature of person. In this chapter, we examine the individual existent as such, identifying its position within the overall divisions of being, recognizing its intrinsic constitution, and distinguishing its different properties and the corresponding formalities by which it is conceived. It is along these lines that Albert both reconstructs the predicamental hierarchy (specifying the sense of relation in God, where relation is ascribed the subsistent act of the individual) and exposes the different uses of the Greek and Latin terms in Trinitarian discourse, in order to establish their precise meaning and the conceptual differences between them. Only after such a specification of our use of language can we approach defining the person in a stable and meaningful manner.

First division of ens

For Albert, being, taken in its broadest analogical sense including created and uncreated beings, is distinguished first of all into being "from another", or dependent being, and being "not from another", that is, independent (or self-subsistent) being. Both realms of this rudimentary division (separating God from creatures) are subsequently divided into relative and non-relative being, and it is with respect to this level of distinction that personality in the Godhead as well as the fundamental entitative composition in creatures is explained.

Following Aristotle, Albert describes relations as constituting their own category of being. The relation which refers one thing to another, even if these things are not opposed or compared to one another according to act[548], is able to be something real, and constitutes therefore a particular mode of being which can be predicated in a

---

[548] Which ordinarily means for Albert the mental act of comparing two objectively comparable realities but which can also be taken in contrast with the relative status of what is objectively possible (whose potency for being is ultimately rooted in the divine knowledge).

special way distinct from the other predicamental modes which predicate being absolutely. The reality of this category of relation shall
turn out to be either accidental (*in inferioribus*) or substantial (*in superioribus*), and, as we shall see, the extension of the concept of relation
places it above every division of being other than that of potency and
act. However, while potency and act are the first principles of the
predicaments, the notions of potency and act themselves include
within their respective concepts a reciprocal reference such that the
two terms are relative to one another, the concept of potency implying that of act, and vice versa. The potency-act division of being, then,
is indissociable from the equally primitive division between absolute
and relative being. Act, considered strictly in itself, of course, concerns what is absolute, while the concept of potency entails a certain
relativity. But it is not the case that what is relative necessarily implies
the imperfection inherent in the concept of potency, and, in order to
be relative, a thing can be indifferently perfect or imperfect; consequently, the notions cannot be identified. Nevertheless, just as the
notion of potency and act precedes every other notion in the division
of being, so the notions of relativity or absoluteness are prior even to
that of substance. Substance as a predicament designating a genus is
composed of being (taken simply as act) and a determining principle
by which it is "this" (and not simply being *simpliciter*). Prior to substance, then, and to being this or that, is *esse "ad"*, since a relation to
something else is already implied in the structure of the principles
making something to be "this" and distinct in being[549]. After, therefore, the notions of *esse ad, esse hoc,* and *esse determinatum ad genus*,
there remains no other fundamental kind of being, except for accidental being which is nothing other than *esse "in"*, which being is
rather a question of *"inesse"* (as opposed to *esse* properly speaking). As
a consequence, the notion of being *ad aliquid* precedes that of accidental being, whence something is able to be predicated *ad aliquid*
without thereby also being predicated *secundum accidens*. Though ac-

---

[549] Cf. especially Albert, *De causis et proc. univ.*, lib. 1, tr. 4, c. 2, ed. Colon., vol. 17/2,
p. 44-45; lib. 2, tr. 1, c. 5, ed. Colon., vol. 17/2, p. 66; lib. 2, tr. 1, c. 17, ed. Colon.,
vol. 17/2, p. 81-82; lib. 2, tr. 1, c. 19, ed. Colon., vol. 17/2, p. 83-84 – where the determination of *esse primum creatum* (necessary for the existence of even a first created being) is attributed to the relationships that *esse* has to nothingness from
which it came and to the First Cause in whom it existed intelligibly prior to its actualization (the potency on the part of *esse primum creatum* to be this or that being
consists here not in something intrinsic, but in the possibilities for the realization of
esse existing in the mind of God); cf. L. Sweeney, "Esse primum creatum in Albert
the Great's Liber de causis et processu universitatis", *The Thomist* 44 (1980), p. 604-
605, 608-609, 612, 615, 634.

cidental being necessarily implies relative being which is conceptually prior to it, relation, however, does not of itself imply anything accidental, as from what is prior we do not necessarily infer what is posterior[550].

Accordingly, being is not divided first into substance and accident but into *ens ab alio* and *ens non ab alio*. And it is only *ens ab alio* which properly divides into substance and accident, since substance, taken as dividing being along with accidents, is a subject in the sense of substrate, but *ens non ab alio* can in no way be a subject of this sort[551]. Analyzing *ens non ab alio*, we see that it may be subdivided into *ens ad aliquid*, when we consider the divine relations, and *ens non ad aliquid*, when we consider the divine substance or essence in itself. With regard to these relations, the *ens ad aliquid* does not *inest* after the manner of an accident, but as identically the same thing as that in which it is, rather equivocally, said to *inest*. *Ens ad aliquid* and *ens non ad aliquid* here differ only according to mode of signification[552], and for this reason, Albert affirms, the mode of relative predication is converted into a substantial mode of predication, as "paternity", for example, is the same as the "Father". "Father", "Son" and "Holy Spirit" are names of relations, but their relativity is had from the fact that they are *ad alte-*

---

[550] *"Modus comparationis in ipsis comparatis est aliquid ut proportio et habitudo, etiamsi numquam comparentur ad invicem secundum actum, et ille modus aliquid entitatis est, et sic cadit in modum praedicandi specialem, divisum ab omnibus aliis modis praedicamentorum, qui praedicant ens absolutum... Et si quis diligenter advertat, secundum rationem praecedit relatio omne praedicamentum tam substantiae quam accidentis; principia enim praedicamenti prima sunt potentia et actus. Statim autem nominata potentia in nomine concipitur et cointelligitur comparatio potentiae ad actum, et in ipso nomine actus cointelligitur comparatio actus ad potentiam et comparatio utriusque ad totum et sic relatio. Unde intellectus relationis est ante intellectum substantiae et ante intellectum accidentis, eo modo quo substantia praedicamentum est et genus, quia sic composita est substantia ex esse et determinante esse ad substantiam et ad id quod est; et sunt isti tres intellectus primi consequentes se, esse scilicet et esse hoc et determinatum ad genus. Et ante hunc secundum intellectum est esse 'ad'; hoc enim cointelligitur in habitudine principiorum facientium hoc esse hoc et distinctum in esse. Et post istos tres intellectus non consequitur, sed accedit intellectus eius quod est esse 'in', qui est intellectus accidentis; 'accidentis enim esse est inesse'. Unde intellectus eius quod est esse ad aliquid, antecedit intellectum accidentis. Et propter hoc dicit Augustinus, quod 'aliquid potest esse praedicatum ad aliquid, quod non est praedicatum secundum accidens'. Prius enim natura est esse 'ad' quam esse 'in'. Et ideo non sequitur, quod praedicatum secundum 'ad aliquid' praedicetur secundum accidens; prius enim natura non infert posterius natura, sed posterius natura infert prius natura"* – Albert, *Sum. theol.*, I, tr. 9, q. 37, sol., ed. Colon., vol. 34, p. 286.

[551] *"Nec prima divisio entis est in substantiam et accidens, sed secunda; sed prima divisio est ens ab alio et ens non ab alio, et postea entis ab alio divisio est in substantiam et accidens. Substantia enim, quae dividit ens cum accidente, est substantia subiectum. Ens autem non ab alio nullius potest esse subiectum; est enim per intellectum ante subicibile et ante accidentale"* – Albert, *Sum. theol.*, I, tr. 9, q. 37, ad 3, ed. Colon., vol. 34, p. 287.

[552] Cf. infra, "ON DISTINCTION ACCORDING TO MODE OF SIGNIFICATION", p. 207.

rum and not inasmuch as they *insunt* in something, which is proper rather to accidents and must be excluded from the divinity. In brief, the notion of relation is independent of and separate from that of accident for all beings in which relation is not founded upon something accidental. Paternity, considered as it is known in nature, is a relation founded upon the act of generation which is an accident in the one generating, and its concept therefore includes accidentality. In God, substance, power and operation are the same thing, even if they express that thing according to differing modes of signification, and relation there is thus founded upon the substance, implying nothing accidental in its concept[553]. In fact, Albert tells us, a relation may be said to be accidental only when it is founded upon or caused by an accident[554].

---

[553] Generation is defined as the procession of one thing from another in like nature, specifically; it is "to substantially produce something similar in species and form to the generator" – Albert, *III Sent.*, d. 4, a. 13, sol., ed. Borgnet, vol. 28, p. 92. The perfection implied by the concept of generation is nothing other than the origin of something distinct in such a similitude of nature (cf. Albert, *I Sent.*, d. 4, a. 2-3). Such a concept of itself is analogous and, as Albert expresses it, "general" in the sense that it can be applied to both God and creatures according to an analogy of proportion. On the concept of generation in general and its application to the divine processions in Albert, see A. Pompei, op. cit., p. 82-154.

[554] "*Sed in divinis relatio non inest ut accidens, sed inest ut idem, non differens ab eo cui inest, nisi secundum modum intelligendi vel significandi... ex illa parte mutatur modum praedicandi relativum in modum praedicandi substantiae; paternitas enim in patre idem est quod pater... Ad dictum Damasceni dicendum, quod pater et filius et spiritus sanctus sunt nomina habitudinis; sed habitudinis illius esse in hoc est quod ad alterum est, et non in hoc quod inest alicui; hoc enim est esse accidentis, quod in divinis non est... intellectus relationis separatus est ab intellectu accidentis in omnibus in quibus non fundatur relatio super aliud accidens... paternitas fundatur super actum generationis... relatio in creaturis in suo intellectu ponit accidens. Sed in divinis substantia, virtus et operatio idem sunt sub diverso modo significandi, et ideo relatio fundata in his... non enim habet esse accidentis relatio, nisi secundum quod ab accidente causatur*" – Albert, *Sum. theol.*, I, tr. 9, q. 37, ad 4, 9 & 11, ed. Colon., vol. 34, p. 287.

The combined divisions of being (taken in its broadest analogous sense)

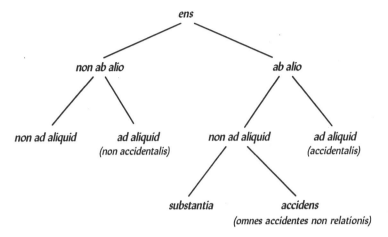

Now, substance may be predicated in two senses, either according to what its name implies which is the act of standing under, or according as it exists *per se* and as the cause of everything else which can be said to exist within it. In the first sense, substance can in no way be predicated of the divinity, since it is a question of being a subject in the sense of substrate which we mentioned above. In the second sense (*res per se ens*), which, for the sake of conceptual clarity, we would prefer to label *"subsistentia"*, substance is maximally and principally said of God and secondarily of all others. Now, relative predication usually means predication according to inherence. But predication according to inherence implies the predicating of something of a subject which is itself distinct from the subject supporting it, and this implies composition. But this cannot occur in the divinity, for which reason the predication of relation in the Godhead takes on, as we have seen, a substantial mode of predication, in the sense that what is predicated is predicated by identity, and not *per inhaerentiam*[555]. In this way, what

---

[555] Distinguishing the mode of signification of a term from the thing signified, the entity of a predicate from the mode according to which that entity is affirmed of the subject, was a speculative step never made by Gilbert of Poitiers, as a result of which he misconstrued the relation between essential and personal predicates in God (cf. infra, "PERSON DISTINGUISHED FROM NATURE OR ESSENCE", p. 290 (especially p. 292-294). That step enabled Albert to express in seminal form the celebrated Thomistic concept of the person as subsistent relation: *"'persona' dicitur relative in supposito; licet non dicat relationem in modo significandi per nomen"* – Albert, *I Sent.*, d. 22, a. 6, sol. & ad 1, ed. Borgnet, vol. 25, p. 576; cf. d. 26, a. 1, ad 3, ed. Borgnet,

is predicated relatively is substantially predicated, and what is predicated substantially is predicated not according to substance as a subject, but as existing *per se.* Thus the divine relations are predicated
according to substance, and this, not as in a subject, but *ut idem*[556]. As
is clear from the statement that "what is relatively predicated is substantially predicated", a sense of relative predication endures, namely
with respect to a relative term's special being, *ad alterum esse* (which
special being is distinctive of the predicament of relation). The relative mode of predication excluded from God pertains to the nature of
the predicament as such (that is, insofar as predicament, *in esse* [≠ according to its distinctive *ratio*]). Thus the reality of the relations in
God remains intact since their predication *ad aliud* maintains its opposition with the substantial mode of predication *ad se* (≠ per se)[557].
[Note that the possibility of the exclusion of the generic mode of
predication while nevertheless retaining the specific mode of predication is a property unique and proper to relation. In predicamental
terms (from which our language used to speak about God derives),
the possibility of denying the generic character of the predicament, its
in esse, while nonetheless retaining its specific character (its constitu-

---

vol. 26, p. 4: "*In divinis autem relatio est relatio, et non accidens, sed potius substantia; et
ideo ibi non est accidens relativum, sed ipsum suppositum relativi realiter seipso relativum*";
cf. A. Pompei, op. cit., p. 227. The divine persons are thus truly substance and truly
relation, since both substance and relation are perfectly verifiable in God; and because substance and relation are themselves identical in God (the latter taking a
substantial mode of predication), the divine person may be defined as the divine
substance, not *simpliciter et absolute,* but insofar as identical to the relation. In other
words, the persons in God are nothing other than subsistent relations: "*substantiale
quod est hypostasis [in divinis], non est simpliciter absolutum, est enim relatum per modum
absoluti dictum*" – Albert, *I Sent.,* d. 26, a. 1, ad 5, ed. Borgnet, vol. 26, p. 5; cf. A.
Pompei, op. cit., p. 298; cf. infra, "THE REALITY OF THE RELATIONS (TRUE NUMBER EVEN IF QUI-
DAM)", p. 408. On mode of signification, cf. infra, "ON DISTINCTION ACCORDING TO MODE OF
SIGNIFICATION", p. 207.

556 "*Substantia dupliciter dicitur, scilicet secundum rationem nominis, quod ab actu substandi
imponitur; et sic substantia solum est, quod omnium et primum subiectum est; et sic in deo
substantia non est, nec aliquid praedicatur secundum substantiam. Alio modo dicitur substantia res per se ens, quod est causa et 'occasio omnibus subsistendi in ipso'; et sic substantia
dicitur de deo maxime et de aliis posterius. Ab ipso enim sicut ab efficiente et in ipso sicut in
continente subsistit omne quod est. Et hoc modo aliquid secundum substantiam dicitur de deo,
sicut id quod dicitur absolute et non 'ad aliquid'... quod omne quod praedicatur per inhaerentiam, praedicatur ut de subiecto, et omne tale compositum est, et hoc modo nihil praedicatur
in divinis. Sed id quod praedicatur per identitatem, non praedicatur per inhaerentiam, quia
inhaerens non est id cui inhaeret... et quod praedicatur in divinis, non praedicatur per inhaerentiam, sed ut idem; et ideo non praedicatur ut de subiecto secundum rationem subiecti,
sed praedicatur ut de eo quod per se existit, et ut idem illi; et ideo praedicatur secundum substantiam, sed non ut de subiecto*" – Albert, *Sum. theol.,* I, tr. 9, q. 37, ad 11 & 13-14, ed.
Colon., vol. 34, p. 288.

557 Cf. A. Pompei, op. cit., p. 227, 296.

tive difference or *ratio*), is something exclusive to the predicament of relation for which a removal of the *ratio generis* does not also imply the destruction of its particular *ratio* (*ad aliud*), as it does in the case of every other accidental predicament the special *ratio* of which always includes intrinsically affecting a subject, since they *"praedicant aliquid inesse ei, de quo praedicantur"*[558]. These considerations permit us to construct the following divisions in both the conceptualization of substance and the kinds of substance (taken in its broadest sense), as well as to schematize the senses of relative predication. (Notice that the parallel breakdown of being on the right is an extract from our previous Boethian reflections).

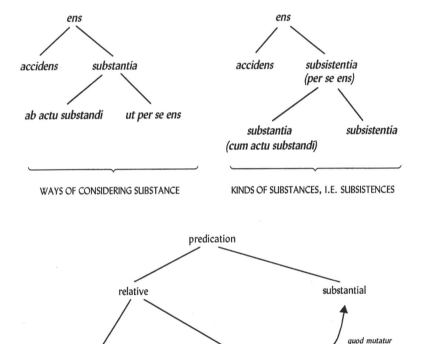

[558] Albert, *I Sent.*, d. 8, a. 31, sol., ed. Borgnet, vol. 25, p. 264; cf. A. Pompei, op. cit., p. 291-293. In this respect, the hierarchical arrangement of Albert – avoiding the subordination of *relatio* to the *inessendi* mode of being – represents a certain improvement over the Aristotelian divisions simply taken.

A closer examination of substance

Properly conceptualizing substance, we have affirmed, is the key to grasping the notion of personhood and every other name used to designate the personal reality. Consequently, we must more thoroughly examine the concept of substance and its related notions [559]. Albert speaks of substance from a variety of points of view. Effectively, this means that the predicament substance can be divided according to the number of perspectives from which it is viewed, or modes in which it is signified. Now, the distinction between "nature" and "person" will depend upon the different ways in which *substantia* can be signified. The most general division among the diverse ways in which substance may be signified corresponds to that between two frequently employed notions in Albert's commentary: those of *substantia essentia* and *substantia supposita*. The first is equivalent to the expression *substantia subiecti*, and the second to *substantia quae est subiectum*, the differences between which Albert explains in his response to the question about the meanings of the Greek "οὐσία", "οὐσίωσις" and "πρόσωπον", and the Latin *"essentia"*, *"subsistentia"*, *"substantia"*, and *"persona"* [560]. Albert's explanation fits in an exceptional way with the diagrammatic exposition earlier presented in the chapter on Boethius. We shall simplify our commentary on this through the use of another diagram:

---

[559] *"Intellectum personae praecedit intellectus usiae, usiosis et hypostasis, ideo primo quaerendum est de his tribus, secundo de persona"* – Albert, *Sum. theol.*, I, tr. 10, ed. Colon., vol. 34, p. 331.

[560] *"In praedicamento substantiae duo sunt consideranda, scilicet substantia subiecti, et substantia quae est subiectum. Substantia subiecti est id quod est naturalis substantiae, quod est praedicamentum, et hoc (ut dicit) accipitur nomine* οὐσίας *apud Graecos, et nomine 'essentiae' apud Latinos. Substantia autem subiecta est in se subsistens nullo indigens, et illa est genera, et species substantiae, quibus accidentia non accidunt, ut dicit Boetius, hoc est, accidentia naturae, ut album, nigrum, et hujusmodi, et haec vocatur 'subsistentia', et* οὐσίωσις*, aut est substans accidentibus, et haec est prima substantia quae propriissime dicitur, hoc est,* ὑπόστασις*, et 'substantia' apud nos. 'Persona' autem et* πρόσωπον *refertur ad proprietatem"* – Albert, *I Sent.*, d. 23, a. 4, sol., ed. Borgnet, vol. 25, p. 592. This explication is founded upon the Aristotelian notion of predicamental substance. In *Met.* IV, c. 8, Aristotle distinguishes substance taken as the quiddity of that which is signified by the definition (οὐσία), and substance taken as subject, the subsistent in the genus of substance (ὑπόστασις). Likewise, in the *Categories* c. 5, Aristotle distinguishes between primary and secondary substance, the first of which is ὑπόστασις (conceptually obtainable by the addition of "individual" to the latter – cf. Albert, *I Sent.*, d. 23, a. 4, sol.; d. 25, a. 2, ad q. 2). Cf. Aquinas, *Sum. theol.*, I, 29, 1, sol. & ad 1-2.

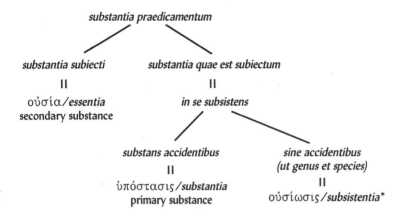

substantia praedicamentum

substantia subiecti   *substantia quae est subiectum*

|| ||

οὐσία/*essentia*   *in se subsistens*
secondary substance

substans accidentibus   *sine accidentibus*
|| *(ut genus et species)*
ὑπόστασις/*substantia* ||
primary substance   οὐσίωσις/*subsistentia**

πρόσωπον/*persona* – *quod pertinet ad proprietatem*

* The value of maintaining this branch, outside of Platonic categories, that is, of continuing to employ the notion after having rejected the notion of subsistent ideas, lies in the fact that it denotes subsisting (or existing) *in se* – this is the formal referent or specification of the term *subsistentia*. For this reason, it is nearly equivalent to the notion of *substantia quae est subiectum*, adding nothing to its notional content, but prescinding from that difference responsible for the constitution of *substantia*. *Substantia*, consequently, is a specified mode of subsisting, adding the notion of standing under to that of *substantia subiectum* taken in its most general sense, that is, without further determination nor precision [561]. Πρόσωπον/*persona* signifies the same reality as that contained under *substantia subiectum*, but from the formal point of view of its incommunicable property.

---

[561] As was demonstrated in Boethius, "substance" and "subsistence" are frequently interchangeable terms, and Albert himself will sometimes treat them as such (cf. *Sum. theol.*, I, tr. 10, q. 43, c. 1, obj. 3, ed. Colon., vol. 34, p. 332). The property of being an occasion for the existence of other things, typically ascribed to substance, moreover, is also ascribed to subsistence, inasmuch as *"sistere"* means to exist as a supposit, other things, namely accidents, existing in it and depending upon it for their existence: *"Augustinus accipit proprie subsistere, scilicet secundum quod suppositum sistit aliud ens in seipso, ut sit; hoc enim est accident, unde accidens potius est esse quam essentia, ut vult Aristoteles in IX primae philosophiae"* – Albert, *Sum. theol.*, I, tr. 10, q. 43, c. 1, ad 1, ed. Colon., vol. 34, p. 334. Here subsistence is being considered according to its substantial mode (and not exclusively according to the minimal formal requirement for subsistence). Indeed, if, after the philosophy of Boethius, every substance is necessarily a subsistence, everything predicable of the former is also predicable of the latter. Accidents, we should note, are ascribed here a minimal sense of existence; they are not truly essences (to which being properly belongs), but are a kind of being, and this, precisely inasmuch as they determine particular modes of being for the subject in which they inhere.

The whole vocabulary problem is resumed by the words of Peter Lombard, whose Sentences remain the fountainhead for Albert's reflections on personhood[562]. Particularly dependent upon the *De duabus naturis in una persona Christi* of Boethius, Saint Albert collocates the Greek and Latin terms according to the standard Ciceronian translation: for the Greek οὐσία stands the Latin *essentia*; for οὐσίωσις, *subsistentia*; for ὑπόστασις, *substantia*; and for πρόσωπον, *persona*[563]. Now, because these terms may be related to one another as more or less determinate/specified notions, it does not follow that the more general terms are superfluously mentioned in a definition (such as that of the person); that is, the implicit inclusion of one term within another does not obviate the need for its employment. While several of these terms may serve to designate an ultimate subject of attribution, namely, *subsistentia, substantia,* and *persona*, no one of them can replace the other two, since each one states something specifically different with regard to the subject of attribution commonly signified; *quia subiectum est multis modis considerare*[564]. The principle that there can be only one ultimate subject and only one ultimate predicate with respect to any nature is left intact. The subject is one and the same; and the ultimate predicate (meaning the fully specific and essentially determinate predicate) must be that term which best specifies and essentially identifies the nature, namely, the essential and ultimate difference. Each of the terms will approach the specification of the ultimate difference to a greater or lesser extent, depending upon its own conceptual precision. Let us proceed to uncover their conceptual differences.

Because the terms ὑπόστασις, οὐσίωσις, and οὐσία, are taken from the act which is proper to those things for which they stand, the same terms are reducible to what is first in the genus of their respec-

---

[562] Cf. Albert, *I Sent.*, d. 23, D, ed. Borgnet, vol. 25, p. 590: *"dictum est a Graecis, una essentia, tres substantiae, id est, una usia, tres hypostases. Aliter enim Graeci accipiunt substantiam quam Latini. A Latinis autem dictum est, una essentia vel substantia, tres personae, quia non aliter in sermone nostro, id est, Latino, essentia quam substantia solet intelligi".*

[563] *"Quatuor vocabulis Graecorum et Latinorum, quae sunt apud Graecos* οὐσία, οὐσίωσις, ὑπόστασις, *et* πρόσωπον, *apud Latinos autem... per ordinem, scilicet essentia, subsistentia, substantia, persona"* – Albert, *I Sent.*, d. 23, a. 4, ed. Borgnet, vol. 25, p. 591. Cf. Boethius, *Contra Eut.*, c. 3, ed. Loeb, p. 86-92.

[564] The objection to which we are responding consists in the following argument: *"in nulla natura potest esse nisi unum subiectum primum, et unum praedicatum ultimum... persona non est nisi subiectum, ergo nullum aliorum potest subiectum, nominare, ergo cum in natura non sit nisi quod est, ex parte cujus sumitur persona, et quo est ex parte cujus sumitur*

tive acts. The rationale operating here is the Aristotelian principle that all causality within a determinate genus is reduced to the first cause in the genus. Since ὑπόστασις/*substantia* denotes that which has the act of standing under, it is taken from the *ratio* of the role proper to prime matter. Philosophically speaking, then, ὑπόστασις refers to prime matter, because prime matter is the first "supporting subject". In like manner, οὐσίωσις/*subsistentia* refers to first form, since it denotes the existent thing itself, without reference to whether or not it also stands under other things; for that which subsists in itself without depending on others in order to be, others eventually rather depending on it for their being, belongs to the formal order, since form does not depend upon matter for its subsistence, but vice versa. Finally, οὐσία/*essentia* names the composite, because it connotes the act of existing which presupposes (in natural things) substantiation in matter[565]. They all signify the same substantial reality (in fact, they are all analogously called substance in the broad sense of the term), but according to different points of reference. With regard to naming persons, ὑπόστασις was chosen because the term is *based upon* that which individuates a thing most distinctly. This most distinct individuation in natural things is accomplished through the ultimate composition of final matter with the final form, resulting in the composite substance. For this reason, ὑπόστασις, though employed to signify person, bears a certain ambiguity, inasmuch as it seems to exclusively signify substance – *substantia supposita*, naturally, but without explicitly indicating the distinguishing factor which makes it a supposit (in distinction from *substantia essentia*), the generic act of which is, in a certain sense, the basis of its signification[566]. "Person" is therefore superior to "ὑπόστασις" in two respects: not only because, as remarked by Albert, the Latin literal translation of hypostasis, *"substantia"*, was rife

---

essentia, videtur quod duo alia superfluunt" – Albert, *I Sent.*, d. 23, a. 4, obj. 4, ed. Borgnet, vol. 25, p. 591; cf. *I Sent.*, d. 23, a. 4, ad 3, ed. Borgnet, vol. 25, p. 593.

[565] *"In philosophia enim 'hypostasis' dicitur prima materia, et 'usiosis' forma prima, et 'usia' compositum... omnis causalitas secundum quodlibet genus causae necessario reducitur ad causam primam in genere illo... cum igitur supponi primo sit materiae primae... substantia, vel hypostasis... ab actu substandi primo sumatur, necessario sonabit a quo est prima ratio substandi, id est, materiam primam, subsistentia autem sonat id quod est in se subsistens nullo indigens... subsistentia sive usiosis accipitur pro forma prima. Essentia autem est illa a qua est esse, et cujus actus est esse... esse autem non est actus essentiae nisi quae est in materia, et ideo illam 'compositum' vocaverunt"* – Albert, *I Sent.*, d. 23, a. 4, sol., ed. Borgnet, vol. 25, p. 592.

[566] The generic act of the *proprietas* is to distinguish which, in the physical order, was understood to be accomplished by matter, according to its receptive role with respect to form.

with ambiguity[567], due to the fact that it was sometimes used to express the natural element beneath the supposit (*substantia suppositi* or *substantia subiecti*) and sometimes to express the supposit of such a nature (*suppositum substantiae* or *substantia supposita*)[568]; but also in virtue of the ambiguity and intensional limit inherent in the notion of hypostasis itself. The name ὑπόστασις does not designate the distinctness as well as does another term like *persona*, which *directly* refers to the *proprietates*, in addition to subsuming the notion of substance and the individuality attached to it. "Hypostasis" already implies distinction, but it does not denote the *ratio* of distinction, which is accomplished by "person"[569].

Concerning the ambiguity over the terms ὑπόστασις and *substantia*, Albert remarks that there is one sense of *substantia* which operates like the Greek ὑπόστασις and is able even in God to be taken in the plural. This precise sense is *substantia* intended according to its subjectival aspect, or "act of standing under"[570].

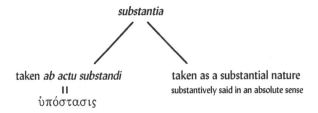

In fact, the name "substance" most properly belongs to the hypostasis because it is given in virtue of the act of "standing under"[571].

---

[567] "*Graeci accipiunt 'hypostasim' pro eo quod maxime est distinctum, et hoc non est nisi ultima compositione compositum... ex ultima materia et ex ultima forma secundum naturam. ... et ideo individuum rationalis naturae vocant 'hypostasim'. ... sed apud nos non superfluit nomen personae, quia id quod respondet hypostasi apud nos, est dubiae significationis, id est, substantia*" – Albert, *I Sent.*, d. 23, a. 4, ad 3, ed. Borgnet, vol. 25, p. 593.

[568] For a discussion of the ambiguities residing in the term *substantia* and its differing uses among Latin authors, cf. A. Pompei, op. cit., p. 232-234.

[569] "*Hypostasis etsi dicat distinctum, secundum usum Graecorum, non tamen dicit rationem distinctionis in ipso nomine, et hanc rationem exprimit persona*" – Albert, *I Sent.*, d. 23, a. 7, ad 3, ed. Borgnet, vol. 25, p. 600.

[570] "*Substantia propter ambiguitatem nominis apud Latinos non recipitur in plurali, apud Graecos autem videtur* ὑπόστασις *esse loco personae, et ideo dicuntur tres hypostases, etsi quandoque inveniatur sicut ab Augustino et Anselmo tres substantiae, sumitur substantia ab actu substandi, et pro hypostasi*" – Albert, *I Sent.*, d. 25, a. 7, sol., ed. Borgnet, vol. 25, p. 637. Cf. *Sum. theol.*, I, tr. 10, q. 43, c. 1, ad 3, ed. Colon., vol. 34, p. 334.

[571] "*Nomen autem 'substantiae' ab actu substandi imponitur, quod proprie convenit hypostasi*" – Albert, *Sum. theol.*, I, tr. 7, q. 30, c. 3, a. 1, ad 3, ed. Colon., vol. 34, p. 234.

In the same response, Albert also divides substance according as it is distinguishable into *quo est* and *quod est* (which stands at the heart of its ambiguity and the diversity of uses it receives from different Latin authors). The first may be taken in two senses. First, as simply in itself, aside from any particular quality, neither universal nor singular in itself – the essence considered absolutely; second, as the common nature predicable of singulars. Considered as *quod est*, substance may also be taken in two ways. First, in relation to the nature under which it subsists, in which case it is called substance (in Boethian terms, but ὑπόστασις or *subsistentia* in the language of Augustine and Jerome); and second, with respect to the particularizing property, where it receives the name person[572]. One will note that for Boethius, Augustine and Jerome, the terms *substantia* and *subsistentia* have different meanings. We shall try to illustrate these various senses and their relations to one another by collocating them in the diagram which follows. As was stated, *substantia*, for Boethius, refers to the *quod est*. For Augustine and Jerome, however, it designates the *quo est*[573]. Moreover, *subsistentia*, as we have seen, represents, according to a primordial[574] Boethian sense, a certain reality subsisting without accidents. For the other Latins, *subsistentia* falls within the category of the individualized, the *quod est* in its most determined sense. Person, on the other hand, signifies the same individualized nature with respect to its distinctive properties and special dignity[575]. The foregoing divisions and comparisons can be schematized as follows:

---

[572] *"In substantia, id est, in natura substantiae duo sunt, scilicet 'quo est', et 'id quod est'. Quo est autem attenditur dupliciter, scilicet prout est in se simplex, non commiscibile alicui particularium, sicut cum dicitur, homo est species, et risibile, et hoc est proprium, et non commune, cum non possit praedicari de aliquo secundum intentionem illam, et hoc dicunt quidam esse essentiam. Accipitur etiam natura communis, ut praedicabilis de singulis, et sic homo est appellativum nomen, si sic accipitur in natura hominis, et sic apud Boetium vocatur usiosis vel subsistentia... Si autem consideratur natura secundum id quod est, dupliciter consideratur, aut per respectum quem ponit ad naturam cui subsistit, et tunc dicitur substantia apud Boetium, et ὑπόστασις, vel subsistentia secundum Augustinum et Hieronymum, aut per respectum ad proprietatem, et tunc dicitur secundum omnes persona et πρόσωπον"* – Albert, I Sent., d. 23, a. 4, sol., ed. Borgnet, vol. 25, p. 593.

[573] *"Substantia quidem secundum eos ponit respectum ad quo est, propter quod etiam dubium facit intellectum apud Latinos, ut quandoque pro essentia, quandoque pro supposito ponatur"* – Albert, I Sent., d. 23, a. 4, sol., ed. Borgnet, vol. 25, p. 593.

[574] We say "primordial", because, as was demonstrated, in the Boethian context, *subsistentia* also has a more precise value of designating anything which exists *in se*. Cf. supra, "SUBSISTENCE AND ITS RELATION TO SUBSTANCE", p. 110 (especially p. 111, 115); "SPECIFIC ASPECTS OF SUBSTANTIA AND SUBSISTENTIA", p. 121-127.

[575] *"Subsistentia autem secundum eos ponit respectum ad individuationem... Sed persona ponit specialem respectum ad distinctionem proprietatis pertinentis ad dignitatem moris vel*

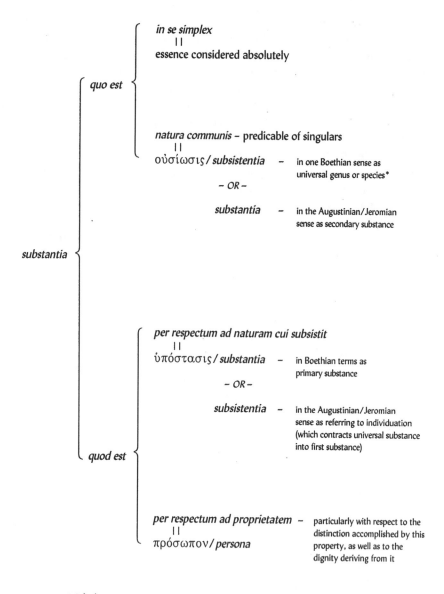

*Οὐσίωσις has been understood in the original Boethian categories of *in se* existent genera and species, for which reason it receives the appellation *subsistentia*. Now, insofar as the word set "οὐσίωσις/ *subsistentia*" represents genera, differences and species as predicable universals constituting the essence of things, it is properly designated as *quo est.* But inasmuch as it stands

naturae" – Albert, *I Sent.*, d. 23, a. 4, sol., ed. Borgnet, vol. 25, p. 593. Cf. infra, "THE DEFINITION OF MASTER LOMBARD AND THE NOTION OF DIGNITY", p. 362.

for the same things as existing *in se,* and can be extended in a metaphysically appropriate way to subsistent forms, it plants itself in the domain of the *quod est,* even though this is not explicitly indicated in the above chart. The fact that the term *subsistentia* is equated with οὐσίωσις is really due to the privileged metaphysical act of subsisting *in se,* and this suggests that that word pair more fittingly belongs with the *quod est,* the *substantia quae est subiectum,* albeit *sine accidentibus* (cf. the first diagram in this section). But because the things to which Boethius would seem to want to attribute subsistent reality are (in this context) abstract forms, it is better to place οὐσίωσις under a division of the *quo est.*

Οὐσία *and* ὑπόστασις *as "substance" in different ways*

As was observed, Albert (following the thought of Praepositinus[576]) distinguishes substance into substance taken as subject, *substantia subiecta,* and substance taken in the sense of the substance of the subject, *substantia subiecti.* Taken as subject, "substance" stands for first substance, which is the subject both of being and of the substance taken as second substance. To this the Greeks assign the name "ὑπόστασις". Taken as *substantia subiecti,* "substance" refers to the substantial property of the substance taken as primary substance, that is, it refers to the secondary substance of which primary substance is the concrete instantiation. This secondary substance is threefold, inasmuch as it designate something generic, something specific or something individual. When considered generically – as, for example, when considering the secondary substance of Socrates at the level of substantiality – the Greeks, according to Albert, assign the name "οὐσία". Considered specifically, *substantia subiecti* receives the name "οὐσίωσις", which is the specific substance of the subject. And, considered individually – i.e. as signifying an individual essence such as "Socratesness" – the individual substance of the subject is given the name "πρόσωπον". All three of these terms refer to the substance as constitutive and formal element, i.e. as secondary substance, and not as the concrete subject which is the primary substance[577]. Now, it

---

[576] The name refers to Gilbert Prevostin (†1210), theologian from Cremon who was Chancellor of the University of Paris from 1206-1209.

[577] *"Dixit emim Praepositinus quod 'alia substantia est subiecta et alia est substantia subiecti. Substantia subiecta est prima substantia, quae est subiectum'... 'Substantia subiecti substantialis proprietas est eiusdem substantiae', hoc est proprietas 'secundae substantiae', cui substat prima. 'Et haec est triplex, scilicet generalis, specialis et individualis; generalis, quae tantum genus est, qua scilicet Socrates est substantia; specialis, quae tantum species est, qua Socrates est homo; individualis, quae nec genus nec speciem, sed individuum tantum constituit, ut qua Socrates est Socrates, et haec ficto nomine dicitur socratitas'. Et pro his dicit in graeco quattuor esse nomina, scilicet 'usia, quae generalis est substantia subiecti, usiosis, quae specialis substantia est subiecti, prosopon, quae individualis est substantia subiecti, hypostasis,*

might seem especially strange to assign the name πρόσωπον to such a reality, but πρόσωπον is not intended here to perform the role of designating the person; that role is conferred rather to the name "ὑπόστασις". In fact, Albert tells us, the use of πρόσωπον here corresponds with what was (inexactly) understood as its strict etymological and cultural origin connected with the idea of a mask, whence the appropriateness of its ascription to the individual essence, which is a kind of "phantom" of the person who exists[578]. Moreover, as it has been explained by Boethius, and accepted by Albert, it is probably in virtue of the dramatic function of a mask placed before one's face as a sign of importance or dignity that πρόσωπον, and the Latin *persona*, were transposed to the realm of personal signification, for the person is the hypostasis which is distinct from every other hypostasis in virtue of a particular property pertaining to dignity[579]. On the other hand, even for the Greeks, both the "special" (or specific) and the individual *substantiae subiecti* may be alternately understood as *substantia subiecta*, inasmuch as they signify the subject in a certain way. That the specific secondary substance be translated as a subject existing in its own right follows, if we accept a Platonic view of universals, from the fact that these οὐσιώσεις are the general and specific forms through which the subject – *id quod est* – is made to be this (as animality makes a substance to be an animal, and humanity makes it to be human), and such forms are said to be complete with their act of existing *non indigens accidentibus ut sit*. According, then, to the rather Platonic perspective assigning subsistent status to these genera and species, they can be said to stand in a certain way for the subject, each representing therefore the *substantia subiecta* (and they are for the same reason also called "*subsistentiae*"). As to the πρόσωπον, the fact that its notion embodies all that is already contained in the general and specific forms of being should be enough to "subjectivize" it in some sense for the Platonist, and its convertibility with the subject itself, when the

---

quae est substantia subiecta'" – Albert, *Sum. theol.*, I, tr. 10, q. 43, c. 1, obj. I, ed. Colon., vol. 34, p. 331.

[578] "*Prosopon autem sive persona proprie dictus est homo larvatus*" – Albert, *Sum. theol.*, I, tr. 10, q. 43, c. 1, obj. II, ed. Colon., vol. 34, p. 332.

[579] "*Larvis pictis ad similitudinem facierum illarum personarum et sibi ante facies circumligatis repraesentabant... personam dicebant transumi ad significandam hypostasim discretam proprietate dignitatis alicuius ab aliis hypostasibus sive individuis. Et ad hoc BOETHIUS inducit duas rationes, unam ex compositione vocabuli, aliam ex accentu; ex compositione, quia componitur a 'pro' quod est ante, et 'sopon', quod est facies, quasi ante faciem vel antefacies; antefacies enim sive anterior facies larva est*" – Albert, *Sum. theol.*, I, tr. 10, q. 43, c. 1, obj. II,

latter is abstracted from its existence alone, does bring it asymptotically close to the person for the realist as well – though the critical difference of the possession and exercise of existence still remains. In any case, the important distinction is that between ὑπόστασις and οὐσία, between that which signifies the substance precisely insofar as subject and that which signifies the substance insofar as a form through which being is possessed. The latter does not name that which is *per se*, and cannot therefore be used to signify the person; the former, understood as signifying according to the act of standing under a common nature and as becoming an occasion for the existence of other things in it, stands for the suppositum. In a general way, just as a ὑπόστασις, which is the substance as supposit, stands beneath a common nature, so does the person; and just as a ὑπόστασις stands beneath accidents, so the person is said to stand beneath the *proprietates*[580].

---

ed. Colon., vol. 34, p. 332. Cf. infra, "THE DEFINITION OF MASTER LOMBARD AND THE NOTION OF DIGNITY", p. 361.

[580] *"Usia in graeco sive essentia in latino est idem quod prima forma simpliciter faciens esse et non esse hoc... Usiosim autem sive subsistentiam dixerunt esse formam generalem vel specialem, qua id quod est, hoc est, ut animalitate animal est et humanitate homo est. Et hi dixerunt, quod subsistentia sive usiosis dicitur esse id quod est, sive subiectum, prout sua substantiali vel speciali forma est quid 'non indigens accidentibus, ut sit'. Et quia subiectum dicit, ideo translatum est aliquando ad significandum personas, sicut pater et filius et spiritus sanctus sunt tres subsistentiae... Usia vero, quia subiectum non dicit nec quod est, non translata est ad significandum personam, sed simpliciter naturam significat... Graeci hypostasim vocant, quod interpretatur suppositum, eo quod ut res naturae sub communi natura posita est... 'est ens in se completum'... substat enim accidentibus. Et ideo hoc etiam dicunt esse translatum ad supponendum pro personis, quia sicut substantia, quae est subiectum, substat naturae communi, ita persona, et sicut substantia, quae est subiectum, substat accidenti, ita persona proprietati"–* Albert, *Sum. theol.*, I, tr. 10, q. 43, c. 1, obj. II, ed. Colon., vol. 34, p. 331-332.

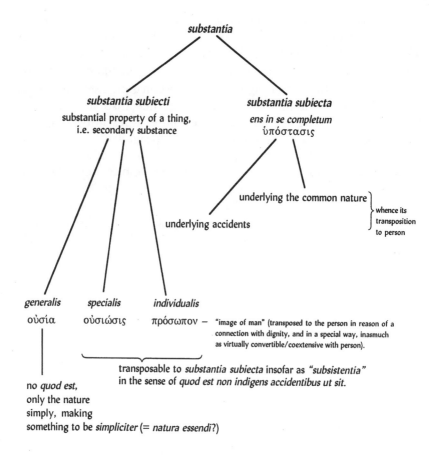

It should be remarked that to treat the οὐσία, οὐσιώσις and πρόσω–
πον here as secondary substances which are in a certain way therefore
universal with respect to their subject would seem to imply a distinction between universal and particular even in the Godhead. Albert
responds to this difficulty by pointing out that it is not Praepositinus'
intention to affirm the presence of genus, species and individual,
strictly speaking, in the Trinity. The universal and the particular,
properly speaking, cannot be admitted in God on account of his
maximal simplicity[581]. Yet a thing can be called "universal" on two ac-

---

[581] "In creatis propter compositionem est universale et particulare secundum rem, universale ex
parte naturae communis, particulare ex parte rei naturae sive suppositi, et haec in divinis
propter omnimodam simplicitatem esse non possunt" – Albert, Sum. theol., I, tr. 10, q. 43,

counts: either inasmuch as it be "in" many things, which is noble and a kind of perfection; or inasmuch as it be "from" many things, which is not dignified since it is taken from, or reclines upon, other things as its subjects. In the latter sense, no notion of something more universal or of something more particular can be correctly had with respect to God. However, in the former sense, the special properties by which each person differs from the others can indeed be *signified* as existing in the persons, and the individual personalities themselves are able to be signified distinctly from the individualized nature as such (i.e. from the *natura appropriata* – in the sense of hypostatically particularized by this or that personal property – taken as the essence of this person [582]); but this is nothing more than a distinction in modes of signification, introducing absolutely no difference *in re* between the referents of such signification [583].

On distinction according to mode of signification

In God, one will speak of personal properties, properties of the person, relations, substance and supposits. None of these things differ, however, according to being, but only according to our way of understanding them and according to the way in which they are predicated of something (*modus attribuendi*) or something is attributed to them (*modus supponendi*). Some may be predicated of a thing while others cannot; and to some a certain thing may be predicated, though not to others [584]. All of these predicative differences are rooted in the man-

---

c. 1, ad 5, ed. Colon., vol. 34, p. 335. Cf. infra, "THE TERMS 'SINGULAR', 'INDIVIDUAL' AND 'PARTICULAR' IN GOD", p. 373.

[582] Or, as we shall soon see, as the concrete nature of the individual considered not insofar as it is individual or determined, but insofar as determin*able*.

[583] *"Praepositinus noluit, quod genus et species et individuum proprie essent in divinis; scivit enim, quod universale et particulare propter indifferentiam maximae simplicitatis in divinis esse non posset. Sed quia in 'universali' duo sunt, unum quidem, quod est 'in' multis, et hoc nobilitatis est et perfectionis, alterum quod est 'de' multis, et hoc ignobilitatis est, quia per hoc innititur alii ut subiecto... 'speciale' autem, quod est in eo quod specie differt ab alio, sicut pater specie proprietatis differt a filio, 'individuale' autem, quod est in uno solo; quae licet re non differant in divinis, differunt tamen modo significandi... praepositio 'sub' non notat inferioritatem ad superius aliquid secundum rem, sed secundum modum significandi tantum, sicut commune re dicitur 'supra' et discretum et determinatum dicitur 'sub', cum tamen re idem sint determinatum et commune. Unde per 'sub' et 'supra' non notatur nisi diversus modus significandi habens et habitum"* – Albert, *Sum. theol.*, I, tr. 10, q. 43, c. 1, ad 1 & 2, ed. Colon., vol. 34, p. 333-334.

[584] *"In divinis ponuntur notiones, proprietates personae, proprietates personales et relationes. Et haec differunt non secundum esse, sed secundum rationem intelligendi sive secundum rationem supponendi et attribuendi... Aliquid enim attribuitur uni quod non attribuitur alteri,*

ner in which a term is understood to signify its referent. The proper point of view from which a name is said of the divine substance determines what it designates about that substance and, consequently, what may or may not be said of the substance so signified[585].

As we shall see in the following sections, the principal *significatum* for both "person" and "hypostasis" is the same; however, in virtue of their diverse modes of signification, one term connotes something which the other term does not. Likewise, whenever several names are used to refer to the same reality, and the result is such that one name is predicable of the other – as, for example, when we affirm that *"persona est hypostasim"* or that *"persona est essentia"* –, the diverse modes of signification proper to each entail diverse modes of supposition and attribution, such that what is predicated of one term is not always predicable of another. Person *is* an essence, but what we say about the person is not always said of the essence[586]. Because "person" does not directly signify the essence as essence, something which is proper to the person, such as being distinct from another person, is negatable of the essence, precisely in virtue of their respective modes of signifying the same reality[587]. The precise mode of signification of a term, then, must be understood in order to respect the logic of predication[588].

---

et uno istorum supposito non necessario supponitur alterum" – Albert, *Sum. theol.*, I, tr. 9, q. 39, c. 2, a. 1, sol., ed. Colon., vol. 34, p. 296.

[585] Cf. Albert, *I Sent.*, d. 5, a. 2, ad 8.

[586] *"Diversus modus significandi causat diversum modum dicendi et diversum modum supponendi et diversum modum attribuendi et non diversum modum rei. Dico autem diversum modum dicendi, quando quidem unum duobus nominibus vel pluribus significatur, sed ratione modi significandi cum significato principali aliquid connotatur in uno, quod non connotatur in alio... licet haec omnia dicant essentiam divinam et significent essentiam divinam, aliud tamen dicitur et connotatur... Diversus autem modus supponendi est, quando quidem, quae dicuntur, eadem sunt re, tamen propter modum significandi diversum supposito uno non supponitur alterum eisdem praedicatis; et sic persona est essentia, tamen supposita persona non supponitur essentia respectu eorundem praedicatorum"* – Albert, *Sum. theol.*, I, tr. 10, q. 44, c. 1, ad 9, ed. Colon., vol. 34, p. 346.*

[587] *"Generare et generari et spirare et spirari non dicunt differentiam personae ad essentiam, sed dicunt differentiam personae ad personam... ex quo persona non supponit essentiam nec dicit eam in recto et ut essentiam, sequitur, quod proprium personae non sit proprium essentiae, sed negetur ab ea propter modum significandi diversum et propter diversum modum supponendi. Et hoc non praeiudicat identitati rei"* – Albert, *Sum. theol.*, I, tr. 10, q. 44, c. 4, ad 1-3, ed. Colon., vol. 34, p. 352. Cf. Boethius, *Utrum Pater et Filius*, 59-60, ed. Loeb, p. 36: *"necesse est quod vocabulum ex personis originem capit id ad substantiam non pertinere"* (cf. Albert, *Sum. theol.*, I, tr. 10, q. 45, c. 1, a. 1, obj. 1, ed. Colon., vol. 34, p. 352; Albert cites the passage but attributes it to the *De Trinitate* of Boethius); cf. Boethius, *Utrum Pater et Filius*, 32-48, ed. Loeb, p. 34-36.

[588] For further clarification of the notion of distinction according to mode of signification, cf. A. F. & D. BARBEDETTE, *Cours de philosophie scolastique*, Berche et Pagis,

If one criticizes the notion of distinction according to mode of signification, claiming, for example, that such a distinction between person and nature in God signals but a verbal or grammatical difference between two things which are exactly the same in reality, we should respond that these things really are identical, but that this does not mean that what one says of the Father, really, must also be said of the nature, really. From the moment we consider what "one says" (or predicates) of these things, we are back at a propositional level where

Paris 1935, "Logique Mineure" §42-47, p. 35-37 [emphasizing the secondary properties of terms according to which their acceptation in a concrete application is determined]; M.-D. CHENU, "Grammaire et théologie aux 12ᵉ et 13ᵉ siècles", *AHDLMA* 10 (1935), p. 5-28; R. GARRIGOU-LAGRANGE, *God: His Existence and His Nature*, trans. B. Rose, Herder Book Co., St. Louis/London 1949, vol. 2, p. 187-267 [dealing with the identification of and distinction between the divine attributes in general in the eminence of the deity]; L. G. KELLY, "Modus significandi: an interdisciplinary concept", *Historiographia Linguistica* VI (1979), p. 159-180; "God and Speculative Grammar", in I. Rosier (editor), *L'héritage des grammairiens latins de l'Antiquité aux Lumières: Actes du Colloque de Chantilly, 2-4 septembre, 1987*, Société pour l'information grammaticale, Paris/Louvain 1987, p. 205-213 [which includes an examination of the application of names to God in consideration of the accidents of the parts of speech by which the *quality* according to which substantives are said is also implied]; CARDINAL MERCIER, *A Manual of Modern Scholastic Philosophy*, 3ʳᵈ English edition, trans. T. L. Parker and S. A. Parker, vol. II, Routledge & Kegan Paul/Herder, London/St. Louis 1962, "Logic" §13-22, p. 145-154 [providing a general introduction to the common scholastic principles of predicate logic]. Cf. also J. BIARD, "Sémantique et Ontologie dans l'Ars Meliduna", in J. Jolivet – A. De Libera (editors), *Gilbert de Poitiers et ses contemporains. Aux origines de la Logica modernorum: Actes du septième Symposium européen d'histoire de la logique et de la sémantique médiévales, Centre d'Études supérieures de civilisation médiévale de Poitiers, Poitiers, 17-22 juin 1985*, Bibliopolis, Naples 1987, p. 121-144 [this work focuses rather on the 12ᵗʰ century problem of signification, particularly concerned with the extensional and intensional aspects of semantics]; H. A. G. BRAAKHUIS, "Signification, Appellation and Predication in the Ars Meliduna", in J. Jolivet – A. De Libera (editors), *Gilbert de Poitiers et ses contemporains. Aux origines de la Logica modernorum: Actes du septième Symposium européen d'histoire de la logique et de la sémantique médiévales, Centre d'Études supérieures de civilisation médiévale de Poitiers, Poitiers, 17-22 juin 1985*, Bibliopolis, Naples 1987, p. 107-120; U. ECO, "Signification and Denotation from Boethius to Ockham", *Franciscan Studies* 44 (1984), p. 1-29; C. H. KNEEPKENS, "'Suppositio' and 'Supponere' in 12ᵗʰ Century Grammar", in J. Jolivet – A. De Libera (editors), *Gilbert de Poitiers et ses contemporains. Aux origines de la Logica modernorum: Actes du septième Symposium européen d'histoire de la logique et de la sémantique médiévales, Centre d'Études supérieures de civilisation médiévale de Poitiers, Poitiers, 17-22 juin 1985*, Bibliopolis, Naples 1987, p. 325-351; H.-J. KONRAD KOERNER/R.H. ROBINS (editors), "Studies in Medieval Linguistic Thought", special edition of *Historiographia Linguistica*, *Historiographia Linguistica* VII, 1/2 (1980); W. E. McMAHON, "Albert the Great on the Semantics of the Categories of Substance, Quantity, and Quality", in *Historiographia Linguistica* VII, 1/2, special edition "Studies in Medieval Linguistic Thought" (1980), p. 145-157; I. ROSIER, *Grammaires médiévales*, Presses universitaires de Vincennes, Saint-Denis 1990; *La parole comme acte: sur la grammaire et la sémantique au XIIIe siècle*, J. Vrin, Paris 1994; cf. also "Signification et référence dans l'Antiquité et au Moyen Age", special edition of *Langages*, in *Langages* 65 (mars 1982).

grammatical principles govern our statements, where, to be precise, the predication must abide by the mode of signification proper to the subject and/or predicate. If we ignore the grammatical nature of our language and focus only on the reality of things while somehow still making statements about the persons and the divinity, we may indeed say that the nature generates, for the nature *as Father* generates, or that the Father is communicated, for the Father *as the divine nature* is communicated; but one should not speak in a way irrespective of the rules of predication and the accepted meanings of terms. In fact, a meaning is assigned to a name not in virtue of how it is logically employed (which lends itself to mere arbitrariness), but in virtue of the reality it signifies and from which its concept is derived, and it is that signification which then determines the logical use (suppositional and attributive value) of the name. In other words, different modes of signifying derive from real attributes of what is signified[589], for which reason the distinction between such attributes is denominated *secundum modum intelligendi*, in the sense of *distinctio secundum ratione ratiocinatae* (*vel cum fundamento in re*), as opposed to the purely logical *distinctio secundum ratione ratiocinantis*[590].

Ways of signifying the divine nature

Because even primary substance can be signified in a diversity of ways, either from its act of substanding or according to its *per se* existence, it follows that the divine substance can be signified in either way – provided, of course, the modes of predication be taken in their proper analogical sense, purified of the imperfections proper to creatures in which *quod est* and *quo est* are distinct (all subjectivality in God pertains exclusively to our mode of conceptualizing and signifying diverse aspects of the same entity in which there is no composition and the differently signified realities are identical *in re*). But, the name used to signify the divine substance will differ according to the mode of signification according to which that substance is represented.

When signified from the point of view of the subjectival act of standing under, the divine substance is designated by the terms sup-

---

[589] Cf. Albert, *I Sent.*, d. 5, a. 1, ad obj. 2, ed. Borgnet, vol. 25, p. 175.

[590] For a discriminating discussion of the various kinds of distinction involved in our talk about God, see A. Muralt, *L'Enjeu de la philosophie médiévale*, E. J. Brill, Leiden/New York/Cologne 1993, p. 47-89; cf. also in this regard R. Garrigou-Lagrange, *God: His Existence and His Nature*, trans. B. Rose, Herder Book Co., St. Louis/London 1949, vol. 2, p. 187-267.

positum or hypostasis; when signified, however, from the point of view of the perseity of its existence, the divine substance is designated by the term divine nature (which is the *ratio* of subsistence for everything in the Godhead)[591]. The fact that a thing signified from the point of view of its *per se* existence receives the name *subsistentia* (in virtue of the strict mode of signification proper to *subsistentia*) does not conflict with Albert's use of the name "divine nature" here. The nature in question here is nothing other than *ipsum esse subsistens*. Therefore, to name the divine substance from the point of view of its *quidditas* is the same as to name it from that of its *per se* act of existence.

As we have just seen, the divine nature, as with every communicable nature, can be taken either as it is in itself, in its simplicity, or according as it exists in the subject having (and identical with) it. But there is more to the analysis. Taken in the first sense, the Latins call the nature the "essence", the Greeks "οὐσία". Taken according as it is had, the nature can again be signified in two ways. First, as a determinate thing of a common and indifferent nature which neither numbers supposits nor is numbered in them, since it is indifferent to being one or many, and this is the Latin "subsistentia" taken as the universal, and the Greek οὐσίωσις – understood after the Boethian explanation of "subsistence" as designating that which has no need for other things such as accidents in order to exist. Such a "nature" is determinate inasmuch as specified by the generic and specific intension of the universal, and, as the composition inherent in the term "sub-sistere" indicates, the nature both "sists" and does so "under" the universal in question, "sisting" in it. To "sist", according to Albert, implies being terminated *in se* such that no further recourse to something other is required to exist; if, on the other hand, a thing's being is accounted for through the positing of another in its definition, then it does not "sist", since it does not possess its own "term", flowing, as it were, to another (such is the case for accidents). *"Subsistentia"* is accordingly said to be a (independent) mode of existence (something which confirms our comments – in the chapter on Boethius – with regard to subsistence as a mode of being when being is taken in an

---

[591] *"Substantia etiam in divinis duobus modis dicitur, scilicet ab actu substandi, et sic suppositum maxime dicitur substantia. Dicitur etiam 'substantia per se ens, alio, ut sit, non indigens', et sic natura divina maxime est substantia. Et hoc secundo modo non possunt esse plures substantiae in divinis. Primo autem modo plures substantiae sunt in divinis sicut plures hypostases et plura supposita, et hoc modo dicitur persona substantia"* – Albert, *Sum. theol.*, I, tr. 10, q. 46, ad 3, ed. Colon., vol. 34, p. 362.

extended analogical sense) [592]. In a second way, the nature taken according as it is had can be signified according as it is distinguishable or determinable on account of the aptitude of the supposit and through the *proprietas*. In this sense, it is called *"substantia"*, in the sense of subject (*substantia subiecta*). But, since substance, according to its strict delineation (setting it off from subsisting things which are not subject to accidents), is an occasion for other things inhering in it, when transferred to God it must be predicated in a more restricted sense, namely, only insofar as signifying that which is complete in itself. Consequently, nature taken in this way designates *ens completum in se determinabile proprietate*, and this is what the Latins call *"substantia"*, and the Greeks "ὑπόστασις" [593]. Now, nature taken as a subject complete in itself can be signified either according to the mentioned aptitude pertaining to the substance by which it is determinable, or according to the *proprietas* by which it is determined. When it is taken and signified according to the determinate and distinct act had through the incommunicable property, that nature is given the name *"persona"* by the Latins, and "πρόσωπον" by the Greeks. The name *persona* or πρόσωπον, then, immediately signifies that whereby the person is distinguished and numbered, which is precisely the incommunicable *proprietas*, unique cause of distinction and number in the Trinity. According, however, as it is considered to be determinable (and not insofar as determined), the nature simply receives the name *"substantia"* or "ὑπόστασις". Hypostasis here is taken according to the Latin understanding of the term equating it with substance taken

---

[592] "*Ratio istorum quattuor nominum est acceptio esse divini secundum nostrum intellectum. Natura enim divina sicut et omnis alia natura communicabilis aut accipitur in se, hoc est in sua simplicitate, aut accipitur, prout est in habente eam... si primo modo intelligatur, latine significatur nomine 'essentiae' et graece usiae. Si autem in habente intelligatur... hoc contingit dupliciter: aut enim significatur ut determinatum sub natura communi indifferenti, quam non numerant supposita nec numeratur in illis, sed indifferens et indifferenti simplicitate est in eis una secundum rem, et sic significatur nomine 'subsistentiae' sive usiosis graece, unde* BOETHIUS *in libro* DE DUABUS NATURIS IN UNA PERSONA CHRISTI *dicit, quod 'hoc subsistit quod non indiget alio, hoc est accidente, ut sit'. Et hoc est secundum compositionem vocabuli; sistit enim, quod in seipso stat proprio termino, et etiam alia sistit, ne fluant ulterius, quod autem fluit ad aliud, ut sit, non sistit, ut accidens; subsistit vero, quod stans sub aliquo sistit in illo, et hoc proprie subsistens est, et modus existentiae suae 'subsistentia' vocatur proprie*" – Albert, *Sum. theol.*, I, tr. 10, q. 43, c. 1, sol., ed. Colon., vol. 34, p. 333.

[593] "*Si autem intelligatur esse divinum in habente, prout illud distinguibile est et determinabile ex aptitudine suppositi proprietate communiter accepta, tunc significatur latine nomine 'substantiae', quae est 'subiectum'. Per hoc enim quod, ut dicit* AVICENNA, *est 'occasio alteri existendi in ipso', translatum in divinam praedicationem significat ens completum in se determinabile proprietate, et hoc vocatur 'substantia' latine et graece hypostasis*" – Albert, *Sum. theol.*, I, tr. 10, q. 43, c. 1, sol, ed. Colon., vol. 34, p. 333.

as that which exists in itself; it is the nature considered as the substantial constituent of the distinct individual – which is not to say essential constituent in the sense of the abstract nature or οὐσία, but rather the substance of this or that individual insofar as the determinable part, that is, the concrete nature, not as it is determined (which is nothing other than the πρόσωπον), but as determinable, that is, considered according as it receives the determination had from the *proprietas*. In this sense, the hypostasis is the same in each of the three persons of the Trinity, for the concrete nature which they are is one and the same. It is in this way that Trinitarian community is said to be had at the level of the nature without implying by that that the community be one of abstraction or of a universal nature. When "ὑπόστασις" is predicated of God, however, in a plural fashion, proper to the Greek use of the term asserting three hypostases, "ὑπόστασις" is intended according to the sense of substance which directly signifies the concrete nature according as it is distinguished or distinct, and not from the point of view of its distinguishability, and in this case "ὑπόστασις" stands for the person[594].

---

[594] "*Si vero accipiatur hoc actu distinctum incommunicabili proprietate, tunc significatur latine nomine 'peronae' et graece nomine prosopon, et haec est causa, quare persona et distinguitur et numeratur in tribus; actu enim distinguens facit numerum in divinis... Hypostasis autem sive substantia determinabilis quidem est proprietate et sic numerabilis; sed quia non est actu determinata, ideo non numeratur secundum Latinos, praecipue prout dicit 'substantiam subiecti' communi proprietate, prout substantia dicitur ens in seipso, non indigens alio, ut sit. Et ideo dicitur pater substantia, filius substantia, spiritus sanctus substantia, et hi tres una substantia. Et si obicitur, quod Graeci dicunt tres substantias sive tres hypostases, dicendum, quod Graeci accipiunt hypostasim ut distinctam, non ut distinguibilem tantum; unde accipiunt hypostasim pro persona*" – Albert, *Sum. theol.*, I, tr. 10, q. 43, c. 1, sol., ed. Colon., vol. 34, p. 333.

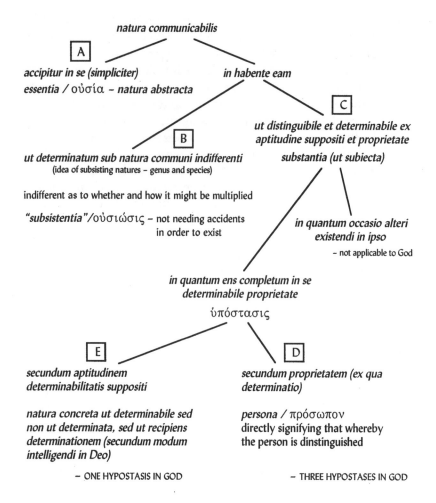

The subject, insofar as determinable only (*ut distinguibile tantum*), if it is still *substantia subiecta,* and not reduced to or confused with *substantia subiecti* (which, in the case of inferiors, is an abstract essence) seems to be very close to *"subsistentia",* since it is now considered only as under a common nature and not insofar as under certain properties which distinguish it. An important implication which can be drawn is that the entire right hand branch (*substantia*) presupposes the left (*subsistentia*); the right hand branch distinguishes itself from the left as a more particular form of subsisting involving properties which, in the case of created substance, entail accidents. Moreover, branch [B] collapses in some sense inasmuch as it is either subsumed into [C] or allocated to subsisting universals not enduring a realist metaphysic. In any case, the [B]-[C] branch is intended to represent *substantia subiecta* as distinguished from *substantia subiecti*, represented by *essentia*/οὐσία. In the Trinity, [E] is the common essence/substance signified concretely – one substance of the three persons taken in the sense of *quid*, as opposed to the same one substance being taken in the sense of *"quo est"* (which would send us back to [A]). This then is the concrete substance considered as common, or the common substance considered as concrete – assuming that such concreteness can be conceived without thereby introducing the notion of the *proprietas* (and if this were not possible, then [E] could not be different from [D] – unless, by leaving concretion behind, it were identified with [A] – and [C] and [D] would become one). But Albert reasserts the validity of branch [E] when addressing how it is that we can affirm three hypostases and one substance in God while maintaining a sense in which hypostasis and substance are the same thing[595]. The concrete substance can be signified either from the point of view of its act of subsistence, independently standing or subsisting in itself[596], no further aspect being considered[597], or from the point of view of its standing under, and subsisting by, a determinate property. It is according to the first sense that we affirm one hypostasis and substance of the three persons; and it is in the second that we say "three hypostases" or "three substances" in God[598].

Combining the observations condensed in the last two charts, we can describe essence or οὐσία, after Albert, as signifying a nature simply, i.e. neither insofar as it be distinguishable nor insofar as dis-

---

[595] Cf. Albert, *Sum. theol.*, I, tr. 10, q. 43, c. 1, obj. 3 & ad 3, ed. Colon., vol. 34, p. 332 & 334; *I Sent.*, d. 25, a. 7, sol., ed. Borgnet, vol. 25, p. 637.

[596] Note that this corresponds perfectly with the Boethian arrangement of subsistence and substance with respect to one another.

[597] *"Sunt tamen quaedam nomina in divinis, quae secundum proprietates nominum secundum modum significandi quoad nostrum intellectum dicunt distinguibile non distinctum; dicunt enim suppositum non cointellecta proprietate distinguente; et sic hypostasis dicit distinguibile, persona autem distinctum"* – Albert, *Sum. theol.*, I, tr. 10, q. 43, c. 1, ad 4, ed. Colon., vol. 34, p. 335.

[598] *"'Substantia' dicitur ut 'substans in seipsa' sive 'subsistens, nullo indigens ad hoc quod sit'; et hoc modo substantia una est trium personarum. Et hoc modo accipit eam Augustinus, et sic accidens non est substantia, et proprietas in divinis non significatur ut substantia. Dicitur etiam a 'substare proprietati determinanti', et sic trahitur ad standum pro persona, et sic dicuntur 'tres hypostases' et 'tres substantiae'"* – Albert, *Sum. theol.*, I, tr. 10, q. 43, c. 1, ad 3, ed. Colon., vol. 34, p. 334. In light of the substanding dimension of substance (*substantia ab actu substandi*), the disputed *"tres substantiae"* formula of Boethius receives its full justification. As noted by A. Pompei (op. cit., p. 234), the same expression is used sometimes by St. Augustine (cf. *De Trin.*, VII, c. 6, n. 9) and can likewise be found in both Anselm and Hilary.

tinct – either in itself or on account of something outside; οὐσία signifies the nature in precision from any differences, additions or accidents able to accrue to it in reason of something outside its own concept. "*Subsistentia*" or οὐσίωσις signifies the nature insofar as distinguishable on account of the addition of something else, and not in
virtue of the nature considered in itself; it signifies the universal able
to be rendered distinct through the addition of differences. Because
"*subsistentia*" does not include the essence of another in order to exist,
and because it underlies something which determines it, "*subsistentia*"
is also able to be referred to and used to name the person[599]. But it is
precisely this subjectival act along with that of independent existence
which characterizes substance considered not insofar as an occasion
for accidents, but from the point of view of its subsisting, as a being
complete in itself[600]. Substance or ὑπόστασις signifies the nature as
distinguishable *ex se* that is, according to its proper notion[601], but not
yet insofar as distinct; ὑπόστασις names a nature from the point of
view of standing under (its disposition and act of standing under being directly signified), and not from that of being determined or distinct, though it is indeed determined[602]. This *actus substandi* proper to
ὑπόστασις can be considered either from the point of view of the
many supposits which underlie a common essence, in which case it is
a question of many things related to something one, according to
which we affirm several substances in the Trinity, or from the point of
view of the nature as such, in which the supposits "*substant*" and
through which they have being and are substances, and in this case
substance cannot be numbered, since substance thus taken is one in
the Trinity (though in men, while still considered concretely, substance is nevertheless multiplied according to the multiplication of

---

[599] "*Richardo… accipit subsistentiam, secundum quod propositio 'sub' dicit habitudinem suppositi ad proprietatem… Unde nomen essentiale est, quod tamen ex adiuncto trahitur ad standum pro persona*" – Albert, *Sum. theol.*, I, tr. 10, q. 43, c. 1, ad 10, ed. Colon., vol. 34,
p. 335.

[600] Thus, even though substance and subsistence are names for the essence, naming
the essence according to the act proper to its subsistent mode of being, they are
appropriately predicated of the person: "*nomen subsistentiae et substantiae nomina sunt
essentialia, quae tamen propter modum significandi possunt trahi ad hoc quod stent pro persona*" – Albert, *Sum. theol.*, I, tr. 10, q. 43, c. 1, ad quaest. 4, ed. Colon., vol. 34,
p. 335.

[601] "*Ex se, hoc est ex propria ratione*" – Albert, *Sum. theol.*, I, tr. 10, q. 43, c. 1, ad quaest. 3,
ed. Colon., vol. 34, p. 334.

[602] "*Distinguibile non distinctum' non ideo dicitur, quod non sit distinctum, sed quia nomine
suo non importat proprietatem, quae demonstrat distinctionem*" – Albert, *Sum. theol.*, I,
tr. 10, q. 43, c. 2, ad 3, ed. Colon., vol. 34, p. 341.

supposits, as Peter and Paul are two men, not one). Finally, person or πρόσωπον signifies the same nature insofar as distinguishable and distinct, i.e. *qua* distinctly individuated[603].

These different modes of signifying the divine being follow upon the different ways according to which we can consider the possession of a common nature, upon the different ways in which the act of standing under is realized or exercised. The variety of modes of signification are based, however, not upon a real difference between the compared names for the nature, but according to their respective *habitudines* to the nature considered *in se* (or to the determining *proprietas* by which a comparison with the nature considered in itself is made possible – as that *proprietas* is the principle of difference)[604].

Thus we recognize a kind of conceptual composition where: οὐσία is comparable to matter, in potency toward certain differentiations achieved through the addition of a difference; οὐσίωσις (taken simply in the sense of the proper specificity of a thing, and not as the *forma totius*) is comparable to the specific form (or *proprietas*) effecting difference; and ὑπόστασις or *substantia* is comparable to the compos-

---

[603] *"Essentia sive usia significat ens nec distinguibile nec distinctum ex se vel ab alio. Subsistentia sive usiosis significat ens ex se nec distinctum nec distinguibile, sed ex alio distinguibile. Substantia vero sive hypostasis significat ens ex se distinguibile, sed non distinctum. Persona vero sive prosopon significat ens ex se distinguibile et distinctum... essentia sive usia numquam stat pro personis nec numeratur nec recipit notionalem distinctionem...* 'ens nec distinguibile nec distinctum ex se vel ab alio', significant primum simplex, quod nullo sibi adveniente distinguitur... sicut et essentia divina nec cum persona nec cum proprietate numeratur... et quod dicunt 'subsistentiam' esse 'ens ex alio distinguibile', intelligunt... in generibus et speciebus, quae quidem ens distinctum est et determinatum non ex se, sed ex alio quod est differentia constitutiva... et ratione huius dicitur 'subsistentia', quia non fluit ad aliud, ut sit. Et per hanc convenientiam, quia substat alicui determinanti se... potest trahi ad standum pro persona... Substantia enim secundum suum nomen subiectum vel suppositum significat, quod apud Aristotelem vocatur prima substantia, et hoc est quod et substat naturae communi et subicibile est accidentibus... Quae habitudo, si consideratur ex parte suppositorum, est plurium habitudo ad unum, et sic accipitur a Graecis, qui dicunt tres substantias; si autem consideratur ex parte naturae, cui substant supposita et qua habent esse ipsa supposita... ut sint et substantiae sint, tunc non potest numerari, quia hoc non est nisi unum... numeratur in suppositis creatis secundum esse naturae communis; Petrus enim et Paulus et Iohannes tres homines sunt, non unus homo... prosopon sive 'persona'... significat 'ens distinctum' discretiva proprietate"* – Albert, *Sum. theol.*, I, tr. 10, q. 43, c. 1, quaest. 3 & ad quaest. 3, ed. Colon., vol. 34, p. 332 & 334-335.

[604] *"Quia vero modus significandi provenit ex habitudine diversa et non ex re diversa... Significatur enim commune ut simplex [A] vel ut in habente, et in habente vel per habitudinem, quam habet ad commune [B], vel per habitudinem, quam habet ad proprietatem [C] secundum solam habitudinem [E], vel secundum actum [D]"* – Albert, *Sum. theol.*, I, tr. 10, q. 43, c. 1, ad 5, ed. Colon., vol. 34, p. 335.

ite resulting from the union of the οὐσία with the specific difference[605].

Hypostasis

Ὑπόστασις signifies the supposit distinguished through the *proprietas*,
and in this way names the substance *qua* "substanding", as that which
is subsistent and perfect in itself, and not as the common nature.
Substance so signified allows for the admission of several hypostases in
the Trinity. When Arius, on the other hand, declares that the Father
and Son differ in substance, he is referring to substance according to
the sense in which it indicates the common nature which is absolutely
and identically predicated of each person[606]. In contrast, hypostasis
(or *suppositum*, to use its Latin equivalent) intends the substantial referent according to a particular respect had toward what is common
and, as we shall see, involves a certain relativity in its notion.

Hypostasis and suppositum are the same thing, each designating
that which "stands under" as a determination of something common –
as the preposition "sub" indicates the relation of what is logically inferior (in extension) to what is logically superior (in extension), of what

---

[605] "Boethius... [in commento super praedicamenta] vocat enim materiam materiale, hoc est
primum genus subiectum formabile differentiis et distinguibile propriis et accidentibus, et hoc
vocat usiam, haec enim potentia est ad formationem propriorum et differentiarum. Et vocat
usiosim differentia formatum; haec enim est forma specifica, prout significatur ut universale
et non ut forma totius. Hypostasis autem sive substantia propter hoc dicitur esse compositum,
quia ambas istas habet compositiones"* – Albert, *Sum. theol.*, I, tr. 10, q. 43, c. 1, ad 7, ed.
Colon., vol. 34, p. 335.

[606] "Hypostasis enim dicit suppositum proprietate distinctum, secundum quod substantia dicitur
a substando, non a communi natura, quae substantia est, eo quod vere substat et res perfecta
est in seipsa... et tamen non differunt nisi proprietate, quia proprietas ipsa tale suppositum
sive talis hypostasis sive etiam talis substantiae est... ARIUS enim dixit aliam esse substantiam
patris et aliam filii, secundum quod substantia communis natura dicitur et quae absolute
praedicatur et non ad aliud"* – Albert, *Sum. theol.*, I, tr. 9, q. 40, c. 1, ad 1-4 & 5, ed. Colon., vol. 34, p. 308. Development of the interrelation between the notions of distinction *ad aliud* (natural distinction effecting incommunicability) and distinction
ad alius (personal or supposital distinction under a common nature) follows in the
ensuing reply: *"'aliud' vel 'alia' notent diversitatem vel alietatem nisi substantiae, quae est
hypostasis, et non illius quae naturae est communis. Et sic est, quando dicimus Petrum alium
a Paulo; non enim notatur quod alius sit in natura humana, sed idem, sed notatur, quod alius sit in persona. Et hoc patet: quotienscumque alius ab alio dicitur, proprie diversitas sive
alietas illorum in aliquo communi designatur. Non enim dicitur homo alius ab asino nisi in
hoc communi quod est animal, in quo communi non ponitur alietas, sed in suppositis illius
communis. Nec dicitur Petrus alius a Paulo, nisi sub hoc communi quod est homo. Et sic dicitur alia persona patris et alia filii in hoc communi quod est deus, quod commune est re et non
ratione tantum"* – Albert, *Sum. theol.*, I, tr. 9, q. 40, c. 1, ad 6, ed. Colon., vol. 34,
p. 308.

is particular to what is common, of what is determinate and distinct to what is indeterminate and indistinct. If hypostasis denotes what is particular and determinate, then whatever is responsible for the determination of what is common to this distinct thing will also have to fall within its notion. The only thing resulting in a determination in God are the *proprietates*, whence the determining *proprietas* must enter into the concept of hypostasis. While the *proprietas* is contained in the notion of hypostasis[607], *proprietas*, does not itself denote the *per se* subsistent thing. It is rather the role of hypostasis to do that, for which reason hypostasis is identical to substance understood as *ens per se subsistens nullo indigens*. But hypostasis names this substantial reality not only from the point of view of its *per se* subsistence, but also from that of its particularity insofar as it is the distinguished and determined thing with respect to the common nature – thus hypostasis, Albert asserts, is *"substantia cum proprietate"*, taking from the notion of substance (according to its broad Boethian sense identified with subsistence) the fact of independently subsisting in itself, and taking from the notion of the *proprietas* the fact of being determined[608]. To collocate this with the previous distinctions, we can say here that hypostasis is "substance" insofar as that which is existing *per se*, which is that which is determinable by the *proprietas* – that is, insofar as hypostasis is identified with the substantial reality which it is. It is "substance with the *proprietas*" insofar as the whole thing determined by the *proprietas* – that is, insofar as a particular determination of the substantial reality which it is, as a *res naturae* distinguished from other *re naturae*

---

[607] Which is not to say that its proper mode of signification explicitates the *proprietas* or principle of distinction. Hypostasis denotes indeed what is particular and determinate, but not necessarily from the point of view of that determinateness, since the name as such (according to its etymology) is restricted in its mode of signifying to the substanding relation, though the thing which a hypostasis is is the distinct thing itself. In respect of the reality as such of the hypostasis, its signification is indistinguishable from that of person (aside from the aspect of dignity which the latter term implies).

[608] *"Hypostasis est idem quod suppositum secundum nominis rationem,... praepositio 'sub' notat habitudinem inferioris ad superius sive particularis ad commune sive determinati et distincti ad commune indeterminatum et indistinctum. Et cum nihil faciat determinatum in divinis nisi proprietas et hypostasis dicat determinatum commune, oportet, quod in intellectu hypostasis sit proprietas determinans. Iterum, cum intellectus non quiescat in proprietate, cum secundum modum suae significationis non dicat ens ut subsistens per se, sed ens indigens alio, ut sit, hypostasis autem dicat ens in se subsistens per se, oportet, quod in intellectu hypostasis sit ens per se subsistens, nullo indigens; et hoc est substantia. Dicit enim* BOETHIUS, *quod substantia est ens per se subsistens nullo indigens, et propter hoc hypostasis est 'substantia cum proprietate'.... ut ex proprietate habeat determinationem, ex substantia autem per se subsistere et nullo indigere"* – Albert, *Sum. theol.*, I, tr. 10, q. 43, c. 2, a. 1, sol., ed. Colon., vol. 34, p. 337.

(whether that distinction follows upon a distinction in essence, i.e. the individual essence, as in creatures, or not, as in the Trinity).

Though hypostasis include an explicit reference to two notions, this does not mean that its notion is not one. Definitionally, it is broken into those components which are entailed by its own notion, just as the concept of man is reduced to those of animal and rational. Every substantial predicate, moreover, which pertains to the definitional components is also contained in the notion of the *definiendum*, as everything entailed by "animal" – such as living, corporate, ensouled, etc. – is intended in the definition of "man". Similarly, the term "substance" is placed in the definition of hypostasis such as to entail its substantial predicates. Hypostasis is a *res naturae*, through an act of nature made to be "this", this determinate thing, subsisting in itself and perfect in natural perfection. In the production of one thing from another, "this" produces "that", as determinate terms of production. Since "this" and "that" signify beings which are determinate and perfect in nature, they are designated by the term *"res naturae"*, res naturae signifying a self-contained determinate being constituted through an operation of nature. Consequently, *res naturae* also entails that by which such determination occurs, and this is precisely the *proprietas*[609]. The *proprietas*, however, is not an additional reality, it is not something added to the determinate thing of nature; it is simply that by which the thing of nature is understood to possess its singular distinct mode of existence, that by which the *res naturae* is distinguished from others. It is that by which the distinct thing of nature is in fact distinct – and in this sense, it is not necessary that the *proprietas* itself be something other than the hypostasis *in re*, though they differ at least in mode of signification. In creatures the *proprietas* – that is, a creature's principles of individuation – are (at least upon first consideration) not identical to the supposit, the individuated thing; but in God there can clearly be no difference *in re* between the individual and the "individualizing" *proprietas* (which, strictly speaking,

---

[609] *"Unumquodque diffinitur et describitur per proximum suum superius, quod substantialiter praedicatur de ipso et quo supposito omnia substantialia praedicata consequentia ad ipsum supponuntur; et hoc patet in diffinitione hominis, qui diffinitur per 'animal', quia animali supposito omnia consequentia supponuntur, ut vivum, substantia corporea animata, corpus et substantia. Et similiter in diffinitione hypostasis, cum ponitur 'substantia'... ut dicit HILARIUS, est 'res naturae', actu naturae ad hoc quod hoc sit, determinata, 'in seipsa subsistens' et naturali perfectione perfecta... hic producit hunc, et primi termini talis productionis designantur per 'hic' et 'hunc'. Et quia 'hic' et 'hunc' dicunt ens ratum et perfectum apud naturam, ideo designantur per hunc terminum 'res naturae'. Unde res naturae dicit primum ens ratum constitutum opere naturae; et id quod sequitur ad illud, est proprietas determinans ipsum"* – Albert, *Sum. theol.*, I, tr. 10, q. 43, c. 2, a. 1, ad 1, ed. Colon., vol. 34, p. 338.

does not "individualize" but accounts for the singular mode of existence proper to the person).

Having isolated the *proprietas* as – along with the act of subsistence – properly characterizing the hypostasis, it seems we may have neglected the category of created persons while focusing uniquely upon the Trinity. But the term *proprietas* has been intended all along as susceptible to being considered in more than one way. While the term *proprietas* refers first of all to individualizing or particularizing factors in the context of the Trinity, it can be used to signify the individualizing/particularizing aspects for any person. In this way, when person or hypostasis is defined as *substantia cum proprietate* we are signaling what is essential to all persons as such. The *proprietas*, Albert tells us, must be understood in the sense of *proprietas incommunicabilis aliis*, according to which the *proprietas* can be found in but one individual and suffices to distinguish one thing of nature from another. In creatures, what is incommunicable and unable to be assumed by another individual is the set of individuating accidents (or whatever else is put forward as a principle of individuation). These individuating aspects, then, are the *proprietas* for the created individual. In God, however, where there can be no true individuation[610], the *proprietas* is identified with nothing other than the relational reality by which one person is distinguished from another. In either case, an incommunicable existence is said to be conferred by an incommunicable reality[611].

Returning to the definition of hypostasis as *substantia cum proprietate*, we must note that "substance" is to be taken in a special way. Certainly, as we have already explained, the term substance denotes *per se* existence, but precisely from what point of view do we signify the *per se* existent thing? The *"cum proprietate"* gives us the answer. Hypostasis, like person, names the subsistent thing which is determinate. That determination is possessed in virtue of the *proprietas*, the notion of which is joined to that of *substantia* in order to denote the determinate thing – the determinate thing being *substantia cum proprietate*.

---

[610] Cf. infra, "THE TERMS 'SINGULAR', 'INDIVIDUAL' AND 'PARTICULAR' IN GOD", p. 373.

[611] *"Dico autem 'proprietas incommunicabilis' alii, quae licet in creatis vocetur accidens individuans, quod sic est in uno, quod impossibile est in alio inveniri, tamen, quia in divinis proprie non est individuatio, loco individuantis ponitur 'proprietas incommunicabilis', quae rei naturae secundum modum intelligendi confert singularis existentiae modum, qua una res naturae separatur ab alia. Et illa duo sunt in intellectu hypostasis; quae quia non sunt duo secundum rem, sed secundum modum intelligendi tantum, ideo intellectus hypostasis non simpliciter est compositus, quia non est compositi, sed simplicis secundum rem... Unde non ex aequo veniunt in diffinitionem eius, sed unum ut ens subsistens ratum in natura, quod est substantia, et alterum ut determinans et incommunicabilis existentiae modum conferens"* – Albert, *Sum. theol.*, I, tr. 10, q. 43, c. 2, a. 1, ad 1, ed. Colon., vol. 34, p. 338.

While the term "person" signifies that determinate thing precisely *as determinate,* "hypostasis" does so according to its special act of substanding. It follows from this that *substantia* of itself does not necessarily signify the determinate thing as such; even if it does refer to the determinate thing of nature, it does not necessarily do so according as it is determinate – to do so, the notion of *substantia* must be united with that of incommunicable propriety. Consequently the *substantia* of our definition, taken by itself, signifies the determinate thing in a way not yet explicitating its determinate mode of existence – it signifies the substance rather *ut determinabile.* This "substance" is not, however, to be confused with the *substantia communis.* We are concerned with the substance being determined by a particular *proprietas,* which, although identical to the common substance *in re,* is not identical in mode of signification. But this determinate substance taken from the point of view of its determinability is neither yet identical in mode of signification with "hypostasis" or "person". The latter name the determinate substance, respectively, as being determined and determinate. Hypostasis, then, also differs from person inasmuch as the first represents a sort of passive undergoing in order to be determined, while the latter signifies according as something is wholly determinate, and not according to the act of determining – i.e. not as being determined. We have three ways of considering the substantial reality:

As *substantia communi – vel essentia*	which is the substantial reality signified as common and not determined.
As the determinate thing taken *as thing*	which can be taken either absolutely – in which case it is the substance *ut determinabile,* which sends us practically back to the essence (though it is a question here of the common essence insofar as concretely instantiated).
	or hypostatically – in which case it is the thing as determined by the *proprietas.* This we signify by the term "hypostasis".
As the determinate thing taken as *determinate*	which we signify by the term "person".

The sense of the term "hypostasis" is thus clarified in the *Summa theologica.* Henceforth the term is not to be understood in the sense according to which it is unnumbered in the Trinity, that is, as the concrete substantial reality of the *quis est* ([E] of the previous diagram), nor in the sense in which it is identical to "person" in its mode of signifying, explicitly naming either distinctness or the principle of distinctness ([D] of the previous diagram), but as the distinct thing according as it is the subject of the actual determination accomplished by the *proprietas* (thus situating "hypostasis" somewhere between [E] and [D]).

The substance as determined by the *proprietas* is the same thing as the substance taken as determinate, however there is a slight difference in mode of signification. The substance as what is determined distinguishes itself as undergoing determination – it is that with respect to which the *proprietas* determines. The substance taken as determinate, signified by the term "person", is not said to undergo the determination of a *proprietas*, for it is precisely "person" because the substance which was determinable has been determined, but not because it itself, according to its own proper mode of signification, is being determined. Person is the determinate thing *as determinate*, hypostasis is the determinate thing as being determined. "Person" signifies the same substance, but insofar as individualized and from the point of view of its individuality, and thus explicitly indicates the principles of individuation (or *proprietas*) making one to be the person he or she is – incommunicable particularity being emphasized.

Possible objections

We encounter an objection to Albert's definition of hypostasis, based upon the fact that his definition entails a quidditative foundation for the *proprietas*. But since the *"quod"* is identical to the *"quis"* and, materially speaking, there really is no *quod est* in the Trinity, the only possible substantial foundation for the *proprietates* could be the *quis*. Thus, when we say that *"substantia cum paternitate"* makes the Father and *"substantia cum filiatione"* makes the Son, it seems that the same thing said to underlie the incommunicable *proprietates* belonging to the different persons of the Trinity will be one same *quis est*, which is impossible[612]. Albert simply responds that this does not follow[613] – the ar-

---

[612] *"Si autem dicat 'quod est', cum in divinis non sit 'quod est' materiale, oportet, quod id quod est, sit idem quod 'qui est', et sit absolutum et sit idem in tribus. Et sic 'quod est' cum paternitate facit personam patris et cum filiatione facit personam filii... Idem ergo videtur substare oppositis proprietatibus... etiam intellectus non admittit, quia sic sequeretur, quod idem mas-*

gument is easy enough to refute on the basis of an articulation of modes of signification. But we might add that the distinction just made between the several senses of substance also responds to the problem. What underlies paternity is the substance of the Father as determined by paternity, that is, the substance taken hypostatically, and this is not identical in *modus intelligendi* to the substance of the Father absolutely considered. Nor is it identical in mode of signification to the *quis* of the Father, for the *quis est* or person consists in both the substance said to underlie the *proprietas* and the *proprietas* itself.

A different objection might be raised that, according as hypostasis was said to denote what is particular and determinate with respect to what is common and indeterminate, it appears that hypostasis is a particularization of something universal. Now we have already seen that, wherever we have something universal and particular, we have a duality of natures, for they are two different things of nature, one universal, one particular[614]. But this situation obtains only for composite substances. In God, there can be no such duality. Consequently, when explaining the community according to which several hypostases share the divine nature, we explicitate it in terms of a community of being – in contrast with the universal (and accidental) community proper to men. But furthermore, when we consider each person as sharing in the community of personhood, and personhood seems to extend in a universal way to several particulars, the community in question is neither one of strict universality, but rather that of a *habitus* or *proportio* to something one[615]. This *habitus* of the individual person with respect to the common notion of person is had, for each person, through the incommunicable *proprietas*. The thing of nature which the Father is is determinable as such, and able to be conceived as determinate, precisely through an incommunicable personal property; likewise, that *res naturae* which is the Son is also determinable, and able to be conceived as determinate, in virtue of an incommunicable *proprietas personalis*[616].

---

culine, qui designatur per 'qui est', esset pater et filius et spiritus sanctus" – Albert, *Sum. theol.*, I, tr. 10, q. 43, c. 2, a. 1, obj. 3, ed. Colon., vol. 34, p. 336.

[613] *"Ad id quod obicitur, quod secundum hoc idem est, qui substat paternitati, filiationi et spirationi, dicendum, quod non sequitur; non enim idem est nisi in communi"* – Albert, *Sum. theol.*, I, tr. 10, q. 43, c. 2, a. 1, ad 3, ed. Colon., vol. 34, p. 338.

[614] *"Id quod est in uno, et quod est in pluribus, non sunt idem re sicut universale et particulare"* – Albert, *Sum theol.*, II, tr. 10, q. 43, c. 2, a. 1, ad 16, ed. Colon., p. 340.

[615] Cf. infra, "SHARING IN THE COMMON NOTION OF PERSON", p. 315 (especially "COMMUNITY OF PROPORTION", p.320).

[616] *"Ubi est universale et particulare, ibi sunt duae naturae re, quarum una est universalis et altera particularis, et una non est alia. Et hoc non potest esse nisi in compositis. Compositio*

As to the predication of "hypostasis" of Father, Son and Holy Spirit, since the hypostatization and *quis est* of each is distinctly constituted in a unique way, it follows that the commonly predicated notion of "hypostasis" or "person" is not univocally said of the three. They are each hypostases in different ways, since the particularization is achieved differently. Nevertheless, they all possess the same proportion to the common nature, namely that of being "particulars" – or, more precisely, singular existents – of that common nature. The name "hypostasis" thus predicates one and the same *respectus* possessed by each of the three persons with respect to the divine nature, a *respectus* to the common nature possessed by each according to proportion[617]:

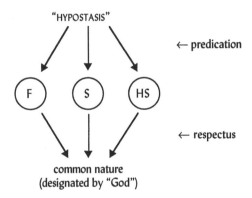

Back to defining hypostasis

When we define hypostasis as *substantia cum proprietate*, "hypostasis" does not signify substance to which something is added, for the notion of addition implies a conjunction of diverse things, and no such

---

autem in divinis non est. Est tamen ibi commune habitudinis sive respectus sive proportionis ad unum, quia sicut res naturae, quae est pater, determinabilis est incommunicabili proprietate, ita res naturae, quae est filius, incommunicabili proprietate determinabilis est et similiter res naturae, quae est spiritus sanctus" – Albert, *Sum. theol.*, I, tr. 10, q. 43, c. 2, a. 1, ad 3, ed. Colon., vol. 34, p. 338.

617 "Praedicatur idem et unum similitudine habitudinis sive proportionis, quod quamvis non sit vere univocum, eo quod non est natura una, sicut nomen unum est in his de quibus praedicatur... res naturae, quae est pater, et res naturae, quae est filius, et res naturae, quae est spiritus sanctus, uno et simili respectu secundum proportionem se habet ad naturam divinam, quae designatur per hoc nomen 'deus', et tali una ratione respectus praedicatur hoc nomen 'hypostasis' de tribus" – Albert, *Sum. theol.*, I, tr. 10, q. 43, c. 2, a. 1, ad 4, ed. Colon., vol. 34, p. 338. Cf. infra, "COMMUNITY OF PROPORTION", p. 320.

diversity can obtain in the simplicity of God, where nothing is nor can be added. The constitutive terms defining hypostasis differ, however according to mode of signification. In the creature, the two terms – it appears upon first consideration – do differ as one thing added to another, in light of composition[618]. Now, in the Trinity, "substance + property" (in the sense of expressing "substance *to which* the *proprietas* is joined") does not signify a real addition, but only a *modus intelligendi* whereby we conceive the substance as determined, and this by an *rationally* distinguishable determinant, whence the hypostasis itself is really the determinate thing without composition. In the realm of natural creatures, despite the composition between nature and designated matter (as a particularizing *proprietas*[619]), something similar may also be said. Individual matter, it may be said, is not something added to my nature or substance, because it actually constitutes (along with the form of the soul) my substance. Consequently, "my hypostasis" ≠ "substance + property", since the substance already includes that property; that substance is composed of "my individualizing *proprietas* + my soul". Hypostasis, then, from this point of view, is identifiable with "substance" *simpliciter* – substance here being taken as constituted of both soul and individuated matter, that is, as "*my* substance". A certain composition can be said to be signified by hypostasis if substance not be taken in that sense but rather as the common substance, i.e. the common human nature. Then hypostasis = substance + individuating properties. But "substance" in this case is not equivalent to "substance as determined" – such as it was understood in the Trinitar-

---

[618]   "*Hypostasis non dicit substantiam aliquo addito, quia cum nihil addatur sibi vel addi possit, oportet quod ubi est additio, ibi sit diversorum coniunctio, nihil autem diversum est in divinis propter indifferentiam maximae simplicitatis; tamen est ibi diversus modus significandi... In humanis enim compositio est, et ideo potest ibi esse additio, in divinis autem omnimoda simplicitas, quae non permittit ibi esse additionem. Unde cum dicitur 'hypostasis est deus', idem est in praedicato et subiecto sub alio modo significandi... Hoc autem non est sic quando dicitur 'Petrus est homo' vel 'Paulus est homo'... natura proprii non est natura communis*" – Albert, *Sum. theol.*, I, tr. 10, q. 43, c. 1, ad 5 & 6, ed. Colon., vol. 34, p. 339.

A fundamental difference lies in the fact that, for God, the constitutive common nature predicated of the hypostasis (as, for example, when we say "*hypostasis est deus*") is identically the same *in re* with the hypostasis, while, in men, the common nature predicated of the hypostasis (as when we say "*Petrus est homo*" or "*Paulus est homo*") is not identical with the proper nature which the hypostasis is. In creatures, the common, absolute nature is not identical to the hypostatic or individual nature, not even *in re* – though the individual nature is only logically distinct from and therefore one *in re* with the common nature as it exists in the individual (which, however, ≠ the common nature absolutely considered).

[619]   We cannot enter here into a discussion of the principle of individuation or singularity. For the sake of the current argument, we simply treat the notion of discrete matter as representative of that principle whatever it might turn out to be.

ian context where we distinguished the term substance (joined to the *proprietas* – i.e. *cum proprietate*) as the thing of nature as being determined, while the *proprietas* was the same *res naturae* as determining. Substance taken in inferiors as the universal nature is rather the common nature as <u>un</u>determined – whence its commonality. Now we may properly speak in this way, and a real composition is seen to occur between substance thus taken (absolutely) and the individualizing properties constituted by designated matter. But there is nothing to prevent us from looking at the hypostasis according to its substance *as hypostatized*, i.e. as individualized, and this is the composite itself. This, it is true, is still, at least according to *modus intelligendi*, distinguishable from its individualizing component; my concrete individual nature, from a certain point of view, is not the same as the matter individuating me. Nevertheless, hypostasis here ≠ "substance + *proprietas*", but rather "substance *cum proprietate*", since the *proprietas* adds nothing to the notion of substance (which, at this particularized level, presupposes the *proprietas*). In the context of the Trinity, Albert remarks: *"hypostasis est 'substantia cum proprietate' – et non 'substantia et proprietas'"*[620]. In the Trinity, this inclusive sense of the hypostatized substance is easier to admit since there can be no kind of composition in God. It seems, however, that, on account of the composition observed in creatures between the common substance and principles of individuation, one has overlooked the fact that, from the point of view of the "substance *as determined*" – and this is what we mean by "hypostasis" – no composition takes place (hypostasis here is nothing other than the person). There is, therefore, no diversity to be admitted between the hypostatized substance and the individualizing conditions, since there is nothing added by the latter to the notion of the former. The individualizing components, as individualizing the common nature (since the individual nature is already individualized) are indeed distinct from the common nature. They are furthermore distinct in reason from the individualized nature, as the individualizing to the individualized, and in this sense they are considered qualitatively, i.e. as specifying the individual within a species. But when they are signified quidditatively – and here is the specific (or individual) difference signified as a whole –, they are convertible with the hypostasis itself, in the same way as an ultimate specific difference is convertible with its

---

[620] *"Dicit enim Boethius, quod substantia est ens per se subsistens nullo indigens, et propter hoc hypostasis est 'substantia cum proprietate' – et non 'substantia et proprietas' –, ut ex proprietate habeat determinationem, ex substantia autem per se subsistere et nullo indigere"* – Albert, *Sum. theol.*, I, tr. 10, q. 43, c. 2, a. 1, sol., ed. Colon., vol. 34, p. 337.

species. The compositely defined reality, were it definable, would be something like "Socratesed (or Socratic) rational-animal", that is, the Socratically qualified substance. This can be signified quidditatively as "the Socratic" wherein what had operated as a qualitative term has now been treated quidditatively in the sense of an ultimate specific difference (specifying or contracting the species man to this individual man) which is convertible with the entire individual primary substance. Since that which "Socratizes" is *materia signata* as principle of individuation, we can speak of this matter either as an individualizing part, signified qualitatively or *ut determinans*, or as a whole, in the sense described above. When signified as a part, "the Socratic" is like *"proprietas"* in the Trinity inasmuch as it determines the substance. Here the substance is distinguishable from "the Socratic" as its bearer; but it is still the individual substance, and not the common human substance, which bears these individualizing conditions. This primary substance, substance as bearer, substance as determined, is identical to "the Socratic" when the latter is signified as a whole, again like the *proprietas* in the Trinity which always signifies as a whole and *ut idem.*

Note that while, in the Trinity, the *proprietas* is, from every point of view, the hypostasis, substantially and essentially, this is not the case for human individuals[621]. In man, the *proprietas* is individual matter, which, taken in itself, cannot be identical to the hypostasis since that hypostasis consists of this soul + this matter[622]. Certainly, the parts of a definition can signify either as a whole or as a part, but the things from which those definitional parts are taken (such as soul and body in the definition of man, or human nature and designated matter in the definition of the human hypostasis) cannot be signified as a whole since they are precisely the parts of the composite being defined (≠ parts of the definition). The parts of the definition of the "individual man" are "individual" and "man" (analogous to "rational" and "animal" in the definition of man). But these are taken from manness (or humanity) and individuality (or designated matter), neither of which can be said to be convertible with the "individual man" composed of

---

[621] *"In divinis proprietas est hypostasis substantialiter et essentialiter, quod non est in humanis, et hoc est propter omnimodam simplicitatem"* – Albert, *Sum. theol.*, I, tr. 10, q. 43, c. 2, a. 2, sol., ed. Colon., vol. 34, p. 341.

[622] The human hypostasis is "human nature + this matter", which can be understood either as "secondary substance + individual matter" or as *substantia prima cum materia signata*, which is the supposit. An appropriate definition would be: "the individually materialized human substance", where either term in the definition (the general or the specific) necessarily implies both the soul and the body and the difference is convertible with the human hypostasis.

them. What was earlier said to signify the whole was "the Socratic", for example, which corresponds to the specifying part of the definition "the individual", i.e. "the individually materialized".

As concerns the predication of the term hypostasis, as was the case in the Trinity, in man too it is a question of proportionality. This is because the hypostasis is the particular underlying the common nature, that is, "the Socratized rational-animal", which is the same as the individual of a rational substance. We are, of course, at the level of defining person, since person is the individual. But – and this is the interesting point of the consideration – no two persons are person in the same way, since the criterion of individualization is realized in different ways, for example through "Socratization" or "Platonization". Consequently, predication of "individual rational animal" is not univocal as in the predication of "rational animal", since the nature "individual rational animal" is not one but diverse. The result is a community of proportionality – we are all hypostases on account of a common *respectus* shared toward the truly common universal nature. And that *respectus* or habitude is precisely that of being particular individualizations of "rational animal" [623]:

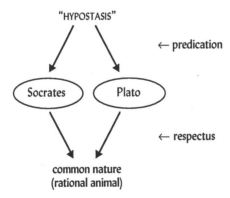

We are all men (in the sense of being human; ≠ in the sense of being human supposits) in the same way, but we are all hypostases or persons in different ways. It is the *proprietas* which is responsible for constituting the hypostasis in a determinate species of personal being, i.e. as a determinate individual. As a consequence, different *proprietates*

---

[623] Cf. infra, "SHARING IN THE COMMON NOTION OF PERSON", p. 315 (especially p. 323-324).

determine different hypostases[624]. The human nature of Christ – or rather Christ himself – is fully human indeed, but he has a particularly unique way of realizing individualization. Human personality or hypostatization is inevitable, but because that event occurs within the dynamics of Christ's divine filiation (that is, the unique *proprietas* of the Word), it follows that no separate hypostasis derives from the individualization of his human nature[625].

The "standing under" proper to primary and secondary substance

Boethius affirmed that substance is called hypostasis inasmuch as it "stands under" certain things. He also informs us that a subsistent reality is capable of "standing under" other things only in the context of particularity, that is, only when the subsisting essence in question is particularized. Thus, as Albert points out, the substance of which Boethius is speaking necessarily refers to primary substance which alone is denominated *ens perfectum et ratum apud naturam*. The "substanding" act of primary substance is nevertheless extended somehow to the substance taken as secondary substance, insofar as secondary substance is in primary substance according to being (for which reason, when we say that Socrates is white, we are also able to say that man is white). Accordingly, the name hypostasis, which signifies according to the act of standing under, is ascribable at once to primary and secondary substance: to the former as that which principally stands beneath other things; to the latter as that which is logically implied (by the presence of primary substance) as a natural (i.e. essential) "substrate". The former – primary substance – is furthermore more properly called hypostasis inasmuch as it underlies the secondary substance itself. Finally, this latter – secondary substance – is able to receive the name hypostasis only insofar as it exists in the subsistent primary substance, where it is only logically distinguishable from the latter, the supposit. Considered in itself and according to its own proper mode of signification, secondary substance is no hypostasis. In

---

[624] *"Constituit enim proprietas hypostasim in determinata specie esse personalis, ut patrem in esse patris et filium in esse filii, et ideo necesse est, quod diversae et oppositae proprietates diversas determinent hypostases"* – Albert, *Sum. theol.*, I, tr. 10, q. 43, c. 2, a. 2, sol., ed. Colon., vol. 34, p. 341.

[625] The elaboration of this perspective shall constitute the heart of our future investigation of personality in Christ.

man, moreover, in contrast with the Trinity, secondary substance thus
considered is really distinct from particular primary substance[626].

The natural referent of "hypostasis", its direct and indirect *significatum*

In response to why saying "three hypostases" does not necessarily entail three natures, given that hypostasis signifies a nature or substance,
Albert clarifies the strict definition of hypostasis. He begins by explicating the different senses in which one thing implies another. Generally speaking there are two ways in which this is able to happen: by
proper implication, or by common association. The former case admits of two possibilities: first, when one concept directly implies another because the second is contained in the concept of the first and
entailed by its being – as when to say "man" necessarily implies "animal" –; second, when whatever is attributed to one is also attributed to
the other – as, for example, when the attribution of numerical plurality to "man" entails its subsequent attribution to "animal", "three
men" entailing "three animals". In both instances, the subject of
proper implication is implied in a direct way. In the case of common
association, on the other hand, what is implied by one thing is not
directly implied, but only obliquely or indirectly. This occurs when
one thing is signified as being *of* another, the other therefore being
indirectly signified. In this way, then – when *substantia* is understood
as standing for "nature" –, we are to understand *substantia* in the proposed definition of hypostasis as the indirectly signified reality *of*
which its direct *significatum* is (the direct *significatum* of "hypostasis",
namely the suppositum, being *of* that nature). But the term *substantia*
in Albert's definition was not meant to directly stand for substance as
nature, but rather for substance as primary substance, that is, as the
subsistent being determined by the *proprietas*. Accordingly, what
seems to be directly signified by the definition *substantia cum proprietate*
is substance, but substance as determined, and in this sense it is acceptable to consider substance as a direct *significatum* of the hypostasis
and therefore as properly implied by the same. On the other hand, if

---

[626] *"Dicit Boethius, 'substantia, cum substat in particularibus, hypostasis dicitur', intelligit de
'prima substantia'... Haec enim non nisi in particularibus accipitur, et illa sola subsistit ut
ens perfectum et ratum apud naturam; et ab illa confertur etiam 'secundae substantiae' substare, secundum quod est secunda substantia in prima per esse, sicut dicimus, quod homo est
albus, quia Socrates est albus; et ideo illa principaliter 'hypostasis', hoc est suppositum, vocatur. In divinis tamen nulla diversitas est inter suppositum et id cui substat sive supponitur,
nisi in modo significandi"* – Albert, *Sum. theol.*, I, tr. 10, q. 43, c. 2, a. 1, ad 7, ed. Colon., vol. 34, p. 339.

substantia intends rather the common nature, then the definition *substantia cum proprietate* requires modification in order to clarify that substance – taken as nature – is but an indirect *significatum* of hypostasis, the direct *significatum* of which is the supposit. The resulting rendition of the definition would be *suppositum naturae communis cum proprietate*[627]. Albert himself affirms that hypostasis says "nature", but only according to common association, that is, as an indirectly signified reality: *"hypostasis dicit 'naturam', dicit enim 'suppositum naturae communis', non quod est natura communis"*[628]. As a consequence, it does not follow that a multiplication of hypostases results in a corresponding multiplication of common natures; rather, several hypostases can imply several supposits of a single substance. Thus Albert reveals the why for what we already knew – namely, that by numbering supposits we are not compelled to number the common nature – because the intelligible content of the terms does not entail such a multiplication at the level of the absolute substance. Finally, although substance (absolute substance, that is) is said to be signified by the term "hypostasis" only indirectly, Albert makes no real error in his formulation of the definition as *substantia cum proprietate*, not only because – as we have seen – "substance" can be taken as determined (particular and primary), but also because, on account of divine simplicity, the suppositum and common substance are one and the same thing[629].

---

[627] Making it clear that the sense of substance mentioned in the definition of hypostasis is determined substance (primary substance in creatures), whence the expression *cum proprietate* in preference to *et proprietas*.

[628] *"Unum dicit alterum tripliciter, proprie scilicet et communiter; proprie dupliciter, scilicet quando unum est in intellectu alterius et actu in ipso ut ens de esse eius, sicut 'homo' dicit 'animal', quia animal est in intellectu hominis et de esse ipsius; secundo, quando quidquid attribuitur uni, attribuitur alteri; et in his duobus modis verum est, quod multiplicato uno multiplicatur et reliquum; unde 'tres homines' sunt 'tria animalia'. Tertio modo dicitur unum dicere alterum large sive communiter, quando scilicet primum dicit significatum ut aliquid alterius, et tunc non dicit in recto, sed in obliquo. Et sic 'hypostasis' dicit 'naturam'; dicit enim 'suppositum naturae communis', non quod est natura communis"* – Albert, *Sum. theol.*, I, tr. 10, q. 43, c. 2, a. 1, ad 8, ed. Colon., vol. 34, p. 339.

[629] *"Si natura communis una et eadem est in suppositis, non sequitur quod si numeratur suppositum, numeretur et natura communis, et... hypostasis dicat substantiam in obliquo, non sequitur, si tres sunt hypostases, quod tres sint substantiae, sed sequitur, quod tres sunt unius substantiae. Et si obicitur, quod in divinis 'hypostasis' est 'substantia' secundum rectum, dicendum, quod hoc est ex modo dicendi vel significandi, secundum quod in divinis, ubi est omnimoda simplicitas. In humanis autem non est sic, quia ibi suppositum non est natura communis per identitatem; aliter enim esset idem communicabile et incommunicabile"* – Albert, *Sum theol.*, II, tr. 10, q. 43, c. 2, a. 1, ad 8, ed. Colon., p. 339. Again, as concerns the Trinity, *"essentia oblique cadit in intellectum hypostasis, nec cadit ut diversum re, sed ut idem sub alio modo significandi"* – Albert, *Sum theol.*, II, tr. 10, q. 43, c. 2, a. 1, ad 15, ed. Colon., p. 340.

The precise denotation of "hypostasis", its distinctive mode of signification

Now we said that it was not in virtue of the act of being distinct that a supposit receives the name hypostasis, but rather in virtue of its disposition of standing under. This was the original reason for identifying the Greek term "hypostasis" with the Latin *"substantia"*, for both signify according to the act of standing under (though *substantia* does more than that and is able to signify according to another act quite distinct from that of standing under). It is time to specify what is most proper to the mode of signification of both of these terms in order to see the difference between them – for they are not identical in all respects. To begin with, "substance" is used as the name of a predicament and as the name of primary substances (which are nothing other – to use a more neutral term – than subsistences). According as the term designates a predicament, "substance" signifies that which is complete with its own act of existence without being referred according to its essence to something else. According, however, as the term refers to primary substance, "substance" signifies that which principally stands under other things after the manner of a substrate (in a logical sense at least)[630]. Now, that which is signified by "substance" according as it is the name of a predicament is not what is signified by the name "hypostasis". Hypostasis rather signifies the same thing as substance only when substance is taken in the second sense. And even if it is the case that "substance" taken in the second sense – as standing under – necessarily implies what is proper to "substance" taken as a predicament (since a nature cannot stand beneath other things as an occasion for their existence unless it itself exists *per se*), it does not mean that what is proper to the mode of signification of "hypostasis" must include both aspects. In fact, according to strict mode of signification, the notion of *per se* existence – subsistence as an ontological perfection – is not included in the concept of "hypostasis". This is why the Greeks could readily affirm several hypostases in the single ontological perfection of the Godhead, while the Latins, because their notion of substance implied the perfection of nature (over and above the act of standing under), in no way wanted to admit several substances in God. Hypostasis, as it were, signifies nothing more

---

[630] Cf. supra, in the chapter on Boethius, "SPECIFIC ASPECTS OF SUBSTANTIA AND SUBSISTENTIA", p. 121.

than the supposit *qua* supposit, *qua* subjectival – and this we designate "*qui est*" or *res naturae*[631].

Qui est signifies the supposit *in ratione suppositi.* It signifies, therefore, the person or *quis est* precisely insofar as that which underlies the *proprietas* of determination; it is the supposit of the person *qua* supposit and not *qua* distinct. It is the function of the name "person" or *quis est* to signify the supposit of the person *qua* distinct. *Qui est*, then, signifies the thing of nature as undetermined in personal being (i.e. it does not signify it as determinate); *quis est* signifies the same *res naturae* as determined in personal being. The *qui est* is in fact determinate, but it names the determined thing according to the logical priority of its being that to which the determination of the determining property applies. *Qui* is the what of the who *qua* who, i.e. *qua* this person – it is the whatness of the person or *quis* as such, the *quod* of the *quis* as *quis* (≠ *quod* of the *quis* absolutely speaking). It is the "hypostatic *quod*", analogous to the substance hypostatically considered – that is, the determinate substance as being determined. *Quis*, on the other hand, is the person or supposit *as determined.*

When we affirm of substance in the Trinity that it is wholly singular and not plural, the sense of "substance" in this case signifies the substance as *quo est* or *quod est*, and not as *quis est* or *qui est*. When, on the other hand, we affirm a plurality of hypostases in God, we are referring to the substance only insofar as it be signified according to the act of standing under, which is the substance as *qui est* – and this is the substance hypostatically conceived, i.e. the substance as being determined by the *proprietas*[632]. Some summarization would be helpful:

[631] "*Hypostasis et substantia sint idem, secundum quod substantia a substare dicitur, tamen modum significandi non habent eundem secundum usum nominum. Substantia enim et nomen est praedicamenti et nomen est substantiae primae. Secundum quod est nomen praedicamenti, dicitur substantia res per se ens, ad aliud non fluens nec alio indigens, ut sit... et hoc non dicit hypostasis. Secundum autem quod dicit primam substantiam, non dicit nisi substare principaliter et maxime; et cum substare non possit, nisi quod per se est alio non indigens, tunc oportet, quod substantia primo modo dicta sit in intellectu substantiae secundo modo dictae; et hoc non est in intellectu hypostasis. Et ideo, licet Graeci dicerent tres hypostases, Latini nullo modo volunt dicere tres substantias... Hypostasis autem non dicit nisi suppositum in ratione suppositi, et hoc est 'qui est' sive res naturae*" – Albert, *Sum. theol.*, I, tr. 10, q. 43, c. 2, a. 2, ad 1, ed. Colon., vol. 34, p. 341.

[632] "*Tamen non dicit substantiam in ratione prima nominis substantiae, sed in ratione secunda, prout res naturae substantia est, et hoc est suppositum in ratione suppositi, prout designatur hoc nomine 'qui est'. Sic autem designatum multiplicatur in personis... Quod enim dicitur, quod substantiale nomen de omnibus in summa dicitur singulariter et non pluraliter, intelligitur de his quae significant substantiam ut 'quo est' vel 'quod est', et non de his, quae significant substantiam ut 'quis est' vel 'qui est'. 'Qui est' enim dicit rem naturae non in specie personali determinatam, 'quis est' autem eandem rem naturae dicit determinatam in specie*

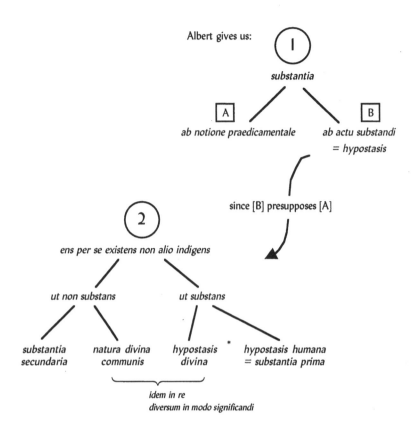

Albert gives us:

(1)

substantia

[A]   [B]

ab notione praedicamentale   *ab actu substandi*
                                  = *hypostasis*

since [B] presupposes [A]

(2)

ens per se existens non alio indigens

ut non substans   *ut substans*

substantia   *natura divina*   *hypostasis*   *hypostasis humana*
secundaria   *communis*   *divina* *   = *substantia prima*

idem in re
diversum in modo significandi

*"Hypostasis" names the substance here only from the point of view of
standing under – it is "the substanding" that it directly signifies. It is
indeed the *per se* existent, but from another point of view.

Strictly speaking, any consideration of *ens per se existens non alio indigens* must
already be limited to primary substance; and neither of the original divisions,
substantia ab notio praedicamentale and *substantia ab actu substandi*, strictly
speaking, pertain to secondary substance. Consequently, we must separate
substance as follows:

secundum esse personale" – Albert, *Sum. theol.*, I, tr. 10, q. 43, c. 2, a. 2, ad 2, ed. Colon., vol. 34, p. 341.

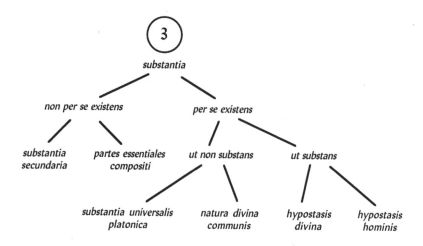

Retaking the previous table specifying the various senses of *substan-tia*[633] and collating it with the last observations pertaining to the differences between *quo/quod*, *qui*, and *quis*, casts additional light on those distinctions:

---

[633] Cf. supra, p. 222 (under "ʜʏᴘᴏsᴛᴀsɪs").

"SUBSTANCE" MAY BE TAKEN AND SIGNIFIED:

As *substantia communis – vel essentia* *"quo est"*	which is the substantial reality signified as common and not determined.
As the determinate thing taken *as thing*	which can be taken either absolutely – in which case it is the substance *ut determinabile*, which sends us practically back to the essence (though it is a question here of the common essence insofar as concretely instantiated). *"quod est"*
	or hypostatically – in which case it is the thing as determined by the *proprietas*. This we signify with the term "hypostasis". *"qui est"*
As the determinate thing taken as *determinate* *"quis est"*	which we signify by the term "person", and which has its constitutive *ratio* from the *proprietas*.

Logical priorities

The notion of hypostasis precedes that of person inasmuch as suppositness – that is, being a distinct thing of nature – is a logical presupposition to the act of a *proprietas* through which personal distinction is apprehended (similar to the way in which the concept of substance precedes that of accident). The suppositness of the Father, for example, is logically prior to the generative act founding the *proprietas* which constitutes the thing which he is (*qui est*) in personal being (*quis est*)[634]. Similarly, the individuality of Peter is logically prior to the notion of his matter as principle of that individuality and as that

---

[634] *"Actus enim generantis non stat nisi in distincto. Et sic hypostasis distincta est etiam ante, secundum rationem intelligendi, quam adveniat ei proprietas demonstrans distinctionem. Est enim per intellectum 'qui est' sive 'hic' ante hunc esse patrem. ... Et verum est, quod proprius terminus generationis est res naturae, et sic distinctus per actum naturae est ante proprietatem determinantem eum in eo quod est 'quis' in persona, non re, sed ratione intelligendi"* – Albert, *Sum. theol.*, I, tr. 10, q. 43, c. 2, a. 2, ad 3 & 7, ed. Colon., vol. 34, p. 341-342. Cf. infra, "ORDER OF NATURE IN THE TRINITY", p. 423 (especially p. 427-428).

which forms a part of his individual. Nonetheless, in the case of Peter, the *proprietas* (*materialis*) is in a certain sense causally prior to the individual it constitutes as such – the same cannot be said for the Trinity [635].

Acts of the supposit

An essence or nature – to follow a more rudimentary division – can be signified in two generally distinct ways. First it may be named abstractly and absolutely, as it is in itself and *simpliciter*, for which we employ the term "essence". Secondly, it may be signified concretely, after the manner of a *"quod est"* (where *"quod est"* is taken in the ordinary sense of indicating an existing subject), and this in two ways: according to operation or inclination to act, which is proper to the supposit as such and not to the essence *per se* (since operation implies a *subject* of operation, a subject which is the subject of a given nature or essence) [636], or according to the very supposital act of standing under the nature, by which the supposit is an *id quod est* or subject. Where the nature is signified concretely, moreover, we use the name "this" or *"hic"*. *"Hic"* designates the concrete subject because its mode of signifying indicates something particularly formed and discernible beneath the common nature [637].

---

[635] *"Quod est in creaturis prius et posterius tempore et causa et effectu, hoc est in divinis secundum modum intelligendi tantum"* – Albert, *Sum. theol.*, I, tr. 10, q. 43, c. 2, a. 2, ad 8, ed. Colon., vol. 34, p. 342.

[636] *"Dicit emim* PRISCIANUS, *quod agere et pati substantiae est proprium, vocans substantiam suppositum"* – Albert, *Sum. theol.*, I, tr. 9, q. 39, c. 2, a. 1, ad 10, ed. Colon., vol. 34, p. 297. To act and to be acted upon is indeed proper to substances, but inasmuch as substances are that from which actions flow and that within which the action of another is passively received. Substances, thus understood, are substance concretely and subjectively considered, that is, hypostases, which properly act and suffer, and not substance which is the essence (neither abstractly nor as this existing *quo est*): *"agere enim et pati, quod (sicut dicit Priscianus) substantiae est proprium, ut de qua egreditur actus, et ut in qua recipitur passio, non intelligitur de substantia quae est usia vel usiosis, sed de substantia quae est hypostasis, quae proprie agit vel patitur"* – Albert, *Sum. theol.*, I, tr. 14, q. 58, m. 1, ad quaest. 4, ad 1, ed. Borgnet, vol. 31, p. 585.

[637] *"Intelligendum regulariter, quod essentia divina secundum modum significandi per nomen tripliciter designari solet. Aliquando enim abstracte et absolute designatur et simpliciter, prout est in seipsa, sicut cum dicitur 'essentia'. Aliquando quasi per modum concretionis designatur sive per modum eius 'quod est'. Et hoc dupliciter, scilicet secundum intellectum et inclinationem ad actum substandi, qui proprie est suppositi et non essentiae sive naturae per se, sicut cum dicitur 'substantia'. Aliquando autem per ipsum actum suppositi substantis, quod sicut id quod est, substat naturae communi... 'Hic' enim de essentia communi non satis convenienter diceretur... 'Hic' enim secundum modum significandi demonstrat aliquid formatum et suppositum sub natura communi. Aliquando significatur ut relata ad actum, sicut cum dicitur natura vel virtus vel vita vel lumen vel sapientia... Rarissime autem invenitur 'essentia*

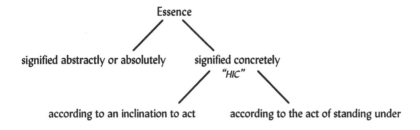

We notice here a distinction within the category of concrete signification between that which is signified concretely in consideration of
(or, more technically, by explicitly indicating) the operations of the
concrete nature, operations which are at least formally distinguishable
as a multiplicity of acts, some immanent, others exteriorly oriented or
ad extra, by which the concrete subject tends, so to speak, to radiate
outward, and that which is signified concretely according to another
kind of act by which the concrete *quod est* is precisely a particular individual of a common nature, a, so to speak, "isolating" act by which the
quod est is a supposital foundation for the common nature. This is
precisely the act of the supposit as standing under, act which determines a particular beneath an umbrella of a more extensive common
nature (as opposed to what we might call the "extroverted" acts directed from the individual agent toward a parameter of other objects). On the one hand, we have the act portrayed as a movement
from the common nature to the individual subject of that nature; on
the other, we have the operations represented as a movement from
the individual subject to a plurality of objects terminating those operations. Only the term of the first kind of "movement" can be the
subject of the second kind of "movement", that is, only supposits are
agents; the particular or person alone is properly said to act[638].

de essentia', eo quod essentia absolute significat commune 'quo est' et non per modum hyposta-
sis sive subsistentis, nec significat naturam ordinatam ad actum, sed absolute in simplicitate
consistens" – Albert, *Sum. theol.,* I, tr. 7, q. 30, c. 3, a. 1, sol., ed. Colon., vol. 34,
p. 232-233.

638 *"Nihil in divinis nec etiam in aliis supponibile est vel substans actu nisi hypostasis vel per-*
sona; et nihil proprie agit sive actum habet nisi particulare vel persona" – Albert, *Sum.*
theol., I, tr. 7, q. 30, c. 3, a. 1, sol., ed. Colon., vol. 34, p. 233.

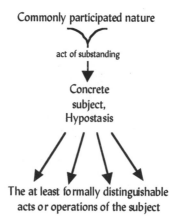

Commonly participated nature

act of substanding

Concrete
subject,
Hypostasis

The at least formally distinguishable
acts or operations of the subject

It is *in virtue* of the act of substanding that a thing is subject and
thereby capable of operations, whence the first "isolating" movement
is ordered to the movement of operations extending to a plurality of
objects and a world which exceeds and is greater than the subject.
This is one of the mysteries of creation (passively considered): a contractive act for the sake of subjective extension, contraction and ex-
pansion. That which is "stood under" is the common nature; as the
supposit of a given nature, a subject is subject and able to act. The
dynamism under observation, then, is precisely the fact succinctly expressed in the maxim: "nature is the principle of operation".

"Person"

The name "person" is not said univocally of divine, angelic and human persons. Person, Albert affirms (following St. Isidore), denotes
what is *"per se una"*. The sense of such unity means that a thing is indivisible in itself and divisible from others. But this notion is more
properly said of creatures than of the divine persons, since the divine
persons are one in essence and undivided *simpliciter*. Nevertheless, we
ascribe the definition even to the divine persons in an analogous way,
inasmuch as *per se* unity pertains to the divine persons through the
distinct personal properties[639]. In light of the Trinity, our understand-

---

[639]   *"Persona dicta de divinis et de angelis et de hominibus non dicitur univoce. Cum enim persona dicatur, ut dicit ISIDORUS, 'per se una', per se autem 'unum sit indivisum in se et divisum ab aliis'... constat, quod in hac perfecta ratione non dicitur de personis divinis; illae*

ing of what universally and univocally belong to the notion of person has to be modified. This does not mean that the traditional conclusions of natural reason with respect to human persons are placed into question, but rather implies that that understanding was limited in its concept of person to but a distinctive class of persons. Removed from the light of revelation, person could signify nothing other than the perfect and determinate thing of nature divisible from all other things of nature in natural being. Only with the Trinity do we learn that persons are also perfect and determinate things of nature distinct from others by reason of incommunicable properties, but indivisible from and united to others in substantial being[640].

In the Trinity, the modes according to which divine personality is realized are themselves distinct, such that no two persons are persons in the same way. Nevertheless, the name "person" is said of every divine person according to a common *ratio*, for person is predicated of the divine persons according as the term signifies a hypostasis which is distinct through a personal property, regardless of the particular kind of personal property in question[641]. Albert cites St. Augustine, remarking that Father, Son and Holy Spirit share in a common notion of person. That common notion able to be predicated of every person of the Trinity furthermore satisfies, in its own analogous way, the broader definition of person also applied to creatures. For, the *"unum"* (in the expression *"per se unum"*) stands for the substance, while the *"per se"* notes the distinction – as one person is *of itself* (through the personal property which it is) distinct from another[642].

---

enim essentialiter unum sunt et simpliciter indivisae... et IOH.XIV (11): 'Ego in patre et pater in me est'... in divinis enim per se unum non est nisi propria proprietate distinctum, essentialiter autem et per se nullo modo ab alio divisum. Et secundum hunc modum persona translatione nominis dicitur de divinis et non proprie" – Albert, *Sum. theol.*, I, tr. 10, q. 44, c. 1, sol., ed. Colon., vol. 34, p. 345.

[640] *"Persona enim semper significabat certum et determinatum et in esse naturati divisum, sed non semper significabat certum et determinatum incommunicabili proprietate distinctum in esse naturante secundum esse substantiale indivisum et aliis unitum; et ad hoc designandum translatum est post quaestionem haereticorum"* – Albert, *Sum. theol.*, I, tr. 10, q. 44, c. 1, ad 10 & ad quaest. 5, ed. Colon., vol. 34, p. 346.

[641] *"In divinis persona dicitur secundum unam rationem in tribus personis; sic enim dicitur persona 'hypostasis propietate personali distincta'"* – Albert, *Sum. theol.*, I, tr. 10, q. 44, c. 1, ad 2, ed. Colon., vol. 34, p. 345. Cf. infra, "SHARING IN THE COMMON NOTION OF PERSON", p. 315.

[642] *"Augustinus VII libro DE TRINITATE: 'Certe, quia pater est persona et filius est persona et spiritus sanctus est persona, ideo dicuntur tres personae', 'quia commune est eis id quod persona est'... unde quod dicitur 'unum', notat substantiam, quod dicitur 'per se' unum, notat distinctionem... cum dicitur 'pater est persona', sensus est: 'unum' et 'per se', hoc est distinctus"* – Albert, *Sum. theol.*, I, tr. 10, q. 44, c. 1, quaest. 3-4, ed. Colon., vol. 34, p. 343; cf.

But even the common notion of person proper to the divine persons is predicated within the context of the Trinity in diverse ways, according as different affirmations imply different kinds of supposition. Sometimes, Albert points out, "person" is predicated *essentialiter*, i.e. as designating what a thing is – as, for example when we say "the Father is a person". Sometimes it is predicated *notionaliter*, i.e. as denoting a difference between two persons based upon the personal property – as, for example, when we say "the Father in his person is different from the Son". Sometimes "person" is said *personaliter*, i.e. as denoting the distinctness of the thing with respect to another, that is, its distinct personal being, as this distinct individual – as, for example, when we say "the person of the Father is other than that of the Son". This latter mode of predication is to say "person" according to its proper mode of signification, that is, it uses the name "person" to denote what pertains precisely to its proper mode of signification – whence the description *"personaliter"*. In the other predicative cases (*essentialiter* and *notionaliter*), "person" is employed to denote more than just what pertains to it according to its proper mode of signification[643]. In all three of these cases, however, the principal signification of "person" does not change. What varies from one case to another is the mode of signification only. Thus, when we say "the Father is a person", "person" does not signify what the Father is *per modum essentiae*, but *per modum qui* (which refers to the *quid* of the *quis*); and when we say "the person of the Father is other than that of the Son", since they cannot be other in essence, and differ therefore only in *proprietate*, it follows that "person" again refers to the same personal reality or *quis*, though in this case according to relative distinction[644].

Augustine, *De trin.*, Bk. 7, c. 4, n. 8 (CC 50, p. 257, v. 81-83). Cf. infra, "THREE BASIC ELEMENTS IN PERSONHOOD – A WORKING DEFINITION", p. 276 (especially p. 281).

[643] *"In divinis persona, ut dicit MAGISTER IN SENTENTIIS, aliquando dicitur essentialiter, aliquando personaliter, aliquando notionaliter: Essentialiter, ut cum dicitur 'pater est persona'...; personaliter, ut cum dicitur 'alia est persona patris, alia filii alia spiritus sancti'; notionaliter, ut cum dicitur 'pater in persona differt a persona filii'"* – Albert, *Sum. theol.*, I, tr. 10, q. 44, c. 1, quaest. 1, obj 2, ed. Colon., vol. 34, p. 343.

[644] *"Et quod obicitur, quod aliquando dicitur essentialiter, aliquando personaliter et aliquando notionaliter, dicendum, quod hoc non variat significationem personae principalem, sed modum significandi tantum. Unde quando dicitur 'pater est persona', 'persona' dicit essentiam non per modum essentiae... sed per modum 'quis est'. 'Quis' enim... dividitur contra 'qualis' et contra 'quantus', et hoc modo 'quis' primo dicit 'quem' et secundario 'quid'... cum dicitur 'pater est persona', intelligitur, quod pater est 'quis' perfecte ens et substantialiter, personali proprietate distinctus. Cum autem dicitur 'pater est... alia persona quam filius', cum non possit esse alius in essentia, oportet, quod sit alius in personali proprietate... et sic per relativum diversitatis cogitur ad standum pro persona"* – Albert, *Sum. theol.*, I, tr. 10, q. 44, c. 1, ad 2, ed. Colon., vol. 34, p. 345.

That principal signification of person as it is predicated in the Trinity allows us to expand, so to speak, our notion of personhood. We have seen that the divine persons, in an analogous way, fit into a definition of person based upon *per se* unity. But, rather than remaining content to fit the doctrine of the divine persons into the terminology of pre-revelatory tradition, a more properly universal definition of person can be had by incorporating what we learn from a consideration of the Trinity. Person is *hypostasis sive substantia, substantialiter et perfecte existens, proprietate personalis determinata*[645]. Person, then, signifies at once substance, hypostasis and the *proprietas*, but each in a way proper to the mode of signification inherent in the name "person". It names the substance, not according as it is generically or communally considered, but according as it exists in this designated individual. This substance – taken from the point of view of its determination –, this *individual* substance, designates more the *quis* than the *quid*. Person names the substance precisely insofar as supposit or hypostasis[646]. But person names this hypostatic substance itself precisely insofar as distinguished from other hypostases through an incommunicable *proprietas*[647]. Hypostasis, we have seen, names the distinct thing of nature, it names the perfect and subsistent determinate thing (which is why it has been defined as *substantia cum proprietate*). According to what is most proper to its mode of signification, it signifies the determinate thing, moreover, precisely from the point of view of its act of substanding, both with respect to the substance commun-

---

[645] *"Est enim persona 'hypostasis sive substantia, substantialiter et perfecte existens, proprietate personali determinata', et ideo per adiuncta trahi potest ad substantiam designandam et ad hypostasim et ad proprietatem"* – Albert, *Sum. theol.*, I, tr. 10, q. 44, c. 1, ad 2, ed. Colon., vol. 34, p. 345.

[646] *"Cum dicitur, quod persona dicit essentiam, non intelligunt isti, quod dicat essentiam per modum essentiae sive per modum naturae unientis personas, sed per modum substantiae, secundum quod substantia a substando dicitur. Sic enim substantia est idem quod hypostasis sive suppositum, sicut dicit Avicenna, quod suppositum sive 'subiectum est ens in se substantialiter completum, occasio alteri existendi in eo'"* – Albert, *Sum. theol.*, I, tr. 10, q. 44, c. 1, ad 7, ed. Colon., vol. 34, p. 345.

[647] *"Persona, licet dicat substantiam, non tamen dicit eam in genere consideratam vel in specie, sed in hoc individuo designatam. Substantia enim in genere designat 'quid' magis quam 'quis'... quaerentes enim 'quid est hoc?', dicimus, quod est substantia... quaerentes autem 'quis est hic?', dicimus, quod est Socrates vel Plato, individuum... et hoc quidem etiam substantia est, sed est substantia sicut suppositum sive hypostasis, quod non designatur nomine naturae communis... translatum est ad designandam hypostasim cum proprietate incommunicabili, ut cum dicitur 'pater et filius et spiritus sanctus sunt tres personae', sensus est: hoc est tres hypostases sive tria supposita propriis et incommunicabilibus proprietatibus a se invicem distincta"* – Albert, *Sum. theol.*, I, tr. 10, q. 44, c. 1, quaest. 5, ed. Colon., vol. 34, p. 343-344.

ally taken and with respect to properties and accidents[648]. Person, however, – besides its obvious essential qualitative inclusion of intelligence –, names that hypostasis according to the distinguishing act proper to the *proprietas* by which the hypostasis is distinct. Thus the *ratio* for the distinctness proper to hypostasis is also contained in the notion of person:

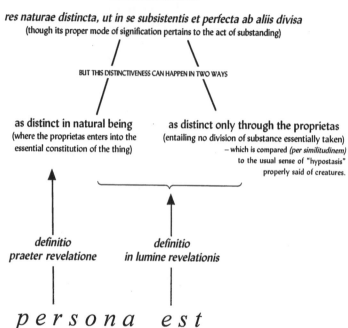

HYPOSTASIS SIGNIFIES

res naturae distincta, ut in se subsistentis et perfecta ab aliis divisa
(though its proper mode of signification pertains to the act of substanding)

BUT THIS DISTINCTIVENESS CAN HAPPEN IN TWO WAYS

as distinct in natural being
(where the proprietas enters into the essential constitution of the thing)

as distinct only through the proprietas
(entailing no division of substance essentially taken)
– which is compared *(per similitudinem)* to the usual sense of "hypostasis" properly said of creatures.

*definitio
praeter revelatione*

*definitio
in lumine revelationis*

p e r s o n a   e s t

In both the Trinity and in men, "person" signifies substance *per modum subsistentiae*. This is the substance which is determinate, or primary substance, in contrast to substance as unifying several persons, i.e. the essence. Such substance, Albert asserts, is the "individual substance" of Boethius, and identical to the "incommunicable substance" of Richard of St. Victor. It is the direct *significatum* of "person". The *per se* subsistent substance, again, can be regarded either according to its act of substanding or precisely according as it is distinct. This, as we

---

[648] *"In divina suppositum est hypostasis, occasio, quod proprietas sit in ea, quae secundum modum significandi non dicit esse per se existentis, sed existentis in hypostasi et non extra ipsam"* – Albert, *Sum. theol.*, I, tr. 10, q. 44, c. 1, ad 7, ed. Colon., vol. 34, p. 345.

have seen, is the proper difference in the modes of signification respectively proper to "hypostasis" and "person". But, signifying the determinate substance precisely insofar as distinct means to signify it from the point of view of its being informed or determined by the *proprietas* (through which distinction is had). For this reason, the *proprietas* is said to be "obliquely" signified by person, inasmuch as distinction (had through the *proprietas*) enters into the concept of person as such [649]:

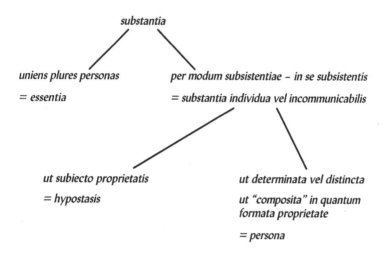

"Hypostasis" does not name the *proprietas* even *in obliquo*; according to strict mode of signification, "hypostasis" abstracts in a certain way from the proprietas. The substance it signifies is indeed *substantia cum proprietate*, but the *cum proprietate* is intended to specify the sense of *substantia* constituting its notion – which considers the "appropriated" substance insofar as *subject of* the appropriation. That is, the *ratio* of "hypostasis" concerns the determined substance in *itself*, as the thing

---

[649] *"Persona enim est 'substantia individua', ut dicit* BOETHIUS, *vel 'substantia incommunicabilis', ut dicit Richardus, et cum talis substantia in recto cadat in diffinitione personae, constat quod persona dicat eam per modum substantiae in se subsistentis, licet non dicat eam per modum essentiae communis, sed per modum suppositi sive hypostasis… in intellectu autem suo super hoc addit distinctum esse proprietate, et ita in obliquo dicit proprietatem distinguentem, et ideo per consequens sive secundario"* – Albert, *Sum. theol.*, I, tr. 10, q. 44, c. 1, ad 8 & ad quaest. 4, ed. Colon., vol. 34, p. 346; cf. ad 3: *"Substantia enim a substando dicitur, ut dicit Aristoteles, per se autem et principaliter substat suppositum; essentia autem dicit per modum essentiantis et unientis supposita"* – Albert, *Sum. theol.*, I, tr. 10, q. 44, c. 1, ad 3, ed. Colon., vol. 34, p. 346.

being determined by the *proprietas* (the *proprietas* itself thus falling outside of its immediate signification).

Now, the idea of abstraction will raise an objection, as that which abstracts from principles of determination is no longer determinate. If personality pertains to determination as such, then the notion of hypostasis, inasmuch as it is distinct from person, is no longer determinate[650]. However, the clause "inasmuch as it is distinct from person" reveals to us precisely the sense in which "hypostasis" may be understood to be indeterminate. Hypostasis and person are unalterably the same thing *in re*, they differ only in mode of signification. But, while hypostasis is always a determinate substance, its mode of signification abstracts as it were from personality, from the act of the *proprietas* as such. In this way, hypostasis is the substance as determinable, since it cannot be regarded as signifying the substance *qua* determinate, the determining *proprietas* being removed from its mode of signification. From the point of view of mode of signification, then, "hypostasis" fails to signify the determined substance as such; and the primordial role of the *proprietas* as determining that hypostasis, as well as the fact that "person" necessarily includes the notion of the *proprietas*, makes is clear that personality lies in determination or distinction, a point we have already emphasized. One must not forget, however, that we can abstract from personality only with respect to the mode of signification. With respect to the *significatum* of "hypostasis", which is the same determinate thing, no abstraction from personality is possible, lest we eliminate the principle whereby the hypostasis is hypostasis, that is, a distinct and perfect thing of nature[651].

The *substantia* said to be directly signified by person is signified not only *per modum subsistentiae* – in distinction from *per modum essentiae* – (as in the chart above), but *secundum quod ab actu substandi dicitur* – which specifies the exact modality according to which the *per se* existent is directly signified by the name person. Person thus directly names the *per se* existing substance precisely *as hypostasis* (*ab actu sub-*

---

[650] *"Abstracto determinante non remanet determinatum; personalitas autem determinans est; ergo abstracta personalitate hypostasis determinata non remanet"* – Albert, *Sum. theol.*, I, tr. 10, q. 44, c. 2, obj. 12, ed. Colon., vol. 34, p. 349.

[651] *"Secundum communem intentionem personae abstracta personalitate per intellectum remaneat hypostasis, quae secundum intellectum substat personalitati, tamen meo iudicio in divinis abstracta personalitate nihil remanet... Hypostasis non remanet, quia proprietas ut proprium accepta [i.e. secundum rem] est ipsa hypostasis"* – Albert, *Sum. theol.*, I, tr. 10, q. 44, c. 3, ad 12, ed. Colon., vol. 34, p. 351.

standi) [652]. Person does not signify the substance as common or as the substantial reality existing *per se* (i.e. the concrete substance viewed in its substantiality or quiddity). Nor does person signify substance as a generic or specific essence. Person signifies substance according as "substance" is said *ab actu substandi*, that is, according to the act of standing under the incommunicable *proprietas* (act which is implied by the mode of signification proper to "hypostasis" and *"suppositum"*). Person may also be said to signify the substance according as the substance is, in some sense, designated by *"quis"* – where it is again a question of the hypostasis, but according as it is distinct (or personal), it is the what of the very person as person [653]. One could confer the following "universal chart" on the different terms by which we name the same substantial reality, in order to situate the senses of "substance" just mentioned.

---

[652] *"Substantia in diffinitione posita non dicitur a natura substantiae, quae subsistere facit, sed ab actu substandi, et sic convenit supposito sive hypostasi... Boethius in illo loco substantiam accipit pro natura, quae substare vel subsistere facit in se et non alio indigere, ut sit, et non accipit eam, secundum quod ab actu substandi dicitur, et hoc modo verum est, quod persona non dicit nec significat substantiam nisi in obliquo"* – Albert, *Sum. theol.*, I, tr. 10, q. 44, c. 1, ad 6 & 11-12, ed. Colon., vol. 34, p. 347. Cf. infra, "ON THE SUBSTANCE WHICH PERSON SIGNIFIES", p. 286; "BOETHIUS' DEFINITION AND THE PRINCIPAL CONSTITUENT OF PERSONALITY", p. 341.

[653] *"Si significat substantiam, ut dicit Richardus, non significat eam ut naturam communem in se substantem et alio non indigentem, ut sit, nec significat eam sub proprietate generali vel speciali, sed significat eam, prout dicitur ab actu substandi ut suppositum et sub proprietate individuali vel quasi-individuali, prout designatur per 'quis'... tamen est 'quid' in esse substantiali... cum enim dicitur 'pater est persona', sensus est: pater est suppositum certa et notabili proprietate distinctum... pater et filius sunt supposita certis proprietatibus distincta"* – Albert, *Sum. theol.*, I, tr. 10, q. 44, c. 3, ed. Colon., vol. 34, p. 351.

Universal chart

THE DIFFERENT TERMS BY WHICH WE NAME THE SAME SUBSTANTIALLY EXISTING
REALITY ACCORDING TO ITS VARIOUS ATTRIBUTES

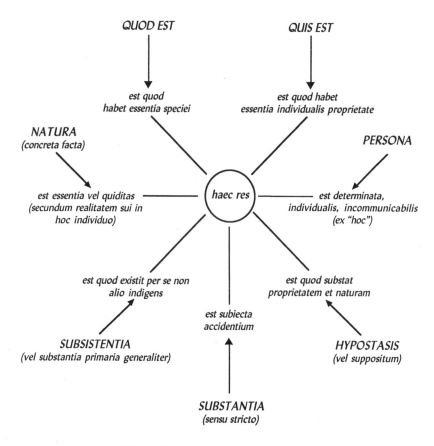

In omnibus, non dicitur quod "haec res" "quo est" est, neque quod "natura communis vel universalis (i.e. substantia secunda)" est. In Trinitate autem non est "quo est" – et igitur "quod est" non vere est, et natura communis non est diversa quam natura concreta ut existente in individuo. Et per hoc quod non sunt accidentes in Trinitate, non habet substantiam sensu stricto (modo subsistentiae) dictam.

Application of these distinctions in speaking about the Trinity

When a given person of the Trinity is named, such as the person of the Father, what is signified is the *substantia supposita,* that is, the substance insofar as supposit. Insofar as supposit, the referent of the personal name is "someone", that is, the substance as this particular person, the *quis est.* To name, however, the substance of the Father is to signify the *substantia essentia,* conceptually referred to as the *quo est,* that is, as logically distinct from the *quis est,* even though they are entirely identical in reality[654]. There is no distinction between the persons who are and the substance which they are[655]. In a similar way, identity must be affirmed with regard to the principles of communicability and the principles of incommunicability in the Godhead, even if, for the sake of founding a plurality of persons in an undifferentiated nature, adequate distinction must be introduced. These opposing principles are adequately distinguished from one another in a logical way (i.e. according to a difference in mode of signification which modality is founded upon the real aspects of the thing)[656]. Now, the principle(s) of incommunicability (i.e., the relations of origin), and therefore the persons constituted by them, are really distinct from one another; what is affirmed, however, is their identity with the *quo est* or nature (the principle of unity). The persons are only logically distinguished from the substance, but really distinct from one another. This is possible because, at the level of "personhood", only the *distinctive* property (*proprietas*) of one person is being compared to another; thus, *as persons,* they are really distinct; but aside from that formal perspective of the distinctive property (which is an immediate *significatum* of "person") there exists no difference at all between the persons (effectively being considered at another level, namely, that of their substance, or *"quo est"*). From the *"quis est"* is understood personality and incommunicability. From the *"quo est"*, the nature and communicability. That *quis est* signifies indeed the nature, but insofar

---

[654] *Quis est* and *quo est,* differ only in mode of signification, but do not signify different things in the Trinity: *"cum dicimus personam Patris, dicitur substantia supposita quae est, quis est in Trinitate, in qua proprie loquendo non est quod est; cum autem dicimus substantiam Patris, dicimus quo; et ut Augustinus notet indifferentiam 'quis est' et 'quo est' in divinis, ideo dicit, quod non aliud dicimus uno et alio, licet dicamus diverso modo significandi... nobilitas simplicitatis divinae tollit diversitatem a quis est et quo est sed non veritatem"* – Albert, *I Sent.,* d. 23, a. 2, ad arg. 2 & ad obj. 4, ed. Borgnet, vol. 25, p. 586-587.

[655] Cf. Augustine, *De doctrina christiana,* Bk. I, c. 5; cf. Peter Lombard: Albert, *I Sent.,* d. 25, a. 7, H, ed. Borgnet, vol. 25, p. 635.

[656] *"In nulla natura idem est principium communicabilitatis et incommunicabilitatis, sed in divina natura sufficit diversus modus intelligendi, et hoc ideo, quia in inferioribus quae composita sunt, diversum est quod est et quo est, et diversum est quis est et quo est; in divinis autem proprie loquendo non est quod est et quo est, sed ibi est verissime quis est et quo est, sed non sunt diversa in re"* – Albert, *I Sent.,* d. 23, a. 2, ad obj. 4, ed. Borgnet, vol. 25, p. 587.

as subject of attribution or supposit[657], and always in conjunction with the *proprietas* through which the person (*quis est*) is constituted[658].

Note that we do not say "*quod est*" with respect to the Trinity, since, properly speaking, there is no *quod est* in God, not only because there can be no distinction between *quod est* and *quo est*, but because the role of attributive subject (notion of the *quod est*) is occupied by the several persons which are more precisely *qui sunt*, and not three *quae sunt*, the latter of which could suggest a plurality of substances. Three *quae sunt*, that is, might be taken as representing three *substantiae essentiae* (*aliud et aliud*), while the notion of three *qui sunt* can only stand for three *substantiae suppositae* (*alius et alius*). "*Quod est*" may never be said of the Godhead, moreover, because there is no separate entity constituted by the divine substance, besides the three persons of the Trinity, to which the term might apply. Thus the three persons in the Trinity are not called "*tria quae sunt*", but "*tria qui sunt*", and the identity between *quod est* and *quo est* is best expressed as one between *quis est* and *quo est* (and likewise with respect to their logical difference[659]).

Person indeed signifies substance: *significatione distinguimus dicentes, quod hoc nomen, scilicet persona, proprie secundum substantiam dicitur, et essentiam significat*[660]. But as has been explained, person signifies more than just the essence; *significat substantiam suppositam cum proprietate*. This is the signified reality, the diverse aspects of which are more or less explicitly denoted, according to different modes of signification, by the different names used to co-signify that reality (such as "hypostasis", "substance", "person", etc.). Moreover, if person only signified substance, the result would be heresy[661]. The fact that more than one

---

[657] Cf. Albert, *I Sent.*, d. 25, a. 3, ad quaest., ed. Borgnet, vol. 25, p. 632: "*persona significet substantiam subjectam*".

[658] "*Ex modo intelligendi 'quis est', accipitur personalitas et incommunicabile, et ex modo intelligendi 'quo est', accipitur natura, et nihilominus quis est significat substantiam suppositam, licet consignificet cum ea proprietatem modi existentiae quo existit persona in divinis*" – Albert, *I Sent.*, d. 23, a. 2, ad obj. 4, ed. Borgnet, vol. 25, p. 587.

[659] *Quo est* and *quod est* are identical in God; yet even there they differ in mode of intelligibility and signification insasmuch as *quo est* is signified as *in eo quod est*, or, to be more precise, *in eo quod quis est*: "*in divinis 'quod est' et 'quo est' idem sint, et quod hoc non sit nisi in divinis... tamen etiam in divinis in modo significandi differunt... et secundum modum illum significandi significatur 'quo est' esse in eo 'quod est' vel in eo quod 'quis est'*" – Albert, *Sum. theol.*, I, tr. 9, q. 39, c. 2, a. 1, ad quaest. 3/ad 6, ed. Colon., vol. 34, p. 300-301.

[660] Peter Lombard: Albert, *I Sent.*, d. 25, a. 2, E, ed. Borgnet, vol. 25, p. 630.

[661] "*Isti dicebant, quod persona non significat nisi essentiam, et supponit eamdem, et connotat distinctionem... Sed videtur, quod ex ista opinione sequatur haeresis sic, Haec persona et Pater, hic secundum istos non fit demostratio nisi essentiae, et essentia Patris est essentia Filii,*

reality is signified by person stands behind the reason for which a plurality of persons can be affirmed in the Trinity[662]. *Plurally said,* person, in the Trinity, does not signify the essence or substance. When we define person, it necessarily signifies the essence; but when we say "three persons", we are signifying the substratum or foundation of multiplicity, which is the *suppositum qua suppositum* (i.e., *qua* distinct and existing *per se,* and not insofar as essence)[663]. This is not to say that the expression "three persons", intending the persons insofar as *suppositi,* does not also signify the essence; but it does so according to a particular mode of signification. Whatever the explicit content of the predicated name, be it "hypostasis", "person" or "substance", the referent is always the very same reality, only viewed from a different perspective and signified according to a unique mode. No one of them, when used to designate that individual we call person, excludes either the community of substance (abstract in man, and entitative in God) or the distinctive quality of the individual as distinct individual[664]. In the statement *"tres personae sunt unus Deus"*, the term *"Deus"* signifies community differently than the term *"sunt"* and differently also than the term *"personae"*. The same community of nature is implied/signified, but not under the same mode of signification. The community signified by *"personae"* (plural) is signified as it be verified *in suppositis*, that is, insofar as the same community of nature is distributed over a plurality of subjects, and it is this multiple distribution which is formal to the signification proper to *"personae"* taken as a plural subject – but the community of nature is also, materially, proper to the signification of *"personae"*. Moreover, there is the simple community proper to the three insofar as they are all supposits. *"Personae"*

---

ergo persona Patris est persona Filii, quod falsum... Sed secundum supra dicta, dicendum quod persona significat substantiam suppositam cum proprietate, ut dicit Dionysius" – Albert, *I Sent.,* d. 25, a. 2, expositio, ed. Borgnet, vol. 25, p. 630.

[662] *"Pluraliter diceretur tres personae, cum quaereretur, quid tres, vel quid tria, ubi non significat essentiam, id est, naturam divinam quae communis est tribus personis, sed subsistentias vel hypostases secundum Graecos"* – Peter Lombard: Albert, *I Sent.,* d. 25, a. 2, E, ed. Borgnet, vol. 25, p. 630-631.

[663] *"'Cum ergo dicimus tres personas, etc.['], ubi non significat essentiam, id est, naturam divinam quae communis est tribus personis, sed subsistentias... in plurali numerum ponit circa suppositum, et non circa significatum"* – Albert, *I Sent.,* d. 25, a. 3 & ad quaest., ed. Borgnet, vol. 25, p. 632.

[664] *"Cum dicitur, tres personae sunt unus Deus, aliter enim dicitur communitas substantiae per ly 'Deus', et aliter per ly 'sunt', et aliter per ly 'isti' vel 'personae', et licet sit una communitas naturae in omnibus importata, non tamen sub eodem modo significandi, quia in ly 'personae' importatur ut in suppositis, et in ly 'sunt' in habitudine suppositi ad naturam, et in ly 'Deus' ut in communi natura secundum rem"* – Albert, *I Sent.,* d. 25, a. 3, sol., ed. Borgnet, vol. 25, p. 632.

explicitly introduces a commonality of sharing in "suppositness"[665], which latter perfection is an explicit articulation, for Albert, of the *term* "person", that is, of the name "person" as it is predicated of real persons (≠ the definition of *a* person)[666]. That the persons really *are* (*sunt*) one God, verifies a relationship or *habitus* on the part of the persons to the nature, each person bearing a certain *habitus* (one of identity) toward the nature, and in this way the copula also signifies the community of substance. Finally, *Deus* indicates that community according to the thing or substance itself.

---

[665] Cf. infra, "SHARING IN THE COMMON NOTION OF PERSON", p. 315.

[666] Explicit articulation refers to the mode of signification of a term; for the mode of its signification signifies the entire reality according to a certain *respectus*, that is, from a certain point of view, explicitly drawing out or emphasizing one aspect among several which belong to the reality signified. Even the term "person" has a mode of signification the *respectus* of which explicitates one of the aspects belonging to the entire reality which is a person. For St. Thomas, the explicitation accomplished by the term "person", as opposed to a term such as "hypostasis" or "substance", is to draw our attention to the aspect of dignity belonging to the reality signified by the terms "person", "hypostasis", "substance". It is true that here the term person is a more precise notion than either hypostasis or substance, since the latter terms can be predicated of many things which are not persons, but the point lies in the fact that the mode of signification of a predicate highlights but one among the many aspects or features which the *definition* of that predicate clearly states. The term "hypostasis" compared with the term "subsistence" (taken substantively) can provide a more transparent example. Neither term – in the context of the Trinity, where hypostasis cannot be taken as a special (substantial) mode of subsisting – is more precise than the other in signification, since they are entirely coextensive. But each one's mode of signification pertains to a particular aspect of the reality which they signify, which aspect is not articulated (though not excluded) by the other term when predicated of the reality. Subsistence signifies a thing according to a certain *respectus* to existence, signifying the thing as existent, while hypostasis does so in respect of the notion of "standing under", designating the subjectival aspect. Looking at "hypostasis", we see that, predicated of the reality, its mode of signification explicitly identifies or singles out one aspect of that reality. But if we consider "hypostasis" *according as it is defined*, then every essential aspect of the reality – including the subjectival act, the fact of being a *res naturae*, the fact of existing *per se* – is clearly articulated or identified. Consequently, a logical distance resides between a term insofar as predicated of a reality and the same term insofar as it is defined (we are touching the difference between signification and meaning). In the former case, what the term explicitly indicates is limited to a certain aspect due to its particular mode of signification. In the latter case, the sense of the term is exposed through the explicit indication of all of the essential aspects, which are its *definiens*. Of course, even though different predicates are limited according to their respective modes of signification, none of the content explicitly imported by one term is excluded when predicating another; each term necessarily includes (at least implicitly) all the aspects pertaining to the object of signification. Note that, throughout this discourse, the notion of "mode of signification" is not dependent upon more or less specific signification, or the signifying as a whole or as a part, but is simply a question of signifying according to a certain *respectus* which emphasizes one aspect over another.

On the name "Deus"

In response to an objection unwarrantedly limiting the possible objects of signification for the name "God"[667], Albert explains that the term "God" can signify more than one thing (or one thing possessing distinct aspects), upon which realities the predication of various predicates may depend, and whence it may be affirmed that "God is three in one"[668]. In the Trinity, *"essentia"* ≠ "supposit". The essence is, however, inevitably supposit insofar as three supposits, to each of which it is identical. When we say "God is three and one", the term God refers to two realities (or to one reality along with a certain aspect), both the essence and the supposits; but it does so by a single name, "God", which signifies the common essence existing *in supposito*, that is, in a supposit or supposits.

In every name, there are two things to be considered: that which is signified, the substantial referent, and that quality or modality according to which the name is used to signify its referent. With regard to *"Deus"*, the substantial referent is the divine essence, but according precisely as that essence is in a supposit (just as "man" signifies humanity as it is concretely in men)[669]. *Deus* therefore signifies the essence according to a particular mode of signification qualifying the *significatum* as *quod est* (and thus does not name the essence *ut quo est*). This it does, moreover, in an indeterminate way with respect to the several persons identically constituted of that *quod est*, such that *Deus* can be predicated indifferently of one person or several[670]. The essence signified by *Deus* is the discrete and concrete thing, which can have the suppositional value of standing either for one person of for the community of three persons. The rules of supposition will determine the validity of the use of the term in a given statement. When,

---

667 *"Cum dicitur, Deus est trinus et unus, aut ly 'Deus' supponit essentiam, aut personam. Si essentiam, ergo essentia est trina, quod falsum est. Si personam, ergo aliqua persona est trina et una, quod falsum est"* – Albert, *I Sent.*, d. 24, a. 8, obj. 3, ed. Borgnet, vol. 25, p. 621.

668 *"Deus est trinus et unus, et ly 'Deus' supponit essentiam in supposito in communi, et ideo gratia essentiae convenit ei unus, et gratia suppositorum trinum, supple, esse"* – Albert, *I Sent.*, d. 24, a. 8, ad 3, ed. Borgnet, vol. 25, p. 621.

669 *"Duo in nomine considerantur, scilicet substantia quae nominatur, et qualitas a qua nomen imponitur. Propter quod etiam dicitur, quod nomen significat substantiam cum qualitate. Et si attenditur substantia quae nominatur hoc nomine, 'Deus'... significat essentiam divinam in habente, sicut hoc nomen, 'homo', humanitatem significat in homine"* – Albert, *Sum. theol.*, I, tr. 13, q. 51, sol., ed. Borgnet, vol. 31, p. 528.

670 *"Hoc nomen, 'Deus', significat essentiam, sed ex modo significandi, quia scilicet significat eam ut quod est, et non ut quo est, indifferenter et in communi supponit personam, et aliquando unam, et aliquando duas, et aliquando tres"* – Albert, *Sum. theol.*, I, tr. 13, q. 51, ad quaest. 2, ed. Borgnet, vol. 31, p. 529.

for example, we say that "the Father is God", the term "God" stands for the concrete reality as *quis est*. Because the Father is not the Trinity, however, does not sanction concluding that God is not the Trinity; for in the proposition "God is not the Trinity", the term "God" no longer has the suppositional value of standing for the *quis est* but rather for the *quod est*. Such a conclusion is censurable for having converted the *quis* in *quid*[671]. God *ut quod* is Triune, but God *ut quis* is not. Adjectively employed as a predicate of one of the persons (as, for example, in "the Father is God"), *Deus* possesses the value of *quis est*; substantively employed as the subject, *Deus* has the value of *quod est*. Simply taken, therefore, i.e. substantively considered, *Deus* is not opposed to Trinity.

Substance, as we have seen, may be designated as *quo est* or essence, *quis est*, and *quod est*. The mode of signification proper to a name signifying as a *quod est*, Albert tells us, lies somewhere between the modes of signification proper to *quo est* and *quis est*. Accordingly, the name *Deus* – which signifies as *quod est* – signifies the hypostasis or supposit in a way different from the name *deitas* (signifying as *quo est*) or *Pater* (signifying as *quis est*). *Deus*, as well as any other strictly hypostatic but non-personal term, signifies the concrete substance according to its act of standing under; *Deus* signifies that which *has* deity[672]. *Persona*, which signifies the substance as *quis est*, differs from a name signifying as *quod est* inasmuch as it names the substance not immediately from the point of view of the hypostatic act of standing under, but from that of incommunicable singularity.

In the qualification of *Deus* as *trinus*, whereby the signification of the name *Deus* is extended to the three hypostases or persons taken collectively, we observe that *Deus* stands for *tres habentes deitatem*, i.e. three supposits commonly possessing the deity. *Deus* refers us to the supposital reality, and it is only through the addition of a term such as *trinus* that the personal reality is signified. *Deus* can be used (according to the predicates we join to it) to signify all three persons in an

---

671   *"Cum enim dicitur, Pater est Deus, et ille non est trinitas, supponit Deus ut quis, et cum infertur, ergo Deus non est trinitas, supponit Deus ut quod, et sic mutatur quis in quod"* – Albert, *Sum. theol.*, I, tr. 13, q. 51, ad quaest. 2, ed. Borgnet, vol. 31, p. 530.

672   *"'Substantia' designatur multipliciter, scilicet ut 'quo est' sive ut essentia, et sic significatur per hoc nomen 'deitas'; aliquando significatur ut 'quis est'... sicut significatur nomine 'suppositi' sive 'hypostasis' vel 'personae'; aliquando significatur ut 'quod est', qui modus significandi quasi medius est inter modum significandi 'quo est' et modum significandi 'quis est', et hoc modo significatur hoc nomine 'deus' – deus enim significat habentem deitatem, et is qui habet, suppositum est sive hypostasis, habitum autem significat substantiam... 'persona' significat substantiam ut 'quis est'"* – Albert, *Sum. theol.*, I, tr. 10, q. 45, c. 1, a. 1, ad 4, ed. Colon., vol. 34, p. 353.

indefinite way, because the term *Deus* stands for the substance *ab actu substandi dicitur*, and not according to that which makes a supposit distinct from another, i.e. the *forma suppositi*. In this way we can say "to God alone be honor and glory", since the exclusion indicated by "alone" pertains to the substantial reality and introduces no opposition between this or that person. The numerical multiplicity expressed by *trinus*, on the other hand, implies a difference (which is the principle of number) by which one supposit is distinguished from another. Such a difference is referred to as the *forma suppositi*, which is nothing other than a singular incommunicable property. *Trinus*, however, though entailing a plurality, does so only with respect to the supposits – by implying different *formae suppositorum* –, and not with respect to the nature (which would require different substantial forms)[673].

As clarified by the last observations, what is predicated of *Deus* determines its suppositional value. In the expression *"Deus generat Deum"*, the term *generare* refers to the subject *Deus* an act proper to but a particular person and thus causes the supposition of the essential term *Deus* to express the supposit which generates, such that *Deus*, that is, stands for the supposit of the Father who alone is the subject of generation. Again, because *Deus* signifies the divine essence concretely, that is, according as it is suppositized, it may be treated as denominating the supposit notwithstanding the fact that it is an essential name. It is the predicated act, that which is attached to the notion of the essence, which entails the special supposition of the term naming the latter. The preposition *"de"*, for example, in the expressions *"Deus de Deo"* and *"Lumen de Lumine"*, because it denotes an origin, when joined to the term *Deus*, makes *Deus* stand for one *having* the divinity, i.e. the supposit of the essence, the person[674]. As a result, no distinc-

---

[673] *"Cum dicitur 'deus est trinus', hoc nomen 'deus' dicit substantiam, secundum quod significatur per 'quod est' et secundum quod ab actu substandi dicitur, et ideo per adiunctum, quod est trinus, trahitur ad standum pro personis sive pro suppositis; sic enim dicit deitatem in habente, habens autem est suppositum; unde tunc indefinite et communiter supponit tres habentes deitatem; aliquando autem per adiunctum trahitur ad supponendum pro determinata persona, ut cum dicitur 'deus generans'... 'soli deo honor et gloria'... et dictio exclusiva exclusionem notat circa oppositum essentiae, non circa oppositum huius vel illius personae... hoc nomen 'deus' communiter potest supponere pro tribus personis indefinite... discretionem ponat circa suppositum et non circa formam suppositi... trinus discretionem ponit circa formam suppositi proximam. Sed non oportet, quod ponat circa formam substantialem"* – Albert, *Sum. theol.*, I, tr. 10, q. 45, c. 2, a. 1, sol. & ad 2, ed. Colon., vol. 34, p. 357. Cf. tr. 10, q. 45, c. 1, a. 2, ad 5: *"cum enim dicitur adiectivum numerale, quod est trium, formam suam numeralem non ponit nisi circa suppositum, et non circa formam, quae est unitas; aliter enim non diceretur 'trium unitas', sed 'trium unitates'"* – ed. Colon., vol. 34, p. 355.

[674] Cf. Albert, *I Sent.*, d. 4, a. 5, ad 2; a. 6, sol., ed. Borgnet, vol. 25, p. 163 & 164.

tion within the essence, but only between hypostatic or supposital terms, is affirmed by such expressions, nor does it follow that the essence is generated or generates. On the basis of these observations, two fundamental errors are avoided, namely those of Joachim of Fiore and Gilbert of Poitiers. The former concluded, in light of the divine simplicity, that the essence generates the essence, while the latter maintained that in all propositions formed with respect to God, personal names alone could be subjects, while every essential name functioned uniquely as a predicate[675]. The solution of St. Albert consists in rightly formulating the kind of distinction to be affirmed between essence and person in God: not after the manner of a subject and its inhering form, but exclusively according to our compositional mode of understanding which successively and distinctly cognizes what is ontologically indistinct. Person and essence, supposit and form, remain absolutely one at the ontological level, wherefore subject and predicate in God are entirely convertible. But, though person and essence in God are identical *in re*, their respective significations are not, whence one generates while the other does not, one is distinct while the other is not[676]. This distinction between signification and reality signified constitutes for A. Pompei the cornerstone of the doctrinal edifice of St. Albert[677].

On the name "Trinity"

A certain difficulty evolves from the previous consideration; for *Trinitas*[678], which is predicated of God, seems to be said substantially, since it does not refer *ad aliud* (i.e. it does not appear to be a relative term). But if said substantially, since everything which is said according to

---

[675] Cf. Albert, *I Sent.*, d. 4, a. 3, ad 5; d. 5, a. 1, ad 2; a. 9, obj. 1. In a polemical opuscule, *Libellus de unitate et essentia Trinitatis*, Joachim of Fiore (1130-1202) contested the Lombardian conception of the Trinity, accusing it of excessively distinguishing essence from person such as to posit a *quaternitas* in the divinity. Overly stating the identity between essence and person, Joachim's theory was condemned at the Fourth Lateran Council (1215) for its tendential tritheism.

[676] Cf. Albert, *I Sent.*, d. 4, a. 8, ad 1-4, ed. Borgnet, vol. 25, p. 170.

[677] Cf. A. Pompei, op. cit., p. 92, 98, 107-108, 110, 241, 277, 282, 284-290, 300-304, 308.

[678] The term "Trinity" is an entirely Christian invention, originating perhaps from the Carthaginian community and first employed in the vocabulary of Latin theology by Tertullian: *"unicum quidem deum credimus, sub hac tamen dispensatione quam oikonomiam dicimus... quae unitatem in trinitatem disponit"* – Tertullian, *Adv. Prax.* 2, 1, 4: CCL 2, 1160-1161 (cf. *Adv. Prax.* 11, 4; 12, 1: CCL 2, 1171; 1172). Cf. R. Braun, *Deus christianorum. Recherches sur le vocabulaire doctrinal de Tertullian*, Paris 1977², p. 151; A. Milano, *Persona in teologia*, Edizioni Dehoniane, Naples 1987, p. 51.

substance is equally predicable of each of the three persons singularly considered, it would follow that the Father is the Trinity, and the Son is the Trinity, and likewise the Holy Spirit, which is unacceptable. It seems, therefore, that *Trinitas* should not be said of *Deus*[679]. The response to the difficulty lies in the fact that *Trinitas* is not substantially predicated of God. The name Trinity, though not itself referred to another, is intrinsically relative forasmuch as what it signifies are the persons who are related *ad aliis*. Thus *Trinitas* is not an essential name, but a relative name[680]. To predicate trinity of God, therefore, does not entail trinity with respect to each person. *Trinitas* is indeed said of the essence, but only according as the essence *res discreta et certa est*; that is, the term *Trinity* is predicable of the essence precisely inasmuch as the subject term of its predication, *Deus*, names the essence *ut in habente*. But this does not make *Trinitas* an essential term *dicitur secundum substantiam*, since it is said of *Deus* only according to the mode of signification proper to *Deus.* Consequently, there is no risk of having to say that the Father or the Son is the Trinity. And because the nature is the same in all three *qui sunt*, that nature – *ut quod est* – is truly triune (three in one), something which could never be said with respect to human natures concretely considered since they are precisely diverse individual natures[681].

The name Trinity signifies at once plurality and unity, and thus names both the persons and the substance: *"tres personas distinctas dicat in recto in unitate essentiae"*[682]. Because "Trinity" names the three persons *in recto*, it appears to be first of all a relative name. But a relative name, if that is all that it is, could not pertain to the substance at all, according as a name derived from personal origin (since relations in the Trinity are precisely relations of origin) does not pertain to the substance[683]. But the sense of "Trinity" is more than simply relative;

---

[679]   *"Omne nomen dictum de Deo, dicitur secundum substantiam, vel secundum ad aliquid... omne quod dicitur secundum substantiam... dicitur de qualibet persona sigillatim in singulari, et de omnibus simul... haec falsa, Pater est trinitas, et similiter falsa est haec, Filius est trinitas, et haec, Spiritus Sanctus est trinitas"* – Albert, *Sum. theol.*, I, tr. 13, q. 51, obj. 2, ed. Borgnet, vol. 31, p. 528.

[680]   *"Hoc nomen, 'trinitas', relativum est intrinsecus, et ideo licet sub hoc nomine, 'trinitas', non referatur ad aliud, tamen sub forma collationis significat personas quae referuntur ad invicem, et ideo non est nomen essentiale, sed ad aliquid"* – Albert, *Sum. theol.*, I, tr. 13, q. 51, ad 2, ed. Borgnet, vol. 31, p. 530.

[681]   *"Quia una est natura deitatis in tribus, ideo praedicatur de eo quod naturam significat ut quod est"* – ibid..

[682]   Albert, *Sum. theol.*, I, tr. 10, q. 45, c. 1, a. 1, obj. 4, ed. Colon., vol. 34, p. 352-353.

[683]   Cf. Boethius, *Utrum Pater et Filius*, 59-60, ed. Loeb, p. 36: *"necesse est quod vocabulum ex personis originem capit id ad substantiam non pertinere"* (cf. Albert, *Sum. theol.*, I, tr. 10,

moreover, its particular relativity is something for which Albert devotes an article to explain. "Trinity" is not a relative name, as though it itself were something beside the Father, Son and Holy Spirit (since the Father is not the Trinity, and nor is the Son or Holy Spirit) which is referred to another. Such a sense of relative corresponds to what Albert calls *relativum extrinsecus*. This kind of relativity is proper to two kinds of names: those in which the relation in question is expressed by the name – *ut concepta* –, examples being "paternity" and "filiation"; and those which signify the relation through stating one of the terms which "exercises" or is said to have the relation – *ut exercitam* –, such as "Father" and "Son", for example. But "Trinity" is not a relative term in either way, for it neither expresses a real relation in God called "Trinity" (which would only add a new, fourth subsistent relation destroying "trinity"), nor states the divine relations by indicating their seat of exercise (which is a logical seat as it were, since the term of a divine relation is identical to the relation itself). "Trinity", for Albert, names the persons (and indirectly the essence) in a relative way as an *intrinsically* relative term (*relativum intrinsecus*). By this he means that the terms of relativity are included in the notion of the name, the name itself not being a term of the relation or relations it designates (and that, as a result of this, differently than the relative terms "paternity" and "filiation", "trinity" is not expressed as a function of a correlative term)[684]. *"Trinitas"* contains within its notion three distinct, mutually related persons. That is the sense of the relativity proper to the name "Trinity". Both the things which are related and that to which they are related are contained within the name, and the name thus points to what is contained within its notion, and not to itself, as to the terms of relation[685]. Note that the idea of "unity" adds to the set

q. 45, c. 1, a. 1, obj. 1, ed. Colon., vol. 34, p. 352 [incorrectly referring the passage to the *De Trin.*]).

[684] Cf. also *De praedicamentis*, tr. 4, c. 5, ed. Borgnet, vol. 1, p. 230-231 (especially 230b): Intrinsic relativity implies the containing on the part of the relative term of both extremes of the relation such that there is only one way of expressing the relation, as, for example, in "similar" and "equal". Extrinsic relativity implies that a relative term does not contain both extremes, but expresses the relation as one of two relatively opposed terms the definition of which depends upon the other, thus depending upon something extrinsic (as "father" is defined in terms of "son").

[685] *"Trinitas nomen relativum est... Est enim relativum extrinsecus et relativum intrinsecus. Extrinsecus dupliciter, scilicet significans relationem ut conceptam, sicut paternitas relationem significat et filiatio et spiratio; et est relativum extrinsecus significans relationem ut exercitam, sicut pater, filius et spiritus sanctus; et hi duo modi relationis extrinsecus habent determinari, sicut paternitas dicitur ad filiationem et pater ad filium. Est et alius modus relativorum, quae sunt relativa intrinsecus, eo quod in intellectu suo claudunt et ea quae referuntur ad invicem, et ea ad quae referuntur... Et tale relativum dicunt esse trinitatem, quia claudit in se tres per-*

of designated relations – over and above that of the persons' relative opposition to one another – that of their essential identity with one another. The label *"relativum intrinsecus"* seems furthermore to be a fitting term inasmuch as the relations thus designated are not so transparent as those expressed by an extrinsically relative term which, in a manner of speaking, "outwardly" expresses either the relation or one of its terms.

A certain relativity of the terms "hypostasis" and "person"

"Hypostasis", according to Albert's treatment of relative terms, is also an intrinsically relative term. It signifies the substance according as it stands under the common nature and the *proprietas* (or simply the *proprietas* in the case of angels). Thus "hypostasis" contains within itself the thing which is related, the substance *ut determinabile*, and the thing to which it is referred, the common nature and the *proprietas* (even if "hypostasis's" mode of signification in not concerned with the proprietas as such). "Person", then, inasmuch as it directly signifies the hypostasis, contains in its concept an intrinsically relative term. Perhaps this could be a way of maintaining the essentially relational character of personhood. The relation in question is not trivial, since it is a question of being related to the common nature as an individual (or supposit) of that nature, as well as being related to the *proprietas* by which individuality – and therefore also being – is possessed.

"Person", moreover, signifies the determinate reality *qua* determinate, in such a way that the *proprietas* indirectly enters into its very signification. Since the *proprietates* in the Trinity are nothing other than relations, some theologians have tried to reduce personhood to a relation[686]. While such a conclusion, as we shall see at the end of this thesis[687], is simply *non sequitur* and unsound, the fact that "person", in the Trinity, indirectly signifies something which is itself relative is, in fact, obvious[688].

---

sonas distinctas et ad invicem relatas. Et ideo non sequitur, ut dicunt, si sic aliquis arguat: 'est relativum, ergo refertur ad aliquid extra se'; claudit enim intra se id ad quod refertur" – Albert, *Sum. theol.,* I, tr. 10, q. 45, c. 1, a. 1, sol., ed. Colon., vol. 34, p. 353.

[686] Cf. in particular, J. Galot, "La définition de la personne, relation et sujet", *Gregorianum* 75/2 (1994), p. 281-299; *La Personne du Christ*, Duculot-Lethielleux, Paris 1969.

[687] Cf. infra, "THE RELATIVE CONCEPTUALIZATION OF J. GALOT", p. 502.

[688] But, even in created persons, by reason of what constitutes the ultimate principle of propriety, the same, it seems, can be said. If being itself, taken as a thing's unique relation to God (cf. in this regard supra, notes 37 & 547; minor paragraph in "THE

The personal name

A personal name is a name used to refer to a single individual and to distinctly designate or call out that individual. Such a name sometimes possesses a particular meaning (in contrast to functioning as but an arbitrary label) according to which the name may be employed either as a proper noun or descriptively. The name "Father", or any personal name, can be taken in two ways: substantively or adjectivally. If it is taken substantively, then it refers to one's very suppositum, for it signifies the nature as determined to a singular being. If, however, the term be taken adjectivally, it serves to predicate of another what belongs to itself as *determining* that thing. In the first case we signify according to a *determinate* mode; in the second, we signify according to a mode of determin*ing* (i.e., qualifying). According to these different

RELATIVE CONCEPTUALIZATION OF J. GALOT", p. 506), is the ultimate principle of individuation (cf. supra, "A WORD ABOUT INDIVIDUALITY AND THE 'PROBLEM OF INDIVIDUATION'", final paragraph, p. 52; note 547; minor paragraph in "THE RELATIVE CONCEPTUALIZATION OF J. GALOT", p. 506), since it is what makes the created *proprietas* (*materia signata*) incommunicable, because it is what makes it individual (and we can guess that Albert tended in this direction when he states that "person" signifies the substance according to its supposital act of standing under the individual or "*quasi individual*" *proprietas* ["*non significat eam ut naturam communem in se substantem et alio non indigentem... sed significat eam, prout dicitur ab actu substandi ut suppositum et sub proprietate individuali vel quasi-individuali*" – Albert, *Sum. theol.*, I, tr. 10, q. 44, c. 3, ed. Colon., vol. 34, p. 351] – perhaps not only because the full sense of individual is to be excluded from something which is "like a part" [and because the *proprietas* signifies *ut determinans* and not *ut determinata*], but because he saw that to call the *proprietas* "individual" might beg a principle of its individuality, and, unless we turn to a supra-essential explanation, such as *esse*, the problem of accounting for individuality seems to continue *ad infinitem* [cf. Albert, *Sum. theol.*, II, tr. 1, q. 4, a. 1, m. 2, ad 2, ed. Borgnet, vol. 32, p. 65; cf. tr. 1, q. 4, a. 1, m. 2, ad 5, ed. Borgnet, vol. 32, p. 66; tr. 12, q. 72, a. 1, m. 2, ad 1, ed. Borgnet, vol. 33, p. 36; *Sum. theol.*, I, tr. 6, q. 24, c. 1, ed. Colon., vol. 34, p. 143-145]), then anything signifying the *proprietas* (*qua* determinate) indirectly signifies *esse*. And since *esse* itself (understood as the actualizing principle of an essence) *is* a relation, then that which signifies the *proprietas* (whether directly or indirectly) is indirectly signifying an extrinsically relative term (*esse*). So, in a sense, "person" is indirectly extrinsically relative, while (because it directly signifies the hypostasis, which is an intrinsically relative term) it is directly intrinsically relative. But, because the thing to which the relation indicated by "hypostasis" is ordered – i.e. because the *terminus* of the relation of substanding – is the *proprietas*, and because the *proprietas* indirectly refers us to another relation, namely *esse*, when we say "person", thereby directly signifying hypostasis indirectly signifying the *proprietas* indirectly signifying *esse*, we directly signify an intrinsically relative term which indirectly (by a double "media tion") signifies an extrinsically relative term. The result (which we mention for the sake of the order) is that we indirectly signify an extrinsically relative term in a direct intrinsically relative way (i.e. directly with an intrinsically relative term). Again, "person" is directly intrinsically relative and indirectly extrinsically relative. "Directly relative" is not meant to say that "person" is a relative term, but rather that it directly signifies an (intrinsically) relative term.

modes of signifying, a proposition may or may not be correctly asserted with respect to certain terms. For example, when we say that the Father is the divine essence, or that that essence is the Father, the proposition is true if "Father" is taken substantively but false if taken adjectivally. Taken substantively, "Father" refers to the hypostasis of the Father in such a way that the sense of the locution is "the essence is the hypostasis which is determined through paternity" or "the hypostasis determined through paternity is the essence". If understood adjectivally, then the form being expressed by "Father" will be predicated of the essence as determining it, in such a way that the rendered sense would be "the essence is that which generates and is therefore determined to be itself through paternity", which is clearly false[689].

Even at the substantive level, the essence is the Father, not through paternity, but rather through the identity of the perfectly simple divine nature. The Father is Father indeed through paternity, and the essence is the Father, but that does not mean that the essence is so itself through paternity. The *determining* paternity refers only to the hypostasis of the Father and not to the nature[690]. Paternity, however *is* the Father, and therefore also the essence; but this sense of identity pertains only to paternity as a determinate relation, and not as *determining*[691]. Substantively, or determinately, hypostasis and the *proprietas* are predicable of the essence, but the *proprietas* does not determine the essence itself, but only the hypostasis. When the person is identified with the essence (as when we say "the Father is the essence"), the signification of the personal name ("Father"), which necessarily designates the *proprietas*[692], is predicated of the essence, but the *proprietas* which it signifies is signified as determining the hypostasis named by

---

[689] *"Pater autem potest accipi dupliciter, substantive scilicet et adiective... Si substantive accipitur, tunc formam, qua ad esse singularis determinatur, ponit circa proprium suppositum et non refert eam ad aliud. Si autem adiective sumitur, tunc formam, quam significat, circa aliud ponit quod est suum substantivum... et ponit eam ut illi inhaerentem et illud determinantem. Unde cum dicitur 'essentia est pater', vel 'pater est essentia', si substantivum est pater, vera est locutio, et paternitas... non refertur ad essentiam, sed ad patris hypostasim sub hoc sensu 'essentia est hypostasis paternitate determinata'... Si autem sit adiectivum, formam suam ponit circa essentiam ut determinantem eam, et est sensus 'essentia est pater', hoc est 'essentia est generans et ideo paternitate determinata', et hoc est falsum"* – Albert, *Sum. theol.*, I, tr. 8, q. 34, c. 2, sol., ed. Colon., vol. 34, p. 264-265. Cf. infra, in the chapter on the *proprietas*, "ESSENCE AND PROPRIETAS", p. 447.

[690] *"Essentia est pater et pater est paternitate pater, et tamen essentia paternitate non est pater, sed potius identitate simplicissmae naturae. Cum enim dicitur 'pater paternitate pater est', paternitas ut determinans refertur ad hypostasim patris et non ad naturam"* – Albert, *Sum. theol.*, I, tr. 8, q. 34, c. 2, ad 5, ed. Colon., vol. 34, p. 265.

[691] Cf. infra, "PROPRIETAS AND PERSON, PERSON AND ESSENCE, ESSENCE AND PROPRIETAS", p. 442.

[692] Cf. the following paragraph.

the personal name, and not as determining the essence of which the signification of the personal name is predicated (note that what is predicated is the signification of the personal name and not the name itself)[693]. An illustration of the point is provided by the phrase *"essentia est pater paternitate"*. In this assertion, the ablative must be understood as determining the predicated thing and not as adverbially modifying the copula[694]. The sense is *"essentia est {pater paternitate}"* (where *"paternitate"* is taken after the manner of an adjective describing *"pater"*), and not *"essentia paternitate pater est"* (where *"paternitate"* be taken as an adverb operating on *"est"*). Actually, the ablative in case is adverbial and not adjectival, for which reason it should pertain to the way *in which* that which is Father is Father. In any case, *"pater paternitate"* must be taken according to a substantive mode of signification (as opposed to adjectival), whence it is correct to say that the essence is the Father insofar as the Father is the *hypostasis* determined through paternity.

The substantive term which is personal, however, signifies something different in a certain way from what it may be said to "name" or "call". If a name is to identify a singular individual in distinction from others, it must signify somehow that thing according to its distinction from every other; a personal name must indirectly signify, therefore, that according to which an individual is distinctly constituted in personal being[695]. The sense of a personal name is thus fuller than a simple term of conventional designation; it does more than point out a given referent. To illustrate the point, consider again the name "Father". "Father" calls out *he who is* the Father – *quis est*; it signifies, however, what is singularly determined through the singular property of paternity – *quod est* (or *qui est* according to the table above). Similarly, the name "Socrates" labels or identifies he who is Socrates; its signification includes the concept of that which, through accidental

[693] *"Hypostasis enim cum proprietate praedicatur de essentia, sed, sicut dictum est, proprietas non determinat essentiam, sed hypostasim... 'pater' praedicat, quod significat, sed non eodem modo. Significat enim proprietatem ut determinantem hypostasim propriam et non ut determinantem essentiam, de qua praedicatur"* – Albert, *Sum. theol.*, I, tr. 8, q. 34, c. 2, ad 9 & 10, ed. Colon., vol. 34, p. 265.

[694] *"Cum dicitur 'essentia est pater paternitate', ablativus, qui determinatio praedicati est, rem praedicati determinat, et ad subiectum, quod est essentia, non refertur, et ideo essentia paternitate non distinguitur"* – Albert, *Sum. theol.*, I, tr. 8, q. 34, c. 2, ad 5, ed. Colon., vol. 34, p. 265.

[695] Cf. Aquinas, *Sum. theol.*, I, 30, 4.

and substantial individuating particularities, is determined in singular being[696].

In the context of the Trinity, as we have seen, one must be careful to avoid the fallacy of confounding the *quis est* and *quod est*, lest one predicate of one term what is predicable only of the other. But this caution only adheres when the intension of *quod est* refers to the essence which the several persons are (as, for example, in the case of "God"). In the event that the *quod est* refer to a given (i.e. determinate) hypostasis *as such*, then there is nothing which cannot be predicated of the *quis est* if it is predicable of the *quod est*. We are recognizing two senses of *quod est* here, one limited to the concrete divine essence (which in a loose sense may be logically referred to as *quo est*), another restricted to determinate hypostatic signification, that is, tied to the persons themselves, where there is no effective difference between this particular *quod est* and *quis est*, except for the just elucidated fact that the former is properly speaking what is signified by the personal name, while the latter is what it *names* or *calls out*[697]. With respect to inferior beings, no such dual sense of *quod est* is possible, since to every hypostatic *quod est* corresponds an identical essential *quod est*, namely the concretized individual nature which the hypostasis is; the essence with respect to which the hypostasis can be said to be distinct is nothing other than the "universal" nature which is rather the *quo est* than a *quod est*.

---

[696] What we are recognizing here is a particular instance of a more general principle of signification and denotation according to which any nominal expression which is more than an arbitrary *vox*, that is, which is assigned in virtue of something proper to the reality it is said to name, denotes the class of individuals of which it is the name while at the same time connoting the properties by reason of which these individuals are recognized as members of the class in question. For a historical survey of the complicated relationship between denotation, connotation, signification and designation, and the confusing lack of uniformity in the use of these terms by different philosophical traditions, see U. Eco, "Signification and Denotation from Boethius to Ockham", *Franciscan Studies* 44 (1984), p. 1-29.

[697] Cf. the above table indicating the ways of signifying substance and signaling the notion of *qui est*.

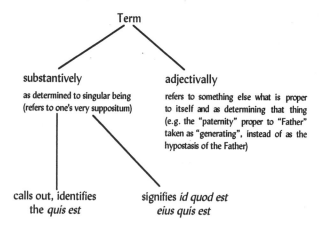

A Christological issue

The name "Father", which is given in virtue of active generation, signifies, for Albert, a *per se* singular existent according to a singular mode of existence. The emphasis upon singular mode of existence is a recognition of the importance of the *proprietas* according to which and through which the person is singularly constituted. "Person", then, signifies more than the singular hypostasis; it signifies simultaneously the fact of *the presence of* a certain modality (and principle of that modality) of singular existence; and the personal name, therefore (since it is tied to a *given* person), signifies not only the singular hypostasis, but also the *particular modality* (along with its principle) according to which the named individual/hypostasis is singularized/hypostatized. The personal name cannot merely signify the hypostasis without the *proprietas*[698].

These last affirmations invite us to consider a hypostasis from two points of view, according as it is with or without a *proprietas*, according as it is the referent of "person" or not. Actually, every hypostasis has some mode of existence such that it cannot be conceived without some kind of *proprietas*; consequently, and as is clear from the context of Albert's solution, *"sine proprietate"* must intend *"sine proprietate singularis"* (in the sense of *a se proprium*) and not simply *"sine proprietate*

---

[698]   *"Hoc nomen 'pater' a generatione activa impositum quantum ad ipsum vocabulum significat 'existens per se solum secundum singularis existentiae modum', paternitate ad eundem modum determinatum; et ideo hypostasim sine proprietate non significat"* – Albert, *Sum. theol.*, I, tr. 8, q. 34, c. 2, sol., ed. Colon., vol. 34, p. 264.

quicquid". But this opens itself to discussion of a Christological question with regard to what part of the just given definition of person the human nature of Christ may be said not to fulfill. The definition underscores existence *per se* and a singular mode of existence. If a certain perseity were necessarily ascribable to every human nature because of its substantiality, perhaps an argument may be made for the second aspect's being at issue with respect to the human nature in Christ. A hypostasis could perhaps have its mode of existence in such a way that its *proprietas* is not a *proprietas singularis*, inasmuch as it may be a *proprietas* belonging to something else. That is, its particular mode of existence might not be a *singular* mode in the fullest sense of the term proper to a self-possessed individual which finds the principle of its individuality within itself. Something like this might arguably be happening in Christ, for whom the "hypostasis" of the human nature may be understood not to possess its own *proprietas singularis*, since it is incorporated into the singularity belonging to the Word. In this case, the singularity of the Word must operate as the *proprietas* for the human nature whereby it is truly made to be an individual substance, but for which reason it cannot be an individual substance of its own right and is therefore neither fully individual or singular in the fullest sense. The humanity in Christ is, nevertheless, singular, and may accordingly be said to avail itself of a *proprietas singularis*, even, therefore, to *have* such a *proprietas*. But such a possession is only a partaking in what belongs by nature only to the Word and not to the human nature in itself. As a result, the one singularity of the God-man is nothing other than the *proprietas singularis* of the Word, whereby the human nature is a *hypostasis sine proprietate singularis sive ipsius*, for which reason it cannot be a person.

Conclusion

Seeking to situate the concept of "person" with respect to the various notions characterizing philosophical discourse about the ontic structure of the most perfect thing of nature, an indispensable series of distinctions and a universally applicable notion of personhood is acquired only when the fruits of pre-Christian reflection on man are coordinated with an analysis of personality in God. The notion of "person" transcends the predicamental order of nature and is properly applicable to God himself. Person is therefore not something belonging exclusively to the realm of created substances but signifies an absolute reality analogically common to *ens ab alio* and *ens non ab alio* alike.

In both God and creatures, person signifies the thing of nature possessing the substantial perfection of *per se* existence (or subsistence). The polyvalent character of the notion of "substance" provides the conceptual room for its verification in the Trinity while nonetheless avoiding any substantial differentiation between the relatively distinguished subsistents. Corresponding with the earliest historical attempts to define the personal reality in God, the name "hypostasis" presents itself as the more adequate term for designating the absolute perfection of the person, since "hypostasis" names the substantial reality from the subjective point of view distinctive of concrete or complete existing substances (primary substance) and cannot be confused with essence as such. The Latin *"persona"*, however, goes beyond "hypostasis" in signifying the distinctive element of personality inasmuch as explicitly denoting distinction as such, more perfectly capturing the incommunicable dimension of perseity.

Considering language, the semantical properties of the diverse names used to designate different aspects of natural perfection manifest a certain hierarchical progression. The nature signified simply, in precision from any differences or determinations, receives the name οὐσία. That nature is called ὑπόστασις when signified as a distinct thing of nature and from the point of view of its distinguishability, an attribute owing to the act of standing under a determining principle proper to substance so signified. The concept of "hypostasis" pertains to the determined substance itself, the *quod est* as being determined by a principle of incommunicable distinction. In virtue of the fact that it denotes the act of substanding, "hypostasis" also signifies the substantial referent according to a respect to what is common, implying a certain relativity in its notion. "Person" or πρόσωπον signifies the same distinct thing of nature precisely *qua* distinctly individuated. While hypostasis is the determinate thing as being determined, person is the determinate thing *as determinate.* The concept of *per se* existence, though distinctive of supposits, is not explicitly included in the notion of "hypostasis" but directly expressed by the name "person" signifying what is *per se una*, indivisible in itself and divisible from others. "Person", of course, names the substance, precisely insofar as hypostasis (i.e. *secundum quod ab actu substandi dicitur*). But "person" signifies this hypostatic reality precisely as distinct from every other hypostasis through an incommunicable property; it names the hypostasis according to the distinguishing act of the *proprietas* by which the hypostasis is distinct, thus containing in its notion the very *ratio* or cause of the distinctness proper to hypostasis. These formal characteristics of the mode of signification proper to "person" entail the possibility of comparing a multiplicity of persons distinguished from one another uniquely on the basis of their respective acts of substanding with respect to a common nature due to a diversity of distinctive *proprietates*. "Person", furthermore, also orients us toward the deontological sphere inasmuch as its notion implies, on account of the etymological origin ascribed to it, the special dignity proper to every intellectual supposit.

II.2. TOWARD DEFINING PERSON

Introduction

With the sense of the various names used to designate the distinct members of the Trinity (and any distinct thing of nature) in place, we can proceed toward establishing a systematic definition of person. Despite the conceptual articulations of the previous section, the name "person" requires further clarification, particularly in light of the mystery of the Trinity where, notwithstanding the absence of absolute number in God, "person" is the object of numerical expressions. As St. Thomas remarks, the difficulty presented by the fact that the name "person" is predicated plurally in God, in contrast to the names proper to the essence, while nevertheless not being a relative term in itself, has led to a diversity of widely discussed opinions concerning its signification[699]. In essence, the simultaneously substantial and notional (distinctive) signification of "person" entails for the theologian the Trinitarian difficulty of reconciling concrete substantial unity with an incommunicable element which is nonetheless identical to the common substance[700]. If we must recognize that number cannot be predicated of the substance in God, we cannot deny that person includes substance in its very notion. This apparently contradictory affirmation forms the central object of Scholastic Trinitarian speculation and constitutes, along with its reciprocally formulated corollary at the heart of the Christological paradox, the meter which must gauge our understanding of personality and according to which the complete definition of person must be constructed. "A definition of person", observes J. Galot, "is unsatisfactory until it contributes to an elucidation of the Trinitarian doctrine and is made in conformity with the mystery of the Incarnation"[701].

Preliminary remark on the personal principle: a tentative hypothesis

The most common characteristic proposed as formal and distinctive of personhood has been rationality. We have seen some theologians (for example,

---

[699] Cf. Aquinas, *Sum. theol.*, I, 29, 4.
[700] Cf. A. Pompei, op. cit., p. 250-253.
[701] J. Galot, "La définition de la personne, relation et sujet", *Gregorianum* 75/2 (1994), p. 282-283.

Richard of Saint Victor) attempt to avoid defining personhood according to a *qualification* of substance, seeking rather to characterize it according to what might be called "subjective" properties, in such a way, for example, that personhood be constituted by a personal property quintessentially incommunicable and which is therefore responsible for constituting an *alius*. But that *alius*, it has been observed, seems to reduce in its constitution to the substance seen as thoroughly individuated, a fact which invites us to reconsider *rationality* as the fundamental source of difference between individual substances enjoying personhood and those which do not. We shall not linger here over whether rationality is precisely that which makes one to be a person, but intend to propose that there is at least another level of consideration in determining whether a certain substance is a person.

Even if rationality is most distinctive of personhood, it does not necessarily follow from this that the humanity of Christ is a person, since it is possible that his human nature fail to be a person on other grounds, namely, insofar as it not be a subject of attribution. The supposition here is that personhood should be defined as "rational subject of attribution" instead of simply "rational substance". But how is it that something could be a substance yet not a subject of attribution[702]? The answer lies especially in what is meant by "substance" and in the various senses according to which it is signified. But without entering into the complex examination of the perfection of substance in Christ, we would like to briefly entertain the following plausibility: it is also possible because, for a given substance, the formally highest ordered reality may be said to determine the subject of attribution[703].

In man, the formally (or ontologically) highest ordered reality is the rational soul, which is intrinsic to his nature, for which reason his very nature (at the individual, concrete level) is identified as the subject of attribution, and therefore also the person. With regard to the substance of Christ's humanity, however, the formally highest ordered reality is God Himself, since the divine nature is united to that humanity in a unique way and not simply related to it externally. That is, the formally highest ordered reality apropos of that substance is something much greater than what is intrinsic to the nature; it is now an integral part of something superior which therefore takes the role of subject of attribution since it is highest in consideration of the entire composite. In an ordinary man, what is highest in his composite is his rational soul, which, because it belongs to the nature, confers attributive subjectivity to the individualized nature as such. The nature's relation with God holding it in existence – which, as we have alluded to elsewhere, might well be the ultimate individuating ingredient in the concrete nature – cannot be the subject of attribution, since what is relative is predicamentally accidental and rooted in something ontologically prior. However, because the relation in question is transcendental[704], and refers particularly to God, and since we may speak of an essence as being "composed" with this relation, then it would fol-

---

[702] This is the fundamental and most pressing question left unresolved since our consideration of the doctrine of Cyril of Alexandria.

[703] By "formally highest ordered reality" we mean the ontologically superior component in a composite.

[704] By "transcendental" we are expressing nothing more than the fact that the relation is so essential to its subject that the subject cannot exist without it.

low that, from this point of view, that relation would be the formally highest reality of the composite being and therefore determine the subject of attribution. But that relation is rooted in the nature which is its subject, whence the attributive subject would still be the nature itself; briefly, the formally highest reality of a composite consisting in an essence and its relation to God does not take us beyond the existing essence itself. Somehow, in the person of the Word, the human nature of Christ is intimately associated with the very divinity which holds it in existence, in such a way that, because of that union, the terms of the entitative relation between the human substance and God are not external one to another, but rather, it may be said that the existing humanity is held in existence by something which is united to it directly, and this through the "medium" of the person of the Word; part of the "composite" is held in existence by another part of the same "composite" to which it is related, which is not the same as to be held in existence by a relation to that with which a thing is not composed, as an ordinary essence is composed with its relation to God, but not with God Himself! And this is the difference which makes the second person of the Trinity the subject of attribution for the humanity of Christ, and for which reason no second person is posited by recognizing the substantial completeness of that humanity which enjoys at once rationality and existence *per se*, but which does not on that account constitute a separate person or *quod est*[705], since it is composed with something ontologically superior which receives the dignity of subject of attribution proper to personhood[706].

Now, it was earlier affirmed that Cyril of Alexandria may be credited with having uncovered the crucial and pivotal issue in articulating the unity of being in the hypostatic union, inasmuch as his conception of ὑπόστασις understood as "subject of attribution" both allowed for its distinction from the individualized concrete nature (a distinction able to be verified really when this latter is taken *qua* nature, and perhaps only according to mode of signification when viewed in its existential integrity) and pointed toward the crucial problem of determining how some really existing, substantial *thing* not also be a subject of attribution[707]. As a consequence, it appeared necessary to seek for a resolution of the difficulty by expanding our notion of subsistence so as to accommodate different forms of real and substantial existence, something which we suggested might be achieved by introducing a distinction, for ex-

---

[705] Or perhaps it is better to say: *ultimum id quod est*, since the human nature seems must indeed constitute some *thing*.

[706] Note that as a consequence of this reasoning, it follows that if we were united to something in a non-accidental way, and that thing is greater than we are, then it would become the subject of attribution of all of our actions. This hypothetical situation is analogous to what occurs with regard to the relation between a substantial whole and an integral part, one of the three fundamental relations cited by St. Thomas as most apt to shed light upon the nature of the hypostatic union.

[707] Cf. supra, "AXIS PLACED IN RELIEF BY CYRIL.", p. 71 (especially p. 73-73). The concept of "thing" here remains, of course, to be spelled-out. Though we do not have room within the scope of this thesis to consider the humanity of Christ in itself, we mention simply that the sense of "*res*" in this context corresponds to a certain attenuated sense of the notion of "*res naturae*" (cf. Albert, *III Sent.*, d. 10, a. 1, ad quaest. 4, ed. Borgnet, vol. 28, p. 190).

ample, between *subsistentia in se* and *subsistentia in alio*[708]. The schema which resulted from this ensemble of reflections turns out to be wholly compatible with and even, in part, explained by the present theory of personhood based upon the notion of subject of attribution (as determined by the ontologically highest ordered reality accruing to the substance in question).

Here are the schematic conclusions from our chapter on Cyril:

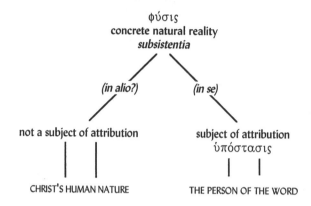

But we are still given no reason for why subsistence *in alio* might preclude a thing's being a subject of attribution [709]. The reason must lie in the fact that the "other" *takes* the role of subject of attribution, and this, on account of a certain principle of priority, which, plausibly, is precisely the principle that the highest "component" determines attributive subjectivity [710]. With respect to those things united to (or within) the humanity of Christ, the person of the Word is ontologically highest, wherefore it retains the privilege of attributive subjectivity. And, because the Word is neither an intrinsic part of nor rooted in the humanity, attributive subjectivity is *not* ascribed to the humanity, for which reason it cannot be a person. Consequently, the schematization can be made more precise:

---

[708] Cf. supra, "AXIS PLACED IN RELIEF BY CYRIL.", p. 75-76.

[709] Unless that which is said to subsist *in alio* is thereby understood to be *incomplete* or but a partial principle of a greater whole – in which case it is clearly not the subject of attribution. But the humanity of Christ is generally recognized to be a complete thing of itself, a substantially perfected entity, whence its subsistence in another does not entail the kind of partiality obviously precluding being a subject of attribution.

[710] Note that this subjectivality which is determined by a principle pertaining to ontological perfection means that a subject of attribution is more than a logical reality. Epistemico-logically speaking, we *identify* it on the basis of its position in the ontological order (that is, we know and affirm that it is the subject of attribution in virtue of the fact that it is highest – satisfying the nominal definition of subject of attribution), but such a *position* is not a description of all that is proper to a subject of attribution (i.e. it is not an expression of its total reality) which is the *id quod est,* subject of initiative, and seat of responsibility for intelligent natures.

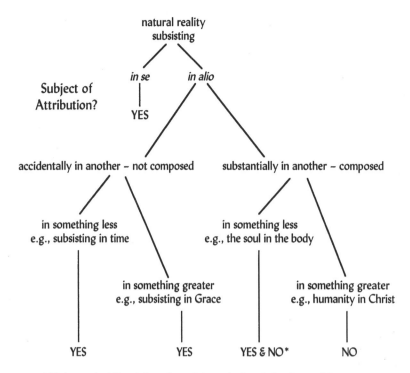

natural reality
subsisting

in se   *in alio*

Subject of
Attribution?

YES

accidentally in another – not composed   substantially in another – composed

in something less   in something less
e.g., subsisting in time   e.g., the soul in the body

in something greater   in something greater
e.g., subsisting in Grace   e.g., humanity in Christ

YES   YES   YES & NO*   NO

* If the early Albertinian view of the priority of the form with respect to
the composite is correct[711], then the form ought to be the subject of attribution; but if the composite is superior (and a form's absolute dependence upon the matter with which it is composed would seem to indicate this), then the form is not the subject of attribution. If the soul be
considered in the state of separation after death, it simply falls, for that
duration, within the branch of subsistence in se.

[711] Cf. Albert, *De anima*, II, tr. I, c. 1 & 3, ed. Borgnet, vol. 5, p. 192-193 & 196, where
Albert argues in favor of form as the entitatively most self-contained and perfect
element of nature (cf. also, *Super Dion. De div. nom.*, c. 5, 5, ed. Colon., vol. 37/1,
p. 306, n. 22-27). The idea of the primacy of form with respect even to the composite is not characteristic of Albert's later hylemorphism and, outside of the *De anima*,
Albert upholds a very different doctrine of the relationship between the essential
parts of a composite and the composite thing itself. For this reason, the negative
response is the more definitive. For a broad analysis of the Albertinian hylemorphic doctrine, see L. De Raeymaeker, "Albert le Grand, philosophe. Les lignes fondamentales de son système métaphysique", *Revue néoscholastique de philosophie* 35
(1933), p. 19-28, for whom the primacy of the composite with respect to the parts is
explicitly maintained both in works antecedent to the *De anima* and in works posterior to it. The texts he cites are: *Sum. de creaturis*, p. 1, tr. 1, q. 2, a. 4, ed. Borgnet,
vol. 34, p. 330; and *Sum. theol.*, II, tr. 4, q. 13, m. 1, ed. Borgnet, vol. 32, p. 160.
However, the passage from the *Sum. de creaturis* points, in our opinion, to the
relatively self-sufficient status of the form, as contrasted with the relative de-

For whatever they are worth, these intuitions cohere with the fuller theory of the "integration of singularity" able to be extracted from the texts of St. Albert. They are better expressed, however, in other terms, namely those of the principle of individuation (i.e. the *proprietas*) and whether the latter is possessed *ex se* or *ex alio*. Furthermore, the most important approach to the question of attributive subjectivality consists not so much in defining "subject of attribution" as in distinguishing the various kinds of ontological reality attributable to substance or nature and the manner in which a nature is rendered a complete subject or hypostasis, and this, along with defining person, remains the central task of the pages which remain.

Four rudimentary senses of personhood

There are for Albert four primitive derivations of the use of the name person to distinguish an individual [712]. The most ancient are those according to which "person" is used in theatrical representations (something already discussed by Boethius) and in the context of civil considerations in respect of the dignity of the legal "party". In both instances, "person", employed as a term descriptive of certain human individuals, intends to emphasize and illuminate the importance of the individual in question enjoining men's noteworthy respect. This aspect of dignity, though certainly not explicative of personhood, is a precise description of every person, and, as an accurate necessary description, reveals something fundamental about the intrinsic structure of persons, namely the quality of the nature indispensable to the constitution of personhood, its intelligence. The remaining two most fundamental senses of "person" derive from the personal reflection of the historically principal contributors to the question: Boethius, according to whom person is the hypostasis or substance of a rational nature; and Richard of St. Victor, for whom person is the *per se* existent according to a singular mode of existence. These latter senses of "person" directly imply something about the ontological structure of the substantial individual of whom the term is predicated and are more than just a qualitative description of that individual. They are,

---

pendency of matter. It is only with the later *Summa theologiae* that an explicit formulation of the primacy of the composite may be affirmed.

[712] "*Sunt enim quatuor rationes personae. Una est, secundum quod 'personae' dicuntur quae repraesentantur in theatris... Est et alia ratio personae quam ponit Boetius in libro de 'Duabus naturis in una persona Christi', quod 'persona est rationalis naturae hypostasis sive substantia individua'*"– Albert, *Sum. theol.*, II, tr. 4, q. 15, m. 2, ed. Borgnet, vol. 32, p. 206.

to be precise, true definitions of persons, to the extent that they explicitly name the essence of the person. It is the content of these two
definitions which becomes the substance of the Albertinian consideration of personhood.

Richard, as we have seen, strongly objected to the use of the term
substantia in defining person in the Trinity. The entire Trinity is an
individual substance, yet the Trinity is not a person. A formal identification of personality with substance would seem to justify either
Arius or Sabellius. On the other hand, withdraw the substantial element from its signification, and "person" risks becoming a mere *modus
loquendi*. Rather than deny the semantical problem, and rather than
avoid it by means of an exaggerated simplification such as that of the
Lombard declaring that "person" is an equivocal term, sometimes
naming the essence, sometimes the hypostasis, and sometimes the
proprietas, Albert tackles the question head on, confronting the demands of both the Boethian and Victorine traditions. If person is a
substantial name, how are we to understand its use in the plural? And
if plurality in God resides exclusively in relations, how are we to avoid
the predication of accidents in God? What is needed is a concept of
person which denotes relation while nevertheless retaining the substantiality expressed in the Boethian definition[713]. The substantiality
of relation is indispensable. Without it, the persons of the Trinity,
who are said *secundum substantiam*, cannot truly be multiplied; for, if
the relations were not identical to the substance, then they could not
be constitutive of the divine persons by way of identity. Such a solution is the only one able to avoid the dangers of both modalism and
tritheism, and it is in virtue of this that the Boethian definition, after
being submitted to the depurations of analogy, retains for Albert a
privileged status in resolving the difficulties connected with the application of the concept of person in the Trinity[714].

---

[713] For a discussion of the implications of these two demands and the contextualization
of Albert's concept of personality with respect to them, see A. Pompei, op. cit.,
p. 217-220, 237-239.
[714] Cf. A. Pompei, op. cit., p. 219-220.

Three basic elements in personhood – a working definition

Three general elements converge to form the Albertinian notion of
personhood: a person, as Albert defines it[715], must be something:

> A) *per se unum*
> B) *secundum existentiae modum*
> C) *in natura intellectuali*

The distinct aspects constitutive of personhood, then, are perseity, a
particular modality of existence and intelligence. The first, though
immediately descriptive of the person as such, is connected with and,
in one sense, derives from the character of "substance" itself. The
second represents the *distinctio*, the importance of which was alluded
to above, and, since, in the context of the Trinity, the *existentiae modus*
performs the essential role of distinguishing personal terms, Albert is
able to affirm that *"si posset, etiam secundum esse et secundum id quod est,
maneret una"*[716], in the sense that the persons are *already accounted for* by
the relations of origin.

The third aspect, namely, intelligence, is of equal importance in
determining personhood and in some respects seems to carry more
weight, since it alone among the three requirements is at once a necessary *and* sufficient condition for the verification of personhood: in
terms of metaphysical extension, every verifiable instance of intelligent life corresponds to a distinct personal entity, since, *"omne autem
communicans naturam intellectualem est persona"*[717]. This is not to say that
it would be a sufficient condition for the *constitution* of personhood,
since the first two elements are indispensable in that regard; however,
the first two, taken by themselves, would still not enable us to declare
a thing a person, while the third aspect, intelligence, according to
Albert, always and everywhere entails personhood (and consequently,
therefore, the other two requirements). Though the large majority of
Albert's concern with isolating the notion of personhood focuses outside of considerations of the qualification of a nature as intelligent (or
rational), the effective convertibility between personhood and that
which participates or communicates in intelligence[718] orients us once

---

[715] *"Constitutio enim personae est ex eo quod sit per se unum secundum quemcumque existentiae
    modum in natura intellectuali"* – Albert, *I Sent.*, d. 23, a. 1, ad 3, ed. Borgnet, vol. 25,
    p. 581.

[716] Albert, *I Sent.*, d. 23, a. 1, ad 4, ed. Borgnet, vol. 25, p. 581.

[717] Albert, *I Sent.*, d. 23, a. 1, contra 7, ed. Borgnet, vol. 25, p. 581.

[718] We say "effective convertibility", since no one would deny the converse that every
    person communicates in some way or another in intelligent nature.

more in the directions pursued by Boethius for whom intelligence serves as the formal qualification rendering a primary substance a person. Now, every definition predicates something *in quid* (the quidditative expression) and something *in quale* (the qualitative element), neither of which elements, taken alone, explicitly says everything contained in the term which they together define[719]. Consequently, it is striking that Albert establishes a perfect identity between person and the intelligent: *"omne autem communicans naturam intellectualem est persona"*[720]. The proposition asserts that everything which is intelligent is a person. The converse, that every person be intelligent will not be disputed, whence the result of convertibility between person and the intelligent. But this means that person is convertible with *one* of the members of its definition, that wherever we find intelligence, there we also find person, and vise versa. The point is interesting because the quidditative part of the definition seems relegated to quasi-superfluity, while intelligence, which, as the qualitative term, effectively operates as a specific difference delimiting a generic category of substance, turns out to be coextensive with the "species" person being defined. But this is not characteristic of definitions. In every definition, the notion of the species is constructed from the notions of the genus and difference, the genus designating what is "material" (at least in a logical sense), otherwise the mention of the genus would prove superfluous. Taken as specific difference, intelligence

---

[719] It is perhaps not without benefit to reiterate some of the logical principles of signification as they are related to definition. In a general way, every definition must include a quidditative term and a qualitative term (the first naming the genus, the second naming the difference). However, the referents of the definitional terms individually naming the substance and quality respectively, when those terms are taken concretely, are not different things, but differ from one another only in mode of signification – that is, the two parts of a definition do not name different *things* but signify the same thing according to diverse qualities or modes. This is possible because every predicable name – whether generic (e.g. "animal"), specific (e.g. "man") or formal (e.g. "rational") – signifies substance along with a certain quality. The substance, or underlying subject of predication, is what the name signifies, while the quality is that by which, or in virtue of which, the name is predicated (i.e. that which specifies the mode according to which the substance is signified): *"In omni nomine significatur substantia cum qualitate; et dicitur substantia id quod nomen significat, qualitas autem id a quo nomen imponitur, quae non sunt diversa in re semper, sed tantum in modo significandi"* – Albert, *Sum. theol.*, I, tr. 6, q. 24, c. 2, ad 4, ed. Colon., vol. 34, p. 146. Consequently, when a name is predicated, it will signify both substance and quality, designating, that is, a referent, and doing so from a particular point of view. When the distinctive points of view of two or more names are different, however, it does not follow that the referent of these names is not the same (though neither name exhaustively signifies the referent). With these points in mind, we can more punctiliously continue in defining the person.

[720] Albert, *I Sent.*, d. 23, a. 1, contra 7, ed. Borgnet, vol. 25, p. 581.

(like rationality in the case of man) indicates the essential structure of a thing, designating a determination taken from the form. If we consider other examples of definition, it seems that the specific difference taken by itself does not always and everywhere designate the species which it defines, for it might also extend to other species outside of the genus of the species being defined. The definition of man (if we take rational in the sense of "having an intellectual nature"[721]) can serve as an example. Man is a rational (or intelligent) animal. Now, it is not the case that the rational (or the intelligent) always and everywhere designates man, since something intelligent could very easily refer to an angel or to God. The point is that a specific difference is not convertible with the species it defines[722]. Nonetheless, intelligence, in the present Albertinian affirmation, operates in a way akin to something like risibility in man, since intelligence is coextensive with personhood, in the same way that the property risible is coextensive with man, though "rational" (understood to mean intelligent) and "man" are not coextensive. It seems that intelligence, for Albert, performs a role with respect to person analogous to that which risibility, for example, plays with respect to man: only *propria*, the fifth of the *praedicabilia* according to Porphyry, are identical in extension with their subject, are predicated reciprocally of the things of which they are the properties[723]. The dissimilarity lies in the fact that risibility, or any other property for that matter, though indicating (in the sense of deriving from) the specific constitution of a thing, does not signify the essence of the thing; there exists no intrinsic necessity joining man and risibility as there exists between person and intelligence which constitutes its essence[724].

Now, in the case of intelligence, if it is a specific difference (in the strict sense naming the properly essential determination of a thing), then its referent cannot be convertible with that of the term person, and if it is similar to a *per se* second mode attribute like risibility, then

---

[721] This is not an unstandard interpretation among the mediaevals, and the acceptation is already attested in the second century: cf. Thomas Aquinas, In VIII *Met.*, Lect. 2 (ed. Cathala, No. 1697); cf. Porphyry, *Isagoge*, ed. A. Busse, CAG, vol. IV, p. 10, 11-15. For Albert, "*omnis rationalis natura est intellectualis, et e converso*" – Albert, *Sum. theol.*, II, tr. 4, q. 15, m. 1, ad 7, ed. Borgnet, vol. 32, p. 205. Cf. infra, "CONTENTIAL EQUIVALENCE BETWEEN BOETHIUS AND RICHARD", p. 351.

[722] "Difference is a consequence of those things whose difference it is, but it is not also convertible with them" – Porphyry, *Isagoge*, op. cit., p. 19, 11-13, trans. E. Warren.

[723] Porphyry, *Isagoge*, op. cit., p. 12, 20-22; 19, 13-15; 20, 10-25.

[724] Cf. Aristotle, *Topics*, A5, 101b37 - 102b8: Property is "a predicate which does not indicate the essence of a thing but yet belongs to that thing alone and is predicated convertibly of it".

it must concomitantly indicate both the generic and specific concepts proper to personhood, neither of which can be identical with intelligence itself. The latter is impossible, because intelligence serves as the specific concept. The former is contradicted by the fact that intelligence is convertible with person. Is it perhaps erroneous to have treated intelligence after the manner of a specific difference? Could it be the case that intelligence, like risibility, is the extension of something more fundamentally essential to the reality having that attribute, that its notion derive from the communication between two different notions which themselves properly define person? If so, then intelligence stems from other principles which constitute the person, and instead of employing the term in the systematic definition of personhood, we should assign to the term "intelligent" the function of nominally labeling "person" insofar as coextensive in signification, and continue to look for a more foundational concept to serve as the specific difference, which when considered in relation to the "matter" of the definition, might suggest or be suggested by the notion of intelligence, just as rationality in man, when considered in its relation with corporal matter, intimates and is inferred by risibility. While the risible without a doubt designates man, in order to adequately answer the question "what is man?", we should still have to respond to the question "what is the essence of that which is risible?". Similarly then, with regard to person, since *omne autem communicans naturam intellectualem est persona*, we perhaps ought to ask ourselves "what is the essence of those things which are intelligent?".

But perhaps the error lies in excluding convertibility between a specific difference and the species. While ordinary definitions respect this rule of logical extension, there is no reason why certain definitions could not consist of a specific difference for which only a single species exists. Rationality, as a specific difference, was seen to be incapable of reciprocal predication with man because of its extension to other species outside of the animal genus. The reason, then, for which a specific difference not be coextensive with the species consists in the fact that the specific difference can be realized in another genus. This may be the key to why intelligence *can* indeed be coextensive with persons, precisely because there is absolutely no (pertinent) genus outside of individual substance (taken in an analogous sense, since we are including God in these considerations) to which such a qualification could be attributed. Consequently, the difference "intelligent" not only includes a quidditative notion (like every specific difference, able to signify as a whole)[725] but is restricted to a single quidditative notion, namely, individual substances, for which reason it cannot extend beyond that genus, thereby acquiring convertibility with the species, since only one such species exists. In fact, there is no genus outside of substance able to be considered, because substance is the highest genus, to which nothing is superior[726]. In this way, person and intelligent always correspond one with the other, since the intelligent has no exterior referent. Nonetheless, this is an accidental reason, due to the mere fact that no competing genus may be found.

The intelligent, then, is indeed coextensive with person, and such a reciprocity does not go against our intuition. But, as specific difference, intelligence succeeds in delimiting the "species" person in an analogous sense, since that "species" (considering person as a universal concept) actually embraces three distinct kinds, or families, of person (divine, angelic, and human). The same analogous character, of course, resides in the predication of all three of the second intentions genus, difference and species, and none of them (substance, intelligence, person) may be understood as univocally predicated of the members of the distinct kinds of persons signaled above.

As stated in part (A) of the proposed working definition, person is something *per se una*. This, we noted, has both a substantial and a non-substantial personal meaning. But something is *per se unum*, as we shall see, only insofar as substance; and person, therefore, is pronounceable only of substances[727]. If the persons in God are indeed substance, this does not mean that we have exhausted the sense of personhood by naming the substance, since the other elements of the definition are equally important[728]. Indeed, the aspect or part from which distinction is had does not pertain to the substance: *"essentia*

---

[725] Every specific difference, in a properly assigned definition, necessarily includes what is commonly possessed by the generic term. This is because the whole essence of the definition is included in the difference. The difference is not an essence distinct from the genus but simply adds a particular mode of being. In fact, "differences have more than their genera" – Porphyry, *Isagoge*, op. cit., p. 15, 24-27. Cf. Thomas Aquinas, In VIII *Met.*, Lect. 2 (ed. Cathala, No. 1519-1555; 1694-1700).

[726] Cf. Porphyry, *Isagoge*, op. cit., p. 5, 1-4.

[727] *"Non convenit nisi substantiae, quia nihil est per se unum, nisi hoc aliquid in substantia"* – Albert, *I Sent.*, d. 23, a. 2, obj. 6, ed. Borgnet, vol. 25, p. 583. Cf. infra, "ON THE SUBSTANCE WHICH PERSON SIGNIFIES", p. 286; "DISTINCTION THROUGH RELATION NEVERTHELESS REQUIRES A SUBSTANTIAL ELEMENT", p. 392; cf. "THE RELATIVE CONCEPTUALIZATION OF J. GALOT", p. 502.

[728] *"Si personae divinae sint, substantia vero indivisa, necesse est vocabulum quod ex personis originem capit, id ad substantiam non pertinere"* – Albert, *I Sent.*, d. 23, a. 2, contra 1, ed. Borgnet, vol. 25, p. 583.

continet unitatem, relatio autem sola multiplicat Trinitatem"[729]. The second part of the definition, concerning a mode of distinction or multiplication, is accomplished in the Trinity by relation alone, while subsistence and perseity is had for the Trinity at the level of the essence. In man, to the contrary, both subsistence and distinction are found already at the level of the substance (primary substance), inasmuch as a man's substance is multiplied according to substantial being and individuated matter (which is an essential part), unique to him alone; for man, both parts (A) and (B) of the definition come from the same source.

That multiplicity central to determining distinct persons in no way derives from substance, neither in God nor in man, when substance is considered from the point of view of its communicability. For this reason, Albert must import something extrinsic to common nature or substance in order to satisfy the *distinctio* requirement of personhood: *"non cadit pluralitas ratione substantiae, sed ratione existentiae proprietatis quae relatio originis est"*[730]. Even in man, the *ratio substantiae* does not supply multiplicity; indeed substance is multiplied, but through that mode of distinction and individuation "contracting" the universal nature, involving the addition of designated matter. *Cadit ergo pluralitas ratione individuationis.* This conclusion captures the heart of the personal requirement expressed in part (B) of the definition and applies to every instance of personal distinction, including God. It also helps to correct the previous statement that parts (A) and (B) both come from substance in the case of man; strictly speaking, part (B), that is, the *distinctio*, derives from man's *individuation*. But since this belongs to the substance insofar as concretized, realized as a primary substance, the *ratio distinctionis* resides in the substance. In God, then, as Albert has put it, plurality is achieved *ratione existentiae proprietatis*; in man, *ratione subsistentiae proprietatis* (evoking substantial composition with accidents, since to be distinct in virtue of subsistence – as Albert employs the term – is to be distinguished by properties *ut in subiecto*[731]); both of these *rationes* are modes of the *ratio individuationis* mentioned just above covering the spectrum for all persons.

Now, the first *definiens* figuring in our tripartite definition of person, namely, *per se una*, entails several aspects[732]. The *"per se"* indicates

---

[729] Albert, *I Sent.*, d. 23, a. 2, contra 2, ed. Borgnet, vol. 25, p. 583.
[730] Albert, *I Sent.*, d. 23, a. 2, ad obj. 1-2, ed. Borgnet, vol. 25, p. 587.
[731] Cf. Albert, *I Sent.*, d. 23, a. 1, ad 2, ed. Borgnet, vol. 25, p. 581.
[732] *"Persona dicitur per se una ... ly 'per se' notat existentiae proprietatem in divinis. Una autem non dicit essentiae unitatem... sed potius unitatem personae quae consequitur ex proprietatis*

the *proprietas existentiae*, that is, the incommunicable property setting one person off from another, establishing the individual as one in number through a property belonging to no other, *non per alium sed per se*. *"Una"* refers to the unity of the person, and not the unity of substance, which unity is due to the numerical distinctness deriving from the incommunicable personal property. This oneness, signaling the distinctive, incommunicable reality of the person, moreover, is *per se*, through itself, since the persons are constituted by distinctive properties (*quae consequitur ex proprietatis distinctione*) with which they are identified. But, according as *"indifferentiam 'quis est' et 'quo est' in divinis"*[733], the perseity of the persons who are identified with the divine essence must equally pertain to the substance, which, as Augustine explains, must necessarily stand behind the notion of their relativity. The *unitas personae* is inseparable from the more fundamental *unitas substantiae*[734]. And this is true *a fortiori* in man for whom the singular person is a distinct substance and whose incommunicability is identical to that of the substance which it is. In man, the *per se* unity of the person is derived from the substance (or a substantial principle); in God, from the properties of origin; in general, *persona enim per se est una sua proprietate personali*[735].

Person signifies substance plus something more

As is evident from the foregoing, "person" possesses a dual signification; there are two realities simultaneously signified or consignified by the term person, namely, a substantial and a distinctive element. From the onset, we are posed the basic question as to whether "person" signifies substance or something else, a problem we already encountered in the Victorine struggle for an alternative to the physical characterization of personhood proper to Boethius. To the question *"utrum [persona] significet substantiam, vel proprietatem?"*[736], the Lombard's response, like that of Albert, tells us that there is something more to the definition of personhood than simply being a kind of substance: *"consideratur etiam in hoc nomine, 'persona', discretio singu-*

---

        distinctione... persona enim per se est una sua proprietate personali" – Albert, *I Sent.*, d. 23,
        a. 2, ad 6, ed. Borgnet, vol. 25, p. 586.
[733]   Albert, *I Sent.*, d. 23, a. 2, ad arg. 2, ed. Borgnet, vol. 25, p. 586.
[734]   Cf. infra, "SUBSTANTIAL FOUNDATION FOR PERSONAL NUMERICAL UNITY", p. 417.
[735]   Albert, *I Sent.*, d. 23, a. 2, ad 6, ed. Borgnet, vol. 25, p. 586.
[736]   Peter Lombard: Albert, *I Sent.*, d. 23, B, ed. Borgnet, vol. 25, p. 579; passim.

laritatis"[737]. Albert clearly affirms that person signifies, in addition to substance, the distinguishing *proprietas* founding that singularity[738]. While six texts cited by the Lombard (taken from Augustine's *De Trinitate*) seem to be in favor of a substantial signification for person, another eight texts (some of which from Boethius and Augustine) incline rather toward a notional conception. The latter is evidently the discretion of Richard of Saint Victor, whom Albert also regularly cites as an authority[739]. Albert, however, chooses a middle path, giving preference neither to the substantial nor to the notional order[740]: person designates substance *plus* a singular property[741].

Since alteriety is dependent upon personal properties, then person, one of the central notions of which is distinction, will depend upon, even signify, these properties[742]. In fact, in the Trinity, the properties are *identified* with the person which we have admitted to be a substance[743]. As is clear from all that has been said, and keeping in mind the substantial foundation of a *per se* act of existing, person has a triple *ratio* and signification. Person, or a personal name, signifies at once, the essence, the hypostasis and the *proprietas* (the former only indirectly, and the latter two directly)[744]. Because God is perfectly simple, these three are related to one another in the Trinity as one *in re* but diverse *in ratione.*

---

[737] Peter Lombard: Albert, *I Sent.*, d. 23, B, ed. Borgnet, vol. 25, p. 579.

[738] *"Licet persona significet substantiam, tamen important etiam proprietatem distinguentem propter quam recipit numerum pluralem"* – Albert, *I Sent.*, d. 23, a. 6, sol & ad 1, 3, 4, ed. Borgnet, vol. 25, p. 599.

[739] *"Persona quod existens per se solum secundum quemdam modum singularis existentiae naturae rationalis, ergo videtur significare singularitatem notionum"* – Albert, *I Sent.*, d. 23, a. 2, contra 7, ed. Borgnet, vol. 25, p. 584.

[740] Cf. Albert, *I Sent.*, d. 23, a. 2, sol., ed. Borgnet, vol. 25, p. 584-586.

[741] *"Cum dicitur Pater, etiam significatur substantia cum singulari proprietate... cadit in praedicamento substantiae theologico ratione substantiae, et in praedicamento relationis ratione consignificati cum substantia"* – Albert, *I Sent.*, d. 23, a. 2, ad obj. 6, ed. Borgnet, vol. 25, p. 587.

[742] *"Alia persona Patris, alia Filii, id est, alia est proprietas qua Pater est Pater, alia qua Filius est Filius, alia qua Spiritus sanctus est Spiritus sanctus. Ita etiam nomine personae quidam proprietates intelligere volunt, cum dicitur tres personae, sed melius est ut subsistentias vel hypostases intelligamus, cum dicimus tres personas"* – Peter Lombard: Albert, *I Sent.*, d. 25, a. 7, L, ed. Borgnet, vol. 25, p. 637.

[743] *"Non enim nomina tantummodo, sed etiam nominum proprietates, id est, personas, vel, ut Graeci exprimunt hypostases, id est, subsistentias confitemur. ... Ecce hic aperte dicit Hieronymus proprietates esse personas, et personas esse subsistentias... personae nomine significari et hypostasim et proprietatem"* – Peter Lombard: Albert, *I Sent.*, d. 25, a. 7, M, ed. Borgnet, vol. 25, p. 638.

[744] *"Nomen personae in Trinitate triplicem tenet rationem. Est enim ubi facit intelligentiam essentiae, et est ubi facit intelligentiam hypostasis, et est ubi facit intelligentiam proprietatis"* – Peter Lombard: Albert, *I Sent.*, d. 25, a. 7, L, ed. Borgnet, vol. 25, p. 637.

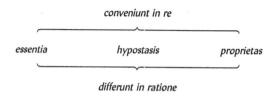

Hypostasis must here be taken according to its subjectival act, *ab actu substandi*, and not as an absolute substantive in the sense of substantial nature, otherwise it would be the same *in ratione* as *essentia*. Now, this association of the act of standing under with substance provides the explanatory foundation for why the person was primitively defined as *"substantia cum singulari proprietate"*[745]. The sense of that definition can be clarified and made more precise by substituting the term *substantia subiecta* for *substantia*. The resulting definitive expression states that person signifies *substantiam subiectam cum proprietate*. From this, three acceptations can be seen to follow, corresponding to each of the defining terms: in virtue of the first term, person can be taken as an essence; in virtue of the second term, hypostasis; and from the third term, as constituted by the *proprietas*[746].

The latter is responsible for the singularity of the person; it is that which distinguishes one person from another. Because distinction is achieved in the Trinity through relation, the divine *proprietates* are the relations of origin. In man, individual distinction is accomplished through (or in the presence of) accidental properties and/or designated matter:

$$
persona = \begin{cases} substantia \\ + \\ proprietas\ singularis \end{cases} \begin{cases} relatio - \text{in the Trinity} \\ \\ accidentes\ vel\ materia \\ designata - \text{in man} \end{cases}
$$

---

[745] *"Licet proprietatem cum substantia consignificet"* – Albert, *I Sent.*, d. 23, a. 2, obj. 2, ed. Borgnet, vol. 25, p. 582.

[746] *"Tres acceptiones personae sic accipi, quod persona significat substantiam subjectam cum proprietate, et ideo gratia significati accipitur prima significatio ejus, quae est essentia, gratia suppositi vel subjecti accipitur secunda, quae est hypostasis, gratia proprietatis tertia"* – Albert, *I Sent.*, d. 25, a. 7, L, expositio, ed. Borgnet, vol. 25, p. 637.

Whether or not it would be better to say that men secure singularizing properties "through *the addition of* designated matter" (as opposed to simply "through designated matter") depends on certain considerations. The expression "through the addition of designated matter" leads one to conceive of the substance to which it is added and which is consignified by the term person as the *common* human nature, in which case person would signify the resulting concrete human nature. The question is whether person, in the case of man, signifies universal human nature plus designated matter (which would seem to be nothing other than the concrete individual human nature) or the concrete human nature plus some singular property:

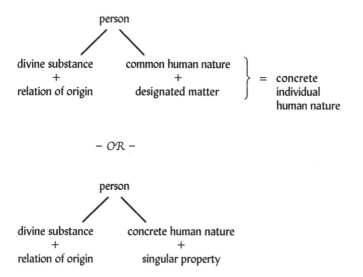

There is nothing to prevent that singular property mentioned in the second case, however, from deriving from the reality of designated matter itself, in which case the two schemata would converge with respect to the direct signification of personhood. Nevertheless, the formal aspect of the signification of person, that is, its particular *manner* of signifying substance insofar as distinct through incommunicable properties, is more explicit in the second schema. Consequently, a clearer definition of person could be had by defining it as an "individual substance (or subsistence) of a rational (or intelligent) nature distinguished by an incommunicable property", even if the latter qualification is implicit in the preceding *significati* (recall that what is proper to and distinctive of the different terms signifying substance is the explicitated content due to their respective modes of signification or points of view) [747].

On the substance which person signifies

The term person is said of something according to substance. As a consequence of the Boethian interpretation of personhood, person falls within the genus of substance, and substance is directly signified by the term person: *cum enim in diffinitione personae substantia cadat in recto, oportet quod persona sit in genere substantiae* [748]. This not only means that substance is the direct *significatum* of "person", but it also implies that "person" cannot be reduced to the category of relation *ad aliquid* (a point we intend to address in more detail near the end of this thesis). [Note that the substance signified by "person" is not the common substance as expressed, for example, by the name *Deus*, but the substance *quae supponitur et distinguitur*. To illustrate the difference, consider the expression *"iste tres sunt unus Deus"*. Here the pronoun *"iste"* and the verb *"sunt"* do not refer to the substance as common (which it is the task of *Deus* to signify), but to the substance as distinctly hypostatized [749]. Attentiveness to these senses of *substantia* avoids confusion over the direct and indirect *significatum* of person. The apparent inconsistency of sometimes affirming person to signify substance directly, sometimes only indirectly, is resolved by the simple stipulation that person signifies the substance taken as supposit (*substantia supposita*) *in recto*, but the common substance (*substantia essentia*) *in obliquo*] [750]. Already in the beginning of distinction XXIII, where Albert embarks in thoroughly elaborating the notion of personhood in an explicit manner, the Lombardian passage under examination declares that the very persons of the Trinity, though indeed constituted through relative opposition, are called persons in a substantial way and not relatively [751]. Neither substance nor the properties or

---

[747] "*Aliter enim significatur substantia, cum dicitur, 'substantia', et aliter, cum dicitur, 'homo', et aliter cum dicitur, 'Socrates'. Primo enim modo significatur in communitate generis. Secundo modo, cum specialitate speciei. Tertio modo, cum singularitate socrateitatis sive individui*"– Albert, *I Sent.*, d. 23, a. 2, contra 7, ed. Borgnet, vol. 25, p. 584.

[748] Albert, *I Sent.*, d. 23, a. 3, obj. 4, ed. Borgnet, vol. 25, p. 583; cf. *I Sent.*, d. 23, a. 2, contra 7, ed. Borgnet, vol. 25, p. 584: "*persona est individua substantia rationalis naturae, in qua 'rationalis naturae' cadit in obliquo*".

[749] Cf. A. Pompei, op. cit., p. 226.

[750] Cf. Aquinas, *Sum. theol.*, I, 29, 4.

[751] "*Ad se quippe dicitur persona, non ad Filium vel Spiritum sanctum, sicut ad se Deus dicitur... quod persona secundum substantiam dicitur, ut cum dicitur, Pater est persona, hic sit*

singularity are excluded from what is signified by person[752]. To attempt to efface the notion of substance from the definition of person by recourse to the notion of incommunicability achieved through extra-essential relations is to beg the question, because such relations or singularizing modes of *existence* necessarily depend upon substantial foundation, even if this in no way involves the notion of composition (as in the case of substantial foundation *in inferioribus*)[753]. If the persons were not substances, they could not even be something said to be relative; to say in any way that personhood is based somehow on being in relation necessarily implies their substantiality.

While person directly signifies substance in a particular way, a variety of other terms also signify substance from their own distinctive points of view. "Person" signifies the substance precisely as *distinctam proprietate incommunicabili*, while "substance", for example, signifies substance according to its common generic notion, "man" according to specific qualification, and "Socrates" according to the singularity of this individual[754]. Each one of these terms, then, including person, signify substance, but according to different modes. It will be the particular mode of signification, along with the content explicitated by what is indirectly signified, which sets one term off from another: while substance is the direct *significatum* of "man", the specifications contained in the terms "animal" and "rational" will give it a different meaning than that contained in the concept "substance", for example. As can be seen from the ablative mention of the *proprietas*, person finds its distinctive meaning through the specification of the fact that the substance (taken as hypostatized) receives its distinction through an incommunicable property. This formally distinctive feature of per-

---

sensus: Pater est divina essentia" – Peter Lombard: Albert, *I Sent.*, d. 23, B, ed. Borgnet, vol. 25, p. 578-579.

[752] *"Persona significationem habet substantiae et proprietatis"* – Albert, *I Sent.*, d. 23, a. 2, sol., ed. Borgnet, vol. 25, p. 584. Albert can thus be said to have conceded *"alla parità il significato essenziale e nozionale del termine 'persona'"* – A. Pompei, op. cit., p. 227.

[753] *"Dicit enim Augustinus in principio libri VII de Trinitate: 'Omnis essentia quae relative dicitur, est etiam aliquid excepto relativo, sicut homo dominus, et homo servus... et si non esset homo, id est, aliqua substantia, non esset qui relative diceretur... Quapropter si et pater non est aliquid ad seipsum, non est omnino qui relative dicatur ad alterum vel ad aliquid'. Ex hoc accipitur, quod persona haec et illa dat intellectum substantiae suppositae, et etiam intellectum proprietatis: ergo et persona...in intellectu suo claudit utrumque"* – Albert, *I Sent.*, d. 23, a. 2, sol., ed. Borgnet, vol. 25, p. 585.

[754] *"Persona significat substantiam primam, distinctam proprietate incommunicabili; aliter enim significatur substantia, cum dicitur, 'substantia', et aliter, cum dicitur, 'homo', et aliter cum dicitur, 'Socrates'. Primo enim modo significatur in communitate generis. Secundo modo, cum specialitate speciei. Tertio modo, cum singularitate socrateitatis sive individui. Et haec*

sonhood forms the basis for identifying a plurality of persons in the Trinity without multiplying the substance, since a multiplication at the level of incommunicable properties is enough to account for a plurality of persons [755]. Consequently, though to affirm *"tres personae"* in creatures is to posit three things distinct according to substance as well as *esse*, in God all that is implied is distinction according to *ex*istential mode or property but not in substance or essence [756]. Trinitarian plurality is thus not referred to the substance, and the divine substance, in contrast to that of creatures, is not divided. Nor does it enter into composition when hypostatized, because, as shall become clearer, the *proprietates* posit nothing absolute and are identical in reality to the essence. In this way, the unity (i.e. communion, and not numerical distinctness) of the persons is centered in the undiversifiable substance, while plurality resides exclusively in the relative modes of origin [757].

The fact that a singular referent is able to be signified by variety of names or that a single name can signify diverse things means that argumentative discourse about personhood must pay close attention to the modes of signification. A good example of faulty argumentation

---

opinio esse videtur Richardi de sancto Victore" – Albert, *I Sent.*, d. 23, a. 2, contra 7, ed. Borgnet, vol. 25, p. 584.

[755] *"Non est aliud Deo esse, aliud personam esse, sed omnino idem, quod hoc verum est; et loquitur de supposita substantia quae non est alia, nec aliud habet esse supposita cum proprietate singularis existentiae, et significata ut natura communis, sed habet alium significandi modum, et ratione illius modi cadit in pluralitatem, et non hoc nomen, 'Deus'"* – Albert, *I Sent.*, d. 23, a. 2, ad arg. 1, ed. Borgnet, vol. 25, p. 586 (cf. Aquinas, *Sum. theol.*, I, 30, 4, sed contra & sol.). *"Richardus... dicens: 'persona significat substantiale esse ex aliqua singulari proprietate... quia sunt ibi plures habentes unum et indifferens esse ex differenti proprietate. Unitas itaque ibi est juxta modum essendi, pluralitas juxta modum existendi; unitas essentiae, quia unum et indifferens esse, plures personae, quia plures existentiae'"* – Albert, *I Sent.*, d. 23, a. 2, sol., ed. Borgnet, vol. 25, p. 585.

[756] *"Et ideo etiam pluralitas consignificata in nomine divino, non est ejusdem rationis cum pluralitate nominis creati; unde cum dicitur, tres personae, sensus est, tres in existentiae proprietate, et non in substantia vel aliquo essentiali distincto; in inferioribus autem tres personae sunt differentes per esse et substantiam, quae dicit id quod est"* – Albert, *I Sent.*, d. 23, a. 3, ad 4, ed. Borgnet, vol. 25, p. 590.

[757] The divine hypostases cannot admit of composition with the nature of which they are supposits, there can be no composition between that nature and their distinctive properties, lest number be introduced into the substance as such. As a result, the use of the name person in the plural can only indicate a multiplicity at the level of the distinct modes of existence, but not at that of the substance: *"persona significet substantiam suppositam cum singulari proprietate in qua secundum existentiae modum admittatur numerus, et non numeretur substantia separata"* – Albert, *I Sent.*, d. 23, a. 2, sol., ed. Borgnet, vol. 25, p. 586. As A. Pompei points out, Albert effectively restricts the content of our created concept of person when applied to God to signifying but the perfection of suppositized substance while excluding the creaturely imperfection of substantial and accidental composition; cf. op. cit., p. 228-229 & note 83.

in regard of the *significatum* of person is given by the argument *in contrario*[758] which wants to claim that "person" does not signify substance because it must signify that which is constitutive of personhood, namely, the *proprietates*, which is not the same as to signify substance. The argumentative weakness lies not so much in the fact that substance and *proprietas* might signify the same reality, as in the fact that it fails to take into account the polyvalent reference of the term person. The *proprietates* do cause number, that is, a multiplication of persons in the Trinity, and this mode of distinction/multiplication is necessarily constitutive of personhood in the Trinity, but that something be constitutive does not mean that it is the only constituent; indeed with respect to person, there are, as we have seen, several constitutive principles[759].

Personal number indifferent to number in substance

Although person signifies substance, it does not imply number with regard to substance, since the notion of person is independent of whether there be one or many substances; what matters is that it be distinguished according to a mode of existence[760]. The distinctness resulting from the principle of personal distinction, or the personal property of each person, constitutes each person in distinct "personal being" (according to a distinct modality by which each person possesses the same essential being). St. Augustine, Albert tells us, expresses these two senses of being in saying that the being of the Father is the same as the being of the Son and of the Holy Spirit, but that being the Father is not the same as being the Son or the Holy Spirit[761]. The indivisible essence is the *res* of the persons (i.e. which each per-

---

[758] *"Proprietas est quae facit in divinis numerum... sed facit numerum personarum, ergo persona est id quod constituitur proprietate; hoc autem non est substantia, quia proprietates substantiam non determinant; ergo videtur, quod persona non dicat substantiam"* – Albert, *I Sent.*, d. 23, a. 2, contra 5, ed. Borgnet, vol. 25, p. 583.

[759] *"Dicendum, quod [persona videtur significare] bene singularitas, large utendo vocabulo singularitas, est ratione proprietatis, sed illud non est tota significatio vocabuli"* – Albert, *I Sent.*, d. 23, a. 2, ad obj. 7, ed. Borgnet, vol. 25, p. 587.

[760] *"Circa substantiam quam significat persona, non ponitur numerus, quia, ut dicit Richardus, non refert ad rationem personae, utrum sint una substantia, vel plures, dummodo sub natura communi distinguantur secundum existentiae modum"* – Albert, *I Sent.*, d. 23, a. 6, ad 2, ed. Borgnet, vol. 25, p. 599.

[761] *"Sicut dicit Augustinus, quod idem est patris esse et filii esse et spiritus sancti esse, quamvis non idem sit esse patrem et esse filium et esse spiritum sanctum"* – Albert, *Sum. theol.*, I, tr. 9, q. 39, c. 2, a. 1, sol., ed. Colon., vol. 34, p. 295 (Augustine, *De Trin.*, l. 5, c. 5, n. 6: CC 50, p. 211, v. 19-22).

son is). That essence is common and not susceptible to distinction, division or appropriation through what is said to give personal being; the principle of personal distinction, that is, cannot also give rise to some kind of multiplicity in the essence[762]. A person generates, the essence not; a person is distinct, the essence not. The essence is neither generated nor generates, and this holds whether the essence is signified abstractly or concretely alike[763], not only because supposits (and not natures) are the subject of operations, but also because of the proper mode according to which the essence is signified (governing the things which may or may not be said of the essence).

Person distinguished from nature or essence

The essence is communicated, something proven by generation and procession in God[764]. But given that essence and person are identical, since there is no opposition of origin or of *quod est* and *quo est* to distinguish them, if one is communicable, the other ought to be, and if one is incommunicable, so ought be the other: if the hypostasis is incommunicable, then the essence which is in the hypostasis, because it has the same being, seems must also be incommunicable[765]. Such is the difficulty facing the theologian. The kind of solution needed must neither exclude the communication of the essence nor the absolute identity between that essence and the incommunicable persons. It is possible, explains Albert, for an essence to be communicated without implying its division. In fact, the essence of itself tends to conserve its unity, but undergoes division only as a result of a lack of simplicity. Were the created nature perfectly simple, it would neither be divisible according to being nor in concept; since, however, that nature is not fully simple, though it remains indivisible *per rationem*, it is divided according to being in the act of generation. In the Trinity, on the other hand, where perfect simplicity prevails, the essence is in no way divided by generation and procession[766], whence (1) the in-

---

[762] "'Persona sit singulariter existens secundum singularis existentiae modum' et essentia divina communis sit re et non susceptibilis distinctionis vel divisionis vel appropriationis per esse, quod dat personis"– Albert, *Sum. theol.*, I, tr. 9, q. 39, c. 2, a. 1, sol., ed. Colon., vol. 34, p. 295.

[763] Cf. Albert, *I Sent.*, d. 4, a. 5.

[764] Cf. A. Pompei, op. cit., p. 93.

[765] Cf. Albert, *I Sent.*, d. 5, a. 1, obj. 1-3 & sed contra 1-4.

[766] "Si essentia creata esset omnino simplex, nec esset divisibilis per esse, nec per rationem; cum autem aliquid habeat de simplicitate et non ad plenum sit simplex, ipsa quidem per rationem remanet indivisa, dividitur tamen per esse in actu naturae qui est generatio; essentia igitur

communicability proper to the communicants does not transfer to the essence, and (2) the communicants themselves remain indivisible according to being. The essence, then, is communicable, while the person is not; the person is incommunicable, while the essence is not. To speak of the person, therefore, is not the same thing as to speak of the essence, as a result of which one cannot be signified in the same way as the other. And, because it signifies something real to say "the person is distinct" and "the essence is not distinguished", the proper distinctiveness of essence *qua* essence and of person *qua* person, is something more than merely logical. The thing signified is at once essential as well as personal; both aspects are true of the same singular referent. The distinction we make, therefore, between the respective modes of signifying is not entirely dependent upon our intellects, but founded on the truly essential and personal reality in God. True, person and nature are identical in God, but this is not based upon what pertains to each according to its *"ratio formalis"*, but rather upon the absolute simplicity of the divine nature excluding every form of real distinction between them[767].

Though the predicates pertaining to the nature are different from those proper to the person, it does not follow that we therefore have

divina quae omnia vincit simplicitate, nec per rationem nec per esse dividitur" – Albert, *I Sent.*, d. 5, a. 1, ad obj. 1, ed. Borgnet, vol. 25, p. 175. As was pointed out above (cf. supra, "FIRST DIVISION OF ENS", p. 192 & note 553), generation, from the point of view of its formal perfection, implies nothing more than the origin of one distinct thing from another in likeness of nature. The limitations inherent in the creaturely mode of generating are thus exterior to the formal notion of generation which, because it indicates but a pure perfection (self-communication according to being) is applicable in an analogous way to God. In a similar way, the procession of the Holy Spirit, though necessarily terminating in a distinct divine person, involves nothing of the accidentality by which love in creatures is distinguished from the nature of the subject, wherefore all three persons of the Trinity *conveniunt* in substantial being according to simplicity of essence (cf. Albert, *I Sent.*, d. 10, a. 2, sol.).

767 "*In divinis non distinguatur persona ab essentia, eo quod inter personam et essentiam non cadat relationis oppositio; nihilominus vere sunt ibi personae, et vere essentia; et ideo non oportet, quod eodem modo significandi etiam secundum rem significetur utrumque; realis enim significatio est, cum dicitur, Persona distincta est; et realis significatio, cum dicitur, Essentia non distinguitur; patet enim ex supra dictis, quod res est essentiale, et etiam personale. Si autem quaeritur, unde hoc contingit, quod idem est a quo non differt differentia, et tamen, non hoc quod convenit uni, convenit alii? Dicendum, quod hoc convenit propter hoc quod est in divinis propter aliud, et non per se, ut si dicatur, Persona non differt aliqua differentia ab essentia, hoc non contingit ei, quia persona est, aut quia essentia est, sed utrique contingit propter aliud, quod est summa simplicitas illius naturae, quae non admittit quod persona cum essentia faciat aliquam compositionem. Sed quia illa simplicitas nec ab essentia tollit id quod convenit ei in quantum essentia est, nec a persona id quod convenit ei in quantum persona est, non sequitur, quod si persona sit incommunicabilis, quod propter hoc essentia sit incommunicabilis, sed secundum antiquos Theologos incidit fallacia accidentis*" – Albert, *I Sent.*, d. 5, a. 1, ad obj. 2, ed. Borgnet, vol. 25, p. 175; cf. A. Pompei, op. cit., p. 95.

two realities in God. There is indeed *"res generans"* and *"res non gener-ans"*, *"res distincta"* and *"res non distincta"*, *"res relata"* and *"res non re-lata"*; but this does not signify the presence of *duae res in divinis*, since all of these are identical to one another[768]. Nor does the opposition in predication (*generans* and *non generans, distincta* and *non distincta*) im-ply that contradictory or incompatible notions are affirmed of the same reality; for these expressions manifest the different modes ac-cording to which the same reality is understood, different modes of signifying one and the same thing, such that the opposition resides in the modes of signifying and not in the reality signified. That which these expressions, in their diverse modes, actually predicate of the reality, the diverse affirmations made with respect to the same thing, do not refer to the subject in the same way, but under two distinct aspects, and in this way no contradiction obtains, since their opposi-tion is not had in the same respect[769].

In accordance with their distinctive modes of signifying, *"non quid-quid convenit uni, convenit et alteri, licet re idem sint"*[770]. To systematically exchange predicates between person and essence amounts to ignor-ing the logical principle of predication *per se* and *per accidens*. In fact, every identity in God, we repeat, is affirmed solely on the basis of the divine simplicity, and not with respect to the *ratio* of the identified terms or attributes. This response to the question *"Unde hoc contingit, quod idem est a quo non differt differentia, et tamen non hoc quod convenit uni, convenit alii?"*[771], represents, according to A. Pompei, the funda-mental innovation operated by St. Albert in establishing the *via media* between the Porretanians and Praepositinus[772]. The general error of

---

[768] *"Non sequitur, Persona est relata, vel distincta, et essentia non relata, nec distincta, ergo sunt duae res. Debet enim addere: et haec res non est illa, et sic sequeretur quod essent duae res"* – Albert, *I Sent.*, d. 5, a. 2, sol. & ad 1-2, ed. Borgnet, vol. 25, p. 176.

[769] *"Nihil prohibet ab eodem secundum rem diversa affirmari et negari, eo quod ipsum accipitur in diversa ratione significandi; modi autem contradictionis tantum significantur, cum dici-tur, res distincta, et res non distincta, quod patet, quia propositiones non sunt contradicto-riae, sed modi contradictionis significantur in praedicato... contradictio non notatur circa idem eodem modo acceptum: cum enim dicit, essentia est res non distincta, ly 'res' tenetur es-sentialiter; cum autem dicit, persona est res distincta, ly 'res' tenetur personaliter; et ideo quia non sumitur ut idem, non est oppositio contradictionis"* – Albert, *I Sent.*, d. 5, a. 2, ad 3, ed. Borgnet, vol. 25, p. 177; cf. A. Pompei, op. cit., p. 95-96.

[770] Albert, *I Sent.*, d. 5, a. 2, ad 8, ed. Borgnet, vol. 25, p. 177.

[771] Albert, *I Sent.*, d. 5, a. 1, ad 2, ed. Borgnet, vol. 25, p. 175.

[772] Cf. A. Pompei, op. cit., p. 108. The thought of Praepositinus (Gilbert Prevostin of Cremona) was earlier encountered in "οὐσία AND ὑπόστασις AS 'SUBSTANCE' IN DIFFERENT WAYS". On the inability of Gilbert to see the necessary kind of distinction, see M. L. Colish, "Gilbert, The Early Porretans, and Peter Lombard: Semantics and Theol-ogy", in J. Jolivet – A. De Libera (editors), *Gilbert de Poitiers et ses contemporains. Aux origines de la Logica modernorum: Actes du septième Symposium européen d'histoire de la*

Praepositinus consisted in espousing one of two extremes with respect to explaining the relation between the persons in God and that by which they are distinguished, i.e. the relations. In diametrical opposition to Gilbert of Poitiers, Praepositinus effectively denied any entitative value of the relations, reducing them to mere *modi loquendi* Unable to conceive the *proprietates* as constitutive of the persons, and seeing no status besides that of personal reality as ascribable to what is in the divinity, Praepositinus declared the relations to be nothing in the persons, subtracting as it were the very means for distinguishing the persons within the unity of being he was defending. As a consequence, each person is understood as distinct and constituted by itself (*seipsa*), while the *proprietates* receive a purely nominal value. The identification between person and *proprietas* is carried in this case to the point of the destruction of the latter[773].

By means of the distinction operated between the principle of identity in God, namely the divine simplicity, and the special *ratio* with respect to which essential names differ from personal names and their respective modes of signifying preclude a total and unqualified sharing of predicates, Albert, Pompei affirms, recovers the grain of truth in the Porretanian doctrine which, while maintaining the divine simplicity, nevertheless introduces a certain degree of objectivity in the opposition between essence and supposit, such that, though they are not two things, neither may be reduced to the other[774]. The kind of distinction intended by the Porretanians was not that between two things in the sense of two really distinguished realities, but that between a reality and its form, such as that between the soul, unique form of the body, and the body organically constituted in its corporal being by the soul, a distinction denominated by many scholastics *"distinctio realis inadaequata"*[775]. The distinction for Gilbert, however, cannot imply composition in God, for the simple reason that concrete *esse* and *quo est* in God are supremely simple[776]. The insufficiency of the Porretanian doctrine consists not so much in having objectively distinguished *quod est* and *quo est* in God – that is, where the two are dis-

---

logique et de la sémantique médiévales, Centre d'Études supérieures de civilisation médiévale de Poitiers, Poitiers, 17-22 juin 1985, Bibliopolis, Naples 1987, p. 229-250.

[773] Cf. A. Pompei, op. cit., p. 335. For an analysis of this error, its comparison with the opposite extreme of Gilbert of Poitiers, and the refutation of both accomplished by St. Albert, see id., op. cit., p. 315-337.

[774] Cf. A. Pompei, op. cit., p. 108.

[775] Cf. A. Hayen, "Le Concile de Reims et l'erreur théologique de Gilbert de la Porrée", *AHDLMA* 10 (1935-1936), Vrin, Paris 1936, p. 63ff; A. Pompei, op. cit., p. 108.

tinguished according to their proper *ratio* (*quod est as such* from *quo est as such*) –, as in refusing the convertibility between essential and personal names on the supposed grounds that substance or essence is incapable of being a subject (and this in light of the grammatical form of propositions). It is particularly this aspect of the Porretanian doctrine that Albert attacks. As exposed by Albert in two objections, Gilbert's position rests upon the presupposition that in every proposition, including those for which the subject and predicate are identical (as is always the case in God), the predicate expresses the *form which is in* the subject[777]. As A. Pompei remarks, such a characterization of that which is signified by the predicate term amounts to reducing the real mode of being of a thing to its mode of predication, as though the being of the reality perfectly corresponded to the manner in which we conceive it[778]. What is apparently lacking in Gilbert's thought, and which is a key resolving element in Albert, is a distinction between predication and mode of predication[779]. While it is true that every predicate expresses a form, it also expresses the modality according to which the formal reality is related to the subject of its predication, a modality which may or may not correspond to the ever verifiable *logical* relation of inherence existing between the subject and predicate of a proposition[780]. Thus the divine essence is not a form *within* the supposit, but a form which is identical in being and in its mode of being with the supposit. Not only does the perfect simplicity of the Godhead preclude any composition between them, but the real identity between them founds their full convertibility, *"et ideo utrumque utrique subjicitur, et utrumque de utroque praedicatur"*[781]. Nevertheless, essence and supposit, person and nature, notwithstanding their absolute identity and unique mode of being, retain their respective and distinctive modes of predication, which distinctive modes are not ratiocinative figments, but have a true *fundamentum in re* inasmuch as the singular referent of each name is truly person and truly essence, *"res est essentiale, et etiam personale"*[782].

---

[776]   Cf. Gilbert, *In De Trin.*, I, 2, 53-55, ed. Häring, p. 89-90 (PL 64, 1269D); *In De heb.*, I, 67-68, ed. Häring, p. 202 (PL 64, 1321B).

[777]   Cf. Albert, *I Sent.*, d. 4, a. 9, obj. 1-2.

[778]   A. Pompei, op. cit., p. 109.

[779]   Cf. A. Hayen, "Le Concile de Reims et l'erreur théologique de Gilbert de la Porrée", *AHDLMA* 10 (1935-1936), Vrin, Paris 1936, p. 60; A. Pompei, op. cit., p. 109.

[780]   Cf. Albert, *I Sent.*, d. 4, a. 9, ad 1-2.

[781]   Albert, *I Sent.*, d. 4, a. 9, sol. & ad 1-2, ed. Borgnet, vol. 25, p. 171.

The distinguishing principle

In contrast to the essence, the persons are themselves distinct. The essence can in no way itself be the cause of this, since it is rather the cause of community and indistinction or identity in substantial or essential being. For this reason, according to Albert, the Saints were compelled to posit *proprietates* in the persons in order to account for personal distinction, which is nothing other than to have formulated a way for designating or signifying the very person (distinct hypostasis) *ut distinguens,* i.e., as the self-distinguishing reality which it also is. Even if the two are one and the same thing, the human intellect cannot capture by a single mode of signification that which distinguishes and that which is distinguished. Our cognitive limitations require, in order to conceptualize that something is distinct, a corresponding conceptualization of that which distinguishes; likewise we cannot conceive of several supposits being one without understanding that something unites them; whence the persons are understood as several distinct realities through the *proprietates,* and as being one through the unifying nature[783].

That no two things can be distinct without that whereby they are made to be distinct is clear enough. To say "distinct", then, necessarily implies some principle of distinction. As a consequence, with respect to the enunciated definition of person, it seems perhaps unnecessary to repeat explicitly with another set of terms what is already implied by one term, as when we say that person is a "singular existent according to a singular mode of *existence*", where the singularity expressed by "singular existent" already implies a certain modality by which that existent is said to be singular. The Boethian definition, because of its simplicity, escapes this criticism. Here the term "individual" necessarily implies that thing *through which* the person is made truly individual, namely, the personal property. Therefore, ulterior definitions of the form "substance (in the full sense of the term entailing supposital individuality) + personal property" (or "subsistence +

---

[782] Albert, *I Sent.,* d. 5, a. 1, ad obj. 2, ed. Borgnet, vol. 25, p. 175; cf. A. Pompei, op. cit., p. 110.

[783] *"Personae distinctae sint, cuius distinctionis essentia nullo modo potuit esse causa, cum ipsa potius sit causa communitatis et indistinctionis et indivisionis et identitatis in esse substantiali vel essentiali; compulsi sunt* SANCTI *ponere proprietates in personis, quae principia sint huiusmodi distinctionis... Non enim capit intellectus, quod secundum modum significandi idem sit distinguens et distinctum, vel quod aliquid sit distinctum sine distinguente, vel quod plures sive plura supposita unum sint sine uniente. Et ideo posuit fides personas esse unum in natura uniente eas et personas distinctas esse proprietatibus"* – Albert, *Sum. theol.,* I, tr. 9, q. 39, c. 2, a. 1, sol., ed. Colon., vol. 34, p. 295.

personal property") would seem to introduce a superfluity, unless the terms in the formula are simply intended to perform the role of place fillers for more specific terms serving to distinguish the several analogically distinct types of persons, viz. divine, angelic and human. That is, in the case of the Trinity, for example, (where "substance" is replaced by "existent" or "subsistent") "personal property" is substituted by *"existentiae modus"*, thereby explicitating what is peculiar to the Trinitarian manner of realizing personhood. In this way, the repetition involved in naming the principle by or through which distinction is achieved (a principle already implicit in the notion of the distinct substance) serves to classify one kind of persons in contrast with other kinds, due to the analogical character of the predication of personhood. While "individual substance" (or "individual subsistent") suffices then to define person, the diverse *rationes* of personhood are made clear by defining person now as *"substantia/subsistentia individualis existentiae modo"*, now as *"substantia/subsistentia individualis materiale signata"*.

Again, from the purely substantive point of view, the composite formula "substance + personal property" introduces a certain redundancy. The individual substance alone (the intelligence of which is an obvious presupposition, since we are not at all concerned with those substances which are not persons) is sufficient to define "person". Nevertheless, the particular kind of personal property must be named for the establishing of a definition of person more properly predicated of a *given kind* of person, and this is where the personal property operates as a specific difference with respect to distinguishing the different kinds of persons, and even for distinguishing individual persons, when the personal property is fully specified (as, for example, by *"principium non de principio"*, or *"paternitas"*).

If substance (which includes the notion of individual) is able to stand for "person" in general, and if "intelligence" is the particular quality setting personal substances off from all other substances, then intelligence is the specific difference of person at the most general and analogical level. But "intelligent substance", taken itself as a single genus, is divided into particular families according to specific kinds of personal properties, which families are divided into particular persons according to unique incommunicable properties. Only at this last and wholly individual level do the properties in question truly become *"proprietates personales"*.

While the essence in God neither distinguishes nor is distinguished, the persons are distinguished from one another, each possessing a discrete personal being, and this in virtue of the *proprietates* to which we attribute neither a single being nor distinct being. We do not attribute one being to the *proprietates*, since the essence alone is signified as unifying. Nor do we attribute distinct being to them, since the person or hypostasis is signified *ut distincto* (whence distinct hypostatic or personal being[784]), while the *proprietates* are signified *ut distinguentes*. The *proprietates*, however, are indeed distinguished from one another, just as, in all genera of being, the differences through which things differ are themselves different from one another[785]. Such differences, however, will not be expressed according to distinctly numbered supposital or hypostatic being, since that is proper to persons whose mode of signification precisely intends the distinct thing of nature. The differences between *proprietates* will rather be expressed by articulating the distinct *ways* in which one person differs from another, as, for example, by paternity or filiation (which relations are clearly distinct from one another, though their mode of signification does not entail two distinct supposital realities)[786].

The predicaments of "who", "how" and "what"

There are three general modes of signifying what is in the Godhead constituting three predicaments: *quis, quae,* and *quod.* We see the same predicaments resumed under the modes of signification *ut distincto* and *ut distinguens* (when it is a question of distinguishing *quis* from *quae* or *quomodo*), *ut appropriata* and *ut approprians,* as well as *ut communis* and *ut supposita* or *ab actu substandi* (when comparing *quod* to *quis*). The first instance, *"quis"*, implies a personal or supposital mode of signification and refers to the person as such; the second, *"quae"*, pertains to the manner in which personal singularity is possessed and refers to the *proprietas;* the third, *"quod"*, signifies absolutely and essentially, referring to the nature. To these predicaments and the respective ways in which they are signified (which modes of signification constitute the very differences between them) corresponds a particular use of language by which the implications inherent in the

---

[784] For the technical use of the notion of "personal being", cf. infra, in the chapter on multiplication of individuals, "PERSONAL BEING", p. 393.

[785] Cf. infra, "DISTINCTION BETWEEN PROPRIETATES AND DISTINCTION BETWEEN THE PERSONS", p. 440.

[786] *"Essentiae enim attribuitur unum facere esse in divinis et nec distingui nec distinguere; personae autem discretam esse, non unam cum alia, sed distingui ab alia; proprietati autem non unam esse nec distinctam, sed distinguere et seipsa discretam esse ab alia proprietate, sicut in omnibus generibus entium primae differentiae, quibus alia differunt, seipsis differunt"* – Albert, *Sum. theol.*, I, tr. 9, q. 39, c. 2, a. 1, sol., ed. Colon., vol. 34, p. 296.

way in which these predicaments are signified is represented; that is, a linguistic convention permits us to identify something owing to a mode of signification. The masculine gender is used to designate the person, the feminine to signify the *proprietas*, and the neuter to signify the substance as such. Father, Son and Holy Spirit, for example, are not *"unus"* but *"unum"*, and they are not *"trium"* but *"trius"*. They are *unum* because they share the same substantial nature; and they are *trius* because they are three hypostases; but they are not *unus,* since they are several and not one person; and they are not *trium,* since they share the same substantial nature[787]. Accordingly, the linguistic property of gender allows us to identify where the unity and plurality is being assigned. Similarly, that through which each person is constituted *unus* may be designated *"una"* (and even when this is substantively conceived and articulated, it does not conflict with the masculine designation of each person, since the feminine is understood to signify *ut quae,* such that its sense is *"una proprietate distincta"*)[788]. Thus,

---

[787] The neuter term is commonly used to designate the common substance on account of its "amorphism", that is, since it is without "form" in comparison with the masculine or feminine forms. The idea is that the common substance is taken as indistinct with respect to the persons who are distinct and therefore stand for the essence as "informed": *"neutrum autem genus, eo quod informe est, refertur ad substantiam quae accipitur ut indistincta; masculinum autem et foemininum, quia dicunt essentiam formatam, referuntur ad personam; et ideo quod sequitur in humanis, non sequitur in divinis"* – Albert, *I Sent.,* d. 9, a. 4, ad 5, ed. Borgnet, vol. 25, p. 277. Such a distinction does not obtain in the case of man, where the common nature is not really common as it is found in this or that man, but only through an intentional operation of the mind.

[788] *"Tria sunt praedicamenta in divinis: 'quis', 'quae', 'quod'; et 'quis' quaerit personam, 'quae' proprietatem, 'quid' vel 'quod' essentiam sive naturam... neutrum... significat essentiam inarticulatam... in neutro genere significant substantiam, et ideo pater et filius et spiritus sanctus sunt 'unum'... In masculino autem genere, etiam si substantiventur per articulum subintellectum, quia trahuntur ad personam, pater et filius et spiritus sanctus sunt 'tres', non duo, non 'unus'. In feminino vero, si articulata et substantivata intelligantur, determinatas dicunt proprietates, sicut una persona 'una' proprietate distincta... Et sicut in inferioribus quodlibet quod est unum, suis terminis intra se contentum est et ab aliis determinatum et divisum, et hoc significat haec dictio 'unum'"* – Albert, *Sum. theol.,* I, tr. 9, q. 40, c. 2, a. 2, sol., ed. Colon., vol. 34, p. 312. We cannot predicate of a plurality in a singular fashion (for example, that "these be one") when speaking in the masculine or feminine gender; though, in the Trinity, we are able to predicate of a plurality in a singular fashion when speaking in the neuter: *"singulariter de pluribus dici non possunt in genere masculino et feminino. Et ideo pater et filius non sunt unus, sed duo, et pater et filius et spiritus sanctus non sunt duo, sed tres, nec sunt 'quis', sed 'qui', nec sunt 'hic' sed 'hi'"* – Albert, *Sum. theol.,* I, tr. 9, q. 40, c. 2, a. 2, ad quaest. 3/ad 8, ed. Colon., vol. 34, p. 313. In Christ, it seems however, we can predicate of a plurality in a singular fashion even when speaking in the masculine, as, for example, would be the case if we were to assert that "these natures are one person (*unus*)", but this depends entirely on the way in which "these natures" are signified in the proposition in question.

whenever we predicate number of subsisting things, the truth or falsity of that predication depends upon how we signify them. The linguistic convention just mentioned signals the kind of signification in question, in order that we be mindful of the mode of signification according to which the statement may be made, and thus understand to what the numerical predication refers. To employ one of these genders in a proposition having numerical implication implies, therefore, the acknowledgment of a particular mode of signification according to which the statement may be made.

Treating the use of feminine and masculine pronouns in God, it is shown that neither the feminine nor the masculine is able to stand for the divine substance, because of the determinate character of such pronouns whose manner of signifying therefore exclusively indicates the hypostases. The pronominal discrimination thus reveals what is distinctive of the hypostasis, namely, singularity and incommunicability[789]. Albert exploits the expression *"Ego et Pater unum sumus"* to demonstrate not only the correspondence of gendered (masculine) signification with supposital signification but also that of grammatical quantity. *Unum*, as a neutral adjective, designates a unity of essence, and not of hypostasis. But because the hypostases thus united are more than one, the term according to which the act of each supposit as such is expressed must also be plural[790].

Realizing personality in different kinds of persons

Different kinds of modes of distinction

As we have seen, different principles supply for personal multiplicity in different kinds of persons; that is, for persons of differing ontological order, different modes of distinction constitute personal singular-

---

[789] *"Pronomina enim talia substantivata substantiam significant quae est hypostasis, et circa illam ponunt discretionem pronominalem, quae est singularitatis et incommunicabilitatis, et haec nullo modo essentiae divinae conveniunt"* – Albert, *Sum. theol.*, I, tr. 14, q. 58, m. 1, ad quaest. 3, ed. Borgnet, vol. 31, p. 584.

[790] *"Cum dicitur, 'Ego et Pater unum sumus', supposita Patris et Filii praemittuntur, quibus per hoc verbum, 'sumus', esse copulatur inesse ut actus. Ideo cum plura sint supposita, necessarium est propter vim grammaticae actum qui est in eis, pluraliter significari, et ideo dicitur: 'Ego et Pater unum sumus', non unum sum. Et quod dicitur 'unum' neutraliter, ostendit essentiae unitatem, et non hypostasis"* – Albert, *Sum. theol.*, I, tr. 14, q. 58, m. 1, ad quaest. 4, ad 1, ed. Borgnet, vol. 31, p. 585. The same gramatical issues are similarly illustrated in a consideration of the expression *"Faciamus hominem ad imaginem et similitudinem nostram"* – *Sum. theol.*, I, tr. 14, q. 58, m. 1, ad quaest. 2 & ad quaest. 4, ad 2, ed Borgnet, vol. 31, p. 584-5.

ity. Personhood is affirmed in God only according to one of several possible *rationes* of personhood, in man according to another[791]. These *rationes* follow upon the distinctive modes by which an entity can be individually determined, the different possible modes of distinction by which angels, men and God are incommunicably constituted as persons.

The Victorine distinction between *"sistere"* and *"existere"* provides the basis for establishing a diversity of ways in which one thing may be distinct from another, though, in place of the vocabulary *"sistere"*, Albert speaks of *"subsistere"*[792]. To subsist means to be distinct through *properties* encountered in the subject, while an existence enjoys its distinctive character from its individual *origin*. The fact that, in God, persons are constituted only according to distinctions in origin, or *ex*istence, could seem to present a difficulty insofar as it was earlier argued that those persons were distinguished only through their distinctive properties (cf. Cappadocians), and the relations of origin were referred to as *proprietates*. These *proprietates*, however, when referring to the principles of incommunicable distinction in the Trinity, should not be understood as *ut in subiecto*, that is, as properties in the strict sense or accidents[793]. Relations of origin and the distinctive marks or *proprietates* constitutive of and identifiable with those relations do not *inhere* in the divine nature; if they did, they would be accidents or properties in the strict sense, and no grounds for distinction in the Trinity can be found here[794]. The case is different for human persons, for whom the necessary distinction, requisite for personhood, is satisfied in more than one way[795]. Here a duality of *rationes* operate to establish personality: differences in substantial properties as well as differences in origin. But does there not seem to be a common element working to accomplish or realize this *ratio personali-*

---

[791] *"Ratio personalitatis conveniat eis, licet non omni eadem ratione qua invenitur personalitas in natura humana et angelica"*– Albert, *I Sent.*, d. 23, a. 1, sol., ed. Borgnet, vol. 25, p. 581.

[792] *"Differentia est inter subsistere et existere: subsistit enim quod per se distinctum est proprietate quae in ipso est ut in subjecto; existit autem quod per se est distinctum ex origine"*– Albert, *I Sent.*, d. 23, a. 1, ad 2, ed. Borgnet, vol. 25, p. 581.

[793] *"Quia distinguuntur modo originis vel relatione quae non est in distincto ut in subjecto, sed potius... praedicat id quod ad alterum est, et non quod ad se est secundum originis modum quo alter est ex altero"*– Albert, *I Sent.*, d. 23, a. 1, ad 2, ed. Borgnet, vol. 25, p. 581.

[794] *"In divinis autem in quibus est plena simplicitas, existentiae modus secundum originem inducit rationem alietatis et personalitatis, et tamen substantia id quod est, manet indivisa"*– Albert, *I Sent.*, d. 23, a. 1, ad 4, ed. Borgnet, vol. 25, p. 582.

[795] *"In humanis autem accipitur distinctio secundum utraque, scilicet substare collationi proprietatum individuantium, et secundum originis modum"*– Albert, *I Sent.*, d. 23, a. 1, ad 2, ed. Borgnet, vol. 25, p. 581; cf. *I Sent.*, d. 25, a. 2, obj. 1, ed. Borgnet, vol. 25, p. 628.

tatis? We ask the question because it has already become clear at this point in the order of Albert's treatise that the different modes of verifying personhood, that is, the different *rationes*, depend upon a central feature common to all of them, namely, distinction[796]. Distinction, understood as a property of real concrete existents, and therefore as demarcating one thing of nature from another according to individuality (for which reason it is synonymous with "individuation"), is the formal element of personality. Distinction, or INDIVIDUATION, we assert, MAKES THE PERSON[797]; the internal principle of individuality is what constitutes the person as such: *"principium enim individuantium est personae singularitas"*[798]. This central and most distinctive feature of personality serves as the exceptional explanatory basis for the unity of person in Christ whose human nature is, according to St. Albert, integrated into the singularity of the Word[799].

Returning to the observation that strict numerical unity is had only through substance, it follows that no plurality of unities can be derived from a multiplicity of accidental qualities. Such multiplicity could only produce something one accidentally, and not *per se*. But we are told that it is in virtue of the *proprietates* that a plurality of persons may be distinguished, both in the Trinity and in the context of men; consequently, the relations responsible for the plurality of personal names in the Trinity as well as the properties deriving from or implied by man's *existere* and *subsistere* cannot be like accidents or ordinary relations which could never account for truly numerically distinct individuals. To the objection that a multiplication of substance alone can account for a *per se* numerical plurality[800], Albert points out

---

[796] *"In humanis autem accipitur distinctio secundum utraque... in divinis autem... existentiae modus... inducit rationem alietatis et personalitatis"* – Albert, *I Sent.*, d. 23, a. 1, ad 2 & 4, ed. Borgnet, vol. 25, p. 581-582.

[797] *"Hoc autem facit personam, quod facit eam esse per se unam; nihil autem facit eam per se unam nisi particulatio formae super hanc materiam [pro tanto principium individuationis]. Cum igitur in Angelis sit esse et quod est, esse distinctum super quod est facit Angelum per se unum esse in angelica natura, et sic facit eam esse per se unam"* – Albert, *Sum. de creaturis,* I, tr. 4, q. 28, a. 1, sol., ed. Borgnet, vol. 34, p. 494.

[798] Albert, *III Sent.*, d. 10, a. 1, ad 1, ed. Borgnet, vol. 28, p. 189. The fact that singularity is the formal constituent of personality for Albert (*"principium enim individuantium est personae singularitas, hoc est, proprietas personalis, a qua persona est"* – ibid.) becomes especially clear when establishing the personal mode of union in Christ, for whom a single principle of singularity guards the unity of hypostasis.

[799] Cf. Albert, *II Sent.*, d. 3, a. 5, ad 2, ed. Borgnet, vol. 27, p. 70; cf. *III Sent*, d. 2, a. 5, sol., ed. Borgnet, vol. 28, p. 27; d. 5, a. 11, sol., ed. Borgnet, vol. 28, p. 110.

[800] *"Si ratione proprietatis nomen habet plurale, quodlibet singulare haberet plurale, quia uni multa accidunt, ut dicit Philosophus; et sic diceremus duos vel plures Socrates ratione grammaticae et musicae quae sunt in Socrate, quod falsum est; ergo numerus ponitur circa substantiam"* – Albert, *I Sent.*, d. 23, a. 3, obj. 5, ed. Borgnet, vol. 25, p. 589.

that, while a multiplication of substance is sufficient (and this is indeed what happens in man), it is not necessary, since a precise notion of incommunicable distinctive "properties" plays the crucial role of multiplying numerical unities, and this can be accomplished, as in the Trinity, at a level not entailing a multiplication of substance, even if substance is a necessary presupposition to the incommunicable distinctive properties[801]. Not just any property is able to provide plurality, but only those for which a variety cannot be proper to one individual, whence, it is argued, they account for personal distinction. This is the special nature of the *proprietates originis*, several of which cannot belong to one and the same person[802]. Since an individual can only possess one such property, this kind of property is sufficient to set one individual off as an ontological unity (and distinct from others if their unique property is distinct). The *proprietas* connected with designated matter is just such a property, an individuating *proprietas* which cannot be multiplied in one man and which at the same time constitutes the individual. Constitutive of distinct persons, these *proprietates* cannot be accidents. In fact, as was said, these *proprietates*, in the Trinity, are

---

[801] *"Non a qualibet proprietate potest accipi pluralitas, sed a proprietate originis secundum existentiae modum, quia de illis non multae conveniunt uni"* – Albert, *I Sent.*, d. 23, a. 3, ad 5, ed. Borgnet, vol. 25, p. 590.

[802] Note here that the fact that a property is such that no other of its kind could pertain to a given individual entails the perfect and complete constitution of the individual inasmuch as such a property would be essential to the individual as such (any other such property disrupting its identity). This manner of constituting the intrinsic unity of the individual is intimately connected with the complimentary concept of the *proprietas* as that which cannot be found in more than one individual, the latter of which characteristics accounts for the "exterior" act of "dividing" one individual from another, i.e. of making one individual distinct precisely with respect to others.

When explaining personal numeration on the basis of existential properties, Albert is not entirely clear, constant or precise in the reason given for their distinguishing role. Properties of origin account for plurality because many cannot belong to one; from another point of view, however, they multiply individuals because they cannot be found in more than one. This is the sense of the suite of Albert's response demonstrating the distinctness of the persons of the Trinity owing to the fact that the property of one cannot pertain to another (a reason ultimately founded upon the opposition between the relations): *"ut Patri convenit non esse ab alio a quo alius, quod non convenit alii... nec natura admittit inesse eidem, cum sint oppositae"* – *I Sent.*, d. 23, a. 3, ad 5, ed. Borgnet, vol. 25, p. 590. Two different perspectives thus emerge with respect to the *proprietates* and their relation to the persons they constitute, the first of which considers a plurality of such properties in comparison with a single person, the second of which reverses the terms by considering a given *proprietas* in its relation to many individuals. Though Albert makes no comment regarding this duality of angles, we deem the two to represent diverse but indissociable aspects of a unique principle of personal numerical unity. We shall

the divine persons themselves, identical to the substance, and thereby *unum* as identified with that substance, each effecting a certain (*non simpliciter sed quaedam tantum*) numerical unity of themselves[803].

The individuation, that is, personal distinction, is had in men from their particular matter (or something pertaining to the determinateness of signate matter) and the proper accidents deriving from that[804]. That which contracts the universal nature and renders it a supposit (*substantiam suppositam*) also results in individuating, distinguishing, the nature as concretized. In other words, substance or nature no longer remains a source of unity because it is composed with individualizing principles and thereby also multiplied.

In the Trinity, the persons are one *in re*, but distinguished according to *rationem* (though this be a real distinction). The converse is true in inferior beings which are considered to be one *in ratione*, but distinguished and even divided *in re*[805]. "*Ratio*" here must be taken in the proper sense. The divine persons can be said to differ only *in ratione* inasmuch as *ratio* is taken to signify relations, which relations in God are real and really distinct from one another[806]. Moreover, in inferior beings, unity is not merely according to reason in the sense of a mind dependent phenomenon, but they are one *in ratione* on account of the common nature (*secundum esse naturae*) whereby they are one *in re secundum quid*[807]. Since there can be no division in the divinity, all multiplicity incurs from extra-substantial sources, while the essence remains one and the basis of the unity amongst the persons.

more fully elaborate the special function and ontological status of the *proprietas personalis* in the section entitled "PROPRIETAS".

[803] "*Praecipue cum... proprietas sit persona subsistens et perfecta, quia in divinis nihil accidentale est, sed proprietas in persona, cujus est proprietas, est persona ipsa subsistens et perfecta*" – Albert, *I Sent.*, d. 23, a. 3, ad 5, ed. Borgnet, vol. 25, p. 590. On the notion of number and the mode according to which it is predicated in God, see infra, "NUMBER IN THE TRINITY AND IN MEN", p. 399.

[804] "*In inferioribus persona significat substantiam suppositam naturae communi, supponitur autem naturae communi per individuationem quam habet ex materia et accidentibus propriis... et quia componitur cum eo quod individuat eam*" – Albert, *I Sent*, d. 23, a. 2, sol., ed. Borgnet, vol. 25, p. 585.

[805] "*Dicit enim Damascenus quod tres personae re conveniunt, et ratione distinguuntur, et in inferioribus e converso est, in quibus ratione consideratur quod unum est, re autem quod est divisum*" – Albert, *I Sent.*, d. 25, a. 7, ed. Borgnet, vol. 25, p. 635.

[806] Cf. infra, "THE REALITY OF THE RELATIONS (TRUE NUMBER EVEN IF QUIDAM)", p. 408.

[807] "*Non enim vult dicere, quod sola ratione distinguantur personae, sed rationem vocat relationem, eo quod in ratione comparationis cujusdam consistit natura relationis, nec intendit, quod natura inferiorum tantum sit ratione una, sed quod secundum quid est una re, et simpliciter pluralitas quaedam, quia secundum esse naturae*" – Albert, *I Sent.*, d. 25, a. 7, sol., ed. Borgnet, vol. 25, p. 635. One "*in re secundum quid*" is not the same as one "*in ratione*" taken as a purely logical operation.

And because of its separation from matter, that community of substance, which has nothing to do with abstraction, is neither composed
nor able to be composed with something destroying its community[808].
Nor is there any composition to be admitted between the divine substance and the personal properties or *proprietates existentiae*, as would
be the case in inferior beings for whom the personal properties are
rooted in the substance in the manner described above when we
spoke about the different senses of *proprietates*[809].

Personal plurality derives only from the modes of distinction
which, in the Trinity, cannot result in *diversity* between persons, that
is, that something substantial be in one person and not in another.
For this reason, relations of origin are the only possible modes of distinction[810].

Distinction, but not diversity in the Trinity

The divine simplicity entails that the distinction of the persons in God
cannot take place by means of an entity entering into composition
with the common essence. Composition excluded, the absolute unicity of substance is preserved, meaning that there is no diversity between the distinct persons who are one identical reality. Nevertheless,
objective distinction must be maintained and expressed without signifying an ontological diversity between the distinguished terms. This is
possible thanks to the distinction between mode of signification and

---

[808] *"Persona in divinis substantiam suppositam, non tamen divisam, nec compositam... et ideo
unitas personarum remanet semper in substantia"* – Albert, *I Sent.*, d. 23, a. 2, sol., ed.
Borgnet, vol. 25, p. 585.

[809] *"In divinis non ea ratione dicitur quod substantia numeretur, sicut fit in inferioribus, et quod
faciat compositionem proprietatis personalis cum substantia supposita quam importat"* – Albert *I Sent.*, d. 23, a. 2, ad 2, ed. Borgnet, vol. 25, p. 586; cf. *I Sent.*, d. 23, a. 1, sol.,
ed. Borgnet, vol. 25, p. 581.

[810] *"Pluralitas personarum vel substantiarum, non potest referri ad aliquid absolutum significatum in hoc nomine, 'persona', quia tunc aliquid de substantia esset in una persona quod non
esset in alia... Pater enim cum Filio omnia habet communia nisi existentiae suae proprietatem"* – Albert, *I Sent.*, d. 23, a. 2, sol. & ad 4, ed. Borgnet, vol. 25, p. 586. On the
basis of substantial unity, the distinction constitutive of personhood in the Trinity
cannot derive from a principle implying either diversity or separation, for the *ratio*
of such division could only reside in a diversity of substantial form or the separation
due to matter. Consequently, in order to provide for distinction without diversity,
alteriety is accounted for by relative properties of origin: *"dicendum, quod diversitas
proprie loquendo, habet oppositionem ad identitatem; identitas autem non est nisi a substantiali, et ideo diversitas non est nisi ubi est divisio per formas substantiales secundum esse diversas; divisio autem est per separationem materiae"* – Albert, *I Sent.*, d. 23, a. 8, sol. & ad
1-2, ed. Borgnet, vol. 25, p. 602. Cf. infra, "NATURAL DIVERSITY AND INDIVIDUATION, ITS EX-
CLUSION IN THE TRINITY", p. 383.

the reality signified, *ratio intelligentiae* and the thing understood. In order to conceptualize distinguished entities in the Trinity, we must have recourse to the *rationes intelligentiae* (upon which mode of signification is based – as the notion of *communicabilitas*, for example, is the *ratio* founding the mode of signification proper to the essence, which signifies *ut communicabile*, according to which signification it is distinguished from hypostasis). These *rationes intelligentiae* (*communicabilitas, incommunicabilitas*, on the one hand, for example, and, on the other hand, *innascibilitas, nascibilitas, paternitas, filiatio*, and every notion, inter-Trinitarian relation or *proprietas*) are the abstract expression of either the logical distinction between common and proper elements in the Trinity or the real distinction between the Father, Son and Holy Spirit; they are the *rationes intelligentiae* of the concrete subsistents and that by virtue of which those subsistents are able to be conceived as distinct. The distinct persons are conceptualized as distinct precisely because the *rationes* by which their distinction is expressed are themselves conceived as diverse: the human intellect, according to its abstractive nature, obtains a concept of the subsistent who is understood as distinct because of the diversity of the concept. Thus the *diversity* of the *rationes* signals a *distinction* between the *res* of which they are the *rationes*, even if these *res* are one thing in reality[811].

The bottom line for personality

We have considered several different ways in which a rational thing of nature may be distinguished. None of these distinctive modes, however, are essential to the concept of personality. The definition of personhood requires only the verification of an incommunicable source of distinction. Already with Boethius' definition of personhood, the term "individual" not only indicates primary substance, but implicitly designates incommunicability[812]. This incommunicability may derive from the substance or from the modes of origin only – the definition of personhood being indifferent to the particular mode, as long as incommunicability is achieved[813]. In the context of the Trinity *"persona significet substantiam suppositam cum singulari proprietate in qua*

---

[811]   Cf. A. Pompei, op. cit., p. 307-309.

[812]   Cf. infra, "BOETHIUS' DEFINITION AND THE PRINCIPAL CONSTITUENT OF PERSONALITY", p. 341; "THE INCOMMUNICABILITY IMPORTED BY 'INDIVIDUAL'", p. 347.

[813]   *"Large sumitur substantia individua pro incommunicabili quocumque modo, sive secundum substantiam sit incommunicabile, sive secundum existentiae proprietatem solam"* – Albert, *I Sent.*, d. 23, a. 2, ad 4, ed. Borgnet, vol. 25, p. 586.

secundum existentiae modum admittatur numerus[814]. This definition
makes it clear that *existentiae* are the modes of distinction, the distinction which constitutes the person. For men, we could substitute the
term *"existentiae"* with *"individuationem quod habet (propinque) ex materia"*, that is, *secundum substantiam*.

Discretio personalis in angelis et considerationes super individuationem

A second instance of explicit and precise definition offered by Albert
for person emerges from his treatment of Angels. To the question as
to whether the notion of person properly belongs to angels, Albert
simply recasts the definition which we have seen, and verifies the fact
that it pertains also to angels[815]. Person is a *per se* existent, of a rational
nature, according to a singular mode of existence. The latter qualification, as we have seen, makes room for a diversity of *rationes* for personhood, since a singular and incommunicable mode of exis-
tence/origin can be had in different ways. While it is true that a
common notion of personhood is required for us to affirm its presence in several distinct kinds of natures, it does not follow that that
notion be common to those natures in the same way[816]. Personality is
commonly "made" and extended; but it is "made" in God by the relations of origin (i.e. relative distinction); in man, by something pertaining to material individuation; in angels, by individuation of the
nature upon a foundation other than matter. Nevertheless, none are
more individual, discrete or distinct than another (even if God can be
said to be more *perfectly* one). The formal key, in all three cases, is
individuation or *distinction*, and it is therefore the commonly formal
element for, that which distinguishes, a person. They all differ, however, as regards the mode of individuation/distinction[817]. With re-

---

[814] *I Sent.*, d. 23, a. 2, sol., ed. Borgnet, vol. 25, p. 586.

[815] *"Dicendum, quod ut dicit Richardus, persona est existens per se solum secundum quemdam
      singularem rationalis naturae existentiae modum... Angelus per se solum existit modo suae
      existentiae in intellectuali natura, ideo quilibet est persona"* – Albert, *II Sent.*, d. 3, a. 5,
      sol., ed. Borgnet, vol. 27, p. 69.

[816] *"Sufficit convenientia proportionis qua ista communis passio referatur ad tres naturas; et
      dicunt, quod illud est suppositum rationalis creaturae [sc. naturae?]... et ideo non oportet,
      quod modus discretionis sit unus"* – Albert, *II Sent.*, d. 3, a. 5, ad 1, ed. Borgnet, vol. 27,
      p. 69-70.

[817] *"Magister Richardus communiter tangit facientia et ostendentia discretionem personalem: in
      divinis enim facit relatio originis, in humanis autem individuatio super hanc materiam, et in
      Angelis individuatio esse naturae Angeli super hoc fundamentum. Et argumentum non
      valet: Pluribus enim distinguitur homo quam Angelus, ergo est magis discretus in persona"* –
      Albert, *II Sent.*, d. 3, a. 5, ad 2, ed. Borgnet, vol. 27, p. 70.

spect to angels, Albert argues that the designation "person" befits them inasmuch as they are distinct things of a rational nature[818], distinctness being the governing notion. According to Albert's subscription to the Victorine account of the principles of singularity, the divine persons were seen to be distinguished *ex origine tantum*, angels *ex proprietate tantum*, and men *ex origine et proprietate*. The principles of distinction in creatures, moreover, must result in wholly distinct individual substances[819]. The sense of *proprietas* employed with respect to men and angels, since it entails distinct substances, must say something more than the sense of *proprietas* identified with relations of origin. In material things, it is designated matter (or the principle of its "designation") which is responsible for individuation; the common nature is individuated *super hanc materiam determinatam*. What, now, in the case of angels, can perform such a role? In spiritual substances, Albert tells us, the nature as *quo est* (= *quod est* as component), according as it is discretely set off through something singularly demonstrated, constitutes a singular mode of existence, making an individual of that spiritual nature[820]. In angels, the essence itself, then, and in itself, appears to be the principle of the distinctive mode of existence constitutive of the individuality proper to personhood (though Albert's formulation seems to presuppose something to the particularized status of the spiritual nature enabling it to be a distinctive principle in itself, something we cannot discuss within the limits of this thesis). Now, that which actually establishes the discreteness of the substance is not the same as that which manifests to us that discreteness. Thus, Richard of Saint Victor must be properly understood when he says that *proprietates tantum* are what distinguish angelic persons, since he has actually identified those things which *demonstrate* their distinction, and not the very principle responsible for *making* the distinction. Just as the individuality and incommunicability in material things is indicated by the collection of accidents consequent upon material

---

818 *"Qui secundum naturam personae sunt distinctae sub hoc communi quod est rationalis natura"* – Albert, *Sum. theol.*, II, tr. 4, q. 15, m. 1, contra 2, ed. Borgnet, vol. 32, p. 204.

819 *"In humanis autem distinguuntur origine et proprietate: nec una substantia est eadem in pluribus personis, sed sunt substantiae individuae a se invicem distinctae"* – Albert, *Sum. theol.*, II, tr. 4, q. 15, m. 1, ad 1, ed. Borgnet, vol. 32, p. 205.

820 *"Sicut enim in materialibus individuatio naturae communis super hanc materiam determinatam et propriam, facit hoc aliquid, et hoc est individuum, ita in natura spirituali in qua differt quod est a quo est, natura... quae significatur per quo est particulata super hoc quod est singulariter demonstratum, facit singularem existentiae modum, et facit hoc aliquid et spiritualis naturae individuum"* – Albert, *Sum. theol.*, II, tr. 4, q. 15, m. 1, ad 1, ed. Borgnet, vol. 32, p. 205.

individuation, so, in angels, non-corporeal properties serve to indicate their singular mode of existence and incommunicability. Properties serve, then, to distinguish persons only in the sense that they manifest the distinctness of each person, though they do not constitute it. Taken in another sense, however, the *proprietates* can be understood to constitute personal distinction, precisely when intended as the very principles of distinction, viz. relations of origin in God, the foundations of singularity in angels, and designated matter (or the principle of its "designation") in man[821].

The constitution of personhood – in a real way in creatures, though only logically in God (with respect, that is, to our concept of person) – takes place at the level of composition. This, because *individuation* determines the person. It was said, shortly above, that, in angels, essential *quod est* is the principle of singular demonstrative discretion; *quod est*, which is "material" with respect to *quo est* (*esse*), is the principle of individuation, through which the substance is divided from others, and by which the person differs substantially from every other person[822]. Here is the *ratio personalis*. For those natures endowed with reason, unity and individuality renders the nature a person: "*Angelus unus, et individuum est, et rationalis naturae est, et ideo persona est*[823]. This emphasis on individuality clarifies why the human soul does not qualify as a person. The individual is what is indivisible and consistent in itself and divided from all others. But the soul is not truly individual, since it is unitable or communicable to others[824]. If one argues that "unitable" does not mean "united", and that the soul, therefore, fails to count as an individual only when it is actually united to another, we could respond by pointing out that, even in the state of separation, the soul is never fully "consistent" in itself, since its es-

---

[821]   "*In Angelis etiam aliud est discretionem substantiae faciens, et aliud est discretam substantiam ostendens. ... Et sicut in corporalibus est collectio accidentium, quae indicat in hoc corporali individuo singularis et incommunicabilis existentiae modum, ita in hoc spirituali individuo quaedam collectio proprietatum est... quae in eo indicant singularis existentiae modum et incommunicabilis. Et quando dicit Richardus, quod proprietate sola distinguuntur personae angelicae, tangit illud quod est ostendens distintionem, et non faciens*" – Albert, Sum. theol., II, tr. 4, q. 15, m. 1, ad 1, ed. Borgnet, vol. 32, p. 205.*

[822]   "*In Angelis autem licet non sit materia corporalis, tamen est ibi diversum quod est et quo est, et quod est in hoc materiale est, quod principium est individuationis naturae communis, et per hoc fit divisio substantiae per quam personae differunt secundum substantiam, quae differentia ostenditur collectione proprietatum incommunicabilium*" – Albert, Sum. theol., II, tr. 4, q. 15, m. 1, ad 2, ed. Borgnet, vol. 32, p. 205.*

[823]   Albert, *Sum. theol.*, II, tr. 4, q. 15, m. 1, ad 3, ed. Borgnet, vol. 32, p. 205.

[824]   "*[Anima] non enim vere individuum est, quod unibile est alteri. Individuum enim est in se consistens unum ab omnibus aliis divisum*" – Albert, *Sum. theol.*, II, tr. 4, q. 15, m. 1, ad 4, ed. Borgnet, vol. 32, p. 205.

sence is irrevocably linked to a given body[825]. In a manner similar to the human soul, the humanity of Christ likewise evades the full attribution of individuality. Because that nature is united to the divine nature in the person of the Word, it is neither *per se una* nor individual in the full sense of the term[826].

This elaboration of the definitive constituent in personhood has broad implication. Such an explanation, moreover, clarifies why "the intelligent" may not be convertible with person after all – assuming we qualify the humanity of Christ as *res intellectualis*. In this way, to say "intelligent thing" will not suffice for personhood, since the stipulation "individual" is needing[827]. But if "the intelligent" necessarily also implies individual (in the full sense of the term), then person and "the intelligent" remain convertible; but then the human nature in Christ cannot be *res intellectualis* in the sense of *res ut individua. Individuatio facit ergo discretionem personalem*, and this event occurs upon the creation of the individual essence rendered suppositum (composite *quod est*) from its intentionally pre-existent state as component or essential *quod est*[828]. In angels, however, the principle of that individuation is not matter but the essential *id quod est*, resembling matter in

---

[825] The human soul is necessarily related to its body according to an essential dependence. Consequently, it cannot be incommunicable, since strict incommunicability depends upon complete individuality and *per se* singularity. As a result, the human soul cannot be a person: *"anima adhuc secundum suam diffinitivam substantiam est endelechia corporis organici physici vitam habentis in potentia, ergo videtur quod essentialis sit dependentia ei ad corpus, igitur non potest esse incommunicabilis alteri incommunicabilitati, ergo anima non est persona"* – Albert, *III Sent.*, d. 5, a. 16, ed. Borgnet, vol. 28, p. 116.

[826] *"Natura enim humana in Christo unita est divinae in una persona Filii, et ideo nec per se proprie una est, nec individua"* – Albert, *Sum. theol.*, II, tr. 4, q. 15, m. 1, ad 5, ed. Borgnet, vol. 32, p. 205. Cf. in this regard and with respect to the soul in the state of separation: infra, "CONSIDERATIONS ON THE SEPARATED SOUL AND THE HUMANITY OF CHRIST; THE CRITERION OF THE OMNINO INCOMMUNICABILIS", p. 365.

[827] Consideration of the separated human soul, which is certainly rational but generally not considered to be a person, would likewise seem to conflict with conceptualizing rationality as a convertible specific difference, vindicating the lengthier definition of Boethius, inasmuch as the notion of individual substance is seen as necessary to the definition of personhood. Being an individual, in the full sense of the term, it seems, is that which is lacking in the case of the separated soul. Cf., however, J.-H. Nicolas who argues that the soul in the state of separation is nevertheless the person, though in an attenuated sense: *Synthèse dogmatique*, §275, (N.B.).

[828] *"Discretionem personalem facit individuatio naturae communis [vel natura ut 'id quo est' vel 'id quod es' ut res ex qua confiatur et efficitur aliquid], quae significatur cum dicitur, quod Angelus est spiritualis et intellectualis natura super id quod est, quod est suppositum et res naturae ejusdem, eductum de non esse ad esse per creationem"* – Albert, *Sum. theol.*, II, tr. 4, q. 15, m. 2, sol., ed. Borgnet, vol. 32, p. 206.

consideration of its passivity with respect to *esse*[829]. From that determination, moreover, the angel receives its discrete being. Supposits receive their discrete being in virtue of the determination deriving from the very principle of individuation (which is the nature itself – as component – in angels)[830]. In angels, then, the nature absolutely considered is both the foundation for *esse* and the principle of singularity/distinction in the constitution of the person. The composition involved in creation is inseparable from the grounds upon which personal distinction is achieved *in inferioribus*. The universally first principle of individuation, furthermore, is not matter, but the essential *quod est*. Even in material things, matter, according to Albert, is not the principle of discreteness and individuation; that discretion is *per hoc quod est id quod est*[831]. The essential *quod est*, as we have seen, operates, in a sense, as its own principle of individuation, that is, as the principle of individuation, or as the foundation (i.e. a metaphysical condition) of that principle, for the supposit, which is nothing other that the *quod est essentialis* in possession of its being. In material things, then, matter is effectively said to individuate the thing precisely because it forms a part of the thing itself. The very created thing (as an essence) is its own foundation of individuation – even if its uniqueness in creation is traceable to one of its constituent parts, namely designated matter – just as it is also the foundation for the being which it receives[832]. In fact, when matter is called the principle of individuation, it is not so called insofar as matter, but in virtue of its subjectivality, which means that the individuating principle consists in being a receptive subject of a participated perfection[833]. Accordingly,

---

[829] "*Sed verum est, quod principium individuationis in eis non est materia, sed id quod est sub quadam convenientia ad materiam*" – Albert, *Sum. theol.*, II, tr. 4, q. 15, m. 2, sol, ed. Borgnet, vol. 32, p. 207.

[830] "*Quod dicitur existens vere ens in natura ex quo est determinato ad quod est, ex qua determinatione discretum esse accipit*" – Albert, *Sum. theol.*, II, tr. 4, q. 15, m. 2, sol., ed. Borgnet, vol. 32, p. 207.

[831] Cf. Albert, *Sum. theol.*, II, tr. 12, q. 72, m. 2, ad 1, ed. Borgnet, vol. 33, p. 36.

[832] Note that this property of being a foundation is indispensable from the essence's role as a principle of individuation and necessarily points toward another element with respect to which the essence is a foundation, namely the thing's act of being which, when signified according to the relation of dependence on the part of *ens* with respect to the First Cause, equally collaborates in the individuation of nature.

[833] "*Materia per rationem materiae non est principium individuationis, sed potius per rationem proprii subjecti est principium individuationis, ut primum subjectum*" – Albert, *Sum. theol.*, II, tr. 1, q. 4, a. 1, particula 2, ad 2, ed. Borgnet, vol. 32, p. 65. In respect of the need for something besides matter in order to explain individuation even in natural substances, cf. Albert, *De praedicabilibus*, tr. 3, c. 4, ed. Borgnet, vol. 1, p. 63; *I Sent.*, d. 19, a. 12, ad 2, ed. Borgnet, vol. 25, p. 528; *I Sent.*, d. 19, a. 17, ed. Borgnet, vol. 25, p. 541; *I Sent.*, d. 24, a. 1 & 3, ed. Borgnet, vol. 25, p. 606, 612-613; *II Sent.*,

the *forma totius individualis*, i.e. the *quod est essentialis individualis* (which, in material things, contains designated matter inasmuch as it represents the *essence of the individual*) is the cause of the individual's discreteness[834], discrete in itself and the cause of every individuality belonging to it[835].

These last considerations both witness to the importance of and attempt to point out the "principle of individuation" in personal constitution. That principle, however, is extremely elusive and entails a complicated reciprocal relationship between the essential principles mentioned above and existential principles – with respect to which the essential principles were, in fact, described as "foundation" – fundamental to the very determinateness of designated matter and subsistent forms. Because the issue or so-called "problem of" individuation requires an in-depth examination, and as the Thomistic tradition itself has consistently vacillated between competing theories, we simply cannot study the question within the scope of this treatise. Nevertheless, confronted with the human nature in Christ, the total and concrete individuation of which seems to be the fundamental Christological dilemma, we have chosen to consecrate a rather elaborated analysis to isolating that principle intended to be presented in the

---

d. 9, a. 7, ad 1, ed. Borgnet, vol. 27, p. 205; *Sum. de creaturis*, II, q. 2, a. 2, ed. Borgnet, vol. 35, p. 15; q. 56, a. 5, ed. Borgnet, vol. 35, p. 486; *Sum. theol.*, II, tr. 1, q. 4, a. 1, m. 2, ad 2, ed. Borgnet, vol. 32, p. 65; *Sum. theol.*, II, tr. 12, q. 72, a. 1, m. 2, ad 1, ed. Borgnet, vol. 33, p. 36; *Super Dion. De div. nom.*, c. 1, 16, ed. Colon., vol. 37/1, p. 8, n. 76 - p. 9, n. 3; c. 4, 111, ed. Colon., vol. 37/1, p. 210, n. 14-15; c. 13, 7, ed. Colon., vol. 37/1, p. 436, n. 16-21 (cf. H. Kühle, "Die Lehre Alberts des Grossen von den Tranzendentalien", in *Philosophia perennis*, Festgabe J. Geyser, Bd. I, Druck und Verlag von Josef Hobbel, Regensburg 1930, p. 137-138); c. 13, 8, ed. Colon., vol. 37/1, p. 436, n. 84 - p. 437, n. 1; c. 13, 16, ed. Colon., vol. 37/1, p. 441, n. 34; cf. also M.-D. Roland-Gosselin, *Le "De ente et essentia" de Saint Thomas d'Aquin*, Vrin, Paris 1948, p. 93-95, 100-101.

[834] *"Secundus [actus formae] est, quod discernit rem sive facit discretam ab aliis"* – Albert, *Sum. theol.*, I, tr. 15, q. 62, ad object., ed. Borgnet, vol. 31, p. 638.

[835] *"Principium primum individuationis universale, non est materia, sed quod est per hoc quod est id quod est, discretum est in se, et causa discretionis omnibus aliis quae sibi insunt, unde per ipsum quod est, quod sibi inest, efficitur discretum et ponitur in numerum et hic et nunc, unde etiam materia in corporalibus per hoc quod est materia, non est principium discretionis et individuationis, sed per hoc quod est id quod est, discretum et divisum ab aliis"* – Albert, *Sum. theol.*, II, tr. 12, q. 72, m. 2, ad 1, ed. Borgnet, vol. 33, p. 36. Cf. the principle appealed to in an objection to Albert's article on plurality and unity in the divinity: *"quia nihil est principium distinctionis et individuationis nisi suppositum, cum hoc solum distinctum sit per proprium"* – Albert, *Sum. theol.*, I, tr. 6, q. 29, c. 1, a. 2, obj. 6, ed. Colon., vol. 34, p. 218. In just what the individuality of the *forma totius individualis* formally consists cannot be discussed in this work, but it is evident that we are approaching the notion of *haeceitas* later developed by Duns Scotus.

context of a Christological study soon to follow our present study on personhood.

Conclusion

Moving toward the construction of a systematic definition of person, we begin by studying the personal phenomenon from the point of view of our general experience and theological knowledge of that reality. Several difficult issues stand in need of clarification on behalf of the Trinitarian implications which demand a concept of person non-disruptive of concrete substantial unity while nevertheless affirming an incommunicable constitutive element. What is required, therefore, with respect to God, is a concept of personality denoting relation while nonetheless retaining the substantiality expressed by the Boethian notion of person.

Three fundamental elements were seen to be inseparable from the most universal concept of personality: perseity, its possession through a singular mode of existence, and its realization in intellectual nature. Persons enjoy that kind of unity incommunicably distinguishing them from every other perfect and complete subsistent individual. The origin of that distinctiveness admits of several *rationes*, deriving in the Trinity from relation alone, and in man from substantial differences associated with individual matter. In either case, it is the individuating conditions which constitute the particular modality according to which the subsistent act of personal being is realized and in virtue of which the person is a *per se* unity in itself. The quidditative character of the person is expressed by the third element designating both intellectual perfection and the nature with respect to which persons are ascribed the subjective perfection of hypostases.

Regarding the signification of "person", we affirmed its simultaneously substantial and notional (or distinctive) denotation. "Person" directly signifies both the substance taken in the sense of hypostasis as well as the distinctive *proprietas* (the principle of the unique mode of existence referred to above). It was also seen to name the essence, but only indirectly. Thus substance is the direct *significatum* of "person", but only *quae supponitur et distinguitur*, that is, only *quod ab actu substandi accipitur*. The distinctive meaning of "person", however, lies in explicitating the incommunicable *proprietas* as that through which the substance directly signified is hypostatized, and it is this formality, focusing on the principle of incommunicable distinction, which provides for an affirmation of several divine persons without implying a like multiplicity with respect to the common nature.

In consideration of God, we learn that personal plurality is indifferent to the verification of but one or many substances. Only as a result of substantial non-simplicity does the natural communication implied in the notion of the possession, on the part of distinct subsistent subjects, of a common nature according to unique existential modes entail a division of essence. In God, essence is communicable, though person is not; to speak of one, therefore, is not to speak of the other, and the formally distinctive character of their respective modes of signifying is a reflection of real aspects of a single reality. Notwithstanding their absolute identity in the Godhead, the distinctive modes according to which we predicate "essence", *"proprietas"* and "person" represent the divine being according as it is, respectively: (a) some-*thing*, (b) possessed in a singular manner, and (c) some *one* or distinct.

Although different kinds of principles were seen to account for personal number among differing kinds of persons, the central and generic feature common to all of them was seen to be the accomplishment of distinction, i.e. individuation. The person is constituted as such, therefore, on the basis of an intrinsic principle of individuality. In God, personality is thus constituted by the relations of origin (which are identical to the persons), while created persons come to be, i.e. are distinguished from one another, on the basis of a principle of individuation either associated with matter (as in the traditional acceptation of the individuation of natural substances, or in a theory of individuation of natural substances recognizing matter as a proximate principle of – or, at the least, as an index of – individuality) or understood to reside within the potential structure of the individual nature lacking matter (as in the case of angels).

II.3. SHARING IN THE COMMON NOTION OF PERSON

Relevance of the problem

Another way of approaching the notion of personhood is to ask the question; "How is it that several persons share in the *ratio* of personhood?", that is, "What is the basis for the community enjoyed by several persons insofar as persons?". For, there is a difference between asking what a thing is (its definition) and asking how the same is predicated of the things participating in it. What is clear is that, even if the name "person" is used for all three of the distinct members of the Trinity, its function is different from that of other names equally predicable of all three (such as *Deus, natura, essentia*, and every essential name) [836]. As Boethius points out, other common names *"de singulis in unum collectis tribus singulariter praedicabuntur"* [837]. Such, however, is not the case with the name "person", for we do not say that Father, Son and Holy Spirit are one person. From this difference, we may conclude that something inherent in the very meaning of "person" determines the manner in which it is commonly attributed to the subjects of personality within a given nature. The question, therefore, of the community of the name person is not of merely grammatical interest, but has equally theological value, inasmuch as its resolution contributes to a greater specification of the real signification of person [838].

How "person" is predicated

Now, if personhood is commonly predicated of the three individuals of the Trinity, it must be so either: (A), as proper to each of the three; or (B), as not proper to what they are. If (B), then personhood would accrue to each person as something accidental, and this is unacceptable. But if (A), namely, being from the *ratio* of what each person is, then either: (C), "person" is convertible with each of the three; or (D), non-convertible. If convertible, however, then any time person

---

[836] Cf. A. Pompei, op. cit., p. 244.
[837] Boethius, *Utrum Pater et Filius*, 18-19, ed. Loeb, p. 34. This property of substantial predicates was already observed in addressing the special signification of the name "Trinity" (cf. supra, "ON THE NAME 'TRINITY'", p. 256).
[838] Cf. A. Pompei, op. cit., p. 244.

were to be predicated, so too would each of the three individuals, as
though wherever there is a person, there too will be the Father, for
example, and the Son. This cannot be. Therefore, person is non-
convertible with the individuals of whom it is predicated. But, if (D),
non-convertibility, then either: (E), person must be a genus or species[839]; or (F), some other explanation must be sought[840]. The alternative explanation must respect the non-convertibility requirement, but
is not obliged to deny strict identity between "person" and the subject
of which it is predicated. This is possible because person can fail to be
convertible with the subject of its predication on account of an inequality positing nothing with regard to the essential being of the subject, contrary to the inequality existing between a universal nature and
its particular realizations, which do not have an ontologically equal
status. The inequality, and consequent inconvertibility, lies in the fact
that person exceeds "Father" and "Son" *secundum rationem tantum*, and
not *secundum esse*[841]. This difference *secundum rationem* is not a difference of universal to particular, since person is not a universal nature
(in the sense of univocally predicable), as though its notion were obtained by abstraction. The community of personhood is a community
according to proportionality (*secundum rationem proportionis*)[842], and

[839] Since, as shall become clear, these things exceed the nature in some way, for which
reason they are not convertible.
[840] *"Si est commune praedicatum de tribus, aut ut ens de ratione trium, aut ut non ens de ratione
trium. Si ut non ens de ratione trium, hoc est accidentale tribus... Si autem praedicatur
communiter, ut ens de ratione trium, aut convertibiliter, aut non convertibiliter. Si convertibiliter, ergo persona convertitur cum Patre, ergo de quocumque praedicatur persona, et Pater,
quod falsum est... Si autem praedicatur ut ens de ratione trium, et non convertitur, necessario erit genus, vel species"* – Albert, *I Sent.*, d. 23, a. 5, obj. 1-2, ed. Borgnet, vol. 25,
p. 594.
[841] *"Nec praedicatur per accidens, sed praedicatur ut idem subjecto de quo praedicatur, et excedens ipsum natura rei, sed secundum rationem tantum... ab illa similitudine imponuntur
hujusmodi nomina relativa, persona, hypostasis, et res naturae, et incommunicabilis, et hujusmodi, et ratione illius proportionis excedunt, licet non in re, et ideo secundum praedicationem non convertuntur cum suis subjectis"* – Albert, *I Sent.*, d. 23, a. 5, ad 1-2, ed. Borgnet, vol. 25, p. 596-597.
[842] One of the central Albertinian conceptual tools for establishing a basis for shared
personhood in the Trinity is the notion of oneness by *proportio*, a notion adopted
from Avicenna and Algazel. In this type of analogy, the oneness in question is that
existing between two or more individuals sharing the same *habitude* or *respectus*, as
the mayor of a city and the captain of a ship share the same kind of relation toward
the townspeople and ship crew respectively. It is with respect to the common art of
governing that the mayor and the captain share a unity of *proportion*, each one in his
own way realizing that singular (perhaps "generic") act of governance. The particular modality by which that art is realized constitutes the proper *habitude* of the
individual said to "govern", and the *habitude* of one individual is "one" with that of

the other on account of their similarity (or identity, at a more generic level): *"his additur ab AVICENNA et ALGAZELE unum proportione, qua scilicet una similitudine habitudinis rector civitatis se habet ad civitatem ut rector navis ad navem. Et dicuntur haec unum habitudine unum... Si secundum veritatem et est uniens diversa, tunc est unitas proportionis diversorum ad unum vel ad diversa similia, quae inquantum similia sunt, sunt unum, sicut habitudo rectoris civitatis dicitur una cum habitudine rectoris navis"* – Albert, *Sum. theol.*, I, tr. 6, q. 24, c. 1, ed. Colon., vol. 34, p. 144-145.

The doctrine of analogy is based upon the similarity and dissimilarity existing between God and creatures and between creatures of differing ontological orders, and it is by reason of these objective relationships that the validity of our knowledge and speech about God is assured. In general, every analogy is a likeness accompanied by an unlikeness (for a general exposition of the question, cf. A. Chollet, "ANALOGIE", *DTC* 1, p. 1142-1154; E. Forment, *Lecciones de Metafísica*, Ediciónes Rialp, Madrid 1992, p. 260-293; P. Secretan, *L'Analogie*, Presses universitaires de France, Paris 1984, especially p. 5-77). We conceptualize and express the similarities (a matter of logical and linguistic analogy) with various terms by which we describe both divine and created being. But the same names applied to God and to creatures do not have entirely the same sense: the properties which they express exist differently in the different referents to which they are ascribed. Analogy stands, therefore, between univocation and equivocation. While the words we use to signify the realities shared by God and creatures originate with creaturely experience, the perfections inherent in the concepts apply primarily and *per se* to God, whom we know by way of causality, excellence and remotion (cf. Aquinas, *Sum. theol.*, I, 13). God, who is "ineffable", is not unnamable: in order to apply a name to God, it is enough to constantly correct our concept by denying the imperfections found in creation while asserting the supereminent realization of the signified reality in God. (Though it cannot provide us with comprehensive knowledge of God, nor ever remove the mystery, analogy nevertheless allows us to speak with meaning about God, in a way which says something positive, and in a way which avoids the fatal extremes of anthropomorphism and agnosticism [comprising the impious reduction of divine revelation to unsuitable jabber]).

As is well known, analogy is distinguished into two distinct kinds: analogy of attribution and analogy of proportion. The first is further distinguished into analogy of intrinsic attribution (corresponding to the ontological analogy between things which participate to differing degrees in a single property) and analogy of extrinsic attribution (corresponding to the kind of real analogy existing between something properly possessing a quality and those things which are causally related to the quality in question). Analogy of proportion (the notion taken up by Albert and which we have described above), however, consists not so much in the unequal sharing of the same perfection as in a resemblance acknowledged by the intellect based upon the sharing of a certain quality or relation. In this form of analogy, when it is a question of speaking about God and created entities, we apply the same term to realities which are entirely different but between which the intelligence is capable of recognizing a common comparative property (i.e. one based upon a relation). The first kind of analogy pertains especially to what theologians have called "pure perfections", perfections which (considered in themselves, and not according to concrete instantiation) are formally present in both God and the creature but which are possessed in an eminent way by God. These perfections are contrasted with what are known as "mixed perfections" the very concept of which implies a certain imperfection and which exist formally only in the creature, since no imperfection may be ascribed to God. Perfections or properties the realization of which implies composition of any sort (even logical composition) are exclusively of this kind (i.e. mixed) and conform to analogy of proportion only.

Now, as *per se* existents (denoting a pure perfection), there exists an intrinsic analogy of attribution between God and creatures, since the supposital perfection of substantial being belongs *formaliter* to both. Person, however, signifies the *ens concretum* according, precisely, to a distinct existential mode. But the unique and concrete mode of existing in a substantial nature (beneath which the supposit is said to stand) represents a mixed perfection in creatures (where *quod est* and *quo est* are really distinguished). Moreover, person itself is not a perfection in which creatures participate or to which God is identical, but designates a concrete substance according as it is related to a common nature. As a result, the analogy by which they are commonly persons is one of proportion. Bearing the said relationship makes one to be a person, and every person shares this relationship in one way or another. When we call two individuals "persons", we affirm that they each have such a relation and effectively relate both individuals to the common reality of possessing such a relation. This *new* relation of referring the individuals to the relation defining personhood is precisely what constitutes the analogy of proportion, in which two or more things share being related to something one. [Note that the relation defining personhood could be any number of things or combination thereof, such as the possessing of rational nature, for example]. Cf. infra, "ANALOGICITY OF THE NAME", p. 338 (in the chapter on "DEFINITIONS OF PERSON"). For a thorough and decisive analysis of the role of analogy in theology, see M. T. L. PENIDO, *Le rôle de l'analogie en théologie dogmatique,* J. Vrin, "Bibliotèque thomiste, 15", Paris 1931; B. MONTAGNES, *La doctrine de l'analogie de l'être d'après Saint Thomas d'Aquin,* Publications universitaires/Béatrice-Nauwelaerts, Louvain/Paris 1963. Cf. also P. AUBENQUE, *Le problème de l'être chez Aristote,* Paris 1962; E. BERTI, "L'Analogia dell'essere nella tradizione aristotelico-tomistica", in AA.VV., *Metafora dell'invisibile,* Brescia 1984; *Origini e sviluppo dell'analogia: da Parmenide a S. Tommaso,* Rome 1987; A. BITBOL-HESPÉRIÈS, *Le problem de l'individuation,* J. Vrin, Paris 1991; O. BURRELL, *Analogy and Philosophical Language,* Yale University Press, London 1973; CAJETAN, *De Nominum Analogia,* critical revised edition, P. H. Hering, Rome 1952 (English trans. E. Bushinski, H. Koren, Pittsburgh 1953); A. DE LIBERA, "Le problème de l'être chez Maître Eckhart: logique et métaphysique de l'analogie", in *Cahiers de la Revue de théologie et de philosophie,* no. 4, Geneva/Lausanne 1980; D. DUBARLE, "La doctrine Aristotélicienne de l'analogie et sa normalisation rationelle", *RSPT* 53 (1969), p. 3-40; C. FABRO, *Participation et causalité chez Thomas d'Aquin,* Louvain/Paris 1961; E. FORMENT, *Lecciones de Metafísica,* Ediciónes Rialp, Madrid 1992, p. 260-293; H. D. GARDEIL, *Introduction to the Philosophy of St. Thomas Aquinas,* trans. J. A. Otto, Herder, New York 1967, vol. 4, "The Doctrine of Analogy", p. 47-72; L. B. GEIGER, *La participation dans la philosophie de saint Thomas d'Aquin,* Paris 1965; P. GISEL – P. SECRETAN (editors), *Analogie et dialectique. Essai de théologie fondamentale,* Geneva 1982; P. GRENET, *Les origines de l'analogie dans les dialogues de Platon,* Paris 1948; J. HABBEL, *Die Analogie zwischen Gott und Welt nach Thomas von Aquin,* Berlin 1949; G. P. KLUBERTANZ, *Saint Thomas Aquinas on Analogy,* Chicago 1960; B. LAKEBRINK, *Klassische Metaphysik,* §6, "Der kantische Analogiebegriff", Freiburg 1967; I. LE ROHELLEC, "L'Analogie de proportion chez S. Thomas d'Aquin. Cognitio nostra analogica de Deo", *Divus Thomas* 30 (1927), p. 298-319; K. LORENZ (editor), *Identität und Individuation,* Frommann-Holzboog, Stuttgart-Bad Cannstatt 1982; V. LOSSKY, "Notion des 'analogies' chez Denys", *AHDLMA* 5 (1930), p. 279-309; H. LYTTKENS, *The Analogy between God and the World,* Uppsala 1952; J. MACQARRIE, *Jesus Christ in Modern Thought,* London 1990; F. MARTY, *La naissance de la métaphysique chez Kant. Une étude sur la notion kantienne d'analogie,* Paris 1982; A. MILANO, "Analogia Christi. Sul parlare intorno a Dio in una teologia cristiana" in *Ricerche teologiche* 4 (1990), p. 29-73; R. MCINERNY, *Aquinas and Analogy,* Catholic University of America Press, Washington D.C. 1996; *Studies in Analogy,* M. Nijhoff, The Hague 1968; *The Logic of Analogy,* The Hague 1961; A. MCINTYRE,

"Analogy", *Scottish Journal of Theology* 12 (1959), p. 1-20; N. W. MTEGA, *Analogy and Theological Language in the "Summa contra gentiles": a Textual Survey of the Concept of Analogy and its Theological Application by St. Thomas Aquinas*, P. Lang, Frankfurt a.m. 1984; M. K. MUNITZ (editor), *Identity and Individuation*, New York University Press, New York 1971; J. PALAKEEL, *The Use of Analogy in Theological Discourse: An Investigation in Ecumenical Perspective*, Editrice Pontificia Università Gregoriana, Rome 1995 [Note: this work provides an extensive bibliography on the Catholic tradition of analogy]; W. PANNENBERG, *Analogie und Offenbarung*, Heidelberg 1955; G. PHELAN, *St. Thomas and Analogy*, Milwaukee 1941; M.-D. PHILIPPE, "Analogon and Analogia in the Philosophy of Aristotle", *The Thomist* 33 (1969), p. 1-74; B. PINCHARD, *Métaphysique et sémantique: la signification analogique des termes dans les principes métaphysiques*, J. Vrin, Paris 1987; E. PRZYWARA, "Die Reichweite der Analogie als katholischer Grundform", *Scholastik* 15 (1940), p. 339-362, 508-532; J. M. RAMIREZ, "De analogia secundum doctrinam aristotelico-thomisticam", *La Ciencia Tomista* 24 (1921), p. 20-40, 195-214, 337-357; 25 (1922), p. 17-38; M. ROQUES, *L'univers dionysien*, Paris 1954; J. F. ROSS, "Analogy as a Rule of Meaning for Religious Language", *InternPhilosQuart* 1 (1961), p. 468-502; C. RUTTEN, "L'analogie chez Aristote", *Revue de philosophie ancienne* 1 (1983), p. 31-48; P. SECRETAN, *L'Analogie*, Presses universitaires de France, Paris 1984; J. A. SAYÉS, *Existencia de Dios y conocimiento humano*, Universidad Pontificia, Salamanca 1980; R. STERTENBRINK, *Ein Weg zum Denken: die Analogia entis bei Erich Przywara*, A. Pustet, Salzburg/Munich 1971; C. THEILEMANN, *Die Frage nach Analogie, natürlicher Theologie und Personenbegriff in der Trinitätslehre: eine vergleichende Untersuchung britischer und deutschsprachiger Trinitätstheologie*, Walter de Gruyter, Berlin/New York 1995.

not that of a common universal nature[843]. Whence:

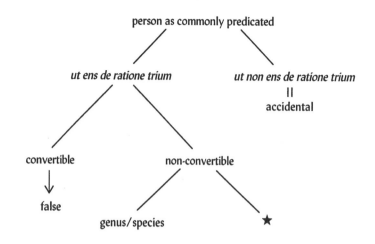

* Person as identical with the subject of which it is predicated, yet not convertible, because exceeding the subject *secundum rationem.*

Community of proportion

Albert analyses the entire question of predicative community according to its different *rationes.* He begins by distinguishing between community of being (*communitas esse*) and community of *ratio*[844] (*communitas rationis*). The first kind of community can only belong to the divinity. Composition, for all created substances, accounts for the fact that their *esse* (or, more precisely, *essentia* – since it is a question of the nature *according to* its being) cannot be common to many. Community in inferior beings, therefore, cannot be had at the level of substantial being, but is rather one of *ratio. Communitas rationis* is also twofold, comprising, on the one hand, that community due to the

---

[843] "*Ad universale exigitur, quod abstrahat ab his de quibus praedicatur... sed hic non est ita, sed tantum similitudo proportionis est in istis nominibus [divinibus] importata*" – Albert, *I Sent.*, d. 23, a. 5, ad 3, ed. Borgnet, vol. 25, p. 597. The universal is what is of many and in many, existing in them and taken from them according to a single concept or *ratio*: "*universale est quod est de multis et in multis, per unam rationem existens in eis, et de eis*" – Albert, *Sum. theol.*, II, tr. 1, q. 3, m. 3, a. 3, ad obj. 2, ed. Borgnet, vol. 32, p. 43.

[844] In the sense of "aspect", "point of view" or "concept".

participation of many in a common nature, which nature is abstracted from its participants and composed in each of them with their respective individualizing features (thus constituting many proper natures), and, on the other hand, that community resulting from a proportion of one thing to another, or, more precisely, several things to something one[845]. That common nature at the base of *communitas secundum naturam communem* is said to exceed those things of which it is predicated because it possesses a broader extension than any one member: it is not, according to its plenitude, in one single particular – for then it would not be universal – and, for this reason, it "exceeds" any singular individual of which it can be predicated. Finally, community of proportion designates that community shared by two or more things based upon a common condition or disposition with regard to something one, just as a governor and a teacher, through their respective arts, bear a certain relation to the art of directing, and have therefore, in proportionate ways, a *habitudo* related to directing. That which makes each of them directors in their own fields is a different art, but they nonetheless share similar *habitudines* to the singular act of directing. The importance of all these distinctions derives from the fact that the notion of personhood shows itself, in the context of the Trinity, to enjoy precisely that kind of community due to a proportion of a plurality of things to something one, and not that due to a universality of abstract nature. In God, there is no universal-particular relationship obtaining between the nature considered as common and the nature of the individual persons. Such a relation holds only for inferiors in whom unique instances of composition result in diverse natures, which are thereby particularized with respect to what is com-

---

[845] *"Duplex est communitas, scilicet esse, et rationis. Communitas autem in esse et essentia eadem numero, non potest inveniri nisi in divinis hypostasibus, et non in aliqua natura creata, quia omne creatum est compositum, et ideo idem numero secundum esse non potest esse in diversis subjectis et distinctis. Communitas autem rationis multiplex est: quaedam enim est secundum naturam communem per eamdem rationem participatam a pluribus, quae natura communis abstrahitur ab unoquoque illorum, et secundum esse in quolibet illorum compositionem habens cum eo quod contrahit eam ad hoc et ad illud; et illa natura facit universale, et secundum totum posse quod habet illa natura, non est in uno, licet sit in eo secundum esse, ideo haec natura excedit quodlibet illorum, de quo praedicatur quoad posse, et quia est in eo secundum totum esse suum, ideo est ratio cujuslibet eorum de quo praedicatur, vel pars rationis ejus, vel simpliciter, ut in genere, vel specie, et differentia, vel secundum quid, sicut est in proprio, et accidente. Est etiam communitas resultans ex proportione aliquorum ad unum... sicut est communitas proportionis regiminis navis et scholae, ad gubernatorem et scholasticum... quia tamen similis est habitudo, ideo respectus ad actum regiminis est eis communis"* – Albert, *I Sent.*, d. 23, a. 5, sol., ed. Borgnet, vol. 25, p. 595-596.

mon in a universal, abstract manner[846]. Universality and particularity
pertains only with regard to natures for which a distinction between
the *quo est* and the *quod est* obtains; for the universal is taken (abstracted) from that which is the *principium quo* (the quidditative principle) of a thing, the constitutive character or essence according to
which several individuals are one, while the particular designates that
which is constituted by what belongs to the *quod est* over and above the
commonly shared essence. But, since there is no difference in God
between *quo est* and *quod est*, there can be no universal or particular in
the strict sense. There is no principle *by which* a divine person is divine and which is itself distinct from that person, as though the person were composed of some extensionally broader nature and a particularizing element[847]. Universality means to be intentionally recognized in many yet distinct from them all according to being (as humanity is predicated of all men, but equivalent to no man). In God,
however, what is common to three persons is identical to each, whose
natural being is identical:

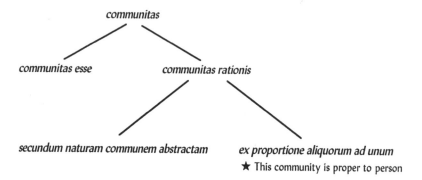

These divisions recapitulate those of the previous diagram, leaving
aside the notion of accidental community, and beginning with community of predication *ut ens de ratione trium*. *Communitas rationis* sur-
rogates here for all pertinent non-convertible predicables in creatures
and all non-substantial predicates in God, while *communitas esse* fills in

<hr>

846   *"Omne particulare sub aliquo communi accipitur, quod plura potentia vel actu habet appel-
lata. Et hoc nullo modo in divinis est; sequeretur enim, quod in divinis esse universale et particulare et compositio ex naturis diversis, quod nullo modo esse potest"* – Albert, *Sum. theol.,*
I, tr. 9, q. 40, c. 2, a. 2, ad 9 & ad quaest. 4, ed. Colon., vol. 34, p. 313.
847   *"Quod universale et particulare non sunt, nisi in quibus differunt 'quo est' et 'quod est';
universale enim est ex parte eius quod 'quo est', particulare autem ex parte eius quod 'quod*

for divine substantial predicates, since this kind of community is proper to God alone, where the divine essence is always and everywhere concomitant with any one of the three persons[848]. The final right hand branch here responds to the anticipated solution yet unspelled out in the previous schematization. It remains now to justify this assignment, in a less *a priori* fashion, by comparatively examining the kinds of community found in both created persons and divine persons.

Beginning with created persons, Albert remarks that Socrates and Plato have community in *humanity*, that is, "man" is common to both of them, on account of the universal rational nature. This is a community of universality, expressed when predicating a common universal nature: "Socrates and Plato are both human beings"[849]. The community which they share, however, insofar as they are said to be "individual men", that is, concrete subjects, is a community of the notion of *supposit*[850]. This latter community, we are told, consists of a common relation to the universal nature: *"haec communitas suppositi nihil aliud est quam similis habitudo eorum ad naturam quae communis est eis"*[851]. Several men are one in nature according to a unity of reason, according to their like possession of the common nature whereby each is called a man. From this community derives another, namely community in supposital act, for each man is a supposit of the human nature. This latter unity is a community of proportion inasmuch as each human supposit is, as a supposit, similarly (but not identically) related to

---

est'... *in deo nihil potest praedicari per modum universalis et particularis"* – Albert, *Sum. theol.*, I, tr. 11, q. 47, c. 3, ad quaest. 4, ed. Colon., vol. 34, p. 369.

[848] One should keep in mind that it is a question here of convertibility with *individuals*, and not of the convertibility one might discover between an ultimate specific difference signified concretely and the *species* which it determines, like that between "the risible" and "man".

[849] Individual creatures are said to be "of the same nature" inasmuch as they share the common nature which is predicable of all of them. That community of nature, however, does not unify the individual natures as such; it is a community *ratione naturae communis*. In God, on the other hand, the individual persons are things of the same nature (*res naturae*) *in re*: *"in inferioribus in natura rationali res eiusdem naturae sunt communes ratione naturae communis, ita in divinis communes sunt re"* – Albert, *Sum. theol.*, I, tr. 10, q. 46, ad 4, ed. Colon., vol. 34, p. 362.

[850] *"Cum enim dicitur, Socrates est homo, Plato est homo, commune est Socrati et Platoni hoc ipsum quod dico homo, et hoc per rationem naturae universalis. Cum autem dico, isti sunt homines, supponuntur Socrates et Plato per nomen demonstrativum, et sic commune est eis, quod sint supposita hominis"* – Albert, *I Sent.*, d. 23, a. 5, sol., ed. Borgnet, vol. 25, p. 596.

[851] Albert, *I Sent.*, d. 23, a. 5, sol., ed. Borgnet, vol. 25, p. 596.

the common nature as something one [852]. Each is a concretization of
the one nature in diverse ways (through unique sets of properties and
in virtue of unique individualizing principles), all of which, however,
are similar and classifiable within a common genus[853]. Community in
manhood, on the other hand, is not a communion of proportion,
since they are not each human in different but similar ways; that is, no
variation in specific nature may be admitted; one man's humanity is
no different than another's. Thus Socrates and Plato have the same
habitude (second kind of commonality) with respect to the common
nature (first kind of commonality) – a habitude of being individuated
supposits of the universal nature (though they are individuated differently) [854].

Now, in the Trinity, we have already seen that person signifies the
substance as subject and supposit, consequently, the community
proper to person must correspond to the second kind of commonality
described above[855]. If the community of person in the Trinity were
one of something universal (like the universal abstract nature in
man), then a distinction between *quo est* and *quis est* would be introduced. Since this cannot be so, there remains the possibility of a
community of proportion with respect to the common nature. Person, then, is not something universal[856] like rationality in which one

---

[852] It is a community of sharing the same relation to the common nature, that is, a
community of proportion or *habitus* toward the common nature as that beneath
which they all stand. The community therefore consists in the sharing of a common relation, and not in the sharing of something which characterizes their being
in an absolute way: *"communitas quae est in ratione suppositi cum dicitur, Petrus est suppositum hominis, et Paulus est suppositum hominis, et sic de aliis, provenit ex proportione
singulorum ad communitatem speciei"* – Albert, *III Sent.*, d. 10, a. 1, quaest. 3, obj. 2, ed.
Borgnet, vol. 28, p. 187.

[853] *"Cum dicitur, Petrus est homo, Joannes est homo, et Thomas est homo, commune est eis quod
est homo, et una ratione est eis commune, ergo quilibet illorum similem alii habet respectum ad
naturam communem quae significatur in homine. Ex ista ergo similitudine respectus
causatur alia communitas proportionis ad unum, scilicet quod sicut unus supponitur
naturae communi, ita et alius, et ex isto accipiunt communitatem suppositi, ita quod unusquisque est suppositum hominis, ergo 'suppositum' dicitur stans sub natura communi"* –
Albert, *III Sent.*, d. 6, a. 2, ed. Borgnet, vol. 28, p. 127.

[854] Thus the object of the proportion is universal. It is the more general embodiment
of the diverse forms of its participation or realization, just as the art of directing is
the general embodiment of its particular forms teaching and governing. This kind
of universality is necessary for common predicability; even the common notion of
person in the Trinity has this logical sense of universality.

[855] *"Quia in divinis persona significat substantiam... ut suppositum, ideo tali communitate
communis est persona tribus"* – Albert, *I Sent.*, d. 23, a. 5, sol., ed. Borgnet, vol. 25,
p. 596.

[856] In the sense of abstract universal, since, in a certain sense, any commonly predicated reality, whether abstract or not, is universal inasmuch as commonly predica-

participates, but designates nothing other than a substance according to the proportion that substance has to something common. This proportionality to something common is what is common to all persons, and an individual instance of such proportionality is precisely what a person is. This instance of proportionality is identical with the subject of which it is predicated, but the term which denotes this instance of proportionality to something common is not convertible with the subject, because its mode of consideration "exceeds" (through broader extension) the subject of which it is predicated, and this, *secundum rationem proportionis*, which *ratio* indeterminately signifies *all* the ways in which such proportionality can be realized (and thus is not strictly identifiable with any single individual) [857].

But there is a fundamental difference between the ways in which the "second kind of community" is realized in the Trinity and in men. In inferior persons, the *ratio suppositi*, and the community of proportion obtained from it, is reducible to the community of universality. In fact, the second kind of community in men is accidental, since it is only due to the fact that the common nature is predicable of each man. And this nature exceeds the subject of which it is predicated – whence it is only on account of the human nature as such, and not on account of the being of individual men themselves, that they enjoy such a community of proportionality; their community is entirely on account of universality of nature. Being a person is based on fulfilling the definition of personhood, which necessitates the inclusion of a certain substantial nature [858]. If many individuals are persons, then they share in personhood precisely to the extent that they also share in the said substantial nature. If the sharing in that nature is reducible to the participation in a universal, a universal which, insofar as universal, exceeds the individual participant, then the community shared as persons is also reducible to and based upon the common

---

ble; but this is not what is meant by the community of universality, which is meant to be taken as that community deriving from the universality proper to abstracted notions.

[857] The *ratio* of proportionality is able to signify indeterminately every instance of actual proportionality in the same way that a genus is said to include, though indeterminately, all that which is contained in the diverse species. Cf. the explanatory comments to the following diagram.

[858] Even community of proportionality is based upon this: *"proportio fundatur realiter in proportionatis ad naturam et in natura"* – Albert, *I Sent.*, d. 23, a. 5, ad 1, ed. Borgnet, vol. 25, p. 596. In fact, all of the elements of personhood for man are not only founded on (or have a final relation to) his substance, but can be traced back to the substantial nature as to their *ratio* or source.

universal nature[859]. In God, however, the persons are not persons or
supposits in virtue of a universal nature which is predicated of them
and which exceeds each one of them taken by himself. There is no
quo est distinct from each of the individual persons upon which to base
their community. Their community, then, is reducible to themselves
alone, or to the substance/nature which they each are[860]. In God, the
ratio of personhood (all that which constitutes it[861]) is not distinct
from the subject of which it is predicated, whence it follows that the
community of personhood is not on account of universality. The several persons, however, are distinct from one another, because the
precise modes in which they realize the *ratio* of personhood (or, in
which they realize the *respectus to* the something one – i.e. the *ratio* of
personhood with all of its constituents) differ. They are commonly
persons, then, by *proportionately* sharing in (or having a *respectus* to) a
non-universal common nature[862]. "Proportionately", because the relation (or *habitudo*) each bears to the common nature is similar, insofar

---

[859] "*Sed differentia est in hoc quod ratio suppositi in inferioribus est universalis per accidens,
       quia accidit Socrati et Platoni esse supposita per hoc quod homo secundum eamdem naturam
       praedicatur de eis*" – Albert, *I Sent.*, d. 23, a. 5, sol., ed. Borgnet, vol. 25, p. 596.

[860] "*In divinis autem persona non est universale, quia re non est excedens subjectum de quo
       praedicatur, cum dicitur, Pater est persona: est enim idem in subjecto et praedicato, differens
       tamen secundum modum significandi*" – Albert, *I Sent.*, d. 23, a. 5, sol., ed. Borgnet, vol.
       25, p. 596.

[861] As the common object of the proportion, and not that which would constitute the
       Father as Father or the Son as Son, since these particular individualizing constitu-
       ents, though identical to the subject of their predication, are not proper to the
       common notion of personhood responsible for predicative community. The com-
       mon predicable notion itself, moreover, is also identifiable with each of the three
       persons inasmuch as each person is the reality signified by that *ratio*, since that real-
       ity is not abstract in God and anything in the divine person *is* the divine person.

[862] They are related to something one which is, logically speaking, universal, but that
       which unites them in reality is not a mere logical (accidental) unity, but the singu-
       lar identical nature which is itself the foundation of the logical union able to be
       considered from the linguistic point of view. The persons of the Trinity all share in
       personhood not because they are each particulars of a common universal nature,
       but because they are each one identical rational nature. Thus they are all persons
       by sharing, fully, in something really one. Men, to the contrary, share in person-
       hood precisely according as they share in "rational individuality" (i.e. that by which
       they are persons, namely by being individual substances of a rational nature), and
       since they share the rational nature only accidentally and as a universal of which
       they are each particularizations, their community in personhood is also accidental
       or that of the universal. Their proportionality is toward something universal. In
       the Trinity, again, the object of proportionality is something concrete and one in
       real being, as an actuality of its own right. We say "of its own right", because the
       "universal" essence man, for example, can be said to have real being when consid-
       ered as it exists in this or that individual man; but such a status is attributed to that
       common essence only insofar as identified *in re* with the individual nature (in which
       case it is only conventionally referred to as "the universal").

as a hypostatization of that nature, but dissimilar insofar as they are hypostatized according to unique modes. Thus the community in question is one of proportionality or habitude, a habitude possessed by each of the three persons with respect to all of the requirements of personhood, namely, *substantia*, perseity, *distinctio singularis*, etc.. The predicate "person", entails this habitude. And, with regard to any of the legitimate predicates we may commonly assign to the persons of the Trinity, that community is based upon a particular habitude which is *distinctive* of the predicate being joined. The community, then, of person, relation, distinction, incommunicability, etc., follows this rule. Father and Son, according to Albert, are said to be relative, supposits, incommunicable, hypostases, persons and even God on the basis of such community[863]. In every case, save the last, the commonality is one of a shared relation or respect to something one, as Father and Son are said to be relative because of their respect to the act of relation; *supposita*, because of their respect to the distinctive act of the *proprietates*; incommunicable, because of their respect to the negative consequence of the act of the distinctive properties; hypostases, because of their respect to the *ratio* of the supposit (which is ordered to the distinctive property as that *in which* the property exists or has its act[864]); persons, because of their respect to the same *ratio suppositi* insofar as ordered to something pertaining to dignity[865]; and, in a unique way, God, because of the respect their supposits bears toward the nature. The last case, commonly naming the Father and Son "God", does not represent a community of proportion, since they are not each God according to a similar respect had with regard to something one, that is, according to sharing *for different reasons* (i.e., in different ways) in the act of a given reality[866]. In the sixth and last affirmation, we are rather at another level of community. It is a question of predicating the essential nature of individuals. For human

---

[863] "*Cum dicitur, Pater et Filius relati sunt, et relativa, vel Pater et Filius sunt duo suposita, vel Pater et Filius sunt incommunicabiles, vel Pater et Filius sunt hypostases, vel Pater et Filius sunt personae, vel Pater et Filius sunt Deus, quia prima harum communitatum sumitur per unum respectum ad relationem actum, secunda per unum respectum ad proprietatis actum, tertia per unum respectum ad negationem consequentem ad actum proprietatis, quarta per unum respectum ad rationem suppositi ordinati ad proprietatem, quinta per unam rationem suppositi ordinati ad actum proprietatis pertinentis ad dignitatem; sexta autem per unum respectum suppositorum ad naturam*" – Albert, *I Sent.*, d. 23, a. 5, sol., ed. Borgnet, vol. 25, p. 596.

[864] A logical ordering, since the two are identical in reality.

[865] The aspect of dignity seems to be all that the term "person" adds to the other notions. Cf. infra, "THE DEFINITION OF MASTER LOMBARD AND THE NOTION OF DIGNITY", p. 362.

beings, this kind of commonality, as has been shown, is that of the universal[867] – Socrates and Plato are called "two men" with respect to a universally common nature. But in the Trinity, the Father and Son are called "God" with respect to a *really* common nature, which is not, indeed, a community of habitude, but *secundum esse*[868]. All the others types of community are instances of community of proportion, a community, however, which is not reducible to that of universality, since the objects of the proportions are not abstract, they are not related to the subject of the proportion (i.e., the participant in this community of proportionality) as the more simple to the less simple[869]. The emphasis on simplicity makes it very clear that Albert's idea of universality entails abstraction, since the abstracted universal will be simpler than and distinct from those things of which it is predicated precisely in virtue of its abstraction: *ad universale exigitur, quod abstrahat ab his de quibus praedicatur*[870]. In the Trinity, no such distinction is possible, consequently there can be no community of universality strictly speaking. The persons in the Trinity share in the common notion or *ratio* of personhood, but this *ratio* is not abstracted, since the divine persons are identical to that *ratio*, that is, to all that constitutes personhood (sharing the very constitutive foundation of their respective personhoods, which foundation is shared as something really identical in each and not universally common). It is true that, in any context, when we say that (A) and (B) share in personhood, we are affirming something at least logically universal (in the sense of predicable). But it is not necessary that, in itself, it be a community of abstraction, since, in the Trinity, the things which constitute/define personhood are not distinct from the persons. The universality of personhood there is due only to our reasoning, *in ratione nostra tantum*[871]. In men, on the other hand, those things defining/constituting personhood are related to the individual persons as

---

[866] As, for example, they share, according to distinct relative modes, in the act of relation.

[867] Again, in the sense of abstract universal, since any commonly predicated reality is in a certain respect universal, since it is predicable of many; but "community of universality" stands for that univocal community deriving from abstracted notions.

[868] Cf. Albert, *I Sent.*, d. 23, a. 5, ad 5, ed. Borgnet, vol. 25, p. 597.

[869] "*Nulla istarum facit commune re nisi una, scilicet sexta; omnes autem aliae sunt communitates proportionis sive habitudinis ad unum in communi rationis, quod commune non est abstractum, ut simplicius a minus simplici*" – Albert, *I Sent.*, d. 23, a. 5, sol., ed. Borgnet, vol. 25, p. 596.

[870] Albert, *I Sent.*, d. 23, a. 5, ad 3, ed. Borgnet, vol. 25, p. 597.

[871] Cf. Albert, *I Sent.*, d. 23, a. 5, ad 3, ed. Borgnet, vol. 25, p. 597.

the more simple to the less simple, because they are truly abstract[872] and not identical to the persons whom they constitute. Person *in itself*, however, is not common to many at all, since, from the point of view of what it is in itself, it is the distinguished and incommunicable. Only its notion, the collection of its *definiens*, to which each individual person bears a proportion, is common – *est commune tantum rationis secundum illam proportionem, non commune realiter*[873].

In man, we have affirmed, the proportionality in question is to something abstract; consequently, our community is one of universality. But we might also consider a human person from the point of view of *his* individual concrete "personhood", in which case the constituents of that personhood are particulars, since it is a question of the individual. If one were to speak of a proportionality here – between the individual person and the definitive elements constituting him thus – it would be a question of community of being and no longer of universality, since the individual is identical to his own individual nature. But this is really an instance of identity, and not community (except in a very stretched logical sense). But this is not a question of proportionate community. For the creature, outside of the community of universality, for essential (non-accidental) community, there is only the possibility of identity, based on the incommunicable individual. All community of proportionality is realized there only at the accidental level, like that existing between a governor and a teacher with regard to directing. For substantial considerations, either we share something at the universal level (which is actually quite far from a truly essential communion[874]), or it is "mine, all mine". Entirely to the contrary in the Trinity, where any and all sharing, whether in terms of a non-substantial common predicate, or in terms of a wholly essence-dependent attribute, expresses itself as an "Ours, all Ours"[875]. In the Trinity, in many cases (for example, with regard to

---

[872] That is, their *concepts* are abstract: the diverse natures in question are able to be considered abstractly.

[873] Cf. Albert, *I Sent.*, d. 23, a. 5, ad 1, ed. Borgnet, vol. 25, p. 596. *"Persona enim nullam unam naturam dicit quae conveniat tribus, et contrahatur in illis ad hanc et illam personam, et ideo in illis est communitas secundum rationem proportionis tantum"* – Albert, *I Sent.*, d. 23, a. 5, ad 5, ed. Borgnet, vol. 25, p. 597.

[874] *"In universali non sit secundum esse communitas"* – Albert, *I Sent.*, d. 23, a. 5, ad 5, ed. Borgnet, vol. 25, p. 597.

[875] *"Dicit enim Iohannes Damascenus, quod 'in creaturis commune consideratur ratione, hypostases autem re. In divinis autem e converso est, quod commune scilitet consideratur re, hypostases autem ratione'"* – Albert, *Sum. theol.*, I, tr. 9, q. 42, c. 2, obj. 6, ed. Colon., vol. 34, p. 325. It is the mystery of God's love that the Trinity's "Ours, all Ours" becomes an "ours, all ours" for all of mankind, in the person of Jesus Christ.

divine intelligence – a substantial predicate), the proportionality is to something identical and in a certain sense convertible with the person or subject of the proportionality *considered in its identity with the predicate* – whence a community of *esse*[876]. But since, in some cases (for example, with respect to the act of relation – a non-substantial predicate), the subject has that proportion in a particular, distinct way (as, for example, the Father realizes relativity in a way distinct from that of the Son), the predicate is not univocally said of the divine persons and there can be no convertibility between the subject (understood according to its identity with the predicate) and the (logically universal) object of the proportionality (or even the predicate signifying that proportionality). With regard to the community of person in the Trinity, it falls precisely into the latter scenario. The general idea of this inherently complicated discourse can be more clearly illustrated by the following summarical diagram:

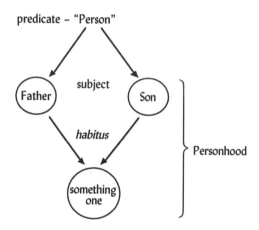

Person = a subject having this habitude. The subject = a person. They are identical in signification, but different in mode of signification. Person signifies personhood (the having of the *habitus*) and the subject of personhood. Person ≠ the habitude, but signifies the habitude possessed by the subject of which it (the name person) is predicated. Every person then is a distinct subject having the same habitus to

---

[876] And there is no real proportionality here, but only in the stretched sense similar to that between an individual man and the distinctive constitution of his individuality (community of being is opposed to *communitas rationis* in either of its forms).

something one. The something one is precisely the *definiens* of the universal concept of person, and the *habitus* in this case would be the possession of (or identity with) those defining realities. The distinction of the subjects can be expressed by what may be called subjectival modality – that is, something on the part of the subject of the predicate which constitutes him as distinct from other subjects of the same predicate, i.e., as distinct realizations of that predicate, or, in other terms, as distinct realizations of the *respectus* to that which defines the predicate. If we take a predicate such as "intelligent", for example, in the Trinity, there are no distinctive ways in which it is realized among the persons. Therefore, there is no multiplicity of subjectival modes upon which to base a community of proportion. The subjectival modality is constitutive of the subjects since it distinctively belongs to each one of them. Moreover, it is precisely that subjectival modality which limits the subject (logically) with respect to the "something one", the logical extension of which embraces (or belongs to) all the subjects having different modes of instantiating the possession of that something one – in that way the something one "exceeds" them (*secundum rationem tantum*). When there is not more than one modality, there can neither be a community of proportionality, because there is nothing to logically distinguish the "something one" (defining the predicate) from the subject – in which case the something one does *not* exceed the subjects, in which case the only possible *respectus* possessed by those subjects is one of substantial identity implying convertibility.

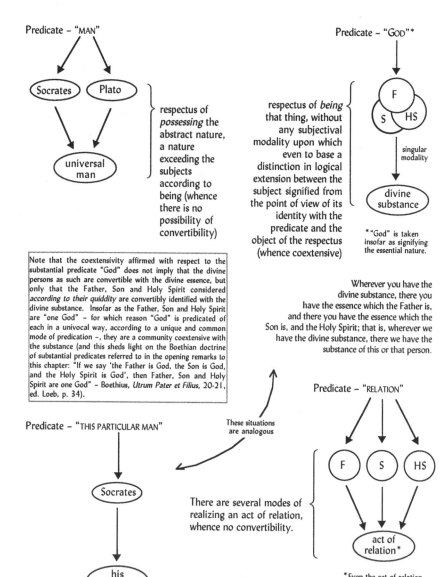

Predicate – "MAN"

Socrates   Plato

universal man

respectus of *possessing* the abstract nature, a nature exceeding the subjects according to being (whence there is no possibility of convertibility)

Predicate – "GOD"*

F
S   HS

singular modality

divine substance

respectus of *being* that thing, without any subjectival modality upon which even to base a distinction in logical extension between the subject signified from the point of view of its identity with the predicate and the object of the respectus (whence coextensive)

* "God" is taken insofar as signifying the essential nature.

Note that the coextensivity affirmed with respect to the substantial predicate "God" does not imply that the divine persons as such are convertible with the divine essence, but only that the Father, Son and Holy Spirit considered *according to their quiddity* are convertibly identified with the divine substance. Insofar as the Father, Son and Holy Spirit are "one God" – for which reason "God" is predicated of each in a univocal way, according to a unique and common mode of predication –, they are a community coextensive with the substance (and this sheds light on the Boethian doctrine of substantial predicates referred to in the opening remarks to this chapter: "If we say 'the Father is God, the Son is God, and the Holy Spirit is God', then Father, Son and Holy Spirit are one God" – Boethius, *Utrum Pater et Filius*, 20-21, ed. Loeb, p. 34).

Wherever you have the divine substance, there you have the essence which the Father is, and there you have the essence which the Son is, and the Holy Spirit; that is, wherever we have the divine substance, there we have the substance of this or that person.

Predicate – "THIS PARTICULAR MAN"

Socrates

his manhood

These situations are analogous

There are several modes of realizing an act of relation, whence no convertibility.

Predicate – "RELATION"

F   S   HS

act of relation*

* Even the act of relation is not something abstract, since, insofar as act, it is one with the concrete substance of the Trinity.

Not wherever you have the divine act of relation, there you have the relation which the Father is, or the relation which the Son is, or the Holy Spirit. Similarly with respect to the predicate "person": *not* wherever you have divine personality, there you also have this or that person. (Note that person, or what is properly contained in its notion, is not convertible with the subject of its predication, not because those contents necessarily refer to a univeral reality really distinguished from the things of which it is predicated (as happens in the case of creatures), but simply because its notion "exceeds" those things *secundum rationem tantum*, according, that is, to an analogically broader application).

In the divinity, all that which is common to the persons is rooted in the divine nature. Each person possesses that nature according to a certain mode, namely, a singular mode of existence determined by a *proprietas*. The community shared by the persons insofar as persons, that is, insofar as having the divine nature through a singular mode of existence, a modality common to each of them, is not a community like that pertaining to the nature. The community of nature is a community *simpliciter*, that caused by the modes according to which the nature is had is a community *secundum quid*, and this for several reasons. First of all, because the particular modality of possession of each person, i.e. the particular *proprietas* of each person, is unlike those of the other persons in species, the community deriving from their comparison to something one, which is the more universal notion of *proprietas* or singular mode of existence taken generically. Secondly, the community deriving from being *"appropriata"* is a community of being a supposit, and in the sense of being distinct, which community is founded upon not being in another and amounts therefore to a community *secundum negationem*. In a similar way, several men share in the common human nature, in virtue of which they are human supposits. Insofar as supposits, they are determinate singular individuals, and a certain community results from that, namely, that each man is this and not that; but this is no community in something really common, but a distributive (or commonly attributed) negation that one man is another. Finally, the singular modes of existence determining the persons are but modes of possessing and sharing that which they share *simpliciter*, and on this account they are modes of community and *secundum quid*[877].

---

[877] *"Ex una communitate, quae secundum rem est, multae causantur communitates tam secundum affirmationem quam secundum negationem, quae sunt modi communitatis et communitatis secundum quid et non simpliciter – sicut cum dico: Socrates et Plato sunt homo; ex hoc enim quod participatione hominis sunt homo, vere commune est eis homo, et ex hoc quod participant hominem, vere efficiuntur supposita hominis, et est eis commune hoc quod dico 'suppositum'; et quia suppositum non est suppositum, nisi quia determinatum est et singulare sive individuum, efficitur eis hoc commune, quod uterque determinatum individuum et singulare est, et quia uterque singulare est, efficitur eis commune hunc non esse illum, quod utrique convenit, et est commune secundum negationem – et omnes isti modi sunt modi communis primi, quod vere commune est: et ita est in divinis, quod nihil ibi vere commune est nisi natura divina, modi autem habendi naturam divinam sunt modi existentiae singularis proprietate determinati... Et si inferatur ex hoc, quod tale commune est commune simpliciter, patet, quod incidit fallacia secundum quid et simpliciter. Natura enim commune est simpliciter in divinis, communitas autem, quae causatur ex modis habendi naturam, est communitas secundum quid" –* Albert, *Sum. theol.*, I, tr. 9, q. 39, c. 2, a. 1, ad quaest. 4, ed. Colon., vol. 34, p. 301.

Conclusion

Noticing that Father, Son and Holy Spirit share in what it is to be a person, and recognizing that the only thing common to these three is the essence, one might be inclined to conclude that "person" therefore says the essence[878]. But there are a variety of things common to the divine persons, and the statement that the only thing common to them is the essence is mistaken. The essence is the only thing common to several persons (at the created or uncreated level alike) according to nature; but something can also be common to many individuals according to the act of the supposit, and not according to nature. Such communities, however, unlike the community based upon nature, will not be univocal. An example of community based upon nature is that of sharing in what it is to be a man: Peter, Paul and Barnabas are all men, and man, according to nature, is common to them all. Here there is unity of essence (even if that essence is abstracted and universal and implies therefore an accidental union between the three). But because Peter, Paul and Barnabas are, according to nature, men, it follows that they are all supposits of that single nature man (otherwise no one of them would be "a man"), and community of suppositness is seen to pertain to them as well. But they are all supposits on account of a particular relation of what substands to what is stood under (the relation being the act of substanding). Each of them has this relation, or does this substanding – with respect to the single nature being stood under –, in similar but not identical ways. Thus the nature of their respective "suppositnesses" is not one, and they are not univocally supposits. Community in suppositness is rather one of habitude or proportion, since each is a supposit according to his relation or proportion to something one – in this case, the stood under nature. Because they share in suppositness according to a common respect to something one which is really and univocally one and itself common according to nature or essence, the community based on this *respectus* is more than a merely analogical community; the term predicated of several individuals having such community (community which is linguistically reflected by the fact that the term is commonly predicated) is predicated according to an analogy of proportion, which is much nearer to univocity than the kind of analogy involved, for example, in the predication of "substance" of both God and man – for God and man are not both called substances because they (or their beings) have a similar relation to something

---

[878] Cf. *Sum. theol.*, I, tr. 10, q. 44, c. 1, obj. 5, ed. Colon., vol. 34, p. 344.

truly one and the same. This community of proportion is precisely the kind of community expressed by naming each the Father, Son and Holy Spirit persons. For personality is not realized in the Father just as it is in the Son or Holy Spirit, and nor is the personality of the Son realized in a way identical to that of the Holy Spirit. But, for all three, personality is realized in a similar fashion and with respect to the really and essentially common nature – as the personality of each, Albert tells us, consists in or is a consequence of a respect had by the hypostasis to a personal property and to the common nature. The fact that the *respectus* is to a personal property is responsible for personality according to its very *ratio*[879]; the fact that the *respectus* is to the really common nature is responsible for the proportionality of the unity in personhood[880].

The personal community of proportion is a species of community *secundum rationem,* distinguished from the intentional community of universality in a way analogous to the community expressed by the concrete predicate *"homo"* when said of several men, pointing only to the fact that they are each a supposit of the common nature, that is, that they share a particular (substanding) relation to the common nature. In like manner, person, taken in the plural, signifies that the individuals of whom it is predicated commonly possess the suppositional relation, that they have it in common to be supposits of the common nature[881]. But there is an important difference, for the common na-

---

[879] In fact, the *proprietates* – because they are not something one, but precisely that according to which the persons differ – are the reason for which personality is not realized in an identical fashion for each of the three persons.

[880] *"Nihil est eis commune per modum naturae nisi essentia... ex uno communi secundum naturam communicato secundum actum suppositis multae consequuntur communitates, quae licet non omnino sint communitates univoci, tamen imitantur univocum. Ex hoc enim, quod Socrates est homo et Plato homo et Petrus homo et commune est eis, quod homo est secundum naturam, sequitur, quod isti tres supposita sunt unius naturae, et commune eis est, quod quilibet suppositum est ex respectu substantis ad id cui substat, qui licet plurium sit ad unum, tamen similis et aequalis est in eis et per consequens unius rationis. Et similiter commune est eis, quod hi tres individua sunt et res naturae sunt. Et hoc vocatur commune habitudinis sive proportionis ad unum, et imitatur univocum, licet vere univocum non sit, quia vere univocum a natura una causatur, quae communis pluribus participatur a singulis. Et hoc modo in divinis commune est hoc quod persona est; quamvis enim non ab una et eadem personalitate pater sit persona, filius sit persona, spiritus sanctus sit persona, sicut ab una et eadem divinitate pater est deus, filius est deus, spiritus sanctus est deus, tamen a simili respectu hypostasis patris ad proprietatem personalem et ad naturam communem et hypostasis filii ad proprietatem suam et naturam communem et similiter hypostasis spiritus sancti causatur communis praedicatio personae de tribus, quae praedicatur de tribus non ut commune naturae, sed ut commune habitudinis sive proportionis ad unum, quod imitatur univocum in hoc quod in pluribus aequalem et coaequaevum ad unum et idem ponit respectum"* – Albert, *Sum. theol.,* I, tr. 10, q. 44, c. 1, ad 5, ed. Colon., vol. 34, p. 347.

[881] Cf. A. Pompei, op. cit., p. 245-246.

ture which is the object of the supposital reference denoted by *"homo"* is an abstract community (for which reason the supposital community of proportion is described as universal *per accidens*) and entails a real distinction between the common nature and its particular hypostatic instantiation. However, because of the supreme divine simplicity, every kind of universality is excluded from God. As a result, the relation of the divine supposit to the *significatum* of "person" is a relation not only of possession (according to the mode of signification proper to "supposit", "nature" and "property", and according to our mode of understanding which *considers* the latter two abstractly) but also of identity (according to the ontological reality, i.e. *in re*). The community of proportion of personality in God is therefore not one of universality, since everything signified by "person" is really identical to (and does not exceed really) the subject of which it is predicated (even if the concepts representing the *significati* to our intellects do so in an abstract mode, a property required by the necessity to establish a real distinction between the concepts themselves). In this way, both the real identity of the divine person with the common nature is preserved along with the special manner in which "person" signifies substance, namely as a unique mode of existence of the substance (where substance as such is only *indirectly* named). "Person", Thomas explains[882], does not signify the individual existent on the part of the nature, but the subsistent reality in that nature, whence the community of personhood lies in commonly having a mode of subsisting in the nature, that is, a divine, human or angelic mode of subsisting. In short, the community expressed by the common predication of "person" is based on a common relation: "person" designates a subject according to a certain relation to nature; and a person is precisely an individual instance of that relation. The proportionality founding the community persons share insofar as persons consists in bearing the hypostatic relation to common nature. "Person" thus signifies the possession of the supposital relation (through the act of an incommunicable property) and the unique mode of subsistence that this implies on the part of the subject of which it is predicated.

---

[882] Aquinas, *Sum. theol.*, I, 30, 4, sol. & ad 3.

II.4. DEFINITIONS OF PERSON

Introduction

Boethius was the first to shed a definitive light on personhood, giving us in systematic form the classical definition of person. The task of later theologians was to adapt that definition, by means of analogy, to the mysteries of the Trinity and Incarnation. That effort, however, was not without misunderstandings which appeared to threaten the very validity of the Boethian doctrine. Besides the precarious thought of Gilbert of Poitiers, the opinion of Richard of Saint-Victor also betrays a certain misconception of Boethius forasmuch as Richard considered his (admittedly original and valid) definition of person to be the only possible definition of person in the divinity[883]. Both definitions express the truth about persons, and theologians after Richard continue to uphold both of them in the theological struggle to reconcile the substantiality of person with the fact that a plurality of persons in God does not entail substantial numeration. In fact, as A. Pompei remarks, the principal difficulty faced by theologians attempting to apply the concept of personhood to the Trinity consisted not so much in having to choose between two competing theories as in simultaneously affirming a substantial signification for person along with its plurality without substantial division[884]. It is in respect of the absolute value proper to personhood that the Boethian definition is ultimately favored for its ability to explicitate the substantial and supposital character of all persons, divine or otherwise.

Treatise in the Sentences: exposition and confirmation of Boethius

A fourfold historical patrimony

We come now to the capital question: *"Quid sit persona secundum diffinitionem? Et, Utrum univocetur in divinis personis et creatis?"*[885]. Albert initially responds by listing the traditionally proposed definitions for personhood.

---

[883] Cf. A. Pompei, op, cit., p. 236-237.
[884] Cf. A. Pompei, op, cit., p. 237.
[885] Albert, *I Sent.*, d. 25, a. 1, ed. Borgnet, vol. 25, p. 624.

These are, first of all, that of BOETHIUS:

    A.   *"Persona est rationalis naturae individua substantia"*[886];

followed by those of RICHARD OF ST. VICTOR:

    B.   *"Personam dicimus aliquem solum a caeteris omnibus singulari proprietate discretum"*[887];

    C.   *"Persona divina est divinae naturae incommunicabilis existentia"*[888];

    D.   *"Persona est existens per se solum juxta singularem rationalis naturae existentiae modum"*[889];

and concluding with a proposition of MASTER LOMBARD:

    E.   *"Persona est hypostasis distincta proprietate ad dignitatem pertinente"*[890].

Analogicity of the name

With respect to the univocity or equivocity of "person" as said of God and creatures, the first thing to keep in mind is that we are dealing with an analogously predicated notion[891], especially when it is a question of speaking about God with respect to whom we must purify our creaturely concepts, even if in God that notion is most perfectly realized[892]. *Nihil est [omnino] univocum Deo et creaturae*[893]: the divine mode of perseity exceeds that of created hypostases not only in degree but in kind; similarly with divine intellection; and the individuality proper to God is most one and distinct because of his perfect simplicity, excluding the forms of composition integral to a creature's individuality. Logically speaking, "person" is first predicated of the creature, from which its concept is derived, but transferable to God by means of the labor of analogy (though, *a parte rei*, "person" is affirmed principally and first of God because he realizes in an eminent way all of the

---

[886] Ibid.
[887] Ibid.
[888] Ibid.
[889] Ibid.
[890] Ibid.
[891] Cf. supra, note 842 in 'HOW 'PERSON' IS PREDICATED" (in the chapter on "SHARING IN THE COMMON NOTION OF PERSON").
[892] *"Si inspiciatur proprietas rei quae est persona, persona magis proprie est in divinis quam in creaturis"* – Albert, *I Sent.*, d. 25, a. 1, sol., ed. Borgnet, vol. 25, p. 626; cf. *I Sent.*, d. 25, a. 2, ad 1, ed. Borgnet, vol. 25, p. 628.
[893] Albert, *I Sent.*, d. 25, a. 2, obj. 2, ed. Borgnet, vol. 25, p. 628.

analogous perfections of personhood) [894]. Though "person" is predicated of the several families of persons (divine, angelic and human)
according to diverse *rationes*, according as the distinctive modes differ
among them [895], this does not derogate the terms of the definition
employed in defining personhood which, if analogously predicated,
are still not equivocal here at the level of a common concept verifiable
in both God and creatures [896]. A universal sense of person is to recognized; abstracting from the modes of distinction proper to God, men
or angels, the personal distinction is satisfactorily applied to all classes
of persons including God and those inferior to God [897]. They are all
persons insofar as they exist *per se* according to intellectual nature;
whether a distinction of persons leaves the numerical unity of essence
intact (as in God) or not (as with creatures) has no effect upon the
concept of person itself. That concept, however, must be precise, and
Albert remarks that the proposed definition of Boethius must be adjusted if it is to universally stand for all persons [898]. The concept of
"person" must be purged of any delimitation to this or that mode of
realizing personality, whence the creaturely connotations in the
Boethian formulation must be eliminated and the distillate sense as-
similated to the Victorine formulation. An alteration in the acceptation of terms results in the effective superimposability of Richard of
Saint Victor's definition for person in the Trinity and Boethius' own
definition:

$$substantia \Leftrightarrow existentia$$
$$individualis \Leftrightarrow distinctum \; proprietate$$
$$naturae \; rationalis \Leftrightarrow naturae \; intellectualis$$

---

[894] *"Dico sine praejudicio, quod convenit per prius et posterius; et res quidem per prius est in Deo
quam in inferioribus, secundum usum autem nominis per prius est in inferioribus"*– Albert,
I Sent., d. 25, a. 2, sol., ed. Borgnet, vol. 25, p. 629.

[895] *"Dicit Richardus, quod in Deo distinguuntur personae proprietate originis tantum, in Angelis
autem proprietatibus naturalibus, non originis, in hominibus autem utroque modo"* – Albert, *I Sent.*, d. 25, a. 2, obj. 1, ed. Borgnet, vol. 25, p. 628. Cf. supra, "DIFFERENT KINDS
OF MODES OF DISTINCTION", p. 299.

[896] *"Nihil est omnino univocum, nec etiam est simpliciter aequivocum id quod invenitur in creatura et in Creatore"*– Albert, *I Sent.*, d. 25, a. 2, ad 2, ed. Borgnet, vol. 25, p. 629.

[897] *"Persona in quantum abstrahit ab hoc et illo modo, ad distinctionem personae divinae sub
natura eadem remanente, refertur distinctio personalis in inferioribus"* – Albert, *I Sent.*,
d. 25, a. 2, ad 1, ed. Borgnet, vol. 25, p. 629.

[898] *"Secundum illam diffinitionem Boetii non competit divinis, nisi exponatur sic, ut substantia
sit existentia, ut dicit Richardus... et individuum dicat distinctum proprietate, et natura rationalis pro intellectuali divina ponatur"*– Albert, *I Sent.*, d. 25, a. 1, sol., ed. Borgnet,
vol. 25, p. 626.

Right interpretation of Boethius

Richard of Saint-Victor never criticized the Boethian definition considered in its application to human persons. In that regard, the im-
peccability of Boethius' definition is unanimously avowed. What the
Victorine objected to was the use of that definition in the theological
explanation of the mystery of the Trinity, particularly in light of the
apparent contradiction occasioned by the fact that the Trinity, which
is not a person, is an individual substance[899]. Not only is Richard concerned by the fact that the individual substance equatable with the
divine nature fails to constitute a person as such, but it seems he furthermore refuses the use of the term in defining person on the basis
of what he understands to be its very denotation. As evidenced by A.
Pompei[900], examination of the alternative suggested by Richard reveals
what it was about the Boethian "substance" that Richard could not
accept. By substituting the term *existentia* for *substantia*, one can de-
duce that the conception Richard wanted to avoid was that proper to
the notion of substance understood precisely as the *subject* of a nature
and a *substrate* for properties. Such a characterization of substance, we
might note, perfectly conforms to the formality assigned to it by
Boethius when distinguishing its signification from that of *subsistentia*
(a reason for which we argued it more fitting to employ the latter
term in the definition of person). Richard's rejection is wholly legitimate: the idea of a real relation between a subject and that of
which it is a subject, something entirely unacceptable in God. But is
this what is being affirmed by the theological use of the Boethian
definition? For Albert, the sense of the Boethian terms is quite different from what Richard rightly condemns. Without yet going into detail, the term *substantia* ought to be taken as signifying primary substance (*subsistentia*) according to its formally distinctive act which is to
be *per se*, and not materially, i.e. according as it is distributed among
various subsistences some of which are subject to accidents and other
kinds of composition (*substantiae*). The further needed concept of
distinction and incommunicability is introduced by the term *individualis*, whence the definition of person, correctly understood, signifies
"quod est distinctum per se in rationale natura", prescinding from the particular mode according to which such distinction is realized[901].

---

[899] Cf. supra, "AN ATTEMPT TO SITUATE PERSONHOOD BEYOND THE CATEGORY OF SUBSTANCE", p. 161 (especially p. 163-163).

[900] Cf. A. Pompei, op. cit., p. 214.

[901] Cf. Albert, *I Sent.*, d. 23, a. 1, sol., ed. Borgnet, vol. 25, p. 581; cf. A. Pompei, op. cit.,
p. 214.

Whether distinction is had from a really distinguishable component – *distinctum proprietate, quae in ipso est ut in subiecto* –, or from a property identical *in re* with the distinct existent, we still have an "individual substance" in the sense just described. [That Richard of Saint-Victor further rejected the use of the term *subsistentia*[902], which, strictly understood, is independent of the limitations of substance, must be ascribable either to: (a) an isolation of the concept of *subsistentia*, where the mere notion of a *per se* act of being is still insufficient for delivering the Trinity from personhood; (b) a confounded or loose acceptation of *subsistentia*, understood as standing for primary substance such as it is yet undistinguished from the proper (and accident related) signification of the term *substantia*; or (c) a failure to seize the full implication of the term "individual" modifying the supposition of the term *substantia*]. As a consequence, the Boethian definition of person is entirely applicable in an analogical way to every domain of persons, provided, of course, it has undergone the necessary conceptual refinement.

Boethius' definition and the principal constituent of personality

The fundamental referent of person is substance, and more precisely, substance as supposit, *substantia supposita*. Such a supposit is a person insofar as *rationalis naturae*, whereupon nature is taken as something common. In creatures, there is diversity between the thing itself or supposit and the nature of which it is a supposit, from which the supposit is understood to be "contracted". Consequently, "person" (or supposit) appears to add something to nature and is, therefore, composite. In God, of course, persons are simple, consequently the definition might seem misleading. But, as Albert explains, something can be simple and non-simple at once, inasmuch as it admit of certain logical priorities and posteriorities[903]. Person, at its most general level, is just such a reality: though the divine person is simple *in re*, its concept is not (in creatures. persons are non-simple, i.e. composed, both with respect to their reality and their concept). In God, therefore, as well as in creatures, the mode according to which we conceive the person presupposes something anterior which enters into its notion,

---

[902] Cf. A. Pompei, op. cit., p. 213 & note 11; M. Bergerson, "La structure du concept latin de personne", in *Études d'hist. litt. et doctr. du XIII' siècle*, II, Paris-Ottawa 1932, p. 130.

namely the intellectual nature of which the person is the supposit. The difference between the substanding subject and the logically antecedent nature is real in creatures, wherefore person is reduplicatively composite (*non simplex, ut non simplex*); in God, however, where there can be no real composition, it suffices to have such a diversity at the purely intelligible level: person is simple in itself, but has *logical* composition[904]. But what, it is time to ask, is the sense of the "components" entering into the definition of person?

Precisely why the term *natura* is employed (in *rationalis naturae*), instead of *essentia* or *substantia*, for example, is due, Albert explains, to the fact that person is a thing of nature: *"persona autem res naturae est"*[905]. *Esse res naturae* entails a twofold respect, namely, being the subject of the nature and being constituted by the nature in question, and it is this respect which is implied in the expression *rationalis naturae*[906]. As Albert clarifies in the *Summa theologica*, the "thing of nature" is distinguished and characterized by the special act which is the emanation of nature, through which "this" comes from "that"[907]. A hypostasis is a *res naturae*, through an act of nature made to be "this", i.e. this determinate thing, subsisting in itself and complete in natural perfection. In the production of one thing from another, "this" produces "that", as determinate terms of production. Since "this" and "that" signify beings which are self-standing and naturally perfect, they are designated by the term *"res naturae"*, the signification of which is precisely the stable and determinate being constituted through an operation of nature[908].

---

[903] *"Simplex autem ut non simplex, est quod re quidem simplex est, sed tamen secundum modum intelligendi habet aliquid prius, et tale est persona"* – Albert, *I Sent.*, d. 25, a. 1, ad quaest. 1, ad 1, ed. Borgnet, vol. 25, p. 626.

[904] *"In veritate omnino simplex, nullam potest habere diffinitionem; sed est simplex, ut simplex, et simplex, ut non simplex... Simplex autem ut non simplex, est quod re quidem simplex est, sed tamen secundum modum intelligendi habet aliquid prius; et tale est persona... quod natura rationalis est de intellectu personae, sicut ens de essentia ejus. ... persona nominat substantiam suppositam, et illa in creaturis diversitatem aliquam rei habet ad naturam cujus est, sive sub qua est. In divinis autem est diversitas secundum modum intelligendi, non secundum rem, et istam diversitatem importat obliquus qui transitivus est"* – Albert, *I Sent.*, d. 25, a. 1, ad quaest. 1, ad 1-2, ed. Borgnet, vol. 25, p. 626-627.

[905] Albert, *I Sent.*, d. 25, a. 1, ad quaest. 1, ad 3-4, ed. Borgnet, vol. 25, p. 627.

[906] Cf. Albert, *I Sent.*, d. 25, a. 1, ad quaest. 1, ad 5, ed. Borgnet, vol. 25, p. 627.

[907] *"Distinguuntur ut res naturae per actum, qui est naturae emanatio, quo hic est ab hoc, et per consequens distinguuntur proprietate"* – Albert, *Sum. theol.*, I, tr. 10, q. 43, c. 2, a. 2, obj. 8, ed. Colon., vol. 34, p. 341.

[908] Cf. Albert, *Sum. theol.*, I, tr. 10, q. 43, c. 2, a. 1, ad 1, ed. Colon., vol. 34, p. 338. St. Thomas, concerning the appropriateness of the term *"naturae"*, makes the further remark that *"naturae"* better than "essence" signifies the personal subject from the point of view of its determination, because of the mode according to which the first

The term *"substantia"*, as alluded to above, must be taken in a very particular way, namely, as *substantia supposita*[909]. Albert distinguishes this sense of substance from a consideration of the divisions of being revealing several ways of speaking about substance[910] and which can be represented as follows:

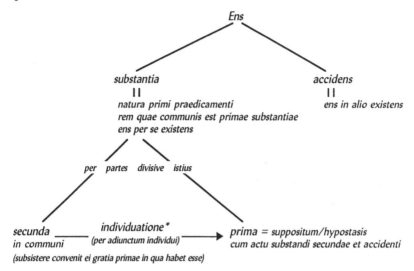

*So "substance", in the definition of person, indirectly indicates the common nature, while "individual" will serve to delimit substance to the hypostasis which is primary substance.

Here the role of "individual" seems quite banal, inasmuch as it merely determines the substance as concretized and particular with respect to

signifies the second; for "nature" is so named (from the point of view of the very origin of the extension of the term φύσις to the essence, whence it is called "nature") in virtue of the fact that it is constituted by something formal, active and specifying; cf. supra, in the Boethian exposition, "DEFINING 'PERSON'", note 295.

909 Cf. supra, "'PERSON'", p. 240 (especially p. 243-247).

910 "'Substantia' dicitur quatuor modis... substàntia divisa contra accidens, et secundum hoc nominat naturam primi praedicamenti, vel rem quae communis est primae substantiae... haec autem substantia nihil aliud est quam ens per se existens, gratia ejus quod est per se existere divisum contra accidens, quod est ens in alio existens... Secundo et tertio dicitur 'substantia' per partes divisive istius... primam dicimus ab actu substandi secundae et accidenti, secundam autem... subsistere convenit ei gratia primae in qua habet esse, et non gratia suiipsius... ly 'albus' refertur ad hominem gratia suppositi quod est substantia prima, et non gratia significati quod est secunda... substantia significet substantiam in communi, vel quod ponatur pro hypostasi... potest stare pro utroque, scilicet pro natura communi quae est ut secunda, et hypostasi quae est ut prima substantia, et per adjunctum individui stabit pro hypostasi" – Albert, *I Sent.*, d. 25, a. 1, ad quaest. 2, ed. Borgnet, vol. 25, p. 627.

the common nature. But "individual" also says something more. For, in the case of the Trinity, the common nature *is* concrete and *not* universal; consequently, the addition of the term individual intends primary substance insofar as the *subject* of the common nature (*cum actu substandi secundae*) and any particularizing qualities accompanying (or identified with) its mode of individuation. This subjective aspect is, moreover, the sense of the expression *res naturae* which Albert alludes to when defending the terms *rationalis naturae* in the definition of person. Whether or not "individual" really adds something to the notion of primary substance/supposit is doubtful from the point of view of the thing (*in re*), but it certainly entails more than merely a particularization or concretization of secondary substance[911]. "Individual" explicitates the subjectival quality of a supposit, and, for this reason, it designates the hypostatic reality proper to a supposit. For this reason, "individual" accomplishes more than a simple negation of community and truly contributes to the constitution of the person[912]. With respect to the substantive to which it is added, the adjective "individual" both restricts the substantive, contracting it or rendering it incommunicable (negative aspect), and implies some real thing about the substantive (positive aspect)[913]. What "individual" implies is already implicit in the notion of primary substance – in fact, it is a question of the act (*actus substandi*) of the supposit – but "individual" explicitates this reality (focusing upon the supposit *qua* supposit)[914]. The negation imported by the concept of incommunicability thus manifests itself as

---

[911] *"Si autem dicit aliquid positive, scilicet individuationem per aliquid distinguens, tunc ex additione se habet ad substantiam"* – Albert, *I Sent.*, d. 25, a. 1, quaest. 4, ed. Borgnet, vol. 25, p. 626.

[912] Cf. Albert, *I Sent.*, d. 25, a. 1, quaest. 4, ed. Borgnet, vol. 25, p. 626.

[913] *"Adjectivum duo facit circa substantivum cui adjungitur: restringit enim ipsum, et ponit rem suam circa ipsum"* – Albert, *I Sent.*, d. 25, a. 1, ad quaest. 3, ed. Borgnet, vol. 25, p. 627. The aspect of a positive quality inseparably bound to the attribute of "indivisibility" is furthermore able to be developed along logico-epistemological lines, precisely according as a certain unity and a unifying mental operation is required in order to conceive of "non-division" and, with particular metaphysical value, according as rational nature (distinctive of persons) can be understood as a sort of "unifying substance" in the sense that only such a nature, capable of consciously relating diverse elements, experiences and *instantiates*, through intellectuality in act (which is the totality of the nature, which *is* rational), the unity immanently expressed by the intention "indivisibility". Cf. C. Vigna, "Sostanza e relazione", in *L'Idea di persona*, V. Melchiorre (editor), Vita e Pensiero, Milan 1990, p. 176-179.

[914] *"Substantia significat essentiam, sed supponit personam; et hoc quod dico 'individua', additur ei ad explanationem suppositi, quod est in illo implicite"* – Albert, *I Sent.*, d. 25, a. 1, quaest. 3, ed. Borgnet, vol. 25, p. 625.

but a *consequence* of the positive quality of the hypostasis[915]; and it is this positiveness which founds and explains the analogicity of the concept of person (in opposition to the thesis that a univocal notion of person can be applied to both God and creatures on the basis of the belief that a negation constitutes the principal element in personality)[916]. But this is not all that the term "individual" explicitates. It also entails the *per se* distinction proper to supposits, that is, it adds to the unrestricted notion of common substance, not only the restriction of being incommunicably "suppositized" (along with the positive notion of "standing under"), but also the very aspect by which the supposit is recognized to be distinct[917]. No substance is brought to the state of an incommunicable supposit except through individuation and the distinctness which this effects. While the term *suppositum* or hypostasis certainly signifies the distinct subject, it does not include that distinction in its name, its formal concept, that is, does not explicitate that distinction, since its mode of signifying does not pertain to the distinction as such. This is why person cannot be defined simply as a *substance* of rational nature. Though *substantia* stands for hypostatized substance, only by virtue of the addition of the term "individual" is the distinction and incommunicability of that hypostasis expressed. "Individual", then, accomplishes a multiple task: it simultaneously implies or explicitates the following determinations:

1.   [in the case of men] the contraction of the common nature to primary substance/suppositum.

2.   [for all persons] the incommunicability implicit in the notion of supposit[918].

3.   [for all persons] the subjectival dimension of the suppositum which possesses the common nature.

915 *"Ad hoc quod ulterius quaeritur de ly 'individua', sine praejudicio dico, quod positive intelligitur; negatio enim consequens positionem relinquit positivum ante se"* – Albert, *I Sent.*, d. 25, a. 1, ad quaest. 4, ed. Borgnet, vol. 25, p. 628.

916 Cf. A. Pompei, op. cit., p. 243.

917 *"Substantia significat substantiam in communi, et adjectivum respicit ipsam secundum id cui convenit per se distinctio quae importatur per ly 'individua', et ideo ponit distinctionem in supposito, et ideo patet etiam quare non superfluit ly 'individua': non enim haberet substantia quo traheretur ad substandum pro supposito incommunicabili, nisi adderetur 'individua'"* – Albert, *I Sent.*, d. 25, a. 1, ad quaest. 3, ed. Borgnet, vol. 25, p. 627-628.

918 *"Incommunicabile importatum per ly 'individuum', quod cadit in ejus diffinitione, et illud ponit circa suppositum, et non circa significatum"* – Albert, *I Sent.*, d. 25, a. 3, ad quaest., ed. Borgnet, vol. 25, p. 632.

4.   [for all persons] the *per se* distinction proper to a supposit.

In sum, "individual" adds a real determinant with respect to *substantia secunda*, the individuating properties entering into composition with the nature to produce the *significatum* of "person". In other respects, it adds nothing *in re*, but explicitly indicates what is only implicitly contained in the other *definiens*, such as the distinctness pertaining to hypostasis (*substantia supposita*)[919]. This is nothing peculiar; it is rather the ordinary character of definitions that the more or less general terms of the definition signify the same reality, but according to different *rationes*, the more specific term determinately signifying what was only indeterminately contained in the more general term. Accordingly, substance cannot designate secondary substance, precisely because this is excluded by the term individual. In a certain sense it signifies secondary substance, namely, insofar as logically contained in the primary substance and identified with the same insofar as individualized. Thus secondary substance is "individualized", but what is individual is that which is individualized, i.e., the primary substance. The adjective "individual", strictly speaking, does not pertain to man *in significato* (that is, in the universal sense of man) but rather, in the words of Albert, to that which principally has accidents, that is, the *suppositum*[920]. In fact, adjectives always express their signification with respect to the *supposit* of the substantive and not with respect to its *significatum*, as can be illustrated by the utterance *"homo musicus"*, where the adjectival restriction is assigned to the human supposit, and not to the definiens of the substantive, as though the essence of man were musical[921]. This enables us to understand just how it is that one can affirm of the Trinity "three individual substances of a rational nature": precisely insofar as "substance" here stands for "hypostasis", the distinction denoted by "individual" referring to the *substantiae supposita*. The *supposita* alone, as the subjects of distinctive unity, provide

---

[919] *"Hypostasis sit suppositum distinctum, non tamen rationem distinctionis importat in nomine, et haec ratio distinctionis significatur, cum dicitur 'individua'"* – Albert, *I Sent.*, d. 25, a. 1, ad quaest. 3, ed. Borgnet, vol. 25, p. 628.

[920] *"Homo habet significatum et suppositum, et non oportet, quod adjectivum ponat implicationem circa utrumque, sed circa illud cujus primo est accidens, et hoc est suppositum, et per consequens non restringitur ly 'homo' in significato, sed potius in suppositis"* – Albert, *I Sent.*, d. 25, a. 1, ad quaest. 3, ed. Borgnet, vol. 25, p. 627.

[921] *"Secundum hoc essentia erit 'individua'; dicendum, quod non: quia adjectivum duo facit circa substantivum cui adjungitur; restringit enim ipsum, et ponit rem suam circa ipsum"* – Albert, *I Sent.*, d. 25, a. 1, ad quaest. 3, ed. Borgnet, vol. 25, p. 627; cf. A. Pompei, op. cit., p. 241.

room for plurality, and not the *substantiae significatum*, to which, in itself, such distinctive unity is not ascribed[922]. Hence personal distinction is wholly independent of what pertains to the essence; individual incommunicability pertains exclusively to the supposit in which alone distinction is placed, while the essence is left undetermined and fully communicable[923]. It is especially this dimension of the Boethian definition which clinches its universal value in resolving the difficulty of predicating personality in both God and creatures. Because the distinction it expresses is not attributed to *substantia essentia* but only to *substantia supposita*, that definition is wholly compatible with an affirmation of three persons in a single substance. As a result, both the distinctiveness of the person as well as the person's substantiality is safeguarded (along with the nobility of intellectual nature) without *imposing* distinction at the level of the essence (the latter kind of distinction perhaps following from the achievement of the former, perhaps not, depending precisely on the conditions of the realization of the first)[924].

The incommunicability imported by "individual"

Individuality, we noted, is responsible for the incommunicability implicit in the notion of supposit. The kind of incommunicability implied by suppositness pertains to the communicability of a common nature, and what "individual" implies in this regard is the "particular" of a nature which does not have predicable inferiors participating in it to which it communicates its nature. We also observed that individuality further implies the *per se* distinctness of a supposit. In this respect, individuality excludes another kind of communicability, namely that proper to things which do not possess an act of existing by themselves but which, because of their incompleteness, depend upon another to be. The first kind of incommunicability can be possessed without possessing the second – as, for example, with substantial parts, which are not present in many communicants, but which are incomplete and do not have an act of existing in themselves. Similarly, the second kind of incommunicability may be possessed without the first – as with the common human nature, which is not a partial principle or

[922] "*Quin hoc sensu possumus dicere tres substantias individuas rationalis naturae, quia substantia stat pro supposito, et hoc bene cadit in pluralitatem, eo quod distinctio (ut jam habitum est) non ponitur circa essentiam quae est substantiae significatum*" – Albert, *I Sent.*, d. 25, a. 1, ad quaest. 3, ed. Borgnet, vol. 25, p. 628.

[923] Cf. infra, "ESSENCE AND PROPRIETAS", p. 447.

incomplete, but which is nevertheless participated in many. What can
be deduced from this is a concept of "degrees of incommunicability"
or "degrees of individuality", according as a thing may be incommuni-
cable/individual in one sense but not necessarily in the other, or
both. A third kind of communicability must also be mentioned,
namely that of assumability. According to Albert, this too is excluded
by the term "individual", guaranteeing the incommunicability necessary for personhood[925]. The incommunicability required for personhood is global, and excludes three kinds of communicability: that of
the universal, that of substantial parts, and that of assumability (which
is proper to the human nature in Christ). Insofar as "individual" is
understood to exclude all three of these, its concept and the manner
in which it may be applied to the human nature in Christ shall play a
crucial role in explaining the mode of the hypostatic union[926]. A person, as we have seen, is rendered incommunicable through the *proprietas* by which it is a supposit, the singular subject of a communicable nature. That *proprietas*, to be precise, is the principle of individuation effecting the distinction between one thing of nature and another from which perfect incommunicability follows[927]. To designate
this effect of the constitutive principle of personality, we use the term
"individual". The term "*hypostasis*", or "*substantia subiecta*", implies
incommunicability in opposition to universal communicability, while
"*individua*" implies incommunicability in opposition to every other
kind of communicability. This gives an extremely important function
to the term "individual" in defining person. Individual, in effect, entails much more than the simple contraction of the universal nature
(secondary substance) to the concrete primary substance; indeed, the
term *substantia*, taken as hypostasis, already accomplishes that role.
Such an implication is not explicitly evident upon an initial examination of the concept individual, and St. Thomas will later defend the

---

[924]   Cf. A. Pompei, op. cit., p. 242.

[925]   "*In ratione personae sit triplex incommunicabilitas, scilicet universalis, partis, et assumptibi-
        lis, unde homo in communi non est persona, et anima quae est pars hominis non est persona,
        et natura humana in Christo non est persona; hypostasis non dicit incommunicabile nisi ad
        oppositionem ad naturam universalis, et aliae duae incommunicabilitates importantur per ly
        'individua'"* – Albert, *I Sent.*, d. 23, a. 6, ad 2, ed. Borgnet, vol. 25, p. 599.

[926]   Cf. infra, "CONSIDERATIONS ON THE SEPARATED SOUL AND THE HUMANITY OF CHRIST; THE CRITERION OF THE
        OMNINO INCOMMUNICABILIS", p. 365.

[927]   "*Incommunicabilitas autem a distinctione ultimo complente et perficiente*" – Albert, *III Sent.*,
        d. 5, a. 15, sol., ed. Borgnet, vol. 28, p. 115.

Boethian definition of person precisely in light of the extensive implication of the term *individualis*[928].

Contiguity with the other definitions

Coming back to our group of proposed definitions, Albert remarks,
that all of the Victorine definitions (which shall be discussed more
thoroughly in the *Summa theologica*) are focused upon that which individuates person. The first (B) designates the universally required discretion common to every class of persons, divine, angelic and human;
the second (C) clearly pertains only to the divine sphere; while the
third (D) is seen to correct the definition of Boethius, substituting
existentia for *substantia* – the notion of person explicitly invokes distinctiveness, and since this distinctiveness derives from the existential
mode of a thing or substance, person is better defined as an existent,
even if it necessarily is also a substance[929]. The emphasis upon the distinctive mode serves to highlight the central feature of personal constitution, namely, as was earlier observed, DISTINCTION. This distinctive
mode of existing does not, of itself, involve any form of division.
Whether or not the distinct entities which are persons are of a single
nature or diverse in nature, is completely extraneous to the *ratio* of
person. What counts is that they exist *per se*, according to whatever
distinctive mode[930]. This perseity was seen to be one of the implications of the term "individual" employed in the "primitive" Boethian
definition. It is precisely when *all* of that implicitly understood in the
use of the term "individual" is taken into account that the human nature of Christ, it can be affirmed, does not enjoy such individuality.
Obviously, the contractive role of individuation cannot be excluded
from that nature, which is certainly not a universal secondary substance, but the aspects of perseity and ontological subjectivity do not
seem readily applicable to it. The existential mode of that nature as
such, it seems, is not *wholly* distinct/"individual". The natural conclu-

---

[928] Cf. especially Thomas Aquinas, *Summa theologiae*, I, 29, 1; III, 2, 2; *De potentia*, q. 9,
a. 2; *Quodl.*, II, q. 2, a. 2.

[929] "*Diffinitiones Richardi omnes dantur per comparationem ad id quod individuat personam.
Et prima dicit hoc in communi secundum quod competit Deo, Angelo, et homini. Secunda
autem divinae tantum. Tertia videtur corrigere diffinitionem Boetii, quod melius dicatur existentia quam substantia. Quarta dicit subjectum personae, et proprietatem in communi*" –
Albert, *I Sent.*, d. 25, a. 1, ad quaest. 4, ed. Borgnet, vol. 25, p. 628.

[930] "*Quod distincti sunt unum natura vel diversi in natura, nihil facit hoc ad rationem personae, sed tantum existere solum per se secundum modum rationalis naturae, et ideo verius est
persona in divinis, ubi non dividitur ab alia, sed distinguitur, quam in inferioribus*" – Albert, *I Sent.*, d. 25, a. 2, ad 1, ed. Borgnet, vol. 25, p. 629.

sion to be drawn from this speculation is that *per se* existence performs the decisive role in determining personality (rationality always being assumed; but since the humanity of Christ is also rational, this natural mode – as opposed to entitative mode – cannot be the criterion we are looking for)[931].

Treatise in the Summa theologica: valuation of Richard of Saint-Victor

Reiteration of the several historically important definitions

Again when Albert explicitly sets out to systematically define person[932], he begins by stating what he considers to be the four principal historically proposed definitions – that of Boethius, two from Richard of Saint-Victor, and one by Peter Lombard (respectively ordered here):

1. Person is the individual substance of a rational nature: *"persona est rationalis naturae individua substantia"*[933].

2. Person is the incommunicable existence of an intellectual nature: *"persona est intellectualis naturae incommunicabilis existentia"*[934].

3. Person is the singular thing existing *per se* according to a rational mode of existence: *"persona est existens per se solum secundum quendam rationalis existentiae modum"*[935].

4. Person is the hypostasis determined through an incommunicable *proprietas* pertaining to dignity: *"persona est hypostasis distincta incommunicabili proprietate ad dignitatem pertinente"*[936].

---

[931]   Cf. infra, "COMPARATIVE EXAMINATION OF 'DIFFERENCES' FOR PERSON", p. 457.

[932]   *Sum. theol.*, I, tr. 10, q. 44, c. 2, ed. Colon., vol. 34, p. 348-351.

[933]   Albert, *Sum. theol.*, I, tr. 10, q. 44, c. 2, ed. Colon., vol. 34, p. 348. This articulation corresponds with Boethius, *Contra Eut.*, III, 4-5 (ed. Loeb, p. 84): *"naturae rationabilis individua substantia"*.

[934]   Albert, *Sum. theol.*, I, tr. 10, q. 44, c. 2, ed. Colon., vol. 34, p. 348. The definition comes from Richard of Saint-Victor, *De Trin.*, IV, c. 22 (ed. Ribaillier, 165c): *"persona divina sit divine nature incommunicabilis existentia"*.

[935]   Albert, *Sum. theol.*, I, tr. 10, q. 44, c. 2, ed. Colon., vol. 34, p. 348. The formulation corresponds with Richard of Saint-Victor, *De Trin.*, IV, c. 24 (ed. Ribaillier, 166a): *"persona sit existens per se solum juxta singularem quemdam rationalis existentie modum"*.

[936]   Albert, *Sum. theol.*, I, tr. 10, q. 44, c. 2, ed. Colon., vol. 34, p. 348. Cf. Peter Lombard, *I Sent.*, d. 25, c. 3, ed. Collegii S. Bonaventurae Ad Claras Aquas, Grottaferrata (Rome) 1971-1981, I, p. 195, v. 26ff. — where the Lombard, in the context of distinguishing the *rationes* of the name "person", directly expounds upon the *proprietas* as a *significatum* of "person" and points to the dignity associated with it via citation of St. Jerome. For Albert, the fourth definition essentially elucidates the *proprietas*: *"quarta vero datur secundum nominis proprietatem; dictum est enim in praehabitis,*

As is suggested by the collocation of four different definitions, each one articulating different proper characteristics of person, none of these designations taken by itself seems to fully and adequately define the being of a person. This is because the concept of the single reality we are trying to define possesses a variety of formally distinguishable predicates. As a result, the various definitional assignments are limited to the formal point of view from which they regard and attempt to describe the reality[937]. We must look at these definitions to see if one is preferable and attempt to evaluate different aspects of each in order to arrive at a synthetic position.

Contential equivalence between Boethius and Richard

Starting with the first definition, we notice that it appears to be restricted in extension to but human persons, since only human persons have a strictly rational nature. Such a definition, then, seems to fail to take into account other classes of persons. On the other hand, one cannot forget that Boethius' aim was to define "person" in the context of natural substances. He did not adapt its articulation to fit divine or angelic persons, but such a thing was not necessary for his treatise. We might add here that the terms "individual" and "substance", in addition to "rational", are equally unfit to be predicated of divine persons when taken in their strictest sense. But the terms of Boethius' definition are easily adaptable to the demands of the ontological expression required by the broader context of persons in general; taken analogously, they are perfectly suited to defining person universally. As concerns the term "rational", Albert affirms that it is able to stand for intellectual nature in general[938], though he admits that the use of "intellectual", introduced by Richard of Saint-Victor, represents an

---

quod persona est facies larvata, quod non fiebat nisi ad designationem certae personae et herilis, quae dignitate praecedebat" – Sum. theol., I, tr. 10, q. 44, c. 2, sol., ed. Colon., vol. 34, p. 349. The earlier considerations to which Albert refers in the above citation, however, are those of his reflection on Boethius' Contra Eut., c. 3, concerning the theatrical origin of the name "prosopon" (q. 43, c. 1, quaest. 2, ed. Colon., vol. 34, p. 332); there the notion of dignity clearly comes into view. In any case, whether compared with Peter Lombard or Boethius, Albert, it seems, develops the notion of dignity in a uniquely emphatic way (cf. infra, "THE DEFINITION OF MASTER LOMBARD AND THE NOTION OF DIGNITY", p. 361.

[937] "Unius rei, sicut unum est esse, sit una diffinitio, tamen secundum plura, quae secundum modum intelligendi sunt in uno et eodem, plures possunt dari assignationes, quae non sunt verae diffinitiones" – Albert, Sum. theol., I, tr. 10, q. 44, c. 2, sol., ed. Colon., vol. 34, p. 349.

[938] Cf. Albert, Sum. theol., II, tr. 4, q. 15, m. 1, ad 7, ed. Borgnet, vol. 32, p. 205: "omnis rationalis natura est intellectualis, et e converso".

improvement in expression[939]. "Rational", that is, should be taken in a sense befitting every spiritual nature, and not as it enters into the definition of man as a difference specifying the genus animal, where "rational" signifies the human *ratio inquirens et discursitans*[940]. "Substance", as we have repeatedly seen, does not have to be taken in an unacceptable way, but can signify rather according to an act able to be recognized in the Trinity as well[941] – nevertheless, a term explicitly articulating the act according to which "substance" is sayable does remain preferable. "Individual", finally, can be employed in a general (and analogous) sense to imply the singular existent – even though, strictly speaking, "individuated" things of nature do not exist in God[942]. Again, Richard of Saint-Victor seems to have overcome certain possible ambiguities residing in the Boethian terms: Richard, Albert maintains, corrects the Boethian terminology by rectifying it to the Trinity, where "intellectual" is better than "rational", "singular" than "individual", and *"existere"* than *"substare"*[943]. Though Albert seems persuaded here that the definitions of Richard of Saint-Victor be restrained to the Trinity, there is no reason for which they cannot be applied to every class of person. Before we turn to the Victorine's definitions, we would like to make an observation about the preposi-

---

[939] *"Ad id ergo quod obicitur contra primam diffinitionem, dicendum, quod ratio compositus intellectus est, et sic rationalis natura pro intellectuali ponitur. Tamen hoc est unum, propter quod corrigit eam Richardus"* – Albert, *Sum. theol.*, I, tr. 10, q. 44, c. 2, ad I.1, ed. Colon., vol. 34, p. 349. *"Omnis rationalis natura est intellectualis, et e converso"* – Albert, *Sum. theol.*, II, tr. 4, q. 15, m. 1, ad 7, ed. Borgnet, vol. 32, p. 205.

[940] Cf. Albert, *I Sent.*, d. 25, a. 1, ad 2; cf. A. Pompei, op. cit., p. 239.

[941] Albert repeats the habitual distinctions here: "substance" does not stand for the essence of nature, which is *quo est*, nor is it named according as substance stands in opposition to accidents; "substance" in the definition stands rather for the supposit or hypostasis, which receives the name "substance" from its act of standing under: *"'substantia' in diffinitione personae non dicit essentiam vel naturam... sed stat pro supposito, quod est hypostasis, quod ab actu substandi substantia dicitur. Et bene conceditur secundum Graecos, quod hoc modo plures personae plures sunt substantiae, sicut apud nos plures personae plura supposita et plures res naturae... substantia apud nos dubiam habet significationem et aliquando ponitur pro natura, qua substat alio non indigens omne quod substat per se, et sic opponitur accidenti, aliquando pro supposito sive prima substantia"* – Albert, *Sum. theol.*, I, tr. 10, q. 44, c. 2, ad 4, ed. Colon., vol. 34, p. 350.

[942] *"Ad aliud dicendum, quod pro certo in divinis non est individuum; individuum enim, ut dicit* PLATO, *est, in quo stat divisio descendentium a generalissimo. Sed individuum in divinis dicitur accommodata significatione idem quod incommunicabile, quod pluribus non convenit"* – Albert, *Sum. theol.*, I, tr. 10, q. 44, c. 2, ad 3, ed. Colon., vol. 34, p. 350. Cf. infra, "THE TERMS 'SINGULAR', 'INDIVIDUAL' AND 'PARTICULAR' IN GOD", p. 373.

[943] *"Illae vero quae sunt Richardi, corrigunt eam quae est Boethii, et determinant ad divina, et ideo dantur per propria divinorum, quorum magis est esse intellectuale quam rationale et singulare quam individuum et existere secundum habitudinem personae ad personam quam substare in seipsa"* – Albert, *Sum. theol.*, I, tr. 10, q. 44, c. 2, sol., ed. Colon., vol. 34, p. 349.

tional aspect of the Boethian definition contained in the expression "of a rational nature" (an observation which is equally valid with respect to the same prepositional character found in the Victorine definition where "rational" is simply replaced by "intellectual"). The reason for the expression is a question of the mode of signification proper to the *definiendum*. Person names the nature, not as the common nature or essence, but as the distinct thing of nature which we call supposit or hypostasis. Naming, thus, the supposit, the perfect thing of nature (*res naturae perfecta et rata*), "person" does say the nature – as that by which a thing of nature is –, but it does so only indirectly. In God these two kinds of "nature" (i.e. the supposital thing of nature and nature as *principium quo*) are diverse in mode of signification. In creatures they are diverse *in re*. Consequently, what may be said of the one cannot necessarily be said of the other[944]. Person, then, can be identified with the one but not the other. For this reason person is said to be "of a rational nature", instead of simply identified with "the rational nature".

Moreover, the expression "of a rational nature" corresponds with the fact that "person", as we have seen, is a concept pertaining to many individuals according to an analogy of proportion. When discussing that proportion, we remarked that the *respectus* in question consisted of a reference of hypostasis to the commonly shared nature (whether that natural community is essential, as in the Trinity, or based upon conceptual universality, as in men). The preposition "of" most appropriately reflects that proportionality, for not only does it indicate that the subject designated by "person" is precisely the supposit[945] (the preceding point), but it designates the object of the proportionality – which is the common nature – and the very kind of proportion as well (that of a similarity based on *possessing* a common nature and being a *particularization of* that nature). Nothing transitive is implied by the preposition "of", and there is no transitivity in the *respectus* it indicates. The expression "of an intellectual nature", then, most befits the Trinitarian persons who are "of one essence" (*unius essentiae*), and not "out of the same essence" (*ex eadem essentia*). The

---

[944] "*Convenientius dicitur persona 'rationalis naturae'... quam 'rationalis natura' vel essentia... Dicit enim HILARIUS, quod aliud est ignis et quod ignis est, et aliud homo et quod hominis est, et aliud deus et quod dei est, et generaliter aliud natura et quod naturae est. Et hoc quidem in creatis aliud est re, in divinis autem aliud modo significandi. Cum ergo persona res naturae sit et rem naturae dicat in recto, naturam autem dicat in obliquo et dicat eam, ut quo est res naturae, et ideo supposita persona non supponatur natura sive essentia*" – Albert, *Sum. theol.*, I, tr. 10, q. 44, c. 2, ad 2, ed. Colon., vol. 34, p. 349-350.

[945] Since the nature as such is only indirectly named.

transitivity expressed by *"ex"* implies diversity; the genitive construction, on the other hand, is said intransitively, noting nothing more than the habitude of the determined reality with respect to the indeterminate[946].

Finally, in relation to the rest of the definition, the centrality of the role of the term *"naturae rationalis"* pertains to definitional structure requiring the placing in relation of a quidditative term and a qualitative term. "Rational (or intellectual) nature" here has the function of specifying – after the manner of a specific difference – the substantial reality. But because a difference, by informing something generic, constitutes a thing in specific nature, and given that in God, because of his simplicity, there can be no such constitution in species or any generic thing able to be specified, "intellectual nature" is not a specific difference in him in the sense of something distinct from what is specified. In God, the intellectual nature is identical to the hypostasis or person, the *quo est* and *quod est* (or *quis est*) are identical. They differ, however, in mode of signification, such that the nature can *signify* as an informing or specifying reality. In this way, "intellectual nature" in God retains the role of specific difference with respect to the supposit it qualifies (and this, precisely according to its mode of signification – and not because of what it is in itself *ut rem*)[947]. Intelligence, then, is a specific difference for person, for the substance (supposit) which is intelligent (which is described as being *"of* a rational" or *"of* an intellectual nature" instead of simply referred to as "rational" or "intelligent", for the reason explained above).

Since intelligence is, in an analogical way, the specific difference for the substance signified by the various terms "hypostasis", "supposit", "person", it follows that what is signified (although according to a particular mode of signification) by these terms is constituted by that difference and therefore identical to that difference when signified as

---

[946] *"Dicit tamen Augustinus VII DE TRINITATE et ponitur in SENTENTIIS DIST. XXV PRIMI LIBRI, quod 'tres personas unius essentiae dicimus, non ex eadem essentia'... ablativus est vehementioris diversitatis quam genitivus... transitiva est et diversitatem notat... constructio genitivi cum recto aliquando intransitiva est et non notat nisi habitudinem determinati ad confusum, cum tamen idem sit re determinatum et confusum"* – Albert, Sum. theol., I, tr. 10, q. 44, c. 2, ad 2, ed. Colon., vol. 34, p. 350.

[947] *"Aut enim est, quae intellectualitate sicut differentia in specie naturae constituitur... tunc natura divina non erit intellectualis; nulla enim differentia in specie naturae constituitur... 'intellectualis natura' intelligitur... secundum quod 'natura' dicitur 'unamquamque rem informans specifica differentia', quam licet deus non habeat ut cum aliquo genere constituentem se in specie, eo quod est in fine simplicitatis, habet tamen ut idem ipsi et ut 'quo est' naturae intellectualis. Licet enim in deo idem sit 'quod est' et 'quo est' secundum rem, differunt tamen*

a whole, as by "the intelligent". For, "person", for example, is said to signify the substance according to its particular mode of signification, and since that substance, *in re*, is convertible with its constitutive difference signified as a whole, person, then, can be said to signify the intelligent, but, again, according to its own mode of signification. We said that the substantial *significatum* is convertible with its specific difference, *in re*, emphasizing the *in re*, because it is precisely at that level that person is manifestly convertible with the intelligent. At the level of the diverse aspects of the substantial *significatum*, with respect to which it may be signified differently, that convertibility is obscured – as is evidenced, for example, by comparing "the intelligent" with "substance insofar as substanding" or "substance as incommunicable". "The intelligent" is indeed that same substance, but "the intelligent" does not name that substance from the point of view of its act of substanding or incommunicability, consequently the mode of signification inherent in terms such as "person" and "hypostasis" or "supposit" is unarticulated by "the intelligent", and while "the intelligent" may well be convertible with "person", it cannot be its definition, since it does not express what is explicit in the notion of person on account of its way of signifying.

The first Victorine definition

Taking up the first definition proposed by Richard of Saint-Victor (no. 2 above), we notice that, besides the substitution of "intellectual" for "rational", the salient addition is the explicit mention of incommunicability. We earlier acknowledged the cardinal importance of this notion. Inasmuch as "incommunicability" is used to specify the kind of existence qualifying for personhood, one can regard it, alternately with the notion of intellectuality, as a difference. Upon first consideration of the proposed definition, we might solely consider "intellectual nature" as the specifying concept, and the "incommunicable existent" as referring as it were to the qualified genus. But, as the formulation of one of the objections to the definition shows, the quidditative and qualitative terms of the definition are able to be cast in reverse orientation, such that "intellectual nature" becomes the generic term, while "incommunicable" becomes the specific difference (incommunicability being understood as a property deriving from an incommunicable mode of existence, such that it is unneces-

modo intelligendi" – Albert, *Sum. theol.*, I, tr. 10, q. 44, c. 2, obj. 5 & ad 5, ed. Colon., vol. 34, p. 348 & 350.

sary to state the term "existence", existence being subsumed by the notion of incommunicability). The objection, which we are about to consider, fails in that it confounds the generic concepts. The quidditative term of the definition, when "intellectual nature" is taken as a difference, is the incommunicable existent. *Existentia* here operates substantively and generically. But, if we reverse the terms of the definition, the expression *"existentia incommunicabilis"* is no longer substantively but qualitatively signified. *Existentia* therefore cannot be the generic term; "intellectual nature" rather performs that role. The objection states that the term "incommunicable" is unfit to define "person" because of the fact that a specific difference, according to Aristotelian logic, must be convertible with the *definiendum*, and, since many things that are not persons are, in virtue of their individuality, incommunicable, "person" and "the incommunicable" cannot be convertible[948]. The objection holds from the strict definitional point of view of convertibility of a specific difference which is truly an ultimate difference. But "incommunicability" as presented by the objector(s) is treated as though it specify the wholesale genus of all individual existents. Yet "incommunicability" cannot be an ultimate difference in this sense, since "incommunicable", in order to specifically designate persons, requires being restricted in extension by the genus to which it is effectively referred – namely "intellectual nature" (if it were referred to the genus of "all existents", then, for personhood, it would be no specific difference at all)[949].

The important conclusion to be drawn from these observations is that seemingly diverse perspectives with respect to what is properly distinctive of person may be adopted. The person may be regarded either as the "incommunicable rational-thing", or as the "rational incommunicable-thing". The term we eventually substitute for "thing" will radically effect our definition of person. It seems, from all that has been said up to this point, that the most suitable candidate for interpolation may be the term "supposit". This would give us a choice between "incommunicable rational-supposit" and "rational incommunicable-supposit". But, since the supposit is necessarily incommu-

---

[948] *"'Incommunicabilis', non videtur convenire soli personae, cum tamen sit ultima differentia in diffinitione posita, de qua dicit Aristoteles in VII PRIMAE PHILOSOPHIAE, quod convertibilis esse debet; omnia enim individua et omnia propria incommunicabilia sunt"* – Albert, *Sum. theol.*, I, tr. 10, q. 44, c. 2, obj. 6, ed. Colon., vol. 34, p. 348.

[949] *"'Incommunicabile' determinatum per hoc quod dicitur rationalis vel intellectualis naturae, soli personae conveniens est et sic ponitur in diffinitione personae ut ultima differentia et convertibilis. Simpliciter autem acceptum maioris communitatis est quam persona"* – Albert, *Sum. theol.*, I, tr. 10, q. 44, c. 2, ad 6, ed. Colon., vol. 34, p. 350.

nicable (and incommunicability is admittedly entailed by individuality and distinctly possessed sets of accidents[950]), the term "incommunicable" is redundant if we employ the term "supposit". We are left with "rational supposit" (or "intellectual supposit"). In this case, the concept of supposit will have the task of explaining why the human soul in the state of separation and the humanity of Christ do not of themselves constitute persons. On the other hand, in light of the previously argued virtual convertibility between "person" and "the intelligent", a term standing for "the intelligent" such as *intellector* might equally meet the task. Since the term *"intellector"* would entirely replace the need for "rational" (or "intelligent"), the result would be "incommunicable *intellector*", where the concept of incommunicability will be responsible for explaining why the separated human soul and Christ's human nature as such are not persons. In both cases, however, – and here is the most interesting part, – it is the *supposital* element which guards the status of both the human nature in Christ and the separated soul (for incommunicability is seen to derive from the status of the substantial reality *qua* supposit). The final choice, then, to put things in more accessible and fully commensurable terms, amounts to a decision between "thinking supposit" and "supposital thinker", where the exclusion of rational entities such as Christ's human nature and the separated soul from personhood occurs at the generic level in the former case and at a specific level in the latter (the exclusion from personhood of all other non-persons occurs in precisely the inverse way). As a consequence, the more restrictive and specifying notion (between "thinker" and "supposit") seems to be put into question. However, it is our opinion that "thinker" is the more restrictive notion, even if it is unable to account for the special cases of Christ and the human soul. These are precisely *special* cases, and should not, therefore, dictate the ordering of the terms in the definition (assuming that the resultant order does not represent a better definition). Accordingly, "thinker" would more appropriately operate as the specific concept, and should therefore be signified qualitatively, rendering as a working definition of person "thinking supposit", or, to put things back into systematic terms, "intellectual supposit"[951].

---

[950] *"Omnia enim individua et omnia propria incommunicabilia sunt"* – Albert, *Sum. theol.*, I, tr. 10, q. 44, c. 2, obj. 6, ed. Colon., vol. 34, p. 348.

[951] We return to the problem of identifying the most formal and specific constituent of personality as regulated by Christological considerations in the last chapter (cf. infra, "COMPARATIVE EXAMINATION OF 'DIFFERENCES' FOR PERSON", p. 457).

The use of the term *"existentia"* to refer to the substantive reality qualified as "intellectual" tells us something about that reality pertinent to personhood (for *existentia* is another formally distinguishable predicate assignable to persons in virtue of the manifold dimensions of personality – that is, in virtue of the content of the concept of "person"). *Existentia* (taken, obviously, as the existent thing, and not as the act of existence), according to its proper conceptual content, denotes a being which is produced or proceeds from another[952]. As such, the concept, though clearly predicable of every other person[953], seems unable to describe the person of the Father (who simply has no origin and receives his being from no one). The difficulty is ironic, since the use of the notion of "existence" to define persons was motivated precisely by a desire to better define person in the context of the Trinity. The fact that *"existentia"*, properly speaking, denotes some kind of origin, presents absolutely no problem for the second and third persons of the Trinity – in fact, their respective modes of origin are precisely what constitute their personalities (and this was the insight inspiring Richard's definition). However, in order to adequate the definition to the Father, the sense of the prepositional *"ex"* will have to be nuanced. Richard will do this by identifying the denoted origin with the personal property: "existence signifies both that something is and that it has being through a certain property"[954]. *"Through a certain property"*, then, is expressed by the *"ex"* in *existentia.* The absence of the term *"proprietate"* in Richard's definition of person, the absence, that is, of an explicit mention of the *proprietas*, does not devaluate his definition (despite what we have said about the mode of signification proper to "person"). Rather, the notion of "origin" implied by *"existentia"* makes the indirect reference to the *proprietas* required by the concept of person. With Richard, Albert is in complete accord. Albert, however, retains the immediate and almost transitive

---

[952] The observation was already made and examined in the section on Richard of Saint-Victor (cf. supra, "HOW PERSONS CAN BE DISTINGUISHED WITHOUT ENTAILING A DISTINCTION OF NATURE", p. 168; "DEFINITION OF THE PERSON AS AN INCOMMUNICABLE EXISTENCE", p.171). *"Existentia enim secundum rationem suorum componentium dicit ens ex alio productum"* – Albert, *Sum. theol.*, I, tr. 10, q. 44, c. 2, obj. 7, ed. Colon., vol. 34, p. 348.

[953] This is our opinion, though Richard of Saint-Victor saw diversity of origin as pertinent almost exclusively with respect to the Trinity. For Richard, difference in origin has nothing to do with the existential realization of angels, for whom he posits a difference in quality only. As for men, Richard acknowledges a difference in both respects, however the substantiality of the qualitative differences, and the fact that difference according to nature already substantially distinguishes men from one another, makes difference of origin of relatively little importance.

sense of the *"ex"* in *existentia,* maintaining not only that the sense of "origin" applicable to the Father must be identified with the personal property, but explaining how it is that (the act of the conceptual foundation for) the personal property still satisfies the requirements of "origin". For Albert, not only must "origin" stand for "a personal property" (to specify the kind of origin), but the personal property even of the Father implies indeed a kind of origin (to retain the original intension of "origin"). How exactly is "origin" predicated of the Father? Insofar as the origination implied by *existentia* can be either active or passive, insofar, that is, as origination is predicable both of what originates (as source) and that which is originated (typically referred to as "having an origin"). Paternity, the personal property of the Father, therefore, implies an origin, in the sense of the active generation by which the Son is originated. This generative act, which founds the personal property of the Father, constitutes the origination proper to the Father; it is origination actively considered, according to which an origin is predicable of the Father[955]. Origin, in the case of created persons, is unproblematic. There existence is readily understood, and the fact that the principles of individuation in creatures directly pertain to their coming to be, and coming to be can occur only through the medium of individualizing aspects, means that individuality or singularity constitutes one's unique mode of existence. The particular modality according to which one "sists" (*sistere*) is nothing other than the distinctiveness proper to personality, and the particular modality of that "sistence" is had from the things pertaining to one's origin. The things pertaining to that origin make that origin unique, and thus the unique origin of a person accounts for his or her personality. Since every person is therefore established in personality on account of his or her origin, the concept of origin is included in the definition of "person", and this by means of the term *existentia.*

---

[954] *"Existentia igitur significat rei esse, et hoc ipsum ex aliqua proprietate"* – Richard of Saint-Victor, *De Trinitate,* IV, c. 19, ed. Ribaillier, 163b; PL 196, 942B.

[955] *"'Existentia' notat originem... sed communiter ad originem activam et passivam, hoc est originem originantem et originem originatam... In deo enim persona est incommunicabile existens incommunicabili proprietate originis determinatum. Et hoc modo Adam habuit originans et similiter angelus effective, quamvis originans illud non fuerit in conformitate naturae cum ipsis; originans enim esse in conformitate naturae cum originato non est de essentia personae secundum se, sed est de essentia huius vel illius personae"* – Albert, *Sum. theol.,* I, tr. 10, q. 44, c. 2, ad 7, ed. Colon., vol. 34, p. 350.

The second Victorine definition

The concept of existential mode alluded to (by *"existentia"*) in Richard's first definition is better expressed by his second definition. In the second definition (no. 3 above), Richard refers to the personal mode of existence in an open-ended fashion, allowing his definition to be fitted to any kind of person, whether distinctively constituted as such solely by means of relations of origin, or qualitatively, or both. If, Albert asserts, the definition seems vague with respect to a given class of persons (viz. human, angelic or divine), that is because it is intended to embrace all persons in an equal way – for which reason the definition is not to be considered vague in respect of the common notion of person[956]. Here the emphasis is placed on the notion of a singular mode of existence as such, and not upon a particular kind of modality (as was intended to be the case in the previous definition, focusing, in virtue of the mode of signification proper to the particular use made of *existentia,* upon those modes of existence pertaining to origin)[957]. The use of the term *"solum"* appears to represent no amelioration with respect to "incommunicable". In fact, Albert has to defend the use of the term by specifying the sense in which it may be said of the divine persons. What is singular, properly speaking, is distinct in being. Singularity is to be excluded in the Trinity if it contradicts sharing in natural being. If, on the other hand, singularity is intended to exclude that one person share in another person's "personal being", such a use is acceptable. In this way, the Father alone (who is never alone in natural being) is Father, and the Son alone (who is never alone in natural being) is Son. The Father's aloneness pertains only to what he is in himself precisely as person (≠ what he is *simpliciter*). This is the "personal being" which cannot be found in another; it is being as it pertains to hypostatic distinction as such[958]. One will notice that, in his second definition, Richard, who is preoccupied with defining person outside of the conceptual sphere bound

---

[956] *"Ponit 'quendam modum', quia in communi diffinit personam et non hanc vel illam... vagum sit quoad hanc vel illam, non tamen vagum est, quin commune determinet"* – Albert, *Sum. theol.,* I, tr. 10, q. 44, c. 2, ad 10, ed. Colon., vol. 34, p. 350-351.

[957] We say "intended" since a restriction of our consideration of the modes of existence exclusively to those pertaining to origin (as opposed to quality) never prevented us from taking angels as well as men into account.

[958] *"Solitarium et singulare, secundum quod excludit consortium in natura divina, in divinis non est... Secundum autem quod dicit exclusionem ab hoc esse personali, in divinis est; sic enim solus pater est pater et solus filius filius, et hoc modo ponitur in diffinitione personae secundum se"* – Albert, *Sum. theol.,* I, tr. 10, q. 44, c. 2, ad III.9, ed. Colon., vol. 34, p. 350. Cf. infra, "PERSONAL BEING", p. 393.

to physical terms, successfully avoids calling that which he is describing "a nature". In this way, he certainly avoids certain ambiguities of supposition with respect to the manner in which the nature may be named. But the very thing he is describing is necessarily "a nature" signified in some way or another, and the substantive *"existens"* certainly corresponds with one of the previously considered instances of "substance".

As pointed out by A. Pompei [959], Albert's professed predilection for Richard's definition of person pertains more to the logical value of the definitional terms as applied to God than to what is metaphysically implied about the nature of the reality defined. *Qua definition*, i.e. with respect to the logical structure and evocation of the terms employed, Richard's definition is preferable to that of Boethius when applied to God. With respect to the *definiendum*, however, which is the very thing being defined, the Boethian definition is not only analogically applicable, but even superior for the completeness of the analogical perfections it implies [960]. For this reason, Albert ultimately rescues the Boethian definition, rectifying its understanding in the light of the observations made by Richard of Saint-Victor, and purifying its concept through the *via analogiae* (whence: the Boethian *substantia*, which is the grammatical subject of distinction and the multiplication which follows from that, should be interpreted in the sense of Richard's *existentia*, open to a variety of, including non-substantial, modes of distinguished existence; while Boethius' *individuum* is to be understood in the sense of Richard's *discretum singulari proprietate*, where the distinctive property is not necessarily bound to the notion of material individuation; and *rationalis naturae* stands simply for intellective nature in general).

The definition of Master Lombard and the notion of dignity

The last definition to be considered, that of Peter Lombard (no. 4 above), Albert tells us, is given according to what is proper to the name "person" as such, inasmuch as *"persona"*, in its original etymo-

---

959 Cf. A. Pompei, op. cit., p. 237-238.
960 *"Si inspiciatur proprietas rei quae est persona, persona magis proprie est in divinis quam in creaturis. Si autem respiciatur usus nominis quod est persona, dico quod secundum illam diffinitionem Boetii non competit divinis, nisi exponatur sic... ut dicit Richardus"* – Albert, *I Sent.*, d. 25, a. 1, sol., ed. Borgnet, vol. 25, p. 626. The distinction operative here is the notable Scholastic distinction with respect to all definitions between the definition itself and the thing defined, introduced precisely in order to conciliate the two definitions of person currently being considered; cf. A. Pompei, op. cit., p. 237-238.

logical sense, referred to the mask received by certain individuals in the context of drama in order to signify their special dignity. Corresponding to this practice, men possessing special dignity in the societal context, such as the emperor and bishops, were also given the name "persons" [961]. The important fact is that dignity itself is proper to the notion of personhood, for if the word referring to that which is a sign of dignity is itself adopted to name the person, then it is done so on account of some dignity intrinsic to persons as such [962]. *Persona*, according to Albert, is a civil name given to men in virtue of the possession of dignitary functions, and its particular designation and mode of signifying therefore pertains to dignity. The term "person", however, adds nothing to the substantial concept of the rational individual, but simply explicitates the dignity belonging to such an individual. It is for this reason that, in view of the prelature distinctive of angels, they must necessarily receive the name person [963]. Saint Thomas himself teaches that the name "person" adds nothing to what is already signified by the term "hypostasis" beside the notion of dignity [964]. But the origin of that ascription, the reason for which we ex-

---

[961] "*Quarta vero datur secundum nominis proprietatem... persona est facies larvata, quod non fiebat nisi ad designationem certae personae et herilis, quae dignitate praecedebat... adhuc in civilibus personae dicuntur homines dignitate praecellentes, ut imperator, praeses, episcopus, praepositus et huiusmodi*" – Albert, *Sum. theol.*, I, tr. 10, q. 44, c. 2, sol., ed. Colon., vol. 34, p. 349.

[962] Cf. Albert, *I Sent.*, d. 23, a. 4.

[963] "*Hoc nomen, 'persona', nomen civile est, et individui homines insigniti praelaturis, 'personae' dicuntur, sicut praeses, tribunus, proconsul, et hujusmodi, sed tales praelaturae sunt in Angelis ad dignitatem pertinentes, quia unus purgat, et alius purgatur, et unus illuminat, et alter illuminatur, et unus perficit, et alter perficitur, ut dicit Dionysius in 'Coelesti hierarchia', igitur personatus sunt in Angelis*" – Albert, *Sum. theol.*, II, tr. 4, q. 15, m. 1, sed contra 2, ed. Borgnet, vol. 32, p. 204.

[964] Cf. Aquinas, *Sum. theol.*, I, 40, 3; I, 29, 2, ad 1-2; I, 30, 1, ad 1; *I Sent.*, d. 23, q. 1, a. 1, ad 4-5; *De Pot.*, q. 9, ad 8. This is not to say, however, that its mode of signifying does not imply something over and above or different from what is expressed by the particular mode of signification proper to "hypostasis". The affirmation here intends to express and explicitly focus on the qualitative side of personality, that is, the fact that a person is a mature/substance/hypostasis having that qualification pertaining to dignity, namely reason. Such importance given to the function (performed by "person") of adding the notion of dignity corresponds to the definitional structure treating rationality or intelligence as a specific difference. The "hypostasis" to which such a dignity is thus added stands for hypostasis according to its extension to all subsistent or individual things/primary substances, some of which are not persons precisely because they lack the perfection of rationality. From this point of view – identifying the proper character of personhood with rationality –, a certain fundamental differentiation may be recognized between individuality (which is proper to every hypostasis) and personality. It is along these lines that J. Maritain presents his reflections on personhood in *La personne humaine et la société*, DDB, Paris 1939. Nevertheless, a subalternate relation between them

plicitly recognized personal dignity, is rooted in the intellectuality of the nature. In the context of the civil ascription of the name "person", we are witnessing what amounts to a convertibility between "person" and "dignified thing". Precisely *what* a person is, however, is not revealed in this observation. Nonetheless, the inseparability between dignity and intelligence ought to transfer the juridical sense of "person" into the ontological sphere. In fact, the intellectual and spiritual nature is what is most dignified in all of creation, and the name person is absolutely restricted only to such individuals [965].

In his response to why the Holy Spirit should not be assigned the property of being "that from which no other thing proceeds" in a similar fashion as when we designate the Father "that proceeding from no other", Albert's argument not only emphasizes the centrality of the notion of dignity with respect to persons, but seems to make dignity a governing principle for the determination of what counts as an authentic *proprietas*, inasmuch as the *proprietates* (whether "personal properties" or "properties of the person" [966]) are that by which a person is known as such, and nothing, according to Albert, can make the person known if not pertaining to dignity. Every *proprietas personalis*, even every *proprietas personae*, must, therefore, in some way or another, imply dignity. Consequently, the property "that from which nothing else proceeds" can neither qualify as a *proprietas personalis* (by which a person is constituted as such) nor even a *proprietas personae* (by which a person is distinctively recognized), because it says nothing about dignity, even tends to suggest a certain non-dignity [967].

This immediate connection with dignity on the part of person, provides the reason according to which Albert defends Saint Bernard for having reduced the unity in Christ to a unity of dignity, inasmuch

---

must always be acknowledged, as every person is individual but not every individual is a person.

[965] *"Dignissima creaturarum est natura spiritualis et intellectualis"* – Albert, *Sum. theol.*, II, tr. 4, q. 16, m. 2, sol., ed. Borgnet, vol. 32, p. 207; *"Intellectualis enim natura semper digna est, et propter hoc hujus solius individuum est persona, et nullius alterius naturae individuum persona est"* – Albert, *Sum. theol.*, II, tr. 4, q. 15, m. 1, ad 6, ed. Borgnet, vol. 32, p. 205.

[966] Cf. infra, "PROPRIETAS PERSONALIS AND PROPRIETATES PERSONAE", p. 450.

[967] *"Persona enim nomen dignitatis est, et ideo nihil innotescit in esse personali, nisi quod innotescit per aliquid ad dignitatem pertinens. Aliquem autem 'non esse ab alio' dignitatis est, sed 'alium non esse ab ipso' non dignitatis est; et ideo innascibilitas notio et proprietas est, 'alium autem non esse ab ipso' nec notio nec proprietas esse potest"* – Albert, *Sum. theol.*, I, tr. 9, q. 39, c. 2, ad 7, ed. Colon., vol. 34, p. 297.

as the union of the humanity to God occurs by assumption into the person[968].

The last definition is also an occasion to better illustrate the relation between "hypostasis" and "person". Person is said to be the hypostasis which is determined through an incommunicable property pertaining to dignity. It appears that "hypostasis" receives, after the manner of a genus, the specifying addition of the incommunicable property, and that, therefore, we could abstract from the specific difference (the incommunicable property) and be left with "hypostasis". This, however, is not true. The incommunicable property cannot be abstracted from the hypostasis, for the hypostasis itself is precisely hypostasis in virtue of the distinguishing property, as that which is determined by the *proprietas*. To remove the distinguishing property would be to remove the very subsistence of the thing, but hypostasis is a determinate subsisting thing. Thus we cannot abstract from the *proprietas* and still be left with the hypostasis[969]. What we can abstract from is something else, the truly specific concept by which a hypostasis is a person, namely rationality. This is why the difference in the Lombard's definition is formulated as "an incommunicable property *pertaining to dignity*". The whole thing is the difference, and can thus be abstracted from only by removing the notion of dignity, which is to leave the qualification "rational" out of our concept of the hypostasis. In this way "person" is said to add something to the notion of "hypostasis".

Questions of rationality aside, we can consider the fact, which we earlier observed, that "person" signifies the supposit with reference to the incommunicable *proprietas*, while hypostasis seems to make no such reference. "Person" is said to signify the thing *ut determinata*, while "hypostasis" *ut determinabile*. This does not mean that hypostasis is undetermined. To the contrary, hypostasis is the same determinate thing as the person. However, the term "hypostasis" names the determinate thing – *secundum modum intelligendi* – according as it receives the determination from the *proprietas*. In reality, there is no composition; according to our understanding there is. This conceptual composition between the (determinate) supposit as *being determined* and the determining principle (*proprietas*) is what is implied by

---

[968] "*Et est dignativa unitas qua limus noster Dei Verbo in unam assumptus est personam...' Ex hoc patet, quod Bernardus unum istud reducit quod est Christus ad unitatem dignativam*" – Albert, *III Sent.*, d. 7, a. 4, ed. Borgnet, vol. 28, p. 152 (referrence to Saint Bernard: *De consideratione*, Lib. 5, c. 8.

[969] Cf. Albert, *Sum. theol.*, I, tr. 10, q. 44, c. 2, obj. 12, ed. Colon., vol. 34, p. 349.

the differing modes of signification ascribed to the terms "hypostasis" and "person"[970]. This is why we acknowledged the possibility of a certain "abstraction", so to speak, from the *proprietas* at the level of the mode of signification (and exclusively at that level)[971].

Considerations on the separated soul and the humanity of Christ; the criterion of the *omnino incommunicabilis*

A final consideration of the human soul and the human nature of Christ throws additional light on these definitions. The incommunicability explicitly expressed in the second and fourth definitions is sufficient to exclude the possibility of falsely concluding that the separated human soul and the humanity of Christ be able of themselves to constitute distinct persons. That incommunicability even sufficiently precludes designating those realities as distinct hypostases or individuals (since it is not rationality, but supposital incommunicability, which is in question).

But with respect to the first and third definitions, there are problems when it comes to the special cases of the separated human soul and the humanity of Christ. Predicating personality of the human soul in the state of separation does not seem to produce any contradiction – for the separated soul is an "individual substance of a rational nature", and it is a "*per se* singular existent having an intellectual mode of existence". Similarly, the human nature in Christ, according to the first definition seems to satisfy the requirements of personhood inasmuch as it is an "individual substance of a rational nature"[972]. The *perseity* of the third definition (*persona est existens per se solum*) does respond to the humanity of Christ, since that humanity subsists in and through the person of the Word. But the third definition seems to fail to adequately classify the separated soul. Though Albert says nothing here to repair the definition, the fact that *per se* existence and

---

[970] "*Diversitas in modo intelligendi, quae non causatur ex diversitate rei, sed ex impotentia intellectus nostri, qui rem, ut est, aliter designare non potest... ea quae ratione nominis addit supra hypostasim, non sunt diversa ab hypostasi re, sed modo significandi tantum; sine quibus perfectum esse personae designari non potest*" – Albert, *Sum. theol.*, I, tr. 10, q. 44, c. 2, ad 11, ed. Colon., vol. 34, p. 351.

[971] Cf. supra, "'PERSON'", p. 244-246.

[972] "*Secundum eas anima separata sit persona, est enim 'substantia individua rationalis naturae' et est 'existens per se solum secundum quendam intellectualis existentiae modum'... natura humana in Christo secundum hoc sit persona, est enim 'rationalis naturae individua substantia'... et sic Christus est duae personae, quod falsum est*" – Albert, *Sum. theol.*, I, tr. 10, q. 44, c. 2, obj. 13-14, ed. Colon., vol. 34, p. 349.

individuality are convertible notions for Albert[973] would, in light of his defense of the first definition (centered on individuality), solve the problem.

With regard to the first definition, Albert explains that "individuality" – just like the "incommunicability" of the second and fourth definition – perfectly delimits personhood in such a way as to exclude both the separated human soul as well as the human nature of Christ from personhood. "Individual", Albert affirms, excludes every mode of communication whether active or potential. Incommunicability is therefore intrinsic to the individual substance as such. What is communicable is, in some way, like a part, and is thus not an individual. Note that we say "not an individual", and not "not individual"; for a part can very well be individual, as an individual part, but it is not itself *an* individual to the extent that its being is that of a part. Consequently, individuality is both opposed to being a part and excludes every kind of communicability. Therefore, the separated soul cannot be a person, because it cannot be an individual – for the separated soul remains in some way *ut forma [vel pars]*. And the humanity of Christ, inasmuch as it is assumed into society or union with another – that is, insofar as communicated – cannot be a person (nor an individual in the full sense of the term)[974]. Thus we have something intelligent (such as the human soul) which is not a person because it lacks the incommunicability consequent upon strict individuality. The result is a reaffirmation that "the intelligent" cannot be considered as convertible with "person" – something we are alerted to only by the human mystery of the soul and the Incarnation. It seems from this that strict incommunicability is the more decisive factor in constituting personhood. However, since the substance in question must be intelligent, it follows that incommunicability alone cannot be a specific difference, since many incommunicable substances are not rational substances. If, however, we place the two notions of rationality

---

[973] *"Hoc autem quod est 'existens per se solum', Boethius elargato vocabulo vocat 'individuum'"* – Albert, *Sum. theol.*, I, tr. 10, q. 46, ad 5, ed. Colon., vol. 34, p. 363. *"Hoc autem facit personam quod facit eam esse per se unam; nihil autem facit eam per se unam nisi particulatio formae super hanc materiam [pro tanto principium individuationis]"* – Albert, *S. de Cr.*, I, tr. 5, q. 28, a. 1, sol., ed. Borgnet, vol. 34, p. 494.

[974] *"'Individua', quod ponitur in diffinitione Boethii, et 'incommunicabile', quod ponitur in diffinitione Richardi, omnem modum communicationis excludit secundum actum et potentiam, communicabile autem 'quiddam' est ut pars, et hoc nec individuum nec incommunicabile est. Et ideo anima separata persona non est, ⟨quia est⟩, 'quiddam' ut forma… ut assumptum in unionem vel societatem alterius; et ideo… natura humana in ipso persona non est, nihil enim horum in se individuum vel singulare et alii non communicans est"* – Albert, *Sum. theol.*, I, tr. 10, q. 44, c. 2, ad quaest. 5 & ad 13-14, ed. Colon., vol. 34, p. 351.

and individuality (or incommunicability) together, there can be no denial of their constituting the concept of personhood. Alternately, person is signified by "individual intellector" or "intelligent individual" (and since the incommunicable individual substance is nothing other than substance as supposit, we are simply restating the "thinking supposit", "suppositial thinker" schema from before).

Communicability and incommunicability between the human nature and the Word

Person has been defined as an incommunicable existent. Several kinds of communicability were seen to be excluded by that assignment. Nevertheless, the person of the Word is certainly in communion somehow with the human nature he assumes. Is this a communication of the person to something else? No, for the certain transitivity implied in the notion of communication entails a distribution of what is communicated to another subject or whole (though not necessarily distinct in being), but the human nature as such is not a subject, neither in itself nor certainly with respect to the person. The only subject capable of receiving (*secundum modum intelligendi*) the act of a communicated perfection is the hypostasis of the Word[975]. The per-

---

[975] The humanity signified in itself is somehow penetrated by the personal property of the Word inasmuch as caused to exist according to such a relative mode and seems in this sense to be a subject of that property. Nevertheless, the moment we say "subject of that property", we no longer signify the humanity in itself, but as hypostatized. This is parallel to the difficulty of seeing my humanity as the subject of my being (or of my principle of individuation), when the very thisness of my human nature is owed to that being (understood as a principle of individuation), which means that "my humanity" already includes its existential act: how can being be communicated to that which already includes being? This difficulty (that is, the need to exist in order to be this) is inversely parallel to the mystery of creation: how, one might ask, does a nature *receive* the act of existence? And this opens up the relevant problem of the instantiation of universals through the addition of something to the universal which – from the implication of the expression – seems must have sufficient reality to be able to receive. But should we not rather say that it is the universal which is received in this composite substance? – what else could it mean to "substand" a nature? But in this latter case at least, the concept of receiving (which implies some sort of change) is wrong; possession is more accurate. In the case of the humanity at hand, the difficulty consists in the fact that we cannot conceive of that humanity formally considered (*ut quo est*) as existing outside of the context of its being hypostatized. But the human nature in itself, *ut quo est*, if truly restrained to being considered in itself, is arguably an abstract entity; in this way at least, we can admit that it is no subject of reception in itself. On the other hand, just as much as filiation can be said to be "in" the Word or to "belong" to Him, so much may it be said to be in the human nature or to belong to it (when this latter is concretely signified, of course), and this is a minimal basis for recognizing the for-

son of the Word as a complete hypostasis is not communicated to the
humanity, but the converse; the humanity is communicated to that
person, and the person is said to be unitable and in communion
therefore *ex parte assumentis*[976]. The humanity is communicated to the
person, entering into its personal identity, precisely at the same time
as the personal property of the person is communicated to the human
nature (according to which the nature is integrated into the singularity and incommunicability of the person)[977]. By virtue of what the

mal communication of the personal property to (or in) the human nature by which
it is rendered concretely distinct.

[976] The humanity's being communicated to the Word is logical with respect to the
person, inasmuch as correlative of the proper essence-act of the humanity taken as
forma totius. Cf. Albert, *III Sent.*, d. 5, a. 3, sol., ed. Borgnet, vol. 28, p. 100.

[977] Note that what is received is a personal property, and a personal property is a principle of relative distinction and not the person *per se.* The personal property as
such is not the being of the person *ut appropriata,* but only *ut approprians* (since the
ut appropriata signifies the distinct thing as distinct, the *quis est* – where "personal
being" is identical to the person as such and incommunicable). "Personal being",
however, if used to designate that *whereby* the person is person – instead of that
which is the person *qua* person (which, by the way, is still distinct from that which is
the person *simpliciter,* its absolute being, whence it is possible to distinguish two
senses of "personal being") –, is personal being signified *ut quomodo.* This is nothing other than the being of the personal property as such. The personal property,
since it signifies *ut approprians,* denotes a *principle* of singularity (and, as a consequence, of incommunicability). But this is not as such the incommunicable thing
itself, and is rather capable of being communicated to the human nature. As that
through which or *according to which* a hypostasis is distinct, the personal property is at
once that modality according to which nature is received (or possessed) by a supposit and that modality according to which a nature is concretized, rendered a supposit. What is being communicated to that nature, therefore, is a *mode* according to
which it can exist (and only through which it does exist). This "modal" aspect of
the personal property is particularly evident in the Trinity where the principles of
distinction/"individuation", the personal properties, are precisely and strictly
modes of origin (*"modi existentiae", "modi obtinentiae"*). In men, no less, that according to which a nature exists is the principle of its concrete being, for which reason
that by which the nature is individual may be defined as a mode according to which
the nature is real. Filiation, which is communicated to the human nature, is that
which fundamentally characterizes the existence of the human nature; to be precise, it is that which "conditions" and specifically (though not generically) defines
the individuating factor for that nature and is therefore that according to which
(*quomodo*) the human nature exists. Of course, the modes of origin in the Trinity as
well as the principles of individuation in men have themselves been repeatedly
identified as incommunicable modes of existence, in the sense that they distinctively set one individual off from all others and cannot be found in another individual. The idea of the communication of filiation to Christ's human nature does
not violate this rule, since the human hypostasis (that is, the human nature which
is necessarily a hypostasis on account of that communication) is identical to that of
the Word whose personal property filiation is. The implication is that whatever a
personal property is communicated to is *idem in persona* with the one of whom it is
the personal property. Thus the personal property remains absolutely incommunicable to any other individual (*alius*). In sum, the complete subsistent thing, the

Word *qua* Word communicates to the humanity, that humanity becomes *idem in supposito* with the Word; by virtue of what the humanity *qua* humanity communicates to the Word, the Word becomes man. The kinds of communicability which must be excluded from the person are those resulting either in being present in a plurality of subjects or being united in such a way as to constitute a *tertium quid*[978]. Neither of these pertains to the personal union in Christ. The kind of incommunicability, on the other hand, which would preclude the assuming of another nature into one's own singularity, must be excluded from personhood[979]. But this is not so much a form of incommunicability as a form of non-receptivity (and appears to be excluded from all substances – *substantiae subiectae* – as such, which are the substrate of accidents and the principle of their being).

Thus it is not contrary to the notion of the person that something be united to it in its very personality. That something, as a consequence of the union, need not be designated as "something *else*", since it is identical (i.e. personally identical) to the person into whose singularity it was united. The term "individual" (in the definition *substantia individua rationalis naturae*), therefore, indicates a divisibility from others excluding that kind of communicability and union

person, is never communicable to another, because a nature cannot be communicated to another nature as such, but only to a subject, and a distinct principle of singularity, a personal property, cannot be communicated to another subject but only to a nature. Nature is communicable to any number of persons, provided there exists at least one principle of personal distinction, one personal property, for each person; the personal property is communicable to any number of natures, as long as those natures do not constitute so many subsistent wholes but convene in a singular subject. For the latter reason, a personal property is not *strictly speaking* communicable, since it is never communicated to another (*alius*) outside of or distinct from its possessor, whereas the communicability of nature extends to distinct individual subsistents, whose distinctiveness as complete individuals most perfectly accounts for the distributive aspect of communication.

[978] *"Communicabile enim dicitur per modum materiae communicatum ad alterum constituendum, sicut corpus communicabile est animae; et hoc communicabile ut pars communicabilis est. Secundo modo dicitur communicabile de pluribus quantum est de se, in quibus est vel potest esse, sicut natura communis. Et illi duo contrariantur personalitati sive singularitati"* – Albert, *III Sent.*, d. 5, a. 3, ad 6, ed. Borgnet, vol. 28, p. 101.

[979] *"Singularitas et incommunicabilitas sunt de intellectu personae, sed non omnis singularitas nec omnis incommunicabilitas, sed singularitas quae contrariatur ad in pluribus esse, et incommunicabilitas quae contrariatur unibilitati ad tertium constituendum... adhuc remansit una singularis persona non praedicabilis de pluribus in quibus esset, nec mutata in aliquod tertium, quin potius assumptum assumpsit in sui incommunicabilitatem et personalitatem aeternam, ut idem esset in persona Deus et homo, et non quaternitas in divinis in numero hypostasium constitueretur"* – Albert, *III Sent.*, d. 5, a. 3, ad 1, ed. Borgnet, vol. 28, p. 100.

proper to potential and active co-principles constituting a *tertium quid* through natural union[980].

Person, as we have seen, is incommunicable in three ways[981]: (a) insofar as not communicable after the manner of a part, as happens with the soul and body; (b) inasmuch as not communicable as a universal predicable of many; and (c) inasmuch as not communicable by reason of being united in the singularity of another[982]. The humanity of Christ, considered as an object of assumption, evidently will not possess the third kind of incommunicability – which is sufficient grounds for labeling it unqualifiedly communicable.

Three properties pertaining to distinction ascribed to personhood

The concept of person includes a triply nuanced distinctiveness: *per se* unity, *per se* singularity, and *per se* incommunicability. Albert describes the difference between these notions according to what he identifies as their causes (though, as we shall observe, they are only formally distinct, and a single cause is sufficient for all three). *Per se* unity is said to derive from the role which matter plays, for (quantified) matter is a principle of division; accordingly, numerical unity is produced as a consequence of material division from others. *Per se* singularity is said to derive from individualizing factors (which would not necessarily be a repetition of the notion of material individuation, since there exist other "particularizing aspects" for both immaterial and material supposits). Finally, *per se* incommunicability derives from what Albert refers to as an ultimate perfecting distinction[983]. Because of the material connotation proper to the concept of division, *per se* unity, as Al-

---

[980] *"Non intendit ut nihil illi in suam singularitatem et personalitatem uniatur... non contraria-tur personalitati, quod aliquid uniatur sibi in personalitatem suam... cum dicitur, individua substantia, ly 'individua' dicit ab aliis separationem quae est contraria unioni et communi-cabilitati potentiae ad actum, et e contra, quia talis communicabilitas est ad tertium constitu-endum, sed non contrariatur unioni alicujus in eamdem singularitatem personae"* – Albert, *III Sent.*, d. 5, a. 3, ad 2 & 3, ed. Borgnet, vol. 28, p. 100.

[981] Cf. supra, "THE INCOMMUNICABILITY IMPORTED BY 'INDIVIDUAL'", p. 347 (especially p. 348).

[982] *"Distinctum proprietate faciente ipsum incommunicabile tribus modis, scilicet quod non sit communicabile ut pars, sicut est anima et corpus, et quod non sit communicabile ut univer-sale, sicut quod praedicatur de multis, et quod non sit communicabile per unionem in singu-laritatem alterius"* – Albert, *III Sent.*, d. 6, a. 2, ed. Borgnet, vol. 28, p. 128.

[983] *"Persona de intellectu suo ponit per se unum, ponit etiam per se incommunicabilitatem ad alterum, quia non est alterius in potentia, nec alterius ut praedicatum... Similiter ponit de se singularitatem. Et ista sunt tria, scilicet unitas, singularitas, et incommunicabilitas. Et uni-tas est a materia, quia idem est unum numero et materia, ut dicit Philosophus. Singularitas autem est ab individuantibus. Incommunicabilitas autem a distinctione ultimo complente et perficiente"* – Albert, *III Sent.*, d. 5, a. 15, sol., ed. Borgnet, vol. 28, p. 115.

bert has described it, will depend upon matter as to its cause. Nonetheless, *per se* unity is an attribute of every subsistent entity, be it material or otherwise, and a materialistic sense of division is not indispensable from its concept (as is already demonstrated by the application
of its notion to all persons). As a consequence, singularity and unity,
or to be one, signify the same thing[984]. Note that *per se* unity does not
have to refer to natural unity, since personal number is also a kind of
unity; thus to recognize a real identity between unity and singularity
does not imply that the divine nature is not common, or that the persons of the Trinity are naturally numbered. Incommunicability designates nothing other than the immediate consequence of perfect
individuality or singularity, for what is *per se* singular is necessarily incommunicable, and *per se.*

Does *per se* unity always imply incommunicability? Is not the divine
nature one *per se* and yet communicable (even in its concreteness)?
Per se unity can refer either to natural or hypostatic unity. Natural
unity may be either that of the abstract nature, or a concrete nature.
If it is that of an abstract nature (possible to creatures alone), then no
hypostatic unity or incommunicability need follow. However, an abstract unity is not something one in reality except for its realization in
concrete instances. If, on the other hand, the natural unity is that of a
concrete nature, then, in the case of creatures, it implies a hypostatic
unity, since the concrete nature is the hypostasis, and cannot be signified as concrete except insofar as hypostatically considered, and
therefore also implies incommunicability. In the case of God, the *per
se* unity of the concrete nature does entail hypostatic unity in reason
of the concreteness in question; however, the hypostatic unity required by that concreteness is not the same as the unity of that concrete nature as such. That is, the nature signified *qua* nature is itself
concrete, whether it be considered according to its identity with the
hypostases or not. The unity of this nature, then, since it is not something abstract, is real and *per se,* though it is not incommunicable, but
rather communicated to several hypostases. In God, then, *per se* unity,
with respect to the nature, does not entail incommunicability. With
respect, however, to the persons, *per se* unity, i.e. personal number,
and incommunicability go hand in hand.

The divine nature, if we signify it as a concrete reality as, for example, in the name "God", is also incommunicable in the sense that it
cannot *belong* to another; but this is because its very concrete reality is

---

[984]   Cf. Aquinas, *III Sent.,* d. 6, q. 1, a. 1, quaest. 1, resp., ed. Moos, p. 224-225.

its triple hypostatization – the hypostases which the concrete nature is. Such an incommunicability thus pertains to the nature only as hypostatically signified, and the divine nature is not incommunicable *per se*, but *in hypostasi* (remaining, as a result, communicable *per se*). Moreover, an additional test for incommunicability lies in discerning that a thing not be *predicable* of many; but "God" is predicable of all three persons – according as it properly names the nature (even if hypostatically signified) –, and thus the reality it directly signifies, the nature, is never incommunicable.

These several properties of personhood, then, in all respects for creatures, and in respect of the hypostases in God, differ only in *modus intelligendi*, as to be one and to be singular or incommunicable are convertible attributes. This is why Albert affirms that the denial of a *per se* singularity of the body-soul conjunction in Christ (when the body and soul are simply considered in themselves) entails the denial, with respect to that natural composition, of the formation of something *per se* one in the concrete sense[985].

An insight into Albert's use of the term "singular" is available from a passage concerning the lack of both universality and singularity with respect to the divine nature. The nature is not singular precisely because it is communicated[986]. This may seem like an obvious conclusion, but we cannot forget that singularity, like individuality, is commonly understood as capable of being predicated of any genus – substances, accidents and partial entities alike, some of which singular things are communicated to the subsistence of another[987]. For Albert, then, the notion of singularity is a more loaded concept. In God there is indeed *per se* unity of nature (*unum per se*), but not singularity. *Unum* and singularity have just been distinguished, and on the basis of communicability. The singular is never communicable. The singular thing for Albert means the independently singular thing, i.e. the singular subsistent thing (thereby excluding accidents and substantial parts), and this *thing* is a supposit (whence the incommunicability and the exclusion of the divine nature). This is to adhere to a strong sense of singularity (corresponding to a strong sense of individuality), which is what Albert must have meant by the expression *singularis per se* (and *unum per se*, and *incommunicabilis per se*).

---

[985] *"Unde cum conjunctum illud ex corpore et anima non sit unum nec fuerit unum per se, nec distinctum per se, sed unitum alii in singularitatem alterius et distinctionem personalem"* – Albert, *III Sent.*, d. 5, a. 15, sol., ed. Borgnet, vol. 28, p. 115.

[986] *"Quod non sit singularis, patet, quia nullum singulare est communicabile pluribus"* – Albert, *III Sent.*, d. 6, a. 1, ad quaest. 2, ed. Borgnet, vol. 28, p. 123.

The terms "singular", "individual" and "particular" in God

In creatures, the nature itself is singularized in order to constitute this individual, this person. If the persons in the Trinity are recognized to be singular existents, this does not entail a "singularization" with respect to the nature. The divine nature is "one", and common, but not "singular". In God, what is "singularized" so to speak by the *proprietates* is the supposit itself, which, although identical with the nature, is that nature *qua* hypostasis, *qua suppositum*, and not *qua natura*. Paternity singularizes the Father, filiation the Son; neither *proprietas* is said to singularize the essence, though the singularized *res naturae* are necessarily *of* that essence. "Singularity", then, though applicable in a certain sense to the notion of person, cannot be said of the divine nature. The reason for this lies especially in the fact that singularity implies individuation (from which incommunicability follows). Individuation, in the strict sense of the term, occurs either as a contraction, by means of particular matter, of an abstractly considered nature, or, as Albert is wont to emphasize, through accidents belonging to but one. As a consequence of such singularization, plurality is excluded, since the accidents (including all the individualizing accidents deriving from individual matter in the case of composite substances[988]) render the subject incommunicable. The resultant incommunicable entity is the individual nature itself. This is not the case in God, where the nature is nowise "contracted" and where nothing is predicated accidentally. Unlike what happens in the creature, Trinitarian incommunicability does not derive from a property distinct from the nature and somehow added to it but from that which is identical to the nature and which is but an expression of it from the point of view of its singular mode of existence *in hypostasi*[989]. As a result, the unity of nature is not a "singularity", which would restrict the nature to this individual, but a unity open to plurality, as long as that plurality be achieved in a way other than strict individuation[990]. Thus,

---

[987] Cf. Aquinas, *III Sent.*, d. 6, q. 1, a. 1, quaest. 1, resp., n. 23, ed. Moos, p. 225.

[988] Cf. Aquinas, *Sum. theol.*, I, q. 3, a. 3, sol.

[989] Cf. Albert, *I Sent.*, d. 19, a. 14 & 17, ed. Borgnet, vol. 25, p. 535 & 541; d. 24, a. 1 & 3, ed. Borgnet, vol. 25, p. 606 & 612-613; *Sum. theol.*, I, tr. 10, q. 43, c. 2, a. 1, ed. Colon., vol. 34/1, p. 337-340; cf. M.-D. Roland-Gosselin, *Le "De ente et essentia" de Saint Thomas d'Aquin*, Vrin, Paris 1948, p. 102.

[990] "'*Singularitas' autem et singularis dicit individuationem per accidentia, quae uni soli conveniunt; et ideo ex consequenti dicit exclusionem plurium. Singularis enim est non plures, eo quod... 'singulare ab accidente incommunicabili efficitur'. Et quia in divinis nec individuatio est nec aliquid praedicatur ut accidens,... nec... unitas consortium plurium excludit et*

since the unity of singularity is had through individuation, and this
excludes a plurality of hypostases, the divine essence cannot have such
a unity; rather, a "uniting unity" is had, where the unity of essence
unifies several persons[991]. Again, the common nature cannot be said
to be singular, precisely inasmuch as it is communicable to several,
and what is singular – in the strong sense employed by Albert implying perseity and independent subsistence – is strictly incommunicable[992].

As was observed in the section on "COMMUNITY OF PROPORTION", the
universal-particular relation pertains only to those natures for which a
distinction may be maintained between *quo est* and *quod est*, for the
universal is taken (abstracted) from that which is the *principio quo* (the
quidditative principle) of a thing, the constitutive character or essence according to which several individuals are one, while the particular designates that which is constituted by what belongs to the *quod
est* over and above the commonly shared essence. However, since
there is no difference in God between *quo est* and *quod est*, there can
be neither universal nor particular in the strict sense. There is no
principle *by which* a divine person is divine and which is itself distinct
from that person, as though the person were composed of some extensionally broader nature and a particularizing element[993]. Nevertheless, we refer to the persons of the Trinity as "individuals" or as
"particular" after a manner of speaking; for, although there is no
principle (material or otherwise) by which the common nature is *rendered* a concrete subsistent, the personal properties of the persons are
distinct from one another, constituting several supposits in distinct

---

ideo unitas illa singularitatis non est: ideo singularitas a divinis excluditur" – Albert, *Sum.
theol.*, I, tr. 9, q. 40, c. 1, sol., ed. Colon., vol. 34, p. 307.

[991] *"Unitas singularitatis per individuationem est et excludit pluralitatem hypostasium, et ideo in
divinis non praedicatur. Unum autem unitatis essentiae dicit unitatem unientis personas, et
ideo hoc non excludit pluralitatem personarum"* – Albert, *Sum. theol.*, I, tr. 9, q. 40, c. 1,
ad 9, ed. Colon., vol. 34, p. 309.

[992] *"Deus', qui nec dicit universale nec singulare. Quod autem universale non dicat, patet, quia
universale est in multis per intentionem, et divisum ab illis per esse; Deus autem habet significatum quidem communicabile pluribus, sed singulare in esse, quia tres personae secundum deitatem habent idem esse. Quod non sit singularis, patet, quia nullum singulare est communicabile pluribus, nec re, nec ratione"* – Albert, *III Sent.*, d. 6, a. 1, ad quaest. 2, ed. Borgnet, vol. 28, p. 123.

[993] *"Universale et particulare non sunt, nisi in quibus differunt 'quo est' et 'quod est'; universale
enim est ex parte eius quod 'quo est', particulare autem ex parte eius quod 'quod est'... in deo
nihil potest praedicari per modum universalis et particularis"* – Albert, *Sum. theol.*, I, tr. 11,
q. 47, c. 3, ad quaest. 4, ed. Colon., vol. 34, p. 369.

personal being, i.e. distinct hypostatic possession of being[994]. What the personal properties accomplish in the Trinity is precisely analogous to what particularization or individuation accomplishes in creatures, namely the constitution of the ontologically perfect *ens* which is the subject of natural being[995]. It is with respect to the *term* of the causality contained in the notions of particularization or individuation that the divine persons may be called particular and individuals.

Conclusion

Defining person, we confronted the principal theological difficulty of having to affirm its substantial signification while nevertheless precluding the necessity of substantial multiplication when persons are numbered. This is achieved by carefully identifying the semantical value of the terms employed in the definitions considered. Though Albert accepts, at times adopts, and frequently refers to the Victorine definition of person able to overstep the difficulties posed by the fact that, strictly speaking, there is neither "individual" nor "rational nature" in God, he rather adheres to the Boethian formulation, specifying, in particular, the senses of its terms and rectifying any apparent inconsistencies pertaining to its attribution to the Trinity, in a way characteristic of his broader Aristotelian metaphysics.

The fundamental referent of person is substance. According to the definition of person, "substance" in a certain sense is distributively multiplied for each and every person; the only acceptable sense, we have seen (in light of the Trinitarian discernments), is substance signified *ab actu substandi*, that is, substance which (because of its mode of signification) is the supposit, and not substance which is the essence (or common nature in God). Only a multiplication of substance as taken in the first way is required for a multiplicity of persons. That is not to say that persons do not also admit of a multiplicity of substance taken in the second way; indeed to every created person corresponds a unique substance from both points of view, i.e., distinc-

---

[994] *"Non quod proprie particularia sint, quia particularia particulant naturam communem, quod non convenit divinis... particularia etiam proprie divisa sunt per materiam et per individuantia, in deo autem nec materia nec accidens est. Sed secundum modum loquendi dicuntur particularia, quia suis proprietatibus personalibus sunt discretae et ab invicem distinctae in esse personali; his enim 'singularis existentiae modum' accipiunt sub 'natura divina intellectuali', cuius sunt supposita sive hypostases"* – Albert, *Sum. theol.*, I, tr. 11, q. 47, c. 3, ad quaest. 4, ed. Colon., vol. 34, p. 370. Cf. infra, "PERSONAL BEING", p. 393.

[995] Cf. Albert, *Sum. theol.*, I, tr. 10, q. 46, ad 1, ed. Colon., vol. 34, p. 362.

tion in hypostasis or suppositum and distinction in natural being or individual essence. Verification of personhood, however, is indifferent as to whether a thing be distinctly constituted in natural being or not (as to whether the common nature is the same according to reason only, or according to reason and reality both), since the necessary and sufficient condition for personhood is supposital distinction alone[996].

"Individual" performs the role of specifying the kind of substance in question, namely primary substance, and insofar as subject. The grammatical value of the term is thus more than that of a negation, but demonstrates a positive quality, namely the subjective integrity of the supposit. Such a substanding character is derived from the principle by which a supposit is individual and the distinction which this effects. The notion of individual thus also names the substantial reality from the point of view of its *per se* distinction (from which incommunicability is understood to follow as an immediate consequence). It is as a result of the inclusion of the term "individual" that the substance named by person cannot be secondary substance or the substance as common, and it is for this reason that personal distinction is independent of diversity in essence. Conjoined with "individual", the concept of "substance" implied in the Boethian definition enjoys an analogically universal applicability giving it a privileged status among the various definitions considered by Albert.

The sense according to which the persons of the Trinity may be called individual substances pertains to their designation as *existens per se solum*. That is, inasmuch as individual implies a *per se* singular existent, it is said of the Trinity, and not insofar as it may be used to signify the individuated thing of a universal nature (where individuation occurs at the level of substantial differences)[997]. In the Trinity, of course, there is no really distinct principle by which common nature is

---

[996] "*Divisa sunt per 'substantiam', quae est 'suppositum', et hoc sufficit ad esse personae. Non sunt autem divisa per substantiam, quae est natura communis; talis enim divisio non exigitur ad esse personae... persona secundum diffinitionem Richardi et Boethii non aequivoce dicitur... conceditur, quod secundum divisionem 'substantiae' dicitur; sed haec est 'substantia', quae est suppositum sive hypostasis et non natura communi... Sicut enim dicit Richardus, nihil interest ad esse personae, utrum natura communis eadem sit ratione tantum et non re vel eadem ratione et re*" – Albert, *Sum. theol.*, I, tr. 10, q. 46, ad 7 & 8, ed. Colon., vol. 34, p. 363.

[997] "*In divinis enim non est proprie individuum, quia nec dividuum, nec est ibi proprie natura rationalis, sed intellectualis... Et ideo Anselmus illam corrigit diffinitionem dicens, quod 'persona est existens aliquis per se solum secundum quendam singularis existentiae et intellectualis naturae modum'. Hoc autem quod est 'existens per se solum', Boethius elargato vocabulo*

rendered a concrete subject of existence. The personal properties in the Trinity, therefore, can only be said to accomplish something analogous to what the principles of individuation achieve in creatures for whom *quod est* and *quo est* are really distinct[998].

Person was defined as "of a rational nature" in order to emphasize the fact that persons are perfect *res naturae*, stable and determinate entities constituted through an operation of nature. The multi-purpose genitive construction serves at once: (a) to position person with respect to nature as such, the latter of which is only indirectly signified in the definition of the former; (b) to express the proportionality according to which person is commonly predicated, referring the hypostatic substance to common nature; and (c) to designate that part of the logically composed personal reality signified as an informing or qualifying part.

In connection with rationality, and on the basis of etymological considerations, the definition of Peter Lombard brings into relief, according to Albert, the intrinsic dignity of the person. That quality is rooted in the intellectual nature itself, however, in such a way that "person" is not understood to add something to the notion of the rational hypostasis, but expresses the fact that the hypostasis is specified by rationality and thus dignified.

With regard to the expression *"res naturae"*, we observed that it is taken from the respect had by a particular to the common nature and signifies the particular according to that respect, which is to be something particular *of* the nature. The term *suppositum* is also taken from the respect of standing under, but *primo et principaliter* from that of standing under the properties and accidents of the nature – and since this necessarily implies standing under the nature, *suppositum* is also said in respect of the act of substanding the common nature. These names, along with hypostasis and person, are always interior to the genus of substance, the *ratio* of which is to subsist *per se*; thus they are each predicable only of that which is complete in itself and subsistent. The terms "particular", "individual" and "singular", on the other hand, ordinarily understood, may be said with respect to any genus and may thus refer to substantial parts or accidents as well. "Individual" is said inasmuch as a thing be indivisible in itself, and this is an

---

vocat 'individuum'; hoc ergo modo est individuum in divina substantia" – Albert, *Sum. theol.*, I, tr. 10, q. 46, ad 5, ed. Colon., vol. 34, p. 363.

[998] The divine persons are thus called "particular" or "individuals" only with respect to the formal effect or term of the causality implied in the ordinary notion of individuation.

intrinsic unity; "singular" is said of a thing inasmuch as it is divisible from others and is thus identical to the unity implied in being *divisum ab alio* (which is an extrinsic unity in the sense of relative to others)[999]. In a general way, however, the concept of individual is also taken to imply divisibility from others, inasmuch as, at the level of concrete existence, indivisibility and singularity go hand in hand. Thus the term "individual" (in the definition *substantia individua rationalis naturae*, where the subject of its denomination is the *per se* thing, entailing individuality in the fullest sense of the term) is understood to indicate a divisibility from others excluding that kind of communicability and union proper to potential and active co-principles constituting a *tertium quid* through natural union[1000]. Every true (or *per se*) individual is incommunicable by that very token. For this reason, the concept of every rational individual (in the full sense of the term) includes the incommunicability proper to personhood[1001].

A threefold kind of incommunicability was conceded as necessary for personhood: that opposed to the communicability of the universal; that opposed to the communicability of substantial or integral parts; and that opposed to assumability. Persons, to be precise, cannot admit of any form of communicability implying either presence in another subject or that kind of union resulting in a third entity. All of these kinds of communicability are understood to be excluded by the addition "individual". While the notion of strict incommunicability satisfactorily precludes the separated soul and humanity of Christ from constituting persons of themselves, that incommunicability shows itself to be an intrinsic property of the individual substance as such, that is, the fully individual natural subject (whose mode of individuality excludes every form of active and potential communicability). As a result, by combing the notions of individuality (or incommunicability) and rationality, personhood is adequately defined.

It is with respect to and as an expression of the first of these notions that Richard of Saint-Victor concretely designates the person with the term *"existentia"*. The fact that *"existentia"* is able to refer to

---

[999] Cf. Aquinas, *III Sent.*, d. 6, q. 1, a. 1, quaest. 1, resp., ed. Moos, p. 224-225.

[1000] *"Cum dicitur, individua substantia, ly 'individua' dicit ab aliis separationem quae est contraria unioni et communicabilitati potentiae ad actum, et e contra, quia talis communicabilitas est ad tertium constituendum"* – Albert, *III Sent.*, d. 5, a. 3, ad 3, ed. Borgnet, vol. 28, p. 100.

[1001] *"Omnia individua incommunicabilitatem personae includunt in suo intellectu"* – Albert, *III Sent.*, d. 10, a. 1, ad quaest. 2, ed. Borgnet, vol. 28, p. 189. Though an explicit mention of incommunicability occurs only in the Victorine formulation, it is clearly entailed by the content of the Boethian definition.

the substantive reality of the person has the particular value of explicitating the fact that persons are constituted as such by reason of their distinct modes of subsisting (identifying the notion of distinction – sometimes tending to be conceptualized as causing personality in an almost efficient sense – with the formal essence of the person as such). It also has the Trinitarian advantage of situating that distinction at the level of properties of origin, as opposed to that of substance. Because the origin denoted in the concept of *existentia* (grammatically indicated by the *"ex"*) is identified with the personal property, the Victorine definition indirectly refers just as much as the Boethian definition to the *proprietas* necessarily contained in the notion of person[1002].

The mode of existence distinguishing one person from another, as is clear from the second Victorine definition, may be constituted in different ways corresponding to the different degrees of ontological simplicity proper to the kinds of persons in question. As a result, Richard's overall contribution to defining person possesses a certain universal value as well. In general and characteristically Albertinian terms, a person's unique mode of existence consists in his or her individuality or singularity. Here we observe a transformation of Victorine language (*"modus existendi"*) into rather Boethian terms; but, as demonstrated by Albert, it is especially the Boethian language which must be interpreted according to Victorine concepts – *"substantia"* to be taken in the sense of *"existentia"*; *"individualis"* in the sense of *"discretum singulari proprietate"*; and *"rationalis naturae"* in the sense of *"intellectualis"*.

[1002] The *proprietas personalis* is the principle of the formal constituent of personality, individuality; it is the cause of the distinction from which perfect incommunicability follows – whence the immeasurable importance of properly conceptualizing that principle. Cf. infra, "PROPRIETAS", p. 433 (especially p. 436-437; 443-444; 461-464).

II.5. MULTIPLYING INDIVIDUALS AND THE ROLE OF RELATION IN THE TRINITY

Pinning down the distinguishing element

If person signifies more than just the essence or substance, but directly denotes the distinctive property of a thing, if person names at once what is common and indistinct along with what is proper and distinct, while both remain in God but a single reality, then what is it that "person" names which distinguishes the person without also introducing distinction in the essence (equally named by "person") [1003]? It is this question which, in the opinion of A. Pompei, radically reorients our search for the content of personhood by directing it less toward the "what" of the person and more toward the distinguishing "cause" of the person (even if the two are one in reality) [1004]. Looking for the *ratio* of distinction precisely in order to explain the possibility of several distinct subsistents in God fundamentally characterizes the entire Albertinian thesis of the necessity of relations in God. Albert, that is, develops his doctrine of the divine relations on the basis of the need to account for the already established distinction between the persons. Thus it is that, after defining person, Albert finally sets out to expose the notion and the role of relation in God as the *principle* of personal distinction [1005].

[1003] *"Circa substantiam illam quam importat, nec ponit proprietatem, nec numerum quem facit proprietas"* – Albert, *I Sent.*, d. 23, a. 2, sol., ed. Borgnet, vol. 25, p. 585.

[1004] Cf. A. Pompei, op. cit., p. 255.

[1005] Such an ordering of considerations reflects not only the methodological discretion of the author, but has its rationale (in particular) in the relation of the human intellect to the very object of its consideration (and to a certain extent in the nature of the object itself). In this light, the overall structure of an author's treatment of the divine persons reflects his convictions about our understanding of those persons as well as about the intrinsic makeup of the same. It would make an interesting study to compare the methodological order of St. Albert with that of St. Thomas. With regard to the distinctive or "multiplying" role of relation in the Trinity, a remarkable similarity exists, for the most part, between the manner in which Thomas and Albert approach the question. However, it is important to be precise about the different senses in which relation may be invoked as a principle of personal distinction.

To the extent that relation is invoked simply as a principle of distinction, without further qualification, the sense of the "principality" involved may be taken in different ways. Relation, in the order of cognition, necessarily follows from, as a logical implication of, distinction, insofar as it is logically antecedent to the notion of distinction (distinction itself being a kind of relation based on lack of identity or sameness). Relation, however, may be understood to be necessitated by distinction in another way, namely as the principle of such distinction in the order of being.

With regard to the cognitive priority, if first we have distinction, then we necessarily have relation. Both Albert and St. Thomas move from distinction to relation in this respect (cf. Aquinas, *Sum. theol.*, I, 28, 1). At this level, in our opinion, Albert's general approach to the divine relations differs little from that of St. Thomas who presents the relations as necessarily included in the concept of origin or procession (implying the issuing of one thing from another and therefore distinction). (This, of course, does not yet show the reality of the relations, for which reason Thomas first considers the nature of the divine processions the conditions of which assure the reality of the relations). With regard, on the other hand, to relation taken after the manner of an efficient principle of distinction, which we must conceptualize according to the mode of natural priority (which manner of conceptualization, however, does not impinge upon the divine simplicity, since the mode according to which we predicate the distinguishing *proprietas* confirms their identity in reality with the distinguished persons, all priority and composition having its place exclusively on the part of the mode according to which we *understand* that which is simple in itself), Thomas and Albert, though in full agreement on the function of relation so considered, and presenting the same argument in its regard (cf. Aquinas, *Sum. theol.*, I, 29, 4), choose in the opinion of A. Pompei (cf. op. cit., p. 189, especially note 4, and p. 255) a reverse order in exposing and discussing the two realities being com pared, namely the distinguishing element (relation) and that which it distinguishes (the person). While St. Thomas (in his *Summa theologica*) moves, in an *a priori* fashion, from the concept of relation in God to a definition of the (logically less simple) divine persons, Albert, Pompei emphasizes, departs rather from the definition of person in search of what, *secundum modum intelligendi*, is the efficient cause of the formal feature of personality. Nevertheless, despite the divergence in methodological progression, both theologians arrive at the same conclusions concerning the function and necessity of relation in distinguishing persons in God. And while this observation of methodological variance holds with respect to Albert's *Sentences* as compared to Thomas' *Summa*, it does not remain consistently demonstrable in other works. Thomas' order of consideration is more similar to Albert's, for example, in *I Sent.* (where heed for a relative account of hypostatic distinction gets underway in d. 26, q. 1, a. 2), *Sum. contra gentiles* (where relation as a retrospective explanatory device appears in IV, c. 24), and, to some degree, even in the *De potentia* (where, despite the structuring of q. 8 and q. 9 rather after the manner of the *Summa*, q. 10 returns to the distinctive notion of relation in the context of procession [taking up in a general way the emblematic argumentative principle iterated in q. 8, a. 1]). Albert himself, moreover, tends to oscillate in (or intermingle) the order in which relations and the divine hypostases come to be addressed in his *Summa theologiae* (something demonstrated by a consideration of divine relations in *Sum. theol.*, I, tr. 9, q. 37 – taken up in our chapter on "ONTOLOGICAL DIVISIONS AND SIGNIFICATION OF TERMS" –, and a systematic attempt to define person in *Sum. theol.*, I, tr. 10, q. 44 – taken up in our chapter on "DEFINITIONS OF PERSON"). Consequently, we cannot so simplistically contrast the Albertinian methodological approach with that of Saint Thomas. A more detailed structural investigation, at once sensitive to the interdependency existing between relative and hypostatic considerations in the Trinity (due to the notional source of relation and the relative cause of hypostatic distinction), and more comprehensively regarding the textual corpus of both men, would constitute a valuable comparative undertaking.

[Interestingly enough, the *Summa* of St. Thomas is very clearly and deliberately structured, and in a more or less unique way. Perhaps the organic nature and comprehensive vision of the *Summa* (over and above its late authorship) indicate that the order chosen there represents Aquinas' most unified and systematic expression of what he sees to be the fundamental line of approach, that is, a more

Natural diversity and individuation, its exclusion in the Trinity

The supposit or person is the distinct (i.e. individual) thing of a rational nature. Distinction as we have seen is constitutive of personality. For every multiplicity of persons, therefore, we must find a basis for supposital distinction according to which such a multiplicity can be affirmed. The principle of distinction can be diverse, depending upon the kind of nature proper to the supposits being distinguished. While material individuation suffices for the particularization of human nature, in God another distinctive principle must provide for personal constitution. The material mode must be excluded from God because of its threefold imperfection, embracing the coming to be of matter, the numerical (and not simply specific) multiplication of nature in diverse supposits, and the receptive potency of matter with respect to the communicated nature. The principle of distinction in the Trinity consists rather in the *proprietates* which, constitutive of the hypostases, nevertheless leave intact the specific and numerical identity of the nature of the supposits for whom there is no difference between *quod est* and *quo est*[1006].

Person, hypostasis, supposit and concrete natural reality (*res naturae*), though recognized both in the Trinity and in men, are in the Trinity differently than in men. In men, one thing of nature is distinguished from another through a division of nature; one man is a distinct *res naturae* because his nature is diverse. In the Trinity, however, one natural reality (person as *res naturae*) is distinct from another through the relations pertaining to origin only and not according to diverse natures – the result is *tres res naturae distincti*, and not *tres res naturarum distinctae*. Similarly, the hypostasis or supposit of human beings is founded upon the naturally distinct act of standing under a common nature, while such natural distinction is excluded in the supposital act proper to divine hypostases.

In men, we have both the common universal nature and the particular nature as a limited instance or contraction of the universal nature. Since this universal nature is common to many men *in ratione tantum*, there is no real natural union between men, the supposits of which, while standing beneath a universal nature, are separate individual natures. In the Trinity, on the other hand, the common nature

---

ideal methodological structure. But we cannot linger on such questions at this time.]

[1006] Cf. supra, "DIFFERENT KINDS OF MODES OF DISTINCTION", p. 299-304 (especially p. 304 & note 810); cf. A. Pompei, op. cit., p. 120.

is the very thing itself, the several hypostases are identically the common nature; they are not limited contractions of something which exceeds them in some way, but possess the fullness of the common nature by perfect and real natural identity. Thus individuals in the Trinity are not constituted through the division of a common nature into particulars, where the concrete realization of the common nature occurs through substantially divided particulars, each hypostasis possessing a distinct substantial being[1007]. For these same reasons, in the *Summa theologica* Albert pronounces a certain predilection for the definitions of personhood proffered by Richard of St. Victor in preference to that supplied by Boethius. The expression "individual substance" is insufficient, he argues, on the grounds that individual substances are, properly speaking, individuals of divided, or at least divisible, natures[1008]. To argue in this way might seem to presuppose the Boethian metaphysical framework where "substance", properly speaking, denotes those subsisting realities which are the support of accidents and which are distinguished from other subsistences which are free from these conditions and possess within themselves everything needed for the act of subsisting. On the other hand, the sense of the criticism might suggest that the term "individual" has the purpose of indicating the particularization of what would otherwise remain universal, since substances here are individual inasmuch as particular instantiations of a broader common nature. What Albert may be rejecting in the Boethian definition, then, is not entirely clear, since he may be referring either to the fact that "substance" implies the limitations and conditions of materiality (substance taken in the strict sense delimiting a category of subsistences), or to the fact that the term "individual", if it is not to be superfluous, must signify the contraction of a common nature by way of substantial division (where "substance" must be understood along more abstract lines, that is, as the essence

---

[1007] "*Res naturae bene est in divinis et suppositum sive hypostasis et etiam persona, licet non eodem modo quo in humanis. In humanis enim res naturae a re naturae distinguitur naturae divisione, in divinis autem non, sed relatione ad originem pertinente. Similiter suppositum in humanis est stans sub natura communi, ita quod sit ibi natura universalis et natura particularis, in divinis autem non, quin immo natura communis est re, non ratione tantum, et suppositum non est particulans naturam, sed totam habens. Individuum autem nullo modo est in divinis… ubi natura communis per esse dividitur, in divinis autem natura communis non dividitur per esse substantiale in personis*" – Albert, Sum. theol., I, tr. 8, q. 34, c. 2, ad 11, ed. Colon., vol. 34, p. 265-266.

[1008] "*Similiter persona est in divinis, sed, ut dicit Richardus, non proprie est 'substantia individua' sicut in humanis, quia substantia individua non est nisi naturae dividuae sive divisibilis. In divinis autem 'persona est existens per se solum secundum singularem existendi*

awaiting its particularization/individuation – whence the meaningful function of the term "individual", since "substance", if taken in the full sense as a kind of subsistence, would already imply the concrete act of existence proper to the individual); or perhaps he is referring to both. As an alternative to the *unrefined* Boethian definition, which, by the way, is entirely acceptable in the context of men, Albert adopts, for the sake of defining person in the broader context embracing the Trinity, the formula of Richard of St. Victor stating that the person is a "*per se* singular existent (subsistent) existing according to a singular mode of existence in an intellectual nature". In this way, person does not entail a division of nature (or the division of a nature, as Albert puts it), neither in the sense of the natural division between the diverse individual natures corresponding to distinct persons, nor in the sense of a multiplication of distinct individuals through a delimitation of a universal abstract nature.

After dismissing from God the various principles of difference according to which creatures are individuated one from another, Albert describes the differences between the Trinitarian persons – which cannot consist in anything generic, specific or substantial – as existential modes, according as a person is said to be from another (*esse ab alio*) or not (*non esse ab alio*). The affirmation states that the *manner* according to which each person is is a distinguishing feature amongst the persons, but this is not to say that they differ according to *esse* simply taken. That there must be some difference between them is clear enough, but the place to which Albert assigns that difference is the *esse personalis* of each person. The persons are distinct in personal being through the incommunicable properties. These incommunicable properties, which are the principle of distinction in personal being, are the very properties through which one person is *non ab alio*, another is *ab alio per generationem*, and a third *a duobus per processionem.* The differences between the persons, which have their principle exclusively in the personal properties, are alternately referred to by Albert as either modes of existence or differences in personal being. The existential modes are precisely unique instances of personal being. The notion of personal being[1009], however, more clearly expresses the diversity of supposits, inasmuch as the term is intended to signify the most perfect kind of being, that possessed by hypostases existing *per se*. Moreover, with respect to the notion of *modus existendi*, in order

---

modum in natura intellectuali', quae non dividitur, sed a singulis tota possidetur" – Albert, *Sum. theol.*, I, tr. 8, q. 34, c. 2, ad 11, ed. Colon., vol. 34, p. 266.
[1009] Cf. infra, "PERSONAL BEING", p. 393.

to sufficiently account for all three persons of the Trinity, a second modality must be introduced; over and above the notion of *modus existendi per esse ab alio* must be added the subsequent modality of *per generationem* or *per processionem (a duobus)*[1010].

Relation as unique source of multiplicity in the Trinity

Revelation tells us that one person is not another and that one person generates another. Yet the persons are one in nature. As a result, the only basis upon which to account for their distinction is the fact that one person generates while the other is generated: distinction, that is, finds its explanation in origin[1011]. In God, personal multiplication is had in virtue of the diversity of the terms of opposition of the relations which are founded upon the different modes of origin[1012]. Without such relations, which are the incommunicable properties constituting each person, no emanation of one thing from another according to diverse modes of origin could be affirmed, and there would be no presence of several things distinct from one another[1013]. The persons are able to be distinguished and constituted by relation precisely because relation introduces no substantial difference between the persons it distinguishes and constitutes[1014].

[1010] *"In divinis non est materia, et ideo nec divisio secundum materiam... Similiter in divinis nec est genus nec species nec differentia nec particulare nec universale... et ideo nihil differt ibi ab alio genere, specie vel differentia substantiali. Sed in divinis differens est existendi modus per esse ab alio et per non esse ab alio... tales existendi modos non possint esse nisi secundum esse perfectissimum, hypostases habentes et in seipsis existentes, sequitur, quod non possunt esse nisi in esse personali distincti per incommunicabiles proprietates, quibus alter est non ab alio et alter ab alio per generationem et tertius a duobus per processionem... in deo non est differentia per accidens neque differentia substantialis, sed differentia, quam facit proprietas relationis, relationis autem dico secundum originem, quae exigit diversitatem suppositi"* – Albert, *Sum. theol.*, I, tr. 10, q. 46, ad 1 & 2, ed. Colon., vol. 34, p. 362.

[1011] Cf. A. Pompei, op. cit., p. 80, for whom the intimate connection between distinction and the origin of the divine persons constitutes the foundation of the Albertinian explanation of the Trinity.

[1012] *"Et sic est in divinis, quod relatio diversitate oppositorum, quae fundatur super diversum modum originis, multiplicat trinitatem"* – Albert, *Sum. theol.*, I, tr. 9, q. 42, c. 2, ad 11, ed. Colon., vol. 34, p. 327.

[1013] *"Si relationes non essent in divinis, quae sunt incommunicabiles proprietates, non esset ponere diversas emanationes et singulares modos existendi... Et si intelligerentur sine his, impossibile esset, quod differrent ab invicem"* – Albert, *Sum. theol.*, I, tr. 9, q. 42, c. 2, ad 13, ed. Colon., vol. 34, p. 328.

[1014] *"Relatio autem originis nihil praedicat absolute inhaerens, sed quod secundum esse quod est, ad alterum est, et ideo nullam facit differentiam"* – Albert, *Sum. theol.*, I, tr. 6, q. 29, c. 1, a. 2, ad 13, ed. Colon., vol. 34, p. 220.

It was St. Augustine who developed the doctrine of relative distinction in the Trinity, in opposition to the Arian claim that substantial alteriety alone could account for three really distinct persons[1015]. In God, he observes, there are predicates of two sorts: substantial and relative. Relation, because its essence is purely referential (*ad alterum*), can in no way divide the singular substance, for it says nothing substantial.

In God, relations are never accidental. Whether it is a question of a relation to creatures or to a consubstantial term, no intrinsic modification of being is implied; no process of change or becoming serves as a foundation for the relation (the accidentality of which process would imply the contingency of the relation)[1016]. Relation in God is rather *eternal* (wherefore, in its being, it can be nothing other than the divine substance). But it expresses a property of the substance (which is the referent of the relative term), not with respect to itself, but with respect to another[1017]. For these reasons, in Augustine's opinion, relation presents itself as the unique means for distinguishing a plurality of persons in a unity of substance, and this becomes the shared doctrine of theologians throughout the centuries to follow[1018].

In a similar fashion, Albert founds the necessity of relation as the sole explanation of distinction in God on the grounds that the divine simplicity absolutely excludes composition or division; outside relation, there is no way to understand hypostasis as adding something to the notion of the essence[1019]. The hypostases in God are not opposed to one another *seipsis*, but by virtue of relation alone (the opposition of which is understood as a consequence of the modes of origin). The importance of relation as the reason for distinction is especially brought out in the context of the controversy over the *Filioque*, where

---

[1015] Cf. Augustine, *De Trin.*, V, c. 3. For an examination of the Augustinian contribution to the notion of person in both its Christological and Trinitarian dimensions, see A. Milano, *Persona in teologia*, Edizioni Dehoniane, Naples 1987, p. 283-318; A. Pompei, op. cit., p. 262-263.

[1016] Cf. Augustine, *De Trin.*, V, c. 4; XV, c. 3, n. 5; cf. A. Pompei, op. cit., p. 262.

[1017] Cf. Augustine, *De Trin.*, V, c. 11.

[1018] *"Tutto ciò rimase la dottrina comune dei secoli posteriori, formulata con più o meno precisione dai dottori. Così Boezio, partendo dalla dottrina di Agostino, può dire per modo di conclusione: 'ita igitur substantia continet unitatem, relatio multiplicat trinitatem'. Ed Anselmo, da parte sua, giunge alla formulazione del celebre assioma che dominerà tutta la speculazione cattolica posteriore, e che fu assunto dagli stessi documenti ecclesiastici: 'in Dio tutto è uno, dove non c'è opposizione relativa"* – A. Pompei, op. cit., p. 263; cf. Bothius, *De Trin.*, c. 6, ed. Loeb, p. 28; Anselm, *De process. Spir. Sancti*, c. 2; cf. DS 1330 (36th edition).

[1019] With regard to Albert's doctrine of relation in general and with respect to its application to God, cf. P. D. Marinozzi, *La relazione in S. Alberto Magno*, Diss., University of Fribourg (Switzerland), 1956; A. Pompei, op. cit., p. 266-296.

Albert demonstrates that the Son and Holy Spirit could not be distinguished amongst themselves were there no relative opposition between them, an opposition which has its explanation in the procession of the one from the other[1020].

With dialectical mastery, Albert illustrates the proper value of our limited creaturely concepts in speaking about the divine mystery, perspicaciously discriminating what, with regard to the natural predicaments of man's experience, may be validly predicated in God, and in what sense. As a natural philosophical category, relation has several distinct characteristics: 1) having the nature of an accident; 2) being a property in some way, according to which it is said to inhere in but a single individual; and 3) being in itself that which is opposed to another. The accidentality pertaining to the first entails composition with its subject, such as cannot be admitted in God. In God, therefore, accidental nature is excluded, yet the nature of property, insofar as *proprietas*, that is, insofar as belonging to a single individual, is retained, along with the latter concept of relation *to another*[1021]. Relation as such, that is, according to its concept, does not imply inherence in another, but only having a respect toward another[1022]. The divine simplicity is thereby left intact, since it could only be derogated by the addition of some being through accidental composition. Relation in God, then, not being an accident, introduces no being the nature of which is diverse from the substance itself[1023]. In this way, personal determination can be accounted for by relation, inasmuch as the determination accomplished in the divine being by relation neither adds to, nor diminishes, nor alters the determinate substance[1024].

[1020] Concerning this argument for the necessity of relation in Albert and, in particular, the origins as responsible for the opposition of terms, cf. A. Pompei, op. cit., p. 267-272. For a succinct and clear analysis of Albert's treatment of Trinitarian procession, see G. Emery, op. cit., p. 68-75, 87-88, 94-108.

[1021] *"Relatio tria habet in se, scilicet naturam accidentis, et quod proprietas quaedam est, et ex hoc habet inesse soli, et habet in se quod ad alterum opponitur relative... est modus accidentis facientis compositionem concretionis cum subjecto in quo est... et talis praedicatio in Deo non potest esse, et ideo in divinis amittit naturam accidentis, et remanet natura proprietatis in quantum est proprietas, scilicet quod est soli convenire, et ulterius remanet ei intellectus relationis ad alterum"* – Albert, *I Sent.*, d. 8, a. 34, sol., ed. Borgnet, vol. 25, p. 269.

[1022] *"Relatio secundum quod relatio est, non dicat aliquod inhaerens, sed ad alterum se habens"* – Albert, *Sum. theol.*, I, tr. 13, q. 52, ad quaest. 3, ad 4, ed Borgnet, vol. 31, p. 538-539.

[1023] *"Non tollit simplicitatem, quia non tolleret nisi per naturam accidentis ut est accidens, quod inducendo diversum ens, id est, ens diversae naturae a substantia"* – Albert, *I Sent.*, d. 8, a. 34, sol., ed. Borgnet, vol. 25, p. 269.

[1024] *"Est etiam determinatio ex relatione... quia nihil addit vel minuit vel mutat in determinato, ut dicit Boetius, nullam inducit compositionem"* – Albert, *Sum. theol.*, II, tr. 1, q. 3, a. 1, ad 3, ed. Borgnet, vol. 32, p. 13.

As a result of the unique character of relation, the very universal divisions of being must be reinterpreted. Relation as such is said to posit nothing diverse in being nor to introduce any alteration in species because it is not necessarily identified with relation taken as a predicament. Every predicament necessarily adds, subtracts or changes something with respect to that to which it is attributed, but the *ratio* of relation does not entail the predicamentality proper to accidental relation[1025]. This is because the kind of being predicated by relation is neither identical to substantial being nor to the being of accidents. Following Aristotle, Albert distinguishes three kinds of being: 1) *esse* which is proper to the subsistent subject, which is absolute and independent being, i.e. *esse simpliciter* or *per se* being; 2) *esse inhaerentis*, which depends upon a subject for its actuality and belongs to accidents, which is also absolute being; and 3) *esse ad aliud* which is neither *per se esse* nor *inesse*, nor reducible to them, but is the special being of relation constituting the *respect* of one substance toward another or of one accident toward another[1026].

Within the latter division Albert distinguishes two kinds of *esse ad*: *esse ad simpliciter* – pertaining to the pure ratio of being referred to another – from which the predicament relation; and *esse ad ab aliquo* – pertaining less to the constitution of a thing than to what accrues to it in virtue of its being compared to another – from which the six predicaments *ubi, quando, agere, passio, situs,* and *habitus*[1027]. Only the first

---

[1025] *"Dicunt relationem non esse differentiam entis vel speciem, nec esse aliquod praedicamentum, eo quod omne praedicamentum species entis est, quod additum alii vel auget, vel minuit, vel mutat in ipso; relatio autem adveniens alicui, ut dicit Boetius, nec addit, nec mutat, nec minuit aliquid"* – Albert, *Sum. theol.,* I, tr. 13, q. 52, sol., ed. Borgnet, vol. 31, p. 535.

[1026] *"Triplex est esse in genere. Est enim esse substantiae subsistentis et nullo indigentis, et hoc est esse absolutum ad nihil dependens, et nullo indigens ut subjecto ad hoc ut sit. Et est esse inhaerentis, subjecto indigentis ad hoc ut sit, et hoc est esse accidentis. Et hoc multiplicatur secundum differentias inhaerendi subjecto. Quoddam enim inhaeret ut mensura subjecti, et est quantitas. Et quoddam inhaeret ut dispositio subjecti, et hoc est qualitas. Et utrumque istorum est esse absolutum... Tertium est esse... quod nec est per se esse, nec est inesse, sed est ad aliud esse, et tale est esse relativorum, et nec reducibile est ad per se esse, nec ad inesse, sed habet praedicandi specialem modum. Propter quod dicit relativum esse speciale praedicamentum, et invenitur tam in substantiis quam in accidentibus, et est in habitudine substantiarum ad invicem substantia, et in habitudine accidentium ad invicem accidens"* – Albert, *Sum. theol.,* I, tr. 13, q. 52, sol., ed. Borgnet, vol. 31, p. 535-536; *"relatio secundum quod relatio est, non dicat aliquod inhaerens, sed ad alterum se habens"* – tr. 13, q. 52, quaest. 3, ad 4, ed. Borgnet, vol. 31, p. 538-539. As observed in the chapter on "ONTOLOGICAL DIVISIONS AND SIGNIFICATION OF TERMS", a similar construal of the fundamental classes of being occurs in tr. 9, q. 37: cf. supra, "FIRST DIVISION OF ENS", p. 189 (especially p. 189-193).

[1027] *"Est autem triplex esse, scilicet esse simpliciter, et ab hoc sumitur praedicamentum substantiae. Et est esse in, et ab hoc sumitur praedicamentum accidentis ut est accidens, ut quantitas et qualitas. Et est esse ad, et hoc dupliciter. Est enim esse ad ita quod ipsum est ad aliud, et ab hoc sumitur praedicamentum relationis. Et est esse ad ab aliquo, quod procedit a compara-*

kind of *esse ad* properly constitutes the (analogous) category of relation, and it is in virtue of the fact that its concept does not imply the
notion of inherence that such an *esse ad* can also be predicated *simpliciter* of the divine persons, even if every natural instance of the predicament exists *in* a subject[1028]. The other predicaments, however,
also find themselves predicated of God according to certain modes of
predication. A consideration of the predicamental divisions and the
manners according to which they may or may not be attributed to
God can throw some light on the special category of relation. In general, the question *de translatione praedicamentorum [Deo]* maintains that
substance and relation alone are properly predicated of God, the
former only insofar as it signify according to *per se subsistent act,* and
not according to the supposital act of standing under, and the latter
only according as it designates reference to another, and not inasmuch as relation is a consequence of the mutability of the quantity or
quality of a substance (in which case the relation is an accident) [1029].

---

tione unius ad alterum; et ab hoc sumuntur sex praedicamenta" – Albert, *Sum. theol.*, I,
tr. 14, q. 56, ad quaest. 1, ad 2, ed. Borgnet, vol. 31, p. 577. For an exposition of
what is considered to be proper to relation in respect of the other accidents also
expressing an *adesse*, see P. D. Marinozzi, *La relazione in S. Alberto Magno*, Diss., University of Fribourg (Switzerland), 1956, p. 94-97. The principle difference consists
in the fact that while relation intrinsically refers the subject to another, the other
six predicaments proceed as a consequence from relations borne by the subject (cf.
the suite of the reply cited here). The being of a relation is thus that of a *forma ab
intrinseco ad aliud* (the sense of inherence being substituted by substantial identity
in God), while the last six predicaments are *formae ab extrinseco.* Such a scenario
underlies the customary designation of these predicaments as "assistant forms", in
contrast to the other accidents (including relation) designated as "inherent forms".

[1028] The great merit of St. Albert consists in having avoided both of the major errors
urged by the double-sided nature of relation, namely, that of introducing composition in the Trinity in virtue of the intrinsic (≈inhering) character of relation, and
that of destroying personal distinction in virtue of the extrinsic referentiality proper
to relation. Unilateral emphasis of the intrinsicalness of the relative predicament
risks either compromising divine simplicity or having to identify the relative being
as such with that of the substance absolutely taken, thereby leaving us without a
concept of a principle of distinction. Restrictive focus, on the other hand, on the
external aspect of relation risks understanding the divine relations either as really
distinct from the persons or as failing to adequately distinguish them. It is precisely
the distinction between *esse in* and *esse ad* that allows the transposition of relation to
the Trinity where the *inesse* proper to predicamental relation is identified with the
divine substance (at the same time evading accidentality and ascribing subsistent
reality to the relations), and where the *esse ad* provides an adequate basis for distinguishing several persons, at once opposed and in a non-absolute way.
  With regard to the impossibility of God being a *subject* for predicaments, cf.
Sum. theol., I, tr. 14, q. 56, ad obj., ed. Borgnet, vol. 31, p. 576.

[1029] *"Praedicamenta duo, scilicet substantiae et relationis proprie in divinam assumuntur...
scilicet quod substantia non a substando dicitur, sed ab eo quod est per se esse... Relatio autem... eo modo quo est dependentia principiorum substantiae ad invicem, quae dependentia*

Analogically, however, certain qualities – namely, those expressing a perfection not repugnant to simplicity –, as well as the predicament of action, are also said of God, while perfections of quantitative expressions and those pertaining to the remaining predicaments are only metaphorically predicable if at all[1030]:

PREDICAMENTAL DIVISIONS

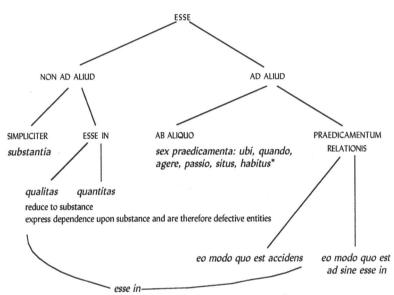

* The six predicaments *ad aliud ab aliquo* fall under *esse in* inasmuch as they are caused by quantity and quality (time and place, for example, being tied to quantity, action and passion to quality)[1031].

ipsis principiis substantiae accidentalis non est, est ante intellectum accidentis, et sic in Deo in quo nihil est secundum accidens, praedicari potest... Secundum autem quod relatio consequens est mutabilitatem compositi, sic est in genere accidentis, et consequens quantitatem et qualitatem, et hoc modo non est in Deo" – Albert, *Sum. theol.*, I, tr. 14, q. 56, sol., ed. Borgnet, vol. 31, p. 575.

1030 *"Multitudo accidentium reducitur ad substantiam. Dico autem accidentium quae praedicant inesse, ut quantitas, et qualitas... dicunt dependentiam ad substantiam, et per consequens entis defectum... Alia autem genera quae dicunt adesse et non inesse, quaedam sunt quae ipso nomine nihil dicunt dependentiae nec imperfectionis, sed potius esse perfectissimum ad quod alia dependent, sicut actio, et haec a divina praedicatione non excluduntur... Quaedam autem inter ea quae dicunt adesse, ipso nomine secundum modum significandi praedicant quid corporale, sicut situs et habitus, et haec in Deo non possunt esse nisi per metaphoram et symbolum, et similiter habitus... Quaedam etiam materialitatem dicunt et imperfectionem, et haec a divina excluduntur praedicatione"* – Albert, *Sum. theol.*, I, tr. 14, q. 56, ad quaest. 2, ed. Borgnet, vol. 31, p. 577.

1031 Cf. tr. 14, q. 56, sol., ed Borgnet, vol. 31, p. 575.

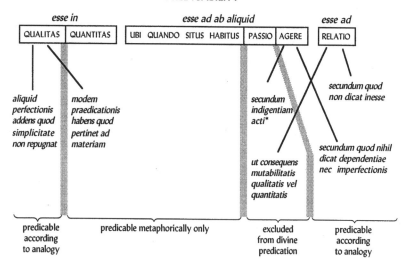

*Action can be considered from two points of view: according as it proceeds from an agent considered as acting; or according as it pertains to the cause of action in creatures which is indigence and implies a movement aimed at filling the need [1032].

Distinction through relation nevertheless requires a substantial element

In opposition to all that has been said about relation as the unique source of distinction in the Godhead stands the assertion that distinct individual beings, and therefore persons, are said to be distinguished according to something absolute and not solely through relations of origin. Such a position is motivated by the belief that the "personal being" by which one person is really distinct from another must be conferred by something absolute which is the cause of the person's individuation. The resulting individuation, that is, the distinctness of the individual, then gives rise to the relation by which it is referred to another, the relation thereby being a *consequence* of an absolute principle of personal distinction [1033]. Of course, the argument is wholly un-

---

[1032] "*Actionis dupliciter considerari potest, scilicet secundum quod est ab agente tantum ut est agens... Sic verum est, quod Deus solus proprie facit et agit, quia est agens simplicissimum et purissimum. Potest etiam considerari secundum quod comparatur ad agens et causam actionis in inferioribus in quibus indigentia causa actionis est. Primo modo non est in genere actio, sed ultra genus, et hoc modo convenit Deo propriissime, quia actio ejus est substantia ejus*" – Albert, *Sum. theol.*, I, tr. 14, q. 56, ad 1, ed. Borgnet, vol. 31, p. 575.

[1033] "*Non distinguantur per relationes fundatas super oppositionem originis, videtur probari ex hoc quod omne quod distinctum esse accipit secundum modum esse individui singularis, ac-*

tenable with respect to God (and, in a certain respect even with re-gard to creatures[1034]). Such a state of affairs, Albert remarks, holds only for those relations which are accidental; that is, real relations are always consequent upon something absolute *in inferioribus*, but not in God, for whom *esse ad aliquid* is an *esse non accidentalis*[1035].

Nevertheless, for every relation there must exist a substance as its foundation (i.e. subject), for which reason Albert, in accord with St. Augustine, affirms that every relative thing is also something other than relative. This something other is substance as a foundation of or ground for relations, though not necessarily to be understood as a substrate of inherence, for, in God, that foundation differs from the relations only according to mode of signification, and not according to essence. In inferior creatures, it differs according to essence, as the relations are accidents inhering in the substance. The foundational something other will, of course, be the supposital reality, that is, the substance taken as subject of attribution, for which reason we may refer to it as "hypostasis" or "supposit". What we are identifying here is the hypostasis insofar as absolute, in contrast to hypostasis insofar as relative. The first is the hypostatic relation according to its substantial reality, while the second is the same hypostatic relation according to its relative opposition. The two differ, of course, only in mode of sig-nification[1036].

Personal being

Distinction between what is *ab alio* and what is *non ab alio* is recognized within the Trinity itself, since the name "Father" implies that some-

---

cipit illud per aliquid absolutum, quod est causa individuationis eius. Et relatio, qua refertur ad illud, est consequens illud distinctum. Ergo esse non accipit a relatione"– Albert, *Sum. theol.*, I, tr. 9, q. 38, obj. 10, ed. Colon., vol. 34, p. 289.

[1034] Namely, as concerns what we consider to be the relative principle of their indi-viduation admitting of a simultaneous priority and posteriority with respect to the individuated substance, a point which, at least with regard to the mutual priority between certain relations and their subjects, is supported by both Albert (cf. *I Sent.*, d. 26, a. 6, ad 6) and Thomas (cf. *Sum. theol.*, I, 45, 3, ad 3).

[1035] *"Dicendum est, quod non procedit, nisi in his in quibus relatio dicit accidens"*– Albert, *Sum. theol.*, I, tr. 9, q. 38, ad 10, ed. Colon., vol. 34, p. 289.

[1036] *"'Omne relativum est aliud quam relativum'; sed in inferioribus est aliud secundum essen-tiam, in quibus relatio est accidens, in divinis autem sufficit, quod sit aliud secundum modum supponendi vel significandi. Est enim hypostasis sive suppositum, quod est aliud in significando vel supponendo, quam sit relativum, quia aliud attribuitur supposito et aliud re-lativo; suppositum enim absolute dicitur, relativum ad aliud"*– Albert, *Sum. theol.*, I, tr. 9, q. 38, ad 11, ed. Colon., vol. 34, p. 290.

thing else is from him, while the signification of the name "Son" implies that he be from another. This distinction, however, does not concern substantial being, since we have seen that the entire Godhead is situated as *ens non ab alio*, and since God's being cannot admit of composition or division. It follows, therefore, that a true procession of one thing *from another* in the Trinity must operate at a level other than substantial being. Yet, if what proceeds is not to be nothing at all, it must also be some kind of being, and Albert will label this *personal being*[1037]. Now, since there are not two kinds of being in God, the notion of personal being will have to pertain, if it truly implies an *esse*, to the singular and simple divine essence or *esse*. How then can it be said that several personal beings are generated or spirated? Because personal being is distinguishable from essential being, not according to being, but according as the same one being is hypostatized in different ways. Thus the divine *esse*, as it is in the Father, *is* the being of the "personal being" of the Father; that is, it is the being implied in the expression "personal being" when attributed to the Father. Similarly, the same divine *esse*, according as it exists in the Son, is the being of the "personal being" of the Son. The "personal being" then may be said to be *ab alio* or *non ab alio*, leaving the substantial being of all three persons intact. Consequently, *"non ab alio esse"* and *"ab alio esse"* distinguish the persons according to personal being. In fact, Albert tells us, these two modes of being are, from a notional point of view, prior to and the cause of the singular modes of existence constituting the persons – and we have just seen that the names indicating these singular modes of existence, namely, "Father" and "Son", imply in their very signification, respectively, *non ab alio esse* and *ab alio esse*[1038].

That personal being signifies something distinct from natural being is clear from the qualification according to which Albert designates the kind of being commonly shared by the three persons of the Trinity and identical to each: *"quia tres personae secundum deitatem ha-*

[1037] *"Significatur etiam necessario 'ordo naturae, quo alter est ab altero', quia in ipso nomine, quod est pater, significatur, quod alius ab ipso sit; et in ipso nomine, quod est filius, significatur, quod ab alio sit. Et in ipsa oppositione significatur, quod in esse personali distincti sunt"* – Albert, *Sum. theol.*, I, tr. 9, q. 38, sol., ed. Colon., vol. 34, p. 289.

[1038] *"'Non ab alio esse' et 'ab alio esse' secundum propriam rationem dicunt id quod antecedit secundum intellectum et causat et confert esse secundum modum existentis, quod existit per se solum secundum singularis existentiae modum; et ab hoc habet, quod distinguit personam secundum esse personale"* – Albert, *Sum. theol.*, I, tr. 9, q. 38, sol., ed. Colon., vol. 34, p. 289.

bent idem esse"[1039]. Personal "being", Albert tells us, is ascribed inasmuch as designating the personal and incommunicable reality of a thing; it directly refers therefore to the very personal state of an individual, the fact of an individual's enduring character as a person, and indirectly to that which makes a person to be the person that he or she is. The personal being of the Father – or, simply, the being of the Father taken according as pertaining to him alone – is precisely that he be Father. Similarly, the "being of the Son" is affirmed precisely insofar as he is Son. The "being" ascribed here is not to be taken in an absolute sense or *simpliciter*, but as signifying the act or existence of an individual according as that individual is distinguished through an incommunicable property (which is precisely what establishes him in personal existence); since the *ratio* of incommunicability in the Trinity is nothing other than the opposition had from the relations of origin, personal being in the Trinity is therefore a "relational being"[1040]. [Note that, abstraction had from the personal relations in God (a personal mode revealed to us only through revelation), God would nevertheless remain everything that a person is: a singular subsistent being of an intellectual nature, discrete from every other substance or subsistence[1041]. The concept of personality, however, would be different, inasmuch as distinction from every other person would obtain only according to discrete natural attributes and according to substance, and no longer according to relations able to distinguish several things of the same substance[1042]].

In response to an objection aimed at dissolving the notion of relation as a viable foundation of personhood, Albert explicitates the role

---

[1039] Albert, *III Sent.*, d. 6, a. 1, ad quaest. 2, ed. Borgnet, vol. 28, p. 123.

[1040] *"Esse personali, inquantum personale est et incommunicabile, hoc enim est esse patris per hoc quod pater est, et esse filii per hoc quod filius est, et esse spiritus sancti per hoc quod spiritus sanctus est... esse personale et persona non est simpliciter absolutum... sed intelligitur 'distinctum incommunicabili proprietate', quae rationem incommunicabilitatis non habet nisi ex oppositione relationis originis"* – Albert, *Sum. theol.*, I, tr. 9, q. 42, c. 2, ad quaest. 3 & ad 12, ed. Colon., vol. 34, p. 327. Summarizing his commentary on Albert's treatment of relation as distinctive and constitutive of the divine persons in *I Sent.*, d. 26, A. Pompei makes a very clear application/formulation of the concept of personal being as it pertains to God: *"l'ipostasi divina è costituita solo da ciò che la distingue opponendola a un'altra, poichè l'essere di essa consiste nell'essere distinta per opposizione"* – op. cit., p. 281.

[1041] *"Si autem fiat abstractio a personalitate quam determinat fides in divinis, tunc adhuc remanet secundum intellectum Deus, ens unus in se rationalis naturae, et discretus suis attributis ab omnibus aliis, et ita manebit in ratione personae"* – Albert, *III Sent.*, d. 5, a. 2, sol., ed. Borgnet, vol. 28, p. 98.

[1042] *"Sed verum est, quod non est eadem ratio personalitatis, quia relationibus non distingueretur a re ejusdem naturae, sed attributis distingueretur a rebus aliarum naturarum"* – Albert, *III Sent.*, d. 5, a. 2, ad 3, ed. Borgnet, vol. 28, p. 99.

of the *proprietates personales* with respect to the difference they effect. The objection states that, if relation is the sole predicamental reality in God able to introduce the distinctions constituting personality, no personal distinction would result at all, since relation can effect nothing more than a difference *in modo se habendi ad aliquid,* and a variety of such modes can exist in one and the same person. While it is true that a mere manner of being constituted or situated with respect to another is insufficient in itself to constitute the perfection of personhood, the personal properties in the divinity, the relations of origin, result in something more, namely, diverse modes of existing in the common divine nature. The persons are not distinguished in personal being merely according as one comes from another or not, but according as they exists in the divine nature (or possess that nature) according to that order. Only in this way are the relative modes in question existential modes, i.e. unique instances of personal being[1043].

Personal being, we observed, refers to the being of the hypostasis *as such.* In a certain respect, therefore, the notion of personal being could be interpreted as signifying the formality of the concept of hypostasis; that is, in such a way that the term "being" in the expression "personal being" operates in a non-technical sense indicating only the proper formality of personhood, i.e. what it is to "be" a person, and not the *esse* belonging to it according as that *esse* is distinctly instantiated. According to this, the expression "personal being" would possess an almost exclusively logical value. On the other hand, the hardy employment of the expression by both Albert and Thomas, particularly in contexts of affirming the reality of the relations which the persons are, encourages an ontological interpretation of "personal being" such as the one we have given above. Both interpretations, in our opinion, are one hundred percent correct.

Relation not only distinguishes, but constitutes the persons

In the preceding paragraphs we established the legitimacy of predicating relation in the Godhead as well as the role of relation in distinguishing the hypostases. But relation in God is not only the principle

---

[1043] *"Relatio, quae est proprietas personalis in divinis et relatio originis. Et ideo non facit solum modum diversum se habendi ad aliquid, sed etiam diversum modum existendi in una natura, quae communis est re, et diversum modum habendi naturam illam"* – Albert, *Sum. theol.,* I, tr. 10, q. 46, ad 9, ed. Colon., vol. 34, p. 363.

of distinction, but the very substantive reality of the distinguished thing (not, of course, insofar as relation – *qua talis* –, but inasmuch as it is *in God*, in whom everything is predicated *ut idem in re*)[1044]. Consequently, taken away the properties of origin in God, the persons themselves disappear. Similarly, in creatures, the principle of their individuation, though not necessarily identical to the individuated substance[1045], nevertheless enters into the essential structure of the individual as such. We shall come back to these dimensions of the personal principle when considering the *proprietas* as such: in God, the relation in its ontological structure, according to which it constitutes and is identical to the persons; in creatures, the principle of individuation considered in its relation to the substance it individuates[1046]. But first we must discuss another concept which, logically speaking, is more immediately connected with the function of the *proprietas* as distinguishing and multiplying, namely, that of "number".

Conclusion

In addition to the *ratio* of subsistence, explaining the possibility of several persons requires identifying the *ratio* of distinction. The basis for supposital distinction and personal singularity with respect to a common nature was shown to be quite different in God and creatures. For the creature, one individual is distinct from another according to a division of nature, while persons in the Trinity are distinguished only through the relations pertaining to origin. It is precisely with respect to the latter feature, peculiar to God, that the Victorine definition of person presents certain advantages over the Boethian definition. Richard's formulation neither entails nor suggests a division of nature, the differences (which are the cause of number) described as purely existential modes.

Whether the differences are essential or *ex*istential, they have their principle in the *proprietas personalis* through which a multiplicity of persons is affirmed. That *proprietas*, in the Trinity, is nothing other than relation (founded on origin), the opposition of which extrinsi-

---

[1044] For an appreciation and penetrating examination of these diverse functions of relation in God, see A. Pompei, op. cit., p. 268, 276, 275-283, 288.

[1045] We say "not *necessarily*" so as to leave room for eventual arguments in favor of a nominalist understanding of individuation according to which individuals are individuated *ex seipsis* and the concept of "individuation", taken as a sort of ontological step, is a pure fiction.

[1046] Cf. infra, "PROPRIETAS AS CONSTITUTIVE OF ALL PERSONS", p. 436.

cally divides one term from another. Relation is the unique source of distinction in the Trinity because it introduces no substantial difference between them. The special *ratio* of relation expresses but a *respectus ad aliud*, and this without necessarily implying the inherent being of accidental *kinds* of relation. As a result, the divine simplicity is not withdrawn by its notion, though it truly add a determination not included in the notion of the essence (wherefore "hypostasis" can truly be said to add something to "essence").

Notwithstanding the purely relational quality of the divine *proprietates*, and the corresponding relative constitution of the different persons, the persons cannot be said to be relations and nothing more; indeed the relative reality was seen to require a substantial term, and the hypostasis is nothing relative at all if it is not also an absolute being of natural perfection. The combination of these aspects is expressed in the notion of "personal being" which signifies the natural hypostatic being according to its distinctive possession and the incommunicable mode.

II.6. NUMBER IN THE TRINITY AND IN MEN

Number in the Trinity is secundum quid

When an enunciation of faith asserts that there are three persons in God, number is obviously affirmed. Number, and unity or oneness, however, depend for their affirmation upon the verification of being, for a thing is said to be one because it has one being, or many, because it has more than one being. Does the numerical affirmation of the doctrine of the Trinity therefore somehow derogate the unity of being in God by positing a plurality of beings? Not if we understand the kind of number predicated of the Trinity and the fact that the kind of number affirmed determines the kind of being entailed. In the Trinity, number is not ascribed *simpliciter*, as in creatures, but *secundum quid.* Number cannot be predicated *simpliciter* of God, for to do so would denote an absolute discreteness of the numbered entities, according to the division of being inferred (or presupposed) by the attribution of number. The result would be a differentiation *simpliciter* between the numbered individuals, that is, a differentiation in substantial being. Such a differentiation, moreover, implies the division of something with respect to which the numbered entities are one, something under which they are commonly (at least analogously) contained, as, for example, two men are precisely different from one another as distinct individuals of the common human species, a species which is divided in the numbered individuals according to being. Since, therefore, the substance by which the divine persons are united is undivided, and the persons of the Trinity are not three gods but one, it follows that number cannot be attributed to God in this way. Number is therefore predicated in God *quidam* or *secundum quid*[1047].

What is the sense of this numbering and from where does it come? The very attribution of number is due to the incommunicable proper-

---

[1047] *"In trinitate... non est simpliciter numerus sicut in creaturis... Omne enim quod in numerum ponitur, sub aliquo communi quod secundum esse divisum est in numeratis, in numerum ponitur, ut Socrates et Plato duo homines, homo et asinus duo animalia, homo et lapis duae substantiae, substantia et accidens duo entia... intelligitur hoc de differentia simpliciter, hoc est de differentia substantiali, quae dividit esse substantiale... cum in divinis substantia uniens personas in personis numeratis non dividatur – pater enim et filius non sunt duo dii, sed unus –, non potest in divinis simpliciter esse numerus, sed numerus quidam, numerus sci-*

ties by which several persons are distinguished. The mode according
to which their distinguishing role is performed in the Trinity is therefore quite different from that according to which the individualizing
principles in created substances effect a division in substantial being.
The *proprietates* in the Trinity distinguish persons in a manner which
divides nothing intrinsic to what the persons are; rather, because they
are relations, and relations establish a relative opposition, no intrinsic
opposition results, whence nothing intrinsic is divided and the persons are distinguished, not for what they are in themselves, but *ab extrinsecis*[1048].

Therefore, since the Father and Son remain *idem in intrinsecis* (one
in substance), number, simply taken, cannot be attributed to them,
for, as we have seen, such number simultaneously unites and divides
numbered things intrinsically, uniting them under a common essence, but dividing them within that essence substantially. Number,
then, is predicable of the Trinity only *quidam*: for they are not distinguished substantially, but only by relative opposition *ad aliud*; they are
several and numbered only insofar as distinguished *ab alio*[1049]. In creatures, the principle of number, that is, that by which one individual is
numerically distinct from another (*numerus numerans*), is distinct from
the distinguished individual (*numerus numeratus*) and introduces an

---

licet personarum, quae penes quiddam numerantur et non simpliciter" – Albert, *Sum. theol.*,
I, tr. 9, q. 42, c. 1, sol., ed. Colon., vol. 34, p. 324.

[1048] *"Talis enim proprietas per hoc quod relatio est et oppositionem relationis habet, nihil intrinsecorum dividit, quia ad nihil intrinsecorum habet oppositionem... si enim aliquis idem sit
pater unius et filius alterius, quamvis oppositas habeat relationes, in seipso non dividitur...
sed dividitur ab extrinsecis... pater non distinguitur nisi a filio et non a substantia divina"* –
Albert, *Sum. theol.*, I, tr. 9, q. 42, c. 1, sol., ed. Colon., vol. 34, p. 324. As a result of
the intrinsic (or substantial) indistinguishability, the differences between the Trinitarian persons and the fact that what is said of one person is not necessarily said of
another do not destroy the simplicity of nature. All such differences are reducible
to relative opposition which posits nothing *in* the subject (whence the numeration
is said to be attributed *ab extrinsecis* and not *ab intrinsecis*): *"non impedit simplicitatem
naturae, quod ea quae conveniunt uni personae non conveniunt alii, quia hoc est propter oppositionem relationis, et non propter naturae divisionem"* – Albert, *III Sent.*, d. 2, a. 12, ad
obj. 2, ed. Borgnet, vol. 28, p. 38.

[1049] *"Numerus autem, qui simpliciter est numerus, intrinseca dividit et communia substantialiter,
ut Socrates et Plato duo homines. Et ideo in divinis non potest esse numerus simpliciter, sed
numerus quidam... non distinguit autem nisi in oppositione ad alium, non ergo in numerum ponit nisi ad alium. Unde pater et filius non sunt duo, nisi inquantum pater opponitur
filio et filius patri... in divinis... non dividunt communem substantiam, sed determinant et
distinguunt ab alio tantum"* – Albert, *Sum. theol.*, I, tr. 9, q. 42, c. 1, sol. & ad 10, ed.
Colon., vol. 34, p. 324-325. The same reasoning is found in *I Sent.* d. 19, a. 12, ad 3
(ed. Borgnet, vol. 25, p. 528-529), where Albert explains that because the number
caused by the notions in God is not a *numerus simpliciter dictus*, no number properly
speaking may be affirmed, even though there is plurality.

additional element by which the being that is common to many is rendered indivisible in a numbered individual. Such a resulting number is a *numerus in esse*[1050]. Every creature is divided from every other according to being, even if many individuals proceed from something one. That something one, which is common to many, is divided through the properties and differences characteristic of and essential to the particulars beneath it. This is unassertible in God where the supreme simplicity maintains essential unity and identity even in the face of particularizing differences[1051]. In fact, the persons

---

[1050] *"Est ibi numerus numerans et numerus numeratus. Et numerus numerans est proprietas personalis per oppoitionem relationis distinguens in esse personali et non in esse simpliciter... in rebus creatis... numerus numerans relatus ad rem est id quod distinguit in esse communi et facit 'unum esse indivisum in se et divisum ab alio' per hoc quod terminat ipsum in se... et tale unum additum uni facit numerum in esse"* – Albert, *Sum. theol.*, I, tr. 9, q. 42, c. 2, sol., ed. Colon., vol. 34, p. 326.

[1051] *"Creaturae enim dividuntur secundum esse, licet procedant ab uno, et dividuntur secundum proprietates et differentias absolutas tam essentiales... illae propter indifferentiam simplicitatis summae remanent una et eadem et unum et idem"* – Albert, *Sum. theol.*, I, tr. 9, q. 41, c. 2, a. 2, ad 7, ed. Colon., vol. 34, p. 320. The concept of division is altogether unacceptable in God, whence our understanding of unity and plurality in God must be purified of the material aspects ordinarily characterizing it. Natural knowledge of the relationship between unity and plurality is complacent with (not obliging us to go beyond) a conceptualization corresponding to the examples of unity and diversity available to human experience and imaginative representation. These examples teach us that that relationship is (at least sometimes, if not always) reducible to a relationship between a whole and its parts, whether it be a question of an integral whole or a potential whole (the universal with respect to its inferiors). In all such relationships, a real diversity (albeit not necessarily real separability) is affirmed between the whole and its parts and the whole is understood as essentially composed. Nothing could be more repugnant to the divine simplicity and perfection which can neither be partial nor composed. Because every part is, as such, essentially imperfect, and because every whole implies composition, neither the concept of part nor that of a whole is permissible in God: *"nulla ratio totius et nulla ratio partis est in divinis; et hoc ideo est, quia omne totum ex suis partibus compositum est, et hoc dico si vere totum est; pars autem imperfecta est ad suum totum; et neutrum illorum competit divinis, quia simplicitas repugnat primo, perfectio autem repugnat secundo"* – Albert, *I Sent.*, d. 19, a. 12, sol., ed. Borgnet, vol. 25, p. 528. Distinguishing a plurality within a unity in God, therefore, compels us to expand our formal concept of the relationship between unity and plurality, so as to make room for another foundation of multiplicity (≠ diversity), namely non-accidental relation (*relatio subsistens*). One might nevertheless be inclined to believe that the exercise of human logic could produce an analogue of the kind of unity-distinction in God which, while admittedly more than merely logical, could perhaps be compared to the classic modern philosophical example of the "duck-rabbit" *gestalt* (which appears to us in different ways). Suggestive as it may be, the "duck-rabbit" *gestalt* is not properly analogous, since the duck and rabbit are not two distinct *things;* they are the same thing, only *viewed* differently (better comparable to modalism). The Father, Son and Holy Spirit, on the other hand, are really distinct existents. Moreover, the rabbit (or duck) is not identical to the whole since the rabbit is a function of the color and shape of the object; that is, the rabbit names the object on the basis of its accidents. In fact, the object

are the relations by which they are constituted according as everything which is in the divine essence *is* that very same substantial essence, and everything which is in the divine person *is* that very divine person[1052]; the *proprietates* said to be "in" and to distinguish the persons in God are the persons and the divine essence itself[1053].

In sum, according as things differ, so they are numbered; if, therefore, two or more things differ *in re*, their numerical distinction entail *numerus in esse, numerus simpliciter*, if two or more things differ not in substance but only in mode of signification (or by relative opposition alone), their numerical multiplicity entails a *numerus quidam* or *secundum quid*[1054]:

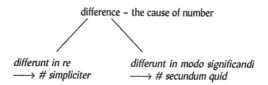

Creatures differ essentially and *simpliciter* from one another. Where there is a plurality of individuals, there is a plurality of being. In God, on the other hand, distinction is had only through relative opposition pertaining to origin, effecting number in *esse personali et notionali tantum*[1055].

itself is "rabbit like", and it is the rabbit *likeness* which we equivocally call "rabbit" (as though it were a real substance as such). Just like "white" and "musical" said of Socrates, "rabbit" and "duck" in the case of the *gestalt* stand for qualities of the object. Though all of these are distinct from one another as really different accidents, none of them are distinct things in themselves. The duck *as duck* is surely distinct from the rabbit, but the duck *as duck* is not the complete thing. The Son *as Son* is, of course, filiation; but filiation *is* the divine essence because the relation here is not an accident *of* the substance (the duck *as duck* is a property *of* the object).

[1052] *"Omne quod est in divina essentia, est idipsum quod divina essentia substantialiter, et omne quod est in divina persona, substantialiter est idipsum quod divina persona. Unde relatio, quae est in persona, est ipsa persona"* – Albert, *Sum. theol.*, I, tr. 4, q. 20, c. 1, ad 8, ed. Colon., vol. 34, p. 100.

[1053] *"Proprietas in personis secundum catholicam fidem et est persona et essentia divina"* – Albert, *Sum. theol.*, I, tr. 9, q. 39, c. 2, a. 1, sol., ed. Colon., vol. 34, p. 299.

[1054] *"Non simpliciter numerus, sed numerus quidam est in divinis relationibus et personis... differentia est causa numeri; et ideo secundum quod differunt, ita numerantur; non autem differunt re, sed modo significandi"* – Albert, *Sum. theol.*, I, tr. 9, q. 39, c. 1, ad quaest. 2, ed. Colon., vol. 34, p. 293.

[1055] *"Quaecumque enim distinguunt in creaturis, eo quod simpliciter et essentialiter differunt, simpliciter faciunt numerum essentiarum ad minus et numerum essentiarum ad minus et numerum secundum esse... In divinis autem... secundum oppositionem relationis originis in*

The nature of the distinctive principle determines the quality of number

For Albert, a thing is a determinate individual, a distinct entity, *divisum ab aliis* and *unum intra se contentum* through, or in virtue of, its *terminus*[1056]. To terminate a thing, therefore, is to give it indivisibility and to distinguish it from all others[1057]. That which terminates the human nature is a *proprietas* added to something one, through which *proprietas*, as was shown above, being is multiplied, *facit numerum in esse*. The *proprietates* of the Trinity also terminate several distinct individuals, *sicut numeri numerati*. But the distinction accomplished by these terminations only renders the persons *qua* persons *divisa ab aliis*, the *proprietates* not determining a distinction in substantial being (nothing absolute being added)[1058]. Indeed, the very distinctness of the personal relative element is due not to some relation it has to the essence, but because of its relation to the other correlative term, to which it is opposed[1059]. Even though the relation is truly identical to the essence, the fact that it is a real thing, a distinct *res*, depends upon its respect to the other person correlative to it. In this way, real personal multiplicity is achieved without disruption of the identity of the essence, since relative opposition, the unique source of distinction in the Trinity, cannot be had with respect to the essence. The personal *proprietas* possesses its distinction in virtue of relative opposition which – because every comparison to the essence pertains strictly to the ab-

---

esse personali et notionali quendam faciunt numerum" – Albert, *Sum. theol.*, I, tr. 10, q. 45, c. 1, a. 2, sol., ed. Colon., vol. 34, p. 354.

[1056] *"Et sicut in inferioribus quodlibet quod est unum, suis terminis intra se contentum est et ab aliis determinatum et divisum, et hoc significat haëc dictio 'unum'"* – Albert, *Sum. theol.*, I, tr. 9, q. 40, c. 2, a. 2, sol., ed. Colon., vol. 34, p. 312.

[1057] That a thing be established in distinct being, that it be numerically distinguished, specifically or individually, means that it has been "terminated" in the sense of complete with respect to ontological perfection. For the Albertinian concept of *terminus*, cf. especially *Metaph.*, lib. 5, tr. 4, c. 3, ed. Colon., vol. 16, p. 274-275; cf. *Super Dion. De div. nom.*, c. 1, 16, ed. Colon., vol. 37/1, p. 8, n. 76 - p. 9, n. 3; c. 4, 111, ed. Colon., vol. 37/1, p. 210, n. 14-15; c. 5, 20, ed. Colon., vol. 37/1, p. 314, n. 46-52; c. 13, 7, ed. Colon., vol. 37/1, p. 436, n. 16-21; c. 13, 16, ed. Colon., vol. 37/1, p. 441, n. 34.

[1058] *"Unum, quod est Socrates, et unum, quod est Plato, sunt duo in esse hominis, quia hoc distinguitur a Socrate et Platone, et ideo sunt duo homines, non unus homo... in divinis... numerus numerans est id quod distinguit in esse personali et facit unum terminatum in se et ab aliis determinatum in esse personali, inquantum personale est, et unum et unum facit duas personas... esse enim substantiale divinum nec distinguitur nec determinatur proprietate aliqua... in esse personali distinguuntur, et distinguens est incommunicabilis proprietas... Numerus autem numeratus hoc numero est pluralitas hypostasum sive personarum... relatio nihil addit rei absolute, addit tamen aliquid quantum ad modum significandi"* – Albert, *Sum. theol.*, I, tr. 9, q. 42, c. 2, sol. & ad 4, ed. Colon., vol. 34, p. 326.

[1059] Cf. A. Pompei, op. cit., p. 201.

solute level (*ut absolutum ad absolutum*), where the only relation is the
logical relation of identity (excluding opposition) – means that the
proprietas can only be distinguished and *connumerata* when taken with
respect to the other person[1060].

Distinct personal being is the term of the *proprietas.* Because the
personal being of a creature also entails a distinct instantiation of
natural being, its terminus involves numerical distinction at the natural or formal level and the principle of that distinction determines the
constitution of the individual essence in the formal causal order. In
God, to the contrary, the principle of distinction is not a principle in
the order of absolute formal causality; it does not determine the ultimate intrinsic actuality of the person, but only its distinctiveness with
respect (and always *in terms of* its respect) to another subject. The intrinsic act of the divine persons is nothing other than the source of
unity. Clearly, then, the persons are not numbered in an absolute
sense, but only relatively; they are not several in regard of their absoluteness, but in regard of their relativity (whence the persons are not
numbered *simpliciter*, even if the relations – from whose number personal number is deduced – *as such* are) [1061].

The notion of "terminus"

A thing is said to be terminated when it has been individuated, made
indivisible in itself and distinct from all others (either according to a
purely personal and non-substantial sense of otherness or according
to substantial diversity). In the *Metaphysica*, Albert defines *terminus* as
a perfection in some way and end of something. He then proceeds to
give four senses in which something may be called term:

[1060] *"Non autem est ibi praedicatio vel comparatio personarum ad essentiam nisi in ratione absoluti de absoluto; quidquid enim comparatur ad essentiam in divinis, comparatur ut absolutum ad absolutum; relativum enim non est ad alterum nisi ad id cui opponitur, et ideo ad essentiam comparatum non est ad alterum; unde ex illa propositione non sequitur, quod Pater
et Filius sint idem, sed quod in omnibus absolutis sint idem, et in his in quibus ad se invicem
referuntur, habent distinctionem"* – Albert, *I Sent.*, d. 19, a. 12, ad 5, ed. Borgnet,
vol. 25, p. 529; cf. A. Pompei, op. cit., p. 201, who notes that Albert's reproach of
Sabellius amounts to a criticism of having extended the modalism of the relations
at the essential level (their *total* real identity) to that of the relative order (cf. Albert,
id., ad 6).

[1061] Cf. Albert, *I Sent.*, d. 19, a. 17, sol., ed. Borgnet, vol. 25, p. 540-541; cf. A. Pompei,
op. cit., p. 204-205.

1.   In the sense of boundary – as that which is last and foremost
      of a dimensive entity, within which the entirety of the entity is
      contained, as, for example, the skin of an animal may be
      called its terminus, or as the entirety of the universe may be
      said to be contained within the heavens as what is foremost
      and the ultimate reaches of the universe.

2.   As the terms of motion – including both that *from which* mo-
      tion begins (*terminus a quo*) and that *toward which* it tends
      (*terminus ad quod* or *ad quem*).

3.   In the sense of final cause – which, taken in its proper exis-
      tence as the resulting end of an action, overlaps with the no-
      tion of *terminus ad quem*, but which, when taken as that which
      determines the movement of a being or intention, is the
      principle of all such things.

4.   As the quiddity of a thing – resolving into a duality of terms
      constituting the definitive substance, namely, that which is
      potential and expressed by the genus, and that which is act
      and expressed by the difference[1062].

It is the fourth sense which deserves our attention, for it represents
precisely the termination in the line of essence of the being of everything (or at least every definable entity[1063]). It is the definition which
expresses the potential and active parts of the essence of a thing.
Consequently, since the definition is the term of cognition, as cogni-

---

[1062] "'*Terminus*', *qui est perfectio quaedam et finis, 'dicitur' multipliciter. Dicitur autem terminus
id 'quod est cuiuslibet ultimum'. Et hoc quidem est quod occurrit in re 'primum, extra quod
nihil est' de re 'et infra quod' sic occurrens in re 'primum' sunt 'omnia' quae sunt rei. ... aliquod ultimum et primum, intra quod contineatur totum, sicut pellis est ultimum et primum
in animalibus, intra quod continetur totum animal, et primum et ultimum caelum est, intra
quod continetur universum. Alio autem modo dicitur ultimum terminus, 'quod est species
mensurae aut' mensurati 'habentis mensuram'... 'ambo' haec dicuntur termini, 'a quo' videlicet incipit motus et actus mensurantis 'et' ad 'quod' pervenit... Tertio autem modo dicitur
terminus, 'cuius causa' fit. Et hic terminus est causa finalis, quae est terminus intentionis,
quando in esse accipitur, licet sit principium omnium, quando accipitur in intentione. ...
Quarto autem modo dicitur terminus 'substantia cuiuslibet' diffinitiva, quae est quiditas sive
'quid erat esse' ipsius. Haec enim est duorum terminorum, potentiae videlicet et actus sive
generis et differentiae*" – Albert, Metaph., lib. 5, tr. 4, c. 3, ed. Colon., vol. 16/1,
p. 274-275.
[1063] That is, every entity which is definable in itself, and not necessarily according as we
are capable or not of defining it. Hence, every created being is included in this notion of termination.

tion is resolved in definition, the definition (or what is contained in it) will be the terminus of the being of the thing itself, according to the principle invoked by Albert that the principles of cognition and being are the same. Thus Albert affirms the quiddity to be both the term of being and of cognition, and that according to which *terminus* is principally said[1064].

If it is correct that *esse*, or its relative aspect[1065] (that is, the source of the incommunicable act of the individual, the principle of individuality) entering into the quiddity of the individual as such is what terminates a thing, then the *terminus* and unity of a thing are not immediately deduced from the form as such[1066]. Form (as a determining co-principle) may be said to give *esse*, but it is the effect of *esse* to terminate and distinguish (existentially) the thing – that is to say, individualization depends upon existential realization[1067]. Note that such a position is not inconsistent with a doctrine of matter as (proximate) principle of individuation, inasmuch as the union of this form with this matter does not occur outside of the context of the composite's existential realization (whence we understand the hylemorphic union as positing a thing in existence)[1068].

[1064] *"In his enim terminatur esse cuiuscumque rei sive entis. ... resolvetur in primi diffinitionem... Si autem diffinitio est 'cognitionis' terminus, oportet, quod etiam sit terminus esse 'et rei', quia eadem sunt principia cognitionis et entis... Terminus autem esse et cognitionis est ipsa quiditas sive substantia diffinitiva, et haec quidem principaliter dicitur terminus"* – Albert, *Metaph.*, lib. 5, tr. 4, c. 3, ed. Colon., vol. 16/1, p. 275. Cf. *Super Dion. De div. nom.*, c. 13, 7, ed. Colon., vol. 37/1, p. 436, n. 16-21: *"negatio consequitur ex actu formae, inquantum est terminus. Habet enim forma duos actus; eadem enim est quae dat esse et terminat materiam, et secundum quod dat esse, facit ens, secundum autem quod terminat, facit indivisum in se et divisum ab aliis, et sic facit unum"* (cf. H. Kühle, "Die Lehre Alberts des Grossen von den Tranzendentalien", in *Philosophia perennis*, Festgabe J. Geyser, Bd. I, Druck und Verlag von Josef Hobbel, Regensburg 1930, p. 137-138); cf. *Super Dion. De div. nom*, c. 11, 7, ed. Colon., vol. 37/1, p. 413, n. 56-65; cf. *I Sent.*, d. 19, a. 12, ad 2, ed. Borgnet, vol. 25, p. 528.

[1065] We are referring to the fact that *esse* is derived according to a relation of dependence upon the First Principle.

[1066] *"Secundum quod dat esse, facit ens, secundum autem quod terminat, facit indivisum in se et divisum ab aliis, et sic facit unum. Et quia terminare est posterius actus et dare esse principalior formae, ideo unum consequiter esse"* – Albert, *Super Dion. De div. nom*, c. 13, 7, ed. Colon., vol. 37/1, p. 436, n. 19-23 (cf. H. Kühle, "Die Lehre Alberts des Grossen von den Tranzendentalien", in *Philosophia perennis*, Festgabe J. Geyser, Bd. I, Druck und Verlag von Josef Hobbel, Regensburg 1930, p. 137-138).

[1067] Cf. Albert, *Sum. theol.*, I, tr. 9, q. 40, c. 2, a. 2, sol., ed. Colon., vol. 34, p. 312: *"Unitas rei forma rei est sub alia et alia ratione – forma enim est, secundum quod dat esse, unitas autem, secundum quod esse terminat et distinguit"*. Cf. *Super Dion. De div. nom*, c. 1, 16, ed. Colon., vol. 37/1, p. 8, n. 76 - p. 9, n. 3: *"unificans, secundum quod est principium esse; forma enim dat esse, et per hoc habet terminare rem, faciens eam divisam ab aliis, indivisam in se, unde res habet 'esse una'; unde non addit 'unum' super esse nisi modum, qui consistit in privatione"*.

[1068] A parallel conception of "matter", in the case of angels, will simply be the grade of potency inherent in the form that it is – where the principle of individuation is intrinsic to the form which is the supposit itself. Of course, Albert thoroughly refuses

Now, a thing is "one" insofar as terminated in itself and distinguished from others; and this occurs, Albert affirms, through the essential constituents of a thing[1069]. That which pertains to the essential constitution of a thing terminates it and makes it one, and that which is itself *unum* is so either through a "terminator" (i.e. principle of termination) distinct from itself (as part from whole) or through a "terminator" identical with itself (as in the case of God, and perhaps, if we follow the tradition, for of all simple or first substances inasmuch as they be terminated or distinguished from one another on the basis of the very substances which they are, the supposit itself being the foundation of essential distinction). For all human natures, including that of Christ, the term of the natural perfection (which is already essentially terminated, at least at the level of the common nature) is the hypostatic act according to which the nature exists as a concrete *res naturae*, that is, existential termination or unity. This perfection, as we have seen in Boethius, is also called subsistence (which properly belongs to the subsistent). Subsistence, therefore, is not the cause of termination, but the effect. Such a termination occurs through the addition of a principle extrinsic to the essence as such considered according to its pure formal perfection (even if it is essential to the individual existent *formaliter accipitur*). That principle is not subsistence, but the cause of subsistence, and subsistence, in the strict sense properly attributed to hypostases alone, is the term or final perfection of the causality.

The very unity of being in Christ, as Albert describes it, is a function of the termination of the human nature in the hypostasis of the

the ascription of spiritual matter to the separated substances, but he nevertheless recognizes a "material" aspect proper to every creature insofar as *receptive* of its being. Cf. Albert, *Sum. theol.*, II, tr. 1, q. 3, m. 3, a. 2, ad quaest. 3, ed. Borgnet, vol. 32, p. 38: "*spiritualia enim ex materia et forma composita non sunt. Sed materiale medium est inter materiam, et non materiam... et hoc modo concedi potest, quod omne compositum, est compositum ex materiali et formali, sed non ex materia et forma, quia quod est, secundum hoc materiale est, et quo est, formale, sed materia proprie non est nisi in corporibus, materiale autem etiam in spiritualibus est, et etiam in accidentalibus, eo modo quo diximus, quod primum formabile in unoquoque genere et subiectum, materiale est respectu omnium aliorum. Et hoc modo partes diffinitionis praecedentes, ad ultimam differentiam materiales sunt: et partes componentes, ad formam compositi materiales sunt*"; tr. 4, q. 15, m. 1, ad 2, ed. Borgnet, vol. 32, p. 205; *S. de Cr.*, II, q. 58, a. 1, ed. Borgnet, vol. 35, p. 500-502; *I Sent.*, d. 2, a. 20, ed. Borgnet, vol. 25, p. 79.

[1069] "*Cum una sit sicut terminata in se et ab aliis determinata et hoc fit essentialibus propriis, quae vel terminus eius sunt determinans ab altero vel seipso determinatus, eo quod simplicia prima seipsis differunt, oportet, quod 'unum' et talis 'terminus esse' secundum suppositum*

Word. The two essences in Christ are united in such a way that only
one hypostatic being results, such that the supposital being of the
concrete human nature is the supposital being of the divine person[1070]. This is possible only because the natures are united in such a
way that the being of one, namely the humanity, is terminated in the
being of the other, the latter being referring to that of the divine nature according as it is hypostatized in the person of the Word[1071]. All
natural being is thus terminated in the being of a supposit, and the
concreteness of a nature is an immediate consequence of the supposital being it receives. Christ's human nature, therefore, does not lack
that terminus by which a thing subsists; rather, the terminus for his
human nature is the supposital being of the Word, instead of the supposital being deriving from the principles of individuation proper to
every other human nature.

The reality of the relations (true number even if quidam)

Those things placed in distinction by the incommunicable properties
through which the divine nature is possessed are numbered in a true
and real manner even if not in absolute being. Albert attributes the
reality of the Trinitarian relations to the truly distinct personal being
following upon the perfection of personal or hypostatic distinction[1072].
The personal property is a principle of real opposition conferring distinct being (in the sense of personal being in the Trinity). The real,
self-contained supposital distinctness implied by these relations can be
contrasted with the kind of distinction or opposition resulting from
the different functions attributable to a point. Whether the point
perform the role of principle, establishing continuity, or terminating
an object, the opposition of the particular relation does not distin-

---

unum et idem sint, differentia tantum in modo significandi" – Albert, *Sum. theol.*, I, tr. 9,
q. 40, c. 2, a. 2, ad 6, ed. Colon., vol. 34, p. 313.

[1070] This understanding has its definitive expression in terms of the "integration of the
human nature into the singularity of the Word": cf. Albert, *II Sent.*, d. 3, a. 5, ad 2,
ed. Borgnet, vol. 27, p. 70; *III Sent.*, d. 2, a. 5, sol., ed. Borgnet, vol. 28, p. 27; d. 5,
a. 11, sol., ed. Borgnet, vol. 28, p. 110. The development of this perspective constitutes the principal objective of our study to follow on the Incarnation.

[1071] *"Qualiter duarum essentiarum sit unum esse hypostasis... non est intelligibile, nisi intelligantur illae essentiae uniri, ita quod esse unius terminetur in esse quod facit altera"* – Albert, *III
Sent.*, d. 6, a. 4, ad quaest., ad 1, ed. Borgnet, vol. 28, p. 131.

[1072] *"Totam divinitatem incommunicabili proprietate possidere... et id in quo ponit distinctionem,
ponit in numerum verum et realem veritate esse personalis et realitete, quia persona est ens ratum et perfectum, et hoc numeratur in divinis"* – Albert, *Sum. theol.*, I, tr. 9, q. 42, c. 2,
ad 5, ed. Colon., vol. 34, p. 327.

guish another truly diverse entity, but merely distinguishes something according to its diverse locale and results therefore only in a diversity according to reason. Such a diversity is not a diversity of supposit, such as that achieved by the relative opposition of the personal properties in the Trinity establishing truly distinct subjects of being[1073]. The opposition means that the terms of the relation are really distinct, since the *proprietas* of one cannot be had in the other. And because relation in God, as we have seen, takes on a substantial mode of predication[1074], the divine relations are not accidents *in* the substance, but identical to the substance (the latter taken according to hypostasis). Because it is divine, the relation cannot have the accidental character proper to relations in creatures, but is identical the very divine substance, and this, however, not "by mode of essence", but "by mode of supposit". That is, relation in God is the divine substance insofar as it is a divine person (formally constituted by the relation as its personal property) who is the divine nature hypostatically signified. Note that relation here is envisaged according as it is constitutive of persons and not simply according as it is relation (pure reference to another)[1075]. In this way, the divine relations have the very subsistent being of the divine nature and the distinctive personal being of the hypostases; they are, in a word, "subsistent relations". When explaining what Damascene meant in contrasting Trinitarian unity *in re* to hypostatic diversity *in ratione*[1076], Albert clearly affirms that the persons are not diversified by the power of our intellects alone, they are not distinct *in ratione tantum*. The *ratio* of Damascene is, according to Albert, affirmed in a general sense able to be taken as designating either the ratiocinative act of our intellects or the act of a thing itself. Referring to the act of the hypostases, that *ratio* designates the *res naturae* which, because it is not numerically unique in an absolute sense and possesses its distinctiveness from relation alone, is said (in a loose

---

[1073] *"In puncto autem, secundum quod est principium, medium et finis, non ponit relationem ad oppositam rem, sed ad oppositam positionem in continuo sive ad oppositum situm; et ideo in puncto non facit diversum ens ratum, ut suppositum a supposito diversum est, sed facit diversum secundum rationem, quae causatur ex diversitate situs, ut DICTUM est, ex qua provenit diversitas actus puncti et non suppositi, secundum quod punctum aliud est actione principians, copulans et terminans, non tamen aliud supposito vel subiecto"* – Albert, *Sum. theol.*, I, tr. 9, q. 42, c. 2, ad 5, ed. Colon., vol. 34, p. 327.

[1074] Cf. supra, "FIRST DIVISION OF ENS", p. 189-195.

[1075] Albert distinguishes relation as relation, as a property of the person, and as constitutive of the person, i.e. as a personal property: cf. *I Sent.*, d. 8, a. 34; d. 26, a. 9; *Super Dion. De div. nom.*, c. 2, n. 25-26; cf. G. Emery, op. cit., p. 100-101, 153; cf. infra, "PROPRIETAS PERSONALIS AND PROPRIETATES PERSONAE", p. 450.

[1076] Cf. supra, "DIFFERENT KINDS OF MODES OF DISTINCTION", p. 303-303.

sense) to be identified *ut ratione*, or *ut relatione* (while the *res* which is
the common nature – and the foundation of the *res naturae* which the
persons are – is identified *ut res secundum esse*) [1077].

Essential oneness and personal number do not conflict

The unity of the divine essence is not opposed to personal plurality.
We know this not only from revelation, but also on the basis of a philosophical reflection concerning the things which may be posited in
the context of the Trinity. A precise notion of relation provides the
basis for distinction. The relations in question cannot add anything
to the substance, for if they were to add something, they would introduce composition [1078]. As we have seen, predicating relation, and especially the relation of origin, through which one thing is from another, states nothing more than that something's being be *ad alterum*,
and consequently adds nothing essential to the being which it situates
ad alterum and divides nothing except those things which its concept
places in opposition [1079]. Because the *proprietates* determine a multiplicity only according to the opposition between them (i.e. only accor-
dong to their correlativity), the kind of number pertaining to the
Trinitarian persons does not exclude the simplicity or unity of the

---

[1077] *"Ratio dupliciter dicitur, scilicet prout est actus ratiocinantis tantum et prout est actus rei...
sicut dicitur universale ratio non ideo, quod tantum sit in nobis sive in nostra ratione, sed
ideo quia est res non in uno absolute accepta, sed quae in collatione accipitur, quae est in
multis et de multis, quam collationem facit ratio. Et hoc modo Damascenus accipit rationem.
Et sic ratio ad rem refertur, sicut res quaedam est, quod conferendo accipitur ut unum in
Socrate et Platone et de Socrate et Platone, et res, in qua est et de qua est realiter, distincte accipitur Socrates et Plato. In divinis autem e converso est, quia natura accipitur ut res eadem
secundum esse in patre et filio, pater autem et filius ut ratione, hoc est relatione, distincti. Et
ex hoc non sequitur, quod personae non differant nisi ratione, quae sit actus ratiocinantis. Et
hoc ignoravit Sabellius"* – Albert, *Sum. theol.*, I, tr. 9, q. 42, c. 2, ad II.6, ed. Colon.,
vol. 34, p. 327.
[1078] *"Nihil addit super substantiam, quia si adderet, compositionem induceret"* – Albert, *Sum.
theol.*, I, tr. 9, q. 38, sol., ed. Colon., vol. 34, p. 289. *"De relationibus enim secundum
originem dicit Boethius, quod nihil diversae essentiae addit relativum vel mutat. Quod autem
nihil addit vel mutat, compositionem non facit"* – Albert, *Sum. theol.*, I, tr. 4, q. 20, c. 1,
ad 1, ed. Colon., vol. 34, p. 98-99.
[1079] *"Dicendum, quod unitas divinae essentiae in nullo repugnat pluralitati personarum. Et
huius causam assignat Boethius, quod relatio et maxime relatio originis, qua alterum est ex
altero, non praedicat, nisi quod esse suum ad alterum est, et propter hoc nihil dividit, ut dicit
Anselmus, nisi ad quod ponit oppositionem. Nullam autem ponit oppositionem ad essentiam... relatio autem originis nihil praedicat absolute inhaerens, sed quod secundum esse quod
est, ad alterum est, et ideo nullam facit differentiam"* – Albert, *Sum. theol.*, I, tr. 6, q. 29,
c. 1, a. 2, sol. & ad 13, ed. Colon., vol. 34, p. 219-220. Cf. supra, 'RELATION AS UNIQUE
SOURCE OF MULTIPLICITY IN THE TRINITY', p. 386 (especially p. 386-388).

essence. Personal multiplicity excludes rather that the essence exist alone and that it be singularized in the sense of restricted to one individual[1080].

On the basis of relation, then, distinct supposits are determined within a single nature. To the objection that distinction in supposit, and therefore in supposital being, entails distinction in natural being[1081], Albert observes two kinds of being pertaining to the supposit which have to be distinguished. Being can be ascribed to something according to the respect obtaining between that thing and something else, *ex ratione relativi*, or it may be ascribed according to the thing's nature, under which the supposit is said to substand. With respect to the first kind of being, it is correct to maintain that a distinction in supposit entails a distinction in the being of the supposit. But this is being *ad alterum* and not absolute being. With respect to the second kind of being, however, distinction of supposit does not necessarily also result in a distinction of being (here being a question of absolute being). This is because, some supposits (the divine supposits) may be distinguished from one another purely on the basis of relative opposition. With respect to the second (absolute) kind of being, relation introduces no opposition, and therefore adds nothing to the natural being on the basis of which to distinguish it from another natural being. Personally unique being, therefore, will be situated in the Trinity at the level of relational being, which concerns nonetheless real being, albeit not absolute. It was the failure to appreciate these distinctions, Albert points out, which led Arius to posit distinction in the natural being of the Father and Son, and Sabellius to conclude from the indivisibility of nature to the impossibility of really distinguished persons[1082].

[1080] *"Si trinitas numerabilis dicatur, hoc intelligitur de numero quodam, scilicet notionum et personarum, et non simpliciter, nec iste numerus excludit simplicitatem vel unitatem essentiae, sed potius solitudinem et singularitatem"* – Albert, *I Sent.*, d. 24, a. 8, ad 2, ed. Borgnet, vol. 25, p. 621.

[1081] *"Distinctum in supposito distinctum est in esse suppositi; in divina natura distincta sunt supposita; ergo distincta sunt in esse suppositorum. Distincta in esse disctincta sunt in essentia, cuius actus est esse; in divina natura distincta sunt supposita; ergo distincta sunt in esse suppositorum, ergo distincta in essentiis"* – Albert, *Sum. theol.*, I, tr. 6, q. 29, c. 1, a. 2, obj. 7, ed. Colon., vol. 34, p. 218.

[1082] *"Ad id quod dicitur, quod distincta in suppositis distincta sunt in esse suppositorum, dicendum, quod duplex est esse suppositi, esse scilicet ex ratione, quod est esse respectivum et relativum, et de hoc verum est, quod probat obiectio, et hoc est esse ad alterum et non absolutum. Et est esse naturae, cui suppositum substat, et de hoc non est verum, quia ad illud esse relatio nullam ponit oppositionem et per consequens nullam ponit in ipso distinctionem. Et quia hoc ignoravit Arius, ideo dixit differre personas in esse naturali, sicut differunt in esse personali. Et quia Sabellius putavit, quod sicut unitas naturae praeiudicat pluralitati naturarum, ita*

An existential distinction of several "qui sunt"

The divine supposits are not distinguished in substantial being, as if
the Father, Son and Holy Spirit were *aliud et aliud* in the way in which
men differ from one another, but they are distinguished through relations of origin constituting distinct modes of existence, by which one
is *alius ex alio*, and not *aliud*[1083].

In God, contrary to what occurs for man, generation does not consist of an antecedent nature and a consequent nature, since in all such
cases the antecedent and consequent natures differ essentially.
Rather, in God, everything is entirely identical *in re*, and that which is
antecedent (in consideration of relations of origin) is equal in essence
with that which is consequent. Nonetheless, that which is antecedent
and that which is consequent differ one from another according to
modus existendi in virtue of the relations of origin (by which they are,
respectively, antecedent or consequent). Consequently, from one
point of view, namely, that of the thing in itself, there is no distinction, while from another point of view, viz. the existential[1084] mode,
distinction obtains. As a result, whatever the divine name we consider, whether personal (such as Father) or common (such as God)
the "what" behind the name is always the same. From which it follows
that wherever there is the Father, there too is God, and wherever is
the Son, there too is God – that is, that which is the Father is God, and
that which is the Son is God. But the converse does not follow, that
wherever there is God, there is the Father, or that whatever is God is
the Son. This is because the common name "God" signifies the same
thing differently than the personal names. While all is one *in re*, in
virtue of the distinctive existential modes distinguishing Father from
Son, the personal names have a restrictive mode of signifying not
identical to that proper to a term such as "God". "Father" (or "Son"),

---

praeiudicaret pluralitati personarum, putans, quod esse personale sit esse absolutum" – Albert, *Sum. theol.*, I, tr. 6, q. 29, c. 1, a. 2, ad 7, ed. Colon., vol. 34, p. 220.

[1083] *"Supposita in natura divina non distinguuntur suis distinguentibus ad esse substantiale
distinctum, ita quod in esse substantiali et absoluto aliud secundum esse divinum sit pater et
aliud filius et aliud spiritus sanctus, sicut Socrates et Plato distinguuntur sub homine, sed relationibus ad originem pertinentibus ad quendam existentiae modum, quo alius secundum
originem sit ex alio et non aliud ab ipso"* – Albert, *Sum. theol.*, I, tr. 4, q. 20, c. 1, ad 1, ed.
Colon., vol. 34, p. 98.

[1084] Existential mode is not intended to signify a mode of existence in the sense of *modus essendi*, but a mode of origin through which one's existence is exercised as one's
own (cf. Richard of Saint-Victor, *De Trin.*, IV, c. 19, ed. Ribaillier, 163a - 164a). Albert is careful to prevent any misinterpretation: *"In divinis autem, ubi relatio non dicit
diversam existentiam, sed tantum diversum existendi modum"* – Albert, *Sum. theol.*, I, tr. 4,
q. 20, c. 1, ad 6, ed. Colon., vol. 34, p. 99.

then, is not convertible with "God", because they differ in mode of signification. Thus, what is attributable to one is not always also attributable to the other. The persons are distinct; the Father is not the Son, and the Son is not the Father. But the nature is the same; what the Father is is precisely what the Son is. If the personal names did not differ from that of the common nature according to a mode of signification, we could never assert these two propositions together. For personal distinction which does not entail natural diversity, and which nonetheless really distinguishes the persons of the Trinity, it is necessary that the persons, though identical to the nature *in re*, be distinguished from that nature according to a *mode of signification* by which the name "person" is assigned. Otherwise, the ensuing convertibility between God and the person would entail the absence of any difference between the persons of the Father, Son and Holy Spirit[1085].

In the human person, on the other hand, it is not repugnant to the nature to be distinguished according to division, in such a way that we find a distinct natural being wherever we have a distinct person. In man, the terms of the relation of origin are really distinct both at a relative level and at an essential level, something which cannot occur in the Trinity where there can be no distinction according to substance due to the perfect simplicity of the divinity[1086].

Even, however, within the Trinity, where substantial distinction is excluded, it does not follow from this that the individual persons are accidentally distinguished or that the persons are persons accidentally. Indeed, the Father's paternity, whereby the Father is a person, is not different from his essence. But the identity between the Father's paternity and his essence does not imply that, because the Father generates, so his essence may be said to generate. For the terms "Father" and "essence" designate the same referent but mean different

---

[1085] *"In deo non est natura antecedens et natura consequens, quia in omni eo in quo est natura antecedens et natura consequens, per aliquid essentiale distincta est natura antecedens a natura consequente... in deo... in quo tamen omnino et omnimodis idem est res, quae antecedit, et res, quae consequitur, quamvis modus existendi secundum relationem, quae nihil addit vel mutat de absolutis, alius sit antecedentis et alius consequentis. Et super illum modum consequentia fundatur, cum dicitur: 'Pater est, ergo deus est'. Et non sequitur e converso; unum et idem enim est in antecedente et in consequente, tamen secundum modum significandi diversum, propter quem id quod attribuitur uni, non attribuitur alteri. Et haec est etiam causa, quare non convertibiliter se habent ad invicem"* – Albert, *Sum. theol.*, I, tr. 4, q. 20, c. 1, ad 2, ed. Colon., vol. 34, p. 99.
[1086] *"In humanis enim natura non repugnat distinctioni et divisioni, quin immo in generante et genito realiter et secundum esse distinguitur et dividitur. Quod nullo modo potest esse in di-*

things – that is, they are identical in extension but different in intension. To confuse what may be predicated of the two would be, in the words of St. Albert, to commit the fallacy of converting the *"quis"* into *"quid"* or *"quid"* into *"quis"*; it would consist in a failure to respect the differences in mode of signification telling us that what may be predicated of the *quid* is not necessarily also predicable of the *quis*. The above mentioned difference in intension is accomplished through diverse modes of signification. While there is no difference of *rem a re*, "Father" differs from the divine nature or *"Deus"* according to the criterion of the distinctness of signification: "Father" signifies distinctly (through the *proprietas* of paternity) what "God" signifies indistinctly[1087]. What may be posited, therefore, of one term may not always be posited of the other, and the attributes of each can differ. The essence may be the same as the Father, but "essence" signifies the thing as common, while "Father", on the other hand, signifies as singular. The term "Father" predicates the notion of substance insofar as hypostasis, and not insofar as substance as essence or nature[1088]. Essence and Father are predicable one of another (provided that they be taken substantively[1089]) because of their identity in virtue of the simplicity of divine nature. This is a concordance in supposition founded upon the identity in *re*. Here Father and essence are identical because they are substantively the same thing. But it does not follow from this that what pertains to Father in virtue of the mode of signification inherent in the term also pertains to "essence", since essence names the same *res* according to another mode of signification. That is to say that, while we may predicate the *"quis"* (hypostasis) of the *"quid"* (es-

---

vinis propter hoc quod natura divina est in fine simplicitatis" – Albert, *Sum. theol.*, I, tr. 7, q. 30, c. 3, a. 1, ad 7, ed. Colon., vol. 34, p. 234.

[1087] *"Pater enim non per accidens est pater, quia paternitas sua est essentia sua... Et quia in tanta simplicitate non est universale et particulare... cum dicitur 'pater est deus', idem penitus est in praedicato et subiecto sub alio modo significandi... 'deus' enim significat indistincte, 'pater' autem distinctum proprietate paternitatis... Unde cum dicitur 'Pater generat; pater est natura divina; ergo natura divina generat', incidit fallacia figurae dictionis; mutat enim 'quis' in 'quid', ac si idem attribuatur ei quod est quid, quod attribuitur ei qui est quis"* – Albert, *Sum. theol.*, I, tr. 7, q. 30, c. 3, a. 1, ad 7 & 9, ed. Colon., vol. 34, p. 234-235.

[1088] *"Non semper eadem sunt suppositione, ita quod supposito uno supponatur alterum; nec eadem sunt attributione, ita quod quidquid attribuitur uni, attribuatur et alteri. Et hoc est propter diversum modum significandi... essentia sit idem patri, tamen significatur ut communis re, pater autem ut singularis;... et pater praedicat substantiam, quae est hypostasis, et non substantiam, quae est usia sive essentia"* – Albert, *Sum. theol.*, I, tr. 8, q. 34, c. 2, ad 6, ed. Colon., vol. 34, p. 265; cf.: *"essentia absolute significat commune 'quo est' et non per modum hypostasis sive subsistentis"* – Albert, *Sum. theol.*, I, tr. 7, q. 30, c. 3, a. 1, sol., ed. Colon., vol. 34, p. 233.

[1089] Cf. supra, "THE PERSONAL NAME", p. 260-264.

sence) or the *"quid"* of the *"quis"*, what we predicate *of* the *quis*, we do not necessarily predicate *of* the *quid*[1090].

How the persons are three "things"

Since the term thing can be taken in either an essential sense or a personal sense, we can affirm one thing in the Trinity, if taken in the first sense, and three things in the Trinity, if taken in the second sense. Father, Son and Holy Spirit are three things in the sense of being three existents established as distinct entities in personal being[1091]. The Father, Son and Holy Spirit are three persons, that is, three distinct realities having in common that which it is to be a person[1092]. This is easy enough to affirm, but what exactly do we mean by saying "three realities"? Master Lombard has no qualms about expressing the personal reality of the members of the Trinity as such, for whom it is licit to say: *"tres personae, id est, tres subsistentiae, tres entes"*[1093]. The key to understanding how it is that we can admit several "beings" in the Trinity, Albert explains, lies in the difference between "being" as it is nominally said and as it is participially said. This difference is eloquently summed up by the words: *ens non est nisi essentia ens*[1094] – where the first instance of *ens* is substantive (nominally said) and the second gerundive and participially said. Albert's explanation[1095] can be condensed in the following diagrammatic representation:

[1090] *"Essentia enim ⟨est⟩ 'quid', hypostasis autem 'quis'; et praedicatur 'quis' de 'quid' ratione identitatis et simplicitatis naturae. Cum autem dicitur 'hypostasis est generans, ergo essentia est generans', procedit, ac si in supponendo et attribuendo idem sint 'quis' et 'quid'"* – Albert, *Sum. theol.*, I, tr. 8, q. 34, c. 2, ad 8, ed. Colon., vol. 34, p. 265.

[1091] *"Hoc nomen 'res' in divinis dupliciter sumitur, scilicet essentialiter, secundum quod dicit AUGUSTINUS... quod 'hi tres sunt una et summa res'. Secundo personaliter, secundum quod dicit, quod pater et filius et spiritus sanctus sunt tres res, hoc est qui sunt entes sive existentes entitate rata in esse personali"* – Albert, *Sum. theol.*, I, tr. 10, q. 43, c. 2, a. 2, ad 9, ed. Colon., vol. 34, p. 342.

[1092] *"Pater et Filius et Spiritus sanctus sunt tres personae, id est, sunt tres id habentes commune quod est persona"* – Peter Lombard: Albert, *I Sent.*, d. 25, D, ed. Borgnet, vol. 25, p. 628.

[1093] Peter Lombard: Albert, *I Sent.*, d. 25, F, ed. Borgnet, vol. 25, p. 632.

[1094] *"Dicit enim Anselmus in 'Monologio', quod essentia, esse, et ens, differunt, sicut lux, et lucere, et lucens, ergo ens non est nisi essentia ens"* – Albert, *I Sent.*, d. 25, a. 4, ed. Borgnet, vol. 25, p. 633. This statement, moreover, contributes to the metaphysical theory stating that there is no such "thing" as *esse*, but only an essence which itself is, *essentia ens* (≠ *essentia cum esse*).

[1095] *"Entes potest teneri participialiter, et sic conceditur, 'tres entes', hoc est, tres qui sunt... Si autem nominaliter sumeretur... secundum modum significandi, quia dicit concretive... ly 'tres' sit substantivum, et ly 'entes' sit activum. Si autem sumatur absolute pro essentia, et sit*

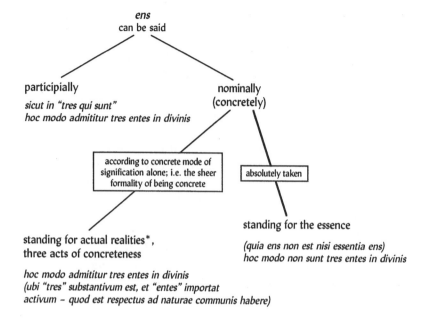

*Cf. Aquinas, *I Sent.*, d. 25, q. 1, a. 4: *tres entes* can be said
here because three relative forms are seen to really exist. The
name "things" can be plurally predicated, due to the several
relative forms, *habentes firmitatem in natura*[1096].

Accordingly, in responding to the question "three what?" or "what
three things?", we observe that, because person signifies *substantiam
subiectivam*, that is, the substance *insofar as* subject, to say three persons means to say three substantive realities, and this is the sense of
tres res[1097] – three substantive referents of being, regardless of the numerical status of that being as such. On the other hand, these three

substantivum, falsa erit locutio" – Albert, *I Sent.*, d. 25, a. 4, sol., ed. Borgnet, vol. 25,
    p. 633.

[1096] "*Est etiam in divinis quaedam forma relativa... secundum quod ab hac relatione sumitur
nomen rei, res pluraliter praedicatur, ut sint ibi plures tales formae relativae, et secundum hoc
dicimus, quod Pater, et Filius, et Spiritus sanctus sunt tres res, non tantum in anima, sed
etiam extra animam, habentes firmitatem in natura*" – Aquinas, *I Sent.*, d. 25, q. 1, a. 4,
ed. Vives, I, p. 319.

[1097] "*Quid subjective essent tres... aliquod substantivum quod diceretur in communi de eis, in
quantum plures sunt, et quia persona significat substantiam subjectam*" – Albert, *I Sent.*,
d. 25, a. 6, sol., ed. Borgnet, vol. 25, p. 635.

are, absolutely speaking, but one thing: *"ita tres subsistentiae dicuntur, et hae sunt una essentia"*[1098].

Substantial foundation for personal numerical unity

Yet, the requirements of numerical unity proper to every individual imply the fact that persons are necessarily substance, that is, that person necessarily signifies substance. This consideration raises the same difficulty of providing for the possibility that several persons not entail several substances. That difficulty is expressed in the context of numerical unity by the objection claiming that because nothing is individuated and rendered numerically one except through substance (according as every predicament besides that of substance signifies an accidental form unable to establish the simple identity of a thing), several persons recognized as several unities are numerically several substances[1099]. While the first principle may not be disputed, the conclusion is unjustified. The fact that the divine persons are three *unities* is indeed due to the substance, but the fact that they are *three* does not imply a plurality of substance. Their plurality is not an absolute plurality, whence they do not represent three diverse realities[1100]. Through the personal names, plurality *simpliciter* is not signified, but only a certain plurality, the kind of plurality which of itself indeed would not constitute something *unum* (*non efficitur unum numero*) absolutely speaking. The persons of the Trinity, however, because they and the relations which constitute them are identical with the divine substance, each are in fact *unum*, insofar as the same undivided substance[1101]. Substance, then, does, in fact, found distinct numerical unity: *"nullum aliud praedicamentum habet individuum nisi substantiae solum"*[1102].

[1098] Peter Lombard: Albert, *I Sent.*, d. 25, a. 6, H, ed. Borgnet, vol. 25, p. 635. Cf. Augustine, *De doctrina christiana*, Bk. I, c. 5.

[1099] *"Nihil individuatur et efficitur unum numero, nisi per substantiam... ergo plures personae quae plures habent unitates, sunt plures substantiae numero. Probatio primae. Omne praedicamentum aliud a substantia, non dicit nisi formam accidentalem; hoc autem non efficitur unum numero"* – Albert, *I Sent.*, d. 23, a. 3, obj. 3, ed. Borgnet, vol. 25, p. 589.

[1100] *"Pluralitas quae est simpliciter multitudo, non est in divinis... et cum non sit simpliciter pluralitas in divinis, nominibus etiam personalibus non est significata simpliciter pluralitas, sed quaedam tantum"* – Albert, *I Sent.*, d. 23, a. 3, ad 3, ed. Borgnet, vol. 25, p. 589-590.

[1101] Cf. Peter Lombard: Albert, *I Sent.*, d. 25, a. 6, H, ed. Borgnet, vol. 25, p. 635; cf. Augustine, *De doctrina christiana*, Bk. I, c. 5.

[1102] Albert, *I Sent.*, d. 23, a. 3, obj. 3, ed. Borgnet, vol. 25, p. 589.

From this principle, another set of conclusions must be examined: *"omne unum numero unitate substantiae est unum, et plura numero pluritate substantiae sunt plura"*[1103]. The first part, (A), claims that "every numerical unity is one through the unity of the substance". Whether or not this is true depends upon how one interprets the prepositional expression "through the unity of substance". The second part, (B), "that a plurality of realities are plural through a plurality of substance", is neither necessary nor always the case – as is demonstrated by the Trinity. The first affirmation (A) seems disaffirmed by the reality of the Incarnation, since the personal unity of Christ Jesus is not realized in virtue of a unity of substances. Therefore it appears (A) must either be rejected or modified. Considering the original premise, *nullum aliud praedicamentum habet individuum nisi substantiae solum,* we might note that only *predicaments*, whether accidents or substance, are taken into consideration. Consequently the conclusion (A) must be revised as: *"omne unum numero praedicamentale unitate substantiae est unum"*. From here, then, in order to deliver ourselves from Monophysitism with respect to the unicity of person in Christ, we must conclude either that person, in some strange way, is not a predicamental, or that the prepositional clause "through the unity of substance" does not demand a synthesis of the two natures in Christ. The former alternative, to treat person as an extra-predicamental reality, presents conceptual difficulty, since the predicament substance forms the generic part of its definition. On the other hand, the idea might provide an efficacious pathway for those who advocate a notion of personhood not based on substance. The second alternative seems more accessible. Christ is a numerical unity. This may indeed be understood to proceed from a unity of substance, since such a unity will not necessarily mean oneness of substance with regard to the united natures in the sense of Monophysitism, but might only imply that the personal numerical unity in question rely upon or exist through the unity of *at least one* substance (the full logical content of (A)). Thus, even in Christ, a unity of substance will make for personal unity (and any other unity for that matter).

The "at least one substance", however, makes room for different theories. One, that there is in Christ an abundant *ratio* for unity, since there are precisely two substances, at least one of which to ground the unity in question. Whatever numerical unity we consider, it must be rooted in some substance; what difference can it make, then, that

---

[1103] Albert, *I Sent.*, d. 23, a. 3, obj. 3, ed. Borgnet, vol. 25, p. 589.

there exist an additional substance, whether or not it also offer itself as a second ground for numerical unity? This interpretation makes no comment about the ontological status of the distinct natures in Christ, the question of their own numerical unity being left untouched. A second interpretation will admit that the only unity of substance required for personal numerical unity be that of the Word, but diminishes the sense of the individual unity and reality of the human nature, reducing the candidates for providing the substantial unity upon which to base personal unity to the divine substance of the Word alone. Accordingly, the unity or singularity of the human nature (if it is not to be denied) is not a reality had of the human nature itself, but the same singularity of the Word, into which it is assumed[1104]. That is, the singularity/unity of the Word *is* the singularity of the human nature, since the human nature is assumed into the singularity of the Word which is then conferred to the human nature which he assumes. Whether this, so to speak, "integration of singularity" is tantamount to an "integration of being" remains to be seen, but the theory is proposed in more or less similar terms by Albert himself when considering the definition of person in the context of angels and introducing a distinction between person in potency and person in act in order to accommodate the notion of assumability imposed by the Incarnation[1105].

Unity, besides its residence in substance, takes its precise *ratio* from form. Form, in the words of Albert, terminates that to which it gives being, and, as that through which a thing is what it is, form has three acts: *dare esse, dare rationem naturae* (from which the definition), *et rem terminare*[1106]. The latter act makes something one, indivisible and distinct from others; thus, *forma* is the cause of "one"[1107]. Now, this sense

---

[1104] Note that the fact that we here portray substantial unity (*unum*) itself as dependent upon a hypostatic principle does not contradict what we have said about hypostatic unity being based upon substance – for, even in the Trinity, the simple nature is not an *ens omnino perfectum* except insofar as hypostatically realized (a formal necessity for the concrete subsistence of any substantial nature). The substantial unity dependent upon hypostatization is none other than that of substance signified *ut subiecta*.

[1105] Cf. Albert, *II Sent.*, d. 3, a. 5, ed. Borgnet, vol. 27, p. 69-70.

[1106] *"Accipit autem rationem unius a forma, non secundum quod forma est, sed secundum quod terminat id cui dat esse; sunt enim tres actus formae sive ejus quo res est id quod est. Primus est dare esse. Secundus autem dare rationem naturae. Et tertius est terminare, et ab isto ultimo actu formae est ratio unius, quia per hoc efficitur in se indivisa, et ab aliis divisa"* – Albert, *I Sent.*, d. 24, a. 1, sol., ed. Borgnet, vol. 25, p. 606.

[1107] *"Dico igitur, quod omne quod est unum, est unum a forma; est autem forma esse et ratio rei. ... Et ab hoc ultimo actu res dicitur 'una'. ... scilicet ut est constitutum ab actu formae... et*

of oneness is proper to the several persons of the Trinity insofar as we are concerned with the substance which they are; but with regard to that unity proper to each person as a *distinct* individual, another *ratio* of oneness is involved. That *ratio* is rooted in the *proprietates*, and not in the form (except in the ideational sense of "form" pertaining to the conceptual foundation of "person", that is, in the sense of what is formal to the complete definition of person, which includes the notion of distinctness). To say that "the Father is one" implies, according to Albert, a distinct *notion* and a distinctness, as we have seen, *secundum quid*. To say, however, "the essence is one" implies indivisibility proper to the oneness possessed through the form, that is, substantial oneness (simpliciter)[1108]. There is no univocity between the unity predicated of the essence and that predicated of the person. In one case, it is a question of the unity convertible with being, in the other, that unity minimally necessary to constitute a plurality in number: *"differunt unum quod convertitur cum ente, et unum quod est principium numeri"*[1109]. This is an important distinction in distancing the notion of what constitutes a person from that which constitutes the individual nature by which that person is defined. The fact that, as we have just expressed it, one notion depends upon the other, in no way undermines the separation between the two; it simply entails a subalternate relation between the two notions[1110]. Now, the essence is distinguished (as something one) through itself, while person is so distinguished through its *proprietas*[1111]. And person *is* the essence, along with certain qualifications and according to a certain mode; the two signify the same thing; hence, there is no priority between them *secundum rem*[1112]. But they signify the same thing differently, according to a relation of priority *secundum rationem intelligendi* – the oneness of the essence pertains to the substance; the oneness of person pertains to the *proprietas*, but this latter oneness presupposes the former.

---

forma terminans est unitas rei" – Albert, *I Sent.*, d. 24, a. 3, sol., ed. Borgnet, vol. 25, p. 612.

[1108] *"Cum dicitur, Pater est unus, sensus est, id est, notione distinctus; cum autem dicitur, essentia una, sensus est, id est, in se indivisa, et ab aliis divisa; ergo non una ratione dicitur essentia una, et persona una"* – Albert, *I Sent.*, d. 24, a. 5, sed contra 1, ed. Borgnet, vol. 25, p. 617-618.

[1109] Albert, *I Sent.*, d. 24, a. 3, ed. Borgnet, vol. 25, p. 610.

[1110] As all persons are a certain kind of nature, but not every such nature is a person.

[1111] *"Unitas cum dicitur de essentia, dicit unitatem essentiae, et cum dicitur de persona, dicit unitatem personae, et licet essentia seipsa distinguatur, persona autem proprietate"* – Albert, *I Sent.*, d. 24, a. 5, sol., ed. Borgnet, vol. 25, p. 618.

"Essentia" signifies the nature according to its form, distinguishing itself (according to mode of signification) from "person" in the same way that *quo est* is distinguished from *quis est*[1113]. This difference is indirectly implied in the expression "three persons in one essence". In contrast, such a difference in mode of signification does not exist between the terms "person" and "God", since "God" is not said after the manner of a *quo est*, but, like person, concretely. Nevertheless, "person" says *suppositum*, whence it is pluralized, while "God" names the substance (albeit concretely), and not the *suppositum*[1114].

According as something is one in reason of the act of the form which gives it being (or is its being), several unities of personality are not affirmed in the Trinity. The principle of personal number is a unity other than that deriving from the act of the form. Number is said of the distinctly numbered realties/unities *secundum quid*. The divine persons are distinct (or many) *through* their *proprietates originis,* only on that account and from that point of view are they distinguished, and not *simpliciter*[1115]. The notion of number enters into the Trinity, only at a non-essential level of unity, *et hoc modo solo numerus positive cadit in divinis, et non numerus quod convertitur cum ente.* The numeral terms (such as "two" and "three") refer to relations and must be understood, therefore, as the consequence of the act of the distinguishing *proprietates,* and not of the form, for which reason they are not predicated essentially[1116].

[1112] *"Non sit prius et posterius secundum rem inter essentiam et personam, tamen est ibi prius et posterius secundum rationem intelligendi"* – Albert, *I Sent.*, d. 24, a. 5, ad 1, ed. Borgnet, vol. 25, p. 618.

[1113] Cf. supra, "PERSON DISTINGUISHED FROM NATURE OR ESSENCE", p. 290 (especially p. 293-294).

[1114] *"Essentia significat naturam per modum formae, et ideo licet sit idem in re cum personis, tamen differt in modo intelligendi, sicut quis est a quo est, et ista diversitas in modo significandi importatur in obliquo, cum dicitur, tres personae unius essentiae; Deus autem non dicit ut quo est... et ideo non talis diversitas in nomine in modo significandi importatur. ... persona dicit suppositum, et illud plurificatur in divinis... Deus autem nominat substantiam concretive, et non suppositum"* – Albert, *I Sent.*, d. 25, a. 5, ad 1-2, ed. Borgnet, vol. 25, p. 633-634. "God" names the substance or nature *ut in supposito* (≠ *ut supposita*). Cf. supra, "ON THE NAME 'DEUS'", p. 253 (especially p. 253-254).

[1115] *"Quarto modo dicitur 'numerus' ex parte rei numeratae secundum quid et non simpliciter, scilicet causata pluralitas a distinguente quocumque modo, sicut etiam dicimus punctum continuans in medio esse duo, eo quod ut duobus utimur uno, scilicet in ratione finis et principii, et dicimus centrum in circulo esse multum in ratione linearum exeuntium ab ipso ad circumferentiam, et hoc modo dicimus personam unam distinctam sua proprietate originis, et duas personas plures distinctas tali originis proprietate, et hoc modo solo numerus positive cadit in divinis... numerus non est simpliciter numerus, sed secundum quid"* – Albert, *I Sent.*, d. 24, a. 1, sol., ed. Borgnet, vol. 25, p. 607.

Notional act as the reason for numerical distinction

Distinction is seen to be a consequence of the personal properties[1117]. Numerical alteriety is thus said to derive from the act of the personal properties. This act, in one sense, is that simply of distinguishing (according to relative opposition). In another sense, it is nothing other than the notional acts corresponding to the notions distinctively denoting the divine persons (i.e. generation and filiation as proper to but one individual and as identical to the Father and Son, respectively). In this way, the notional acts are the cause of numerical distinction in the Trinity insofar as constituting the persons in unique ways[1118]. In another way, the notional acts are able to be described as responsible for numerical distinction, precisely as responsible for the relations which the persons are – but this, not with respect to the relation as constitutive of the person, but with respect to the relation *qua* relation (as expressing pure reference to another)[1119]. Relative opposition is, from this point of view, the consequence of notional act in God; consequently, an order can be established, moving in causal priority[1120] from notional act to relative opposition, and from relative opposition to numerical distinctness:

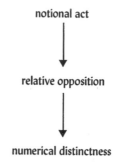

notional act

↓

relative opposition

↓

numerical distinctness

[1116] *"Talia nomina dicunt relationem, sunt enim consequentia actum proprietatis distinguentis"* – Albert, *I Sent.*, d. 24, a. 4, ad 1, ed. Borgnet, vol. 25, p. 616.

[1117] Note that the consequentiality here obviously concerns the order of our comprehension of the divine mystery which is simple and without movement or causality in itself.

[1118] *"Distinctio' igitur in divinis est actus notionem consequens, in quantum est proprietas personalis; sic enim distinguitur una persona ab alia"* – Albert, *I Sent.*, d. 24, a. 7, ed. Borgnet, vol. 25, p. 620.

[1119] Divine relation, as was mentioned, can be considered in three different ways; as a reference *ad aliud*; as a property of a person; and as a *proprietas personalis* constituting the person (who is the subject of and logically prior to the notional acts). Cf. Albert, *I Sent.*, d. 8, a. 34; d. 26, a. 9; cf. G. Emery, op. cit., p. 100-101.

[1120] Again, all anteriority and posteriority is *secundum rationem intelligentiae tantum.*

Order of nature in the Trinity

Notional principality, that is, the principles of origin which are notional, as opposed to essential (as in the case of the principles causing the existence of creatures), gives rise in God to an order of nature. This order results from the fact that the Father is the principle *from whom* the Son is said to proceed, while the Father with the Son are the principle *from whom* proceeds the Holy Spirit, according to a communication of identical nature. Accordingly, the Father is *"principium non de principio"*, the Son *"principium de principio"*, and the Holy Spirit *"principium de utroque principio"*[1121]. "Principle", then, in this context, stands for the notions by which the persons proceed and are distinguished from one another in an order of nature[1122].

The expression "order of nature" must be understood correctly, so as not to introduce the notions of posteriority and priority, cause and effect, temporality, etc. in the Trinity[1123]. The sense of the expression rests upon the diverse ways in which "nature" may be said in God, and a consideration of these distinct ways of signifying "nature" furthermore sheds light on the sense of the expression *"res naturae"* and on the sense of the inclusion of the term "substance" ("nature") in the definition of person. For Albert, if we are to accept the Augustinian position affirming an order of nature amongst the persons in the

---

[1121] *"Ex distinctione personarum ex relatione originis causatur ordo naturae in divinis... ordo talis causatur ex hoc quod 'pater est principium non de principio, filius autem principium de principio et spiritus sanctus principium de utroque principio'"* – Albert, *Sum. theol.*, I, tr. 9, q. 41, ed. Colon., vol. 34, p. 314.

[1122] *"Principium in divinis dicit notionem, qua procedit persona a persona et distinguitur in ordine naturae"* – Albert, *Sum. theol.*, I, tr. 9, q. 41, c. 1, a. 2, sol., ed. Colon., vol. 34, p. 316. The manner in which the term "principle" belongs to each of the persons of the Trinity is specified by Albert in such a way as to unify the matter of Trinitarian theology around this central concept (cf. G. Emery, op. cit., p. 42). Albert makes an elaborate and carefully nuanced use of the term, which may receive either a notional or essential sense. The notion has various applications in respect of the immanent and *ad extra* operations proper to God. While the Father, source of all of the divinity, is principle without principle, and the Son principle from principle, the Holy Spirit, who is *de utroque principio*, is not a principle of another divine person, but only with respect to creatures: *"per appropriationem convenit Patri esse altissimum, eo quod ipse principium est totius divinitatis, ut dicit Augustinus, eo quod ipse principium est non de principio; Filius autem principium de principio; Spiritus sanctus autem non est principium respectu alicujus personae, sed respectu creaturae tantum, et est de utroque principio, scilicet, Pater et Filio"* – Albert, *I Sent.*, praefatio, ed. Borgnet, vol. 25, p. 2; cf. *I Sent.*, d. 29, a. 3, ed. Borgnet, vol. 26, p. 77-78. For an analysis of Albert's treatement of the notion of "principle" and the relation between its different senses, see G. Emery, op. cit., p. 94-108.

[1123] There is no inequality or *gradus* with respect to the possession of the divine nature by the persons. Cf. Albert, *I Sent.*, d. 31, a. 14 & ad quaest. 1, ed. Borgnet, vol. 26, p. 119; *De incarn.*, tr. 5, q. 2, a. 5, ed. Colon., vol. 26, p. 216-217.

Godhead, the term "*naturae*", can only be taken in a way extraneous to the first and proper conceptualization of the notion of "nature". In an immediate sense, an order of nature designates natural priority and inequality; this is an order *simpliciter*, and this must be excluded from God. Thus, what is meant by the term "*naturae*" is something other than a strict and *simpliciter* order in nature and remains an order *secundum quid*[1124]. Just what is meant becomes clear when Albert distinguishes two senses according to which we signify nature in God. In a first and obvious way, nature can be signified according as it intends the absolute nature, or nature according to its first and strict conceptualization. In a second way, nature is signified as that by which or out of which that which proceeds proceeds. According to this sense, nature stands for the supposit which generates or produces – even if that supposit so operates in virtue of the nature it is and which is the principle of its operation. "*Ordo naturae*" is predicable in the divinity only when nature is signified in this second sense, which, although unable to be abstracted from the nature taken in the first sense, directly refers rather to the acting subject of the nature, or person[1125]. The inseparability between the two concepts of nature, or, rather, the dependency of the latter (supposital) sense upon the former (absolute) sense of "nature" elucidates the constitutional structure of person inasmuch as subject *of a given nature*, inasmuch as its concept is necessarily defined as underlying the nature, and inasmuch as it necessarily *is* a nature.

From the order of nature results a numerical plurality in the Trinity, according as the nature is the principle of the substantial emanation of one individual from another. The emanations are substantial, giving rise to perfect individual *res naturae* (since nothing is accidental in God), in contrast to the kind of emanation proper to the notional acts of the human soul, where the emanation of the intellect from the soul, intelligence from the intellect, and the will from both, produce nothing substantial or suppositally independent, but rather effect di-

---

[1124] "*Non dicitur ordo simpliciter, sed naturae sive originis, ut per hoc quod dico 'naturae', extrahatur ordo extra rationem propriam et primam, ita quod non sit ordo simpliciter... et relinquitur secundum aliquid et non simpliciter. Unde est ibi ordo aliquis et non ordo simpliciter*" – Albert, *Sum. theol.*, I, tr. 9, q. 41, c. 2, a.1, ad 1, ed. Colon., vol. 34, p. 317.

[1125] "*Natura in divinis dicitur duobus modis. Dicitur enim id quod est natura, et dicitur natura, unde natura, hoc est vis, 'ex qua pullulat pullulans'... Primo modo dicitur natura absolute et est... indistincta in divinis, et hoc modo non est ordo naturae in divinis. Secundo modo natura supponit pro persona consignificando notionem determinantem modum pullulationis, quo natura communicatur personae pullulanti a persona, ex qua fit pullulatio, et sic est in divinis ordo naturae*" – Albert, *Sum. theol.*, I, tr. 9, q. 41, c. 2, a. 1, ad 4, ed. Colon., vol. 34, p. 317.

verse potencies in the same person. The order of nature in God originates from the most perfect principle of emanation by which one thing proceeds from another, constituting the most perfect things of nature, hypostases which possess the entire nature in a perfect way through incommunicable properties in reason of which they are most truly persons[1126].

The singular personal modes of existence which the persons are cannot be had outside of the rational nature, nor can they be distinguished except through the act of the principle communicating the nature. Filiation, by which the Son is distinguished in personal being, is precisely a relation of origin specifying the communication of nature. Personal distinction, then, cannot be understood outside of such an "order of nature" which, while referring directly to the personal properties as relations of origin (having a certain order amongst themselves), is nevertheless founded upon the communication of nature resulting from these relations (or the act upon which these relations are founded). Inversely, as the acts of the principles communicating the divine nature (such as generation) follow upon the relations of origin constituting the persons as such, the very "order of nature" cannot be understood outside of a distinction of persons[1127].

This last observation points to a certain complexity in the logical order between the notional acts and the relations or persons. In specifying the manner in which the notional acts compare to the essence and persons, Albert explains that the acts must be referred to a power understood as the principle of the acts. When a power produces the entire being of a thing, it is necessary, moreover, that that power be rooted in the very nature of the one producing. Thus generation and spiration have their principle in a power of generation and a power of spiration, both of which are rooted in the nature (the

---

[1126] *"Ex ordine naturae numerus est in divinis, inquantum natura principium pullulationis est et emanationis substantialis unius ab alio, eo quod in divinis nihil est per accidens... substantiali enim emanatione non emanat mens de anima nec intelligentia de mente nec voluntas de utroque, sed ut potentiae naturales; et in talibus est ordo naturae secundum quid et non simpliciter, propter quod personas efficere non potest, sed facit differentiam potentiarum in una persona... In divinis autem ordo naturae est secundum perfectissimam rationem naturae, quae perfectissime principium est pullulandi et emanandi, quo alter procedit ex altero; et ideo in divinis constituit perfectissime rem naturae et hypostasim, quae, cum incommunicabili proprietate naturam possideat, perfectissime habet nomen personae et veritatem"* – Albert, Sum. theol., I, tr. 9, q. 42, c. 2, ad 9, ed. Colon., vol. 34, p. 327.

[1127] *"Singulares enim existentiae modi personales non sunt nisi in natura rationali, ut dicit BOETHIUS, nec distinguuntur nisi per actum principii communicantis naturam illam, quem actum semper comitatur relatio originis; et ideo talis ordo naturae sine distinctione personarum esse non potest, nec distinctio personarum intelligi potest sine tali ordine naturae"* – Albert, Sum. theol., I, tr. 9, q. 41, c. 2, a.3, ad 2, ed. Colon., vol. 34, p. 322.

first rooted in the nature *qua* nature, the second in the nature insofar as will)[1128]. In this way, the concept of a notional power enters into our intelligence of the Trinitarian mystery, as an intermediary between what pertains to the essence as such and what pertains to the strictly personal realm[1129]. Insofar as *power*, the power to generate concerns the nature, since every power is rooted in the nature. But when that power to generate is considered according to its *act*, it is grasped from the point of view of its *notional* quality corresponding to the personal domain: the power as such is essential, whereas generation pertains to the notional and personal order[1130]. Accordingly, the power to generate, because it signifies at once power in a general sense (rooted in the essence of the three persons) as well as power under the formality of generation (going beyond the essential notion of power by considering what is proper to the notional act)[1131], signifies both some *thing* in God – namely, the essence, the *quid est* (which is the power to generate insofar as power) –, and *someone*, or a personal property, forasmuch as it implies the generative act (insofar as it is a power *to generate*)[1132]. The same duality of signification can be expressed in a superior way by a single concept, by considering the power to generate, taken in its integrity, as rooted in the nature according as the nature is the person of the Father; that is, when the nature in which the power is rooted is conceptualized according to its identity to the Father, thus capturing the notional signification inherent in the expression *"potentia generandi"* (by tying its notion to the Father)[1133]. Having established the concept of a principle of the no-

---

[1128] Cf. Albert, *I Sent.*, d. 7, a. 2, ad 4; d. 11, a. 4-5, ed. Borgnet, vol. 25, p. 208 & 341-344. The present consideration of the relationship between the notional acts and the personal relations is dependent upon the study of G. Emery: *Les actes notionnels et la création: potentia et principium*, op. cit., p. 94-108 (especially p. 95-97, 100-101). On the concept of the generative power in God, its entitative content and the different ways in which that reality can be viewed, its essentiality and its notional dimension, see A. Pompei, op. cit., p. 111-115.

[1129] *"Potentia generandi secundum rationem intelligendi medium est inter pure essentiale, et pure personale"* – Albert, *I Sent.*, d. 7, a. 2, sol., ed. Borgnet, vol. 25, p. 207; cf. d. 11, a. 4-5, ed. Borgnet, vol. 25, p. 341-344. Cf. in this regard, A. Pompei, op. cit., p. 113-114.

[1130] Cf. G. Emery, op. cit., p. 96; A. Pompei, op. cit., p. 115.

[1131] Cf. Albert, *I Sent.*, d. 7, a. 4, ed. Borgnet, vol. 25, p. 210.

[1132] Cf. Albert, *I Sent.*, d. 7, a. 2, ed. Borgnet, vol. 25, p. 206-208; cf. G. Emery, op. cit., p. 96-97.

[1133] *"In divinis secundum modum intelligendi quem habere possumus, potentia generandi radicatur in natura secundum quod est persona"* – Albert, *I Sent.*, d. 7, a. 2, ad 4, ed. Borgnet, vol. 25, p. 208. Here we seem to reiterate in some fashion the earlier observed "intermediary" (or "in-between") realm of the *qui est* (the *quid* hypostatically signified); cf. supra, "THE PRECISE DENOTATION OF 'HYPOSTASIS', ITS DISTINCTIVE MODE OF SIGNIFICATION", p. 233 (especially p. 233 and chart on p. 237).

tional act, thus moving our understanding from the power of the essence to the personal properties, by reason of the proper character of the notions implied in the notional powers, Albert illustrates the dependency (*secundum modum intelligendi tantum*) of the notional act upon the essence, while intimating (in our opinion) a certain priority of the personal properties or persons with respect to the notional act itself, inasmuch as the notional power as such (taken in its integrity) implies the nature according to its identity with the person, which is to imply the person already in the very power to generate which logically precedes the generative act. Equipped with these distinctions, we are in a better position to appreciate the conceptual order established by Albert[1134] between the notional acts and the persons themselves.

Do the notional acts produce the persons, or do the persons vehicle the acts? Or, to put the question in other terms (in reverse respectivity), does the Father generate because he is Father, or is he Father because he generates? To this question, Albert responds that the Father generates because he is Father[1135]. The response rests upon the metaphysical doctrine that persons or supposits are the subjects of actions[1136]; thus the personal subject must precede the action according to reason, whence the person of the Father is antecedent in our understanding to the generative act. What then of the relative opposition said to result *from* the notional acts? And just how can these acts be the cause of numerical distinction when the latter was said to be founded upon the personal properties? In order to make sense of the apparent circularity, it is necessary to distinguish in God two sense of relation: one in which relation is taken precisely as constitutive of the person, that is, as a personal property belonging and identical to a single person; and one in which relation is considered only from the point of view of its relative *ratio, ad aliud*[1137]. That which may be un-

[1134] As pointed out by G. Emery (op. cit., p. 100), the Albertinian explanation is not original and can already be found in Alexander of Hales (cf. *Summa*, lib. I, pars 2, inq. 2, tr. 2, sect. 1, quaest. 2, m. 1, c. 3, ed. Quaracchi, t. 1, n. 407, p. 600). The same explanation shall be assumed by St. Thomas (cf. *I Sent.*, d. 27, q. 1, a. 2; in general, d. 23-27, 33), though Bonaventure rejects it in favor of an inverse explanation (cf. *I Sent.*, d. 27, p. 1, a. un., q. 2).

[1135] Albert, *I Sent.*, d. 27, a. 2, ed. Borgnet, vol. 26, p. 36-37.

[1136] Actions belong to persons, not to natures. Cf. Albert, *Sum. theol.*, I, tr. 7, q. 30, c. 3, a. 1, ad 3 & 8, ed. Colon., vol. 34, p. 234-235: *"actum, qui personae est proprie... personam, cuius sit actus, cum tamen omnis actus certae personae sit"*.

[1137] Cf. (on relation *as relation*) Albert, *I Sent.*, d. 8, a. 34 (ed. Borgnet, vol. 25, p. 268-269); d. 27, a. 2 (ed. Borgnet, vol. 26, p. 3638); (on relation as constitutive)

derstood as produced by the notional act is relation only insofar as relation, and not relation insofar as the *proprietas* constitutive of the person. This is why the diagram in the previous section indicates relative opposition as the result of the notional act able to account for numerical plurality in the Trinity. Accordingly, to say that the Father is Father because he generates, that is, that the generative act causes Paternity (with respect to our mode of understanding), would be to focus exclusively upon the relative content as such of the paternal relation[1138]. On the other hand, it is the person which must be grasped as the subject of the notional act prior to conceptualizing its exercise, whence we affirm that the Father generates because he is Father, that is, Paternity, as identical to the Father, exercises (and is thus the explanation for) the generative act, privileging as it were the relation *qua* constitutive of the person. In sum, our minds perceive the persons (i.e. the relations *in quantum proprietates personales*) prior to the generative and spirative acts, which acts are conceived as productive of and prior to the relations (which the persons are) *qua* relations.

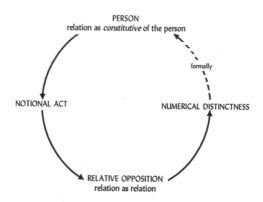

Conclusion

A numeration of distinct individuals entails distinct instances of being, according to the convertibility between *unum* and *esse*, and according as a thing be one or many on account of one or many beings. The quality of the number affirmed thus indicates the kind of distinction

Albert, *I Sent*, d. 26, a. 5 & 9-11 (ed. Borgnet, vol. 26, p. 9-11 & 17-23); cf. G. Emery, op. cit., p. 100.
[1138] Cf. Albert, *I Sent.*, d. 27, a. 2, ed. Borgnet, vol. 26, p. 36-38.

with respect to being. In God, where there can be no differences in being absolutely considered, the only kind of number is that which is predicated *secundum quid*, or *quidam*.

The cause of number is difference, and difference is introduced by an incommunicable *proprietas*. In creatures, the *proprietas*, the principle of number, introduces an additional element with respect to the unity of nature, an element which is really distinct from the common nature as such, whence the "appropriated" persons differ *in re*. In God, on the other hand, the *proprietates* are identical both to the persons and the common nature, introducing nothing by which one person may be distinct in concrete being from another (though they are really distinguished at another level, according as the divine *proprietates* distinguish really but *ab extrinsecis*).

The distinctive function of the *proprietas* in God is due to relative opposition. Because relative opposition cannot be had with respect to the essence, the *proprietas* and the person it constitutes are only distinguished and numbered with respect to another relative term and person. It is for this reason that the persons are not numbered in regard of their absoluteness, but only *qua* relative.

Though they are not numbered in absolute being, the divine persons are really distinct and thus truly numbered. This is because the opposition of relation excludes the possibility of its being present in more than one term (that is, it cannot be predicated of its co-relative). As relations, therefore, the divine persons are clearly distinct. But what is the ontological status of these relations? If those relations are not founded upon or identical to some real being, then the relatively distinguished entities will not be the terms of real relation and lose the basis for their real distinction. The divine relations are identical *in re* with the very divinity; and, as constitutive of the very persons as such, they are the divine substance hypostatically signified: thus they possess the subsistent being of the Godhead and hypostatic perfection (the very meaning of "subsistent relations").

Though the persons are really distinguished and numbered, no distinction or number obtains with regard to nature. But the numbering of persons without numbering natures implies a distinction even in God between person and nature, even if they are one *in re*. The two are distinguished precisely according to a mode of signification (founding the possibility of simultaneously affirming that the Father is not the Son while their nature is yet the same). A personal name and an essential name designate the same referent but mean different things: one signifies as *"quis"*, the other as *"quid"*. In God, number is affirmed only with regard to the *quis est*, in which respect we may speak of three "things" in the Trinity, each of which is a distinct relative form grounded in a common nature.

While the number ascribed to a plurality of *qui sunt* is indifferent to the number pertaining to the essence, the unity of every *quis est* nevertheless depends upon the substance as the foundation or *ratio* of its reality. Consequently, since discrete instances of unity constitute plurality, even the *plurality* of supposits presupposes the unity of substance, whether as a single substance common to each supposit (in the case of God) or as many substances resulting in *diversely* constituted hypostatic unities (in the case of creatures).

Yet the role of nature in constituting personal unity and several persons is not limited to the essential causality of supplying absolute perfection, but includes a sort of final causality inasmuch as distinct things of nature (persons) result precisely from operations (which are immanent acts in God) ordered to the communication of nature. This communication of nature, which is one of the intrinsic ends of natural generation and of the notional acts proper to the persons of the Trinity (the other intrinsic end of which is the realization of perfect hypostases) accounts for the notion of "order of nature" (predicable of the Trinity only with respect to nature taken as supposit). Numerical distinction in the Trinity, on the one hand, is a result of this order of nature, inasmuch as the persons are distinguished only through the act of the principles which communicate the nature (filiation, paternity and spiration). On the other hand, that order of nature itself is consequent upon the numerically distinct persons who alone are subjects of the operations by which the nature is communicated. Thus the *proprietates* as constitutive of the persons from whom operations flow enjoy a certain conceptual priority with respect to the same *proprietates* as relatively opposing and distinguishing the persons. Yet the distinctive numeration itself is understood to follow from the *proprietates* as relations. From either point of view, it is a non-substantial predicate which explains the notional acts and the distinction which these effect[1139], whence the number involved is nowise *simpliciter*.

No difference in essence or substantial being implied, number in the Trinity is indeed a number *quidam*. And it is because of the fact that number there is achieved by a difference (the essence of which difference as such is purely relational) resulting in a diversity *in esse*

[1139] Predicates such as "Father" (who is the subject of operation), "generation", and even *"potentia generandi"* to the extent that that power is conceptualized as rooted in the nature according as it is identical to the Father.

personali, and not in *esse simpliciter,* that the plurality in question receives the appellation *Trinitas,* as opposed to *triplicitas* proper to the
case of several creatures differing in substantial being[1140].

[1140] *"In divinis nullus sit numerus realis, qui differentiam faciat in essentia et esse substantiali,
tamen ibi est numerus quidam, proprietatum scilicet et propriorum personalium, qui identitati
substantiali non repugnat... in divinis divisio sive differentia quaedam est quae est proprietatis personalis in esse personali et non in esse simpliciter... quendam numerum et non simpliciter numerum... in eis est trinitas, in aliis triplicitas dici debet"* – Albert, *Sum. theol.,* I,
tr. 10, q. 45, c. 1, a. 2, sol. & ad 1-2, ed. Colon., vol. 34, p. 354.

II.7. PROPRIETAS

Persons differ only through their proprietates – a summary

Through his *proprietas*, the Father is other (*alius*) than the Son, the paternal *proprietas* distinguishing the hypostasis of the Father from that of the Son. Similarly, and reciprocally, the filial *proprietas* distinguishes the Son from the Father[1141]. Now, to state that the Father is father *through the proprietas* seems both to make the *proprietas* more simple than the Father, as well as to imply composition between *"quod est"* and *"quo est"*[1142]. However, the fact that the person and the *proprietas* differ only according to mode of signification means that there is no difference *secundum rem* by which composition could obtain. The respective modes of signification correspond to different modes of predication, the one (Father) predicated *ut "quis"* and the other (*proprietas*) predicated *ut "quomodo"*[1143].

From the fact that the Father and Son differ from one another solely on account of their *proprietates*, it does not follow that they are not therefore also distinct in hypostasis. Even though they differ only through their respective *proprietates*, the distinction achieved means that they are, precisely as distinguished realities, distinct according to hypostasis. The hypostasis is, in fact, identical to the *proprietas*; but the *proprietas* is the substantive reality *ut distinguente*, while hypostasis is the same reality *ut distincto*[1144]. In effect, from the very nature of the properties of origin, implying mutual opposition, several such properties cannot be found within the same subject, whence their numeration suffices to enumerate hypostases. The same properties of origin, moreover, because they are not accidents, are the very subsistent per-

---

[1141] *"Alius est in persona vel personaliter Pater, id est, proprietate sua Pater alius est quam Filius... Paternali enim proprietate distinguitur hypostasis Patris ab hypostasi Filii, et hypostasis Filii filiali proprietate discernitur a Patre"* – Peter Lombard: Albert, *I Sent.*, d. 25, a. 7, K, ed. Borgnet, vol. 25, p. 636.

[1142] Cf. *Sum. theol.*, I, tr. 9, q. 39, c. 2, a. 1, obj. 3-4, ed. Colon., vol. 34, p. 299.

[1143] *"Si secundum rem poneretur distinctio inter distinguens et distinctum, tunc verum esset, quod obicitur. ... sed ad diversum modum intelligendi tantum vel significandi... unum enim praedicatur ut 'quis', alterum autem, ut 'quomodo' se habet quis ad aliquem"* – Albert, *Sum. theol.*, I, tr. 9, q. 39, c. 2, a. 1, ad 4, ed. Colon., vol. 34, p. 300. Cf. supra, "THE PREDICAMENTS OF 'WHO', 'HOW' AND 'WHAT'", p. 297; infra, "MODES OF PREDICATION", p. 437.

[1144] *"Et quod dicitur, quod filius differt a patre sola proprietate, verum est, quod ut distinguente sola proprietate differt, sed ut distincto differt etiam hypostasi; et ideo verissime filius est ut alius in hypostasi a patre genitus"* – Albert, *Sum. theol.*, I, tr. 8, q. 35, c. 1, ad 2, ed. Colon., vol. 34, p. 267.

sons, wherefore the multiplicity of *proprietates* in the persons of whom they are the properties equally entails a multiplicity (and therefore distinction) of the persons to whom they are identical [1145].

Note that the sense of *"proprietas"* employed in the context of the Trinity is not to be understood according to what pertains to inferior creatures; that is, no *proprietas* is predicated after the manner in which it is ordinarily predicated in creatures, namely, as an accident, since nothing in God is accidental [1146]. *"Proprietas"* is intended rather only in the sense that it is an ultimate distinctive feature proper to but a single individual whose act it is. It is, according to this mode of predication, also convertible with the individual it distinctively demarcates, in the same way as a specific difference is convertible with the species it serves to define [1147].

Difference between hypostasis and proprietas

Objectively speaking, there is no difference in the Trinity between the persons or hypostases and the *proprietates*, for the Father and Son *are* paternity and filiation, respectively. Although the grammatical quality of the distinct pair of terms employed when we consider, for example, "Father" and "paternity", seems to suggest that the referent of one is concrete while the referent of the other is abstract, the distinctness of these terms simply follows from their diverse modes of attribution, and not from any difference between the things to which they refer. The hypostasis being the thing as *distinct*, we signify it *per modum concretionis*; the *proprietas* being the thing as *distinguishing*, we signify it *per modum abstractionis*. We are obliged to signify one concretely and the

---

[1145] "Non a qualibet proprietate potest accipi pluralitas, sed a proprietate originis secundum existentiae modum... tales enim proprietates (ut dicit Anselmus) nec natura admittit inesse eidem, cum sint oppositae, nec ratio capit qualiter uni possint convenire, et ideo numerus talium sufficit hypostasibus divinis, praecipue cum (ut dicit Hylarius) proprietas sit persona subsistens et perfecta, quia in divinis nihil accidentale est, sed proprietas in persona, cujus est proprietas, est persona ipsa subsistens et perfecta ut dicit Damascenus" – Albert, I Sent., d. 23, a. 3, ad 5, ed. Borgnet, vol. 25, p. 590; cf. A. Pompei, op. cit., p. 229.

[1146] Cf. infra, "KINDS OF PROPRIETATES", p. 448.

[1147] "Quod autem est proprietas, non dicitur a modo proprii in inferioribus, quia, ut dicit Boethius, hoc est de genere accidentium et in deo nihil est per accidens, sed est per modum eius quod sit ultimum, quod soli convenit et convertibile est cum eo cuius est actus, sicut ARISTOTELES in VII PRIMAE PHILOSOPHIAE dicit de differentia ultima... diffinitio propter ultimam talem differentiam convertibilis sit et propria. Et talis proprii actum habet proprietas personalis et non illius quod est unum de quinque praedicabilibus" – Albert, Sum. theol., I, tr. 9, q. 39, c. 2, a. 1, ad quaest. 4, ed. Colon., vol. 34, p. 298.

other abstractly on account of the weakness of our intellectual capacities, which, for the sake of conceptualizing a unique referent from two different points of view, must signify according to diverse modes of signification, whence the multiplicity of terms suggesting a difference between their respective referents[1148]. There, however, is no difference, since that whereby *"proprietas"* is abstract and "hypostasis" concrete does not refer to the *esse* of the thing, but is a feature of our intentionating, referring therefore only *ad modum intelligendi*[1149]. Thus, when we say that the *proprietas* signifies abstractly, we do not say "abstractly" as though *proprietas* had an abstract being distinct from that of the Father, but insofar as it has a separate mode of signification[1150].

For the *proprietas* and hypostasis to be identical *in re* in creatures, the *proprietas* could not differ in reality from the very supposit which exists, but would rather represent the completely singularized individual form in conjunction with its being (especially if the latter be understood to enter into the constitution of the essential individuality itself), according, however, to its distinguishing role with respect to the universe of ontological possibilities – that is, with respect to its function of making this individual thing a unique ontological referent in the real world –, as opposed to according as it simply be this distinct thing. If, on the other hand, that to which we ascribe the name *proprietas*, as that which is responsible for hypostatic distinction, is identified with either an accidental feature or a *part* of the essence (as, for example, in the case of the theory of material individuation), then no such identity may be affirmed. In creatures, it seems, the principle of hypostatic distinction and the hypostasis itself are related to one another after the manner of *quo est* and *quod est* respectively, according to composition, and as distinct from each other not only *secundum modum intelligendi*, but really[1151].

[1148] *"In divinis enim paternitas est pater. Et talis modus loquendi propter inopiam nostri intellectus est, qui non potest significare, quod in supponendo et attribuendo diversum modum habet proprietas ab hypostasi, in qua est – eo quod hypostasis distincta est, proprietas autem distinguens –, nisi significet unum per modum abstractionis et alterum per modum concretionis"* – Albert, *Sum. theol.*, I, tr. 9, q. 39, c. 1, ad 8, ed. Colon., vol. 34, p. 293.

[1149] *"Non refertur ad esse, quo scilicet proprietas abstracta sit et hypostasis concreta, sed ad modum intelligendi"* – Albert, *Sum. theol.*, I, tr. 9, q. 39, c. 1, ad 8, ed. Colon., vol. 34, p. 293.

[1150] *"Cum enim dicitur 'paternitas est pater', eadem notio significatur, sed diversis modis, scilicet ut abstractum et concretum; nec per abstractum significatur ut abstractum esse habens extra patrem, sed ut separatum modum significandi habens, quando accipitur ut principium distinctionis a modo eiusdem, quando accipitur ut in distincto distinctum denominans"* – Albert, *Sum. theol.*, I, tr. 9, q. 39, c. 2, a. 1, ad quaest. 1, ed. Colon., vol. 34, p. 296.

[1151] In fact, the very reason for the identity between substance and relation or *proprietas* in God lies not in the fact that relation is *relation*, but in the fact that it is relation *in God* (where everything is simple).

Proprietas as constitutive of all persons

Since hypostases are constituted by that which distinguishes them (either entirely as in God, or partially as with creatures), their very being as hypostases (their "personal being"[1152]) depends upon the distinguishing *proprietas*. In God, hypostatic being depends upon nothing else (lest the divine persons were to be distinguished from one another at the level of substance); in creatures, on the other hand, the being of the hypostasis is additionally constituted by a difference in substantial being. Over and above its role of distinguishing, in God, and on account of his supreme simplicity, relations are the very distinguished things, constitutive of and identical to the persons they oppose. As a result, if the distinctive relations of origin were removed, the very divine persons would cease to be. In an analogous way, if in creatures the principle of their individuation were taken away, with it their very substantial being would come to end. The principle is evident: if the principle of distinction is eliminated, so is distinction itself; and where distinction is abolished, nothing remains except the unity of essence. To continue to speak of three hypostases in God in abstraction from relative opposition can only mean one of two things: either the hypostases are three different substances (Arianism), or a single substance in which the three hypostases are really only one *res naturae* (Sabellianism)[1153].

Not only does distinction depend upon an indispensable principle of distinction, but the very distinguishing principle constitutes that which it distinguishes. The principle of personal distinction, that is, enters into the very being of the distinguished reality and is not an extrinsic cause of hypostatic being. In this way, the argument for the inseparability between the *proprietas* and the hypostasis (without destroying the latter) is clarified: over and above the mere necessity of an antecedent cause (real causality in the creature, and logical priority in God), something holding our attention to the efficient order, we affirm the sustained being of the hypostasis as formally dependent

---

[1152] Cf. supra, "PERSONAL BEING", p. 393 (especially p. 395-396).

[1153] *"Si forte dicas, quod remanet hypostasis seipsa distincta ab alia, hoc est haeresis Arii apertissima; quia tunc essent tres substantiae divisae per id quod substantiae sunt, et per hoc tres dii essent. Si autem dicas, quod remanet hypostasis, sed non potest numerari, sed remanet in ratione alicujus unius. Contra: Illud unum, aut idem numero erit in omnibus personis, aut diversum. Si idem, tunc tres essent una hypostasis, quod falsum est. Si diversum, ergo proprietas essentialiter dividit ipsum, sicut fit divisio in inferioribus, quod falsum est"* – Albert, *I Sent.*, d. 26, a. 5, sed contra 2, ed. Borgnet, vol. 26, p. 9; cf. A. Pompei, op. cit., p. 279.

upon the same principle[1154]. This observation has enormous implication for Christology. The being of the hypostasis is nothing other than to be distinct. Wherever (and, to capture the logical convertibility, if and only if) there is a principle of true and numerical distinction (as opposed to generic or specific, and regardless of whether that numeration is *quidam* or *simpliciter*), there is a hypostasis. If, then, there is but a single principle of individuality for an entire ensemble of natural principles, there can be but a single hypostasis. The entire personal unicity of Christ is explained in precisely such terms, for in him we find but one ultimate principle for both the distinctive mode of existence of his divine hypostasis and the individuation of his humanity[1155].

Modes of predication

In the Trinity, we recognize at once the substantial unicity (*unum quod*) of three individuals (*plures qui*) and their real distinction achieved through incommunicable properties (*principia quibus*). Particularly in the context of examining the principles of personal constitution, it is important, therefore, to distinguish the difference between the several just identified realities and the predicative modes according to which the terms used to designate them are understood. As we have seen, there are diverse ways of attributing that which distinguishes and that which is distinguished, according as one is taken as distinguishing, and the other as distinct[1156]. The former is predicated *ut quomodo*, the latter *ut quis*[1157].

Following these discriminations, we observed Albert distinguish three ways of predicating: "what", "who" and "how" (*"quid"*, *"quis"* et *"quomodo"*, or, alternately, *"quod"*, *"quis"* and *"quae"*)[1158]. When we ask "what is the Father?" (*quaeratur per quid*), our response shall be "God", or some other essential name. If, on the other hand we ask the ques-

---

[1154] *"Cum ergo per intellectum... proprietas sit ante hypostasim, ut distinguens eam, et suum esse est esse distinctum, et nihil aliud, oportet quod remota proprietate, nihil remaneat de hypostasi"* – Albert, *I Sent.*, d. 26, a. 5, sol., ed. Borgnet, vol. 26, p. 10.

[1155] Explaining this shall be the fundamental goal of our following study on Christ.

[1156] *"Diversus modus esse in attribuendo eius quod distinguit, et eius quod distinguitur, secundum quod unum accipitur in ratione distinguentis et alterum in ratione distincti"* – Albert, *Sum. theol.*, I, tr. 9, q. 39, c. 2, a. 1, ad 3, ed. Colon., vol. 34, p. 300.

[1157] *"Ad diversum modum intelligendi tantum vel significandi... Unum enim praedicatur ut 'quis', alterum autem, ut 'quomodo' se habet quis ad aliquem"* – Albert, *Sum. theol.*, I, tr. 9, q. 39, c. 2, a. 1, ad 4, ed. Colon., vol. 34, p. 300.

[1158] Cf. supra, "THE PREDICAMENTS OF 'WHO', 'HOW' AND 'WHAT'", p. 297.

tion "who in God is the principleless source of all the others?" (*quaera-tur per quis*), we would respond by saying "the person of the Father". Finally, if we pose the question "how is it that he is Father?" (*quaeratur per quomodo*), we shall answer "through paternity" or "through genera-tion", indicating the relation or property by which the Father is Fa-ther[1159].

In response to the more general question "how is it that the Father is distinct" (as opposed to the more specific question concerning his Fatherhood), several properties are able to be named (e.g. *ut princip-ium non de principio*, or *paternitate*), the nature of which properties al-lows us to recognize and distinguish two ways of predicating *quomodo*: indeterminately (or confusedly) and determinately[1160]. Note that the question "how is it that the Father is distinct?" is not exactly the same as "what is it that makes him distinct?", or, more precisely, "in what does his distinction consist?". Although the latter interrogative is concerned with how it is that the Father is a distinct person, it never-theless questions *per quid*, and the response to this, if it is to respond *per quid*, must indicate something entitative, which, in this case (since it cannot be a question of the commonly shared divine being), can only be what Albert has referred to as "personal being". A thing's per-sonal being is that in which his personal distinction consists; that per-sonal being, however, is had through the personal property, which is the "how" of the "what" corresponding to personal being.

Having identified three general modes of predication with regard to ques-tions concerning personhood, and having subdivided one of these into two, we recognize four figures of speech with respect to which we must follow the rules of predication and avoid committing syntactical errors. Albert describes the impropriety consisting in falsely identifying properties of non-correspond-ing supposition as inattentiveness to the ramifications of the above mentioned predicative modes. A characteristic example of such an error is the identifica-tion of *paternitas* with *innascibilitas*. While the Father is *innascibilis* (since he is principle without principle), and the Father is paternity, it does not follow from this that *innascibilitas* is paternity. Such an affirmation would be to

---

[1159] *"Inventi sunt tres modi praedicandi, 'quid' scilicet et 'quis' et 'quomodo'. Si enim in divinis quaeratur per 'quid' ut 'quid est pater?', respondetur 'deus' vel aliud nomen essentiale. Si au-tem quaeratur 'quis'… respondetur 'persona pater'. Si autem quaeratur per 'quomodo', ut 'quomodo se habet pater ad filium?', respondetur relatio vel proprietas vel notio ut 'paternitate vel generatione'"* – Albert, *Sum. theol.*, I, tr. 9, q. 39, c. 2, a. 1, ad quaest. 1, ed. Colon., vol. 34, p. 296.

[1160] *"Ipsae notiones significantur quattuor modis, scilicet confuse et determinate, ut 'principium non de principio' et 'paternitas', quae determinatum principium significat. Similiter 'princi-pium de principio' et 'filiatio'"* – Albert, *Sum. theol.*, I, tr. 9, q. 39, c. 2, a. 1, ad quaest. 1, ed. Colon., vol. 34, p. 296.

commit the fallacy of moving from the confused (or indeterminate) to the determinate, as though the two were convertible notions. But they are not convertible, precisely because of the simple difference in intension between the terms, the comprehensions (that is, the content, or individual notes) of which are diverse, even if their extension is the same. Similar errors result when confusing names assigned to the persons of the Trinity according to particular modes of predication, as, for example, when we move from the affirmations "whatever the Father is, so is the Son" and "the Father is Father" to the conclusion "the Son is Father". In this case the fallacy committed consists in moving from predication according to *quid* to predication according to *quis*, converting *quid* in *quis*; for the Father is not Father on account of "what" he is, but for that "whom" he is[1161]. Another fallacy of speech is identified in that of converting *quis* in *quomodo*, an example of which would be to conclude that the Father generates the Holy Spirit, under the assumption that however the Father communicates himself to the Son, so he must communicate himself to the Holy Spirit[1162]. To convert any of these modes of predication into another results in erroneous judgment, as is evidenced, once again, in identifying Father and Son because of the fact that they are each common active spiration, or in having already moved from the fact that whatever is in the Father is the Father, and whatever is in the Son is the Son, to the affirmation that they are each therefore common spiration – in both of which cases one "flip-flops" between *"quid"* and *"quomodo"*[1163].

[1161] Which we are to understand as the purely relational reality by which he is Father, and not as the absolute nature which he is (and shares with the other persons of the Trinity); this is the sense of Albert's "personal being".

[1162] *"Unde si aliquis arguat: Pater per hoc quod est principium non de principio, est innascibilis, et pater est paternitas per hoc, quod alius generando est de ipso... ergo paternitas est innascibilitas, ergo innascibilitas est paternitas, incidit fallacia figurae dictionis a confusa ad determinatam. Si autem sic arguat: Quidquid est pater, est filius, sed pater est pater, ergo filius est pater, incidit fallacia figurae dictionis ex hoc quod mutatur 'quid' in 'quis'; pater enim est pater per hoc quod 'quis' est, et non per hoc quod 'quid' est. Si vero sic arguat: Quomodocumque se habet pater ad filium, communicando sibi naturam et naturalia, sic se habet ad spiritum sanctum, communicando naturam sibi et substantiam; sed ad filium se habet generando, ergo ad spiritum sanctum generando, incidit eadem fallacia ex mutato modo in modum vel ex eo quod mutatur 'quis' et 'quomodo'"* – Albert, *Sum. theol.*, I, tr. 9, q. 39, c. 2, a. 1, ad quaest. 1, ed. Colon., vol. 34, p. 296.

[1163] They are each common spiration, but *ut quomodo* and not *ut quid*. *"Si autem aliquis sic arguat: Quidquid est in patre, est pater, et quidquid est in filio, est filius, et sic communis spiratio est pater et communis spiratio est filius; ergo pater est filius: secundum praedicta constat, quod incidit fallacia figurae dictionis ex hoc quod mutatur 'quid' in 'quomodo'. Non enim est spiratio in patre ut 'quid' secundum modum significandi, sed ut 'quomodo' se habens ad spiritum sanctum, et eodem modo est in filio"* – Albert, *Sum. theol.*, I, tr. 9, q. 39, c. 2, a. 1, ad 2, ed. Colon., vol. 34, p. 297. In virtue of a common term of relative opposition, active spiration on the part of a plurality of supposits is one principle corresponding to a singular mode of existence: *"commune enim esse pluribus suppositis non excludit singularem existentiae modum in relativis ex relatione ad unum singulare oppositum... pater et filius sint unum principium; quamvis non sint idem principium"* – the Father and Son are one principle *ut quomodo*, they are not the same principle *ut quid* – *"... eo quod 'idem, cum sit eius quod est idem, idem', etiam dicitur ad suppositum, suppositum autem patris non est suppositum filii"* – Albert, *Sum. theol.*, I, tr. 9, q. 39, c. 2, a. 1, ad 8 & 10, ed. Colon., vol. 34, p. 296.

The majority of such fallacies, consisting in predicating one notion of another by means of the verb "to be", without respect for the opposition or diversity in modes of signification, amount to ignoring qualifications inherent to a notion on the basis of its supposition or predicative mode, qualifications which are not expressed in the mere definitions of the terms being predicated. These fallacies can be ranged, in more general modern terms, amongst the categories of the "fallacy of ambiguity", the "fallacy *secundum quid*", and (less frequently) the "fallacy of equivocation". A fine example of the illicit disregard for syntactical qualification, and which corresponds to the first two categories of fallacy just mentioned, is supplied by Albert in concluding question 39: if one argues from the fact that the Father is *innascibilitas* and paternity is not *innascibilitas* (something recently shown above) to the conclusion that paternity is not the Father, he commits, according to Albert, the fallacy of the accident, in the same way that one errs by arguing that animal is a genus, and man is not a genus, therefore man is not animal[1164]. More precisely, the error committed consists in what is called the converse fallacy of the accident (also called the fallacy of moving *a dicto secundum quid ad dictum simpliciter*), invalidly going from a qualified statement to an unqualified one, or in dropping a conjunct from a distributed term. The distributed term here is "animal" which, in the first premise, includes, in virtue of its mode of signification, its qualification as a secondary concept: animal taken only *in a certain sense* is a genus. This qualification is omitted in the concluding proposition, whence the illegitimacy of the argument[1165].

Distinction between proprietates and distinction between the persons

The *ratio proprietatum* in the Trinity has been shown to consist exclusively in relative opposition. Now, relation of itself predicates nothing intrinsic as though it inhered in the essence or person, because the only thing proper to relation as such is that it be referred *ad aliud*, in such a way that it may be said to predicate extrinsically to the essence. This does not mean, however, that the divine relations are nothing but logical notions by which we compare one thing to another. If such were the case, then the persons, who differ only through the *proprietates* (relations of origin), would differ only logically from one an-

---

[1164] *"Una notio de alia non potest praedicari per hoc verbum 'est',... propter scilicet oppositos vel diversos modos significandi hanc notionem vel illam. Dico autem oppositos ut peternitas et filiatio, diversos autem ut paternitas et innascibilitas... Et si fiat tale argumentum: pater innascibilitas est; paternitas non est innascibilitas; ergo paternitas non est pater, fallacia accidentis est, sicut hic: animal est genus; homo non est genus; ergo homo non est animal"* – Albert, *Sum. theol.*, I, tr. 9, q. 40, c. 1, a. 3, ad 5, ed. Colon., vol. 34, p. 306.

[1165] Note that the fallacy stems from a failure to adequately take into consideration mode of signification. It is not a question of supposition here because the ambiguous term "animal" is distributed – that is, it represents (or stands for) all of the members of the class it denotes – both in the first premise (where it is the subject) and in the conclusion (where it is the predicate of a negative proposition).

other, which is Sabellianism. Furthermore, and along the same lines but inversely, if the *proprietates* differed from one another absolutely, then so would the persons; but the persons are identical in all things but the relations of origin which, as was stated, predicate nothing intrinsic to the essence. According as the *proprietates* differ from one another, so will the persons; the former differ only by relative opposition, so then too do the persons. But, for the persons to differ really from one another, the relations have to be real and the *proprietates* have to be more than mere notions, but things, *res*. They are things, and they are that through which the persons differ. But they cannot be things different from the persons which they distinguish, otherwise the persons would not be identical in all things except relative origin. Thus they are indistinguishable from the persons themselves, not because they are mere *rationes*, but because the persons cannot differ amongst themselves as several *diverse* things, *ut aliud et aliud* (diversity, over and above the notion of distinction, implying qualitative or substantial difference). The unity and simplicity of nature in the divinity necessitates not only that the persons be substantially identical, but also that the *proprietates* by which they are distinguished be so both with respect to the persons and to each other. Any diversity between the *proprietates* and the persons will find its sole source in the opposed modes of signification and attribution already referred to – person is predicated *ut "quis"*, relation *ut "quomodo" se habens* – and this is sufficient[1166].

[1166] *"Relatio enim ut relatio non praedicat aliquid intrinsecum ut inhaerens essentiae vel inhaerens personae, eo quod relatio secundum suum esse est 'ad aliud' se habere, et sic praedicat ut extrinsecus existens. Propter quod dixit, quod proprietas nec essentia est nec persona nec est proprie res, sed ratio ex comparatione rei ad rem sumpta. Sed quia ex hoc [sequitur], cum secundum Augustinum personae non differant nisi proprietatibus, quae sunt relationes, et proprietates non sint nisi in ratione, ut dicit, sequitur necessario, ut personae non differant nisi ratione tantum, ut dixit Sabellius, videtur mihi, quod temerarium sit ita dicere. Si enim personae differunt re, cum non differant nisi proprietate, oportet, quod proprietas sit res. Dicit enim Damascenus, quod personae in omnibus idem sunt, praeterquam in ingeneratione, generatione et processione... Sed hoc verum est, quod re non differunt ab ipsis personis, in quibus sunt, sed hoc non est nisi propter indifferentiam simplicitatis, et non propter hoc quod non sint res, sed rationes tantum... personae seipsis differunt, quia differunt proprietatibus, quae sunt hoc quod ipsae personae... ad diversitatem illam sufficit oppositus modus significandi et attribuendi et diversus modus praedicandi; persona enim praedicatur ut 'quis', relatio ut 'quomodo' se habens"* – Albert, *Sum. theol.*, I, tr. 9, q. 39, c. 2, a. 1, ad 8 & 9, ed. Colon., vol. 34, p. 301.

Proprietas and person, person and essence, essence and proprietas

Proprietas and person

Proprietates, in a general sense, signify *ut quomodo,* and in such a way
they do not denote the per se existent – as is the case with a term such
as "hypostasis", "person" or "trium" (the latter denoting a numerical
multiplicity of existents); they merely state *how* there exists what is one
or two or three. The *proprietas personalis* is that by which (*principium
quo*) one person is from another; it is that which determines a thing in
personal being.   Hypostasis, or the supposit, is that which is determined as this or that person. Though they are one and the same
thing in reality, the *proprietas* as *proprietas* is not signified as existing *per
se,* nor can it be, since to be signified as a *per se* existent is proper only
to *suppositum.* Consequently, the *proprietas,* insofar as *proprietas,* can
never be signified as existing *per se,* "hypostatizing" as it were the *proprietas* considered abstractly: we do not say that paternity generates, or
that filiation is generated or that procession proceeds (to do so would
be to convert *"quomodo"* in *"quis"*) [1167].

In fact, the *proprietas* possesses rather the mode of signification of a
notion (the general function of which is to reveal how one person is
distinct from another, naming a *proper* element or the *ratio distinctionis* [1168]). The distinction between the proper signification of the *proprietas* and that of the person is therefore manifested in the use of
personal verbs and adjectives (such as *generat* and *generans*) which

---

[1167] *"Cum dicitur trium, intelligitur, quod quilibet trium est per se existens sive subsistens in
seipso... tres in una natura existentes... Proprietas autem secundum modum significandi
proprietatem non dicit existens per se solum... sed dicit quiddam quod est unius vel duorum
vel trium, et non ponit numerum per se existentium... proprietas enim est, quo est persona a
persona, eo quod proprietas determinans est in esse personali... hypostasis autem sive suppositum est sicut determinatum, ut sit haec persona vel illa... proprietas autem ut proprietas, licet
idem sit cum tali supposito relatiter, tamen non significatur ut per se existens"–*Albert, *Sum.
theol.,* I, tr. 9, q. 39, c. 2, a. 2, ad 12 & a. 3, sol, ed. Colon., vol. 34, p. 304-305.

[1168] Notions, properties of the persons and personal properties are the abstract expression of the reason for the real distinction between the concrete subsistent subjects.
They posit real distinctive principles in the hypostases without entailing real composition or any diversity from the hypostases themselves, since their abstract mode
of signifying means that they do not signify those principles as things able to objectively inhere in the subjects they distinguish, but only as the ratio for that distinction (cf. A. Pompei, op. cit., p. 309). *"In ultima analisi, i termini astratti hanno una
duplice funzione: manifestativa e costitutiva-distintiva.   Come manifestativi, essi sono
l'espressione concettuale (intelligentiae ratio) del concreto distinto e costituito, sono cioè la 'ratio distinctionis' o 'nozione'; in quanto distintivi-costitutivi, essi sono entitativamente i dis-
tinti concreti e i costituiti (substantia individua-persona): è cioè la relazione sussistente-pro-
prietà personale"*–ibid.

cannot be said of notions: acts (signified by the verbal expressions) are the exclusive domain of hypostases and therefore cannot be predicated of notions, since the latter signify *ut ratio distinguens* and not *ut res distincta ens per seipsam*, while the participial personal adjectives, because they express the modes of origin (*qualiter una persona emanat a persona*) *ut agens*, and not *ut ratio agentis* (that is, as the *ratio* of the agent in his distinction, the *ratio personae*), are equally impredicable of notions such as the *proprietas*[1169]. [Note that the *proprietas* is a more specific concept than that of *notio*. The *notiones* differ from the *proprietates* as superior to inferior in extension, according as every *proprietas* is a notion, but not vice versa. The specificity of *proprietas*, distinguishing it from other notions, consists in the fact that a *proprietas* can never be found in more than one person][1170].

It is precisely inasmuch as the *proprietas* differs from the person according to *modus intelligendi et attribuendi* that we speak of them as *in* the persons. But, insofar as identical to the persons and the divine substance in reality, they *are* the persons. Indeed, there can be no diversity in the divinity inasmuch as every diversity entails composition. As a consequence, it cannot properly be said that the *proprietates* are *in* the persons; for, as Aristotle explains in IV *Physica*, nothing can be in itself, and every preposition is transitive and implies diversity[1171].

[1169] *"Personalia non dicuntur de notionibus, quia personalia adjectiva ut hujusmodi, aut conveniunt personae in se, ut distinctum esse, et tunc non possunt convenire notioni propter oppositum modum significandi, quia notio significatur ut ratio distinguens, non ut res distincta ens per seipsam; aut personalia sunt quibus persona emanat a persona, ut generat, spirat, quae significant actum personalem, vel adjective dicuntur de personis, ut sunt generans, spirans, secundum quod adjective tenentur illa participia, et tunc non possunt convenire notionibus, quia notio non significatur ut agens, sed potius ut ratio agentis actu illo; actus enim hypostasum sunt et individuorum, et tali modo non significatur notio"* – Albert, *I Sent.*, d. 33, a. 7, sol., ed. Borgnet, vol. 26, p. 154; cf. A. Pompei, op. cit., p. 306.

[1170] *"Proprietas personalis et proprietates personae se habent sicut superius et inferius, quia omnis proprietas personalis est etiam proprietas personae, sed non convertitur. Proprietas autem personae et relatio se habent sicut excedentia et excessa, quia quaedam relatio est proprietas personae, ut paternitas, et quaedam non, ut communis spiratio... omnis proprietas personalis est relatio, sed non convertitur... tam proprietas personae quam personalis se habent ad notionem, ut superius et inferius, quia omnis proprietas... est notio, sed non convertitur"* – Albert, *I Sent.*, d. 26, a. 9, ad quaest. 1, ad 2, ed. Borgnet, vol. 26, p. 18; cf. infra, "PROPRIETAS PERSONALIS AND PROPRIETATES PERSONAE", p. 450 (especially p. 452); cf. A. Pompei, op. cit., p. 310-311, 314; cf. Aquinas, *Sum. theol.*, I, 32, 2-3.

[1171] *"Nulla potest esse in eo diversitas, eo quod omnis diversitas rei inducit compositionem in tantum... quod proprietates non essent in persona, sed essent ipsa persona, eo quod ARISTOTELES probat in IV PHYSICORUM, quod nihil est in seipso, praepositiones enim, ut dicit PRISCIANUS, transitivae sunt et diversitatem notant, et si diceretur proprietas esse in persona, notaretur diversitas inter proprietatem et personam, quae nulla est... 'in personis proprietas', respondet dicens impropriam esse locutionem et sensum esse... 'in personis, quae sunt pro-*

Rather, the *proprietates* are identical to the persons and the very divine essence, since that which unites and that which distinguishes are the same *in re* at the heart of the highest, most perfect simplicity[1172]. Nevertheless, while the *proprietates* are not truly in the persons, they signify and are predicated as in the persons. This mode of being *in* is described as the mode of being of the distinguishing thing in that which is distinguished (to which it is nevertheless identical in reality)[1173].

While distinctive of the hypostases because of their opposition (*proprietas in quantum relatio*), the *proprietates*, as we have observed, are equally *constitutive* of the persons (*proprietas in quantum proprietas*[1174]). Consequently, analogous to the relation between a species and its specific difference, the *proprietas* is logically antecedent to the hypostasis, whence the following order obtains: first is posed the constitutive *proprietas*, followed by the hypostasis, followed by the notional act which depends upon the hypostasis inasmuch as hypostases alone are subjects of operation[1175]. Of course, the *proprietas* and the divine person are really identical (*quia quidquid in Deo est, Deus est*[1176]); the *proprietas* is at once that which distinguishes (*ratio personae*) and that which is distinct. But we have the right to distinguish them mentally in virtue of their distinct modes of signification. The logical anteriority of the *proprietas* with respect to the hypostasis pertains to the *proprietas* signified *ut distinguens*, and not *ut distincta*[1177].

---

priae'... proprietas sit essentia et deus" – Albert, *Sum. theol.*, I, tr. 9, q. 39, c. 2, a. 2, sol., ed. Colon., vol. 34, p. 303.

[1172] *"Proprietas in personis secundum catholicam fidem et est persona et essentia divina... uniens et distinguens in summe simplicibus idem sunt re... persona et essentia, quae idem sunt re"* – Albert, *Sum. theol.*, I, tr. 9, q. 39, c. 2, a. 1, sol. & a. 2, ad 6, ed. Colon., vol. 34, p. 299 & 303. Cf. *Sum. theol.*, I, tr. 7, q. 30, c. 3, a. 1, sol., ed. Colon., vol. 34, p. 234: *"est enim persona 'ens distinctum proprietate', et essentia ens non distinctum; et tamen essentia est persona et persona essentia, et pater est persona proprietate distincta, paternitate scilicet".*

[1173] *"In personis secundum modum intelligendi, quia licet realiter loquendo relatio nihil sit in persona in divinis, tamen secundum modum intelligendi distinguens est in distincto, et supposita persona, relatio non supponitur* – Albert, *I Sent.*, d. 26, a. 6, sol., ed. Borgnet, vol. 26, p. 13; cf. Albert, *I Sent.*, d. 27, a. 2, ad quaest. 1, ed. Borgnet, vol. 26, p. 37; cf. A. Pompei, op. cit., p. 305.

[1174] The distinction between the *proprietas in quantum relatio* and the *proprietas in quantum proprietas* signals the dual function of the *proprietas* on the one hand, the *proprietates* are distinctive of the persons, and this precisely insofar as they are relatively opposed; on the other hand, the *proprietates* are constitutive of the persons, and this inasmuch as each is a *proprium* unable to be found in more than one person. Cf. in this regard, A. Pompei, op. cit., p. 299, 313-314.

[1175] Cf. A. Pompei, op. cit., p. 299; cf. Albert, *I Sent.*, d. 26, a. 2, ad obj., ed. Borgnet, vol. 26, p. 6.

[1176] Cf. DS, vetus num. 391; cf. Aquinas, *Sum. theol.*, I, 28, 2.

[1177] The same relationship between the *proprietas* and person can be expressed in terms of incommunicability: the former is that which causes or constitutes the incommu-

From the point of view of intension, lastly, person is described as the supposit of an essence: *persona enim suppositum essentiae est.* Person, then, in its concept, contains the essence (or, more precisely, the notion of being qualified by the essence); and, just as whatever is predicated *per se* (and not per accidens or by mode of indifference or indetermination[1178]) of that which is contained in the concept of another is also predicated of that other, so whatever may be predicated of a thing of essence (to concretely and quidditatively render the qualifying genitive *essentiae*) is predicable of the person as well. (To be clearer, a person is *an* essence or nature, essence or nature taken concretely). The notion of *proprietas*, since it does not signify *ut quid vel quis*, neither names the essence directly nor indirectly (though since a *proprietas* is *of* the person – *proprietas enim non est essentiae, sed personae*[1179] –, its concept does name the person, but only as something external to its essence, similarly as a subject is included in the notion of an accident). Essence is not included in its concept, and thus what is predicated of a thing of essence (the concrete *ens*) is not necessarily also predicated of the *proprietas*. Moreover, even though person indirectly enters into the concept of the *proprietas*, the latter cannot be said to signify according to the personal mode, for if it did, it would signify the *per se* existent (which has already been excluded), and it would follow that whatever is predicated of the person *per se* (which, of course, would include anything predicable of a thing of essence *per se*)

---

nicability of the latter which is itself the incommunicable thing. Of course, they are one in reality, and each is incommunicable, the *proprietas* the incommunicable thing *ut faciens incommunicabilitatem*, person the incommunicable thing *ut incommunicabilis.* Cf. Albert, *I Sent*, d. 33, a. 7, ad 2, ed. Borgnet, vol. 26, p. 155: *"Conveniant in hoc quod utrumque est incommunicabile, tamen in ratione incommunicabilitatis differunt... unum ut id quod est incommunicabile, reliquum ut faciens ipsam incommunicabilitatem in eo, et ideo non oportet ut conveniens uni, conveniat et alteri".*

[1178] If we consider the example of man, the concept of which includes "animal", it is clear that whatever we predicate of "animal" *per se,* such as sentience and locomotion, is also predicated of man. But we say *"per se"*, because not everything predicable of "animal" is predicable of man. The concept of animal, due to its genericity, is *indifferent* to a great variety of perfections which do not enter into its concept *per se,* but which are indeterminately contained (inasmuch as they are not excluded). Thus many things can be predicated of animal which are not predicable of all of its realizations at the specific level, such as "eight legged" and "winged" which we do not predicate of man; though whatever is predicated of animal *qua* animal, and not in virtue of the perfection it is capable of being qualified by because of this or that animal, is predicable of every animal, including man.

[1179] Albert, *Sum. theol.,* I, tr. 9, q. 39, c. 2, a. 2, ad 14, ed. Colon., vol. 34, p. 304.

would also be predicable of the *proprietas*, but this has been denied[1180]: *"proprietates secundum quod per se significantur, non significantur ut res, sed potius ut rationes personarum"*[1181]. What is predicable, therefore of the person is not always also predicable of the *proprietas*, even if the *proprietas* is responsible for what the person is and therefore of what may be predicated of the person. As an analogy, consider something round: touching a plane at but one point is not attributed to roundness, but to the round thing, even if roundness is what makes the thing to be round and receive such an attribution. In a like manner, what is predicated of the person in virtue of its distinctness or supposital act is not predicable of the *proprietas* as such[1182].

Person and essence[1183]

Though person and essence are one in the ontological order, person remains distinct and incommunicable, while the essence is indistinct and communicable. This real identity notwithstanding their distinct modes of supposition (whence the diversity, even opposition, of their respective predicates) is due to the divine simplicity. Apart from God, natural communication includes a real composition between a common and individual element. As a consequence of this real composition, the individual nature is distinct both from the common nature as such and that of another individual. In God, on the other hand, the communication of nature results only in the addition of new predicates proper to the persons but not to the essence[1184]. The persons or hypostases and the essence are really identical but cannot be "subjected" to the same predicates[1185]. This difference in mode of supposition between per-

---

[1180] *"Ea quae sunt in intellectu alicuius, per se praedicantur de ipso, ut de homine animal et substantia et ea quae conveniunt animali et substantiae per se. Similiter, quia persona de intellectu suo ponit essentiam, persona enim suppositum essentiae est, ideo praedicata de essentia praedicantur de persona. Proprietas autem, quantum est de intellectu suo, non ponit essentiam nec in recto nec in obliquo; et ideo proprietas non recipit praedicata de essentia, quae modum essentiae dicunt; proprietas enim non est essentiae, sed personae"* – Albert, *Sum. theol.*, I, tr. 9, q. 39, c. 2, a. 2, ad 14, ed. Colon., vol. 34, p. 304.

[1181] Albert, *I Sent.*, d. 26, a. 5, sol., ed. Borgnet, vol. 26, p. 10.

[1182] *"Id enim quod non potest esse nisi per se existentis et perfectum esse habentis in seipso, nullo modo potest convenire vel attribui ei quod non potest significari ut in seipso existens et perfectum esse in seipso habens, sed ut in quodam existens et in quodam esse habens... Similiter tangere in puncto planum non attribuitur rotunditati, sed rotundo, licet rotunditas rotundum ad hoc determinet"* – Albert, *Sum. theol.*, I, tr. 9, q. 39, c. 2, a. 3, ad 3, ed. Colon., vol. 34, p. 305-306.

[1183] This paragraph is a succinct reiteration of what we have already thoroughly discussed, but serves as a logical bridge to the next paragraph.

[1184] *"Est enim persona 'ens distinctum proprietate', et essentia ens non distinctum; et tamen essentia est persona et persona essentia"* – Albert, *Sum. theol.*, I, tr. 7, q. 30, c. 3, a. 1, sol., ed. Colon., vol. 34, p. 234.

[1185] *"Non addat re, sed modo intelligendi, qui modus intelligendi realiter significatur, cum dicitur, hypostasis est distincta, vel hypostasis est incommunicabilis... quia aliquid addi alii, duobus*

son and essence is not to be understood as merely logical, but as a distinction having a real foundation in the thing; though the personal and essential realities are one in reality, they nevertheless conserve their proper modes of supposition which cannot be confused[1186].

Essence and proprietas

The personal entity is identical to the essential entity, though the former signifies *ut distincto*, the latter *ut communis*. That distinctiveness proper to the personal mode of signification derives from the *proprietas* understood as *in* the person according to *modus intelligendi*. The same *proprietas*, in virtue of the real identity between person and nature, is in the essence in the same way. However, it cannot be said to determine or to distinguish the essence; for the *proprietas* in the personal-essential reality only determines and distinguishes that reality according to its relative opposition, an opposition implying that several co-relative *proprietates* cannot be within the same subject, whence the distinguishing role of the *proprietas* pertains to the personal-essential reality only according to its supposital (subjectival) aspect. The *proprietates* distinguish only by means of the opposition owing to their *relativity* and *correlativity* (opposition being had only insofar as the *proprietates* are *ad alterum*), and because relative comparison is not referred to the essence as such, but only to a distinct correlative,

modis congnoscitur, scilicet quia facit compositionem, vel quia convenit ei quod alii non convenit, et in inferioribus est utroque modo... in divinis autem alterum tantum est, quia additum non inducit compositionem, eo quod realiter est idem, sed inducit diversam suppositionem... quia supposito uno non supponitur alterum, eo quod aliquid convenit uni quod non alii" – Albert, *I Sent.*, d. 26, a. 3, ad quaest., ed. Borgnet, vol. 26, p. 7; cf. A. Pompei, op. cit., p. 300.

[1186] *"È così che Alberto spiega quel modo di dire 'multum vulgatum', secondo cui natura e persona si distinguono 'logicamente'; distinzione questa che evidentemente egli intende per ciò che noi chiamiamo 'distinctio virtualis' o 'rationis ratiocinatae cum fundamento in re'... fondata tuttavia sulla realtà dell'essenza e della persona che, sebbene identiche a causa della semplicità divina, conservano tuttavia i loro modi inconfondibili e propri di supporre"* – A. Pompei, op. cit., p. 302; cf. Albert, *I Sent.*, d. 34, a. 2, sol., ed. Borgnet, vol. 26, p. 166: *"In divinis autem natura non potest significari ut diversa a persona, quia idem est; tamen realiter aliquid convenit ei, quod non convenit personae, et e converso; et ideo dicunt Doctores, quod supposita natura, non supponitur persona, et super illud fundatur intelligentiae ratio. Et nota, quod ab hoc loco trahitur illud multum vulgatum, quod distinguitur secundum intelligentiae rationem"*. Cf. supra, "PERSON DISTINGUISHED FROM NATURE OR ESSENCE", p. 290 (especially p. 291, 294). With regard to the rules governing the convertibility of personal names and the essence in the presence of complex propositions involving adjectival or adverbial qualifications, cf. supra, "THE PERSONAL NAME", p. 260 (especially p. 260-262).

the *proprietates* do not determine the essence, but rather the persons who are so compared and distinguished from one another[1187].

Kinds of proprietates

When we encounter an individual, we normally come into immediate contact with diverse properties of the thing according to which we are able to recognize the individual in its singularity. Individual substances can possess a great variety of such properties distinctively belonging to it an no other. In every case except God, that is, for angels and men, the property by which one may recognize the individual as distinct can be taken in the sense of a quality (as opposed to original mode and implicitly including quantity as the cause of many of the perceptible attributes in material things). A *"proprietas"*, understood in this sense, has the nature of an accident. Despite the fact that it provides us with a means of distinctively identifying a given individual, the accidental character of such a *proprietas*, entails that it be unable in itself to account for personal distinction. Such is the implication of certain objections and responses emphasizing the need for a non-accidental individuator for personal distinction[1188].

Instead of denying the accidental quality of such a *discretio* of these *proprietates*, Albert draws our attention to the fact that they derive from something more fundamental and non-accidental truly able to account for personal distinction. Such *proprietates* are said to show the singularity of the person but they do not make the person singular. This, because something deeper constitutes the singularity of the person, namely, in the case of angels, what has been referred to as their *fundamentum*, the distinctive ontological limiting factor entering into composition with *esse*[1189]. Sometimes, however, as in the case of angels, we are unable to apperceive this particular *fundamentum* responsible

---

[1187] *"[Proprietates] non determinant nisi per hoc quod habent; oppositionem autem non habent, nisi per hoc quod ad alterum sunt; et cum illa comparatione non referantur ad essentiam, sed ad extra, patet quod non determinant essentiam, sed personam quae comparatur ad illam personam quae distinguitur ab ipsa"* – Albert, *I Sent*, d. 33, a. 6, ad 2, ed. Borgnet, vol. 26, p. 152; cf. A. Pompei, op. cit., p. 305. Cf. supra, "THE PERSONAL NAME", p. 261-262.

[1188] *"Quod discretio personalis est, aut origine tantum, ut in Deo, aut proprietate tantum, ut in Angelis, aut proprietate simul et origine, ut in homine... Angelorum autem discretio personalis non est nisi sola proprietate, ergo non differunt Angeli nisi per accidens"* – Albert, *II Sent.*, d. 3, a. 5, obj. 2-3, ed. Borgnet, vol. 27, p. 69; cf. *III Sent.*, d. 6, a. 2, ed. Borgnet, vol. 28, p. 128; *III Sent.*, d. 10, a. 1, quaest. 2, obj. 1 & ad quaest. 2, ad 1, ed. Borgnet, vol. 28, p. 187 & 189.

[1189] Cf. supra, "DISCRETIO PERSONALIS IN ANGELIS ET CONSIDERATIONES SUPER INDIVIDUATIONEM", p. 306-310.

for the individuation of the being, and we must consequently come to a knowledge of it *through* the properties of a thing, properties which are not, strictly speaking, the source of the singularity proper to personhood, though they are a sign of it, inasmuch as an extension of it[1190]. The *discretio* of personhood, then, lies precisely in the singularity constituted by a certain incommunicable *fundamentum*, distinguishable in some sense from the *ratio* of the essence or of the being (in the sense of simple act) of the individual. This situation holds true even with respect to God, where the *ratio* of or foundation for distinction is relative opposition, while the essence or divine being remains one. To the extent that they are intended as identifiable distinctive qualities of a thing, properties serve to enable us to distinguish persons, but do not represent the grounds for that distinction, though they may directly derive from that ground. When one engages the term *proprietas* in the context of personal distinction, the sense must be understood to mean not only that whereby we recognize a things distinctiveness, but also the very ground of distinction itself[1191].

A variety of predicates are such that they may be applied to but one person of the Trinity, in such a way that the use of these predicates will serve to distinctively identify one person in exclusion of the others. But these distinctive predicates do not necessarily capture the essential personal property whereby the person is the distinct individual that he is. An analogous example would be the set of fingerprints absolutely unique to one human individual and apt to permit his or her identification with complete certitude, but which cannot be considered to be the fundamental essential quality by which that person is distinct in personal being. In the Trinity, diverse names may be substituted for "Father" and "Son", such as "generator" and "begotten", "paternity" and "filiation", or "principle without a principle" and "principle having a principle". But, while the extension of these sets of terms is identical, they do not all express with equal precision that which *constitutes* the persons in their distinctive existential mode. To express this difference, one names the collection of properties which are unique to a given person but which do not establish it according to distinct personal being "properties of the person" (*proprietates personae*), while that singular property by which the person is constitutively

---

[1190] "*Revera proprietates ostendunt singularitatem personae et non faciunt, sed facit eam fundamentum esse particulans, et individuans ipsum esse per se super se, sed quia in Angelis est hoc elongatum a cognitione, ideo cognoscimus ipsum proprietatibus*" – Albert, *II Sent.*, d. 3, a. 5, ad 3, ed. Borgnet, vol. 27, p. 70.

distinct from all others is called the "personal property" (*proprietas personalis*). In men, the former shall consist in the unique collections of accidents setting one man off from another, while the latter, the *proprietas personalis*, shall be something intimately bound with each person's individual essence. In the Trinity, a *proprietas personae* will not differ from the *proprietas personalis* as accidental qualification from essential determination, but only according to their respective modes of signifying.

Proprietas personalis and proprietates personae

Something will be called a *proprietas* of the person when it belongs to that person alone or confers to him distinct being pertaining to no other person. When that property confers distinct being in the order of nature, i.e., is responsible for the person's being a distinct *res naturae*, it is called the *proprietas personalis*[1192]. If, on the other hand, the distinction resulting from the property is not strictly a distinction in the order of nature, but the property simply distinguishes the person according to this or that unique attribute, then it receives the denomination *proprietas personae*. Properties of the person, then, are said to be in the person in the sense of in that which has distinct being, while personal properties are in the person as that which confers distinct being[1193]. The personal property thus distinguishes the person as a principle of distinction, through which the person possesses its being distinctly, and for which reason it is said to "confer" distinct being. Properties of the person, on the other hand, serve to demonstrate or show the distinctness of the person, and as such are not principles of distinction but consequent upon distinct being. The last statement must be understood correctly. *As such*, that is, as demonstrative of the distinctness of the person, a *proprietas personae* is consequent upon distinct personal being; that is, from the point of view of its epistemic relation to cognition (since it permits us to recognize something as a person), it will be conceived as consequent to realization of the distinction. But this does not mean that it is actually posterior to distinc-

---

[1191] Cf. the Cappadocian perspective above in "INTEGRATION OF THESE CONCEPTS IN THE WRITINGS OF BASIL THE GREAT ~ GREGORY OF NYSSA", p. 39.

[1192] "*Si quidem distinctum esse facit in ordine naturae, dicitur proprietas personalis*" – Albert, *Sum. theol.*, I, tr. 9, q. 39, c. 2, a. 1, ad quaest. 1, ed. Colon., vol. 34, p. 296.

[1193] "*Proprietas enim personae est in persona sicut in eo quod habet esse distinctum; personalis enim proprietas est in persona sicut in eo cui confert esse distinctum*" – Albert, *Sum. theol.*, I, tr. 9, q. 39, c. 2, a. 1, ad 12, ed. Colon., vol. 34, p. 298.

tion; in fact, the property in question might very well be the *proprietas personalis* responsible for the distinction itself. It is simply a question of conceptualizing the property from the point of view of its role as indicator (as opposed to conceptualizing a property from the point of view of its role as principle of distinction, in the case that it be the *proprietas personalis*)[1194]. With the Cappadocian Fathers we already encountered the perspectives considering the *proprietates*, now as consequent upon the being of the persons, now as constitutive thereof. Albert systematically delineates where the distinction and identity lies between the concepts:

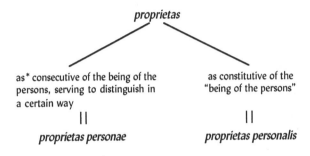

*We say "as" since it is a question of the same *proprietas* which in both cases is identical *in re* though different in mode of signification, as indeterminately and determinately signifying the person.

Finally, a property designating the relation of one distinct thing of nature to another, or designating the way in which one distinct thing of nature is referred to another, whether it be a *proprietas personalis* or a *proprietas personae*, is called *relatio*[1195]. As a result, every *proprietas personalis* implying inter-hypostatic reference has a double aspect: that according to which it is a *proprietas*, and that according to which it is a

[1194] *"Proprietas enim personae est in persona sicut in eo quod habet esse distinctum; personalis autem proprietas est in persona sicut in eo cui confert esse distinctum... proprietas personalis distinguit personam sicut principium distinctionis distinctum esse conferens; proprietas autem personae ostendit distinctionem non sicut principium distinctionis, sed sicut consequens distinctum esse secundum rationem intelligendi et sicut notificans distinctum esse et distinguens ab hoc, et non simpliciter"* – Albert, *Sum. theol.*, I, tr. 9, q. 39, c. 2, a. 1, ad 12 & 13, ed. Colon., vol. 34, p. 298.

[1195] *"Proprietas autem dicitur per hoc quod uni soli convenit vel distinctum esse facit personale vel distincti est proprium et illi soli convenit. Et si quidem distinctum esse facit in ordine naturae, dicitur proprietas personalis. Si autem distincto convenit ex hoc quod sic vel sic distinctum est, dicitur proprietas personae. Si autem dicit relationem distincti ad distinctum sive modum, quo unum distinctum refertur ad alterum, tunc dicitur relatio"* – Albert, *Sum. theol.*, I, tr. 9, q. 39, c. 2, a. 1, ad quaest. 1, ed. Colon., vol. 34, p. 296.

relation, which aspects differ, however, only in mode of signification (according as it belongs to but one person or according as it distinguishes the person from others) and not *in re*[1196].

Though a plurality of *proprietates* can exist in a single person without resulting in a numerical diversity of persons or *per se* existents, what accounts for personal multiplication in the Trinity is the opposition of relation, since the correlative opposite cannot be one with the term to which it is opposed. If such a relation obtains with respect to the *proprietas*, we call it the *proprietas personalis*, from which personal distinction is obtained[1197]. Nevertheless, the principle of distinction is not the *proprietas qua proprietas*, but the *proprietas* insofar as opposed to a correlative term. "To generate" and "to spirate", for example, signify personal properties, but they signify them according to act, and not according to relative opposition. Insofar as act, the personal properties do not accomplish distinction[1198]. In fact, as act, the *proprietates* are no principle of anything in the divinity, since there is nothing in the divinity besides that sole same act (which is the essence). The Father, then, does not differ from the Son because he has an exclusive act of generating, but because he is relatively opposed to the Son as generator to generated; there is no generative *act* which can be said to be possessed by one person and not another. Paternity, however, is not different from generation: it simply designates the same reality from a different point of view. While designating the same *proprietas*, "generation" does so according to act, while "paternity" signifies precisely *ut proprietatem* (that is, as *proprietas* in the sense of that through which persons are distinguished), and this because paternity is relatively opposed to filiation[1199].

[1196] *"Duo sunt in proprietate personali, unum scilicet, quo est proprietas, alterum, quo est relatio; quae duo licet non sint duo secundum rem, sunt tamen duo secundum modum significandi"* – Albert, *Sum. theol.*, I, tr. 9, q. 39, c. 2, a. 1, ad quaest. 4, ed. Colon., vol. 34, p. 298.

[1197] *"Plures enim proprietates sunt in una persona et non faciunt numerum personarum sive per se existentium... Haec est etiam causa, quare propter tres notiones, quae sunt in patre, non dicitur pater trinus, et propter duas, quae sunt in filio, non dicitur filius binus... talis multiplicatio non est ex proprietate, secundum quod proprietas est, sed ex proprietate personali, secundum quod oppositionem habet ad correlativum sibi oppositum"* – Albert, *Sum. theol.*, I, tr. 9, q. 39, c. 2, a. 2, ad 12, ed. Colon., vol. 34, p. 304.

[1198] *"Generare et spirare proprietates personales dicunt ut actus, proprietates autem personales per oppositionem relationis distinguunt personas et determinant"* – Albert, *Sum. theol.*, I, tr. 7, q. 30, c. 3, a. 1, sol., ed. Colon., vol. 34, p. 233.

[1199] *"Paternitas non differt a generatione, quin immo generatio eandem proprietatem dicit quam paternitas; sed dicit eam ut actum, paternitas autem ut proprietatem, et haec duo non faciunt differre rem a re, sed faciunt differentiam in modo significandi"* – Albert, *Sum. theol.*, I, tr. 7, q. 30, c. 3, a. 1, ad 7, ed. Colon., vol. 34, p. 234.

The particular proprietates of the Trinity

Each Trinitarian person possesses a variety of properties strictly bound to the person which he is. We have seen that "properties of the person", by which an individual can be singularly identified, are not identical to the "personal property", the latter of which alone constitutes the personal being of the individual thing of nature. For the sake of contextualization, we should briefly mention, in addition to the personal property, the principal properties distinctively tied to personal distinction. Three such properties belong to the Father, two of which belong to him alone and one of which is shared with the Son. Those distinctive of or coextensive with the Father are the properties of paternity and *innascibilitas*. The first is the personal property of the Father, while the second, though adequately and uniquely identifying the person of the Father, does not positively identify the personal property. Finally, the property said to be shared with the Son is active spiration, as Father and Son, taken together, constitute the active principle of spiration. This property, since it is shared with another person, cannot serve to adequately distinguish the Father. To the Son belong two such properties. One is properly the Son's and distinctive of his person, namely filiation in virtue of passive generation; the other is the just mentioned common (active) spiration. Lastly, one property pertains to the Holy Spirit, and this is called passive spiration, which is strictly distinctive of his person[1200].

Determinate and indeterminate signification

The complex names for the divine persons based on principality (such as *"principium non de principio"* ascribed to the Father, and *"principium de principio"* ascribed to the Son) designate, in each case, a duality of notions, only one of which is properly distinctive of the person – as the first part of the title ascribed to the Father, *"principium"*, signifies his paternity while the second part, *"non de principio"*, stands for

---

[1200] *"Tres sunt relationes sive proprietates patris, duae soli patri convenientes, scilicet innascibilitas et paternitas; tertia patri et filio communis, inquantum unum sunt in spirando, quae dicitur communis spiratio activa; duae convenientes filio, una propria, filiatio scilicet, alia communis filio et patri, quae dicta est communis spiratio; una in spiritu sancto, quae dicitur spiratio passiva"* – Albert, *Sum. theol.*, I, tr. 9, q. 39, c. 1, ad 10, ed. Colon., vol. 34, p. 293. *"Et ideo notiones quinque sunt, tres scilicet in patre, una in filio propria, una in filio et patre, quae secundum quod est in duobus, non facit numerum, et sic in patre et filio non sunt nisi quattuor, et una in spiritu sancto"* – *Sum. theol.*, I, tr. 9, q. 39, c. 2, a. 1, ad 1, ed. Colon., vol. 34, p. 296.

his *innascibilitas,* and the first part of the name given to the Son, *"principium"*, signifies the notion of active spiration while *"de principio"* stands for filiation[1201]. Nevertheless, they do so in an indeterminate and confused way. To name "paternity" indirectly through the notion of *principium* fails to name the *proprietas personalis* in a distinct and determinate manner; similarly, to designate *innascibilitas* by means of the notion of *non de principio,* since *innascibilitas* is necessarily implied by it, is to indeterminately signify that *proprietas personae*[1202].

When defending the legitimacy of designating the several persons by means of negative predication, Albert concedes that the negations do not explicitly name the *proprietates personales,* but vindicates their utility and appropriateness, while pointing out, in addition, that they are not purely and simply negations but always retain something positive and thus possess an affirmative aspect. A negation, such as that expressed by *"quis a quo non sit"*, though it cannot directly signify the personal property in the sense of explicitating a singular mode of existence, nevertheless designates a unique property of the person, *proprietas personae,* and thereby indicates a particular mode proper to the singular existence which the person is[1203]. From this we can gather that the *proprietas personalis* must designate a singular mode of existence, which is not equivalent to the designation of a mode of singular existence. The first explicitates the unique *mode,* while the second only accentuates the singularity of the existence. The second is sufficient to singularly identify one individual and therefore does specify something/someone one, but it does not name the particular (positive) modality by which that person is distinguished. The negative ex-

---

[1201] *"Cum dicitur 'principium non de principio', stat pro patre consignificans notionem paternitatis et innascibilitatis, paternitatis in eo quod dicitur 'principium', innascibilitatis in eo quod dicitur 'non de principio'. Et cum dicitur 'principium de principio', stat pro persona filii consignificando notionem filiationis in eo quod dicitur 'de principio', et notionem spirationis in hoc quod dicitur 'principium'. Et cum dicitur 'principium de utroque', principium stat pro persona spiritus sancti consignificando notionem processionis a patre et filio et consignificando relationem ad creaturam in hoc quod dicitur 'principium'"* – Albert, *Sum. theol.,* I, tr. 9, q. 41, c. 1, a. 1, sol., ed. Colon., vol. 34, p. 315.

[1202] *"Dupliciter contingit dicere notionem, scilicet determinate et distincte et indeterminate et confuse: determinate ut pater et paternitas, filius et filiatio, spiritus et spiratio; confuse autem et indeterminate sicut principium... 'principium de principio', circumloquitur persona filii; et per hoc quod dicitur 'principium', communiter et confuse dicit processionem activam spiritus sancti, per hoc autem quod dicitur 'de principio', confuse dicit filiationem"* – Albert, *Sum. theol.,* I, tr. 9, q. 41, c. 1, a. 2, sol., ed. Colon., vol. 34, p. 316. Cf. *Sum. theol.,* I, tr. 9, q. 39, c. 2, a. 1, sol., ed. Colon., vol. 34, p. 296.

[1203] *"'Quis a quo non sit' non dicat singularis existentiae modum, tamen dicit singularis existentis modum; et ideo non est proprietas personalis, sed proprietas personae; dicit enim modum eius qui est 'principium non de principio'"* – Albert, *Sum. theol.,* I, tr. 9, q. 39, c. 1, ad 2, ed. Colon., vol. 34, p. 292.

pression *"quis a quo non sit"* or *"principium non de principio"*, however, does name or isolate the thing as being something, because it is not a simple negation, but retains a genus; that is, a generic being is signified, while a particular form or determination of that genus is denied. Accordingly, the phrase *"pater innascibilis sive non exiens ab alio"* posits the Father in existence, but denies the particular forms or modes of existence proper to every other existent. In fact, the negations in question are negations – in the genus of existence, as Albert puts it – of modes of being in the order of nature, whereby they suffice to delimit something in being. Consequently, through such negations, the *esse* of the *proprietas personalis* is, indirectly, also affirmed of the subject[1204]. One affirms positively what the other affirms negatively (and implicitly), and the negative predication is made possible only in virtue of the positive reality signified by the *proprietas personalis*[1205].

The personal property in men

Essentially constitutive of the person

Whether the above stipulation as to the intension of *"proprietas"* – namely, that it be convertible with (as a constitutive difference of) the singular individual whose very act it is – is intended to apply to every *proprietas personalis*, including those of men, can only be gathered from the context. Clearly, in the case of the Trinity, the *proprietas* is no accidental reality, and this discretion serves to vindicate the role of the *proprietas* as distinguishing the very personal being of the persons. In inferiors, however, it seems that any "property" will necessarily fall into one of the non-substantial predicaments, whence it is not so evident how the *proprietas personalis* might be capable of constituting the personal being of the person (which cannot be something accidental[1206], and which cannot be naturally consecutive to the person). The

---

[1204] *"Est negatio in genere existentis in esse ordinis naturae; et ideo negatio illa ponit et fundatur in esse... Et esse proprietatis tali negatione determinatum affirmatur de subiecto, cum dicitur 'pater est secundum esse personale aliquis non ens ab alio'"* – Albert, *Sum. theol.,* I, tr. 9, q. 39, c. 1, ad 5, ed. Colon., vol. 34, p. 293.

[1205] *"Ipsae notiones significantur... scilicet confuse et determinate, ut 'principium non de principio' et 'paternitas'"* – Albert, *Sum. theol.,* I, tr. 9, q. 39, c. 2, a. 1, ad quaest. 1, ed. Colon., vol. 34, p. 296. Cf. *Sum. theol.,* I, tr. 9, q. 41, c. 1, a. 2, sol., ed. Colon., vol. 34, p. 316.

[1206] At least not in the sense of a contingent accident, and perhaps not as an accident at all (proper or otherwise). The person is made to be distinct and incommunicable through the *proprietas* *"distinctum proprietate"*. But, because accidents are excluded

problem making itself felt is expressed in the objection stating that a property, and any property, is, at least logically, posterior to the being of that of which it is the property, and that, therefore, it is not possible for the "personal property" to constitute an individual in its personal being[1207]. The difficulty can be avoided, however, by arguing that the "particularizing property" in inferior persons actually is convertible with the person, according to the sense of *"proprietas"* already indicated, that is, according as that *proprietas* be understood as the "specific difference" of the individual, and in this way the *proprium* in question consists of something non-accidental, even constitutive of the person as such. To fail to distinguish the senses in which *"proprietas"* may be predicated, and to limit it to implying accidentality results, therefore, in equivocation[1208].

The *proprietas*, then, indeed, gets at something fundamental to the very being of the person, and it is a question of the singular difference which is fully constitutive of personhood, and in this sense must be convertible with the person, in the same way that the specific difference is convertible with the species (that is, in the same way that an ultimate specific difference is convertible, since no part of a definition is convertible with the *definiendum* except for such a difference)[1209]. We must bear in mind, however, that such a difference is convertible with the species it demarcates only inasmuch as it be signified substantively or quidditatively and as a whole, while, insofar as specifically *distinguishing*, it is signified qualitatively and as a property or part of the species.

---

from the role of distinguishing substances according to individuality – that is, since accidents, though they permit us to distinguish one substance from another, nonetheless do not constitute one substance's distinction from another –, the *proprietas* cannot be an accident. Cf. Albert, *III Sent.*, d. 6, a. 2, ed. Borgnet, vol. 28, p. 128: *"quod stat sub natura communi, distinctum quidem est per materiam... distinguibile est per accidentia individuantia... substantia erit distincta per materiam hanc, distinguibilis autem per accidentia et non distincta per ea".* Cf. supra, "DIFFERENT KINDS OF MODES OF DISTINCTION", p. 299 (especially p. 301-301).

[1207] *"Proprium autem sive proprietas secundum rationem intelligendi est post esse eius cuius est proprium. Non ergo potest esse, quod proprietas personalis personam constituat in esse personali"* – Albert, *Sum. theol.*, I, tr. 9, q. 39, c. 2, a. 1, obj. 11, ed. Colon., vol. 34, p. 295.

[1208] Cf. Albert, *Sum. theol.*, I, tr. 9, q. 39, c. 2, a. 1, ad 11, ed. Colon., vol. 34, p. 298.

[1209] Since the *proprietates* distinguish one person from another, and since that which accomplishes distinction is called a "difference", the *proprietates* are rightly called "differences": *"nec per substantialem differentiam nec per accidentalem differunt personae... ibi enim differentia dicitur, quidquid unum ab alio distinguit; et quia proprietates distinguunt personas, translato nomine proprietates differentiae dicuntur"* – Albert, *Sum. theol.*, I, tr. 9, q. 40, c. 1, ad quaest. 2/ad 10, ed. Colon., vol. 34, p. 309.

Comparative examination of "differences" for person

Whether the earlier considered convertibility between person and the intelligent is most foundational in regard of establishing a thing's personal being is unclear, especially in light of the humanity of Christ which, at least on first consideration, we should want to call rational. If rationality is the key, and sufficient, personal determinant, then we must avoid saying that Christ's humanity is rational, by affirming that it is only the person of the Word who is made (humanly) rational – where we do not even attribute "rational" to the human nature of Christ in the sense that it be a rational thing, since as thing (in the most concrete substantive sense) it is identical to the unique personal subject. Let us note that such a standpoint actually rests upon stripping Christ's humanity of the subjectival status of being that of which rationality is predicated; that is, even if rationality is a convertible specific difference for personhood, and we must therefore deny such a qualification of Christ's human nature, this is only possible in virtue of a denial of a certain mode of existence proper to *id quod plene est.* Is it correct to single out rationality as the constitutive difference for person? Already we are obliged by Christ's humanity to look for another, perhaps definitionally subordinate, but ontologically prior, criterion: namely, the subjectival status (and suppositional privileges which accompany it) proper to *id quod plene est,* which we can call, for the sake of conceptual clarity, perseity. Yet, since true rationality, one might argue, entails perseity, "the rational" would guard its role as a convertible specific difference. On the other hand, it seems hardly possible to minimize the mode according which we attribute rationality to Christ's human nature when taking into account the presence of the rational soul, wherefore the role of perseity seems to take precedence. Perseity, however, is obviously an insufficient perfection from which to derive the ultimate specific difference for person, since there are a great variety of *per se* existents which are not persons. Moreover, in the attempt to categorically descend from the most general notion of *ens* to person, it is not clear as to the order of division with respect to the perfections of rationality and perseity:

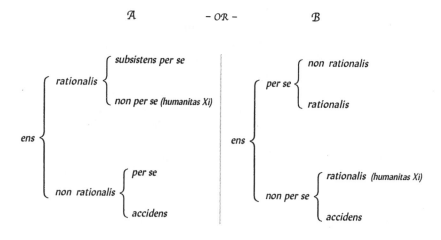

Of course, the problem already resides in the non-univocal use of the term *ens*, and especially when predicated of the non per se (which seems to imply accidentality, since the propermost concept of substance implies perseity[1210]). The confusion furthermore arises from speaking about Christ's humanity itself as a substance, since it is neither a primary substance in the independent way typical of primary substances nor a secondary substance in the sense of abstract. The most natural division would be the following, where, however, we might observe, neither perseity nor rationality are able of themselves to supply the ultimate specific difference for personhood, for "the rational" is no longer convertible with "person" if Christ's humanity is taken as a rational thing:

[1210] Cf. Aristotle, *Categories*, c. 2.

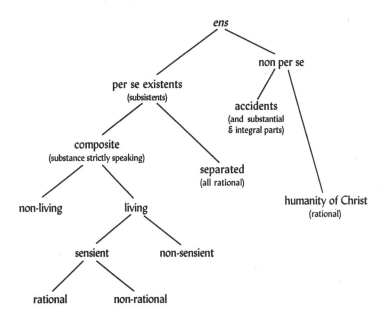

On the other hand, precisely with respect to the generic concept of the *per se* existent, rationality does indeed operate as a specific difference (in a non-convertible way[1211]). And since the *per se* existent is the individual or primary substance (the supposit), the specific and generic parts of the definition of person are most adequately expressed by the Boethian formulation qualifying individual substance as rational:

[1211] Since the humanity of Christ cannot be completely ignored, given that an authentically convertible difference is convertible anywhere and everywhere, and not just with respect to a delimited class of beings.

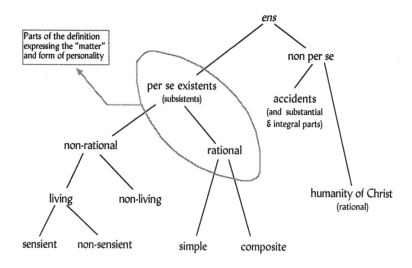

But all of this is an attempt to designate a difference capable of constituting personhood at a general level, for every kind of person. In other words, the perfections we have considered until now could not of themselves constitute *a* particular person, but are constitutive of personhood universally considered. Thus rationality and perseity may be in some sense constitutive differences in the definition of person, but they are not constitutive differences of particular persons. But it is just such constitutive differences of individual persons which are the personal properties. And these constitutive differences shall indeed turn out to be convertible with the unique individuals they particularize. Moreover, we have seen that the *proprietas personalis* consists of different things in different kinds of persons. As a result, there is nothing to prevent us from calling designated matter, for example, the "personal property" for man, and "this designated matter" the personal property of "this man". Here we are at an entitative level which is not accidental and which is convertible in a certain way with the person, inasmuch as "this body", where body signifies as a whole, is the person[1212]. A fuller definition of person, then, would include, in addition to the perseity entailed in substantial being and rationality, the notion of a wholly unique and singular property (in virtue of which individual persons are multiplied with respect to the more gen-

---

[1212] Cf. Aquinas, *De ente et ess.*, c. 2.

eral notion of person)[1213]. But the nature of such a property cannot be specified in the definition, lest we limit the definition to one family of persons or to but a single person, as, for example, when specifying designated matter as the personal property, which limits our scope to human persons (in a similar way, we could restrict our definition of person to divine persons by including the notion of relations of origin).

The appropriating proprietas and the appropriated thing

The *proprietas*, as was mentioned, was conceptualized in order to give a cognitive handle to the distinctness of the persons (as distinction, in order to be understood, necessitates a principle of distinction). However, the actual identity between the *proprietas* and the person it distinguishes means that the two terms signify the same *res* according to diverse points of view, viz: *ut distinguens* and *ut distincto*, respectively. The *proprietas*, then, is able to designate the person itself, as when we say that the Father is paternity, and, in this case, the *proprietas*, paternity, is signified as *id quod est appropriatum*, as opposed to *approprians vel id quod appropriat.* This twofold way of signifying the *proprietas*, namely, *ut approprians* (which is proper to the concept taken in itself) and *ut appropriata* (pertaining to it insofar as substantively identified with the hypostasis it delimits) corresponds, according to Albert, with the alternate uses of the term as it is found in St. Augustine and St. Hilary, respectively[1214]. Albert provides an example to illustrate the senses by distinguishing Socrates – an individual, concretized, "appropriated" (made "proper" or uniquely particular) human nature – from socratesness (*socratitas*) – the entirety of the individualizing elements making Socrates to be *this* man, "appropriating" his nature[1215].

[1213] As is accomplished, for example, by the second Victorine definition and that of the Lombard ablatively mentioning the incommunicable property or existential mode.

[1214] Cf. Albert, *Sum. theol.*, I, tr. 9, q. 39, c. 2, a. 1, quest. 1 & sol., ed. Colon., vol. 34, p. 298-299.

[1215] "*Huius exemplum est, quia Socrates est proprium sicut appropriatum, socratitas autem, quae est collectio omnium appropriantium Socratem, est proprium sicut approprians. Augustinus igitur in assignatione sua ponit propria, quae sunt sicut appropriantia secundum modum significandi posita, Hilarius vero ponit propria, quae sunt sicut appropriata. Non sunt diversa inter se nisi secundum modum intelligendi, et non secundum rem. Et cum dicitur 'Pater est, qui genuit vel qui semper pater est', hoc idem est secundum rem 'pater semper paternitate pater est et paternitate genuit', nec differunt nisi... quod unum dicit proprium appropriatum et alterum approprians. Et haec re in divinis non differunt, quia propter indifferentiam simplicitatis, quae est in divinis, approprians est appropriatum et e converso*" – Albert, *Sum. theol.*, I, tr. 9, q. 39, c. 2, a. 1, sol., ed. Colon., vol. 34, p. 299-300.

Each are the same *proprium*, the former as appropriated, the latter as appropriating. Albert points out that in the perfect simplicity of the divinity convertible identity obtains between the appropriated and the appropriating. This remark suggests that such is not the case in inferiors, as, for example, we cannot identify an individual man with the principle of his individuation, that principle being understood as a material constituent of his nature. On the other hand, the very example proposed asserts an identity between Socrates as an individual human nature and his "appropriating" principle(s), the latter of which must then be understood as his individual human nature *as* appropriating. The discrepancy derives from the diverse ways of considering the individuating principles of human nature. Considered from the point of view of what individuates a man with respect to the common and conceptually abstract human nature, seeing as designated matter suffices for this, we identify this matter, which is not convertible with the man of whom it is a part, as the principle of individuation. Considered from the point of view of the individually exercised act of existence proper to this man, we identify the individual essence, consisting of this matter and everything else proper to the individual which he is, as principle of individuation. In the first case, the *proprietas*, by which the common nature is contracted to this individual, is simpler and partial with respect to the individual; in the second case, the *proprietas*, by which the subject individual nature is the individual nature that it is, is indistinguishable from its subject when considered from the point of view of what it is, though it is distinguishable (in concept only) when considered from the point of view of its distinguishing role, i.e. what it *does* for the supposit (which is nothing other than to signify the supposit *ut quomodo*, as opposed to *ut quid vel quis*):

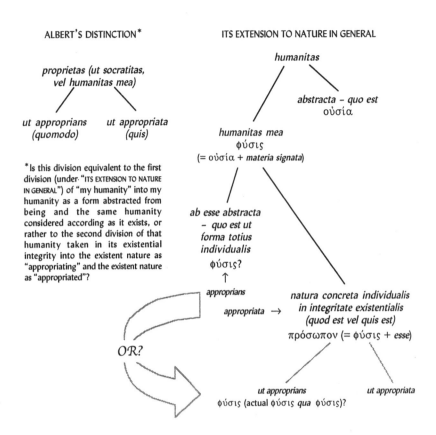

ALBERT'S DISTINCTION*

proprietas (ut socratitas,
vel humanitas mea)

ut approprians   ut appropriata
(quomodo)   (quis)

*Is this division equivalent to the first division (under· "ITS EXTENSION TO NATURE IN GENERAL") of "my humanity" into my humanity as a form abstracted from being and the same humanity considered according as it exists, or rather to the second division of that humanity taken in its existential integrity into the existent nature as "appropriating" and the existent nature as "appropriated"?

ITS EXTENSION TO NATURE IN GENERAL

humanitas

abstracta - quo est
οὐσία

humanitas mea
φύσις
(= οὐσία + materia signata)

ab esse abstracta
- quo est ut
forma totius
individualis
φύσις?
↑
approprians

appropriata →

natura concreta individualis
in integritate existentialis
(quod est vel quis est)
πρόσωπον (= φύσις + esse)

ut approprians   ut appropriata
φύσις (actual φύσις qua φύσις)?

OR?

The question is whether Albert intends *socratitas* as the individual nature in abstraction from its act of existence or as the individual nature in its complete existential integrity. Based on his description of *socratitas* as the collection of that which individualizes Socrates, this *proprietas, socratitas*, seems to be the existing principle(s) of individuation, which are nothing other than what the individual Socrates is, only considered from a different point of view, namely, insofar as *principle of* his distinctness – i.e. *ut approprians*. The question we must ask ourselves, however, is whether *socratitas ut approprians* (that is the existing principle[s] of individuation *insofar as principle* of individuation – and thus, somehow, *quod est ut quo est*) is at all distinct (even logically) from *socratitas ut forma totius individualis ab actu existendi abstracta*. Perhaps the difference lies in this: the latter is simply *quo est*, while the former is *quod est ut quo est*, the one notion arrived at by prescinding from the act of existence, the other arrived at by considering the discrete existent from the point of view of that which distinguishes (presupposing here an identity between *quod est* and *quo est* even at the level of creatures when the *quo est* is a question of the undefinable individual nature)[1216]. All of these considerations become extremely important in addressing the problem of distinguishing the human nature from the personal subject in Christ, where the human nature itself can be regarded either as such and as a natural *quo est* in its own right or according to its concrete mode of existing derived from the hypostatic property of the Word[1217].

Conclusion

Because the *proprietas* is the very reason for the distinctiveness formal to personality, analyzing the notion in itself and comparing it with the distinct thing it is understood to determine draws a vast range of considerations into a panorama. Conceived in an analogous way as a "principle of individuation", the *proprietas* functions for all persons after the manner of a constitutive difference in constituting individual persons. With regard to creatures, we observed that the distinctive principle and subject of distinction are related to one another accord-

---

[1216] The newly introduced notion of *quod est ut quo est* may be explained in the following terms. *Quod est* insofar as *quo est* is the concrete existent form (which is identical to the supposit according to individual act) considered not insofar as it is or is concrete, but insofar as formal, according to which it is viewed as a potency with respect to being even though it necessarily includes that being in order to be concrete and to be at all (for which reason it is an *actual* potency and not said to be *in* potency to being but only *a* potency with respect to the being it has [and from which it is being distinguished as such, similarly to the way in which we obtain a concept of the supposit *denominative accipitur*]). What we are identifying here is the *quo est qua* concretely existing, the individualized nature *in actu* (whence its possession of being and designation as *quod est*, since it is the real substance of the supposit, that is primary substance), but according to what is proper to it *in quantum natura*. Such a substance is certainly identical *in re* with the supposit, but differs from the latter according to the mode of its signification. It singles out the natural or formal aspect of the unique referent which is at once a specific or particular kind of thing as well as an existent. Both of these attributes truly characterize the referent, whence it may be signified from the point of view of either, and what is predicated of the term possessing a formal mode of signification (the *quod est* as *quo est*, or the *forma totius individualis realis*) is not always also predicable of the term having a subjective mode of signification (the *quod est ut quod est* [properly in possession of being], or the *individuum seipsum*).

[1217] In this latter case, the human nature in Christ possesses both a hypostatic signification (expressing the unity of person) and that of a *quod est ut quo est* insofar as *substantia concreta ut determinabile* (cf. supra, "HYPOSTASIS", p. 221-222; "THE PRECISE DENOTATION OF 'HYPOSTASIS', ITS DISTINCTIVE MODE OF SIGNIFICATION", p. 234, 237). These considerations will have an important role to play in our subsequent study on the Incarnation and the unity of person in Christ.

ing to a difference in being, as what is more simple to what is less simple, *quo est* to *quod est*, implying composition and an absolute diversity between subsisting subjects. Contrary to what obtains in creatures, a divine *proprietas* differs from the person only according to mode of signification, the first predicated *ut quomodo*, the second *ut quis*. The ontological identity of the relations with the substance safeguards for the several hypostases constituted by the distinctive relations the unity of substantial being in which the constitutive differences are themselves identified. Nevertheless, the hypostases constituted by these relations are truly distinct, in virtue of the fact that the relations, although identical to the substance, are opposed to one another, precluding the presence of more than one within the same subject, whence a diversity of hypostases.

Persons differ among themselves precisely according to the differences between their *proprietates*. If the principles of individual distinction imply natural division, then the instances of personal being effected will represent separate natural realities. Because the *ratio proprietatum* in the Trinity was shown to be nothing other than relative opposition, the *proprietates* do not differ from one another at an absolute level, whence the persons they constitute differ only in a relative way. For, divine simplicity not only precludes that the *proprietates* differ in reality from the persons whom they distinguish, but also that the *proprietates* as constitutive of the persons differ really from one another (even if they do differ really *as relations*, i.e. as relatively opposed).

The determination imported by the *proprietates* pertains only to supposits and not to the essence, since they determine only as they are opposed, and they are opposed only insofar as relative and correlative (the opposition consisting in the fact that one relative property cannot be shared by a co-relative subject). Such opposition has nothing to do with the essence but resides exclusively between co-related terms (the persons).

Naming that *whereby* the substantial subject is distinct, the *proprietas* signifies as distinguishing, and not as distinct, for which reason it is conceived abstractly (even if there is no difference in being according to which the *proprietas* is simpler than the concretely signified hypostasis – in God, the *proprietates* being identical to the persons they oppose).

The *proprietas* as such is not signified as existing *per se*, since such a characteristic belongs to supposits alone (distinct subjects of being) and the proper mode of signification common to all notions (including the *proprietas*) designates a thing according to the manner of its distinction, that is, as manifesting personal distinction. What sets the *proprietas personalis* off from other notions is, first of all, the fact that it is a *proprietas* unable to be found in more than one individual[1218], and, secondly, the fact that it is the precise cause (and not just a sign) of the singularity proper to the hypostasis.

Certain *proprietates* demonstrate the distinctness of a person, but fail to denote the principle of that distinction. Such are the "properties of the person" which indeterminately signify the reason for personal distinction (corresponding to one of two forms of predication *quomodo*). Those predicates *determinately* signifying that whereby a person is a distinct hypostatic unity are *proprietates personales*; they are the constitutive differences producing numerical (i.e. individual) distinction; they are what confers distinct personal being. Such a *proprietas* precisely denotes a thing's singular mode of existence, and not just a given (albeit proper) mode of that singular existence; while a variety of proper predicates are able to correctly indicate that in which a subject's distinction consists, only by naming a true *proprietas personalis* do we precisely respond to the question "*How* is it that a person is distinct?".

An inseparability between the *proprietas* and the persons they constitute was demonstrated by Albert. The hypostasis is formally dependent upon the *proprietas* for its very hypostatic being. At the same time, every instance of perfect and complete (i.e. ontologically independent) distinction entails a unique hypostatic being. The result is a logical convertibility between principle of numerical distinction and personal being or hypostasis. Such an observation, we affirmed, constitutes the core explanatory instrument in addressing the personal unity in Christ.

Regarding the intrinsic constitutive value of the *proprietas* with respect to individual subsistents, Albert speaks, finally, of a dual sense in which the *proprietas personalis* may be signified, depending on whether we signify it according to its proper notion or according as it is substantively identified with the distinct thing it determines. In the first way, we signify the principle of numerical distinction *ut approprians*; in the second, *ut appropriata*. While the latter way of signifying that principle, namely as identical to the distinguished thing, is evidently le-

---

[1218] This assumes that we maintain the traditional fivefold notional discretion in God which includes a nomination common to more than one person, namely active spiration; cf. Aquinas, *Sum. theol.*, I, 32, 2-3.

gitimate in God (in light of the divine simplicity), in a certain sense, even in inferiors the *proprietas*, when taken as the formal principle of the individually exercised act of existence, is perhaps indistinguishable from its subject when considering *what* it is, which is possibly nothing other than the essence itself *qua* actually this – though it is always logically distinguishable from the subject with respect to its distinguishing *role* (possibly expressive of but a notional value)[1219].

Whether or not a certain identity between principle of distinction and distinguished reality may be affirmed in creatures, the creature remains a composition between potency and act[1220] and one person is substantially distinct from another (facilitating the conceptualization of personal plurality). In God, nothing of the sort may be affirmed. Rather person, *proprietas*, essence and supposit, are all one *in re* and no person differs from another absolutely speaking, the respective differences between them reducing to diverse modes of signification. Contemplating the mystery of the Trinity, we must constantly coordinate that which we signify diversely with a "remedial" mode of predication honoring supreme simplicity. All of this is necessary if we wish to speak about God, with respect to whom we must constantly correct and purify our temporal and composite human concepts, finding within them those pure perfections able to be transferred by analogy to the most perfect and simple divine reality. When confronted with the difficulty of speaking of personality in the most simple Godhead, when the structure of the person, according as it is conceived by us, presents itself as complex and composed, we are offered several choices: either (a) we abandon our conception of person in God, because it appears to be incompatible with the divine simplicity, denying that there is any form of distinction whatsoever between person and proprietas, whence the persons are distinguished not according to the

---

[1219] We cannot enter here into an analysis of the relationship between the individual and the formal principles of its concrete actual individuality, something which beseeches an equally complicated consideration of the relation between the actual essence and its existence (especially if the latter is proposed as the principle of individuation), but await another occasion to do so, when we address the Christological problem of the status of the individuality of the human nature in Christ and the mode of its individuation.

[1220] This holds even were an actual essence and its being considered as being only logically distinct, since actual essence as such still represents a limited form of being dependent upon the first cause, that is, the whole essence-reality admitting for its sustenance in reality a relation to God with which it cannot be identical (unless one were to destroy the absolute status of the essence). Again, these (rather Suarezian) considerations cannot be developed here.

fictive principle invoked in our definition, but *a seipsae*, or (b) we conceptualize the structure of the divine persons in direct correspondence with our understanding, such that person and the relative principle constituting it receive the objective value of *quod est* and *quo est* respectively, the latter (along with the essence) informing the former; or (c) we follow a middle path respectful of the motives, but refusing the extremism, of both [1221]. The first choice was that of Praepositinus, the second attributed to Gilbert of Poitiers, while the third is proper to St. Albert. Only the last choice affords a theological solution to the problem. While the first pays homage to the divine simplicity (respecting the demands of the object), it utterly dissolves the conception of a diversity of formally distinguishable aspects within the same reality, neglectful of possible differences in modes of attribution and supposition [1222]. The second choice, though rightfully assigning value to the structure of intelligence and its cognitive content, makes the fundamental error of superimposing the order of knowing upon the order of being. The choice of Albert, as we have seen, demonstrates the possibility of objectively recognizing relations in God and the presence of several persons constituted by these relations along with the essence without undermining the simplicity of that essence, illustrating that the intellect can licitly conceive of a certain structure within the person even if it cannot attribute the differences according to which the elements within that structure are conceived (for example, the difference between what is abstract and what is concrete) to the objective reality. In this light, "the unquestionable merit of Albert is that of having demonstrated once and for all how the use of dialectics, balanced by profound metaphysical conceptions, is able to become a most valid instrument in the hands of the theologian. This was more of less lacking amongst Albert's predecessors. Their oscillation between conceptualism and exaggerated realism rendered them incapable of specifying the path to follow" [1223].

[1221] Cf. A. Pompei, op. cit., p. 289-290.

[1222] *"Compellunt nos [haeretici] discernere in nominum intentionibus; et cum noster intellectus sit materialis, et non valeat accipere simplex nisi per modum compositionis, sicut consuevit in inferioribus, accipit eodem modo in superioribus, non dicens quidem rem compositam, sed discernens inter ea quae sunt eadem res, secundum modum attribuendi et supponendi"* – Albert, *I Sent.*, d. 33, a. 1, sol., ed. Borgnet, vol. 26, p. 140.

[1223] A. Pompei, op. cit., p. 278.

III. SYNTHESIS AND OVERVIEW

1.   OVERALL HISTORICAL PERSPECTIVE

2.   FINAL CONCLUSION

III.1. OVERALL HISTORICAL PERSPECTIVE

The two central inquiries presented in our INTRODUCTION were: "In what does the formal constitution of person consist?", and "How is person defined?". There we observed that a response to these questions must begin with the givens of Christian faith and move toward correctly distinguishing person and nature within the context of the Church's reflection on the divine mysteries of the Trinity and Incarnation. Just how has this reflection progressed across the centuries?

Cappadocian theology of the person

Basil the Great, alongside the other Cappadocians, led the way in this effort, by formalizing an *a posteriori* conception of language complemented with a theory of names by which to distinguish common from proper designation and absolute from relative signification [1224], and, later, by specifying the sense of the Trinitarian language as it was found in what appeared to be contentiously single-sided formulas within different Churches [1225], clarifying the difference between οὐσία and ὑπόστασις [1226]. Briefly, the basic element which differentiates nature from person, and which renders the former the latter, is the particular property of a thing. As we saw in our survey of Cappadocian theology, Basil, Gregory of Nazianzus and Gregory of Nyssa alike, all define hypostasis as the concrete reality standing beneath the common nature in virtue of the latter's reception of definite particularities. Person, or hypostasis, then, is the distinct and particular thing in contrast to universal nature; it is also that which subsists. Basil also supplies us with the fundamental doctrine of the incommunicability of this hypostasis, understood as following upon the inconciliable

---

[1224] Cf. Basil the Great, *Contra Eunomius*, II, 4, 9, 17, 22, 28; cf. B. Sesboüé (editor), *Histoire des dogmes, Le Dieu du Salut*, Desclée, Paris 1994, p. 285-290.

[1225] The homoiousian Churches, either non-Nicene or neo-Nicene, held firmly to tri-hypostatic Trinitarian formulations but had not yet accepted the "consubstantial" of the old-Nicene Churches, while it still remained for the old-Nicene Churches to profess three perfect hypostases. Cf. B. Sesboüé (editor), *Histoire des dogmes, Le Dieu du Salut*, Desclée, Paris 1994, p. 297-299.

[1226] Cf. Ps-Basil, *Ep.* 38, *Lettres*, I, p. 81-92; Basil the Great, *Ep.* 52, 3, *Lettres*, I, p. 135-136; *Ep.* 125, 1, *Lettres*, II, p. 31; *Ep.* 210, 3-5, *Lettres*, II, p. 192-196; *Ep.* 236, 6, *Lettres*, III, p. 53-54. Cf. supra, "INTEGRATION OF THESE CONCEPTS IN THE WRITINGS OF BASIL THE GREAT ~ GREGORY OF NYSSA", p. 39.

ἰδιωμάτα themselves. The logical precision of Gregory of Nyssa furthermore clarifies that the substance rendered person through the
ἰδιώμα is nothing at all in reality without the particularity resulting
from that. The result of these explanations is a wholly physical understanding (and definition) of personhood; person is not distinguished
from the concrete individualized nature[1227].

Cyrillian intuition

In the writings of Cyril of Alexandria we encounter a certain (though
limited) advancement in identifying the proper characteristic of personhood. By choosing the word "characteristic" (which is not the
same as cause or principle), we already indicate one of the limitations
(≠ inaccuracy) in his explanation. In order to avoid having to affirm a
duality of subjects in Christ, Cyril develops what we would like to describe as a referential notion of hypostatic unicity. Person, or hypostasis (taken in the sense of synonymous with πρόσωπον[1228]), is distinguished from the concrete natural reality as such inasmuch as it is the
unique object of predication, the subject of attribution. Now, while
this subjectivality is indeed distinctive of the person, it is rather a consequence than a cause of personhood; it is more like a *proprium* of the
ontologically formal constituent of personality. Being a subject of
attribution certainly implies something about the ontological make-up
of a thing, for there must be a metaphysical basis to justify the use of
our language; but Cyril says nothing in its regard. And, though it was
perhaps neither required of nor possible for Cyril to identify that basis, the difference signaled by him between nature and person in no
way precludes the natural reality from sharing the predicative privileges of person, from having, that is, the same ontological perfection:
the only difference we are obliged to confess is that the natural reality
as such, i.e. *qua* natural, is not a subject of attribution, and therefore
not a person. The observation is crucial, but the implications of the
doctrine cannot be misconstrued: the alteriety expressed is indifferent

---

[1227] Though but latent in the doctrine of Basil, there is perhaps an implicit reference to
the fact that person, as the subsistent, is somehow distinguishable from nature according as person (though identical to the concrete nature) is signified as the possessor or subject of being – that is, according as "person" signifies the same concrete nature *qua* possessing the substantial act of existence. Such an explanation,
however, does not appear until the Scholastic period, particularly in St. Albert.

[1228] Cf. Cyril of Alexandria, Ἐπιστολὴ Κυρίλλου πρὸς Νεστόριον τρίτη: DEC 55,
13-15; cf. supra, "AXIS PLACED IN RELIEF BY CYRIL OF ALEXANDRIA", p. 74-75.

to identity at another level. We cannot agree with the opinion, therefore, that Cyril transposes the concept of person from non-personal
natural categories to a personal category, transcending somehow the
technical limitation of the Cappadocian school[1229].

Boethius and the "classical" definition of person

The achievements of later systematic and detailed analyses of personhood (mostly proper to the Scholastic period) are indebted in a special way to one man: Anicius Manlius Severinus Boethius. It is
Boethius who imparts to us the "classical" definition of person as "the
individual substance of a rational nature". If we take intellection for
granted, then, contrary to the logical structure of the definition assigning the specific difference to rationality, something else appears
as the fundamental principle of personality. What is key in the definition, and as emerges only from a thorough analysis of Boethius' entire
theological corpus, is the concept of individuality. This is not significantly different from the concept of the particularities as expounded
by the Cappadocians. What is original in Boethius, however, besides
his systematic presentation of person and the use of a more carefully
distinguished vocabulary, is the fact that he explicitly distinguishes
subsistent existence in itself from the substantial mode of existence
proper to creatures, whereby person is able to have a trans-categorical
application. The distinction between person and nature nevertheless
remains at the level of individuating properties. The latter are manifestly bound with the production of an essence in reality. Though
some have accused Boethius of philosophical regression for having
returned to the concretized nature (an opinion we do not share), an
entirely different problem resides in his definition. As F. L. B. Cunningham points out[1230], there are many ways of understanding individuality, and a thing is called individual in very different senses. The
kind of individuality characteristic and constitutive of personality –
something Boethius does not spell out – is that which implies at once
a perfectly self-contained entity (not depending upon another for its
existence) and complete natural integrity (the substance's constituting a specific nature of itself).

[1229] Cf. J. A. Sayes, *Jesucristo, Ser y Persona*, Aldecoa, Burgos 1984, p. 28-40.
[1230] Cf. F. L. B. Cunningham (editor), *Christ and His Sacraments*, The Priory Press, Dubuque (Iowa) 1958, p. 104-105.

Richard of Saint-Victor

The concept of incommunicability is closely connected with the last mentioned requirement for personality. Though the notion is already present in Basil the Great, it is Richard of St. Victor who may be described as the doctor of personal incommunicability (and of the supreme communicability of divine nature). Unless the sense and extension of "individual" is carefully mapped-out, the term could be taken in a way detrimental to both Trinitarian and Christological dogma: because the divine nature is said to be individual, it might seem that the divine nature of itself satisfies the definition of person, thus producing a quaternity of persons in God; similarly, in Christ, if "individual" is applied to the human nature as such, it would seem, on the basis of the Boethian definition, to imply another person. For Richard, the Boethian definition is insufficient, and, in order to dissociate the concept of person from that of nature, Richard formulates his definition of person by distinguishing two senses of the term *"existentia"*, one of which pertains to nature or quiddity, the other of which pertains to person and incommunicable origin[1231]. Personality amounts, for Richard, to a mode of subsisting constituted by an incommunicable property (a property pertaining to origin or qualitative difference)[1232]. Absolute incommunicability accounts for the unique and undefinable expression of the personal name, alone by which one or another person is adequately denominated in his or her singularity. Richard's attempt to sever from Boethian categories in defining person possesses, in virtue of the notion of *"existentia"*, the exceptional value not only of sanctioning the distinction of *alius* and *alius* independently of that between *aliud* and *aliud,* but of emphasizing non-physical dimensions involved in the "incommunicabilization" of an entity. His theory thus points to the possibility of a non-physical determinant in the explanation of individuality. Nevertheless, persons themselves, who are the possessors of individuality and the subjects of distinctive modes of existing, are not removed from the substantial category which is expressive of their quiddity and the principle of the being distinctively exercised by several *qui sunt.*

[1231] Cf. Richard of Saint-Victor, *De Trin.*, IV, c. 10, ed. Ribaillier, 159d; cf. supra, "HOW PERSONS CAN BE DISTINGUISHED WITHOUT ENTAILING A DISTINCTION OF NATURE", p. 168.

[1232] Cf. Richard of Saint-Victor, *De Trin.*, IV, c. 18-19, ed. Ribaillier, 162d - 163d; cf. supra, "DEFINITION OF THE PERSON AS AN INCOMMUNICABLE EXISTENCE", p. 171.

Through the thirteenth century and Albert the Great

Unanimously to this point, personality has been perceived as rooted in an incommunicable property by which the person is itself (the na- ture rendered) incommunicable or individual in the fullest sense of the term (a sense which necessarily entails incommunicability). Whether clothed in the language of incommunicability or that of in- dividuality, the theories are in general agreement that the cause of personality is a singular property – whether absolute or relative (any of the so-called "modal properties" falling into one or the other of the two) – joined to common nature, resulting in a mode according to which the latter (taken as particularized and therefore in a supposital sense) is. Person and nature as such are distinguished only according to the possession or lack of such a *proprietas*, respectively; but there are no grounds for affirming any real distinction between person and the nature *with its proprietas*. If they differ at all, they will have to do so at another level. Here lies the genius of St. Albert whose complex analy- sis of the concepts surrounding the problem of personality elucidate the logical dimensions of the problem. Epitomizing the definitions of Boethius and Richard, Albert, better than any of his contemporaries, explicitates the difference between person and nature and elaborates the various ways of signifying a concrete nature, upheld as *idem in re* with person. "Person", for Albert, signifies that which is individual precisely *qua individual*. It is indeed *ens ratum et perfectum*, precisely because wholly terminated, both naturally or specifically (i.e. by its form) and in particular determination (by its *proprietas*). But it differs from this essence or nature *modo intelligendi, et modo supponendi, et modo attribuendi, et modo dicendi tantum*. This perspective is wholly compati- ble with the givens of the faith and altogether respectful of the phi- losophical tradition. What it entails with respect to the Christological problem remains to be explored. Certainly Christ's human nature is not *of itself* a person. But the fundamental implication of the Albertin- ian position is that the humanity *in se* is not fully individual[1233]. This is

---

[1233] The response to the fundamental Christological problem largely resides in an analysis of individuation. Christ's human nature does not of itself constitute a per- son because, as Albert argues, it is integrated into the singularity of the Word; not possessing its own singularity, it cannot be of itself a person. The premise being presupposed is that singularity, or individuality, is what constitutes personhood. It is, of course, the very fact of individuation which, as made clear by the precursors of St. Albert, renders something subsistent, as a subsisting member of a given species; subsistence and personhood go together. But the *cause* of personhood is individua- tion, and not subsistence. The issue of individuation and the modality of its realiza-

not explicitly drawn out by Albert, but it is nevertheless latent in his principles and further evidenced by describing the human nature of Christ *as such* as in potency to being a person on the grounds that it is in potency to singularity[1234].

Thomas Aquinas and beyond

The thought of St. Thomas on the matter adds little of original value to understanding the exact constituent of personality, quite simply because he is firmly seated within the prevailing tradition. Thomas must be praised rather for further clarifying the distinctive marks of personality once constituted[1235]. Taking the Boethian definition as a point of departure – whence the role of individuality predominates[1236] –, person is the substantial and concrete whole[1237] alone properly said to possess being[1238]. It is a subject complete in itself, thus enjoying the

---

tion with respect to the humanity of Christ shall constitute a pivotal point in our study of the hypostatic union to follow.

[1234] Cf. Albert, *II Sent.*, d. 3, a. 5, ad 2, ed. Borgnet, vol. 27, p. 70. Unfortunately, with the exception of A. Pompei (op. cit.), little to no research has been conducted on the Albertinian concept of personality, and its application to the Christological mystery is almost entirely neglected; cf. supra, "PRINCIPAL STUDIES", p. 183.

[1235] We do not wish to suggest that Thomas had nothing original to contribute to the notion of personal constitution, but mention simply that his originality does not principally pertain to the struggle of determining the *intrinsic formal principle* of personality. In general, Thomas and Albert assert practically identical doctrines concerning the divine persons, especially as regards their Trinitarian theology; and both authors consciously stand upon the shoulders of a long and consistent (albeit insufficient) tradition. What Thomas does manage to draw out more emphatically than Albert is the ontological character of the subsistent perfection proper to persons as seen in the light of *esse* and the act of existence. Considering their explicit textual exposition, Thomas offers much more than Albert concerning the position occupied by the created person in the hierarchy of participated being and the incommensurable value of properly possessing being for oneself (as well as for the sake of a transcendent finality already intimated by the self-containment of personal first act). These elements, however, are implicitly contained in the Albertinian corpus.

[1236] Not only is person individual, but it differs from nature as such precisely according to the lack or presence of individuating conditions: *"haec anima et haec caro et hoc os sunt de ratione huius hominis. Et idea hypostasis et persona addunt supra rationem essentiae principia individualia"* – Aquinas, *Sum. theol.*, I, 29, 2, ad 3, ed. Leonine, vol. 4, p. 330; cf. *Sum. theol.*, III, 2, 2; 7, 13; I-II, 1, 7; II-II, 58, 2; *III Sent.*, d. 5, q. 2, a. 3.

[1237] Cf. Aquinas, *III Sent.*, d. 5, q. 3, a. 2-3 (ed. Moos, p. 206-9): *"persona habet rationem completi et totius... ratio partis contrariatur rationi personae (a. 2)... ad rationem personae exigitur ulterius quod sit totum completum (a. 2, ad 3)... quae maximam completionem importat (a. 3)"*.

[1238] Cf. Aquinas, *Quodl.* II, q. 2, a. 2; *Sum. theol.*, III, 2, 2 & ad 3; III, 2, 3; *De Pot.*, q. 7, a. 4; In V *Met.*, Lect. 10 (ed. Cathala, No. 903-904).

property of incommunicability, since it does not and cannot form part of a larger whole. Person is also the most dignified thing of nature, not because it properly possesses being, but in virtue of its rational nature[1239]. For these distinctive marks, person, Thomas affirms, is what is most perfect in all of nature[1240]. Other fundamental traits of the Thomistic conception of (created) personality include the notion not only of an ontological composition (according as supposit adds something to nature), but of a composition realized at the operative level, as well as the notion of an intrinsic orientation toward further actualization by means of intersubjective dynamism. These are especially emphasized by adherents of a more or less "personalistic" viewpoint, such as W. N. Clarke[1241] and, in particular, E. H. Wéber[1242].

[1239] Cf. Aquinas, *Sum. theol.*, I, 29, 3; *De Pot.*, q. 9, a. 1, ad 3.

[1240] *"Persona significat id quod est perfectissimum in tota natura, scilicet subsistens in natura rationali"* – Aquinas, *Sum. theol.*, I, 29, 3, ed. Leonine, vol. 4, p. 331.

[1241] Cf. W. Norris Clarke, "Person, Being, and St. Thomas", *Communio: International Catholic Review*, XIX, n. 4 (1992), p. 601-618.

[1242] Cf. E. H. Wéber, *La personne humaine au XIIIᵉ siècle*, Vrin, Paris 1991; *Le Christ selon saint Thomas d'Aquin*, Desclée, Tournai 1988. Attentive to the historical development of explanations of the hypostatic union, Wéber presents the fundamental distinction between person and nature as that between the concrete whole (the subject) and the bare essence lacking those "complements" by which (through their addition) it is suppositized (cf. *Le Christ selon saint Thomas d'Aquin*, p. 149; *La personne humaine au XIIIᵉ siècle*, p. 499500). The particular position of Wéber is characterized by what he considers to perform the "complementary" roll with respect to nature, that is, what he understands to be added to nature in order that it be hypostatized. What is added to nature, according to Wéber, is the operative powers by which, in his own words, the nature is "dynamized", open toward becoming, in a continual progressive manner, what transcends its individual limits, according as the intelligible and volitional object of these powers is infinite and transcendental, the universal true and good (cf. *La personne humaine au XIIIᵉ siècle*, p. 500-506; *Le Christ selon saint Thomas d'Aquin*, p. 121-123, 127-133, 151). The accent is consistently placed on the notion of the progressive fulfillment of nature understood as taking place at the level of the supposit and in virtue of the principles of the supposit as opposed to those of the nature; it is a dynamism extrinsic to nature establishing relationships with the universe about (cf. *Le Christ selon saint Thomas d'Aquin*, p. 149-151). The personal accomplishment in question is achieved therefore at the operational level (cf. *La personne humaine au XIIIᵉ siècle*, p. 502). All of this is a meritorious exposition as intended to express the intrinsic capacity of intelligent nature for something greater than itself and the fundamental *status viae* of the created person on his or her way to perfection, a perfection acquired in time and which pertains to *second act*. However, to the extent that Wéber seems to want to reduce personality to the "para-essential" transcendental realm of becoming by means of intentional operation, something wholly posterior to the intrinsic natural constitution of the subject who acts, he diverges from the primary essence of personality rooted in first act. Wéber is, of course, sensitive to the distinction between first and second act (cf. *Le Christ selon saint Thomas d'Aquin*, p. 125-6; *La personne humaine au XIII siècle*, p. 504, 506); he is simply more concerned with the ultimate fulfillment of intellective nature. On the other hand, his discussion of the distinction between the

Among the countless volumes dedicated to the metaphysical doctrine of St. Thomas, that of L. J. Elders, *La métaphysique de saint Thomas d'Aquin dans une perspective historique*[1243], has the particular value of presenting the major features of the Thomistic conception of personality within the context of Thomas' philosophy of substance in a clear and simple fashion. As a consequence of the limits of the Thomistic treatment of the *principle* of personality (something expressly remarked by H. Diepen in *La critique du baslisme selon saint Thomas d'Aquin*[1244]), Elders ultimately directs our attention to Thomas' commentators. Unfortunately, the conclusions which emerge from the detour represent little to no advancement. To say that "a person is that which, as a being endowed with reason, possesses and exercises being in an entirely unique and incommunicable way"[1245] is fine enough. But what is it that renders it such? Just what is it that constitutes or causes the subjective mode in question? If the mode itself receives the name "subsistence", then the cause will have to be the "principle of subsistence"; to call the cause in this case "subsistence" would only be vicious, or at best very confusing. If, on the other hand, "subsistence" is used to designate the cause of personality (a cause able to account for the formality of the incommunicable mode of existence), then the term should not be used to designate the personal (subjective) mode itself (unless the causality in question is limited to that of the formal cause somehow identical to its formal effect; but then the formal cause must still be explained). According to Eld-

essence of the soul and its powers (based on the Thomistic understanding of potency and act as cutting equally across every category – cf. Aquinas, *Sum theol.*, I, 77, 1; cf. *Le Christ selon saint Thomas d'Aquin*, p. 121) offers new insight into the extra-essential elements capable of accounting for the personalization of intelligent nature as such. The intellective and volitional powers, however, like the essence as such, will nevertheless petition an explanation for their individuality, an explanation which seems must remain outside of the natural realm to which the powers themselves belong. As a final remark, we might mention that some of the citations used to develop his perspective on the teaching of St. Thomas offer little to no support for Wéber's claims (two simple examples are the conclusion drawn from the citation corresponding to note 20 on p. 500 of *La personne humaine au XIII*ᵉ *siècle*, and the passage corresponding to note 114 on p. 133 of *Le Christ selon saint Thomas d'Aquin* in order to justify the preceding paragraph); the works should be seen rather as an *interpretation* of the Master.

[1243] L. J. Elders, *La métaphysique de saint Thomas d'Aquin dans une perspective historique*, Vrin, Paris 1994.

[1244] Cf. H. Diepen, "La critique du baslisme selon saint Thomas d'Aquin", *RT* 50 (1950), p. 105. With respect to the restricted scope of Thomas' treatment of the corresponding issue of the unity of being, cf. J.-H. Nicolas, "L'unité d'être dans le Christ d'après saint Thomas", *RT* 65 (1965), p. 253.

ers, "to subsist" is "to be a subject"; "subsistence" designates the *exercise* of existence and the fact of being a subject[1246]. Both Cajetan and John of Saint Thomas, however, treat "subsistence" as that which causes a thing to be a subject of existence, either as an ultimate perfective term[1247] or as a substantial mode[1248] by which the individual essence exists as a subject. Just how this positive entity, "subsistence", referred to alternately as term or mode, must be understood is not so clear (the problem is somewhat analogous to our vacuous understanding of "gravity" taken as a force [≠ "phenomenon of gravity", of which we have immediate experience]: we know that it is, and what it does, but not what it is in itself). Subsistence, for Cajetan, precedes existence; it is the final preparatory step toward self-possessed being. L. J. Elders, however describes subsistence as the possession of being by and for oneself; it is the subjective exercise of being. As Elders himself concedes, such an understanding of subsistence necessarily includes the notion of being[1249]. But the result of this is that subsistence cannot at all be prior to being. Subsistence, as formulated by Elders, is rather posterior (in thought at least) to being; for it is a subjective mode of its possession[1250]. The confusion, of course, is occasioned by the fact that the term "subsistence" is employed according to different senses: for Elders, it stands for the personal mode of being; for the commentators, it designates the principle of that mode.

The specificity of that mode, the particular character of personality, is spelled-out by Elders as self-possession and subjective exercise of being. Subsistence (as treated by the commentators), Elders tells us, is responsible for being's coming to an essence in such a way that it not only realizes the essence, but is possessed and intrinsically exercised by the essence[1251]. Problems with this explanation already begin

---

[1245] L. J. Elders, *La métaphysique de saint Thomas d'Aquin dans une perspective historique*, Vrin, Paris 1994, p. 288.

[1246] *"Cet 'être un sujet' (subsister)... désigne l'exercice de l'existence et le fait d'être un sujet"* – L. J. Elders, *La métaphysique de saint Thomas d'Aquin dans une perspective historique*, Vrin, Paris 1994, p. 287.

[1247] Cf. Cajetan, *In De ente*, q. 12, ed. Marietti, p. 154; cf. L. J. Elders, *La métaphysique de saint Thomas d'Aquin dans une perspective historique*, Vrin, Paris 1994, p. 287.

[1248] Cf. John of Saint Thomas, *Cursus theol.*, III, q. 3, disp. 6, a. 1, n. 9ff; cf. L. J. Elders, *La métaphysique de saint Thomas d'Aquin dans une perspective historique*, Vrin, Paris 1994, p. 287.

[1249] L. J. Elders, *La métaphysique de saint Thomas d'Aquin dans une perspective historique*, Vrin, Paris 1994, p. 288.

[1250] Such a rendition closely resembles the Suarezian concept of subsistence; cf. infra, "THE SYSTEM OF SUÁREZ", p. 492.

[1251] L. J. Elders, *La métaphysique de saint Thomas d'Aquin dans une perspective historique*, Vrin, Paris 1994, p. 287-288.

to make themselves felt. First of all, what difference are we to understand between being's coming to an essence in order to realize it and
being's coming to an essence in order to be possessed and intrinsically exercised by it[1252]? Secondly, subsistence is spoken of here as
though it affected the act of being, when in reality it can only affect
the essence which becomes a subject of being. If subsistence makes
the act of being to be received in a certain way, then it is because the
receiving essence is intrinsically constituted in a certain way, since that
which is received is received according to the mode of the receiver,
and the intrinsic mode of the receiver (i.e. the ontological make-up of
the receiver) determines the receptive mode. Subsistence, it was affirmed, causes being to be received in a certain way: not as had by a
quo est or something which is not in complete possession of being, but
as fully possessed, as it belongs to a *quod est, id quod habet esse*. With respect to the essence, this means that subsistence makes the essence
able to possess being *per se*. Philosophically speaking, that which possesses being in itself is the complete and perfect thing of nature, the
individual, or complete primary substance. "Subsistence", from this
point of view, need translate as nothing other than the principle of
individuation. Of course, one will advance against this opinion, on
the basis of Revelation, the conviction that perfect individuality not be
enough to enable the autonomous possession of being. But, as we
have stated above, the objection is rooted in what appears to be an
illegitimate conclusion drawn from Christological dogma: though it is
indeed true that Christ's human nature is of itself nowise a person,
and though we nevertheless confess his individual human nature, this
is *NOT* to say that individual human nature and person are diverse realities, for the individuality of that nature is not necessarily had of itself[1253].

[1252] The question is particularly acute when, in either case, a complete substantial nature is in question.

[1253] In its most general form, the argument of the post-Thomistic tradition claims that
concrete individual nature and person must be distinct realities because otherwise
the human nature of Christ (which is concrete) would constitute another person.
But the premise is ungrounded. What must first of all be settled is the principle of
hypostatic constitution. Once the singular cause of personal distincion in Christ is
recognized, then and only then can the question of its relation to the causes of
concretization/individuality be resolved. Even were concrete nature equivalent to
person, this does not mean that the concretization of Christ's nature entails a separate person, for the same personal principle by which the natures are *idem in hypostasi* can supply for its concreteness as well, whence there is no multiplicity of principles of concrete existence as well.

It is the theological mystery of the Incarnation which gives rise to the philosophical notion of subsistence as a means for explaining the lack of personality with respect to Christ's human nature. However, the first problem inherent in discussions of this notion resides in the formulation of the terms which are distinguished from one another on the basis of this "subsistence". In a general way, person or supposit is said to be distinguished from human nature. But this is insufficient, since nature can be signified in diverse ways. The tradition recognizes that Christ's human nature is individual. But it then concludes that, because Christ's humanity is not a person, individual human nature is not necessarily personal. Is this legitimate? Christ's humanity in some sense of the term is certainly not a person, but this does not affirm what the conclusion presupposes, namely, that Christ's humanity *concretely signified* is not a person. The sense in which Christ's humanity is not a person can be specified as follows: Christ's human nature *as such* (or *of itself*) is not a person. No one will disagree with this (equally traditional) formula. However, what often fails to be taken into account is the relation between *individual* human nature and human nature *as such*. If the two are convertible, then the tradition's conclusion in respect of Christ's individual human nature stands without question, along with the corresponding need for the concept of subsistence. If, on the other hand, they are not convertible notions, then it is possible to identify concretely signified (individual) human nature and person – and this without jeopardizing the unicity of person in Christ, for the individual human nature *qua* individual is, arguably, convertible with the person of the Word (whose personality consists in nothing other than a unique principle of individuality or distinction). The thought of St. Thomas is entirely open to such a position; for that nature which Thomas consistently distinguishes from person is nature in itself (so much so that it seems at times to refer to nothing other than abstract or universal nature). The difficulty is to specify just what it is that the Word assumes and, ultimately, to explain the sense of *"natura in atomo"*. The position we maintain may be viewed as a systematization of the doctrine of Maximus Confessor who identifies Christ's concrete natures with his person[1254]. But most medieval thinkers subsequent to Thomas adopt a strategy dis-

---

[1254] Cf. Maximus Confessor, *Ambiguum ad Thomam* 5: PG 91, 1052D; *Epistola 15*: PG 91, 573A; cf. Pierre Piret, "Christologie et théologie trinitaire chez Maxime le Confesseur, d'après sa formule des natures 'desquelles, en lesquelles et lesquelles est le Christ'", in *Maximus Confessor, Actes du Symposium sur Maxime le Confesseur*, Editions Universitaires, Fribourg 1982, p. 215-222.

missing personality from the individual human nature of Christ[1255] (transforming the problem of personality into an inquiry over what metaphysical element renders concrete individual nature a hypostasis). The principal "theories of subsistence" come from Scotus, Capreolus, Cajetan and Suárez.

The Scotistic theory of personality

For Scotus (1265-1308), personality is conceived as a negative modality of the substance by which every form of communicability to another hypostasis is excluded (the requirements for personhood involve a twofold negation: both the denial of actual dependency upon – in the sense of substantial composition with – another reality; as well as the denial of any aptitudinal dependency)[1256]. A singular and com-

---

[1255] For a general view of the possible theories by which this is accomplished, theories of "subsistence", see: E. Forment, *Ser y Persona*, 2ª edición, Publicacions i Edicions de la Universitat de Barcelona, Barcelona 1983, p. 1-13; H. D. Gardeil, *Introduction to the Philosophy of St. Thomas Aquinas*, trans. J. A. Otto, Herder, St. Louis 1967, vol. 4, p. 168-169; F. L. B. Cunningham (editor), *Christ and His Sacraments*, Priory Press, Dubuque (Iowa) 1958, p. 106-109 (this latter work is not without gross, sometimes abusive, over-simplifications).

[1256] Cf. Scotus, *Op. Ox.*, III, d. 1, q. 1; d. 5, q. 2, n. 4-5; d. 6, q. 1; *Quodl.* XIX, a. 3. For Scotus' views on personhood, cf. BASTIT, M., *Les principes des choses en ontologie médiévale: Thomas d'Aquin, Scot, Occam*, Éditions Bière, Bordeaux 1997; BETTONI, EFREM, *Duns Scotus: the basic principles of his philosophy*, translated and edited by B. Bonansea, Catholic University of America Press, Washington D.C. 1961; *Vent' anni di studi scotisti (1920-1940): saggio bibliografico*, L. Necchi, Milan 1943; BOTTE, PETRUS CHRYSOLOGUS, "Ioannis Duns Scoti doctrina de constitutivo formali personae Patris", in *De doctrina Ioannis Duns Scoti. Acta Congressus Scotistici Internationalis Oxonii et Edimburgi 11-17 septembris 1966 celebrati*, III, Rome 1968, p. 85-104; BURGER, MARIA, *Personalität im Horizont absoluter Prädestination: Untersuchungen zur Christologie des Johannes Duns Scotus und ihrer Rezeption in modernen theologischen Ansätzen*, Aschendorff, Münster 1994; "Univozität des Seienden – Univozität der Person: Zwei Grenzbegriffe", in L. Honnefelder (editor), *John Duns Scotus. Metaphysics and Ethics*, Brill, Leiden 1996, p. 317-326; "Zwischen Trinitätslehre und Christologie. Der Personbegriff bei Johannes Duns Scotus", in Aertsen, J. A./Speer, A. (editors), *Individualität und Individualität im Mittelalter*, Walter de Gruyter, Berlin/New York 1996 (*Miscellanea Mediaevalia* 24), p. 406-415; BUSCAROLI, S., "L'haecceitas scotista e la singolarità personale: cenni per una lettura teoretica", *Teoresi* 34 (1979), p. 297-360; CARDAROPOLI, G., "Cristologia e antropologia in Duns Scoto e nella teologia contemporanea", in Casamenti, S. (editor), *Etica e persona. Duns Scoto e suggestioni nel moderno*, Edizioni Francescane Bologna, Bologna 1994, p. 261-280; COCCIA, A., "Duns Scoto, persona e libertà", *Miscellanea francescana* 77 (1977), p. 169-174; CONTI, ALESSANDRO D., "I presupposti metafisici del concetto di persona in Scoto", in S. Casamenti (editor), *Etica e persona. Duns Scoto e suggestioni nel moderno*, Edizioni Francescane Bologna, Bologna 1994, p. 87-99; CROSS, RICHARD, *Duns Scotus*, Oxford University Press, New York/Oxford 1999; FRANK, WILLIAM A., *Duns Scotus, metaphysician* (William A. Frank and Allan B. Wolter, editors), Purdue University Press, West Lafayette (Indi-

plete rational nature, therefore, is a person by reason of the fact that it is not assumed into the hypostatic unity of another. Because Christ's humanity has been assumed by the person of the Word, it is not a person, even though it possesses every perfection which would constitute a person were there no union. If the human nature were separated from the Word, without acquiring any positive entity, it

ana) 1995; GILSON, E., *Jean Duns Scot: introduction à ses positions fondamentales*, J. Vrin, Paris 1952; GRAJEWSKI, M., *The formal distinction of Duns Scotus; a study in metaphysics*, Catholic University of America Press, Washington D.C. 1944; HARTMANN, N., "Person in Einsamkeit und Gemeinsamkeit. Überlegungen zum Personbegriff bei Joh. Duns Scotus", *Wissenschaft und Weisheit* 47 (1984), p. 37-60; HAYEN, A., "L'Etre et la Personne selon le B. Jean Duns Scot", *RPL* 53 (1955), p. 525-541; HOERES, W., "Wille und Person bei Scotus", *Wissenschaft und Weisheit* 29 (1966), p. 188-210; HOFFMANN, TOBIAS, "Individuation bei Duns Scotus und bei dem jungen Leibniz", *Medioevo* 24 (1998), p. 31-87; HONNEFELDER, L., WOOD, R., DREYER, M. (editors), *John Duns Scotus: Metaphysics and Ethics*, E. J. Brill, Leiden/New York 1996; LAURIOLA, G., "Il concetto di persona in Duns Scoto come scelta ermeneutica", in Sileo, L., (editor), *Via scoti. Methodologia ad mentem Joannis Duns Scoti. Atti del Congresso Scotistico Internazionale*, vol. 2, (March 9-11, 1993), Edizioni Antonianum, Rome 1995, p. 967-984; LIME, V., "Liberté et autonomie de la personne chez Duns Scot", *Études franciscaines* 3 (1952), p. 51-70; MANNO, AMBROGIO G., *Introduzione al pensiero di Giovanni Duns Scoto*, Levante editori, Bari 1994; MARCHESI, A., "Singolarità irripetibile e continua perfettibilità della persona umana, fondata nella volontà libera secondo Duns Scoto", in *Deus et homo ad mentem I. Duns Scoti*, Societas Internationalis Scotistica, Rome 1972, p. 371-377; MCGINLEY, J., *Miasma: "haecceitas" in Scotus, the esoteric in Plato, and other related matters*, University Press of America, Lanham (MD) 1996; MÜHLEN, HERIBERT, *Sein und Person nach Johannes Duns Scotus. Beitrag zur Grundlegung einer Metaphysik der Person*, Dietrich-Coelde-Verlag, Werl 1954; PEREZ DE TUDELA Y VELASCO, J., *Identidad, forma y diferencia en la obra de Juan Duns Scoto: una aproximacion al problema del fundamento*, Departamento de Metafisica, Facultad de Filosofia y Ciencias de la Educacion, Universidad Complutense, Madrid 1981; PRENTICE, R., *The basic quidditative metaphysics of Duns Scotus as seen in his De primo principio*, Antonianum, Rome 1970; SCHAFER, ODULF, *Bibliographia de vita, operibus et doctrina Iohannis Duns Scoti, doctoris subtilis ac Mariani, saec. XIX-XX*, Herder, Rome 1955; SEILLER, L., "La notion de personne selon Scot. Ses principales applications en christologie", *La France Franciscaine*, 20 (1937), p. 209-248; SHIRCEL, C., *The univocity of the concept of being in the philosophy of John Duns Scotus*, Catholic University of America Press, Washington D.C. 1942; TWEEDALE, M., *Scotus vs. Ockham: a medieval dispute over universals*, texts translated into English, with commentary, E. Mellen Press, Lewiston (NY) 1999; VOS, ANTONIE, *Johannes Duns Scotus*, Uitgeverij J. J. Groen En Zoon, Leiden 1994; WERNER, HANS-JOACHIM, "Unmitteilbarkeit und Unabhängigkeit. Zur anthropologischen Bedeutung zweier personaler Bestimmungen nach Duns Scotus", in Aertsen, J. A./Speer, A. (editors), *Individuum und Individualität im Mittelalter*, Walter de Gruyter, Berlin - New York 1996, p. 389-405; WETTER, F., *Die Trinitätslehre des Johannes Duns Scotus*, Aschendorff, Münster 1967; WOLTER, ALLAN B., *The philosophical theology of John Duns Scotus* (A. Wolter and M. McCord Adams, editors), Cornell University Press, Ithaca/London 1990. Cf. supra, note 140 for additional bibliography relevant to the Scotistic theory of individuation. A special thanks to Tobias Hoffmann for bibliographical assistance on Duns Scotus.

would thereby constitute a person of its own[1257]. Critics of this theory begin by noting that personality signifies a perfection much greater than what is expressed by a *de facto* negation. Indeed, every supposit in general includes a positive perfection by which it subsists *in se*. Moreover, the notion of incommunicability – not being drawn (or drawable) into the unity of another being –, would express no perfection at all were it not for the fact that it presupposes the positive entity constitutive of distinct subsistence. It seems, furthermore, ironic that Scotus advocates such a theory when considering his lucid rejection of Henry of Ghent's double negation argument concerning the principle of individuation[1258]. The Christological danger of the position, if sometimes exaggerated, cannot be taken lightly: if Christ's humanity lacks nothing positive, then why, the question remains, is it not a human person (even if it is assumed)[1259]? And, if there is no positive entity in which the two natures share as a basis for union, then it is difficult to see how the union can be real and intrinsic[1260]. Interestingly enough, the resulting Scotistic identification of individual nature with person at the positive level, as much as lending itself in support of a reprehensible hypostatic duality[1261], lends itself in support of an iden-

---

[1257] Cf. regarding Scotus' negative "way" and its implicated positive counterpart, M. Burger, "Zwischen Trinitätslehre und Christologie. Der Personbegriff bei Johannes Duns Scotus", in *Individuum und Individualität im Mittelalter*, Walter de Gruyter, Berlin/New York 1996 (*Miscellanea Mediaevalia* 24), p. 406-415.

[1258] Cf. Henry of Ghent, *Quodl.* V, q. 8 (Paris 1518), I, f. 166rM; cf. Scotus, *Lectura*, d. 3, p. 1, q. 2, n. 39-53, ed. Vatican, p. 240-244; *Ordinatio* II, d. 3, p. 1, q. 2, n. 43-58, ed. Vatican, p. 410-417.

[1259] Herein lies a significant disparity between the explanations of Scotus and Aquinas. Even if they affirm the same thing about the humanity of Christ as automatically constituting a person once removed from the union – a fact which signifies for both of them the just recognition of the complete integrity of the human nature –, Scotus can supply no account of the "depersonalization" of the humanity as such.

[1260] Cf. F. L. B. Cunningham (editor), *Christ and His Sacraments*, Priory Press, Dubuque (Iowa) 1958, p. 107.

[1261] The reproach is a battle cry of many Thomists who frequently misrepresent Scotus. Nevertheless, objectively speaking, the Scotistic exposition on personality is subject to many of the criticisms leveled against it by H. Diepen in *La critique du baslisme selon saint Thomas d'Aquin, RT* 50 (1950), p. 82-3. Diepen situates the origin of the entire debate over the unity of being in Christ between two poles: that which tends to deny the consubstantiality of Christ's human nature with our own on the basis of the fact that some positive reality is lacking to Christ's human nature in respect of our own, and that which tends toward recognizing the presence of two sons and two persons in Christ on the grounds that every positive reality required in the constitution of a man is possessed by the human nature belonging to Christ. The former pertains to the theory of the "ecstasy of being" defended by the so-called "classical" Thomistic school; the latter is attributed to doctrines proper to defenders of Scotus. Parallel to, and as an immediate consequence of, the position one adopts in regard to these poles (whether at either extreme or, if possible, somehow in the

tification of Christ's concrete human nature with the person of the Word, provided one make the necessary assertion that this individual nature is hypostatically one with the Word, something far from Scotus' intendment.

The theory of Capreolus

Capreolus (1388-1444), considered by many to be the most faithful interpreter of Thomas, follows the Aquinate in associating personality with substantial or suppositable being in an inseparable way[1262]. According to Capreolus, being itself (*esse substantialis*) is the fundamental constituent of personality[1263]. In opposition to the Scotistic doctrine of negation, Capreolus formulates his definition of person maintaining that something positive is added by the notion of person to that of the individual nature, namely *"esse actualis existentiae", esse actus entis*[1264].

---

middle, or – as is characteristic of our own position – by going around the horns [since we accept neither position *at all*, but rather maintain both that *nothing* is lacking to the human nature and that it could constitute no personal reality of itself]) emerges a theory of the unity of being. The real implications of Scotism (as well as Capreolism) go beyond the structure of personality in itself right down to the existential act(s) proper to the nature's in Christ. What former Thomists concerned with the principle of subsistence have condemned as a virtual Christological dihypostasism in the Scotistic understanding of personality, contemporary Thomists concerned with the unity of being in Christ refer to as implying a *duplex esse* in Christ. For the less "classical" strain of Thomists in favor of the theory of the "integration of being", the Scotistic outcome ought to correspond to their own intuitions on the integrity of the human nature in Christ (even if dihypostasism must be avoided at all costs). For those deferential to the theory of the "ecstasy of being", the implications of Scotism are unthinkable and only too readily stamped with the label *assumptus homo*. For an excellent outlay of the debate over the unity of being in Christ, particularly as manifest during the period of concentrated speculative Christological discussion in the first twenty years of the latter half of this century, as well as a bibliographical repertoire of the authors engaged in that debate, see J. P. Torrell, "Le thomisme dans le débat Christologique contemporain", in *Saint Thomas au XXᵉ siècle, Actes du colloque du Centenaire de la "Revue thomiste"*, Saint-Paul, Paris 1994, p. 379-387.

[1262] *"Quia ponit unum subsistens, et humanitatem non accidentaliter divinae personae advenire, oportet quod ponat unum esse. Impossibile est enim quod unum aliquid habeat duo esse substantialia; quia unum fundatur super ens. Unde si sint plura esse, secundum quae aliquid dicitur ens simpliciter, impossibile est quod dicatur unum. Sed non est inconveniens quod esse unius subsistentis sit per respectum ad plura, sicut esse Petri est unum, habens tamen respectum ad diversa principia constituentia ipsum. Et similiter suo modo unum esse Christi habet duos respectus, unum ad naturam divinam, alterum ad humanam"* – Aquinas, *III Sent.*, d. 6, q. 2, a. 2, ed. Moos, p. 239 (cf. also *Quodl.* IX, a. 3; *Sum. theol.*, III, 17, 3).

[1263] Cf. Capreolus, *Defensiones theologiae divi Thomas Aquinatis*, III, d. 5, q. 3, a. 3, ed. Paban-Pègues, Alfred Cattiere, vol. V, Turin 1904, p. 105-107.

[1264] Capreolus, *Def. theol.*, III, d. 5, q. 3, a. 3, op. cit., p. 105ᵃ.

Important distinctions are drawn between the essence as composed with an extrinsic act and the essence as intrinsically dependent upon that act (the elaboration of which distinction is facilitated by the introduction of the notions of *"compositio cum his"* and *"compositio ex his"*), and person formally considered and person denominatively considered[1265]. Because person is formally constituted by the substantial act of being proper to individual substance, the nature along with its own existence' suffices for personhood. Capreolus' *"princeps thomistarum"* has been sustained by numerous modern authors, in particular Cardinal Billot[1266]. Applied to the Christological problem, the humanity is simply understood to lack its own existence, since it is supplied by the personal being of the Word. Though the position accounts with logical ease for the traditional formulation of the hypostatic union as a union in or according to the subsistence of the Word[1267], it collides against the difficulty of explaining the reality of the humanity as such[1268]. Furthermore, the fact that the possession of being (in the subjective sense) is a sufficient condition for the affirmation of personality does not necessarily mean that supposital existence is the cause of personality. Existence is an inseparable property of personhood, but there are perhaps other factors which enable for the realization of such a property, factors which directly effect what may be described as the essence of personality in distinction from its properties. And, even if the existential realization of a nature is what renders it incommunicable, the immediate principle conferring incommunicability does not have to be *esse* in itself, but could be a *modality* of that *esse*, as seems to be implied in the Boethian notion of "particularizing

---

[1265] See E. Forment, *Ser y Persona*, 2ª edición, Publicacions i Edicions de la Universitat de Barcelona, Barcelona 1983, p. 135-183. A thorough and detailed analysis of the personal doctrine of Capreolus, consistently compared to contending medieval theories of personality, is presented in this work.

[1266] Cf. L. Cardinal Billot, *De Verbo incarnato*, 9th edition, Rome 1949, p. 66-86.

[1267] Cf., in particular, Council of Florence, *Bulla unionis Coptorum*: *"anethematizat etiam Theodorum Mopsuestenum atque Nestorium asserentes humanitatem Dei Filio unitam esse per gratiam, et ob id duas in Christo esse personas, sicut duas fatentur esse naturas, cum intelligere non valerent unionem humanitatis ad verbum hypostaticam extitisse, et propterea negarent Verbi subsistentiam accepisse"* (DEC 574, 23-33).

[1268] This issue directly concerns the unity of being in Christ and demonstrates how one's concept of person determines his or her perspective on the unity of being (the mode of union being taken for granted as professed by the teaching of the Catholic Church).

aspect" (the individuating factor conditioning/defining the reception of being for a given nature)[1269].

Cajetan and subsistence as substantial mode

The theology of Cajetan (1469-1534) introduces a new system for approaching the Christological problem, namely, that based on the concept of substantial modes[1270]. In the Cajetanian theory of personality, subsistence (i.e. personality) is constituted by a substantial mode really distinct from the nature by which the nature is completed in the substantial order[1271]. This substantial mode, "subsistence", is the for-

---

[1269] Cf. supra, "ONTOLOGICAL PRINCIPLES BEHIND SUBSISTENTIA AND SUBSTANTIA", p. 115; "BRIEF COMPARISON WITH THE 'CLASSICAL' NOTION OF SUBSISTENCE", p. 117; and note 358 (on Cajetanian doctrine) in "SPECIFIC ASPECTS OF SUBSTANTIA AND SUBSISTENTIA", p. 121.

[1270] Cf. A. Michel, "HYPOSTASE", *DTC* 7, p. 422.

[1271] Cf. Cajetan, *In III^am*, q. 4, a. 2. For bibliographical information on Cajetan, see M.-J. Congar, "Bio-bibliographie de Cajétan", *Revue Thomiste* 17, special edition "Cajétan" (Nov., 1934 - Feb., 1935), p. 3-49; Marcel Nieden, *Organum dietatis: die Christologie des Thomas de Vio Cajetan* ("Studies in Medieval and Reformation Thought" LXII) Brill, Leiden/New York 1997. See also: BAÑEZ, D., *Scholastica Comentaria in Primam Partem Summae Theologicae S. Thomae Aquinatis*, ed. L. Urbano, F.E.D.A., Madrid/Valencia 1934; BOBIK, J., "The 'Materia Signata' of Cajetan", *NSchol* 30 (1956), p. 127-153; BRAUN, BERNHARD, *Ontische Metaphysik: zur Aktualität der Thomasdeutung Cajetans*, Konigshausen und Neumann, Wurzburg 1995; DEGL'INNOCENTI, U., "Animadversiones in Caietani doctrinam de corporum individuatione", *Divus Thomas* (Piacenza) 51 (1948), p. 19-45; "Del Gaetano e del principio d'individuazione", *Divus Thomas* (Piacenza) 52 (1949), p. 202-208; "L'opinione giovanile del Gaetano sulla costituzione ontologica della persona", *Divus Thomas* 44 (1941), p. 154-166; FORMENT GIRALT, E., *Persona y Modo Substancial*, Promociónes Publicaciónes Universitarias, Barcelona 1984; GARRIGOU-LAGRANGE, R., "De personalitatem iuxta Caietanum", *Angelicum* 21 (Oct.-Dec. 1944), p. 410-460; GAZZANA, A., "La 'materia signata' di S. Tommaso secondo la diversa interpretazione del Gaetano e del Ferrarese", *Gregorianum* 24 (1943), p. 78-85; GUIL BLANES, F., "La distinción cayetanista entre abstractio formalis y abstractio totalis", *Sapientia* 10 (1955), p. 44-53; HEGYI, JOHANNES, *Die Bedeutung des Seins bei den klassischen Kommentatoren des heiligen Thomas von Aquinas: Capreolus, Silvester von Ferrara, Cajetan*, Verlage Berchmanskolleg, Pullach bei München 1959; KUC, P. L., "La métaphysique de l'être chez Cajetan", in *Miscellanea Mediaevalia* 2, "Die Metaphysik im Mittelalter", Walter de Gruyter, Berlin 1963, p. 661-666; MUÑIZ, FRANCISCO P., "El constitutivo formal de la persona creada en la tradición tomista", *La Ciencia Tomista* 212 (1945), p. 5-89; 219 (1946), p. 201-293; PETERSON, L., "Cardinal Cajetan (Thomas De Vio) (B. 1468; D. 1534) and Giles of Rome (B. CA. 1243/47; D. 1316)", in *Individuation in Scholasticism, The Later Middle Ages and the Counter-Reformation, 1150-1650*, J. J. E. Gracia (editor), State University of New York Press, New York 1994, p. 431-455; PINCHARD, BRUNO, *Metaphysique et semantique: la signification analogique des termes dans les principes metaphysiques* (followed Latin text and annotated translation of *The Analogy of Names*), Librairie Philosophique J. Vrin, Paris 1987; QUARELLO, D., "Il problema scolastico della persona nel Gaetano e nel Capreolo", *Divus Thomas* 55 (1952), p. 34-63; REILLY, JOHN P., "Cajetan: Essentialist or Existentialist?", *NSchol* 41 (1967),

mality which "terminates" the substance in such a way that it belongs to one individual alone and cannot belong to another, that is, which makes it incommunicable. Completed by such a mode, the substance receives the ultimate perfection of existence, in an independent, autonomous way. Thus essence, subsistence and existence are three distinct realities superimposed on one another in a single subject. Subsistence is a perfection subsequent to that of the individual nature but antecedent to that of existence. It renders the substance so independent and incommunicable that it cannot be assumed by another supposit, terminating the nature in itself and disposing it to be actuated by its own existence. It is thus understood as a positive intrinsic perfection which existence cannot supply but which is itself completed in actuality (along with nature) by the crowning perfection of existence. Person, from this standpoint, is intrinsically constituted by nothing other than the individual nature terminated by the substantial mode of subsistence. Existence itself does not enter into the formal constitution of personality, but pertains to person only as a (necessary) consequence of the perfection of subsistence [1272].

The idea of a substantial mode has its own limitations. While theologians insist that Cajetan and his followers have every reason to assert a real objective distinction between concrete nature and hypostasis, the opinion is simply not necessary. The gratuitous introduction of a third element in order to account for such a distinction is moreover insufficient to account for the constitution of the supposit. The immediate effect of the substantial mode in question is to render the nature incommunicable. But this incommunicable thing, if we consider it in abstraction from or prior to its existence (which is to consider it according to *subsistentia tantum*), is yet an unrealized nature. Is it not, therefore, like an *idea*, and therefore potentially multipliable into many? An entity which is already determined according to natural singularity is nowise a supposit until it exists *in se* [1273]; furthermore, by the very fact that an entity exists *in se* it becomes a supposit, a dis-

---

p. 191-222; *Cajetan's Notion of Existence*, Mouton, The Hague (Netherlands) 1971; RIVA, FRANCO, *Analogia e univocità in Tommaso de Vio 'Gaetano'*, Vita e Pensiero, Milan 1995; THOBE, URBAN A., *Comparison of the Commentaries of Cajetan and Saint Albert the Great on the Isagoge of Porphyry with Regard to the Predicable Accident and a Comparison of Their Doctrines with Regard to the Inseparable Accident*, master's thesis at the University of Notre Dame, 1961.

[1272] Cf. Cajetan, *In III^{am}*, q. 4, a. 3, ad 1.

[1273] That is to say, Cajetan certainly cannot exclude existence and still have a supposit or subsistent; there can be no natural priority of subsistence with respect to existence.

tinct subsistent[1274]. Such a mode, therefore, whether taken as antecedent to being (as is the case for Cajetan) or as posterior (as apparently the case with Suárez whom we shall consider next), seems insufficient to account for hypostatization. Just what is it supposed to add to the complete individual substance which already possesses everything needed for existing *in se* and *per se*, and which, if existing *in se*, is already suppositized? And what is this pure "term" described by Cajetan as having neither an extrinsic nor an intrinsic causal function, as adding something to nature, since – according to the hypothesis – it is a positive entity, and as adding nothing, because it is but a term[1275]?

In Cajetan's unprecedented concept of "subsistence", just how are we to understand this thing which is something in-between essence and existence? Why, moreover, should we invoke such a thing to "terminate" the essence which is already confined, limited, as an essential type or instance? What else does it mean to terminate a thing if not to limit it, or to delimit it, which is to define it? But the essence is all of this in itself: as a finite essence, it is wholly limited, *a fortiori* if we consider it, as does Cajetan, according to its individuating conditions. Particularly in the latter case, it is perfected and defined, forasmuch as its proper form specifies its every substantial and individual characteristic (even the designated matter, which is taken as "interminate"[1276] in order to be a principle of individuation for form, receives its "termination" – accurately translated in English by the term "definition" – from the particular form to which it is actually united). It is precisely in this sense that Albert the Great defines *"terminus"* in terms of form, according as that which specifies, terminates and perfects a thing[1277]. There seems to be little apparent value in the Ca-

---

[1274] Thus whatever makes a thing exist *in se* is exactly what makes a thing a subsistent and vice versa; whatever confers personality (subsistence) confers *per se* existence; personality cannot be a perfection prior to existence except perhaps in a logical fashion, as the existence in question must be understood as the existence of some*thing* (the whatness of that thing preceding within our intellect the thought of it as existing). But, if our notion of the subsistent were to necessarily include that of existing *per se*, then such a logical priority fails as well.

[1275] Cf. Cajetan, *In III^m*, q. 4, a. 2, *comm.*, n. 10.

[1276] For the discussion of "signate" and "interminate" matter, cf. Aquinas, *De ente et ess.*, c. 2; *In Boeth. De Trin.*, q. 4, a. 2; *Sum. theol.*, I, 76, 6, ad 2; *De nat. mat.*, c. 3-7; Capreolus, *De nat. mat. et dimens. intermin.*, c. 3; *De verit.*, q. 5, a. 9; Cajetan, *In De ente et ess. s. Th.*; Ferrariensis, *Sum. c. gent.*, l. 1, c. 21, n. 4. A perspicacious exegesis of the notion of "interminate dimensions" is given by J. Owens, "Thomas Aquinas", in *Individuation in Scholasticism, The Later Middle Ages and the Counter-Reformation, 1150-1650*, Jorge J. E. Gracia (editor), State University of New York Press, New York 1994, p. 181-186, 193 (note 39).

[1277] Cf. supra, "THE NOTION OF 'TERMINUS'", p. 404.

jetanian concept of "subsistence" – unless the "term" of Cajetan can be understood in terms of (or made to fit somehow in a doctrine of) a supra-essential principle of individuation, in the sense of an existential principle (e.g. the existential relation) which renders the individual individual and singularly defined. But then, contrary to Cajetan, the complete individual cannot be considered in abstraction from such a principle (or relation) which enters into its essential constitution insofar as individual (for which reason, moreover, that principle is no longer something which comes *between* the individuated, terminated essence and its existence, even if it can somehow be conceived in abstraction from and as logically prior to the formal act of the existence of the individual).

The previous rejection of the notion of causality[1278] reveals something about the spontaneous origin of the perfection of subsistence. Personality is neither substance nor form nor any other cause entering into a substance's constitution as such, but the formal *effect* of one or another of its causes (namely, the cause or causes pertaining to the individuality of the substance). As a formal effect, personality necessarily follows upon the principles of the nature: *"modus ergo quo personalitas sequitur naturam vel naturae principia, est quo terminus actionis et rei factae naturaliter adest in fine actionis rei factae, nisi adsit impedimentum"*[1279]. Absence of personality consists therefore in either the lack of completeness on the part of the substance and from the point of view of its substantial principles, or in an impediment preventing the realization of the formal effect of those principles: *"sublato impedimento, non oportet quaerere aliam causam donantem complementum; quoniam ipsa natura secundum se habet in se sufficiens consecutivum sui termini"*[1280]. Now, to refuse any distinction between subsistence and the substance which it is said to terminate would be to confuse cause and effect[1281], but to distinguish them as separable perfections or as one entity added to another would not be compatible with the principles just laid down. Despite the fundamental defects of the line-point anal-

---

[1278] Stated just above with regard to either an intrinsic or extrinsic causal role (cf. Cajetan, *In III^{am}*, q. 4, a. 2, *comm.*, n. 10).

[1279] Cajetan, *In III^{am}*, q. 4, a. 2, *comm.*, n. 28.

[1280] Ibid.

[1281] The principles of the substance can be said to cause subsistence formally, while the terminus subsistence, if synonymous with individuality, is a formal cause of the hypostatic act of the substance.

ogy[1282], contrary to the opinion of H. Diepen[1283], Cajetan, we believe, does not understate the distinction. The *terminus* of subsistence, in the final analysis, is distinguished from the singular nature as "this personality" from "this person" (*sicut terminus est terminato quasi idem*), and it is possessed by the nature (*est enim aliquid eius*) as the person *has* personality (or the rational has rationality)[1284]. Personality, or subsistence, is the formality of the person; the terminus is equivalent to the formal reality of that which is terminated. From what has been said about personality following upon the principles of the nature, the terminus is the formal result of the act of the principles constituting the nature: "*substantia originative importat principia individuantia, formaliter vero est terminus*"[1285]. The principles of individuation therefore make a thing to be individual, but the "individuality" which "accompanies" that is, for Cajetan, the terminus constitutive of personality which may or may not be impeded. But individuality is nothing more than the individual as such abstractly considered; it directly, though abstractly, signifies the *effect* of the individuating principles: such a personality cannot be blocked unless the principles themselves are deprived of their function. Terminus here is a necessary result of the natural/substantial principles *in the very line of the nature*; its only claim to distinction is its abstract content when compared to the nature in the concrete, the *terminata*.

In defense of a salvageable variant of the Cajetanian theory, we observe that subsistence abstractly considered could indeed be understood as a substantial mode, provided this not be understood as distinct from – in the sense of able to be added to (as though naturally extraneous to) – the concrete nature. The substantial mode would be a modality inseparably connected to the concrete actuality of the nature. Now, it is true that existence in itself is unable to supply the perfection of subsistence, i.e. that perfection by which a thing is constituted as a complete thing of itself properly entitled to being after the

---

[1282] See in this regard the critique of Cajetan's theory in A. Michel, "HYPOSTASE", *DTC* 7, p. 418; the remarks of H. Diepen, "La critique du baslisme selon saint Thomas d'Aquin", *RT* 50 (1950), p. 109-110.

[1283] Cf. H. Diepen, "La critique du baslisme selon saint Thomas d'Aquin", *RT* 50 (1950), p. 109-110.

[1284] "*Ex hoc quod realitas personalitas est terminus ultimus naturae, patet primo difficultas de identitate et diversitate eius a natura singulari. Est enim quodammodo idem, et quodammodo non idem; sicut terminus est terminato quasi idem, et quasi non idem. Est enim aliquid eius, scilicet terminus, et non est illud; ut patet de puncto et linea*" – Cajetan, *In IIIᵖᵐ*, q. 4, a. 2, comm., n. 12.

[1285] John of Saint Thomas, *In Iᵖᵐ*, disp. 4, a. 1, n. 34; cf. Aquinas, *Sum. theol.*, III, 6, 1, ad 2.

manner of a subject. Indeed, the proper character of being is to actu-
ate and nothing else; nothing in its concept explains or assures incommunicability. But this does not mean that something with respect
to its *cause* cannot assure incommunicability, and it is precisely the
causal dimensions of an existing essence which can be invoked as a
principle of incommunicability and as constitutive of the substantial
mode proper to persons[1286].

The system of Suárez

In contrast to the Cajetanian doctrine of a substantial mode which
precedes existence in the constitution of the person, existence presupposing the formally complete supposit, the doctrine of Suárez
(1548-1617), as generally understood, proposes a substantial mode
constitutive of the supposit presupposing the substantial existence of
the nature[1287]. An *existing* nature is said to be completed by the addi-

---

[1286] Cf. supra, note 358. If subsistence is a mode of the substance which formally causes
it to be a person, then it may well be nothing other than individuality considered as
properly belonging to the substance itself. The *cause* of such a mode is thus the
cause of the incommunicability understood as the formal perfection of personality;
it is the principle of incommunicability/individuality and the explanation for the
mode in question.

[1287] On the Suarezian theory of personality and subsistence, see: ALCORTA, J. I., "Prob-
lemática de la existencia en Suárez", *Revista de Filosofía* (Madrid) 7 (1948),
p. 693-726; *La teoría de los modos en Suárez*, Inst. Luis Vives de Filosofía, C.S.I.C., Madrid 1949; ARBOLEYA, E., *Francisco Suárez, S.J.: situación espiritual, vida y obra, metafísica*, Universidad de Granada, Granada 1946; BAENA, JOSÉ GUSTAVO, *Fundamentos
metafísicos de la potencia obediencial en Suárez*, Secretaria Departamental de Educación
Pública, Medellín 1957; BAERT, E., *Aufstieg und Untergang der Ontologie: Descartes und
die nachthomasische Philosophie*, Universitätsverlag Rasch, Osnabruck 1997; BEUCHOT,
M., *La esencia y la existencia en la filosofía escolástica medieval: su repercusión en la filosofía
analítica actual*, Universidad Nacional Autónoma de México, Mexico 1992; COUJOU,
J., *Suárez et la refondation de la métaphysique comme ontologie: étude et traduction de l'Index
détaillé de la métaphysique d'Aristote de F. Suárez*, Editions de l'Institut supérieur de phi-
losophie/Editions Peeters, Louvain/Paris 1999; COURTINE, J.-F., "Le principe
d'individuation chez Suárez et chez Leibniz", *Studia Leibnitiana*, suppl. 23 (1983),
p. 174-190; *Suárez et le système de la métaphysique*, Presses universitaires de France,
Paris 1990; CRONIN, T., *Objective Being in Descartes and in Suárez*, Garland Publications, New York 1987; DAY, FRANCIS T., *The Concept of Being in the Metaphysics of Suárez*,
Ph.D. Diss., Fordham University, Fordham 1951; FORMENT GIRALT, E., *Persona y
Modo Substancial*, Promociónes Publicaciónes Universitarias, Barcelona 1984; GIA-
CON, C., *Suárez*, second edition, La Scuola Editrice, Brescia 1945; GNEMMI, A., *Il
fondamento metafisico. Analisi di struttura sulle Disputationes metaphysicae di F. Suárez*,
Vita e pensiero, Milan 1969; GRABMANN, M., "Die Disputationes Metaphysicae des
Franz Suárez", in *Mittelalterliches Geistesleben*, 3 vols., M. Hueber, Munich 1926-1956,
vol. 1, p. 525-560; GRACIA, J. J. E., "Suárez' Criticism of the Thomistic Principle of
Individuation", in *Atti. Congresso di S. Tommaso d'Aquino nel suo VII Centenario,*

tion of a substantial modal perfection rendering it incommunicable[1288]. While Cajetan was able to conceive subsistence as a modality disposing nature for the subsequent reception of its own existence, Suárez, because of his denial of the real distinction between an actual essence and its existence, can conceive of a substantial mode only as

Rome 1977, p. 563-568; *Suárez on Individuation*, Marquette University Press, Milwaukee 1982; "What the Individual Adds to the Common Nature According to Suárez", *NSchol* 53 (1979), p. 221-233; HELLÍN, JOSÉ, *La analogia del ser y el conocimiento de Dios en Suárez*, Graficas Uguina, Madrid 1947; HONNEFELDER, L., *Scientia transcendens: die formale Bestimmung der Seiendheit und Realität in der Metaphysik des Mittelalters und der Neuzeit (Duns Scotus, Suárez, Wolff, Kant, Pierce)*, F. Meiner, Hamburg 1990; IBARZ, JOSÉ MARIA ORTÍZ, *La participación como razón constitutiva del mundo: el constitutivo formal del ente finito según F. Suárez*, Promocciónes Publicaciónes Universitarias, Barcelona 1991; ITURRIOZ, J., *Estudios sobre la metafísica de Francisco Suárez*, Ediciónes Fax, Madrid 1949; "La noción de subsistencia y suposito en Suárez", *Estudios Eclesiásticos* 64 (1943), p. 33-75; LOMBARDO, M., *La forma che dà l'essere alle cose: enti di ragione e bene trascendentale in Suárez, Leibniz, Kant*, IPL, Milan 1995; MAHIEU, L., *François Suárez, sa philosophie et les rapports qu'elle a avec la théologie*, Desclée de Brouwer, Paris 1921 (reprint in 1973); McCORMICK, JOHN F., "A Suarezian Bibliography", in *A Symposium on Suárez*, James V. Kelly (editor), Jesuit Education Association, New York 1939, p. 212-214; McGANN, T., "Suárez y el personalismo", *Pensamiento* 56 (1958), p. 487-502; MUGICA BERRONDO, P., *Bibliografia suareciana, con una introducción sobre el estado actual de los estudios suarecianos por Eleuterio Elorduy*, Universidad de Granada (Catedra Suárez), Granada 1948; MURRAY, M., *The Theory of Distinctions in the Metaphysics of Francis Suárez*, Ph.D. Diss., Fordham University, Fordham 1944; NEIDL, W., *Der Realitätsbegriff des Franz Suárez nach dem Disputationes metaphysicae*, Hueber, Munich 1966; PALMA, J., *La potencia obediencial activa en el plano metafísico segun Suárez*, José Maria Ventura Hita, Granada 1955; QUILES, I., *Francisco Suárez, S.J.: su metafísica*, Ediciónes Depalma, Buenos Aires 1989; ROIG GIRONELLA, J., "La noción de sustancia", *Pensamiento* 18 (1962), p. 387-406; 19 (1963), p. 23-52; "La Oposición Individuo-Universal en los Siglos XIV-XV, Punto de Partida de Suárez", in *Miscellanea Mediaevalia* 2, "Die Metaphysik im Mittelalter", Walter de Gruyter, Berlin 1963, p. 667-678; "La síntesis metafísica de Suárez", *Pensamiento* 4 (1948), p. 169-213; ROSANAS, J., "El principio de individuación, según Suárez", *Ciencia y Fe* 6 (1950), p. 69-86; ROSENBERG, J. R., *The Principle of Individuation. A Comparative Study of St. Thomas, Scotus and Suárez*, Ph.D. Diss., Catholic University of America, Catholic University of America Press (*Philosophical Studies* 121), Washington D.C. 1950; SEIGFRIED, H., *Wahrheit und Metaphysik bei Suárez*, H. Bouvier, Bonn 1967; SIEGMUND, G., *Die Lehre von Individuationsprinzip bei Suárez*, Fuld. Actiendr., Fulda 1927; SPECHT, R., *Francisco Suárez, Über die Individualität und das Individuationsprinzip*, 2 vols., Meiner, Hamburg 1976; SSEKASOZI, E., *A Comparative and Critical Analysis of the Metaphysical Theories of William of Ockham and Francis Suárez as Regards the Principle of Individuation*, Ph.D. Diss., University of Kansas, Kansas 1976; STENGREN, G., *Human Intellectual Knowledge of the Material Singular according to Francis Suárez*, Ph.D. Diss., Fordham University, Fordham 1965; TRELOAR, J., *Francis Suárez: A Metaphysics for Body and Soul*, Ph.D. Diss., Michigan State University, Lansing 1976; VOLLER, C., *Francis Suárez, On the Various Kinds of Distinctions*, Marquette University Press, Milwaukee 1947, reprint 1976; VOS, A. F., DE, "L'aristotélisme de Suárez et sa théorie de l'individuation", in *Actas. Congreso Internacional de Filosofía, Barcelona, 1948*, Istituto Luis Vives de Filosofía, Madrid 1949, vol. 3, p. 505-514; WHITCOMB, P., *Existence and Essence in Scholastic Metaphysics*, Ph.D. Diss., University of Kansas, Kansas 1981.

[1288] Cf. Suárez, *De incarnatione.*, disp. 11, s. 3, n. 10; *Disp. met.*, disp. 34, s. 4, n. 23-24.

coming to the already existent nature; if it is a perfection posterior and added to the individual concrete nature, then it is also posterior and added to the existence of that nature. Subsistence, for Suárez, is a positive entity really distinct from the essence to which it is added. Because subsistence is really distinct from the essence, on the basis of the denial of the real distinction, it follows that it is also really distinct from existence. While the actual essence and its existence are utterly inseparable, subsistence, Suárez affirms, is separable from the existing nature, without the nature's losing its actuality[1289].

This latter assertion would seem to confirm the fact that subsistence is truly posterior in the order of nature to existence, for a withdrawal of the former appears in no way to retract, diminish or alter the latter. If such is the case, then the Suarezian theory will be rife with difficulties in maintaining the substantial, non-accidental character of subsistence. However, recommendable as such an interpretation might seem, it is not imposed by the text. An existing nature which were to relinquish its subsistent mode of existing could indeed retain its actuality while nevertheless admitting of a radical alteration/decline of its existence (in the sense of a diminishing of the quality or kind of that existence). To say, therefore, that the actual entity of the nature remains is not to affirm that it go unchanged; for, that which remains will be an actuality proper to the nature *according, precisely, to a non-subsistent mode*. As a result, the substantial being of a thing, which being is a manner of existing proper to subsistents, will be constitutively tied to, inseparable from, even caused by, the modal perfection of subsistence. To say that it is separable implies the separability of a thing's proper substantial being, meaning that it be replaced by a non-substantial, or non-subsistent, being. Though such an explication may not be what Suárez had in mind, it nevertheless accords with his general presentation and offers itself as a viable interpretation (or adaptation) of his theory. To the extent that the substantial/existential mode is naturally posterior to the existence of the actual essence, the theory faces a certain contradiction, due to the fact that every reality added to a substance already constituted in its being is added in an accidental manner, unless it participate in the substantial being of the substance itself (which cannot be the case for a perfection understood as added to the substance's being as a completion of it[1290]). To the extent, however, that the modality may be understood as itself entering into the conditions for the realization of the

---

[1289] Cf. Suárez, *Disp. met.*, disp. 34, s. 4, n. 15; *De incarnatione*, disp. 11, s. 3.

essence, i.e. as participating in the causes of existence, a different understanding of subsistence emerges, one which situates personality at the level of the principles of the actual essence (as opposed to the level of accidental adjunction presupposing the constitution of the actual essence).

One of the keys to understanding the Suarezian theory is his notion of existence in itself. Existence, he tells us, signifies nothing other than the possession of reality *extra causis*; it is indifferent to the *kind* of actuality it implies, whether existing *in se* or in another[1291]. The former mode of existence is implied by the notion of subsistence, which is to exist in a manner independent of another subject, opposed to *inexistence*, existing in a subject. As a result, existence as such may be described as "incomplete" prior to – or, more precisely, in abstraction from – the modality by which it is determined. It is in this sense, in our opinion (if we attempt to defend his doctrine), that Suárez can assert that existence is incomplete until terminated by the mode of being *in se* or the mode of being *in alio*, that it remains in a quasi-potential state prior to the addition of the mode according to which it is completed[1292]. From this point of view, and if the sense of "terminated" is synonymous with "determined", Suárez' thesis seems incontestably acceptable: every act of created being is determined by, limited to, the nature of which it is the act (*a fortiori* if they are only logically distinct). But the mode cannot determine being; the mode *is* the determination *in actu*. Rather, the determination brought about by the form (i.e. the specific form) or nature constitutes the modality for the being (subsistent if the nature is substantial and unassumed; inherent, or "inexistent", if the nature is accidental or assumed). In this way, the termination called a substantial mode is a determination deriving from the specificity of the nature. Such an understanding has the further advantage of mitigating the apparent logical posteriority of subsistence with respect to being. The substantial mode could be a mode which qualifies or conditions the very advent of the nature's existence, the very realization of the essence. Subsistence would thus be simultaneous with being, a modality of the essence's actuality. In fact, existence of any kind is the kind it is in virtue of its intrinsic quality, its kind, its mode: existence cannot precede its own mode. Note: the fact that we treat subsistence here as a mode of existence (as opposed to a mode of the substance) matters

---

[1290] Cf. Suárez, *Disp. met.*, disp. 34, s. 4, n. 23.
[1291] Cf. Suárez, *Disp. met.*, disp. 34, s. 4, n. 23.
[1292] Cf. Suárez, *Disp. met.*, disp. 34, s. 4, n. 23.

little in light of the identity between the actual essence and its existence.

With these observations in place, we are better equipped to grapple with the prevailing criticisms brought against the Suarezian theory[1293]. To the censure attacking the accidentality and posteriority of the substantial mode, we have already responded by proposing an alternative acceptation of the Suarezian thesis. We cannot assume that the substance is already constituted in its being prior to the reception of the substantial mode; for the mode in question is the necessary condition for the realization of the essence, or the realization of its existence (which must be some kind of existence). Subsistence cannot be said to "complete" a being already fully constituted without it; it enters rather into the *causes* of being, thus preceding the substance in nature. It does not add a *new* mode of being posterior to substantial being; it is rather that according to which the substance is at all, i.e. *simpliciter* (and as a *per se* existent).

A second objection is raised on account of the presupposed identity between the concrete nature and its existence. If the nature is its own existence, then, by its very reality, the nature exists in itself and by itself. This seems to imply that every real nature is self-subsistent. However, the implication is not necessary. To exist *in se* and *per se* can be taken simply as assigning one or another existential state to the actual nature, and as inseparable from it; that is, a given nature exists, of its very self, in one way or another. But this does not imply that that nature exist according to self-subsistence, even though the existence it enjoys is inseparable from the nature it is. In other words, a non-self subsistent being (i.e. dependent being) can be said to follow (logically) from the real nature *in se* and *per se*: the *per se* existence here is non-self subsistent; through itself, the nature exists, but it does not subsist as a subject of existence[1294]. Accordingly, Suárez could continue to speak of subsistence as that modality distinguishing the *per se* existence of a non-self-subsistent nature from that of a self-subsistent nature. There is, therefore, no contradiction in qualifying a nature as existent *in se* and *per se* while nevertheless not self-subsistent; such a state of affairs is not equivalent to simultaneously existing *in se* and *per se* and not existing *in se* and *per se*. Rather, a thing exists in

---

[1293] Cf. in this regard the critique of Suárez' system in A. Michel, "HYPOSTASE", *DTC* 7, p. 421-423.

[1294] A precise delineation of the senses of *per se, in se, a se*, etc. – such as that attempted by Maurice Blondel in his celebrated *L'Être et les êtres* (Paris 1935) – would prove in-

itself and by itself in a non-self-subsistent way; that is, it is its own existence, but that existence is "inexisting" existence[1295]. The inseity and perseity of its existence do not imply self-subsistence, but only the kind of existence proper to its current natural (or supernaturally effected) status. Nonetheless, if the nature is self-subsistent or sustained by another, then the nature is identical to its self-subsistent or "inexistent" reality; the mode, as we have observed, appears to derive immediately from the nature in itself. The self-subsistent nature (the supposit) exists, therefore, *according to subsistence* in itself and through itself; the mode of the existence (which latter is identical to the nature) stems from the nature itself. To claim, therefore, that a substantial nature is not self-subsistent is to assert something about the nature itself and its intrinsic reality (and not simply to deny the nature some perfection independent of its very ontological makeup). (With this, moreover, we salvage the notion of the analogicity of being. That analogy is not lost, but reduced to an analogicity of essence: the limitation of the essence determines the perfection of the being. The created essence's being is always contingent, and not necessary, since that being is constrained to, identified with, the limited perfection represented by the essence[1296]).

What, then, does this imply with respect to the humanity of Christ? To accuse Suárez of contradiction for simultaneously assigning to that nature existence *in se* and non-subsistence amounts to a shallow criticism. The humanity considered in itself is certainly not self-subsistent but nevertheless possesses its own (arguably identical) existence (even if this existence is of a diminished or subordinated analogical sort). Depending upon the accepted criteria for concrete reality, the humanity so signified may or may not represent the concrete individualized human nature. If, as we would like to maintain, the concrete reality of a substantial nature is had through a principle by which a

---

valuable to the project of exploring the metaphysical parameters opened up by Suárez.

[1295] The analogicity of being thus expresses itself according to the analogicity of essences, according as the being of a supposit is identical to the supposit, and the being of a *quo est* identical to the *quo est.*

[1296] To the question "How does God differentiate the creature from himself?", one can respond by stating that he simply produces the essence according to its intrinsic delimitation. The essence is of itself a limited kind. Of course, it does not come to be of itself, but is produced by God. But that production does not have to mean the joining or composing of the essence with existence – except in a logical sense. For the possible essence, which is the essence considered in abstraction from its being, is not a real subject to which *esse* is joined. Creation proceeds *ex nihilo*, not from a

thing subsists (or is hypostatized), then the concrete human nature of Christ is the human nature according to the subsistence it enjoys through the Word. In virtue of the unique subsistent, the unique subject, this nature (hypostatically signified, i.e. signified according to subsistence) *is* the person of the Word[1297]. As a result, the human nature concretely envisaged is *not* non-self-subsistent, for it is one with the supposit which subsists of itself. Now, the reality Suárez is concerned with is that of the essence in its concrete actuality, and not that of something which is real (and therefore actual) but in a non-concrete or partial way. Accordingly, from the point of view of the criteria of concreteness we have adopted, it would be wrong to claim that the human nature in Christ is non-subsistent, since, as concrete, its existence is that of this person. Here the identity between the actual essence and its existence translates as an identity between the concrete human nature and the subsistent act of the Word[1298]. Of course, Suárez, like all of the authors of the diverse theories of subsistence we have considered, intends the human nature strictly from the point of view of its non-subsistence. To do so, without entering into contradiction, he would either have (a) to uphold the idea of self-existing non-subsistence as explained above (that is, a non-subsistent nature possessing of itself a certain being to which it is identical), while nonetheless ascribing concreteness to such a nature of attenuated being (and it is precisely here that we recognize a crucial problem interior to the system), or (b) envisage that nature not according to its concrete actuality. To maintain that the substantial mode "subsistence" is *added* to nature in order that the latter be self-subsistent, the nature to which the mode is added must be understood as not yet actual if, as is our belief, its actuality is precisely a subsistent actuality, that is, if the fully actualized concrete nature enjoys the perfection of subsistence (if its reality is not to be a subsistent actuality, then the substantial mode "subsistence" cannot be added to it). The nature so considered is the nature prior to or in abstraction from its existential perfection (a pure possible for Suárez); we are back to considering the "substantial mode"/"existential mode" as entering into the causes of the realization of the nature.

---

possible, as though act were somehow united to it. If such were the case, the possible would have to be real, and thus not a possible at all, but actual.

[1297] A demonstration of this doctrine shall be given only in our following study on the Incarnation.

[1298] Note, the formality of this act is the <u>subsistere</u>, that is, the subsistent act of the person as such in hypostatic distinction (which we may call, following St. Albert, *esse personalis*, in contradistinction from the *esse simpliciter* constitutive of the divine nature).

As a final remark about all of these systems, without unduly criticizing the inventiveness of proposing a substantial mode (metaphysical novelty and multiplication of entities), we shall simply point out that none of them are verifiable in the texts of Saint Thomas (whose doctrine most of them aim to interpret) [1299]. A distinction between subsistence and substantial existence, furthermore, is not affirmed (nor explicitly denied) in the *opera* of the Angelic Doctor.

Modern reflections

With the advent of modern philosophy, considerations of personality underwent a radical transformation. The Scholastic concept of a personal principle possessing a real and concrete value is altogether lost and replaced with criteria of the psychological order (as, for example, those of "consciousness" or "thought") [1300]. In post-Kantian idealism, the notion of a principle of personality loses its importance and ceases to be a philosophical problem forasmuch as the person is but a transient phenomenon in the evolutionary process of the absolute (Fichte, Schelling, Hegel). The empiricist movement finally strips the notion of objective value by denying the existence of an underlying substrate as a foundation for the objects of our perception, themselves reduced to either pure appearances or perceptions (Locke, Hume,

---

[1299] Cajetan's interpretation of St. Thomas, over and above the introduction of the concept of substantial mode, is certainly not without its measure of inventiveness. Not only is his theory of the "elimination of being" not to be found in Thomas, but the notion of an individualized nature which is not subsistent is another Cajetanian innovation in Thomism. While the first has been the object of recent and well reasoned objection (cf., for example, J.-H. Nicolas, *Synthèse dogmatique*, §284, 321-322; *L'Unité d'Etre dans le Christ d'après Saint Thomas* in *RT* 65 [1965], p. 229-260; M.-V. Leroy, "L'union selon l'hypostase d'après saint Thomas d'Aquin", *RT* 74 [1974], p. 205-243; H. Diepen, *La critique du baslisme selon saint Thomas d'Aquin*, in *RT* 50 [1950], p. 82-118, 290-329), the latter has seemed to pass as a principle beyond question. We disagree.

[1300] Cf. Descartes, *Les principes de la philosophie* I, n. 8, where personality is reduced to thought and to the self-consciousness of the soul as to its constitutive principle; Kant, *Critique of Pure Reason* (especially the beginning of the "Dialectic" and the third "Paralogism"), where the "I" is not even the thinking substance, but thought in itself and the very psychological acts upon which the soul reflects (self-identity reduces to a "unity of consciousness" described as an "identity of function" whereby the mind unifies many things, connecting experience within a single consciousness; here "subject" is an active operation of construction, a "categorial apparatus"; the unity of apperception serves as but a logical subject of or point of reference for experience; the "I" is but a "bare consciousness accompanying all concepts", and "person" is described as the consciousness of the very identity in question).

Berkeley). We shall not linger over the theological inadequacies and philosophical inconsistencies inherent in modern philosophy's renovation of the concept of personality, but note that it is only with the revival of the Scholastic tradition that personality recovers its legitimate status as a philosophical issue of *ontological* value[1301].

[1301] And this, despite the fact that contemporary philosophy is stamped with the theme of personality as its proper domain, philosophy, as it were, taking over what was originally the task of the theologian, while theology is seen as approaching the question in uncreative repetitive ways (cf. A. Milano, *Persona in teologia*, Edizioni Dehoniane, Naples 1987, p. 20-22).

The contemporary approach to the question of personality typically formulates the problem in terms of "personal identity". The expression, however, receives two very different senses or applications. On the one hand, it is sometimes taken as an achievement of the characteristics of consciousness proper to man, in the sense that it is itself constituted by reason of the unifying act of intelligence and memory able to coherently relate past and present experience into a consistent whole (thus "personal identity" is a mind dependent phenomenon). On the other hand, "personal identity" is sometimes understood as the trans-phenomenal endurance of a subject which resists the changes and dissolution proper to its perceivable properties threatened by time. This latter understanding, of course, has no direct value for questions related to personality in the Trinity, since there is absolutely no change or succession in God (however, the notion of "subject" and the unity which this implies can be employed in an analogous way in accounting for divine personality). While the first sense of "personal identity" falls properly within the domain of psychology, the latter is synonymous with the Scholastic conception of substance as the principle of unity for any given entity.

With respect to the "identity" of the persisting subject, modern philosophy has attempted to substitute the Scholastic account of its principle with a variety of other candidates. Memory is frequently advanced as the reason for "personal identity", since it alone manifests a temporally successive unity of experience to the human mind. But memory itself must stem from something more foundational to the very entity (man) of whom it is the memory. Ordinary experience teaches me not that I *am* a memory, but that I *have* a memory. Memory is something I *exercise*, it is an *operation* and, as such, requires a *principle* of operation. As a result, proposing memory as an explanation for "personal identity" merely begs the question. Another, less popular, opinion regards materiality itself (independent of the notions of "substance" or "nature" or "essence") as responsible for everything proper to men including their "personal identity". This position, as a consequence of its rejection of "nature", also denies the reality of the soul. However, the problem with such a perspective is that the very empirical elements recognized to constitute this or that individual lose their *own* consistency on the basis of the premise presupposed. If their is no underlying (and unobservable) principle of unity for an observable reality, but only outwardly manifest properties, then this or that man, animal, plant or fluid is no longer one in reality, but only conventionally referred to as "one", since there is no unifying principle by which it is one total being. To the contrary, according to the materialistic point of view, such things are *conglomerates* of a multitude of empirically acknowledged material unities. What is even more destructive of the theory, however, is the fact that, if there can be no natures in the metaphysical sense of the term, then *even these aggregated constituents* lack an intrinsic unity (and we either continue to dissect the perceived individual *ad infinitem*, without ever knowing what it or any of its components are, or we deny that it is anything at all). If, on the other hand, we ascribe some sort of subsistent or enduring status to

As to current theological inquiry, contemporary theology of the Incarnation consists for the most part in a study of Redemption, the mysteries of the life of Christ, and the psychology of the God-man[1302]. The relatively few works centering on the speculative issue of personality characteristically aim either at a historical exposition of Scholastic positions or, if inspired by more or less "personalistic" tendencies emphasizing subjectivity and the "I", at an integration of the contributions of phenomenology and modern psychology[1303]. Some authors whose works fall into the latter category have attempted to approach personality from original, authentically ontological points of view. Two, in particular, have published works bearing an important relation to our study: J. Galot, *La personne du Christ*, Duculot-Lethielleux, Paris 1969; "La définition de la personne, relation et sujet", *Gregorianum* 75 (1994), p. 281-299; and J. A. Sayes, *Jesucristo, Ser y Persona*, Aldecoa, Burgos 1984. The first is important for characterizing personality in terms of relation, and this, in a formal, constitutive way; the second, for emphasizing the value of "subject" in defining personhood and for identifying the personal principle as a point of junction

the perceivable qualities of a thing themselves – such as in the theory maintaining that such qualities are the only real things (whose existence we may legitimately affirm) – then we have either (a) returned to a concept of the substance, insofar as these *passiones* of a thing are now treated as existing in their own right and not within another as in a subject (i.e. as *per se* existents), or (b) reduced all reality to mere appearance (effectively restricting it to having but an intentional value, which is no ontological value at all).

The principal contribution of current philosophy of the person consists not in breaking new territory with respect to the fundamental ontology of personality, but in expounding the moral, social and psychological dimensions of the human being, the ramifications of which are expressed in terms of transfigurative relationships, interiority, conscious acts of loving and knowing, responsibility, etc..

[1302] Cf. J. P. Torrell, "Le thomisme dans le débat Christologique contemporain", in *Saint Thomas au XXᵉ siècle, Actes du colloque du Centenaire de la "Revue thomiste"*, Saint-Paul, Paris 1994, p. 380-382, 387.

[1303] Outside of the speculative field, the modern personalistic propensity expresses itself in a spiritually rich manner and with hermeneutical originality particularly in biblical studies of the Christian socio-redemptive structure. Cf., as recent examples illustrating the importance of the notion of the individual, the community, and the formation of a "people" (chosen by God, constituted through "alliance", represented and unified in different historical figures): P. Beauchamp, "Persona, elezione e universalità nella Bibbia", in *L'Idea di persona*, V. Melchiorre (editor), Vita e Pensiero, Milan 1996, p. 33-50; G. Angelini, "La figura della 'persona' nel quadro dell'alleanza", in *L'Idea di persona*, V. Melchiorre (editor), Vita e Pensiero, Milan 1996, p. 51-62. For a general evaluation of "personalistic" anthropologies, their evolutionary or dynamic conceptualization of personality (presented largely as a form of self-realization through freedom of choice), and their sharp contrast with the metaphysical project of ascertaining the precise ontological constitution of the

for both of the natures in Christ. Both authors share certain fundamental perspectives with our own theory, however the thought of both
differs from ours in vital metaphysical ways. We would like to briefly
consider the theological position of J. Galot within this overview, but
wish to reserve our analysis of J. A. Sayes for another occasion (when
we present the sequel to this thesis).

The relative conceptualization of J. Galot

Chief amongst the defenders of the importance of relation in defining personhood is J. Galot who, in several publications [1304], advances a
perspective according to which the person is essentially constituted by
relation as such; person, that is, is relation according to predication *in
quid*. The picture painted by Galot roots the very reality of the person
in nothing other than relation *qua* relation. Such a position is far
from anything we have affirmed about relation which, as a principle
of opposition, distinguishes a plurality in God, and, as identical to the
substance, constitutes complete hypostases. From our own perspective, relation *as such* is but a principle of the distinctness formally constitutive of personhood, a distinctness, moreover, which amounts to
nothing at all without the real being understood to come from the
divine substance by which the distinguished terms truly subsist and
with which they are identical. J. Galot, as we shall see, adopts an entirely different understanding of the divine relations and of relation in
general with which we cannot agree, an understanding originally
motivated by what effectively amounts to a misconstrual of the
analogical relationship between the divine attributes and created perfections. From the fact that persons in God are subsistent relations, it
follows, according to Galot, that created persons must also be so defined, due to the fundamental analogy between God and his creature [1305]. While it is true that whatever is formal to personality as such
must be equally verifiable in both divine and created persons, it is
simply incorrect to affirm that the modality according to which that
formality is realized must be the same in both. Furthermore, Galot's

---

person, cf. E. Forment, *Lecciones de Metafísica*, Ediciónes Rialp, Madrid 1992,
p. 330-348.

[1304] Cf. in particular, J. Galot, *La Personne du Christ*, Duculot-Lethielleux, Paris 1969; "La
définition de la personne, relation et sujet", *Gregorianum* 75/2 (1994), p. 281-299.
From here onward, we shall abbreviate the latter work as "La définition de la personne".

[1305] Cf. J. Galot, *La Personne du Christ*, p. 32-33; "La définition de la personne", p. 282,
288-289.

attempt to move from the divine realization of a given perfection to a conclusion about the manner in which it is found in creatures is in some ways irrespective of the very structure of human understanding. With respect to the origin of our concepts and the attribution of names (such as "person"), the terms we employ pertain first of all to creatures, even if they express pure perfections and even when revelation authorizes their ascription to God. The fact that such perfections are more fully realized in God, in whom they exist in a supreme and infinite way, changes nothing about the analogy of proportion according to which we arrived in the first place at speaking about God with such terms, the broad analogical sense of which alone is predicable of both created and uncreated being.

Taking as his point of departure the Chalcedonian definition of faith, obliging the human intelligence to recognize a difference between nature (i.e. an existing nature) as such and the person who possesses that nature, in order to preserve the perfect humanity of Christ while nevertheless being able to deny its personality, Galot thoroughly refuses to consider the nature or any properties of the nature as constitutive of personality, lest the human nature, he fears, be deprived of some absolute perfection[1306]. Because personality, he maintains, is a relative perfection, the absence of human personality in Christ implies no privation of an absolute perfection from that human nature. Now, structuring personality on relation may successfully secure the integrity of Christ's human nature (and our own theory of personality based on a relative principle of individuation assures the perfection of Christ's human nature in a similar way) as well as emphasize the subjectivity of the person who is the bearer of relations, but, if that is all there is to personality, then it is the integrity of the person itself which is jeopardized. If, in order to protect the natural integrity of human nature in Christ, personality itself is reduced to nothing of the absolute order, then the cost of distinguishing person from nature amounts to an effective destruction of the former. Consciously and explicitly coordinating the personal mystery in Christ with the mystery of three persons in God – one of the strongest merits of Galot's theology –, he develops his notion of person as relation on the basis of the concept of person emerging from Trinitarian reflection. Unfortunately, his notion is deduced not from what is essential to person as such, but from other elements pertaining to the divine persons in virtue, ironically, of their divine nature.

Person, Galot claims, is defined in Trinitarian theology by relation, a conclusion deriving from the fact that the three persons cannot have a diversity of perfection, from the fact that they cannot differ absolutely[1307]. Already the conclusion goes beyond the strict implication of the premises. Though the divine persons, in order not to be diverse, can only be distinct from one another on a relative basis, this does not mean that those persons are defined by relation as such. The persons are *distinguished*, and therefore constituted according to personal number, by relation, but their persons are not necessarily defined by relation. To the premise stating that "the plurality of persons in God only exists to the extent that there are relations entailing a certain opposition"[1308], we remark that it is precisely the *plurality* the existence of which depends upon relative opposition, not the entire constitution of the persons as such. It may be that they result from relations, but it is not from these relations *in themselves* (i.e., insofar as relations) that the persons are persons. For the person is the distinguished *thing of nature*, and it is only the distinction which proceeds from relation *qua* relation. The persons, therefore, are not constituted by relation *qua* relation insofar as *persons*, but only insofar as "Father", "Son" and "Holy Spirit" understood according to their relative opposition and, therefore, distinction[1309]. Moreover, the distinctive function of the relations is not sufficient for relation to enter into the *definition* of person, for the definition is not concerned with this or that form of personality, but with what formally constitutes personhood as such. As pointed out by St. Thomas, what makes the Father, Son and Holy Spirit persons is their *distinction*; in the Trinity, however, that distinction *results from* relations[1310]. Perfect distinction is thus formal to personality; the fact that such distinction obtains through relation is of secondary importance to the definition of person as such.

The question to be asked is: just what is that distinction which makes something to be a person? It cannot be any kind of distinction – like the modality of Sabellius, for example (which fails to recognize a plurality of persons) –, but must be a distinction of reality, one which is concrete, individual. By individual we mean being distin-

---

[1306] Cf. J. Galot, *La Personne du Christ*, p. 5-26, 31; "La définition de la personne", p. 289-292; cf. J. A. Sayes, *Jesucristo, Ser y Persona*, Aldecoa, Burgos 1984, p. 92-94.

[1307] Cf. J. Galot, "La définition de la personne", p. 281; *La Personne du Christ*, p. 30.

[1308] J. Galot, *La Personne du Christ*, p. 30.

[1309] As J.-H. Nicolas equally attests, the persons in God are not constituted by relation as such, but distinguished from one another on that account; cf. J.-H. Nicolas, *Synthèse dogmatique*, §121.

[1310] Cf. Aquinas, *Sum. theol.*, I, 29, 4.

guished as *an* individual (*alius*), which is the perfect individual, for many things called "individual" do not qualify as persons precisely because they do not constitute *an* individual. Naturally, this pushes us toward the notion of individuality in the sense just described, which really entails existence *in se*, as constitutive of the person. But why should this be so maladroit? In the Trinity, it is not sufficient in order to have a plurality of persons that there be a plurality of relations, but it is precisely because of the fact that these relations are *subsistent* relations, and this because whatever is in God *is* God, that they also account for a plurality of persons[1311]. For this additional reason it seems correct to say, in conformity with the doctrine of St. Basil, that "the divine Persons are not equated with the (relational) particularities insofar as *persons* but only insofar as *divine* Persons"[1312]. The situation is stated most clearly by J.-H. Nicolas: "The divine person is constituted in the divine nature by a relation *insofar as the relation is identified with the nature*, that is, by the relation insofar as subsistent. The person is distinguished from the other persons, in the same nature, *by the same relation insofar as relation, insofar as AD*"[1313].

From this point of view, it is entirely illicit to exclude a substantial basis for the subsistent nature of the relations[1314]. It is precisely the nature of the divine nature that makes these relations to be subsistent,

---

[1311] Cf. Aquinas, *Comp. theol.*, c. 55.

[1312] Cf. supra, "INTEGRATION OF THESE CONCEPTS IN THE WRITINGS OF BASIL THE GREAT", p. 43-44.

[1313] J.-H. Nicolas, *Synthèse dogmatique*, §121. One might object that such a depiction of the constitutive function of relation appears to be inconsistent with what was earlier affirmed, namely that relation constitutes the person insofar as *proprietas* However, the assertion that relation constitutes the person insofar as identical to the divine substance is entirely coherent with what was stated before. Insofar as *proprietas* relation is constitutive of the person according to the person's distinct/personal being, while, insofar as identified with the nature, relation is constitutive of the person with respect to its being *simpliciter*. The first pertains to the what of the person as hypostatically signified and restricted to this person (the conceptualization of which is facilitated by the notion not only of personal being but of *qui est*). But this "whatness" is nothing other than the substantial being of the Godhead as hypostatically possessed according to a unique mode of existence. Relation insofar as *proprietas* is everything the person is, only viewed as proper to the person itself; relation insofar as divine substance is everything the person is viewed simply as quiddity and nothing more. Each of these conceptualizations of relation differ from relation *qua* relation which has rather a *distinguishing* than constituting role. Furthermore, the citation from Nicolas emerges only in the context of disproving the theory that relations possess their own subsistence as such. That is, the author wishes to insist upon the *substantial* foundation for the reality and subsistence of relations, whence the person (which is this subsistent thing) is constituted by relation only insofar as the latter be identifiable with the subsistent divine substance. Cf, supra, "PROPRIETAS AS CONSTITUTIVE OF ALL PERSONS", p. 436; "PROPRIETAS AND PERSON", p. 442.

according to the principle that whatever is in God is God, which is a function of the simplicity of his nature.

The result of this argument points toward subsistence as constituting the person. Of course, if we ask what is subsistence, and respond in consideration of all of its causes, then, because it may be formally described as a mode of being, we may return, in the case of creatures at least, to the concept of relation as responsible for its reality inasmuch as "being" is sustained through a relation with the Creator who holds all things in being (in fact, even the Being which God is is *self*-sustaining). We ultimately arrive at this fundamental relation, naturally progressing from the notion of a thing's mode of being to that of the distinctiveness of its essence (which, if it possesses a mode of existing *in se*, will be a complete individual), to the cause of the (actualization of the) composition of that essence with its actuality or being[1315]. Relation to God, then, may be invoked to explain person, not only as a source of complete distinctness (in the event that it play a fundamental role in individuation), but also according to its role in constituting the reality of an essence (*ens ab alio*). However, the impetus for this way of explaining created personality seems to proceed from first recognizing subsistence, i.e. the perseity proper to the individual, as the characterizing aspect of person (taking intelligence, or any other necessary attribute for granted), relation entering into the picture only as an explanatory device with respect to the formal constituent of personality, a fully distinct act of being (which is received).

Our author intends to demonstrate not merely the intrinsic relativity of personhood, but that persons are essentially relations by appealing, furthermore, to conciliar statements. Citing a passage from the XIth Council of Toledo – "*quae cum relative tres personae dicantur*"[1316] –, he draws the conclusion that persons are relatively defined[1317]. But that is not what the council affirms. In the passage under consideration, it is a question: (1) of pronouncing a *plurality* of persons, and not of the meaning of "person" as such; and (2) of *relative terms*: we say "Father" or "Son" relatively (≠ saying "person" relatively). When Galot asserts that "the persons are therefore defined as relative to one another"[1318], the proposition would be entirely acceptable were he simply to mean that the "Father" is defined as relative to the "Son", and vice versa. On the other hand, if what he means is that "person" is defined as

---

[1314] Cf. J. Galot, *La personne du Christ*, p. 33: "*nous faisons abstraction des théories diverses qui ont interprété la notion de 'relation subsistante' en y faisant rentrer la substance ou nature*".

[1315] That is, subsistence is formally described as a mode of being, which mode of being (along with being itself) and the individuality which it implies have their cause and explanation in a relation to God, a relation responsible for the realization of the essence in act.

[1316] XIth Council of Toledo (675), DS 528.

[1317] Cf. J. Galot, "La définition de la personne", p. 287; *La Personne du Christ*, p. 28-29.

[1318] J. Galot, "La définition de la personne", p. 287.

relative, and this is just what he means[1319], then the assertion cannot be accepted.

Thoroughly isolating the signification of person to the relative order, and understanding this as necessary in order to assure the absolute equality of the divine persons, Galot sees every attempt at defining person in absolute terms as verging upon tritheism[1320]. However, when attacking the absolute characterization of personality with respect to the Trinity, he does not consider its most rigorous and refined versions. In his criticism of theological explanations taking recourse to an absolute element[1321], Galot sweepingly rejects the entirety of such positions due to certain inadequacies encountered in their formulation as presented by several modern authors whose theology is far from representative of the long-standing tradition defining person in terms of nature along with a distinctive element. Moreover, with respect to these weaker versions, Galot insufficiently discerns, in our opinion, what is worthy of merit from what is outright inadmissible. While it is true that the Father cannot be identified with the divine essence in the sense that the essence itself constitutes his personality without reference to the Son, and while it is true that the fundamental equality of the persons entails that nothing absolute can characterize one person in distinction from the others[1322], such observations, which suffice to refute the false part of a theory presenting the Father as absolute principle of the Trinity[1323], do not overturn what is accurate in it when that theory explains that relation is not sufficient of itself to account for the fact that the divine relations are subsistent subjects[1324]. In his article consecrated to defining person, Galot typifies absolute concepts of the person in terms of non-standard modern versions of it. The problem, for example, of affirming a quaternity in God on the basis of a substantial or absolute concept of personality is an ancient point of discussion and not a doctrinal hazard recently advocated by followers of J. E. Kuhn. In the face of such heterodox efforts to define personhood in absolute terms, it is perhaps not so surprising that J. Galot regards relative and absolute conceptualizations of person as essentially divergent and incompatible. Nevertheless his mutually ex-

---

[1319] *"Cette manière de définir la personne..."* – J. Galot, "La définition de la personne", p. 287.

[1320] Cf. J. Galot, "La définition de la personne", p. 286-287, 291.

[1321] Cf. J. Galot, "La définition de la personne", p. 283-286.

[1322] Cf. J. Galot, "La définition de la personne", p. 286.

[1323] Cf. G. Girones, *La Divina Arqueología (Del primer principio teológico en el tratado de la Trinidad)*, Faculdad de Teología, Valencia 1991, p. 23-43.

[1324] Ibid.

clusive classification of the two approaches[1325] represents an extreme oversimplification. A relative and an absolute notion of the person are far from necessarily incompatible: a person is not said to be absolute and relative in the same respect. The two conceptualizations are falsely pitted against one another; indeed the greatest minds of the Church have retained the relative aspect of personality while nonetheless maintaining an absolute concept[1326].

Another weakness in the relative understanding of personality as espoused by J. Galot lies in what appears to be a tendency to define the primary act of the person in terms of second act, inasmuch as the relational dimension he elaborates pertains to the intersubjective relations naturally subsequent to the ontological constitution of the individual subsistent (the real term of relation)[1327]. As J. A. Sayes argues[1328], Galot's conception of the relative element in personality is the purely phenomenological reality of subjective interrelation between an "I" and a "you". Such a position is unsatisfactory for its lack of an objective ontological foundation. Moreover, the relational element understood to be constitutive of personhood in that case is one between two already constituted subjects, and not – to contrast the position with our own – that relation which we have associated with the being of a concrete nature (by which it is individuated and thus rendered person). The relation Galot is getting at presupposes the ontological constitution of personhood; the relation we have spoken of *is* the ontological constituent of personhood (though this does not mean that relation itself must enter the analogical definition of person, even if its proper effect of distinguishing does).

Galot's appeal to the domain of second act corresponds to an omission in his account of personality of the very element which, in nature, is metaphysically prior to relation (and which is logically prior in God), namely substance or οὐσία, with respect to which everything else is. Our author wants to deny that our understanding of relation depends upon an antecedent understanding of being in itself[1329], a

---

[1325] Cf. J. Galot, "La définition de la personne", p. 286.

[1326] C. Vigna, a major contemporary advocate of the essentially relative structure of personality and human nature, clearly states the impossibility of prescinding from an absolute foundation for relative perfection (cf. op. cit., p. 183, 192) and, contrary to any incompatibility between substantial and relative descriptions of personhood, erects a concept of personality based upon their inmost inseparability (cf. op. cit., especially p. 182, 187-202).

[1327] Cf. J. Galot, *La Personne du Christ*, p. 39-41, 58; cf. "La définition de la personne", p. 297.

[1328] Cf. J. A. Sayes, op. cit., p. 94.

[1329] Cf. J. Galot, *La Personne du Christ*, p. 50.

metaphysical error motivated by a legitimate concern for the psychological dimension of the blossoming of personality through second act[1330]. But relation of the sort envisaged by Galot is always posterior, at least logically, to the reality of the subject (and relation of any sort, including the transcendental relation to the First Cause, is always in some respect posterior to the subject of which it is the relation). There can be no separation of the concept of relation from that of its subject, and this even if we confess the two to be identical in reality as in the case of God. "Where there is not some thing that is related, there is no relation. In other words, if the I and the you do not have their own autonomous reality, if they are not two absolute things, they cannot be related"[1331]. Relation is not of itself an autonomous entity.

Nevertheless, Galot explicitly attributes to relation in itself a kind of subsistence which is independent of and distinct from that of the nature or substance[1332]: *"c'est la subsistance de l'être relationnel comme tel"*[1333]. First of all, no kind of subsistent being may be ascribed to God distinct from that of the nature without implying another *esse simpliciter*. And if a being distinct from that of the nature is ascribed to each of the three relations in God, then we would have four beings in the Godhead, three relative beings distinctly subsisting beside one absolute being. [Note that if the "subsistence of relational being as such" is intended to mean something like the "personal being" we earlier discussed, then it could not be affirmed that this being is distinct from that of the essence in the sense of *independent* of natural being; for, "personal being", as the being of the person according to its distinctive constitution as such, is distinguished only from the "personal being" of another person, but not from the being of the substance which also constitutes it. "Personal being", as we have seen, indicates the personal alteriety characteristic of the divine substance hypostatically signified, an alteriety exclusively between hypostases and not with respect to the substance[1334]]. Not only is such a characterization of relation impossible on account of introducing another *esse* in God, but it furthermore inconsistently loads the concept of relation with something extrinsic to its signification. Relation as such says *ad aliud* and nothing about subsisting, merely ephemerally inhering, or any other mode of being. The being of relation is rather a function of that

[1330] Cf. J. Galot, "La définition de la personne", p. 297.
[1331] J. A. Sayes, op. cit., p. 94.
[1332] Cf. J. Galot, "La définition de la personne", p. 295-296.
[1333] J. Galot, "La définition de la personne", p. 296.
[1334] Cf. supra, "PERSONAL BEING", p. 393.

upon which it is founded. Moreover, "to subsist" is not a relative notion, and therefore says something absolute, whence Galot is ascribing
to relation *as such* an absolute value, the very thing he wants to deny.
Galot's concept of relation is flawed. He wants to invest it with an intrinsic and independent act of subsistence, absolutizing it as it were,
such that the notion no longer has anything to do with relation as ordinarily conceived where the reality of the relation necessitates both
the distinctness of the terms of relation as well as their absolute reality. Even when used to speak about God, we cannot forget that,
though predicated as identical with the persons and the nature, relation's analogous notion was taken from *human* categories of understanding and cannot be stripped entirely of its conceptual origin. No
matter how purified and distanced from material conditions an
analogous notion of relation may be, its formal *ratio, ad aliud esse,*
which signifies nothing about real existence, requires for its objective
reality a source of being and foundation distinct from the formal
characteristic of relation.

In an attempt to avoid a substantial explanation of the subsistence
of the divine relations, Galot cites A. Malet who asserts: "relation in
God is subsistent, not because it is identical to the essence, but because it is identical to the supposit"[1335]. The assertion, however, is of
no avail; for the supposit is nothing other than the substance signified
according to the act proper to primary substance. If Galot and Malet
want to affirm that the relations are identical to the supposit only according to the formal concept of the supposit, that is, only with respect to the act of substanding, this is unreasonable; for then there
would be nothing to distinguish the notion of supposit from person,
the latter of which expresses in its concept the distinctiveness derived
from relation, over and above the act of substanding expressed by
"supposit"[1336].

The concept of subsistence as applied to the divine relations has
given rise to two very distinct philosophical currents, one of which,
commonly accredited to Billot, but which is clearly present in St. Albert and Thomas, holds that the relations are subsistent precisely in-

---

[1335] A. Malet, *Personne et amour dans la théologie trinitaire de saint Thomas d'Aquin,* Vrin,
Paris 1956, p. 92; cf. J. Galot, *La Personne du Christ,* p. 36, note 5.
[1336] If the substance-relation identity is strictly limited to the act of substanding, then
the subsisting relations which the persons are are *nothing more* than particular acts
of substanding and unable to be signified otherwise, there remains no possibility of
signifying the persons constituted by these relations differently than we signify the
mere formal act of substanding proper to the hypostasis *qua* hypostasis (cf. supra,
"THE PRECISE DENOTATION OF 'HYPOSTASIS', ITS DISTINCTIVE MODE OF SIGNIFICATION", p. 233).

sofar as identical to the nature (concerning the *esse in* of relation), the other and more recent of which maintains that the relations, of their very relative nature (concerning the *esse ad*), are constitutive of the persons and subsist as three relative subsistents, a position proper to Galtier, Billuart and Galot[1337]. The latter perspective, as we have seen in Galot, attempts to assign subsistence to relation *as such*, in its *esse ad*. But we have already seen that relation as such is not signified as constitutive of the persons, but rather as distinctive (according to the concept of its opposition which renders the relations of origin *proprietates* of the persons)[1338]. With Billot, we agree that to subsist is to exist *in se*, as a result of which the "relational subsistence" of Galot converts a relative notion into an absolute notion – unless one were to claim that "to subsist" is able somehow to imply but a purely relative perfection, but then another relation would accrue to the relation said to subsist *qua* relation, namely that of subsistence, which cannot be said to be the same as the subsisting relation in question (such as Paternity), lest the very concept of paternity include the notion of subsisting. And if one were to argue that "to subsist" does not mean to exist *in se*, but can mean to exist in some other fashion, then the fact that the subsisting relation in this case does not exist of itself means that it subsists in dependence upon another principle, contrary to the presupposition of the adherent to the second philosophical trend. If it is not necessary that the principle of subsistence be something absolute – and here we perhaps differ with Billot who holds that that principle is absolute; though, if he is simply referring to the formal principle of subsistence (the intrinsic act of a thing), there is no divergence between us, since our relative principle in creatures, with respect to simple being, is of the efficient order –, the subsistent thing itself must be (just as the subsistent relations in God *are* the divine substance). Moreover, if the relations were subsistent insofar as relations, i.e. with respect to their *esse ad*, the very divine persons would be opposed to one another at the level of subsistence, making each person absolutely distinct from the others as an immediate consequence of their distinction at the relative level.

Expressly defending himself against the critical evaluation of J. A. Sayes, Galot, besides accurately observing that nature itself cannot be

---

[1337] Cf. A. Michel, "RELATIONS DIVINES", *DTC* 10, p. 2152-2154; cf. J. A. Sayes, op. cit., p. 95-96.

[1338] Cf. Albert, *I Sent.*, d. 8, a. 34; d. 26, a. 9; cf. J.-H. Nicolas, *Synthèse dogmatique*, §121; G. Emery, op. cit., p. 100-101; A. Pompei, op. cit., p. 268, 276, 275-283, 288; cf. supra,

the source of personal reality, an observation which is fully accurate only if taken to mean that nature cannot supply for the reality of the person according to its numerical unity (*qua* personally distinguished), unjustly accuses Sayes of having adopted a position radically opposed to the spirit of Chalcedonian theology, claiming that "he wishes to root the concept of hypostasis in that of substance, in a reverse way from the road paved by theology when it distinguished hypostasis from nature"[1339]. Without entering into a discussion of the perspective of Sayes, we simply remark that the theological tradition has always identified substance and hypostasis *in re*, but distinguished their mode of signifying in virtue of what hypostasis adds to the notion of substance simply taken. Galot's conclusion that "to consider the nature as the '*constitutivo ontológico*' of the person is to remove from the person its characteristic reality" simplistically overlooks the fact that nature is never presented as the *only* constitutive of personhood, nor even as the distinctive element. The statement is simply unfounded, as St. Albert and everything we have presented in this thesis thoroughly confirms.

In some respects, Galot admits that nature enters into the constitution of the complete person, and he is aware of the difference between *what the person is* (in its entirety) and what is *formally distinctive* of personality[1340]. The traditional definition of person corresponds, he observes, to the totality of the human being with which the person is identical. However, when it comes to recognizing the necessary distinction between person and nature, according to Galot, another *definition* of person is required[1341]. This conviction, however, seems to proceed from a certain logical confusion, inasmuch as the formal supposition and mode of signification of the name "person" is confounded with its definition[1342]. The author's ultimate recourse to the notion of subject of operation, we cannot neglect, also puts his theory of personality back on ontological grounds: "considerations of the psychological order and the progress of investigation in this area do not change the essential content of the concept of person... conceived as a unity of a subject of activity"[1343]. But Galot does not seem

---

"RELATION NOT ONLY DISTINGUISHES, BUT CONSTITUTES THE PERSONS", p. 396; "PROPRIETAS AS CONSTITUTIVE OF ALL PERSONS", p. 436.

[1339] J. Galot, "La définition de la personne", p. 296, note 27.
[1340] Cf. J. Galot, "La définition de la personne", p. 290.
[1341] Ibid.
[1342] Since Galot would cast the definition of person uniquely in terms of what pertains to the particular mode of signification proper to the name "person".
[1343] J. Galot, "La définition de la personne", p. 293.

to retain the ontological foundation and reality of this subject when he denies that this subject, considered in itself, has an absolute reality[1344]. Besides the metaphysical liabilities of such a position, it seems to exhibit the logical solecism alluded to above. "Considered in itself" does not mean "considered according to that formality by which its concept is distinct from that of the nature". In itself, the person is both something absolute and relative (or distinct); it is but the signification of person as determined by its *proper mode of signifying* which names something not named by the nature, wherefore the signification of person is distinguished from that of nature precisely according to the formality indicated by its *mode* of signifying.

Nevertheless, the notion of several distinct "subjects" in God requires great caution, since, as illustrated by R. Radlbeck, if its concept includes something absolute, one is tempted to assert an absolute difference between the persons resulting in tritheism[1345]. Galot therefore emphasizes the need for a balance between a concept of person as subject and a concept of person as relation[1346]: on the one hand, we must avoid the modalistic risk inherent in the doctrine of K. Barth and K. Rahner (affirming three modes within a single divine subject) by presenting the Father, Son and Holy Spirit as three subjects; on the other hand, in order to avoid any semblance of tritheism, we must uphold a single divine substance, restricting personal distinction to the purely relational level[1347]. Unfortunately, Galot carries his intuition too far when he identifies the person in itself with nothing other than relation, removing the absolute element from the constitution of the three divine subjects. The concept of subject does not present difficulties on account of an inherent reference to the absolute, but strictly on the basis of what being a subject normally implies, namely composition. In this respect, the Father is not the *subject* of paternity; he *is* paternity; and there is no real subject of paternity because that relation is identical to (and not *in*) the substance. The problem is not that there is an absolute element, but consists rather in the fact that there can be no "subject—in a subject" relation in God (one of the reasons for which Richard of St. Victor avoids the *substan*tial definition

---

[1344] Cf. J. Galot, "La définition de la personne", p. 295.

[1345] Cf. R. Radlbeck, *Der Personbegriff in der Trinitätstheologie der Gegenwart untersucht am Beispiel der Entwürfe Jürgen Moltmanns und Walter Kaspers*, Pustet, Regensburg 1989; cf. J. Galot, "La définition de la personne", p. 291.

[1346] On the modern debate concerning the value of the notion of subjectivity in defining personhood, see A. Bertuletti, "Il concetto di persona e il sapere teologico", in *L'Idea di persona*, V. Melchiorre (editor), Vita e Pensiero, Milan 1996, p. 3-31.

[1347] Cf. J. Galot, "La définition de la personne", p. 291.

of Boethius [1348]). The three persons are truly "subjects" of the divine nature in the sense that they are its concrete hypostatization; but they cannot be subjects in a sense which might really distinguish them from the nature of which they are the subjects. An affirmation of three subjects therefore numbers nothing absolute, but places number on the hypostatic possession of the absolute. Nevertheless, as is clear from the last clause, the absolute element is necessarily implied as that of which a subject is a subject [1349]. It is along just such lines that one affirms that the divine persons, while directly constituted by relation, are also constituted indirectly by the nature or essence: *per relationem in recto, per essentiam in obliquo* [1350].

A final ground for rejecting a theory of personality defining persons as relations lies in what appears to be an immediate and inadmissible implication of that theory. If there were no Trinity of persons in the Godhead, that is, if God were a single subject (as inevitably conceived prior to Christian revelation [1351]), it would follow from a thesis unqualifiedly basing personhood on subsisting relationship that this God is not a person. But certainly God is a person, even were he not to exist triunely; indeed "an impersonal God is a contradiction" [1352]. St. Albert and St. Thomas alike distinctly affirm that "God would still be such a person, even if he was not Father, Son and Holy Spirit" [1353]. "If there

---

[1348] Cf. supra, "RIGHT INTERPRETATION OF BOETHIUS", p. 340.

[1349] One will note that, just as it is unnecessary to subscribe to Rahner's Trinitarian monosubjectivism in order to preserve monosubstantiality, so in the Christological context, and again contrary to Rahner, the subjective singularity of the incarnate Word nowise entails a unicity of nature or substance in Christ (cf. K. Rahner, *Kirchliche Christologie zwischen Exegese und Dogmatik*, Schriften zur Theologie II, Benziger, Einsiedeln 1970, p. 210-211; K. Rahner - W. Thüsing, *Christologie systematisch und exegetisch*, Herder, Fribourg-Basel-Vienna 1972, p. 57-58; cf. J. Galot, "La définition de la personne", p. 292). As pointed out by J. Galot, to affirm a single subject in no way implies a single nature or operation; one must distinguish between the subject of operation and the nature as such (*by which* the subject acts), between the subject and the conscious and voluntary activity belonging to it (cf. J. Galot, "La définition de la personne", p. 292-293).

[1350] Cf. J.-H. Nicolas, *Synthèse dogmatique*, §121.

[1351] St. Albert as well as St. Thomas affirm that no knowledge of the Trinity can proceed from a natural knowledge of creatures: knowledge of the Trinity is only accessible through revelation and faith (cf. Albert, *I Sent.*, d. 3, a. 18; Aquinas, *Sum. theol.*, I, 32, 1, ad 2).

[1352] F. L. B. Cunningham (editor), *Christ and His Sacraments*, from *Theology: A Basic Synthesis for the College*, 3 vol., vol. III, Priory Press, Dubuque (Iowa) 1958, p. 122.

[1353] "*Creare personae actus est, prout persona est rationalis naturae individua substantia; et haec persona adhuc esset Deus, etiamsi non esset Pater et Filius et Spiritus sanctus*" – Albert, *I Sent.*, d. 36, a. 11, ad 1, ed. Borgnet, vol. 26, p. 223; cf. Aquinas, *I Sent.*, d. 29, q. 1,

were not three distinct persons in the sense of the faith, God would still be a certain person distinct in himself from other essences and natures of things"[1354]. Note that one cannot argue on the basis of this last statement of Albert that God remains a person on account of the relations obtaining between himself and creatures; for not only are these relations merely logical on the part of God, but creation itself is a purely contingent event and can be entirely abstracted from without detriment to God's eternal being, adding nothing to his ontological perfection. That perfection requires personality, not only because it must embrace every perfection, including that of concrete supposital existence, but because, without personality, no action whatsoever could be attributed to God, since actions pertain to supposits: "whoever thinks of God, necessarily thinks of him as someone possessing the deity or intellectual nature, without which he does not think of God as a perfect being in itself, nor as perfectly powerful, nor as perfectly wise"[1355].

On the other hand, even in the case that our God was not a unity of several, one could perhaps find some logical room to force a theory of relative personality. Even if God were a single subject, as conceived for example by the Jews, one might take recourse to the relation of

---

a. 4, ad 2 (cf. also Bonaventure, *III Sent.*, d. 5, a. 1, q. 4 & ad 1-4); cf. G. Emery, op. cit., p. 63-64.

[1354] Albert, *I Sent.*, d. 2, a. 12, ad 1, ed. Borgnet, vol. 25, p. 68: *"imo si non essent tres personae in rationibus quibus distinctae sunt in fide, adhuc Deus esset quaedam persona seipsa ab aliis essentiis et naturis rerum distincta".*

[1355] Bonaventure, *III Sent.*, d. 5, a. 1, q. 4, ad 1-4; cf. G. Emery, op. cit., p. 64. Concerning the concept of three persons relatively opposed in God, we must recognize a certain paradox able to be pitted against our own argument. Even though we cannot know its truth without revelation, this does not imply that it is metaphysically possible for God not to be Triune; metaphysical inaccessibility to the human intelligence does not imply metaphysical non-necessity. In this way, one could perhaps maintain – though this too could never be proven – that it is impossible (in an absolute sense and not just *de facto*) for God not to be Triune, that it is impossible, therefore, to have supreme perfection without intersubjective relationships. In this sense, we cannot say "if God were not Triune he would still be a person", for, according to the thesis, it would be impossible to have an adequate notion of God in abstraction from the relations. In such a case, that which is destroyed by the removal of the relations would be nothing other than personality. With respect to the issue of activity, one might thus argue that the fact that God cannot be thought of without the supposital perfection implied by activity (immanent or otherwise) implies that he cannot be thought of without relation; take away all relation, and he cannot act. To subtract intersubjective relation from our concept of God would thus leave us with an imperfect, inert concept of the divine nature in itself. Of course, this is not how Albert, Bonaventure and Thomas approach the question, but the quandary seems worthy of consideration. In any case, admission of the necessity of relation for the constitution of personal perfection will in no way mitigate what has already been said about the necessity of an absolute element.

identity, inasmuch as even this God is related to himself according to
the classical principal of identity. (Note that a thesis basing personhood on subsisting relations is not *necessarily* a thesis basing personhood on relative opposition[1356], hence, even cases of relation which do
not involve opposite relations – such as the relation of identity – are
not necessarily excluded). Of course, such a relation is a purely logical entity and explains nothing of the ontological structure of personhood.

Before concluding with a citation of Augustine and Thomas, we would
like to mention that the best known philosophers and theologians
who have recently accentuated the importance of relation in understanding the integral reality of person do not repudiate its substantial
value nor abate the significance of perseity in specifying its distinctive
notes. In fact, even modern attempts to glorify the status of relation
to the point of renouncing absolute elements in defining personality
inevitably return, against their very resolution, to natural conceptualizations and a language betraying the primacy of absolute being. In an
article by W. Norris Clarke[1357], the relative perfection of the person
and of being in itself as such is professed as sharply opposed to the
traditional Boethian definition of the person, vitiated for its narrow-
minded static perspective[1358]. The article rightly accentuates the dynamic and intrinsically self-communicative nature of *ens*, but misrep-
resents the tradition (in particular, Thomism) to the extent that emphasizing the relative perfection of personal being is understood to
conflict with an essence-centered understanding of the same, and
simply errs on divine liberty with respect to creative contingency
(while sacrificing systematic precision when denominating the persons of the Trinity in virtue of a failure to distinguish notional love
from essential love, and both from the personal property of the
Son)[1359]. The self-diffusive notion of being should indeed be integrated into our concept of the highest expression of being which is
the person, and who is, therefore, essentially relational. But this does
not mean that person is defined as relation; it only points to the fact
that every person is necessarily a subject of relation (something which,
as we have observed, could not occur if the person were nothing more

---

[1356] Cf. Aquinas, *Sum. theol.*, I, 30, 2.
[1357] Cf. W. Norris Clarke, "Person, Being and St. Thomas", *Communio: International Catholic Review*, XIX, n. 4 (1992), p. 601-618.
[1358] Cf. W. Norris Clarke, op. cit., p. 601-602.
[1359] Cf. W. Norris Clarke, op. cit., p. 613-616.

than an *esse ad*). Clarke's invocation of J. Ratzinger[1360] only reinforces the importance of a substantial structure of personality: "it is made apparent how being that truly understands itself grasps... that it only comes to itself by moving away from itself"[1361]. Person is here described as a *kind* of being, and therefore designatable as a "nature". It is this kind of nature, individually taken, of course, which is self-communicable. The appeal to J. Pieper[1362], furthermore, ultimately demonstrates the presence of a more fundamental root of the relational overflow of personality, the being of the person as first act, on the basis of which its existence is self-perfecting through time: "The higher the form of intrinsic existence, the more developed becomes the relatedness with reality... And the deeper such relations penetrate the world of reality, the more intrinsic becomes the subject's existence... These two aspects combined – dwelling most intensively within itself, and being *capax universi*, able to grasp the universe – together constitute the essence of the spirit"[1363]. The existential fulfillment Pieper is speaking of concerns the second act necessarily consequent upon the kind of being which the spirit is. This is indicated, moreover, by the term "becomes", implying a passage from potency to act. In fact, the essence of the spirit is not described as actually grasping the universe, but as *capax universi*, which is a capacity rooted in the nature and its powers. Clarke himself implicitly expresses both the distinction which must be recognized, as well as the inseparability between second act and first act when commenting the Thomistic affirmation that "every substance exists for the sake of its operations"[1364]. "Being as substance", he affirms, "naturally flows over into being as relational, turned *towards others* by its self-communicating action. *To be* is to be *substance-in-relation*"[1365], where substance, we might add, is the necessary pre-requisite (according to metaphysical priority) for relation. "It follows that to be a person as such is to be a being that tends by nature to pour over into active, conscious self-manifestation and self-communication to others, through intellect and will"[1366]. The person is an absolute reality, a being of nature, which tends, *on account of its nature*, to share itself with other distinct individuals. And its distinctness is a presupposition to such interaction. Indeed, like all being,

---

[1360] Cf. W. Norris Clarke, op. cit., p. 603.
[1361] J. Ratzinger, *Introduction to Christianity*, Herder & Herder, New York 1970, p. 137.
[1362] Cf. W. Norris Clarke, op. cit., p. 610.
[1363] J. Pieper, *Living the Truth*, Ignatius Press, San Francisco 1989, p. 83.
[1364] Aquinas, *Sum. theol.*, I, 105, 5; cf. *Sum. c. Gent.*, III, c. 113.
[1365] Cf. W. Norris Clarke, op. cit., p. 607.
[1366] W. Norris Clarke, op. cit., p. 609.

the person is intrinsically active and self-communicating[1367], but what is communicated to other persons is everything but its distinctive character; a person never communicates its personality to another individual, for then the person *as such* according to first act would be participated by several and no longer be one.

In conclusion, let us simply furnish the following words of St. Augustine and St. Thomas: "When, in the Trinity, we speak of the person of the Father, we mean nothing other than the substance of the Father. ... For He is called a person in respect to Himself (*ad se dicitur persona*), and not in respect to the Son or the Holy Spirit. ... We do not say three persons out of one essence as though therein essence were one thing and person another"[1368]. Person is therefore an absolute term, not a relative term[1369]: "it signifies relation not as such, but by way of a substance, which is a hypostasis"[1370].

[1367] Clarke gathers an entire series of texts from Aquinas expressing this theme; cf. W. Norris Clarke, op. cit., p. 603-604.

[1368] Augustine, *De Trin.*, VII, 6, 11.

[1369] Cf. B. Sesboüé, *Histoire des dogmes*, tome I: *Le Dieu du Salut*, Desclée, Paris 1994, p. 308.

[1370] Aquinas, *Sum. theol.*, I, 29, 4, ad 1; cf. *De Pot.*, q. 8, a. 3, ad 8.

III.2. FINAL CONCLUSION

Encapsulated results and value of this study

Consecrated to the diverse groups of examined authors and chronologically ordered, the INTRODUCTION placed in relief a series of considerations at the heart of the analysis of personality: (a) the enormous problem of semantics in the signification of the object of our ontological discourse relative to the person; (b) the different levels at which we must look for unity and multiplicity in the mystery of personality in God; (c) the specificity of the notion of hypostasis expressing a concrete act of existence as well as a perfect substantial totality; (d) the structural continuity between hypostasis and nature of which it represents the particular and subjective realization; (e) the different manners according to which nature or substance can be envisaged; (f) the great import of the notion and perfection of subsistence and its distinction from substantiality strictly speaking; (g) the necessity and nature of an incommunicable principle of each act of *per se* existence; (h) the possibility offered by the oecumenical councils of identifying in Christ the two concretely signified natures with the person, that is to say, insofar as hypostatized.

It is from these givens that we have sought to establish, on the basis of Albertinian reflection – a basis which is justified by the incomparably vast and profound work of Albert dedicated to the problem of personality –, the precise signification of the name "person", the essence of personality, the right definition of person, the elements which come together in its constitution, and a possible approach to personal unity in the unique subject of Christ. Sifting through the metaphysical meanders of the Universal Doctor, we have brought to light, to the extent to which it was possible, the exact acceptation of our language with regard to hypostatic realities in order to understand the acquired sense of the predicate "person", in order to better seize the ontological constitution of this subject which acts by means of or according to nature, and in order to clarify the principles anchored in the key problem of the multiplication of persons and the differentiation between the cause of numerical distinction and the substantial being of the individual (in this case rational). Along these lines, we underscored: (a) the capital role of mode of signification and of propositional supposition in theological discourse; (b) the intensional notes which differentiate the different names for the same reality which contains in itself a multiplicity of attributes; (c) the analogical character of our language when applied to divine realities; (d) the essential traits of every person; (e) the reciprocal indifference of substantial numeration in relation to personal numeration; (f) the elusive but very instrumental notion of "personal being"; (g) the diversity and community, at the generic, specific and individual levels, of the multiple principles of personal distinction known as *proprietates personalium*; (h) the special character of relation vis-à-vis divine hypostatic distinction; (i) the *distinctive* and *constitutive* dimensions of the divine relations as well as of every *proprietas personalis*; (j) the crucial necessity of discerning the formal principle of individuation in order to identify the intrinsic cause of hypostatization, something indispensable to an appreciation of the personal unicity of Christ; (k) the possibility of explaining the personal unity in Christ according to a participation of the humanity in the unique *proprietas personalis* of the Word as the reason for its own concretization; (l) the logical structures, the ontological content, and the advantages or disadvantages of the principal definitions of person proposed over history.

As for Saint Albert, we hope to have illuminated: (a) his profound elaboration of the sense of the different names for the reality which a person is; (b) his analysis of the diverse modes of personal distinction and their indissociability from the problem of individuality/singularity; (c) his doctrine concerning the logical relations between the different components of the definition of person and the illustration of these relations offered by the analogy of proportion; (d) the categorical importance he accords to the term "individual" and the grand import of this attribution; (e) the manner in which Albertinian thought lends itself to original interpretations regarding the ontological character of the principle of hypostatic distinction according to the different modes of its consideration.

The final historical overview by which we have attempted to draw this study together facilitates observing the continuity of the theology of the Church with regard to the distinction and identity between "person" and "nature" and a rupture with this tradition occasioned by certain post-Thomist scholars. In this regard, by rapidly examining the theories of "subsistence" advanced by Duns Scotus, John Capreolus, Cajetan and Suárez, we hope to have shed light on the non-necessity of a variety of presuppositions and conclusions there inherent and to have marked the importance of considering a "substantial mode" or "existential mode", not as superadded to the real substantial whole, but as entering into the very causes of the *realization* of a nature placed in the state of concrete existence (a thesis which lends itself to the explanation of the personal unity in Christ indicated above). Lastly, we acknowledged the need to reject a false modern and popular conception of the relational being of the person which undermines the integrity of its first act (that is, of its primordial ontological structure).

The conclusions reached allow us to unify the ensemble of historical results under a *uniform* conception of personality as well as of the rapport between person and nature. We are able to unite the primitive intuitions of the Fathers of the Church as well as the speculations of the Commentators in the melting pot of Aristotelio-Boethian metaphysics by means of Albertinian formalities:

On the one side (the efficient): "τὸ ἰδιάζον", *"particularitas"*, *"proprietas"*, *"causa modi substantialis"*;

On the other side (the formal): "τὰ ἀκοινώνητα" (the "λόγος ὑποστάσεων"), *"individualitas"*, *"incommunicabilitas"*, *"modus substantialis"*;

And on another side (that of the concrete whole): "ὑπόστα-σις", *"substantia individualis"*, *"existentia incommunicabilis"*, *"natura cum subsistentia"*.

All of these elements, within their respective orders, can, as we have tried to show, harmoniously agree *without abandoning the goals of those who uttered them.*

It is especially in this sense that the Christological confrontation, notwithstanding the enlargement of our conceptual baggage, has as a result a metaphysical rarefaction in the sense that we recognize fewer really distinct entities; for it leads us to seek the reasons for identity and distinction in the different layers interior to the same object (a fact which imposes upon us so many logical distinctions).

In this regard, we discovered in our analysis certain basic elements for the formulation of an "ancient-new" theory, so to speak, of the modality of personal unity in Christ. Regarding the dynamics of communicability and incommunicability between the human nature of Christ, his person and the principle of his personal being, we have sketched, on the basis of everything concluded with regard to the formality of personality, the profile of a personal unicity which translates as an identity between two natures *hypostatically* signified by reason of the unique relative principle of their hypostatization, in other words, by reason of their unique enhypostatization (a perfection required by the substantiality of the natures in question).

What, then, are the essential affirmations which this study allows us to make? Without repeating the already mentioned facts, we would like to signal eight negative diagnoses and eleven positive deductions.

ON THE NEGATIVE SIDE, WE BELIEVE THAT:

(1) based on our analysis of the treated authors, we have found no tradition anterior to the 14th century which affirms a real distinction between person and nature taken according to its concrete actuality;

(2) those who distinguish person and nature up to that time have not sufficiently specified the sense of "nature" according to which their affirmations have been formulated;

(3) no attempt at eliminating the notion of substance, even directly signified, has succeeded throughout the reflection on personality;

(4) the pretended opposition between natural categories and the so-called "personal" categories must be rejected as a myth, for every operation, every relation and attributive subjectivity rests upon an absolute and subsistent foundation, upon the being of (or identical to) a concrete and complete nature;

(5) the rejection of the Boethian definition is unfounded, provided that the notion of substance assumes its adequate signification implied in the enunciation "individual";

(6) almost the entire tradition seems to have practically neglected, in the context of the person, the investigation of the formal principle of created personality commonly recognized as principle of individuation/particularity;

(7) it is especially at the dawn of the commentators of Saint Thomas that one finds a dialectical analysis of the manner according to which a substantial entity is able to form part of a composite whole, however that does not take place with respect to the principle of numerical

unity (which is generally admitted without discussion) but in reference to a new entity called "subsistence";

(8) in our opinion, by reason as much of their internal logic as of their presuppositions, the so-called "classical" theories of subsistence fail to achieve their ends.

ON THE POSITIVE SIDE, WE HAVE DEMONSTRATED OR EMPHASIZED THAT:

(1) it is only by means of the revelation of the Living God that, in ontological terms, the question of personality poses itself in an acute manner, and it is theological reflection alone, interior to the Christian tradition, which is able to adequately respond to this enigma[1371];

[1371] The notion of person which emerges from our theological investigation of the Trinity serves, moreover, to balance and refine our concept of person as applied in the anthropological context. Naturally, everything we have affirmed about the divine persons has its origin in the value of language as derived from a rational organization of our experience with the creature; and that language is subsequently transposed to divine realities by reason of the similitude existing between God and the creature, a transposition which implies a contextual adjustment of our concepts. But the fruits of theological reflection themselves further provide for an illumination of the transcendent perfections observed within the creature. Theology's disclosing the importance of individuality – understood not as a self-contained enclosure, but as a foundational principle of interrelation and enduring ontological constitution –, for example, demonstrates the inestimable value that contemplating the mysteries of God has for our philosophical appreciation of man. The analogicity of the transposable notions allows for the scientific evidence of one domain to influence our reasoning within the other, particularly as we move from conclusions about personality in the Trinity to anthropological considerations of person, since the perfections constituting the universal foundation of all personality taken in its most analogical sense exist most eminently in the divine personal-essential reality. Nonetheless, despite the similarities in virtue of which the name "person" has a transcendental application, the precise connotation of the term as applied within either the theological or anthropological domain can only be ascertained when analyzed within the special context of the given domain and with respect to the scientific principles proper to each domain. Thus, for example, the rules of divine simplicity govern our understanding (and the predicative mode) of the ascription of a principle of concrete existence, that is a principle by which common nature is hypostatized. Only after the attributions are validated according to the internal rationality of the respective disciplines (attributions which, with respect to God, nevertheless presuppose a certain dependency and inseparability from the primordial significations derived from our familiarity with the creature) do we then proceed to find a common ground on the basis of which to construct a more univocal notion of person. Naturally, the differences between the realization of personality in men and its realization in the Trinity are always kept in the foreground when speaking about God, even if those differences can be left out of our consideration when limiting ourselves to the anthropological domain (thanks to the fact that none of the predicative qualifications unique to Trinitarian discourse need be retained when turning our attention back to the creature, wherefore any

(2) the etymology and original usage of Trinitarian language, especially for what concerns the name "hypostasis", unveils a significative polyvalence which, in its turn, reveals and rests upon the ontological strata of a unique referent;

(3) personal number flows as an immediate consequence of the difference constitutive of every nature possessing being by itself, namely every substantial nature;

(4) just as natural identity between two existents admits (and presupposes) a distinction of the same at another level, so supposital (or hypostatic, or personal) identity between two things admits (and even presupposes) a distinction of the same at another level, such that person and nature are indeed identical and non-identical according to the mode of signification according to which we understand the latter;

(5) for every person, its ontological structure embraces a substantial element and a distinctive element, a source of the perseity of its existence and a source of the numeration of such an act;

(6) the *manner* according to which the human nature of Christ concretely exists becomes the explicative key to its non-personality in itself, an observation which recapitulates both the *modus obtinentiae* of Richard of Saint-Victor and the Cajetanian or Suarezian *modus substantialis*;

(7) the principle of personal distinction is as *constitutive* as distinctive, remaining an intrinsic cause of the hypostatic being without which the enhypostatization of a nature would disappear;

transposition from God to the creature already presupposes having isolated an analogically universally applicable notion). For recent perspectives affirming the reciprocal influence between anthropology and theology (particularly as regards the power of theology to illuminate human personality), see H. U. von Balthasar, "On the Concept of Person", *Communio* 13 (Spring 1986), p. 18-26; "The Theological Concept of Person", in *Theo-Drama*, vol. 3, p. 208-220; A. Ramos, "Foundations for Christian Anthropology", *Anthropotes* 5 (1989), p. 225-257; J. Ratzinger, "Concerning the Notion of Person in Theology", *Communio* 17 (Fall 1990), p. 439-454; K. Schmitz, "Selves and persons: A difference in loves?", *Communio* 18 (Summer 1991), p. 183-206.

(8) it is the individuating conditions which constitute the modality according to which the subsistent act of personal being is realized and which account for its *per se* unity;

(9) taking into account all of the implications of the term "individual" in the Boethian definition, containing the exclusion of every kind of communicability, it becomes legitimate to affirm that the humanity of Christ *as such* is not individual;

(10) the name "person" signifies the substance insofar as hypostatized, but it denotes precisely its *distinction* or complete individuality in virtue of an incommunicable property; it designates the hypostasis *according to the act of distinction* received from the *proprietas personalis;*

(11) as for the subsistence theories of the late Middle Ages, if this new entity known as habitual subsistence could be invoked as a mode of the nature insofar as concrete, that is, as a formal expression of the individuality of the nature, we would see in this a means for safeguarding a doctrine of the substantial mode.

Finally, what perspectives can our study be said to open up? Perhaps the most important thing from the historical point of view is the necessity to reconsider the continuity between the constant tradition of the Church up to the late Middle Ages and the innovative philosophy which follows. In comparison with the nucleus of personality attested here, a study of the precise motives, of the noetic framework and of the origin of the presuppositions which occasioned the novelty of the Commentators remains a task of inestimable value. Although it dominated the theological mentality of the western world from its birth, in front of the insufficiency of this last tradition (dismantled by great minds of our century), it seems fitting to us to reevaluate the metaphysical possibilities intrinsic to the ancient tradition and to cogitate upon the non-necessity of exiting its proper philosophical framework.

In second place, it becomes pertinent to submit several aspects of the Nestorian, Boethian and conciliar doctrine to a new examination. There is room for a re-reading of Nestorius which focuses our attention on his conception of φύσις and the operative distinction between the concrete nature as such and the same insofar as form. The unfolding of this distinction could be placed in comparison with that of Albert between individuating conditions insofar as effecting distinction and the same conditions insofar as constitutive of the *ens concretum*, as well as with the Albertinian idea of individuation as explained by the potential aspect of the entire *quod est* (a thesis applied even to material beings). Regarding Boethius, we believe that it would be profitable to develop the content of the Boethian idea of "particularities" which account for the subsistent and to advance an interpretation which conceives of them as a mode of the substantial mode of being, a modality according to which a nature is actualized. For what concerns the oecumenical councils, our sketch suffices in our opinion to manifest the latitude at our disposition for exploiting the speculative riches surrounding personhood which lie hidden in those councils in a potential form.

In the third place, it seems necessary to us to deepen our philosophical appreciation of the attribute of individuality. In this regard, it would be useful to study the relation between individuality and incommunicability, their different degrees and, especially, the measure of their mutual implication[1372]. One could also maintain the need to better value and better exploit the Thomistic conception of the role of individuality in the constitution of the person[1373].

We should also mention the opportuneness of examining more deeply the methodological differences, manifested as much in the responses given as in the questions posed, which distinguish the Albertinian treatment of personality from that of Saint Thomas.

But from the theological point of view, the most important invitation of our thesis appears to be a Christological approach pushing

---

[1372] As mentioned earlier, studies of individuality and the problem of individuation are extensive, however the precise relationship between the notion of individuality and that of incommunicability stands in need of much greater elaboration, particularly in light of the theological considerations raised in this thesis. For a general bibliography concerning the principle of individuation, cf. supra, "A WORD ABOUT INDIVIDUALITY AND THE 'PROBLEM OF INDIVIDUATION'", note 140. Concerning the relationship between individuality and communicability, cf. supra "TERMINOLOGICAL SUBSTITUTIONS OR DIFFERENT CONCEPTUAL CONTENT" (under Richard of Saint-Victor), p. 172; 'BOETHIUS' DEFINITION AND THE PRINCIPAL CONSTITUENT OF PERSONALITY", p. 341; "THE INCOMMUNICABILITY IMPORTED BY 'INDIVIDUAL'", p. 347; cf. also Jorge J. E. Gracia, "Individuals as Instances", *The Review of Metaphysics* 37, no. 1 (September 1983), p. 37-57.

[1373] The major passages in St. Thomas which deal with individuality in connection with personal constitution are: *Sum. theol.*, I, 13, 9; *Sum. theol.*, I, 29 (especially a. 3-4); *Sum. theol.*, I, 30, 4; *Sum. theol.*, I, 40, 3; *Sum. theol.*, I-II, 1, 7; *Sum. theol.*, II-II, 58, 2; *Sum. theol.*, III, 2, 2; *Sum. theol.*, III, 3, 1; *Sum. theol.*, III, 3, 6; *Sum. theol.*, III, 7, 13; *Sum. theol.*, III, 16, 12; *Sum. contra gentiles*, IV, c. 10; *Sum. contra gentiles*, IV, c. 14; *Sum. contra gentiles*, IV, c. 37-38; *Sum. contra gentiles*, IV, c. 40-41; *Sum. contra gentiles*, IV, c. 49; *III Sent.*, d. 2, q. 1, a. 3; *III Sent.*, d. 5, q. 1, a. 3; *III Sent.*, d. 5, q. 2, a. 3; *III Sent.*, d. 5, q. 3, a. 2-3; *III Sent*, d. 6, q. 1, a. 1-2; *III Sent.*, d. 6, q. 2, a. 1-2; *III Sent.*, d. 10, q. 1, a. 1-2; *De potentia* q. 9; *De veritate*, q. 2, a. 6.

us toward the development of a viable theory of the unity of the concretizing or particularizing act at the heart of the personal dynamics
of the Incarnate Word. There again we shall find the crucible which
permits our concept of personality to be purified. As long as one has
failed to take into account the problem of the modality of this union
in connection with the givens of personality in itself, one will not yet
have the understanding necessary to make a definitive pronouncement on the mystery of the person. It is our hope to have opened up
some avenues for consideration, to have raised various questions, and
to have offered points of reference capable of contributing to the elucidation of this profound mystery.

Closing remarks

We have surveyed, from the fourth century to the present day, a variety of systematic points of view concerning the nature of the intelligent subject called "person". From the Cappadocians through Albert the Great and St. Thomas, we witness a coherence in doctrinal
progression spurred by the problem of personal multiplicity in God.
In light of the relation between the creature and its Creator, the perfections of participated being are able to be transferred by means of
the depurations of analogy to God himself, in such a way that a variety
of predicates are authentically able to define persons of every ontological order. Observing the analogical equivalence between the
members of each column, person can be defined by joining any one
member from each of the three columns (A), (B), and (C):

A	B	C
INDIVIDUALIS	*SUBSTANTIA*	*NATURAE RATIONALIS*
DISCRETUM	*SUBIECTUM*	*NATURAE INTELLECTUALIS*
INCOMMUNICABILIS	*EXISTENTIA*	*RATIONALIS*
PER SE	*RES NATURAE*	*INTELLECTUALIS*
DISTINCTA	*NATURA*	*CUM DIGNITATE*

It is by spelling out the sense in which the analogical notions are employed – their mode of predication and mode of signification (corresponding to a real ontological perfection of the referent of the
grammatical subject) – that our theology of the Trinity and Incarnation is justified. Though any A-B-C combination is sufficient to define
the person, only by conscious referral to the other notions does a
definition take meaningful shape. Particularly in this regard, Albert
reveals the complimentarity between the definition of Boethius and

that of Richard of St. Victor, each one bringing into focus, according to its own methodological point of view, the same fundamental aspects of personality while uniquely supplying for the limitations of the other.

In the eyes of the Scholastics, there is no adverse opposition between the Boethian and Victorine definitions of person[1374]. Rather than opting for this or that formula, their fundamental concern was simply to discern the precise sense and signification of person in light of the conceptual difficulties presented by its transposition to the uncreated order of the divine nature. The labor of St. Albert with respect to Trinitarian doctrine achieved just such an end, revealing the absolute perfection of the person in general. Drawing several philosophical perspectives on personhood into a coherent whole, Albert illustrates the person's *per se* act of existing, its substantiality, its distinctness and incommunicability, and all of the elements collocated above. He furthermore integrated the Augustinian insight into the role and necessity of relations in providing for the numerable and distinctive element in the constitution of divine personality, thus liberating personal multiplication from that of substantial nature. Particularly in this sense, Albert can be said to have significantly contributed to the historical advancement of the understanding of personality, inasmuch as he precisely identifies the subject of the distinctive function of relation, distinguishing it as such from the very nature with which that subject is identical *in re*: "*persona significationem habet substantiae et proprietatis, sed circa substantiam illam quam importat [persona], nec ponit proprietatem, nec numerum quem facit proprietas*"[1375]. His notion of the distinctive *proprietates* in God demonstrates, furthermore, how a careful metaphysics of relation alone can avoid the errors of either implicitly admitting some sort of real distinction between *quo est* and *quod est*, between the principle of distinction and the distinguished thing in God, or denying the reality of the relations at all[1376].

The Albertinian solution rests upon a differentiation between person and nature expressed in terms of "*modus significandi*", a linguistic principle he extensively exploits. Notwithstanding their real identity

---

[1374] Cf. A. Pompei, op. cit., p. 350.

[1375] Albert, *I Sent.*, d. 23, a. 2, sol., ed. Borgnet, vol. 25, p. 584-585; cf. A. Pompei, op. cit., p. 350-351.

[1376] Both of which errors are excluded, respectively, by the following phrases typical of the Albertinian corpus: "*proprietas quae est persona*" and "*proprietas est ante personam secundum rationem*" – the first expressive of the constitutive function of relations in God (identified with the persons *in facto esse*), the second of their distinctive function (conceptually prior to the persons).

in God, person generates and nature does not, persons are distinct, nature not, and this, because they do not signify the same thing in the same respect. Person and essence in God are identical due to the simplicity of the divine nature (and exclusively on that account), yet their respective *rationes formales* are different. Albert thus finds a *via media* between exaggerated realism and nominalism, though the nature of the distinction maintained by Albert is not entirely clear. Is the Albertinian difference between person and essence identical to the *distinctio formalis* used chiefly by the Scotists, or the Thomistic *distinctio virtualis*[1377]? However it be interpreted, the fact that there is some real foundation for the distinction affirmed is clear, and the value of distinguishing person and nature in God according to mode of signification seems to extend in a particularly efficacious way to the created order when nature is considered according to its concrete particular mode of existing. To look at the personality associated with a perfect substantial nature in this light opens the door to an alternative explanation of the notion of habitual subsistence, providing a wholly different means for distinguishing nature from person in Christ while nevertheless maintaining an orthodox sense of their hypostatic identity. That alternative has a first and momentous representative in Maximus Confessor and is, in our opinion, virtually contained in the doctrine of the Universal Doctor; developing it shall be the goal of our subsequent study on the Incarnation.

In the final analysis, shifting one's attention from the Trinity to Christ may not entail the need to go beyond the categories of metaphysical discourse inherited by Albert and Thomas. To the contrary, it might simply demand a more refined and formalistic appreciation of the traditional response to the problem of personality. Expressing all of its dimensions together, that problem requires specifying the signification of the terms involved in its discussion, assigning the ontological status of the person with respect to the predicamental order, distinguishing person from nature, identifying the formally constitutive element of personhood, discerning the ontological status of the latter and its relation to the essence of the person as well as to the person itself, comparing the distinctiveness and the formally distinctive prop-

---

[1377] The real difficulty is generated by the fact that the Albertinian distinction expresses itself in the logical (as opposed to metaphysical) terms of the nature of attribution and logical supposition (an example of the latter being *"Deus generat"*, where *"Deus"* stands for the person of the Father and not for the divine substance); cf. A. Pompei, op. cit., p. 348-349.

erty of one person to that of another, and exposing the implications of these with respect to the possibility of one person communicating in either the personal or natural act of another. We hope to have satisfactorily touched upon all of these issues, though we cannot pretend to have exhausted any of them. In fact, the object we have set out to define exceeds in many ways the very capacities of human reason. Even guided by revelation, we cannot comprehend the Trinity, nor can we form a truly adequate concept of the person independent of reduplicative qualifications owing to the analogicity of its notion. Who, moreover, could claim to have comprehensively comprised the reality of personhood by means of a definition? Made in the image and resemblance of the divine mystery, man, and every form of intelligent life, is a mystery unto itself. The irreducible value of the individual is something practically imperceptible by the metaphysician inevitably plunged in the world of essences and universals. Yet the individual, as manifested in the revelation of God's incomprehensible love for every one of his children, is that which is most precious and worthy of respect. "Person", affirms St. Thomas, "is that which is most perfect in all of nature" [1378], and the effort to unfold the meaning of that name, the metaphysical implications of applying it to God, and the ramifications it entails for moral behavior in the sphere of human actions is one of the cardinal responsibilities and privileges of the Christian theologian.

[1378] Aquinas, *Sum. theol.*, I, 29, 3.

BIBLIOGRAPHY

ANCIENT AND MEDIEVAL AUTHORS:

ALBERT THE GREAT, *De causis et processu universitatis a prima causa*, ed. A. Borgnet, vol. 10, Paris 1891.

— *De incarnatione*, ed. Coloniensis, vol. 26, 1958.

— *De praedicabilibus*, ed. A. Borgnet, vol. 1, Paris 1890.

— *De praedicamentis*, ed. A. Borgnet, vol. 1, Paris 1890.

— *Metaphysica*, ed. Coloniensis, vol. 16, 1960-1964.

— *Scripta super quattuor libros Sententiarum*, ed. A. Borgnet, vol. 25-30, Paris 1893-1894.

— *Summa de creaturis*, ed. A. Borgnet, vol. 35, Paris 1896.

— *Summa theologiae* (*Summa de mirabili scientia Dei*), ed. A. Borgnet, vol. 31-33, Paris 1895; for *pars prima* through tractatus 12, ed. Coloniensis, vol. 34, 1978.

— *Super Dionysium De divinis nominibus*, ed. Coloniensis, vol. 37/1, 1972.

ARISTOTLE, *Categories*, in *The Basic Works of Aristotle*, R. McKeon (editor), Random House, New York 1941.

— *Metaphysics*, in *La Métaphysique*, introduction and notes by J. Tricot, Vrin, Paris 1986; in consultation with *The Basic Works of Aristotle*, R. McKeon (editor), Random House, New York 1941.

— *Physics*, in *The Basic Works of Aristotle*, R. McKeon (editor), Random House, New York 1941.

AUGUSTINE, SAINT, *De doctrina christiana*, trans. J. F. Shaw, in the collection: Nicene and Post-Nicene Fathers, ed. P. Schaff, Eerdmans Printing, Grand Rapids, Michigan 1988.

—   *De Trinitate*; trans. A. W. Haddan, in the collection: Nicene and Post-Nicene Fathers, ed. P. Schaff, Eerdmans Printing, Grand Rapids, Michigan 1988.

BASIL THE GREAT, *Adversus Eunomium* (Ἀνατρεπτικὸς τοῦ ἀπολογητικοῦ Εὐνομίου): PG 29, 498-774.

—   *De Spiritu Sancto* (Του ἁγίου Βασιλείου πρὸς Ἀμφιλόχιον ἐπίσκοπον Ἰκονίου τῆς Λυκαόνων πεπὶ του ἁγίου Πνεύματος ἐν κεφαλαίος τριάκοντα): PG 32, 67-218.

—   *Epistola 9*, Μαξίμῳ φιλοσόφῳ, ed. Y. Courtonne, *Saint Basile, Lettres*, Collection des Universités de France, Paris 1957, vol. I; PG 32, 267-272.

—   *Epistola 38*, Γρηγορίῳ ἀδελφῷ περὶ διαφορᾶς οὐσίας καὶ ὑποστάσεως, ed. Y. Courtonne, *Saint Basile, Lettres*, Collection des Universités de France, Paris 1957, vol. I; PG 32, 325-342.

—   *Epistola 52*, Κανονικαῖς, ed. Y. Courtonne, *Saint Basile, Lettres*, Collection des Universités de France, Paris 1957, vol. I; PG 32, 391-396.

—   *Epistola 125*, Ἀντίγραφον Πίστεως ὑπαγορευθείσης παρὰ τοῦ ἁγιωτάτου Βασιλείου, ᾗ ὑπέγαψεν Εὐστάθιος ὁ Σεβαστείας ἐπίσκοπος, ed. Y. Courtonne, *Saint Basile, Lettres*, Collection des Universités de France, Paris 1957, vol. II; PG 32, 545-552.

—   *Epistola 210*, Τοῖς κατὰ Νεοκαισάρειαν λογιωτάτοις, ed. Y. Courtonne, *Saint Basile, Lettres*, Collection des Universités de France, Paris 1957, vol. II; PG 32, 767-778.

—   *Epistola 236*, Ἀμφιλοχίῳ Ἐπισκόπῳ, ed. Y. Courtonne, *Saint Basile, Lettres*, Collection des Universités de France, Paris 1957, vol. III; PG 32, 876-885.

—   *Hom. 24*, Κατὰ Σαβελλιανῶν, καὶ Ἀρείου, καὶ τῶν Ἀνομοίων: PG 31, 599-618.

BOETHIUS, ANICIUS MANLIUS SEVERINUS, *Commentaria in Porphyrium a se translatum*, PL 64, 71-158.

—   *Contra Eutychen et Nestorium*, ed. H. F. Stewart - E. K. Rand, *Boethius, The Theological Tractates, The Consolation of Philosophy*, London/Cambridge 1953.

—   *De Trinitate (Trinitas unus Deus ac non tres dii)*, ed. H. F. Stewart - E. K. Rand, *Boethius, The Theological Tractates, The Consolation of Philosophy*, London/Cambridge 1953.

—   *Quomodo substantiae in eo quod sint bonae sint cum non sint substantialia bona*, ed. H. F. Stewart - E. K. Rand, *Boethius, The Theological Tractates, The Consolation of Philosophy*, London/Cambridge 1953.

—   *Utrum Pater et Filius et Spiritus Sanctus substantialiter praedicentur*, ed. H. F. Stewart - E. K. Rand, *Boethius, The Theological Tractates, The Consolation of Philosophy*, London-Cambridge 1953.

CAJETAN, *In de ente et essentia D. Thomae Aquinatis*, ed. Marietti, Turin 1934 (ed. De Maria, Rome 1907).

—   *In III^{am} Summa theologiae*, in Thomas Aquinas, *Summa theologiae*, ed. Leonine, vol. 4-12, Rome 1888-1906.

CAPREOLUS, *Defensiones theologiae divi Thomas Aquinatis*, ed. Paban-Pègues, Alfred Cattiere, 7 vols., Turin 1900-1908.

CYRIL OF ALEXANDRIA, *Adversus Theodoretum*: Acta Conciliorum Oecumenicorum, ed. Schwartz, Walter de Gruyter Co., Berlin 1927.

—   *Epistola 39 (ad Joannem Antiochenum)*: PG 77, 173-182.

—   Ἐπιστολὴ Κυρίλλου πρὸς Νεστόριον τρίτη: *Conciliorum Oecumenicorum Decreta*, ed. G. Alberigo, Istituto per le Scienze Religiose, Bologna 1973, in *Decrees of the Ecumenical Councils*, ed. N. P. Tanner, Sheed & Ward, Georgetown 1990.

—   Κυρίλλου ἐπιστολὴ δευτέρα πρὸς Νεστόριον: *Conciliorum Oecumenicorum Decreta*, ed. G. Alberigo, Istituto per le Scienze Religiose, Bologna 1973, in *Decrees of the Ecumenical Councils*, ed. N. P. Tanner, Sheed & Ward, Georgetown 1990.

GILBERT OF POITIERS, *Expositio in Boecii librum Contra Euticen et Nestorium*, ed. N. M. Häring, in *The Commentaries on Boethius by Gilbert of Poitiers*, Pontifical Institute of Mediaeval Studies, Toronto 1966, p. 231-364. Also in *AHDLMA* 21 (1954), J. Vrin, Paris 1955, p. 250-357.

— *Expositio in Boecii librum De bonorum ebdomade*, ed. N. M. Häring, in *The Commentaries on Boethius by Gilbert of Poitiers*, Pontifical Institute of Mediaeval Studies, Toronto 1966, p. 181-230. (PL 64, 1313C-1334A).

— *Expositio in Boecii librum De Trinitate*, ed. N. M. Häring, in *The Commentaries on Boethius by Gilbert of Poitiers*, Pontifical Institute of Mediaeval Studies, Toronto 1966, p. 51-180. (PL 64, 1255B-1300C).

GREGORY OF NAZIANZUS, *Ep. 101*, Πρὸς Κληδόνιον πρεσβύτερον κατὰ Ἀπολλιναρίου: PG 37, 175-194.

— *Oratio 31*, Θεολόγικος πέμπτος. Περὶ τοῦ ἁγίου Πνεύματος: PG 36, 133-172.

— *Oratio 33*, Πρὸς Ἀρειανοὺς, καὶ εἰς ἑαυτόν: PG 36, 213-238.

— *Oratio 37*, Εἰς τὸ ῥητὸν τοῦ Εὐαγγελίου "Ὅτε ἐτέλεσεν ὁ Ἰησοῦς τοὺς λόγους τούτους", καὶ τὰ ἐξῆς: PG 36, 281-308.

— *Oratio 39*, Εἰς τὰ ἅγια Φῶτα: PG 36, 335-360; *Sources Chrétiennes*, 358.

— *Oratio 41*, Τοῦ αὐτοῦ εἰς τὴν Πεντηκοστήν: PG 36, 427-452.

— *Oratio 42*, Συντακτήριος, εἰς τὴν τῶν ρν' ἐπισκόπων παρουσίαν: PG 36, 457-492.

GREGORY OF NYSSA, *Ad Theoph. adv. Apoll.* (Ἀντιρρητικὸς πρὸς τὰ Ἀπολλιναρίου): PG 45, 1123-1278.

— *Contra Eunomium* (Πρὸς Εὐνόμιον ἀντιρρητικὸς λόγος), I: PG 45, 247-464.

HIPPOLYTUS, *Contra Noetum*, ed. P. Nautin, Paris 1949.

JOHN OF SAINT THOMAS, *Cursus theologicus*, ed. Vives, Paris 1886 (vol. 4); ed. Solesmes, 1931 (vol. 4, 1953).

NESTORIUS, *Liber Heraclidis*. F. Nau, *Le Livre d'Héraclide de Damas*, ed. Letouzey and Ané, Paris 1910.

— Νεστορίου ἐπιστολὴ δευτέρα πρὸς Κύριλλον, *Conciliorum Oecumenicorum Decreta*, ed. G. Alberigo, Istituto per le Scienze Religiose, Bologna 1973, in *Decrees of the Ecumenical Councils*, ed. N. P. Tanner, Sheed & Ward, Georgetown 1990.

PETER LOMBARD, *Magistri Petri Lombardi Sententiae in IV libris distinctae*, 2 vols, ed. Collegii S. Bonaventurae Ad Claras Aquas, Grottaferrata (Rome) 1971-1981.

PORPHYRY, *Isagoge*, translation, introduction and notes by E. W. Warren, Pontifical Institute of Medieval Studies, Toronto 1975.

PSEUDO-ALBERTUS MAGNUS, *Questiones Alberti de modis significandi*, translated and edited by L. G. Kelly, in "Amsterdam Studies in the Theory and History of Linguistic Science", John Benjamins B.V., Amsterdam 1977.

RICHARD OF SAINT-VICTOR, *De Trinitate*. ed. J. Ribaillier, *Textes philosophiques du Moyen Age*, VI, Vrin, Paris 1958; PL 196; *Sources Chrétiennes*, 63.

SUÁREZ, F., *De incarnatione*, ed. Vives, vol. 17-18, Paris 1860.

— *Disputationes metaphysicae*, ed. Vives, vol. 25-26, Paris 1861; in consultation with ed. S. Romeo/S. Sánchez, 5 vols., Biblioteca Hispanica de Filosofia, Madrid 1960.

— *On the Essence of Finite Being As Such, On the Eistence of That Essence and Their Distinction, De essentia entis finiti ut tale est et de illius esse eorumque distinctione*, trans. N. Wells, Marquette University Press, Milwaukee 1983.

TERTULLIAN, *Adversus Praxean*. CCL II, 1159-1205.

THOMAS AQUINAS, SAINT, *Compendium theologiae*, ed. Leonine, vol. 42, Rome 1979.

— *De ente et essentia*, ed. Leonine, vol. 43, Rome 1976.

— *De principiis naturae*, ed. Leonine, vol. 43, Rome 1976.

— *De unione verbi incarnati*, ed. Parma, vol. 8, 1856 (ed. Leonine, vol. 24/2).

— *In Duodecim Libros Metaphysicorum Aristotelis Expositio*, ed. Cathala–Spiazzi, Turin 1950 (*Sententia super Metaphysicam*, ed. Parma, vol. 20, 1866; ed. Leonine, vol. 46).

— *In Boet. de Trinitate*, ed. Leonine, vol. 50, Rome 1992.

— *Quaestiones disputatae De potentia*, ed. Marietti, Turin 1965.

— *Quaestiones disputatae De veritate*, ed. Leonine, vol. 22, Rome 1972-1976.

— *Questiones de quodlibet*, ed. Leonine, vol. 25, Rome 1996.

— *Scriptum super libros Sententiarum*, ed. Moos, 4 vols., Paris 1933.

— *Summa contra gentiles*, ed. Leonine, vol. 13-15, Rome 1918-1930.

— *Summa theologiae*, ed. Leonine, vol. 4-12, Rome 1888-1906.

MODERN AND CONTEMPORARY AUTHORS:

ALLAN, W., ADAMS, M. MCCORD (editors), *The Philosophical Theology of John Duns Scotus*, Cornell University Press, Ithaca/London 1990.

ANGELINI, G., "La figura della "persona" nel quadro dell'alleanza", in *L'Idea di persona*, V. Melchiorre (editor), Vita e Pensiero, Milan 1996, p. 51-62.

ANZULEWICZ, H., "Grundlagen von Individuum und Individualität in der Anthropologie des Albertus Magnus", in Aertsen, J. A./Speer, A. (editors), *Individuum und Individualität im Mittelalter*,

Walter de Gruyter, Berlin/New York 1996 (*Miscellanea Mediaevalia* 24), p. 124-160.

— "Neuere Forschung zu Albertus Magnus, Bestandsaufnahme und Problemstellungen", *Recherches de théologie et philosophie médiévales* 66 (1999), p. 163-206.

— "Zur Theorie des menschlichen Lebens nach Albertus Magnus. Theologische Grundlegung und ihre bioethischen Implikationen", *Studia Mediewistyczne* 33 (1998), p. 35-49.

AUER, J., *Person. Ein Schlüssel zum christlichen Mysterium*, Pustet, Regensburg 1979.

BAILLEUX, E., "Le personnalisme de saint Thomas en théologie trinitaire", *RT* 61 (1961), p. 25-42.

BALTHASAR, H. U., VON, "On the Concept of Person", *Communio* 13 (Spring 1986), p. 18-26.

— "The Concept of Nature in Catholic Theology", in *The Theology of Karl Barth*, Communio Books/Ignatius Press, San Francisco 1992, p. 267-291, 301-325.

— "The Theological Concept of Person", in *Theo-Drama*, vol. 3, "The Dramatis Personae: The Person in Christ", trans. G. Harrison, Ignatius Press, San Francisco 1992, p. 208-220.

— *Theologik*, vol. 2: *Wahrheit Gottes*, Johannes Verlag, Einsiedeln 1985.

BARBEDETTE, A. F. & D., *Cours de philosophie scolastique*, Berche et Pagis, Paris 1935.

BASTIT, M., *Les principes des choses en ontologie médiévale: Thomas d'Aquin, Scot, Occam*, Ed. Bière, Bordeaux 1997.

BEAUCHAMP, P., "Persona, elezione e universalità nella Bibbia", in *L'Idea di persona*, V. Melchiorre (editor), Vita e Pensiero, Milan 1996, p. 33-50.

BEINHAUER, R., *Untersuchungen zu philosophisch-theologischen Termini in "De Trinitate" des Boethius*, VWGÖ, Vienna 1990.

BERGERSON, M., *La Structure du Concept Latin de Personne du XIIIe Siècle*, in Etudes d'Histoire de Doctrine et Litterature du Moyen Age, IIe séries, Institut d'Etudes Médiévales d'Ottawa, Paris 1932, p. 121-161.

BERTULETTI, A., "Il concetto di persona e il sapere teologico", in *L'Idea di persona*, V. Melchiorre (editor), Vita e Pensiero, Milan 1996.

BÉRUBÉ, C., *La connaissance de l'individuel au Moyen Age*, Presses de l'université de Montréal, Montréal 1964.

BIARD, J., "Sémantique et Ontologie dans l'Ars Meliduna", in J. Jolivet – A. De Libera (editors), *Gilbert de Poitiers et ses contemporains. Aux origines de la Logica modernorum: Actes du septième Symposium européen d'histoire de la logique et de la sémantique médiévales, Centre d'Études supérieures de civilisation médiévale de Poitiers, Poitiers, 17-22 juin 1985*, Bibliopolis, Naples 1987, p. 121-144.

BILLOT, L., *De Verbo incarnato*, 9th edition, Rome 1949.

BLARER, J., *Alberti Magni "De antecedentibus ad logicam"*, Diss., University of Fribourg (Switzerland), 1951; also in *Teoresi* 9 (1954), p. 177-242.

BRAAKHUIS, H. A. G., "Signification, Appellation and Predication in the Ars Meliduna", in J. Jolivet – A. De Libera (editors), *Gilbert de Poitiers et ses contemporains. Aux origines de la Logica modernorum: Actes du septième Symposium européen d'histoire de la logique et de la sémantique médiévales, Centre d'Études supérieures de civilisation médiévale de Poitiers, Poitiers, 17-22 juin 1985*, Bibliopolis, Naples 1987, p. 107-120.

BRUDER, K., *Die philosophischen Elemente in den Opuscula Sacra des Boethius: ein Beitrag zur Quellengeschichte der Philosophie der Scholastik*, F. Meiner, Leipzig 1928.

BURGER, MARIA, *Personalität im Horizont absoluter Prädestination: Untersuchungen zur Christologie des Johannes Duns Scotus und ihrer Rezep-

tion in modernen theologischen Ansätzen, Aschendorff, Münster 1994.

— "Univozität des Seienden – Univozität der Person: Zwei Grenzbegriffe", in L. Honnefelder (editor), *John Duns Scotus. Metaphysics and Ethics,* Brill, Leiden 1996, p. 317-326.

— "Zwischen Trinitätslehre und Christologie. Der Personbegriff bei Johannes Duns Scotus", in Aertsen, J. A./Speer, A. (editors), *Individuum und Individualität im Mittelalter,* Walter de Gruyter, Berlin/New York 1996 (*Miscellanea Mediaevalia* 24), p. 406-415.

BURGER, MARIA / LUTZ-BACHMANN, M., "Person", in *Lexikon des Mittelalters,* vol. 6, 1900-1903, Munich 1993.

BUSCAROLI, S., "L'haecceitas scotista e la singolarità personale: cenni per una lettura teoretica", *Teoresi* 34 (1979), p. 297-360.

CARDAROPOLI, G., "Cristologia e antropologia in Duns Scoto e nella teologia contemporanea", in Casamenti, S. (editor), *Etica e persona. Duns Scoto e suggestioni nel moderno,* Edizioni Francescane Bologna, Bologna 1994, p. 261-280.

CATAN, J. R., "Aristotele e S. Tommaso intorno all' 'actus essendi'", *Rivista di Filosofia Neoscolastica* 73 (1981), p. 639-695.

CATECHISM OF THE CATHOLIC CHURCH, Ignatius Press, San Francisco 1994.

CHÂTILLON, J., "Richard de Saint-Victor", in *D.S.* XIII, Paris 1987, p. 593-654.

CHENU, M.-D., "Grammaire et théologie aux 12e et 13e siècles", *AHDLMA* 10 (1935), p. 5-28.

CHIEREGHIN, F., "Le ambiguità del concetto di persona e l'impersonale", in *L'Idea di persona,* V. Melchiorre (editor), Vita e Pensiero, Milan 1996, p. 65-86.

CLARKE, W. NORRIS, "Person, Being, and St. Thomas", *Communio: International Catholic Review,* XIX, n. 4 (1992), p. 601-618.

COLISH, M. L., "Gilbert, The Early Porretans, and Peter Lombard: Semantics and Theology", in J. Jolivet – A. De Libera (editors), *Gilbert de Poitiers et ses contemporains. Aux origines de la Logica modernorum: Actes du septième Symposium européen d'histoire de la logique et de la sémantique médiévales, Centre d'Études supérieures de civilisation médiévale de Poitiers, Poitiers, 17-22 juin 1985*, Bibliopolis, Naples 1987, p. 229-250.

CONNELL, R. J., *Substance and Modern Science*, Center for Thomistic Studies, University of St. Thomas, Houston 1988.

— *Substance, Structure and Operation: an Essay in Natural Philosophy*, University of St. Thomas, St. Paul (MN) 1985.

— *The Empirical Intelligence*, Edwin Mellon Press, Lewis/Queenston 1988.

COOPER, L., *A Concordance of Boethius. The Five Theological Tractates and the Consolation of Philosophy*, Cambridge 1928.

COPLESTON, F., *A History of Philosophy*, vol. II-III, Image Books, New York 1948.

COURCELLE, P., "Étude critique sur les Commentaires de Boèce (IX-XV siècles)", *AHDLMA* 13 (1939), p. 5-140.

— *La Consolation de la philosophie dans la tradition littéraire. Antécédentes et postérité de Boèce*, Études Augustiniennes, Paris 1967.

COUSINS, E., *The Notion of Person in the "De Trinitate" of Richard of Saint Victor*, unpublished Diss., Fordham University 1966.

CRAEMER-RUEGENBERG, I., *Albertus Magnus*, C. H. Beck, Munich 1980.

— *Die Substanzmetaphysik des Boethius in den Opuscula sacra*, Diss., University of Cologne, 1969.

CROCCO, A., *Introduzione a Boezio*, Empireo, Naples 1975.

CUNNINGHAM, F. L. B. (editor), *Christ and His Sacraments*, from *Theology: A Basic Synthesis for the College*, vol. III, Priory Press, Dubuque (Iowa) 1958.

— *God and His Creation*, from *Theology: A Basic Synthesis for the College*, vol. I, Priory Press, Dubuque (Iowa) 1958.

CUSMARIU, A., "Subsistence Demystified", *Auslegung* 6 (1978), p. 24-28.

DEN BOK, N., *Communcating the Most High. A Systematic Study of Person and Trinity in the Theology of Richard of St. Victor († 1173)*, Brepols, Paris/Tournai 1996.

DENZINGER, H. - SCHÖNMETZER, A., *Enchiridion Symbolorum, Definitionum et declarationum de rebus fidei et morum*, 36th edition, Herder, Rome 1976.

DERISI, OCTAVIO N., *La Persona. Su esencia, su vida, su mundo*, Universidad Nacional de La Plata, La Plata 1950.

— "El Constitutivo Esencial de la Persona", *Sapientia* 31 (1976), p. 259-268.

DESCOQS, P., "Individu et Personne", *ArPh* 14 (1938), p. 235-292.

— "La nature métaphysique de la personalité", *ArPh* 14 (1938), cahier 3, p. 102-138. (Part of "Métaphysique", *ArPh* 14, 1938, p. 423-578 [vol. 14, cahier 3, p. 1-156]).

DIEPEN, H., "La critique du baslisme selon saint Thomas d'Aquin", *RT* 50 (1950), p. 83-118, 290-329.

— *La Théologie de l'Emmanuel*, DDB, Paris 1960.

DRONKE, P. (editor), *A History of Twelfth-Century Western Philosophy*, Cambridge University Press, Cambridge 1988.

DÜRR, K., *The Propositional Logic of Boethius*, North-Holland Publishing Co., Amsterdam 1951 (reprinted in 1969 and in 1980 by Greenwood Press, Westport, Conn.).

ECO, U., "Signification and Denotation from Boethius to Ockham", *Franciscan Studies* 44 (1984), p. 1-29.

ELDERS, L. J., *La métaphysique de saint Thomas d'Aquin dans une perspective historique*, Vrin, Paris 1994.

— *La philosophie de la nature de saint Thomas d'Aquin*, trans. J.-Y. Brachet, Pierre Téqui (éditeur), Paris 1993.

ELSÄSSER, M., *Anicius Manlius Severinus Boethius, Die theologischen Traktate*, Felix Meiner Verlag, Hamburg 1988.

— *Das Person-Verständnis des Boethius*, Diss., Julius-Maximilians-Universität zu Würzburg, Munster 1973.

EMERY, G., *La Trinité créatrice*, Vrin, Paris 1995.

ÉTHIER, A.-M., *Le De Trinitate de Richard de Saint-Victor*, Institut d'Etudes Médiévale, Ottawa/Paris 1939.

FESTUGIERE, A. J., *Ephèse et Chalcédoine. Actes des Counciles*, Paris 1982.

FORMENT GIRALT, E., *Lecciones de Metafísica*, Ediciónes Rialp, Madrid 1992.

— *Persona y Modo Substancial*, Promociónes Publicaciónes Universitarias, Barcelona 1983.

— *Ser y Persona* (2nd edition), Promociónes Publicaciónes Universitarias, Barcelona 1984.

GAIDOZ, J., "Saint Prosper d'Aquitaine et le Tome a Flavien", *RevSR* 23 (1949), p. 270-301.

GALOT, J., "La définition de la personne, relation et sujet", *Gregorianum* 75/2 (1994), p. 281-299.

— *La Personne du Christ*, Duculot-Lethielleux, Paris 1969.

GARCÍA MORENTE, M., "El clasicismo de Santo Tomás", in *Escritos desconocidos e inéditos*, M. García Morente (editor), BAC, Madrid 1987, p. 174-190.

GARDEIL, H. D., *Introduction to the Philosophy of St. Thomas Aquinas*, trans. J. A. Otto, 4 vols., Herder Book Co., New York 1967.

GARRIGOU-LAGRANGE, R., *God: His Existence and His Nature*, 2 vols., trans. B. Rose, Herder Book Co., St. Louis/London 1949.

GEYER, B., *Prologomena* to the edition of the *De Bono*, ed. Coloniensis, vol. 28, Münster 1951.

GEIGER, L. B., *La participation dans la philosophie de St. Thomas d'Aquin*, Paris 1942.

GILSON, E., *Jean Duns Scot: introduction à ses positions fondamentales*, J. Vrin, Paris 1952.

GIRONES, G., *La Divina Arqueología (Del primer principio teológico en el tratado de la Trinidad)*, Faculdad de Teología, Valencia 1991.

GOICHON, A. M., *La philosophie d'Avicenne et son influence en Europe médiévale*, Adrien-Maisonneuve, Paris 1944.

GRABMANN, M., "Die Schrift 'De ente et essentia', und die Seinsmetaphysik des heiligen Thomas von Aquin", in *Mittelalterliches Geistesleben*, M. Grabmann/Max Hüber (editors), Munich 1926 (reprinted in 1956), vol. 1, p. 314-331.

GRACIA, JORGE, J. E., "Boethius and the Problem of Individuation in the Commentaries on the 'Isagoge'", in *Atti, Congresso internazionale di studi boeziani* (Pavia, 5-8 Ottobre 1980), edited by L. Obertello, Editrice Herder, Rome 1981, p. 169-182.

— *Individuality. An Essay on the Foundations of Metaphysics*, State University of New York Press, New York 1988.

— "Individuals as Instances", *The Review of Metaphysics* 37, no. 1 (September 1983), p. 37-57.

— (editor), *Individuation in Scholasticism, The Later Middle Ages and the Counter-Reformation, 1150-1650*, State University of New York Press, New York 1994.

— *Introduction to the Problem of individuation in the Early Middle Ages*, second revised edition, Philosophia Verlag, Munich 1988.

GRILLMEIER, A., *Christ in Christian Tradition. From the Apostoloc Age to Chalcedon (451)*, trans. J. Bowden, John Knox Press, 2nd edition, Atlanta 1975.

HACKETT, JEREMIAH, "Albert the Great", in Gracia Jorge, *Individuation in Scholasticism*, University of N.Y. Press, New York 1994, p. 97-115.

HADOT, P., "Forma essendi. Interpretation philologique et interpretation philosophique d'une formule de Boèce", *Les études classiques* 38 (1970), p. 143-156.

— "La distinction de l'être et de létant dans le "De hebdomadibus" de Boèce", in *Miscellanea Mediaevalia* 2, "Die Metaphysik im Mittelalter", Walter de Gruyter, Berlin 1963, p. 147-153.

HALL, D. C., *The Trinity: an Analysis of St. Thomas Aquinas' "Expositio" of the "De Trinitate" of Boethius*, E. J. Brill, Leiden/New York 1992.

HALLEUX, A. DE, "'Hypostase' et 'Personne' dans la Formation du Dogme Trinitaire (ca 375-381)" in *Patrologie et oecuménisme*, University Press, Louvain 1990, p. 113-214.

HARDY, R., *Christology of the Later Fathers*, Westminster Press, Philadelphia 1954.

HARTMANN, N., "Person in Einsamkeit und Gemeinsamkeit. Überlegungen zum Personbegriff bei Joh. Duns Scotus", *Wissenschaft und Weisheit* 47 (1984), p. 37-60.

HAYEN, A., "Le Concile de Reims et l'erreur théologique de Gilbert de la Porrée", *AHDLMA* 10-11 (1935-1936), Vrin, Paris 1936.

— "L'Etre et la Personne selon le B. Jean Duns Scot", *RPL* 53 (1955), p. 525-541.

HEFELE, *Histoire des conciles*, trans. Delarc, Le Clere, Paris 1912.

HENNINGER, M. G., *Relations, Medieval Theories 1250-1325*, Clarendon Press, Oxford 1989.

HENRY, A. M. (editor), *God and His Creation*, trans. W. Storey, Fides Publishers, Chicago 1955.

— (editor), *The Historical and Mystical Christ*, trans. W. Storey, Fides Publishers, Chicago 1958.

HOFMANN, P., "Analogie und Person. Zur Trinitätsspekulation Richards von St.-Victor", *Theologie und Philosophie* 59 (1984), p. 191-234.

HONNEFELDER, L., WOOD, R., DREYER, M. (editors), *John Duns Scotus: Metaphysics and Ethics*, E. J. Brill, Leiden/New York 1996.

HUFNAGEL, A., "Das Person-Problem bei Albertus Magnus", in H. Ostlender (editor), *Studia Albertina. Festschrift für Bernhard Geyer zum 70. Geburtstage*, "BGPTM, Suppl. 4", Aschendorff, Münster 1952, p. 202-233.

— "Der Mensch als Person nach Thomas von Aquin", in *Tommaso d'Aquino nel suo settimo centenario: atti del Congresso Internazionale Roma-Napoli 1974*, vol. 7, Edizioni domenicane italiane, Naples 1974, p. 257-264.

JACOBI, K., "Einzelnes – Individuum – Person. Gilbert von Poitiers' Philosophie des Individuellen", in Aertsen, J. A. / Speer, A. (editors), *Individuum und Individualität im Mittelalter*, Walter de Gruyter, Berlin/New York 1996 (*Miscellanea Mediaevalia* 24), p. 3-21.

JOLIVET, J., "Trois variations médiévales sur l'universel et l'individu: Roscelin, Abélard, Gilbert de la Porrée", *Rev. Méta. Morale* 97 (1992), p. 111-155.

JOLIVET, J. – DE LIBERA, A. (editors), *Gilbert de Poitiers et ses contemporains. Aux origines de la Logica modernorum: Actes du septième Symposium européen d'histoire de la logique et de la sémantique médiévales, Centre d'Études supérieures de civilisation médiévale de Poitiers, Poitiers, 17-22 juin 1985*, Bibliopolis, Naples 1987.

KARAYIANNIS, V., *Maxime le Confesseur, essence et énergies de Dieu*, Beauchesne, Paris 1993.

KASPER, W., *Der Gott Jesu Christi*, Mainz 1982.

KELLY, L. G., "God and Speculative Grammar", in I. Rosier (editor), *L'héritage des grammairiens latins de l'Antiquité aux Lumières: Actes du Colloque de Chantilly, 2-4 septembre, 1987*, Société pour l'information grammaticale, Paris/Louvain 1987, p. 205-213.

— "Modus significandi: an interdisciplinary concept", *Historiographia Linguistica* 6 (1979), p. 159-180.

KELLY, J. N. D., *Early Christian Doctrines*, Harper and Row, New York 1960.

KNEEPKENS, C. H., "'Suppositio' and 'Supponere' in 12th Century Grammar", in J. Jolivet – A. De Libera (editors), *Gilbert de Poitiers et ses contemporains. Aux origines de la Logica modernorum: Actes du septième Symposium européen d'histoire de la logique et de la sémantique médiévales, Centre d'Études supérieures de civilisation médiévale de Poitiers, Poitiers, 17-22 juin 1985*, Bibliopolis, Naples 1987, p. 325-351.

KREMPEL, A., *La doctrine de la relation chez S. Thomas, exposé historique et systématique*, Vrin, Paris 1952.

KUC, P. L., "La métaphysique de l'être chez Cajetan", in *Miscellanea Mediaevalia* 2, "Die Metaphysik im Mittelalter", Walter de Gruyter, Berlin 1963, p. 661-666.

KÜHLE, H., "Die Lehre Alberts des Grossen von den Tranzendentalien", in *Philosophia perennis*, Festgabe J. Geyser, Bd. I, Druck und Verlag von Josef Hobbel, Regensburg 1930, p. 129-147.

LEROY, M.-V., "L'Union selon l'hypostase d'après saint Thomas d'Aquin" in *RT* 74 (1974), p. 205-243.

LIBERA, A. DE, *Albert le Grand et la philosophie*, Librairie Philosophique J. Vrin, Paris 1990.

— "Philosophie et théologie chez Albert le Grand et dans l'école dominicaine allemande", in *Miscellanea Mediaevalia* 20, "Die Kölner Universität im Mittelalter", Walter de Gruyter, Berlin/ New York 1989, p. 49-67.

LLUCH-BAIXAULI, M., "Bibliografia commemorativa de Manlio Severino Boecio", *Scripta Theologica* 21 (1989), p. 213-225.

— *La teologia de Boecio en la transición del mundo clásico al mundo medieval*, Ediciones Universidad de Navarra, Pamplona 1990.

LOOFS, F., *Nestoriana*, Halle, 1905.

LORENZ, D., *I fondamenti dell'ontologia tomista, Il trattato "De ente et essentia"*, Edizioni studio domenicano, Bologna 1992.

LUTZ-BACHMANN, M., "'Natur' und 'Person' in den 'Opuscula Sacra' des A.M.S. Boethius", *Theologie und Philosophie* 58 (1983), p. 48-70.

MAIOLI, B., *Gilberto Porretano: dalla grammatica speculativa alla metafisica del concreto*, Bulzoni, Rome 1979.

MALET, A., *Personne et amour dans la théologie trinitaire de saint Thomas d'Aquin*, Vrin, Paris 1956.

MARENBON, J., "Gilbert of Poitiers", in *A History of Twelfth-Century Western Philsophy*, P. Dronke (editor), Cambridge University Press, Cambridge 1988.

MARINOZZI, P. D., *La relazione in S. Alberto Magno*, Diss., University of Fribourg (Switzerland), 1956.

— *La relazione trascendentale in S. Alberto Magno*, Pax et Bonum, Rome 1964.

MARITAIN, J., *Court traité de l'existence et de l'existant*, 2nd edition, Flammarion, Paris 1964.

— *La personne humaine et la société*, DDB, Paris 1939.

McINERNY, R., *Boethius and Aquinas*, Catholic University of America Press, Washington D.C. 1990.

MEERSSEMAN, P. G., *Introductio in Opera Omnia B. Alberti Magni O.P.*, Carolum Beyaert, Bruge 1931.

MERCIER, CARDINAL, *A Manual of Modern Scholastic Philosophy*, 3rd English edition, trans. T. L. Parker and S. A. Parker, vol. II, Routledge & Kegan Paul/Herder, London/St. Louis 1962.

MICAELLI, C., "'Natura' e 'Persona' nel 'Contra Eutychen et Nestorium' di Boezio: osservazioni su alcuni problemi filosofici e linguistici", in *Atti, Congresso internazionale di studi boeziani* (Pavia, 5-8 Ottobre 1980), edited by L. Obertello, Editrice Herder, Rome 1981, p. 327-336.

— *Studi sui trattati teologici di Boezio*, M. D'Auria, Naples 1988.

MICHEL, A., "UNION (HYPOSTATIQUE)" in *DTC* 7, 437-568.

MILANI, M., *Boezio: l'ultimo degli antichi*, Camunia, Milan 1994.

MILANO, ANDREA, *Persona in teologia*, Edizioni Dehoniane, Naples 1987.

MOINGT, J, *Théologie trinitaire de Tertullien*, 4 vol., Aubier, Paris 1966-1969.

MÜHLEN, H., *Sein und Person nach Johannes Duns Scotus. Beitrag zur Grundlegung einer Metaphysik der Person*, Dietrich-Coelde-Verlag, Werl 1954.

MURALT, A., *L'Enjeu de la philosophie médiévale*, E. J. Brill, Leiden/New York/Cologne 1993.

NÉDONCELLE, M., *La Personne Humaine et la Nature*, Presses Universitaires de France, Paris 1943.

— "Les variations de Boèce sur la personne", *RevSR* 29 (1955), p. 201-238.

— "Prósopon et persona dans l'antiquité classique. Essai de bilan linguistique", *RevSR* 22 (1948), p. 277-299.

NICOLAS, J.-H., "L'Unité d'Etre dans le Christ d'après Saint Thomas", *RT* 65 (1965), p. 229-260.

— *Synthèse dogmatique, complément: de l'Univers à la Trinité*, Imprimerie Saint Paul, Fribourg 1993.

— *Synthèse dogmatique: de la Trinité à la Trinité*, 2nd edition, Éditions Universitaires, Fribourg 1986.

NICOLAS, M.-J., "La Doctrine Christologique de S. Léon le Grand", *RT* 51 (1951), p. 609-660.

NIEDEN, M., *Organum Dietatis: die Christologie des Thomas de Vio Cajetan*, Brill, Leiden 1997.

NIELSEN, L. O., *Theology and Philosophy in the Twelfth Century: A Study of Gilbert Porreta's Thinking and the Theological Expositions of the Doctrine of the Incarnation During the Period 1130-1180*, E. J. Brill, Leiden 1982.

OBERTELLO, L., *Severino Boezio*, 2 vols., Accademia ligure di scienze e lettere, Genova 1974.

— (editor), *Boezio, La consolazione della filosofia. Gli opuscoli teologici*, Milan 1979.

OFFERMANN, H., *Der christologische und trinitarische Personbegriff der frühen Kirche. Ein Beitrag zum Verständnis von Dogmenentwicklung und Dogmengeschichte*, Bern/Frankfurt 1976.

OTT, LOUIS, *Précis de théologie dogmatique*, trans. M. Grandclaudon, Éditions Salvator, Tournai/Paris 1954.

OWENS, J., "Thomas Aquinas", in *Individuation in Scolasticism, The Later Middle Ages and the Counter-Reformation, 1150-1650*, Jorge J. E. Gracia (editor), State University of New York Press, New York 1994, p. 173-194.

PATFOORT, A., *L'Unité d'Etre dans le Christ d'après S. Thomas, A la Croisée de l'Ontologie et de la Christologie*, Paris-Tournai 1964.

PENIDO, M. T. L., *Le rôle de l'analogie en théologie dogmatique*, "Bibliotèque thomiste, 15", Paris 1931.

PETERSON, L., "Cardinal Cajetan (Thomas De Vio) (B. 1468; D. 1534) and Giles of Rome (B. CA. 1243/47; D. 1316)", in *Individuation in Scholasticism, The Later Middle Ages and the Counter-Reformation, 1150-1650*, J. J. E. Gracia (editor), State University of New York Press, New York 1994, p. 431-455.

PHILIPPE, M.-D., *Introduction à la philosophie d'Aristote*, Editions Universitaires, Campin (Belgium) 1991.

PIEPER, J., *Living the Truth*, Ignatius Press, San Francisco 1989.

PIRET, PIERRE, "Christologie et théologie trinitaire chez Maxime le Confesseur, d'après sa formule des natures 'desquelles, en lesquelles et lesquelles est le Christ'", in *Maximus Confessor, Actes du Symposium sur Maxime le Confesseur*, Editions Universitaires, Fribourg 1982, p. 215-222.

—   *Le Christ et la Trinité selon Maxime le Confesseur*, Beauchesne, Paris 1983.

POMPEI, A., *La dottrina trinitaria di S. Alberto Magno, O. P.. Esposizione organica del Commentario delle Sentenze in rapporto al movimento teologico scolastico*, Diss., University of Fribourg (Switzerland), Rome 1953.

PORTALUPI, E., "Das Lexicon der Individualität bei Thomas von Aquin", in Aertsen, J. A./Speer, A. (editors), *Individuum und Individualität im Mittelalter*, Walter de Gruyter, Berlin/New York 1996 (*Miscellanea Mediaevalia* 24), p. 57-73.

POTTIER, BERNARD, *Dieu et le Christ selon Grégoire de Nysse*, Culture et Vérité, Brussels 1994.

PURWATMA, M., *The Explanation of the Mystery of the Trinity Based on the Attribute of God as Supreme Love: A Study on the "De Trinitate" of Richard of St. Victor*, Rome 1990.

QUASTEN, J., *Patrology*, Spectrum Publishers, Brussels, vol. I (1950); vol. II (1953); vol. III (1960).

RAEYMAEKER, L. DE, "Albert le Grand, philosophe. Les lignes fondamentales de son système métaphysique", *Revue néoscholastique de philosophie* 35 (1933), p. 5-36.

RAMOS, A., "Foundations for Christian Anthropology", *Anthropotes* 5 (1989), p. 225-257.

RATZINGER, J., "Concerning the Notion of Person in Theology", *Communio* 17 (Fall 1990), p. 439-454.

— *Introduction to Christianity*, Herder & Herder, New York 1970.

REALE, GIOVANNI, *Storia della filosofia antica*, Vita e Pensiero, Milan 1992.

RIBAILLIER, J. (editor), *Textes philosophiques du Moyen Age*, VI, Vrin, Paris 1958.

RICHARD, M., "L'Introduction du mot "Hypostase" dans la Théologie de l'Incarnation", *Opera Minora*, vol. II, 42, p. 243-269.

RIJK, L. M., DE, "Boèce logicien et philosophe: ses positions sémantiques et sa métaphysique de l'être", in *Atti, Congresso internazionale di studi boeziani* (Pavia, 5-8 Ottobre 1980), edited by L. Obertello, Editrice Herder, Rome 1981, p. 141-156.

— "Gilbert de Poitiers: ses vues sémantiques et métaphysiques", in J. Jolivet – A. De Libera (editors), *Gilbert de Poitiers et ses contemporains. Aux origines de la Logica modernorum: Actes du septième Symposium européen d'histoire de la logique et de la sémantique médiévales, Centre d'Études supérieures de civilisation médiévale de Poitiers, Poitiers, 17-22 juin 1985*, Bibliopolis, Naples 1987, p. 147-171.

RODRIGUEZ, J. J. ACOSTA, "Los conceptos esse e id quod est en Boecio", *Ciudad de Dios* 202 (1989), p. 613-656.

ROIG GIRONELLA, J., "La Oposición Individuo-Universal en los Siglos XIV-XV, Punto de Partida de Suárez", in *Miscellanea Mediaevalia* 2, "Die Metaphysik im Mittelalter", Walter de Gruyter, Berlin 1963, p. 667-678.

ROLAND-GOSSELIN, M. D., *Le "De ente et essentia" de Saint Thomas d'Aquin*, Vrin, Paris 1948.

ROSENBERG, J. R., The Principle of Individuation. A Comparative Study of St. Thomas, Scotus and Suárez, The Catholic University of America Press, Washington D.C. 1950.

ROSIER, IRÈNE, *Grammaires médiévales*, Presses universitaires de Vincennes, Saint-Denis 1990.

— *La parole comme acte: sur la grammaire et la sémantique au XIIIe siècle*, J. Vrin, Paris 1994.

SALET, G., *Richard de Saint-Victor, La Trinité* (*Sources chrétiennes* 63).

SANGUINETI, JUAN JOSÉ, "La persona humana en el orden del ser", in *Tommaso d'Aquino nel suo settimo centenario: atti del Congresso Internazionale Roma-Napoli 1974*, vol. 7, Edizioni domenicane italiane, Naples 1974, p. 340-345.

SARANYANA, J., "Sobre la Contribution de Alberto Magno a la Doctrina del 'Actus Essendi'", in *Miscellanea Mediaevalia* 14, "Albert der Grosse. Seine Zeit, sein Werk, sein Wirkung", Walter de Gruyter, Berlin/New York 1981, p. 41-49.

SAYES, J. A., *Jesucristo, Ser y Persona*, Aldecoa, Burgos 1984.

SCHEEBEN, M. J., *The Mysteries of Christianity*, trans. C. Vollert, Herder, London 1947.

SCHMIDT, M. A., *Gottheit und Trinität nach dem Kommentar des Gilberts Porreta zu Boethius De Trinitate*, Basel 1956.

SCHMITZ, K., "Selves and persons: A difference in loves?", *Communio* 18 (Summer 1991), p. 183-206.

— "The Geography of the Human Person", *Communio* 13 (Spring 1986), p. 27-48.

SCHNACKENBURG R. - SMULDERS P., *La christologie dans le Nouveau Testament et le dogme*, Mysterium Salutis, n. 10, Éditions du Cerf, Paris 1974.

SCHOONENBERG, P., "Trinity – The Consummated Covenant: Theses on the Doctrine of the Trinitarian God", *Studies in Religion* 5 (1975), p. 111-116.

SCHULTHESS, P. - IMBACH, R., *Die Philosophie im lateinischen Mittelalter: ein Handbuch mit einem bio-bibliographischen Repertorium*, Artermis & Winkler, Zurich/Düsseldorf 1996.

SCIPIONI, L. I., *Ricerche sulla Cristologia del 'Libro di Eraclide' di Nestorio. La formulazione e il suo contesto filosofico*, Fribourg 1956.

SEIFERT, J., *Essere e persona*, Vita e Pensiero, Milan 1989.

SEILLER, L., "La notion de personne selon Scot. Ses principales applications en christologie", *La France Franciscaine* 20 (1937), p. 209-248.

SESBOÜÉ, B., *Histoire des* Dogmes, tome I: *Le Dieu du Salut*, Desclée, Paris 1994.

— *Jésus-Christ dans la tradition de l'Église*, Desclée, Paris 1982.

STURLESE, L., *Die deutsche Philosophie im Mittelalter*, Verlag C. H. Beck, Munich 1993, p. 324-388; *Storia della filosofia tedesca*, Florence 1996, p. 69-124.

SWEENEY, L., "Are Plotinus and Albertus Magnus Neoplatonists?", in *Graceful Reason: Essays in Ancient and Medieval Philosophy Presented to Joseph Owens, CSSR*, L. P. Gerson (editor), Papers in Mediaeval Studies 4, Pontifical Institute of Mediaeval Studies, Toronto 1983, p. 177-202.

— "Esse primum creatum in Albert the Great's Liber de causis et processu universitatis", *The Thomist* 44 (1980), p. 599-646.

THONNARD, F.-J., *Précis de Philosophie en Harmonie avec les Sciences Modernes*, Desclée & Cie, Tornaci (Belgium) 1950.

TOCCAFONDI, E. T., "Il concetto di ente nella metafisica tomista", in *Miscellanea Mediaevalia* 2, "Die Metaphysik im Mittelalter", Walter de Gruyter, Berlin 1963, p. 365-370.

TORRELL, J.-P., "Le thomisme dans le débat christologique contemporain", in *Saint Thomas au XXᵉ siècle, Actes du colloque du Centenaire de la "Revue thomiste"*, Saint-Paul, Paris 1994, p. 379-393.

TURIENZO, S. A., "Aspectos del Problema de la Persona en el Siglo XII", in *Miscellanea Mediaevalia* 2, "Die Metaphysik im Mittelalter", Walter de Gruyter, Berlin 1963, p. 180-183.

TYN, T., *Metafisica della sostanza, partecipazione e analogie entis*, Edizioni studio domenicano, Bologna 1991.

VAN ELSWIJK, H. C., *Gilbert Porreta: sa vie, son oeuvre, sa pensée*, Spicilegium sacrum Lovaniense, Louvain 1966.

VIGNA, C., "Sostanza e relazione", in *L'Idea di persona*, V. Melchiorre (editor), Vita e Pensiero, Milan 1996, p. 175-203.

WALD, BERTHOLD, "Aristoteles, Boethius und der Begriff der Person im Mittelalter", *Archiv für Begriffsgeschichte* 39 (1996), p. 161-179; also in Aertsen, J. A./Speer, A. (editors), *Individuum und Individualität im Mittelalter*, Walter de Gruyter, Berlin/New York 1996 (*Miscellanea Mediaevalia* 24), p. 371-388.

WÉBER, E. H., *La personne humaine au XIIIᵉ siècle*, Vrin, Paris 1991.

— *Le Christ selon saint Thomas d'Aquin*, Desclée, Tournai 1988.

WEISHEIPL, J. A., *Friar Thomas d'Aquino*, Doubleday, New York 1974.

— "The Concept of Nature: Avicenna and Aquinas", *Thomistic Papers* 1 (1984), p. 65-81.

— "The Concepts of 'Nature' and 'Person'", in *Commentary on the Gospel of St. John of St. Thomas Aquinas*, Magi, New York 1980, I, appendix III, p. 458-468.

WELLS, NORMAN J., "Capreolus on Essence and Existence", *The Modern Schoolman* 38 (1960), p. 1-24.

WULF, M. DE, *Histoire de la philosophie médiévale*, 3 vols., Louvain 1905.

INDEXES, LEXICONS, DICTIONARIES:

Dictionaire de Théologie Catholique, Letouzey, Paris, 1930-1953.

Enciclopedia filsofica, 2nd edition, Centro di studi filosofico di Gallarate, Stampa Romagraf, Rome 1979.

Encyclopedia of Philosophy, ed. Edwards, P., Macmillan Publishing Co., New York 1967.

Lexicon Scholasticorum Verborum, in *Summa theologica [Thomae Aquinatis],* ed. Marietti, vol. 6, Taurin 1937.

Tabula Aurea, in *Thomae Aquinatis Opera Omnia,* ed. Vives, vol. 33-34, Paris 1880.

INDEX OF NAMES

ABBREVIATIONS

ACO
: *Acta Conciliorum Oecumenicorum*, ed. E. Schwartz, De Gruyter, Berlin 1959-1984.

ACPQ
: *American Catholic Philosophical Quarterly*, Washington D.C..

AHDLMA
: *Archives d'histoire doctrinale et littéraire du moyen âge*, Paris.

ArPh
: *Archives de philosophie*, Paris.

CCL
: *Corpus Christianorum. Series Latina*, Turnhout, Brepols.

D.S.
: *Dictionaire de spiritualité*, Beauchesne, Paris.

DEC
: *Conciliorum Oecumenicorum Decreta*, ed. G. Alberigo, Istituto per le Scienze Religiose, Bologna 1973, in *Decrees of the Ecumenical Councils*, ed. N. P. Tanner, Sheed & Ward, Georgetown 1990.

DS
: Denzinger-Schönmetzer, *Enchiridion Symbolorum, definitionum et declarationum de rebus fidei et morum*, 36th edition, Herder, Rome 1976.

DTC
: *Dictionaire de théologie catholique*, Letouzey, Paris.

InternPhilosQuart
: *International Philosophical Quarterly*, New York.

NSchol
: *The New Scholasticism*, Washington D.C..

PG
: *Patrologia graeca*, J. P. Migne, Paris.

PL
: *Patrologia latina*, J. P. Migne, Paris.

Rev. Méta. Morale
: *Revue de métaphysique et de Morale*, Vineuil.

RevSR	*Revue des Sciences Religieuses*, F.-X. Le Roux & Co., Strasbourg - Paris.
RIPh	*Revue Internationale de Philosophie*, Brussels.
RPL	*Revue philosophique de Louvain*, Louvain.
RSR	*Recherches de Science Religieuse*, Paris.
RT	*Revue Thomiste*, Toulouse.
SC	*Sources chrétiennes* (Lyon), Le Cerf, Paris.
Scripta Theol.	*Scripta Theologica*, Pamplona (Navarra).

FOR THE WORKS OF ST. ALBERT

De anima	*De anima.*
De causis et proc. univ.	*De causis et processu universitatis a prima causa.*
De incarn.	*De incarnatione.*
De praedicabilibus	*Super Porphyrium de V universalibus seu Super Isagogen Porphyrii.*
De praedicamentis	*De praedicamentis seu In categorias Aristotelis.*
I Sent.	*Super I Sententiarum.*
II Sent.	*Super II Sententiarum.*
III Sent.	*Super III Sententiarum.*
Metaph.	*Metaphysica.*
Sum. de creaturis	*Summa de creaturis (Summa de mirabili scientia Dei I).*

Sum. theol.	*Summa theologiae (Summa de mirabili scientia Dei II).*
Super Dion. De div. nom.	*Super Dionysium De divinis nominibus.*

Beiträge zur Geschichte der Philosophie und der Theologie des Mittelalters – Neue Folge

Ausführliche Prospekte auf Wunsch. Verlag Aschendorff, Postanschrift: D-48135 Münster
Internet: http://www.aschendorff.de/buch

Aschendorff